national STATISTICS

United Kingdom National Accounts
The Blue Book 2007

James Sosimi

Office for National Statistics

palgrave macmillan

This publication is also available at the National Statistics website: www.statistics.gov.uk

For any other use of this material please apply for a Click-Use Licence for core material at www.opsi.gov.uk/click-use/system/online/pLogin.asp or by writing to:

Office of Public Sector Information

Information Policy Team

St Clements House

2–16 Colegate

Norwich NR3 1BQ

Fax: 01603 723000

E-mail: hmsolicensing@cabinet-office.x.gsi.gov.uk

First published 2007 by
PALGRAVE MACMILLAN
Houndmills, Basingstoke, Hampshire RG21 6XS and 175 Fifth Avenue, New York, NY 10010, USA
Companies and representatives throughout the world.

PALGRAVE MACMILLAN is the global academic imprint of the Palgrave Macmillan division of St. Martin's Press, LLC and of Palgrave Macmillan Ltd. Macmillan® is a registered trademark in the United States, United Kingdom and other countries. Palgrave is a registered trademark in the European Union and other countries.

ISBN 978-1-4039-9398-4
ISSN 0267–8691

This book is printed on paper suitable for recycling and made from fully managed and sustained forest sources. Logging, pulping and manufacturing processes are expected to conform to the environmental regulations of the country of origin.

A catalogue record for this book is available from the British Library.

10 9 8 7 6 5 4 3 2 1
16 15 14 13 12 11 10 09 08 07

Printed and bound in Great Britain by Hobbs the Printers Ltd, Totton, Hampshire.

A National Statistics publication

National Statistics are produced to high professional standards set out in the National Statistics Code of Practice. They are produced free from political influence.

About the Office for National Statistics

The Office for National Statistics (ONS) is the government agency responsible for compiling, analysing and disseminating economic, social and demographic statistics about the United Kingdom. It also administers the statutory registration of births, marriages and deaths in England and Wales.

The Director of ONS is also the National Statistician and the Registrar General for England and Wales.

Contact points

For enquiries about this publication, contact the Editor
Tel: 020 7533 6045
E-mail: john.dye@ons.gsi.gov.uk

For general enquiries, contact the National Statistics Customer Contact Centre.
Tel: 0845 601 3034
(minicom: 01633 812399)
E-mail: info@statistics.gsi.gov.uk
Fax: 01633 652747
Post: Room 1015, Government Buildings, Cardiff Road, Newport NP10 8XG

You can also find National Statistics on the Internet at: www.statistics.gov.uk

Contents

Chapter 10: Non-financial balance sheets

Chapter 11: Public sector supplementary tables

Chapter 12 : Statistics for European Union purposes

Part 5 UK Environmental Accounts

Chapter 13: Environmental Accounts

Supplementary information

Preface

The annual National Statistics *Blue Book* publication contains the estimates of the domestic and national product, income and expenditure of the United Kingdom.

The presentation of accounts is based on the *European System of Accounts 1995* (ESA95), which is itself based on the *System of National Accounts 1993* (SNA93). The SNA93 has been adopted worldwide.

Quarterly estimates

Quarterly estimates of the main components of the National Accounts for the last few years are published in National Statistics *First Releases* and, in more detail with commentary, in the *United Kingdom Economic Accounts* (UKEA).

A number of long run quarterly and annual estimates consistent with the Blue Book are available in the online publication *Economic & Labour Market Review* (ELMR). The latest estimates are also given in summary form in the *Monthly Digest of Statistics* and the quarterly income, capital and financial accounts for each sector are published regularly in *Financial Statistics*.

National Statistics Online

(www.statistics.gov.uk)

Users can download time series, cross-sectional data and metadata from across the Government Statistical Service (GSS) using the site search and index functions from the homepage. Many datasets can be downloaded, in whole or in part, and directory information for all GSS statistical resources can be consulted, including censuses, surveys, periodicals and enquiry services. Information is posted as PDF electronic documents or in XLS and CSV formats, compatible with most spreadsheet packages.

Time series data

The Time series data facility on the website provides access to around 40,000 time series, of primarily macro-economic data, drawn from the main tables in a range of our major economic and labour market publications. Users can download complete releases, or view and download customised selections of individual time series.

Comments and enquiries

National Statistics looks forward to receiving comments on its publications.

Suggestions for improvements or alterations to the *Blue Book* can be sent in writing to:

John Dye

Blue Book Editor

D3/11, 1 Drummond Gate

LONDON SW1V 2QQ

Tel: 020 7533 6045 Fax: 020 7533 5189

Email: gdp@ons.gsi.gov.uk

Enquiries regarding National Accounts should be directed to the following:

National accounts:
Geoff Tily
020 7533 5919
geoff.tily@ons.gsi.gov.uk

Sector and financial accounts:
Michael Rizzo
020 7533 5653
michael.rizzo@ons.gsi.gov.uk

Household final consumption expenditure:
Ann Harris
020 7533 6058
ann.harris@ons.gsi.gov.uk

General government and public sector:
Martin Kellaway
020 7533 5987
martin.kellaway@ons.gsi.gov.uk

Gross capital formation:
Neil Wilson
020 7533 5934
neil.wilson@ons.gsi.gov.uk

Exports and imports of goods:
Caroline Lakin
020 7533 607
caroline.lakin@ons.gsi.gov.uk

Exports and imports of services:
Tom Orford
020 7533 6095
tom.orford@ons.gsi.gov.uk

Gross value added by industry:
Simon Woodsford
01633 813126
simon.woodsford@ons.gsi.gov.uk

Input-Output supply and use tables/Production accounts:
Sanjiv Mahajan
020 7533 5954
sanjiv.mahajan@ons.gsi.gov.uk

Households and NPISH sector:
Ann Harris
020 7533 6058
ann.harris@ons.gsi.gov.uk

Non-financial corporations:
Brian Hopps
020 7533 5498
brian.hopps@ons.gsi.gov.uk

Financial corporations:
Richard Dagnall
020 7533 6055
richard.dagnall@ons.gsi.gov.uk

Rest of the world:
Perry Francis
020 7533 6075
perry.francis@ons.gsi.gov.uk

Capital stock and non-financial balance sheets:
Neil Wilson
020 7533 5934
neil.wilson@ons.gsi.gov.uk

Environmental accounts:
Ian Gazley
020 7533 5904
ian.gazley@ons.gsi.gov.uk

The *Blue Book* is a collaborative effort. National Statistics is grateful for the assistance provided by the various government departments and organisations that have contributed to this book.

Design and artwork by ONSdesign:

Andy Leach

Shain Bali

Tony Castro

Michelle Franco

An introduction to the United Kingdom National Accounts

The *Blue Book* presents the full set of economic accounts, or National Accounts, for the United Kingdom. These accounts are compiled by the Office for National Statistics (ONS). They record and describe economic activity in the United Kingdom and as such are used to support the formulation and monitoring of economic and social policies.

This edition of the *Blue Book* presents estimates of the UK domestic and national product, income and expenditure covering the calendar years 1998–2006. The tables of the main aggregates are extended to cover 1992–1997 on a consistent basis. Data for 2005 and 2006 are not yet available for the production account, the generation of income account, Input-Output Supply and Use Tables and for the full detailed industrial analysis of gross value added and its income components.

The accounts are based on the *European System of Accounts 1995* (ESA95)[1], itself based on the *System of National Accounts 1993* (SNA93)[2], which is being adopted by national statistical offices throughout the world. The UK National Accounts have been based on the ESA95 since September 1998. The 1998 edition of the *Blue Book* explains the main changes; a more detailed explanation of changes can be found in *Introducing the ESA95 in the UK*.[3] A detailed description of the structure for the accounts is provided in a separate National Statistics publication *UK National Accounts Concepts, Sources and Methods*.[4]

This introduction gives a brief overview of the accounts, explains their framework and sets out the main changes included in this edition of the *Blue Book*. Definitions of terms used throughout the accounts are included in the glossary. Explanations of more specific concepts are provided within the relevant parts.

The *Blue Book* comprises five parts:

- **Part 1** provides a summary of the UK National Accounts along with explanations and tables that cover the main national and domestic aggregates, for example gross domestic product (GDP) at current market prices and chained volume measures and the GDP deflator; gross value added (GVA) at basic prices; gross national income (GNI); gross national disposable income (GNDI); and where appropriate their equivalents net of capital consumption; population estimates; employment estimates and GDP per head; and the UK summary accounts (the goods and services account, production accounts, distribution and use of income accounts and accumulation accounts). It also includes details of revisions to the data.

Transitional nature of this year's Blue Book

The annual *Blue Book* is the major annual update of the UK National Accounts. It would normally include:

- incorporation of new and revised methods
- updating, or benchmarking, the estimates to take account of the major annual business surveys and administrative data from HM Revenue & Customs
- production of balanced current price GDP through balancing Input-Output Supply and Use Tables
- any classification changes necessary to bring the national accounts into line with public sector finances

The effect of the annual exercise is usually larger revisions than at other times of the year, with revisions to levels and growth going back much further in time. The UK is most unusual among major industrialised countries in overhauling its accounts in such a comprehensive manner on an annual basis. Most other countries work to five-yearly or even ten-yearly updates.

To free up resource necessary to allow delivery of modernised National Accounts systems and methods in next year's annual *Blue Book*, ONS agreed, after consultation with the Bank of England and HM Treasury, that the annual updating of the GDP accounts through the Input-Output Supply and Use framework would not take place this year. An article (Modernising the UK's National Accounts) was released earlier this year describing the implications of this reduced scope on this year's *Blue Book* dataset:

- postponing implementation of some methodological improvements
- the latest annual benchmark data, including the Annual Business Inquiry and estimates from HM Revenue & Customs will not be fully incorporated
- not striking a balanced picture of the economy based on these new data for 2005 (the latest normally balanced year) and not updating the preliminary balance for 2004

It should be noted that most of the text relating to methodology and processes used in producing the UK National Accounts has been retained in this year's publication for information purposes even where those numbers are not included.

- **Part 2** includes analyses of gross value added at current market prices and chained volume measures, capital formation and employment, by industry. Input-Output Supply and Use Tables which are usually included in this section will not be available this year
- **Part 3** provides a description of the institutional sectors as well as explaining different types of transactions, the sequence of the accounts and the balance sheets. Explanation is also given of the statistical adjustment items needed to reconcile the accounts. This part comprises the fullest available set of accounts showing transactions by sectors and appropriate sub-sectors of the economy (including the rest of the world).
- **Part 4** covers other additional analyses. It includes tables showing the percentage growth rates of the main aggregates and supplementary tables for capital consumption, gross fixed capital formation, capital stock, non-financial balance sheets, public sector data, and GNI and GNP consistent with the ESA79 compiled for EU budgetary purposes.
- **Part 5** covers environmental accounts.

Overview of the accounts

In the United Kingdom priority is given to the production of a single estimate of GDP using the income, production and expenditure data. The income analysis is available at current prices, expenditure is available at both current prices and chained volume measures and value added on a quarterly basis is compiled in chained volume measures only. Income, capital and financial accounts are also produced for each of the institutional sectors: non-financial corporations, financial corporations, general government and the households and non-profit institutions serving households sectors. The accounts are fully integrated, but with a statistical discrepancy, known as the statistical adjustment, shown for each sector account (which reflects the difference between the sector net borrowing or lending from the capital account and the identified borrowing or lending in the financial accounts which should theoretically be equal). Financial transactions and balance sheets are also produced for the rest of the world sector in respect of its dealings with the United Kingdom.

The basic framework of the UK National Accounts

The accounting framework provides for a systematic and detailed description of the UK economy. It includes the sector accounts, which provide, by institutional sector, a description of the different stages of the economic process from production through income generation, distribution and use of income to capital accumulation and financing; and the Input-Output framework, which describes the production process in more detail. It contains all the elements required to compile aggregate measures such as GDP, gross national income (previously known as gross national product), saving and the current external balance (the balance of payments). The economic accounts provide the framework for a system of volume and price indices, so that chained volume measures of aggregates such as GDP can be produced. It should be noted that, in this system, value added, from the production approach, is measured at basic prices (including other taxes *less* subsidies on production but not on products) rather than at factor cost (which excludes all taxes *less* subsidies on production). The system also encompasses measures of population and employment.

The whole economy is subdivided into institutional sectors. For each sector, current price accounts run in sequence from the production account through to the balance sheet.

The accounts for the whole UK economy and its counterpart, the rest of the world, follow a similar structure to the UK sectors, although several of the rest of the world accounts are collapsed into a single account because they can never be complete when viewed from a UK perspective.

The table numbering system is designed to show the relationships between the UK, its sectors and the rest of the world. A three part numbering system (for example, 5.2.1) has been adopted for the accounts drawn directly from the ESA95. The first two digits denote the sector; the third digit denotes the ESA account. In this way for example, table 5.2.1 is the central government production account, table 5.3.1 is the local government production account and table 5.3.2 is the local government generation of income account. Not all sectors can have all types of account, so the numbering is not necessarily consecutive within each sector's chapter. For the rest of the world, the identified components of accounts 2-6 inclusive are given in a single account numbered 2. The UK whole economy accounts consistent with the ESA95 are given in section 1.6 as a time series and in section 1.7 in detailed matrix format with all sectors, the rest of the world, and the UK total identified.

The ESA95 code for each series is shown in the left hand column. The ESA95 codes use the prefix 'S' for the classification of institutional sectors. The ESA95 classification of transactions and other flows comprises transactions in products (prefix P), distributive transactions (prefix D), transactions in financial instruments (prefix F) and other accumulation entries (prefix K). Balancing items are classified using the prefix B. Within the financial balance sheets, financial assets/liabilities are classified using the prefix AF and non-financial assets/liabilities using the prefix AN.

What is an account? What is its purpose?

An account records and displays all of the flows and stocks for a given aspect of economic life. The sum of resources is equal to the sum of uses with a balancing item to ensure this equality. Normally the balancing item will be an economic measure which is itself of interest.

By employing a system of economic accounts we can build up accounts for different areas of the economy which highlight, for example, production, income and financial transactions. In many cases these accounts can be elaborated and set out for different institutional units and groups of units (or sectors). Usually a balancing item has to be introduced between the total resources and total uses of these units or sectors and, when summed across the whole economy, these balancing items constitute significant aggregates.

The integrated economic accounts

The integrated economic accounts of the UK provide an overall view of the economy. The sequence of accounts is shown in Figure 1 below. Figure 1 presents a summary view of the accounts, balancing items and main aggregates and shows how they are expressed.

The accounting structure is uniform throughout the system and applies to all units in the economy, whether they are institutional units, sub-sectors, sectors or the whole economy, though some accounts (or transactions) may not be relevant for some sectors.

The accounts are grouped into four main categories: goods and services account, current accounts, accumulation accounts and balance sheets.

The goods and services account (Account 0)

The goods and services account is a transactions account which balances total resources, from output and imports, against the uses of these resources in consumption, investment, inventories and exports. Because the resources are simply balanced with the uses, there is no balancing item. The goods and services account is discussed in detail in Chapters 3 and 12 of *UK National Accounts Concepts, Sources and Methods.*[4]

Current accounts: the production accounts and the distribution of income accounts

Current accounts deal with production, distribution of income and use of income.

The production account (Account I)

The production account displays the transactions involved in the generation of income by the activity of producing goods and services. In this case the balancing item is value added (B.1). For the nation's accounts, the balancing item (the sum of value added for all industries) is, after the addition of taxes less subsidies on products, gross domestic product (GDP) at market prices or net domestic product when measured net of capital consumption. The production accounts are also shown for each institutional sector.

The production accounts are discussed in detail in Chapters 4 and 13 of *Concepts, Sources and Methods.*[4]

Distribution and use of income account (Account II)

The distribution and use of income account shows the distribution of current income (in this case value added) carried forward from the production account, and has as its balancing item saving (B.8), which is the difference between income (disposable income) and expenditure (or final consumption). There are three sub-accounts which break down the distribution of income into the primary distribution of income, the secondary distribution of income and the redistribution of income in kind.

Primary incomes are those that accrue to institutional units as a consequence of their involvement in production, or their ownership of productive assets. They include property income (from lending or renting assets) and taxes on production and imports, but exclude taxes on income or wealth, social contributions or benefits and other current transfers. The primary distribution of income shows the way these are distributed among institutional units and sectors. The primary distribution account is itself divided into two sub-accounts – the generation and the allocation of primary incomes – but the further breakdown in the ESA95 of the allocation of primary income account into an entrepreneurial income account and an allocation of other primary income account has not been adopted in the United Kingdom.

The secondary distribution of income account shows how the balance of primary incomes for an institutional unit or sector is transformed into its disposable income by the receipt and payment of current transfers (excluding social transfers in kind). A further two sub-accounts – the use of disposable income and the use of adjusted disposable income – look at the use of income for either consumption or saving. These accounts are examined in detail in Chapters 5 and 14 of Concepts, Sources and Methods.[4]

Aggregated across the whole economy the balance of the primary distribution of income provides national income (B.5) (which can be measured net or gross), the balance of the secondary distribution of income in kind provides national disposable income (B.6), and the balance of the use of income accounts provides national saving (B.8). These are shown in Figure 1.

The accumulation accounts (Accounts III and IV)

The accumulation accounts cover all changes in assets, liabilities and net worth (the difference for any sector between its assets and liabilities). The accounts are structured to allow various types of change in these elements to be distinguished.

The first group of accounts covers transactions which would correspond to all changes in assets/liabilities and net worth which result from transactions, for example, savings and voluntary transfers of wealth (capital transfers). These accounts are the capital account and financial account which are distinguished in order to show the balancing item net lending/ borrowing (B.9).

A UK summary accounts, 2005

Total economy: all sectors and the rest of the world

£ million

		RESOURCES							USES	TOTAL
		UK total economy	Non-financial corporations	Financial corporations	General government	Households & NPISH	Not sector -ised	Rest of the world	Goods & services	
		S.1	S.11	S.12	S.13	S.14+S.15	S.N	S.2		
	Current accounts									
I	**PRODUCTION / EXTERNAL**									
0	**ACCOUNT OF GOODS AND SERVICES**									
P.7	Imports of goods and services							370 968		370 968
P.6	Exports of goods and services								326 790	326 790
P.1	Output at basic prices	..	..	..	291 748	..				..
P.2	Intermediate consumption								..	..
D.21-D.31	Taxes *less* subsidies on products	137 347					137 347			137 347
II.1.1	**GENERATION OF INCOME**									
B.1g	**Gross domestic product, value added at market prices**	**1 233 976**	**..**	**80 407**	**152 479**	**..**	**84 509**			**1 233 976**
B.11	External balance of goods and services							44 178		44 178
II.1.2	**ALLOCATION OF PRIMARY INCOME**									
D.1	Compensation of employees	686 195				686 195		1 584		687 779
D.21-D.31	Taxes *less* subsidies on products	133 087			133 087			4 260		137 347
D.29-D.39	Other taxes *less* subsidies on production	17 543	18 051	1 482	–	–1 990		3 272		14 271
B.2g	Operating surplus, gross	320 794	242 623	39 697	12 605	77 791	–51 922			320 794
B.3g	Mixed income, gross	75 675				75 675				75 675
	Statistical discrepancy between									
di	income components and GDP	–916					–916			–916
D.4	Property income	607 948	95 746	355 033	10 282	146 887		160 169		768 117
	Adjustment to property income									
-P.119	for financial services (FISIM)			–51 922			51 922			
II.2	**SECONDARY DISTRIBUTION OF INCOME**									
	National income,									
B.5g	balance of primary incomes, gross	1 258 722	174 994	23 749	144 068	916 827	–916			1 258 722
D.5	Current taxes on income, wealth etc	201 872			201 872			584		202 456
D.61	Social contributions	188 767	3 612	80 106	104 549	500		–		188 767
	Social benefits									
D.62	other than social transfers in kind	213 858				213 858		1 690		215 548
D.7	Other current transfers	200 220	7 248	32 464	104 847	55 661		22 796		223 016
II.3	**REDISTRIBUTION OF INCOME IN KIND**									
B.6g	Disposable income, gross	1 247 635	140 899	46 102	253 561	807 989	–916			1 247 635
D.63	Social transfers in kind	198 984				198 984				198 984
II.4	**USE OF INCOME**									
B.7g	Adjusted disposable income, gross	1 247 635	140 899	46 102	86 162	975 388	–916			1 247 635
B.6g	Disposable income, gross	1 247 635	140 899	46 102	253 561	807 989	–916			1 247 635
P.4	Actual final consumption								1 061 355	1 061 355
P.3	Final consumption expenditure								1 061 355	1 061 355
	Adjustment for change in households' net equity									
D.8	in pension funds	31 210				31 210		–67		31 143
	Accumulation accounts									
III.1.1	**CHANGE IN NET WORTH DUE TO SAVING AND CAPITAL TRANSFERS**									
B.8g	Saving, gross	186 347	140 899	14 959	–15 340	46 745	–916			186 347
B.12	Current external balance							30 452		30 452
D.9	Capital transfers receivable	43 899	19 021	321	15 532	9 025		2 224		46 123
D.9	Capital transfers payable	–42 150	–1 257	–321	–36 508	–4 064		–3 973		–46 123
III.1.2	**ACQUISITION ON NON-FINANCIAL ASSETS**									
	Changes in liabilities and net worth									
	Changes in net worth due to saving and									
B.10.1.g	capital transfers	188 096	158 663	14 959	–36 316	51 706	–916	28 703		216 799
P.51	Gross fixed capital formation								211 862	211 862
-K.1	(Consumption of fixed capital)									
P.52	Changes in inventories								4 071	4 071
P.53	Acquisitions less disposals of valuables								–377	–377
	Acquisitions less disposals of									
K.2	non-produced non-financial assets									
	Statistical discrepancy between									
de	expenditure components and GDP								1 243	1 243
III.2	**FINANCIAL ACCOUNT**									
B.9	**Net lending(+) / net borrowing(-)**	–28 961	21 233	8 168	–42 251	–13 952	–2 159	28 961		–
	Changes in liabilities									
F.2	Currency and deposits	594 201	–	588 529	5 672	–		371 280		965 481
F.3	Securities other than shares	184 545	12 166	136 278	36 157	–56		91 059		275 604
F.4	Loans	530 496	119 671	292 245	6 264	112 316		159 036		689 532
F.5	Shares and other equity	58 577	10 421	48 156		–		122 744		181 321
F.6	Insurance technical reserves	55 963		55 963						55 963
F.7	Other accounts payable	15 258	5 819	2 032	3 623	3 784		–1 096		14 162

A UK summary accounts, 2005

Total economy: all sectors and the rest of the world

continued £ million

		USES							RESOURCES	TOTAL
		UK total economy	Non-financial corporations	Financial corporations	General government	Households & NPISH	Not sector -ised	Rest of the world	Goods & services	
		S.1	S.11	S.12	S.13	S.14+S.15	S.N	S.2		
	Current accounts									
I	**PRODUCTION / EXTERNAL**									
0	**ACCOUNT OF GOODS AND SERVICES**									
P.7	Imports of goods and services								370 968	370 968
P.6	Exports of goods and services							326 790		326 790
P.1	Output at basic prices								..	..
P.2	Intermediate consumption	..	..	..	140 817	..	51 922			..
D.21-D.31	Taxes *less* subsidies on products								137 347	137 347
B.1g	**Gross domestic product, value added at market prices**	**1 233 976**	**..**	**80 407**	**152 479**	**..**	**84 509**			**1 233 976**
B.11	External balance of goods and services							44 178		44 178
II.1.1	**GENERATION OF INCOME**									
D.1	Compensation of employees	686 805	443 406	39 228	139 874	64 297		974		687 779
D.21-D.31	Taxes *less* subsidies on products	137 347					137 347			137 347
D.29-D.39	Other taxes *less* subsidies on production	17 543			17 543			3 272		14 271
B.2g	Operating surplus, gross	320 794	242 623	39 697	12 605	77 791	–51 922			320 794
B.3g	Mixed income, gross	75 675				75 675				75 675
di	Statistical discrepancy between income components and GDP	–916					–916			–916
II.1.2	**ALLOCATION OF PRIMARY INCOME**									
D.4	Property income	581 604	163 375	319 059	29 449	69 721		186 513		768 117
-P.119	Adjustment to property income for financial services (FISIM)									
B.5g	National income, balance of primary incomes, gross	1 258 722	174 994	23 749	144 068	916 827	–916			1 258 722
II.2	**SECONDARY DISTRIBUTION OF INCOME**									
D.5	Current taxes on income, wealth etc	201 912	33 607	8 710	997	158 598		544		202 456
D.61	Social contributions	188 753				188 753		14		188 767
D.62	Social benefits other than social transfers in kind	215 548	3 612	48 963	161 979	994				215 548
D.7	Other current transfers	209 591	7 736	32 544	138 799	30 512		13 425		223 016
B.6g	Disposable income, gross	1 247 635	140 899	46 102	253 561	807 989	–916			1 247 635
II.3	**REDISTRIBUTION OF INCOME IN KIND**									
B.7g	Adjusted disposable income, gross	1 247 635	140 899	46 102	86 162	975 388	–916			1 247 635
D.63	Social transfers in kind	198 984			167 399	31 585				198 984
II.4	**USE OF INCOME ACCOUNT**									
B.6g	Disposable income, gross									
P.4	Actual final consumption	1 061 355			101 502	959 853				1 061 355
P.3	Final consumption expenditure	1 061 355			268 901	792 454				1 061 355
D.8	Adjustment for change in households' net equity in pension funds	31 143		31 143						31 143
B.8g	Saving, gross	186 347	140 899	14 959	–15 340	46 745	–916			186 347
B.12	Current external balance							30 452		30 452
	Accumulation accounts									
III.1.1	**CHANGE IN NET WORTH DUE TO SAVING AND CAPITAL TRANSFERS**									
D.9	Capital transfers receivable									
D.9	Capital transfers payable									
B.10.1.g	Changes in net worth due to saving and capital transfers	188 096	158 663	14 959	–36 316	51 706	–916	28 703		216 799
III.1.2	**ACQUISITION OF NON-FINANCIAL ASSETS**									
	Changes in assets									
P.51	Gross fixed capital formation	211 862	131 525	7 043	7 130	66 164				211 862
-K.1	(Consumption of fixed capital)	–131 093	–71 335	–4 530	–12 605	–42 623				–131 093
P.52	Changes in inventories	4 071	4 292	48	–6	–263				4 071
P.53	Acquisitions less disposals of valuables	–377	–171	–299	16	77				–377
K.2	Acquisitions less disposals of non-produced non-financial assets	258	1 784	–1	–1 205	–320		–258		–
de	Statistical discrepancy between expenditure components and GDP	1 243					1 243			1 243
B.9	**Net lending(+) / net borrowing(-)**	–28 961	21 233	8 168	–42 251	–13 952	–2 159	28 961		–
III.2	**FINANCIAL ACCOUNT: changes in assets**									
F.1	Monetary gold and SDRs	–8			–8			8		
F.2	Currency and deposits	685 762	61 551	559 893	–1 195	65 513		279 719		965 481
F.3	Securities other than shares	150 565	–1 870	149 549	3 075	–189		125 039		275 604
F.4	Loans	413 768	36 118	370 162	5 097	2 391		275 764		689 532
F.5	Shares and other equity	78 733	69 604	38 019	–3 422	–25 468		102 588		181 321
F.6	Insurance technical reserves	55 305	965	107	44	54 189		658		55 963
F.7	Other accounts receivable	14 004	1 190	3 425	5 526	3 863		158		14 162
dB.9f	Statistical discrepancy between non-financial and financial transactions	11 950	1 752	10 216	348	1 793	–2 159	–11 950		–

Figure 1 Synoptic presentation of the accounts, balancing items and main aggregates

Accounts							Balancing items		Main aggregates 1
	Full sequence of accounts for institutional sectors								
Current accounts	I.	Production account	I.	Production account I			B.1	Value added	Domestic product (GDP/NDP)
	II.	Distribution and use of income accounts	II.1.	Primary distribution of income accounts	II.1.1.	Generation of income accountII	B.2 B.3	Operating surplus Mixed income	
					II.1.2.	Allocation of primary income account	B.5	Balance of primary incomes	National income (GNI, NNI)
			II.2.	Secondary distribution of income account			B.6	Disposable income	National disposable income
			II.3.	Redistribution of income in kind account			B.7	Adjusted disposable income	
			II.4.	Use of income account					
			II.4.1.	Use of disposable income account			B.8	Saving	National saving
			II.4.2.	Use of adjusted disposable income account					
Accumulation accounts	III.	Accumulation accounts	III.1.	Capital account			B.10.1 B.9	(Changes in net worth, due to saving and capital transfers) Net lending/Net borrowing	
			III.2.	Financial account			B.9	Net lending/Net borrowing	
Balance sheets	IV.	Financialbalance sheets	IV.3.	Closing balance sheet			B.90	Financial net worth	
	Transaction accounts								
Goods and services account	0	Goods and services account							National expenditure
	Rest of the world account (external transactions account)								
Current accounts	V.	Rest of the world account	V.I.	External account of goods and services			B.11	External balance of goods and services	External balance of goods and services
			V.II.	External account of primary income and current transfers			B.12	Current external balance	Current external balance
Accumulation accounts			V.III.	External accumulation accounts	V.III.1.	Capital account	B.10.1 B.9	(Changes in net worth due to current external balance and capital transfers) Net lending/Net borrowing	
					V.III.2.	Financial account	B.9	Net lending/Net borrowing	Net lending/Net borrowing of the nation
Balance sheets			V.IV.	External assets and liabilities account	V.IV.3.	Closing balance sheet	B.90	Net worth	
							B.10 B.90	Changes in net worth Net worth	

1/ Most balancing items and aggregates may be calculated gross or net.

The second group of accounts relates to changes in assets, liabilities and net worth due to other factors (for example the discovery or re-evaluation of mineral reserves, or the reclassification of a body from one sector to another). Within this second group, the other changes in assets accounts, has not been implemented in the United Kingdom except for the general government financial account (see Tables 11.4–11.6).

Capital account (Account III.1)

The capital account concerns the acquisition of non-financial assets (some of which will be income creating and others which are wealth only) such as fixed assets or inventories, financed out of saving, and capital transfers involving the redistribution of wealth. Capital transfers include, for example, capital grants from private corporations to public corporations (for example, private sector contributions to the extension of the Jubilee line). This account shows how saving finances investment in the economy. In addition to gross fixed capital formation and changes in inventories, it shows the redistribution of capital assets between sectors of the economy and the rest of the world. The balance on the capital account, if negative, is designated net borrowing, and measures the net amount a unit or sector is obliged to borrow from others; if positive the balance is described as net lending, the amount the United Kingdom or a sector has available to lend to others. This balance is also referred to as the financial surplus or deficit and the net aggregate for the five sectors of the economy equals net lending/borrowing from the rest of the world.

Financial account (Account III.2)

The financial account shows how net lending and borrowing are achieved by transactions in financial instruments. The net acquisitions of financial assets are shown separately from the net incurrence of liabilities. The balancing item is again net lending or borrowing.

In principle net lending or borrowing in the capital account should be identical to net lending or borrowing on the financial account. However in practice, because of errors and omissions, this identity is very difficult to achieve for the sectors and the economy as a whole. The difference is known as the statistical discrepancy (previously known as the balancing item).

The balance sheet (Account IV)

The second group of accounts within the accumulation accounts completes the full set of accounts in the system. These include the balance sheets and a reconciliation of the changes that have brought about the change in net worth between the beginning and the end of the accounting period.

The opening and closing balance sheets show how total holdings of assets by the UK or its sectors match total liabilities and net worth (the balancing item). In detailed presentations of the balance sheets the various types of asset and liability can be shown. Changes between the opening and closing balance sheets for each group of assets and liabilities result from transactions and other flows recorded in the accumulation accounts, or reclassifications and revaluations. Net worth equals changes in assets less changes in liabilities.

Rest of the world account (Account V)

This account covers the transactions between resident and non-resident institutional units and the related stocks of assets and liabilities. The rest of the world plays a similar role to an institutional sector and the account is written from the point of view of the rest of the world. This account is discussed in detail in Chapter 24 of *Concepts, Sources and Methods*.[4]

Satellite accounts

Satellite accounts are accounts which involve areas or activities not dealt with in the central framework above, either because they add additional detail to an already complex system or because they actually conflict with the conceptual framework. The UK has begun work on a number of satellite accounts and one such – the UK environmental accounts – links environmental and economic data in order to show the interactions between the economy and the environment. Summary information from the environmental accounts is presented in Part 5. More detailed information on the environmental accounts is available from the National Statistics website at www.statistics.gov.uk/environmentalaccounts.

Some definitions

The text within Sections 1–3 explains the sources and methods used in the estimation of the UK economic accounts, but it is sensible to precede them with an explanation of some of the basic concepts and their 'UK specific' definitions, namely:

- the limits of the UK national economy: economic territory, residency and centre of economic interest
- economic activity: what production is included – the production boundary
- what price is used to value the products of economic activity
- estimation or imputation of values for non-monetary transactions
- the rest of the world: national and domestic

A full description of the accounting rules is provided in Chapter 2 of *Concepts, Sources and Methods*.[4]

The limits of the national economy: economic territory, residence and centre of economic interest

The economy of the United Kingdom is made up of institutional units (see Chapter 10 of *Concepts, Sources and Methods*[4]) which have a centre of economic interest in the UK economic territory. These units are known as resident units and it is their transactions which are recorded in the UK National Accounts. The definitions of these terms are given below:

The UK economic territory is made up of:

- Great Britain and Northern Ireland (the geographic territory administered by the UK government within which persons, goods, services and capital move freely)
- any free zones, including bonded warehouses and factories under UK customs control
- the national airspace, UK territorial waters and the UK sector of the continental shelf

It excludes the offshore islands, the Channel Islands and the Isle of Man, which are not part of the United Kingdom or members of the European Union.

Within the ESA95 the definition of economic territory also includes:

- territorial enclaves in the rest of the world (like embassies, military bases, scientific stations, information or immigration offices, aid agencies, etc., used by the British government with the formal political agreement of the governments in which these units are located)

but excludes:

- any extra territorial enclaves (that is, parts of the UK geographic territory like embassies and US military bases used by general government agencies of other countries, by the institutions of the European Union or by international organisations under treaties or by agreement)

Centre of economic interest and residency

An institutional unit has a centre of economic interest and is a resident of the UK when, from a location (for example a dwelling, place of production or premises) within the UK economic territory, it engages and intends to continue engaging (indefinitely or for a finite period; one year or more is used as a guideline) in economic activities on a significant scale. It follows that if a unit carries out transactions on the economic territory of several countries it has a centre of economic interest in each of them (for example, BP has an interest in many countries where it is involved in the exploration and production of oil and gas). Ownership of land and structures in the UK is enough to qualify the owner to have a centre of interest here.

Within the definition given above resident units are households, legal and social entities such as corporations and quasi corporations (for example, branches of foreign investors), non-profit institutions and government. Also included here however are so called 'notional residents'.

Travellers, cross border and seasonal workers, crews of ships and aircraft and students studying overseas are all residents of their home countries and remain members of their households. However an individual who leaves the UK for a year or more (except students and patients receiving medical treatment) ceases to be a member of a resident household and becomes a non-resident even on home visits.

Economic activity: what production is included?

As GDP is defined as the sum of all economic activity taking place in UK territory, having defined the economic territory it is important to be clear about what is defined as economic activity. In its widest sense it could cover all activities resulting in the production of goods or services and so encompass some activities which are very difficult to measure. For example, estimates of smuggling of alcoholic drink and tobacco products, and the output, expenditure and income directly generated by that activity, have been included since the 2001 edition of the *Blue Book*.

In practice a 'production boundary' is defined, inside which are all the economic activities taken to contribute to economic performance. This economic production may be defined as activity carried out under the control of an institutional unit that uses inputs of labour or capital and goods and services to produce outputs of other goods and services. These activities range from agriculture and manufacturing through service producing activities (for example, financial services and hotels and catering) to the provision of health, education, public administration and defence; they are all activities where an output is owned and produced by an institutional unit, for which payment or other compensation has to be made to enable a change of ownership to take place. This omits purely natural processes.

The decision whether to include a particular activity within the production boundary takes into account the following:

- does the activity produce a useful output?
- is the product or activity marketable and does it have a market value?
- if the product does not have a meaningful market value can a market value be assigned (that is, can a value be imputed)?
- would exclusion (or inclusion) of the product of the activity make comparisons between countries or over time more meaningful?

In practice the ESA95 production boundary can be summarised as follows:

The production of all goods whether supplied to other units or retained by the producer for own final consumption or gross capital formation, and services only in so far as they are exchanged in the market and/or generate income for other economic units.

For households this has the result of including the production of goods on own-account, for example the produce of farms consumed by the farmer's own household (however, in practice produce from gardens or allotments has proved impossible to estimate in the United Kingdom so far). The boundary excludes the production of services for own final consumption (household domestic and personal services like cleaning, cooking, ironing and the care of children and the sick or infirm). Although the production of these services does take considerable time and effort, the activities are self-contained with limited repercussions for the rest of the economy and, as the vast majority of household domestic and personal services are not produced for the market, it is very difficult to value the services in a meaningful way.

What price is used to value the products of economic activity?

In the UK a number of different prices may be used to value inputs, outputs and purchases. The prices are different depending on the perception of the bodies engaged in the transaction, that is, the producer and user of a product will usually perceive the value of the product differently, with the result that the output prices received by producers can be distinguished from the prices paid by purchasers.

These different prices – purchasers' (or market) prices, basic prices and producers' prices – are looked at in turn below. They differ as a result of the treatment of taxes less subsidies on products, and trade and transport margins. Although the factor cost valuation (see explanation in Part 1) is not required under the SNA93 or the ESA95, ONS will continue to provide figures for gross value added at factor cost for as long as customers continue to find this analysis useful.

Basic prices

These prices are the preferred method of valuing output in the accounts. They reflect the amount received by the producer for a unit of goods or services, minus any taxes payable, and plus any subsidy receivable on that unit as a consequence of production or sale (that is, the cost of production including subsidies). As a result the only taxes included in the price will be taxes on the output process – for example business rates and vehicle excise duty – which are not specifically levied on the production of a unit of output. Basic prices exclude any transport charges invoiced separately by the producer. When a valuation at basic prices is not feasible then producers' prices may be used.

Producers' prices

Producers' prices equal basic prices plus those taxes paid per unit of output (other than taxes deductible by the purchaser, such as VAT, invoiced for output sold) less any subsidies received per unit of output.

Purchasers' or Market prices

These are the prices paid by the purchaser and include transport costs, trade margins and taxes (unless the taxes are deductible by the purchaser).

Purchasers' prices equal producers' prices plus any non-deductible VAT or similar tax payable by the purchaser plus transport costs paid separately by the purchaser and not included in the producers' price.

'Purchaser's prices' are also referred to as 'market prices', for example 'GDP at market prices'.

The rest of the world: national and domestic

Domestic product (or income) includes production (or primary incomes generated and distributed) resulting from all activities taking place 'at home' or in the UK domestic territory. This will include production by any foreign owned company in the United Kingdom but exclude any income earned by UK residents from production taking place outside the domestic territory. Thus gross domestic product is also equal to the sum of primary incomes distributed by resident producer units.

The definition of gross national income can be introduced by considering the primary incomes distributed by the resident producer units above. These primary incomes, generated in the production activity of resident producer units, are distributed mostly to other residents' institutional units. For example, when a resident producer unit is owned by a foreign company, some of the primary incomes generated by the producer unit are likely to be paid abroad. Similarly, some primary incomes generated in the rest of the world may go to resident units. Thus, when looking at the income of the nation, it is necessary to exclude that part of resident producers' primary income paid abroad, but include the primary incomes generated abroad but paid to resident units; that is,,

Gross domestic product (or income)

less

primary incomes payable to non-resident units

plus

primary incomes receivable from the rest of the world

equals

Gross national income

Thus gross national income (GNI) at market prices is the sum of gross primary incomes receivable by resident institutional units/sectors.

National income includes income earned by residents of the national territory, remitted (or deemed to be remitted in the case of direct investment) to the national territory, no matter where the income is earned; that is,

Real GDP (chained volume measures)

plus

trading gain

equals

Real gross domestic income (RGDI)

Real gross domestic income (RGDI)

plus

real primary incomes receivable from abroad

less

real primary incomes payable abroad

equals

Real gross national income (real GNI)

Real GNI (chained volume measures)

plus

real current transfers from abroad

less

real current transfers abroad

equals

Real gross national disposable income (real GNDI)

Receivables and transfers of primary incomes, and transfers to and from abroad are deflated using the index of gross domestic final expenditure.

Gross domestic product: the concept of net and gross

The term gross refers to the fact that when measuring domestic production we have not allowed for an important phenomenon: capital consumption or depreciation. Capital goods are different from the materials and fuels used up in the production process because they are not used up in the period of account but are instrumental in allowing that process to take place. However, over time capital goods do wear out or become obsolete and in this sense gross domestic product does not give a true picture of value added in the economy. In other words, in calculating value added as the difference between output and costs we should include as a current cost that part of the capital goods used up in the production process; that is, the depreciation of the capital assets.

Net concepts are net of this capital depreciation, for example:

Gross domestic product

minus

consumption of fixed capital

equals

Net domestic product

However, because of the difficulties in obtaining reliable estimates of the consumption of fixed capital (depreciation), gross domestic product remains the most widely used measure of economic activity.

Symbols and conventions used

Symbols

In general, the following symbols are used:

.. not available

\- nil or less than £500,000

£ billion denotes £1,000 million.

Sign conventions

Resources and Uses

Increase shown positive

Decrease shown negative

Capital account

Liabilities, net worth and Assets:

Increase shown positive

Decrease shown negative

Financial account

Assets: net acquisition shown positive

net disposal shown negative

Liabilities: net acquisition shown positive

net disposal shown negative

Balance sheet

Assets and liabilities each shown positive

Balance shown positive if net asset, negative if net liability

References

1. *Eurostat (1995) European System of Accounts 1995 (ESA95).* ISBN 92 827 7954 8

2. UN, OECD, IMF, EU (1993) *System of National Accounts 1993 (SNA93).* ISBN 92 1 161352 3

3. Office for National Statistics (1998) *Introducing the ESA95* in the UK. ISBN 0 11 621061 3. The Stationery Office: London.

4. Office for National Statistics (1998) *National Accounts Concepts, Sources and Methods.* ISBN 0 11 621062. The Stationery Office: London.

Articles

Akritidis L (2002) Accuracy assessment of National Accounts statistics. *Economic Trends*, No. 589.

Baxter M (1998) Developments in the measurement of general government output. *Economic Trends*, No. 537.

Fletcher D and Williams M (2002) Index of Production redevelopment. *Economic Trends,* No. 587.

Jenkinson G (1997) Quarterly integrated economic accounts – The United Kingdom approach. *Economic Trends*, No. 520.

Jones G (2000) The development of the annual business inquiry. *Economic Trends*, No. 564.

Powell M and Swatch N (2002) An investigation into the coherence of deflation methods in the National Accounts. *Economic Trends*, No. 588.

Pritchard A (2003) Understanding government output and productivity. *Economic Trends*, No. 596.

Ruffles D, Tily G, Caplan D and Tudor S (2003) VAT missing trader intra-community fraud: The effect on balance of payments statistics and UK National Accounts. *Economic Trends*, No. 597.

Sheerin C (2002) UK Material Flow Accounting. *Economic Trends*, No. 583.

Skipper H (2005) Early estimates of GDP: information content and forecasting methods. *Economic Trends*, No. 617.

Soo A and Charmokly Z (2003) The application of annual chain-linking to the Gross National Income system. *Economic Trends,* No. 593.

Tuke A and Beadle J (2003) The effect of annual chain-linking on Blue Book 2002 annual growth estimates. *Economic Trends*, No. 593.

Calendar of economic events: 1980–2006

1980

Jan Steel strike begins

Mar Medium Term Financial Strategy announced

Jun Britain becomes a net exporter of oil

Agreement to reduce UK's budget contribution to EEC

Oct Dollar exchange rate peaks at $2.39 per £

Nov Ronald Reagan elected US President

1981

Jan Bottom of worst post-War slump in Britain

Feb *The Times* sold to Rupert Murdoch

Mar Budget announces windfall tax on banks

Jul Cuts in university spending announced

Aug Minimum Lending Rate (MLR) suspended

1982

Feb Laker Airlines collapses

Mar British naval task force sent to Falklands

Jun Ceasefire in Falklands

Jul Hire purchase controls abolished

Aug Barclays Bank starts opening on Saturdays

Sep Unemployment reaches 3 million

Nov Channel 4 Television begins transmission

1983

Jun £450m EC budget rebate granted to UK

Jul £500m public spending cuts announced

Sep 3% target set for public sector pay

Oct European Parliament freezes budget rebate

1984

Mar Miners' strike begins

Jun Robert Maxwell buys *Daily Mirror*

Fontainebleau Summit agrees permanent settlement of UK's contribution to EEC

Oct Bank of England rescues Johnson Matthey

Nov British Telecom plc privatised

Dec Agreement to hand over Hong Kong to China in 1997

1985

Jan FT Index reaches 1,000 for the first time

Mar End of year-long miners' strike

Dollar exchange rate bottoms out at $1.05 per £

Dec NatWest, Barclays and Lloyds Banks announce 'free banking'

1986

Jan Michael Heseltine resigns from Government over Westland Helicopters affair

Feb Single European Act signed

Mar Budget cuts basic rate of income tax to 29% and introduces Personal Equity Plans (PEPs)

Greater London Council abolished

Apr Chernobyl nuclear reactor disaster

Bus services deregulated

The Independent newspaper founded

Nov 'Big Bang' deregulates dealing in the City

Dec British Gas privatisation

1987

Jan Prosecutions for insider dealing in Guinness case

British Airways privatisation

Mar Budget reduces basic rate of tax to 27%

Oct "Hurricane" strikes Britain

'Black Monday': collapse of stock market

1988

Mar Budget reduces basic rate of tax to 25%; top rate to 40%

BL sold to BMW

Jun Barlow-Clowes collapses

Jul Piper Alpha oil rig disaster

Sep Worst ever UK trade deficit announced

Nov George Bush elected US President

Dec Salmonella outbreak in Britain

1989

Mar Exon Valdez oil spillage disaster in Alaska

Apr Chinese authorities quell dissidents in Tiananmen Square

Jul Blue Arrow report from DTI

Oct Nigel Lawson resigns as Chancellor

Nov Ford takes over Jaguar

Fall of Berlin Wall

1990

Mar Budget introduces tax-exempt savings accounts (TESSAs)

Apr BSE ('mad cow disease') identified

New Education Act brings in student loans

Community Charge ('poll tax') introduced

Aug Kuwait invaded by Iraq

Oct Official reunification of Germany

UK enters Exchange Rate Mechanism

Nov John Major replaces Mrs Thatcher as PM

Privatisation of electricity boards

1991

Jan NHS internal market created

Gulf War begins

Feb Gulf War ends

Mar Air Europe collapses

Budget restricts mortgage interest relief to basic rate: Corporation Tax reduced and VAT increased

Jul BCCI closed by Bank of England

Nov Maastricht agreement signed with UK opt-outs

Dec Mikhail Gorbachev replaced by Boris Yeltsin as President of the Soviet Union

1992

Jan Russia agrees to join the IMF

Feb 'Delors Package' raises EC's spending limits to 1.37% of GDP to aid poorer member states

Mar Budget raises lower rate of income tax to 20%

Midland Bank agrees merger with Hong Kong and Shanghai Bank

Apr Conservatives win General Election

May Swiss vote in a referendum to join the IMF and IBRD

Reform of EC Common Agricultural Policy agreed, switching from farm price support to income support

Sep 'Black Wednesday': UK leaves Exchange Rate Mechanism

Oct North American Free Trade Agreement (NAFTA) signed

Nov Bill Clinton defeats George Bush in US presidential election

Dec Plan for National Lottery announced

1993

Jan Council Tax announced as replacement for Community Charge

University status given to polytechnics

Mar Budget imposes VAT on domestic fuel

Nov Parliament votes to relax Sunday trading rules

First autumn Budget cuts public expenditure and increases taxes

Dec Uruguay Round of tariff reductions approved

1994

Jan European Economic Area formed linking EU and EFTA

Apr Eurotunnel opens

Aug IRA ceasefire begins

Oct Brent Walker leisure group collapses

Nov First draw of National Lottery

Dec Coal industry privatised

1995

Jan EU expanded to include Sweden, Finland and Austria

World Trade Organisation succeeds GATT

Feb Barings Bank collapses

Sep Net Book Agreement suspended

1996

Jan Gilt 'repo' market established

Mar Rebates worth £1 billion paid to electricity consumers after break-up of National Grid

May Railtrack privatised, reducing public service borrowing requirement (PSBR) by £1.1 billion

Aug CREST clearing system initiated

Sep Privatisation of National Power and PowerGen reduces PSBR by further £1.0 billion

1997

Apr Alliance and Leicester Building Society converts to bank

May Labour Party wins General Election

Chancellor announces operational independence for the Bank of England, decisions on interest rates to be taken by a new Monetary Policy Committee

Jun Halifax Building Society converts to a bank
Norwich Union floated on the stock market

Jul Gordon Brown presents his first Budget, setting inflation target of 2.5%

Woolwich Building Society converts to a bank

Bristol and West Building Society converts to a bank

Aug Stock market falls in Far East, Hang Seng Index ending 20% lower than a year earlier

Economic and financial crisis in Russia

Dec The first instalment of the windfall tax on utilities (£2.6 billion) is paid

1998

Apr Sterling Exchange Rate Index hits its highest point since 1989

Mortgage payments rise as MIRAS is cut from 15% to 10%

The New Deal for the unemployed is introduced

Jun The Bank of England's 'repo' rate is raised by 0.25% to a peak of 7.5%

Economic and Fiscal Strategy Report announces new format for public finances, distinguishing between current and capital spending

Aug BP merge with Amoco to create the UK's largest company

Oct The Working Time Directive, setting a 48 hour week, takes effect

Dec The second instalment of the windfall tax on utilities (£2.6 billion) is paid

Ten of the eleven countries about to enter the euro harmonised interest rates at 3.0%

1999

Jan Introduction of Euro currency

Mar Allocation of new car registration letters switched from yearly in August to twice yearly

Budget, energy tax announced

Apr Introduction of ISAs replaces PEPs and TESSAs

Introduction of national minimum wage

Advanced Corporation tax abolished

Jun The Bank of England 'repo' rate reduced to low point of 5%

Nov Jubilee Line extension completed

Dec Pre-budget statement

Year 2000 preparations (Y2K)

2000

Jan Confounding expectations, the millennium passed without any major problems

Feb House price growth peaks at 15% in January and February

Oil price rises to highest level in ten years

The UK company Vodafone takes over the German company Mannesman for £113 billion

Apr Government announces issue of 3G mobile phone spectrum licences

May Share prices in so-called internet companies start falling

Competition commission finds that UK car prices high relative to EU prices

BMW sells Rover and Ford shuts Dagenham plant

Jun Inward investment in the UK hits record levels, with a large proportion made up of take-over deals

Jul Hauliers and farmers stage large scale protests over the price of fuel

Aug European banking regulators investigate £117 billion of new loans made to telecommunications companies, reflecting concerns that banks have overlent to the sector

Nov George W Bush elected US President

Dec US GDP growth slows sharply, following prolonged expansion

2001

Jan The Federal Reserve cuts interest rates twice in one month, by half a percentage point each time

Feb The FTSE share price index falls below the symbolic 6000 points mark

Apr It emerges that Japan's bad debt problems are even worse than feared

May In the UK, business insolvencies are at a six year high

Jun Pharmaceutical company Glaxo sheds 18,000 staff, 7% of its UK workforce

Sep Terrorist attacks in United States. The World Trade Centre in New York is destroyed

Oct The US attacks Afghanistan

Argentina devalues its currency and defaults on its debt of $155 billion, the biggest default in history

Railtrack collapses after the Government refuses to give further subsidies

Nov Bank of England cuts interest rates from 4.5% to 4.0%

Dec In the third quarter of 2001, US GDP shrinks for the first time in eight years

Enron, the 8th largest company in the United States, collapses leading to concerns about accountancy practices, banking involvement and financial market regulation

2002

Jan Euro notes and coins enter circulation

Apr UK tax rises announced to fund NHS

Jun WorldCom collapsed - the biggest corporate failure in history

Network Rail took over the running of the railways

Aug IMF announced a $30 billion loan for Brazil, its biggest ever bailout of a struggling economy

Oct UK housing boom peaks as house price inflation reaches 30%

Nov US Federal Reserve cuts rate to 1.25%, a 40 year low in reaction to fears that the economy is running out of steam

Slowing UK economy forces doubling of the estimate of public borrowing

Dec ECB cuts interest rates for the first time in more than a year, from 2.75% to 2.5%

Stock markets around the world fell sharply over the second half of the year, with the FTSE100 dropping below 4000

2003

Jan Sweden pushes back its preferred date of euro entry from early 2005 to 2006

The FTSE 100 drops by nearly 50 per cent since its peak in 1999, reaching its lowest level since 1995

UK economic growth at its lowest level since 1992, at 1.8% per annum

UK manufacturing jobs fall to their lowest level since records began

Feb UK interest rates reduced by 0.25% to 3.75% due to weak internal and external demand

Mar Iraq war begins

Jul UK interest rates reduced by 0.25% to 3.5%, its nadir since May 1954, due to weak demand

Nov UK interest rates raised by 0.25% to 3.75%

2004

Feb UK interest rates raised by 0.25% to 4.0%

Mar Gordon Brown delivers his eighth Budget statement

May UK Interest rates rise 0.25% to 4.25%

Price of oil breaches $40 barrier

Petrol prices reach 80p a litre

June Federal Reserve of US rises interest rates by 0.25% to 1.25%

UK Interest rates rise 0.25% to 4.5%

July Chancellor Brown releases 2004-05 Spending Review

Atkinson Review of gov't output measurement published

Aug Bank of England raises interest rates 0.25% to 4.75%

Nov George Bush wins US election

2005

Jan Sir Tony Atkinson presents his report on the 'Measurement of government output and productivity in the National Accounts'

Mar Federal Reserve Committee raises interest rates by 0.25% to 2.75%

May Labour win general election

June Oil reaches near $60 a barrel- due to proposed strike in Norway

July G8 Summit in Gleneagles, Scotland

UK wins right to host Olympics in 2012

Aug Bank of England cuts interest rates by 0.25% to 4.5%

Hurricane Katrina hits the US

US crude oil prices breach $70 a barrel

Oct UK House price inflation hits 9 year low of 2.2% in October according to ODPM

Dec ECB raises interest rates by 0.25% to 2.5%

Fed raises interest rates for the 13th consecutive time by 0.25% to 4.25%

2006

Jan Ukraine / Russia gas dispute leads to cuts in gas supplies to Europe

Fed raises interest rates by 0.25% to 4.50%

Mar ECB raises interest rates by 0.25% to 2.5%

FTSE breaks 6000 barrier

Gordon Brown delivers Budget statement

Fed raises interest rates by 0.25% to 4.75%

May Fed raises interest rates by 0.25% to 5.00%

Oil prices have rise above $73 a barrel

State pension age to rise to 68 from 2044

June Oil reaches $74 a barrel in response Iran nuclear dispute

ECB raises interest rates by 0.25% to 2.75%

Fed raises interest rates by 0.25% to 5.25%

July Israel-Lebanon conflict pushes barrel of oil to $78 a barrel

Japan's Central Bank raises interest rate form 0.0% to 0.25% - the first increase in six years

G8 summit held in Russia

Aug Bank of England raises Interest rates by 0.25% to 4.75%

ECB raises interest rates by 0.25% to 3.00%

Sep At $64.55, Oil prices fell to their lowest level since the end of March

Greece announces 25 per cent increase in annual GDP after a new GDP calculation is applied

Oct ECB lifts repo rate by 25 basis points to 3.25%

World output increased by 5.2% in the year to the second quarter

Nov Bank of England raises Interest rates by 0.25% to 5.00%

Dec The pound surges against the dollar - Sterling is at its highest level since Black Wednesday

The European Central Bank increase interest rates by 25 basis points to 3.5%

OPEC agrees to cut oil production from the 1st February 2007

Part 1

Main aggregates and summary accounts

Chapter 1

National Accounts at a glance

Gross domestic product

In 2006 the output of the economy as measured by the chained volume measure of gross domestic product (GDP) was 2.8 per cent higher than in 2005, compared with a rise of 1.8 per cent in 2005 over 2004. The chained volume measure of GDP rose by 71.1 per cent between 1984 and 2004.

Money GDP (at current market prices) increased by 5.3 per cent between 2006 and 2005, compared to a 4.2 per cent increase in 2005 over 2004. Since 1984, money GDP has grown by a factor of 4.0.

Annual changes GDP chained volume measures

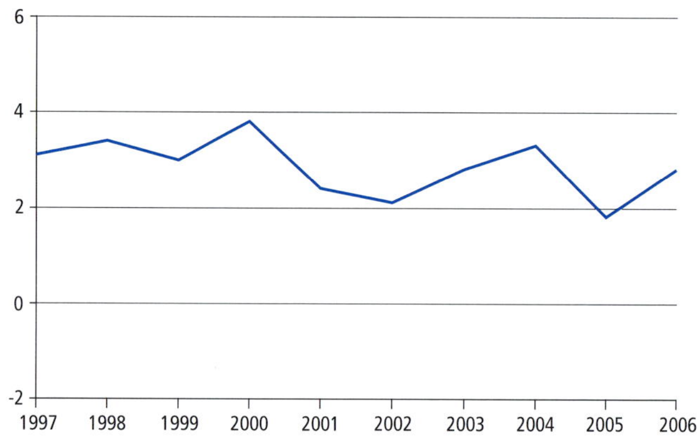

Gross domestic product deflator

This graph shows changes in the implied GDP deflator based on expenditure at market prices.

The annual rate of growth in the GDP expenditure deflator is 2.4 per cent in 2006 over 2005. This is the third consecutive year where growth of the GDP deflator has remained below 3.0 per cent.

Annual changes in the GDP market prices deflator

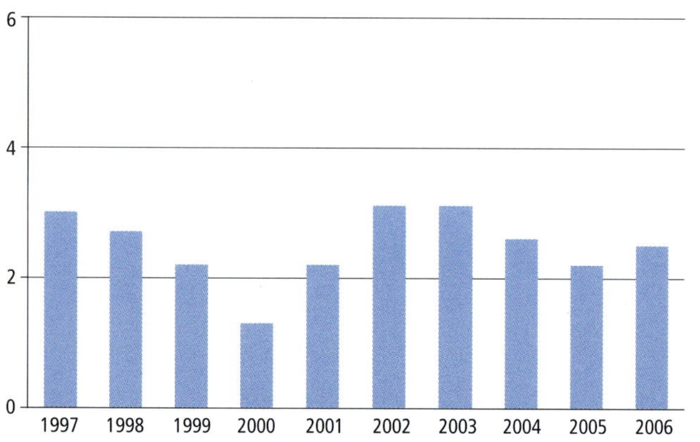

GDP: contribution of expenditure components to growth in 2006

The growth in real GDP of 2.8 per cent in 2006 can be split amongst the various expenditure components. This table shows what effect the change in each component would have had if all other components had remained unchanged. The rise in gross fixed capital formation has been the strongest positive influence on growth. In contrast, net trade in goods and services showed a small negative influence on growth.

Contributions to annual growth in the chained volume measure of GDP, 2006

Component	Change in GDP	
	£m	%
Household and NPISH final expenditure	15,802	1.3
General government final expenditure	5,832	0.5
GFCF	16,013	1.0
Changes in inventories	147	0.0
Net exports	-4,196	-0.4
Other[1]	-171	0.0
Total	33,428	2.8

1 Comprises acquisition of valuables and the statistical discrepancy between the expenditure measure and the average measure of GDP

Gross final expenditure at current prices: share by category of expenditure

Gross final expenditure (GFE) measures the sum of final uses of goods and services produced by, or imported to, the UK. In 2006, just under half of the total GFE was attributed to households and NPISH final consumption (48 per cent). Exports of goods and services accounted for around 21 per cent and the remainder was split between general government consumption (17 per cent) and gross capital formation (14 per cent).

GFE at current prices: share by category of expenditure

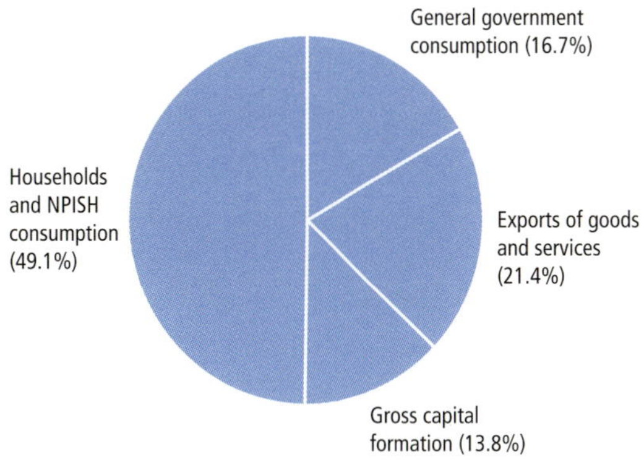

GDP at current prices: share by category of income

The income approach to GDP measures the income earned by individuals and corporations in the production of goods and services. In 2006, over half (56 per cent) of GDP at current market prices was accounted for by compensation of employees, which is largely comprised of wages and salaries. Total operating surplus, which includes corporations' gross trading profits accounted for just over one fifth (23 per cent). Taxes and subsidies on production and imports, included to convert the estimate to market prices, accounted for 12 per cent of the remainder.

GDP at current market prices: share by category of income

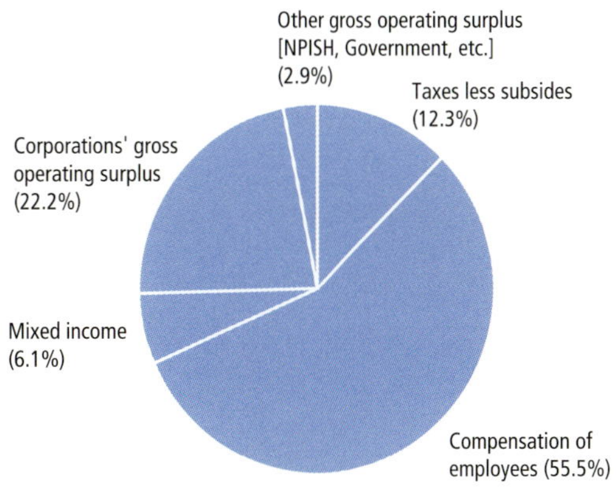

Gross value added at basic prices, by industry

In 2006 compared to 2005, the output of the production sector was unchanged, while the service sector rose by 3.6 per cent. The output of the agriculture, hunting, forestry and fishing sector rose by 2.8 per cent.

GVA at basic prices, by industry

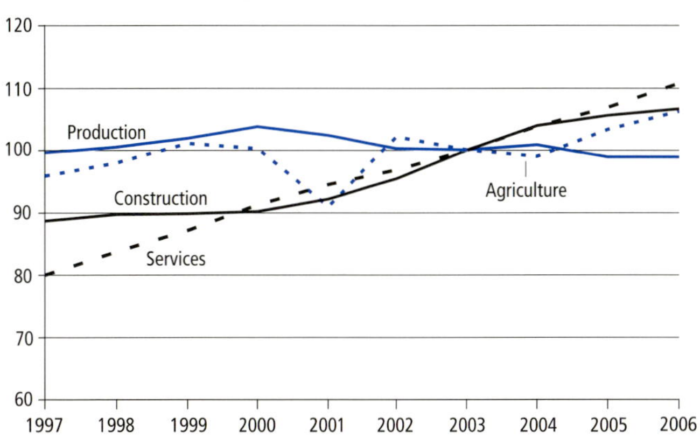

Gross value added at basic prices, by industry, 2003

In 2003, the latest base year, about three quarters of total gross value added was from the services sector, compared to about a fifth from the production sector. Most of the remainder was attributed to the construction sector.

Gross value added at basic prices, by industry, 2003

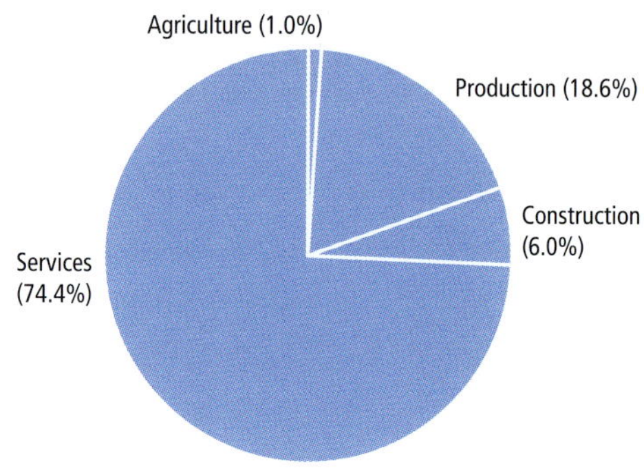

GDP per head

GDP chained volume measures per head rose by 2.3 per cent in 2006 compared to 1.9 per cent in 2005.

GDP per head

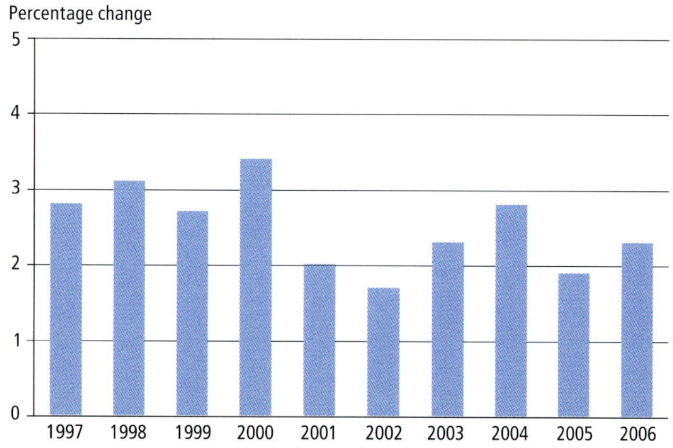

GDP and real household disposable income

Real household disposable income (RHDI) is the total resources available to the households sector after deductions. RHDI rose by 1.1 per cent in 2006, while the chained volume measure of GDP rose by 2.8 per cent.

Comparison of GDP and real household disposable income

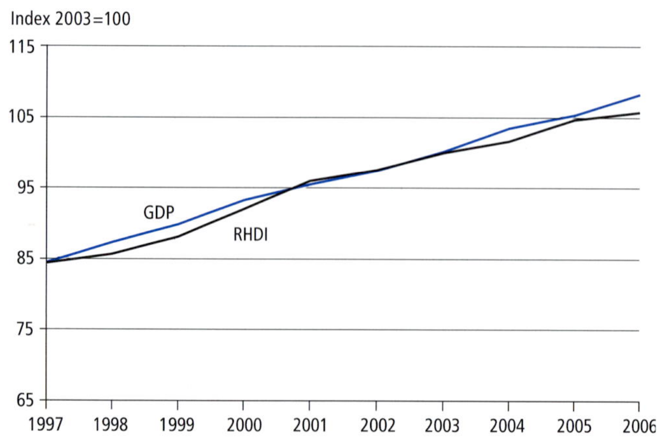

Main aggregates and summary accounts

Please note, that due to the restricted nature of this year's annual process some tables and analysis will not be available in this edition of the *Blue Book* (the reasons why this process is necessary are detailed in the introduction of this publication). This will primarily be reflected in areas where data is reliant on the Input-Output Supply and Use balancing system. Most of the text relating to methodology and processes used in producing the UK National Accounts has been retained in this years publication for information purposes.

UK GDP and national income (Tables 1.1, 1.2, 1.3, 1.4)

Gross domestic product at current prices

The three approaches and the need for balancing

Gross Domestic Product (GDP) is arguably the most important aggregate or summary indicator for purposes of economic analysis and comparisons over time. It measures total domestic activity and can be defined in three different ways:

- GDP is the sum of gross value added of the institutional sectors or the industries *plus* taxes and *less* subsidies on products (which are not allocated to sectors and industries). It is also the balancing item in the total economy production account
- GDP is the sum of final uses of goods and services by resident institutional units (actual final consumption and gross capital formation), plus exports and less imports of goods and services
- GDP is the sum of uses in the total economy generation of income account (compensation of employees, taxes on production and imports *less* subsidies, gross operating surplus and gross mixed income of the total economy)

This is also the basis of estimating GDP. The use of three different methods which, as far as possible, use independent sources of information avoids sole reliance on one source and allows greater confidence in the overall estimation process.

The resulting estimates however, like all statistical estimates, contain errors and omissions; we obtain the best estimate of GDP (that is, the published figure) by reconciling the estimates obtained from all three approaches. On an annual basis this reconciliation is carried out through the construction of the Input-Output Supply and Use Tables for the years for which data are available, and for subsequent periods by carrying forward the level of GDP set by the annual balancing process by using the quarterly movements in production, income and expenditure indicators.

For years in which no input-output balance has been struck a statistical discrepancy exists between estimates of the total expenditure components of GDP and the total income components of GDP after the balancing process has been carried out. This statistical discrepancy is made up of two components which are shown in the accounts, namely:

- **the statistical discrepancy (expenditure adjustment)**, which is the difference between the sum of the expenditure components and the definitive estimate of GDP, plus
- **the statistical discrepancy (income adjustment)**, which is the difference between the sum of the income components and the definitive estimate of GDP (with sign reversed).

As outlined in the framework above, the different approaches to the measurement of GDP provide various breakdowns useful for a wide range of economic analyses. These approaches are described in more detail below.

The income approach

The income approach provides estimates of GDP and its 'income' component parts at current market prices. The sources and methods of this approach are described in detail in Chapter 14 of *Concepts, Sources and Methods*.[1]

As it suggests, the income approach adds up all income earned by resident individuals or corporations in the production of goods and services and is therefore the sum of uses in the generation of income account for the total economy (or alternatively the sum of primary incomes distributed by resident producer units).

However some types of income are not included – these are transfer payments like unemployment benefit, child benefit or state pensions. Although they do provide individuals with money to spend, the payments are made out of, for example, taxes and national insurance contributions. Transfer payments are a redistribution of existing incomes and do not themselves represent any addition to current economic activity. To avoid double counting, these transfer payments and other current transfers (for example taxes on income and wealth) are excluded from the calculation of GDP although they are recorded in the secondary distribution of income account.

In the UK the income measure of GDP is obtained by summing together:

- gross operating surplus
- gross mixed income
- compensation of employees (wages and salaries and employers' social contributions)
- taxes on production and imports

  less any subsidies on production

Mixed income is effectively the operating surplus of unincorporated enterprises owned by households, which implicitly includes remuneration for work done by the owner or other members of the household. This remuneration cannot be identified separately from the return to the owner as entrepreneur.

As most of these incomes are subject to tax, the figures are usually obtained from data collected for tax purposes by HM Revenue & Customs. However, because there is some delay in providing good quality estimates by this method, other sources are used to provide initial estimates.

The operating surplus and mixed income are measures of profit that exclude any holding gains. (Holding gains result when, although no new goods or services have been produced, the value of inventories and fixed assets has increased simply as the result of an increase in the price of the item.)

National Statistics aims to cover the UK economy as comprehensively as possible. It is recognised that some income is not declared to the tax authorities, and to allow for this adjustments are routinely made to the GDP income measure. In 2004 the adjustment for undeclared income was about £18 billion, approximately 1 $^{2}/_{3}$ per cent of GDP.

Although the income approach cannot be used to calculate chained volume measures directly (because it is not possible to separate income components into prices and quantities in the same way as for goods and services) some estimates are obtained indirectly. The expenditure-based **GDP deflator at market prices** (also known as the **index of total home costs**) is used to deflate the current market price estimates to provide a chained volume measure of the total income component of GDP for balancing purposes.

Data on the income components can be found in Table 1.2.

The expenditure approach

The expenditure approach measures total expenditure on finished or final goods and services produced in the domestic economy or, alternatively, the sum of final uses of goods and services by resident institutional units *less* the value of imports of goods and services.

The total is obtained from the sum of final consumption expenditure by households, non-profit institutions serving households and government on goods and services, gross capital formation (capital expenditure on tangible and intangible fixed assets, changes in inventories and acquisitions *less* disposals of valuables) and net exports of goods and services.

This approach can be represented by the following equation:

$$GDP = C + G + I + X - M$$

Where: C = final consumption expenditure by households and NPISH sectors,

G = government consumption expenditure,

I = investment or gross capital formation,

X = exports and M = imports.

The data for these categories are estimated from a wide variety of sources including expenditure surveys, the government's internal accounting system, surveys of traders and the administrative documents used in the importing and exporting of some goods.

To avoid double counting in this approach it is important to classify consumption expenditures as either final or intermediate. **Final consumption** involves the consumption of goods purchased by or for the ultimate consumer or user. These expenditures are final because the goods are no longer part of the economic flow or being traded in the market place. **Intermediate consumption** on the other hand is consumption of goods and services which are used or consumed in the production process. Gross capital formation is treated separately from intermediate expenditure as the goods involved are not used up within the production process in an accounting period.

Exports include all sales to non-residents, and exports of both goods and services have to be regarded as final consumption expenditure, since they are final as far as the UK economy is concerned.

Imports of goods and services are deducted because although they are included directly or indirectly in final consumption expenditure they are not part of domestic production. What remains is what has been produced in the United Kingdom – gross domestic product using the expenditure approach.

Data on the current price expenditure components can be found in Table 1.2.

As well as GDP at current prices the expenditure approach is used to estimate chained volume measures of GDP. The chained volume measure shows the change in GDP after the effects of inflation have been removed (see UK GDP Chained Volume Measures below).

GDP at market prices (£ million)

	Current prices	Chained volume measures
1995	723,080	889,041
1996	768,905	913,800
1997	815,881	942,154
1998	865,710	973,748
1999	911,945	1,003,370
2000	958,931	1,041,517
2001	1,003,297	1,066,217
2002	1,055,793	1,088,108
2003	1,118,245	1,118,245
2004	1,184,296	1,154,685
2005	1,233,976	1,175,916
2006	1,299,622	1,209,344

The reference year for the chained volume measure series in this edition of the *Blue Book* is 2003; the chained volume measure of GDP for 2003 is referenced to, and therefore equal to, the annual current price estimate of GDP for 2003.

Two methods are used to remove the effects of inflation to obtain these chained volume measures. For some series, price indices for particular goods and services – such as components of the retail prices index (RPI) or the producer price index (PPI) – are used to 'deflate' the current price series. For other series, chained volume measures are assumed to be proportional to the volume of goods or services. Chained volume measures of GDP and its main expenditure components can be found in Table 1.3; the calculation of these chained volume measures are explained below.

The production approach

The production approach to the estimation of GDP, which is also referred to as the output approach, looks at the contribution to production of each economic unit; that is the value (at basic prices) of their total output *less* the value of the inputs used up in the production process. The sum of these gross values added, *plus* taxes and *less* subsidies on products for all producers, is GDP at market prices: the production account balancing item. The following paragraphs give a brief overview of the methodology. It should be noted that the production approach concentrates on the basic price concept.

In theory, chained volume measures of value added should be estimated by double deflation; that is, deflating separately the inputs and the outputs of each economic unit (valued in chained volume measures) and then subtracting one from the other. But, because it is hard to get reliable information from companies, double deflation is only used in the estimation of output for the agriculture and electricity industries. So, for most industries movements in the chained volume measures for gross value added are estimated by the use of output series. For industries whose outputs are goods, output can be estimated from the physical quantities of goods produced or from the value of output deflated by an index of price.

Apart from the use of output to estimate chained volume measures of Value Added, which accounts for around 80 per cent of the total of the production measure, a number of other kinds of indicator might be used as a proxy for the change in gross value added. For example, they may be estimated by changes in inputs, where the inputs chosen may be materials used, employment or some combination of these.

In the short-term it is reasonable to assume that movements in value added can be measured this way. However, changes in the ratio of output and inputs to gross value added can be caused by many factors: new production processes, new products made and inputs used; and changes in inputs from other industries will all occur over time. Aggregated over all industries the impact of these changes will be lessened. In the longer term all indicators are under constant review, with more suitable ones being used as they become available.

The estimate of gross value added for all industries (the proxy for the quarterly production measure of GDP) is finally obtained by combining or 'weighting together' the estimates for each industrial sector according to its relative importance (as established in the Input-Output Supply and Use Tables). For each year these weights are based on Input-Output data for the immediately preceding year, except for the most recent years where the weights are based on Input-Output data for 2003. This use of previous years' weights is a feature of the move to annual chain-linking, introduced in this edition of the *Blue Book* (see 'UK GDP Chained Volume Measures' below). Data can be found in Table 2.4.

Headline GDP

The chained volume measure of **gross domestic product at market prices** provide the key indicator of the state of the economy; this is sometimes called 'headline' GDP. The chained volume measure of gross value added at basic prices (GVA), another useful short-term indicator of growth in the economy, is the headline measure for the production approach. It is compiled in a way which is relatively free of short-term fluctuations due to uncertainties of timing. The construction of chained volume measures of **gross domestic product at factor cost** however, requires an adjustment for the relevant taxes and subsidies which can be subject to erratic changes. As a result the factor cost measure is less suitable as an indicator of short-term movements in the economy.

The figure below shows the distinction between market prices, basic prices and factor cost measures.

ESA95 code	
	Gross domestic product, at market prices
D.211	*Less* value added taxes (VAT) on products
D.212, D.214	*Less* other taxes on products (e.g. alcohol duty)
D.31	*Plus* subsidies on products
	Gross value added, at basic prices
D.29	*less* taxes on production other than taxes on products (for example, business rates, vehicle excise duty paid by businesses and operating licences)
	Gross value added, at factor cost

GDP at market prices includes taxes on production, whilst GDP at basic prices includes only those taxes on production, such as business rates which are not taxes on products and GDP at factor cost excludes all taxes on production. A more detailed explanation of taxes follows.

Taxes

Taxes on production and imports including taxes on products (D.2), along with subsidies (D.3) (which can be regarded as negative taxes) make up the factor cost adjustment which represents the difference between GDP at market prices (sum of final expenditures) and GVA at factor cost (sum of incomes). This adjustment has to be added to the sum of incomes to obtain GDP at market prices. The basic price adjustment, which is the sum of **taxes on products (D.21)** ***less*** **subsidies on products (D.31)**, is the difference between GVA at basic prices and GDP at market prices. Details of the taxes which comprise **taxes on production** are included in Table 11.1.

Taxes on production and imports (D.2) are taxes paid during the production or import of goods and services. They are paid irrespective of whether profits are made. They comprise taxes on products (D.21) and other taxes on production (D.29).

Taxes on products (D.21) are taxes paid per unit of good or service produced, sold, leased, transferred, exported or imported. They are included in the prices paid to suppliers of goods and services, so they are included in intermediate consumption at purchasers' prices (except for deductible VAT). Fuel duty is an example.

Deductible VAT differs from other **taxes on products.** It is levied like other taxes on products but producers are reimbursed by government for the amount they pay when goods and services are bought. Intermediate consumption at **purchasers' prices** is the price paid less deductible VAT refunded. The value of sales or production at **producers' prices** also excludes any deductible VAT charged.

Suppliers are required to pay to government any **taxes on products** included in their prices. So the supplier's net revenue from selling the good is the selling price less the taxes on products included in the selling price. This is the **basic price**. It is the price at which market output is measured since it represents the producers' actual revenue.

Other taxes on production (D.29) are taxes which producers have to pay but they are not paid when goods and services are bought and so are not included in intermediate consumption. They are levied separately and are usually linked to the use of fixed capital or to the right to undertake certain regulated activities. Examples are non-domestic rates, vehicle excise duty, and various licence fees where the fee is much higher than the cost of administering the licence and so, in effect, is classified as taxation.

Other aggregates – Gross national disposable income

IIn the discussions so far we have yet to consider the measure which represents the total **disposable income** of the country's' residents. Gross national income (GNI) represents the **total income** of UK residents and is the balancing item of the UK allocation of primary income account. It can also be derived from GDP by adding net employment income and net property income from the rest of the world. However there are two other areas which affect UK residents' command over resources.

First, there are flows into and out of the country which are not concerned with economic production. These are current transfers from abroad and current transfers paid abroad. They include transactions with the European Union, overseas aid and private gifts. An estimate of gross national disposable income (GNDI) is reached by adjusting GNI by the amount of net income received. GNI and GNDI are shown in Table 1.1.

Second, disposable income is affected by the terms of trade effect. Some of the expenditure by UK residents is on imported goods and services; some of the income earned by residents is from exports of goods and services. If UK export prices fall relative to the price of imports then the terms of trade effect would move against the UK; that is, residents would have to sell more exports to be able to continue to buy the same amount of imports. The purchasing power of UK residents would be diminished to this extent. Similarly, if UK export prices rose relative to prices of imports then the effect would be opposite: the purchasing power of residents would rise. An adjustment is made specifically for the terms of trade effect in calculating the chained volume measure of GNDI, also shown in Table 1.1.

UK GDP chained volume measures (Tables 1.1, 1.3, 1.4)

When looking at the change in the economy over time, the main concern is usually whether more goods and services are actually being produced now than at some time in the past. Over time, changes in current price GDP show changes in the monetary value of the components of GDP and, as these changes in value can reflect changes in both price and volume, it is difficult to establish how much of an increase in the series is due either to increased activity in the economy or to an increase in the price level. It is therefore useful to measure GDP in real terms (that is, excluding price effects) as well as at current prices. In most cases the revaluation of current price data to remove price effects (known as deflation) is carried out by using price indices such as component series of the retail prices index or producer price index to deflate current price series at a detailed level of disaggregation. In the 2003 edition of the *Blue Book* a new method of measuring GDP in real terms, **annual chain-linking**, was introduced to replace fixed base chain-linking which was used in previous editions of the *Blue Book*. The real GDP time series produced by annual chain-linking are referred to as **chained volume measures**.

In the UK economic accounts the expenditure approach is used to provide current price and chained volume measures of GDP. Because of the difficulties in accounting for changes in labour productivity it is not possible to obtain direct chained volume measures of GDP from the income data. However, an approximate aggregate measure is calculated by deflating the current price estimates using the GDP deflator derived from the expenditure measure for balancing purposes. The production measure of GDP is largely based on output measures.

The introduction of annual chain-linking

The fixed-base chain-linking method, which was used in editions of the *Blue Book* prior to 2003, produced 'constant price' estimates of GDP whereby the price structure prevailing in 1995 was used to compile data from 1994 onwards. For years prior to 1994 more appropriate pricing structures were used and, in order to link all of the 'constant price' estimates to produce continuous time series, a process of chain-linking was used whereby blocks of constant price data with different price bases were linked together. In the link years, figures were calculated with reference to two consecutive base years to obtain a linking factor so that the whole time series could be shown with reference to the latest base year. This system of fixed-base chain-linking is described in more detail at pages 36 to 38 of the 2002 edition of the *Blue Book*.

In the 2003 edition of the *Blue Book*, the fixed-base chain-linking method was replaced with an annual chain-linking process which produces 'chained volume measures' of GDP. Chained volume measures are calculated by applying the price structure prevailing in the previous year for each year, except the most recent available years where chained volume measures are calculated by applying the price structure prevailing in 2003. The year 2003 is therefore the 'latest base year' for chained volume measures published in this edition of the *Blue Book*. Thus estimates for 2004, 2005 and 2006 are based on 2003 prices, estimates for 2003 are based on 2002 prices and so on. These 'previous years prices' data are chain-linked to produce continuous time series called 'chained volume measures', in a similar fashion to the fixed-based chain-linking described in the above paragraph.

These chained volume measure series are shown in £ million and referenced onto the 'latest base year' which is 2003 in this edition of the *Blue Book*. Current price data therefore equals chained volume measures annually in 2003. The process of annually chain-linking 'previous years prices' data onto a continuous time series referenced onto the latest base year results in a loss of additivity in the annual data prior to the latest base year. Thus chained volume measures prior to 2003 are non-additive in this edition of the Blue Book. Usually the 'latest base year' and therefore the 'reference year' will move forward by one year. However, in the 2007 edition of the *Blue Book*, the 'latest base year' will continue to be 2003 due to the restrictions outlined above. In the 2008 edition of the *Blue Book* the 'latest base year' will move on two years to be 2005.

In the expenditure measure of GDP all of the components are annually chain-linked, as described above, and the chained volume measure of total GDP is aggregated from these. The output approach involves weighting together the detailed components using the contribution to current price GVA (or weight) in the immediately preceding year and annually chain-linking to produce a continuous time series. The application of annual chain-linking to the output measure of GDP is described in detail in an article published in the October 2001 edition of *Economic Trends*.[1]

Annual chain-linking provides more accurate measures of growth in the economy than that provided by the old method of fixed-base chain-linking because more up to date, and therefore more appropriate, price structures are used. The move to annual chain-linking is also consistent with international guidelines laid down in the *System for National Accounts 1993 (SNA93)*.

Index numbers and price indices

Some chained volume measure series are expressed as index numbers in which the series are simply scaled proportionately to a value of 100 in the reference year. These index numbers are volume indices of the 'base weighted' or 'Laspeyres' form. (see Chapter 2 of *Concepts, Sources and Methods*[2]) Aggregate price indices are of the 'Paasche' or 'current-weighted' form. They are generally calculated indirectly by dividing the current price value by the corresponding chained volume measure and multiplying by 100. Examples are the GDP deflator and the households' consumption deflator.

Value indices are calculated by scaling current price values proportionately to a value of 100 in the reference year. By definition such a value index, if divided by the corresponding volume index and multiplied by 100, will give the corresponding price index.

Population, employment and GDP per head (Table 1.5)

Population and employment data are supplementary to the system of accounts. The estimated population of the UK is as at 30 June and includes all those resident in the UK, whatever their nationality. They include members of both UK and non-UK armed forces and their dependants stationed in the UK and exclude members of H.M. armed forces stationed in the rest of the world. This is recognised as not being in strict accord with ESA95 requirements, which are for all UK armed forces and dependants, wherever stationed, to be included and all non-UK ones to be excluded. At present, this is the most appropriate estimate available; it is used to calculate GDP per head. For the latest year, in this case 2006, population estimates are not available at the time of publication. As such, a population projection produced by the Government Actuary's Department has been used.

The total employment data are from the UK Labour Force Survey (LFS) which is recognised as the most appropriate source for coherent national aggregate labour market estimates. The LFS is a household survey which uses definitions which are consistent with the International Labour Organisation recommendations and have been adopted by all EU member countries. The coverage of the LFS is people living in private households and, from 1992, student halls of residence and NHS accommodation; it is not precisely consistent with either the home population data or the ESA95 requirements.

The employment data in the table are estimates of people according to their economic and employment status. They are not comparable with estimates of jobs, as shown in Table 2.5, as some people have more than one job. The total employment figures include people on government sponsored training and employment programmes and, from 1992, unpaid family workers.

UK summary accounts (Tables 1.6.0 – 1.6.9)

The UK summary accounts show the full set of accounts for the UK total economy. The accounts comprise the goods and services account, the production account, the distribution and use of income account and the accumulation accounts. The structure of the accounts is explained in the introduction. Due to the restrictions outlined above, the latest years are not available for all of these tables.

UK summary accounts by sector (Tables 1.7.1 – 1.7.9)

The framework

As can be seen in Table 1.7, the UK sector accounts can be used to show the economic accounting framework in considerable detail by elaborating the accounts in three different dimensions:

- the institutional sectors
- the types of transaction
- the national and sector balance sheets

The institutional sectors

The first dimension involves the breakdown of the current account into institutional sectors grouped broadly according to their roles in the economy. Examples of these roles are: income distribution, income redistribution, private consumption, collective consumption, investment, financial intermediation, etc. Most units have more than one role but a natural classification is to distinguish between corporations, government and households. The rest of the world sector is also identified as having a role although it is obviously not part of the domestic economy.

The types of transaction

The second dimension is that of the type of transaction which relates to the particular account within which the transaction appears. These can be grouped broadly according to purpose, whether current, capital or financial.

Summary of the UK institutional sectors

Sectors and sub-sectors	ESA95	code
Non-financial corporations	**S.11**	
Public		S.11001
National private and foreign controlled		S.11002/3
Financial corporations	**S.12**	
Central bank		S.121
Other monetary financial institutions		S.122
Other financial intermediaries		S.123
Financial auxiliaries		S.124
Insurance corporations and pension funds		S.125
General government:	**S.13**	
Central government		S.1311
Local government		S.1313
Households	S.14	
Non-profit institutions serving households (NPISH)	**S.15**	
Rest of the world	**S.2**	

The balance sheets

To complete the full set of accounts the system includes balance sheets and a reconciliation of the changes that have brought about the change between the beginning and the end of the period. At present the UK does not compile the latter except for the general government sector which are available in the ONS Public sector finances First Release.

In theory the net lending or borrowing from the capital account for each sector should equal the net borrowing or lending from the financial account. In practice, because of errors and omissions in the accounts, a balance is rarely achieved and the difference is known as the **statistical discrepancy** although, across all accounts, when an Input-Output balance is available, these sum to zero. Consolidating the current and accumulation accounts would provide a balanced account which would look like many of the presentations of commercial accounts.

Assessment of Quality

ONS is commited to providing users with ways to assess the fitness for purpose of official statistics and has developed Quality Reports for key outputs in order to communicate quality information, as outlined in an article published in June 2005.[3] Quality Reports are structured around information on the six Eurostat dimensions of quality: relevance, accuracy, timeliness and punctuality, accessibility and clarity, comparability and coherence. The package considers both static and dynamic quality measures and where possible provides both qualitative and quantitative anlaysis. A Summary Quality Report for GDP was published in June 2005[4] and a dedicated area for Quality Information on Economic Statistics created on the National Statistics website.[5]

Accuracy and reliability

One key aspect of quality for many users is accuracy. National Statistics strives to publish timely, consistent, and coherent estimates of GDP that accurately represent productive activity in the economy. The basis of these estimates is strengthened by the inter-relationships within the system, and the subsequent requirement that the many (and often independent) data sources are internally consistent. However, it remains very difficult to comment on the accuracy of GDP.

Estimates of GDP are built from numerous sources of information, including business surveys, household and other social surveys, administrative information and survey data from HM Revenue & Customs. Data is collected monthly, quarterly, annually and in some cases from ad hoc surveys. Some of the resulting estimates that feed into GDP will be firmly based whilst others may be weaker.

Assessing the accuracy of an estimate involves assessing the errors associated with that estimate. Sampling errors can be calculated for estimates derived from random samples. At present, sampling errors are calculated for several surveys that feed into GDP, but for other surveys there remain technical problems to be solved before reliable estimates of error can be formed. A program of work is currently underway which will lead to the publication of sampling errors for all major ONS business surveys.

In addition to sampling errors, accuracy is also affected by non-sampling errors such as limitations in coverage and measurement problems. Though there is limited information about non-sampling errors it is likely that for some surveys non-sampling errors are the more important source of error. Data validation by survey statisticians, additional consistency checks and the inclusion of coverage adjustments where survey sources are known to have shortcomings reduce non-sampling error and improve the quality of the accounts.

Even if the sampling and non-sampling errors of all individual data sources were known, the complexity of the process by which GDP is estimated is such that it would be difficult to build up an overall estimate of accuracy from the component series. The process of bringing together the three approaches to GDP into one measure, which uses detailed supply and demand balances, brings in extra information about the accuracy of the raw data and its consistency with other sources. This adds significantly to the accuracy of the overall estimate of GDP, but this cannot be measured scientifically.

One alternative approach to measuring the quality of GDP estimates is to use evidence from analyses of revisions to growth rates, outlined below. The purpose is to assess the reliability of GDP estimates, referring to the closeness of early estimates to subsequently estimated values.

Assessing the reliablity of the initial estimates of GDP

In order to achieve timeliness, National Accounts estimates are published first as preliminary quarterly estimates, approximately 25 days after the end of the quarter in question. Some components of this preliminary estimate contain a large proportion of estimation, as survey data available at this point is limited. An article in the April 2005 edition of *Economic Trends* provides analysis on the information content, and the proportion of model based forecasts at this and other early stages of the compilation process.[6] This preliminary estimate of growth is therefore often subject to revisions when more comprehensive data become available. In addition, methodological changes in the National Accounts processes might lead to further revisions of the estimates. Looking at the size and direction of revisions is an important way of assessing the reliability of early estimates. This information is also used internally to guide the production of subsequent figures, but the historical level of revisions should not be used by users as a measure of the reliability of current estimates.

In revisions analysis, the revisions to initial estimates of growth rates of GDP are tested to discover if the mean revision is statistically significantly different from zero.

Following an announcement in the March 2004 edition of *Economic Trends*,[7] ONS now publishes information on revisions in the background notes of its First Releases. Text about possible future revisions is included, along with a table showing the mean revision over the last five years. A modified t-statistic is used to determine whether there is statistical evidence that this mean revision is statistically significantly different from zero (if the test is not significant this implies that the observed revisions might have occurred by chance). The table also shows the average absolute revision to the key variables over this period (the average size of revisions over the last five years) as a further indication of the reliability of the latest figures. A summary of the revisions analysis published to April 2005, and the user feedback received was published in May 2005.[8]

Following a second announcement, in *Economic Trends*[9] this revisions analysis is now supported by revisions triangles on the National Statistics website. These are spreadsheets that show how an estimate has evolved over time. The provision of these triangles allows users to produce their own revisions analysis and fully investigate the reliability of national accounts estimates. Revisions triangles are available for GDP and its key components at: www.statistics.gov.uk/statbase/Product.asp?vlnk=13560&More=n

More in-depth revisions analysis is published regularly by ONS in *Economic & Labour Market Review*. The latest results were published in April 2007;[10] relating to data from 1993 to 2002 (the latest data have been published in the last three Blue Books). It looks at revisions to estimates for quarterly GDP growth and its production, expenditure and income components, by stages of the GDP compilation process, where different methods or different data are used at each stage. The stages are as follows:

- **Preliminary Estimate (M1)** – Month One, published around 25 days after the end of the quarter when the estimate is prepared on the basis of a limited proportion of survey data from short-term indicator surveys on the production side
- **UK Output, Income and Expenditure (M2)** – Month Two, published around 55 days after the end of the quarter when the estimate is based on more complete data on the production side, and early information from the expenditure and income approaches
- **Quarterly National Accounts (M3)** – Month Three, published around 85 days after the end of the quarter when fuller survey data for the components of each of the production (output), expenditure and income measures are available from short-term indicators and other surveys, but production remains the main source
- **Blue Book One (BB1)** – the first time the estimate appears in the Blue Book, typically after new and more comprehensive annual data sources have become available, around three to twelve months after publication of the corresponding M1 estimate
- **Blue Book Two (BB2)** – the stage at which Input-Output Supply and Use balancing is usually applied to the estimate for the first time, around twelve to eighteen months after it is first published. As outlined above, this process will not take place this year
- **Post Blue Book Two (Post-BB2)** – the Input-Output Supply and Use balancing is run for the second time, and longer run methodological changes may be introduced to the current data and back series, including revised benchmark data. As outlined above, this process will not take place this year

In selecting the sample period for revisions analysis it is necessary to balance the number of years on which the test is based against the need for the stages to be consistent. The M1 estimate was first published in 1993, so analysis of revisions between M1 and M3 is not possible before this. Similarly, the latest year of data to have appeared in three *Blue Books* is 2003. The main result is that the average mean total revision to real quarterly GDP growth is statistically significant for the period under consideration, by 0.18 per cent. The breakdown by stage is outlined below.

Revisions at each stage of the quarterly constant price GDP growth estimate

1994 Q1 – 2003 Q4	Mean Revision
Month Three (M3) *less* Month One (M1)	0.01
Blue Book One (BB1) *less* M3	0.05*
Blue Book Two (BB2) *less* BB1	0.02
Post Blue Book Two (Post-BB2)	0.10*
Total revisions	0.18*

* Shows that the mean revision is statistically significant.

The results of the revisions analysis by stages showed that the only individual stage with a mean revision statistically significantly different from zero was post *Blue Book* 2. A large proportion of the revisions occur at this later stage of the compilation process. These revisions in the later stages could be caused by changes in methodology. Revisions in the early stages would mostly be due to data replacing early forecasts and models, and more comprehensive data becoming available.

The revisions analysis is also applied to the output, expenditure and income components of GDP. However, only some output components have been published at M1 during the period analysed, all expenditure components are not published until at least the Month Two (M2) stage and most income components are first published at M3 during this time period. Additionally the data for components was only available from 1996 at the earliest, which meant the data windows and revision periods differed from that analysed in the GDP revisions analysis.

Of the components across all three measures, only revisions to gross fixed capital formation, imports and exports are statistically significant. Further investigation of the components of imports and exports showed that the revisions followed a similar trend and thus offset each other to a certain extent.

Summary of the revisions to expenditure components

1996 Q1 – 2003 Q4	% of GDP (2003)	Mean Revision
Household Final Consumption Expenditure	62.8	0.00
Non-Profit Institutions Serving Households Final Consumption Expenditure	2.4	-0.40
General Government Final Consumption Expenditure	21.0	0.00
Gross Capital Formation	16.1	1.30*
Total Exports	25.7	0.81*
Total Imports	-28.4	0.63*

* Shows that the mean revision is statistically significantly different from zero.

Summary of the revisions to output components

1996 Q1 – 2003 Q4	% of GVA (2003)	Mean Revision
Agriculture	1.0	0.47
Production	18.5	0.20
Construction	6.1	0.06
Services	74.4	0.19
Distribution, Hotels and Catering	15.3	0.29*
Transport, Storage and Communications	7.8	0.43*
Business Services and Finance	27.7	0.27
Government and Other Services	23.5	0.06

* Shows that the mean revision is statistically significant different from zero.

Summary of the revisions to income components

1996 Q1 – 2003 Q4	% of GVA (2003)	Mean Revision
Compensation employees	55.6	0.29*
Public non-financial corporations	0.7	-2.39
Private non-financial corporations	18.2	0.13
Financial corporations	3.6	6.04
Other income	9.2	-0.91
Taxes on productsless subsidies	12.7	0.06

* Shows that the mean revision is statistically significant different from zero.

National Statistics regularly looks at revisions to initial estimates and although no correction factors are applied to data series, the information is used in the GDP balancing procedure to identify areas where improvements to early models might be made. Regular monitoring of the revisions to estimates continues, and the results are published in *Economic & Labour Market Review.*

Balances

Further assessment of the reliability of the consolidated economic and sector accounts can be gained by examination of the capital and financial accounts – which should, in theory, show a balance between the net lending/borrowing in the capital account and financial account for each sector. However, because of errors and omissions in the accounts, such a balance is rarely achieved. The resulting statistical discrepancy items required to equate these accounts are shown in this publication (see Table D at Part 3).

These discrepancies provide a measure of reliability as they reflect errors and omissions in the accounts. Some components of the accounts (for example, estimates for general government) provide excellent coverage and are very reliable whilst others (for example life insurance and pension funds) are less fully covered. A detailed table, which looks specifically at the reliability of components of the sector financial accounts, is published in *Financial Statistics Explanatory Handbook*. However, because of the many sources of information that feed into the economic accounts it is not possible to generalise these 'reliability measures' to the aggregate estimates.

Spurious accuracy and rounding to the nearest £ million

One final point must also be made about the reliability of the statistics. In most of the published tables no attempt is made to round estimates beyond the nearest £ million. In some instances this shows figures which appear to have more precision than evidence warrants.

The reasons for this presentation are as follows:

- rounded figures can distort differences over time or between items
- some of the estimates in the tables are fairly precise and, if such an estimate is small, rounding would unnecessarily distort what it shows; yet if such series were not rounded to the nearest £ million the major aggregates of which they are components would appear precise even though other components were heavily rounded
- not rounding beyond the nearest £ million aids users who prepare derived statistics, by avoiding the accumulation of rounding errors which can occur when a number of rounded numbers are manipulated
- in presenting numbers to the nearest £ million, the rounding is usually such that the components add to the total at current prices, so that the accounts balance. In particular the quarterly estimates, both before and after seasonal adjustment, add up to the calendar year totals. However, there are some small differences between the sum of component series and the total shown, due to rounding

Changes since last year's *Blue Book*

An analysis of revisions in current prices since last year's *Blue Book* is shown in Table B. Estimates for private investment in own-account computer software have been revised back to 1970 reflecting the adoption of an improved methodology in accordance with the recommendations of Eurostat and the OECD.

The new methodology is a supply-side approach whereby investment in own-account software is measured using the costs of production. This previous method was based on an historic demand-side survey, updated using assumptions about labour input, by sector. It was recognised, however, that these estimates were likely to understate the activity actually taking place.

In the absence of full supply and use balancing this year, however, the new estimates have been incorporated into the accounts using a simplified approach which does not involve a detailed allocation of the production of own-account software across industries. This simplification is possible because all three measures of GDP are affected equally, that is, it is a balanced revision. Thus GDP levels are revised up through additions to production (value added), income (gross operating surplus) and expenditure (gross fixed capital formation intangible fixed assets). This has been implemented at the aggregate level in years up to and including 2004 (revisions to the detailed industry breakdown of value added is not possible without supply and use balancing).

From 2005, however, a balanced implementation is not possible for *Blue Book* 2007. Whilst revisions have been made to the income and expenditure measures, these will not be automatically reflected in the production measure. This is because the quarterly production measure is constructed using volume indices which are aggregated using industry weights obtained from the supply and use balance in the base year (currently 2003). Since the supply and use balance has not been updated to reflect the own account software change, neither have the weights. This will be addressed in *Blue Book* 2008.

The impact of the new methodology is to increase levels of current price GDP in all years back to 1970; the revision in 2006, for example, is £8.3 billion. The effect on GDP volume growth is less than 0.1 percentage points a year, although the effect on growth is not smooth over the period; increased growth during the 1990s is followed by more variable effects on growth since 2000.

For further background: a summary of the main findings of the OECD task force on computer software is presented in Ahmad (2003: Measuring investment in software, STI Working paper, OECD). ONS's implementation of this method is described by Chamberlin, Clayton and Farooqui (May 2007: New measures of UK private sector software investment).

www.statistics.gov.uk/elmr/05_07/downloads/ELMR_0507Chamberlin_Clayton_Farooqui.pdf

References

1. Tuke A and Reed G (2001) The Effects of Annual Chain-linking on the Output Measure of GDP. *Economic Trends* No. 575.

2. Office for National Statistics (1998) *National Accounts Concepts, Sources and Measures*. The Stationery Office: London.

3. Jenkinson G (2005) *Publishing Quality Information for National Accounts Outputs.*

4. Robinson H (2005) *Summary Quality Report for GDP Data Releases.*

5. Quality Information for Economic Statistics webpage: www.statistics.gov.uk/about/_ns/economicstatistics_qualityreports.asp

6. Skipper H (2005) Early estimates of GDP; information content and forecasting methods. *Economic Trends* No. 617.

7. Jenkinson J (2004) ONS Policy on Standards for Presenting Revisions Analysis in Time Series First Releases. *Economic Trends* No. 604.

8. George E and Obuwa D (2005) *Revisions Analysis published by National Accounts: A summary to April 2005.*

9. George E and Jenkinson G (2005) Publication of Revisions Triangles on the National Statistics website. *Economic Trends* No. 614.

10. Robinson H (2005) Revisions to Quarterly GDP Growth and its Production, Expenditure and Income Components. *Economic Trends* No. 625.

Other articles

- Jones F (1998) Rebasing the National Accounts. *Economic Trends* No. 535.
- Penneck S and Mahajan S (1999) Annual Coherence Adjustments in the National Accounts. *Economic Trends* No. 551.
- Brueton A (1999) The Development of Chain-linked and Harmonised Estimates of GDP at Constant Prices. *Economic Trends* No. 552.
- Andrews T (2000) Improvements to Economic Statistics. *Economic Trends* No. 555.
- Akritidis L (2002) Accuracy Assessment of National Accounts Statistics. *Economic Trends* No. 589.
- Tuke A and Beadle J (2003) The effect of annual chain-linking on Blue Book 2002 annual growth estimates. *Economic Trends* No. 593.
- Ruffles D, Tily G, Caplan D and Tudor S (2003) VAT Missing Trader Intra-Community Fraud: the effect on Balance of Payments and UK National Accounts. *Economic Trends* No. 597.
- Tily G (2006) Improvements to timely measures of service sector output. *Economic Trends* No. 630.

For further reading and access to all these articles see the National Statistics web page dedicated to revisions analysis at:

www.statistics.gov.uk/about_ns/economic_revisions.asp

B Revisions since ONS Blue Book, 2006 edition

£ million

	1998	1999	2000	2001	2002	2003	2004	2005
National accounts aggregates								
At current prices								
Gross domestic product at market prices	4 914	5 378	5 704	6 310	7 026	7 949	7 769	9 261
less Basic price adjustment	–	–	–	–	–	–	–	–509
Gross value added at basic prices	4 914	5 378	5 704	6 310	7 026	7 949	7 769	9 770
Expenditure components at current prices								
Domestic expenditure on goods and services at market prices								
Households	–	–	–	–	–	–	–	92
Non-profit making institutions serving households	–	–	–	–	–	–	–	1 060
General government	–	–	–	–	–	–	–	1 371
Gross fixed capital formation	4 914	5 378	5 704	6 310	7 026	7 949	7 769	6 019
Changes in inventories	–	–	–	–	–	–	–	350
Acquisitions less disposals of valuables	–	–	–	–	–	–	–	–
Total exports	–	–	–	–	–	–	–	4 492
Statistical discrepancy (expenditure)	–	–	–	–	–	–	–	305
Total imports	–	–	–	–	–	–	–	4 428
Income components at current prices								
Compensation of employeees	–	–	–	–	–	–	–	2 187
Gross operating surplus								
Public non-financial corporations	–	–	–	–	–	–	–	847
Private non-financial corporations	3 958	4 344	4 547	5 120	5 642	6 466	6 465	7 072
Financial corporations	956	1 034	1 157	1 190	1 384	1 483	1 304	1 702
FISIM	–	–	–	–	–	–	–	–203
General government	–	–	–	–	–	–	–	–
Household sector	–	–	–	–	–	–	–	–650
Mixed income	–	–	–	–	–	–	–	–437
Taxes on production and imports	–	–	–	–	–	–	–	–208
less subsidies	–	–	–	–	–	–	–	–1 050
Statistical discrepancy (income)	–	–	–	–	–	–	–	1

1.1 UK national and domestic product
Main aggregates: index numbers and values

Current prices and chained volume measures (Reference year 2003)

			1993	1994	1995	1996	1997	1998	1999
	INDICES (2003=100)								
	VALUES AT CURRENT PRICES								
B.1*g	Gross domestic product at current market prices ("money GDP")	YBEU	57.7	61.2	64.7	68.8	73.0	77.4	81.6
B.1g	Gross value added at current basic prices	YBEX	58.2	61.5	64.8	69.0	73.0	77.4	81.1
	CHAINED VOLUME MEASURES								
B.1*g	Gross domestic product at market prices	YBEZ	74.0	77.2	79.5	81.7	84.3	87.1	89.7
B.6*g	Gross national disposable income at market prices	YBFP	71.7	74.8	75.9	78.3	81.9	85.8	87.6
B.1g	Gross value added at basic prices	CGCE	74.8	77.8	79.8	82.0	84.5	87.5	90.2
	PRICES								
	Implied deflator of GDP at market prices	YBGB	78.0	79.2	81.3	84.1	86.6	88.9	90.9
	VALUES AT CURRENT PRICES (£ million)								
	Gross measures (before deduction of fixed capital consumption) at current market prices								
B.1*g	**Gross Domestic Product ("money GDP")**	YBHA	**645 500**	**684 067**	**723 080**	**768 905**	**815 881**	**865 710**	**911 945**
D.1+D.4	Employment, property and entrepreneurial income from the rest of the world (receipts *less* payments)	YBGG	–191	3 348	2 166	556	3 314	12 320	1 270
-D.21+D.31	Subsidies (receipts) *less* taxes (payments) on products from/to the rest of the world	-QZOZ	–4 725	–3 349	–5 220	–3 116	–2 919	–3 651	–3 438
+D.29-D.39	Other subsidies on production from/to the rest of the world	-IBJL	215	286	293	261	208	241	338
B.5*g	**Gross National Income (GNI)**	ABMX	**640 799**	**684 352**	**720 317**	**766 606**	**816 484**	**874 620**	**910 115**
D.5,6,7	Current transfers from the rest of the world (receipts *less* payments)	-YBGF	–734	–2 309	–2 649	–1 902	–3 209	–4 966	–4 435
B.6*g	**Gross National Disposable Income**	NQCO	**640 065**	**682 043**	**717 668**	**764 704**	**813 275**	**869 654**	**905 680**
	Adjustment to current basic prices								
B.1*g	**Gross Domestic Product (at current market prices)**	YBHA	**645 500**	**684 067**	**723 080**	**768 905**	**815 881**	**865 710**	**911 945**
-D.21 +D.31	Adjustment to current basic prices (*less* taxes *plus* subsidies on products)	-NQBU	–66 922	–72 645	–79 331	–83 316	–90 570	–97 116	–105 956
B.1g	**Gross Value Added (at current basic prices)**	ABML	**578 578**	**611 422**	**643 749**	**685 589**	**725 311**	**768 594**	**805 989**
-K.1	*Net measures (after deduction of fixed capital consumption) at current market prices*	-NQAE	–81 312	–83 649	–86 160	–90 145	–91 935	–95 051	–101 055
B.1*n	Net domestic product	NHRK	564 188	600 418	636 920	678 760	723 946	770 659	810 890
B.5*n	Net national income	NSRX	559 487	600 703	634 157	676 461	724 549	779 569	809 060
B.6*n	Net national disposable income	NQCP	558 753	598 394	631 508	674 559	721 340	774 603	804 625
	CHAINED VOLUME MEASURES (Reference year 2003, £ million)								
	Gross measures (before deduction of fixed capital consumption) at market prices								
B.1*g	**Gross Domestic Product**	ABMI	**827 886**	**863 623**	**889 041**	**913 800**	**942 154**	**973 748**	**1 003 370**
TGL	Terms of trade effect ("Trading gain or loss")	YBGJ	–12 587	–17 410	–24 157	–21 525	–12 770	–7 253	–5 461
GDI	Real gross domestic income	YBGL	815 299	846 213	864 884	892 275	929 384	966 495	997 909
D.1+D.4	Real employment, property and entrepreneurial income from the rest of the world (receipts *less* payments)	YBGI	–240	4 128	2 582	643	3 762	13 715	1 386
-D.21+D.31	Subsidies (receipts) *less* taxes (payments) on products from/to the rest of the world	-QZPB	–4 116	–3 987	–5 441	–4 955	–2 014	–2 848	–2 701
+D.29-D.39	Other subsidies on production from/to the rest of the world	-IBJN	191	262	267	233	183	215	298
B.5*g	**Gross National Income (GNI)**	YBGM	**812 764**	**849 652**	**863 298**	**889 308**	**931 614**	**977 454**	**996 838**
D.5,6,7	Real current transfers from the rest of the world (receipts *less* payments)	-YBGP	–924	–2 847	–3 158	–2 200	–3 643	–5 528	–4 842
B.6*g	**Gross National Disposable Income**	YBGO	**811 861**	**846 813**	**860 146**	**887 121**	**927 980**	**971 927**	**992 000**
	Adjustment to basic prices								
B.1*g	**Gross Domestic Product (at market prices)**	ABMI	**827 886**	**863 623**	**889 041**	**913 800**	**942 154**	**973 748**	**1 003 370**
-D.21 +D.31	Adjustment to basic prices (*less* taxes *plus* subsidies on products)	-NTAQ	–85 385	–90 868	–96 324	–99 676	–103 014	–105 165	–107 873
B.1g	**Gross Value Added (at basic prices)**	ABMM	**742 756**	**773 010**	**792 949**	**814 354**	**839 379**	**868 852**	**895 795**
-K.1	*Net measures (after deduction of fixed capital consumption) at market prices*	-CIHA	–93 284	–93 081	–92 781	–95 182	–97 450	–101 125	–105 781
B.5*n	Net national income at market prices	YBET	723 458	761 333	775 586	798 285	837 790	879 460	893 158
B.6*n	Net national disposable income at market prices	YBEY	722 614	758 519	772 455	796 139	834 177	873 931	888 326

1.1 UK national and domestic product
Main aggregates: index numbers and values

continued

Current prices and chained volume measures (Reference year 2003) £ million

			2000	2001	2002	2003	2004	2005	2006
	INDICES (2003=100)								
	VALUES AT CURRENT PRICES								
B.1*g	Gross domestic product at current market prices ("money GDP")	YBEU	85.8	89.7	94.4	100.0	105.9	110.3	116.2
B.1g	Gross value added at current basic prices	YBEX	85.2	89.5	94.3	100.0	105.9	110.4	116.3
	CHAINED VOLUME MEASURES								
B.1*g	Gross domestic product at market prices	YBEZ	93.1	95.3	97.3	100.0	103.3	105.2	108.1
B.6*g	Gross national disposable income at market prices	YBFP	90.7	93.7	97.1	100.0	103.4	104.3	106.2
B.1g	Gross value added at basic prices	CGCE	93.6	95.6	97.3	100.0	103.3	105.2	108.2
	PRICES								
	Implied deflator of GDP at market prices	YBGB	92.1	94.1	97.0	100.0	102.6	104.9	107.5
	VALUES AT CURRENT PRICES (£ million)								
	Gross measures (before deduction of fixed capital consumption) at current market prices								
B.1*g	**Gross Domestic Product ("money GDP")**	YBHA	**958 931**	**1 003 297**	**1 055 793**	**1 118 245**	**1 184 296**	**1 233 976**	**1 299 622**
D.1+D.4	Employment, property and entrepreneurial income from the rest of the world (receipts *less* payments)	YBGG	4 540	11 664	23 443	24 646	26 596	25 734	18 555
-D.21+D.31	Subsidies (receipts) *less* taxes (payments) on products from/to the rest of the world	-QZOZ	–4 098	–3 920	–2 890	–2 596	–1 640	–4 260	–4 496
+D.29-D.39	Other subsidies on production from/to the rest of the world	-IBJL	335	582	519	592	592	3 272	3 275
B.5*g	**Gross National Income (GNI)**	ABMX	**959 708**	**1 011 623**	**1 076 865**	**1 140 887**	**1 209 844**	**1 258 722**	**1 316 956**
D.5,6,7	Current transfers from the rest of the world (receipts *less* payments)	-YBGF	–6 253	–3 426	–6 711	–8 130	–9 920	–11 087	–10 697
B.6*g	**Gross National Disposable Income**	NQCO	**953 455**	**1 008 197**	**1 070 154**	**1 132 757**	**1 199 924**	**1 247 635**	**1 306 259**
	Adjustment to current basic prices								
B.1*g	**Gross Domestic Product (at current market prices)**	YBHA	**958 931**	**1 003 297**	**1 055 793**	**1 118 245**	**1 184 296**	**1 233 976**	**1 299 622**
-D.21 +D.31	Adjustment to current basic prices (*less* taxes *plus* subsidies on products)	-NQBU	–112 248	–114 234	–118 470	–124 738	–132 362	–137 347	–144 663
B.1g	**Gross Value Added (at current basic prices)**	ABML	**846 683**	**889 063**	**937 323**	**993 507**	**1 051 934**	**1 096 629**	**1 154 959**
-K.1	*Net measures (after deduction of fixed capital consumption) at current market prices*	-NQAE	–106 372	–110 434	–116 007	–119 239	–128 427	–131 093	–133 936
B.1*n	Net domestic product	NHRK	852 559	892 863	939 786	999 006	1 055 869	1 102 883	1 165 686
B.5*n	Net national income	NSRX	853 336	901 189	960 858	1 021 648	1 081 417	1 127 629	1 183 020
B.6*n	Net national disposable income	NQCP	847 083	897 763	954 147	1 013 518	1 071 497	1 116 542	1 172 323
	CHAINED VOLUME MEASURES (Reference year 2003, £ million)								
	Gross measures (before deduction of fixed capital consumption) at market prices								
B.1*g	**Gross Domestic Product**	ABMI	**1 041 517**	**1 066 217**	**1 088 108**	**1 118 245**	**1 154 685**	**1 175 916**	**1 209 344**
TGL	Terms of trade effect ("Trading gain or loss")	YBGJ	–8 007	–9 966	–2 932	–	1 226	–6 950	–11 474
GDI	Real gross domestic income	YBGL	1 033 510	1 056 251	1 085 176	1 118 245	1 155 911	1 168 966	1 197 870
D.1+D.4	Real employment, property and entrepreneurial income from the rest of the world (receipts *less* payments)	YBGI	4 880	12 256	24 081	24 646	25 981	24 398	17 121
-D.21+D.31	Subsidies (receipts) *less* taxes (payments) on products from/to the rest of the world	-QZPB	–3 686	–3 393	–2 624	–2 596	–1 762	–2 140	–2 664
+D.29-D.39	Other subsidies on production from/to the rest of the world	-IBJN	305	590	707	592	661	669	664
B.5*g	**Gross National Income (GNI)**	YBGM	**1 034 615**	**1 065 447**	**1 107 294**	**1 140 887**	**1 180 791**	**1 191 893**	**1 212 991**
D.5,6,7	Real current transfers from the rest of the world (receipts *less* payments)	-YBGP	–6 722	–3 600	–6 894	–8 130	–9 691	–10 511	–9 870
B.6*g	**Gross National Disposable Income**	YBGO	**1 027 891**	**1 061 855**	**1 100 401**	**1 132 757**	**1 171 100**	**1 181 382**	**1 203 121**
	Adjustment to basic prices								
B.1*g	**Gross Domestic Product (at market prices)**	ABMI	**1 041 517**	**1 066 217**	**1 088 108**	**1 118 245**	**1 154 685**	**1 175 916**	**1 209 344**
-D.21 +D.31	Adjustment to basic prices (*less* taxes *plus* subsidies on products)	-NTAQ	–112 020	–116 584	–121 657	–124 738	–128 660	–130 432	–133 966
B.1g	**Gross Value Added (at basic prices)**	ABMM	**929 802**	**949 755**	**966 449**	**993 507**	**1 026 025**	**1 045 484**	**1 075 378**
-K.1	*Net measures (after deduction of fixed capital consumption) at market prices*	-CIHA	–109 621	–112 575	–117 430	–119 239	–126 566	–126 926	–118 869
B.5*n	Net national income at market prices	YBET	926 314	953 482	989 809	1 021 648	1 054 226	1 064 967	1 094 122
B.6*n	Net national disposable income at market prices	YBEY	919 584	949 906	982 918	1 013 518	1 044 535	1 054 456	1 084 252

1.2 UK gross domestic product and national income

Current prices

£ million

			1992	1993	1994	1995	1996	1997	1998	1999
	GROSS DOMESTIC PRODUCT									
	Gross domestic product: Output									
B.1g	Gross value added, at basic prices									
P.1	Output of goods and services	NQAF	1 102 334	1 162 863	1 247 189	1 334 533	1 425 859	1 506 744	1 597 123	1 681 412
-P.2	*less* intermediate consumption	-NQAJ	–552 037	–584 285	–635 767	–690 784	–740 270	–781 433	–828 529	–875 423
B.1g	**Total Gross Value Added**	ABML	**550 297**	**578 578**	**611 422**	**643 749**	**685 589**	**725 311**	**768 594**	**805 989**
D.211	Value added taxes (VAT) on products	QYRC	41 339	42 208	45 806	47 984	50 919	54 964	56 541	61 512
D.212,4	Other taxes on products	NSUI	29 033	30 853	33 507	38 068	39 972	43 076	46 999	50 512
-D.31	*less* subsidies on products	-NZHC	–5 893	–6 139	–6 668	–6 721	–7 575	–7 470	–6 424	–6 068
B.1*g	**Gross Domestic Product at market prices**	YBHA	**614 776**	**645 500**	**684 067**	**723 080**	**768 905**	**815 881**	**865 710**	**911 945**
	Gross domestic product: Expenditure									
P.3	Final consumption expenditure									
P.41	Actual individual consumption									
P.3	Household final consumption expenditure	ABPB	377 780	399 875	419 825	441 085	472 711	501 290	534 153	567 994
P.3	Final consumption expenditure of NPISH	ABNV	10 889	14 012	15 303	16 408	18 129	19 372	20 837	21 874
P.31	Individual govt. final consumption expenditure	NNAQ	74 878	75 600	78 970	82 313	87 519	90 004	94 783	102 742
P.41	Total actual individual consumption	NQEO	463 547	489 487	514 098	539 806	578 359	610 666	649 773	692 610
P.32	Collective govt. final consumption expenditure	NQEP	56 684	58 041	59 142	60 585	61 107	60 550	61 626	66 778
P.3	Total final consumption expenditure	ABKW	520 231	547 528	573 240	600 391	639 466	671 216	711 399	759 388
P.3	Households and NPISH	NSSG	388 669	413 887	435 128	457 493	490 840	520 662	554 990	589 868
P.3	Central government	NMBJ	79 842	82 903	85 503	87 958	92 468	93 889	97 145	103 580
P.3	Local government	NMMT	51 720	50 738	52 609	54 940	56 158	56 665	59 264	65 940
P.5	Gross capital formation									
P.51	Gross fixed capital formation	NPQX	103 913	103 997	111 623	121 364	130 346	138 307	155 997	161 722
P.52	Changes in inventories	ABMP	–1 937	329	3 708	4 512	1 771	4 621	5 026	6 060
P.53	Acquisitions less disposals of valuables	NPJO	17	–29	113	–121	–160	–27	429	229
P.5	Total gross capital formation	NQFM	101 993	104 297	115 444	125 755	131 957	142 901	161 452	168 011
P.6	Exports of goods and services	KTMW	144 211	163 800	180 758	204 151	225 158	234 019	232 034	239 782
-P.7	*less* imports of goods and services	-KTMX	–151 659	–170 125	–185 375	–207 217	–227 676	–232 255	–239 175	–255 236
B.11	External balance of goods and services	KTMY	–7 448	–6 325	–4 617	–3 066	–2 518	1 764	–7 141	–15 454
de	Statistical discrepancy between expenditure components and GDP	RVFD	–	–	–	–	–	–	–	–
B.1*g	**Gross Domestic Product at market prices**	YBHA	**614 776**	**645 500**	**684 067**	**723 080**	**768 905**	**815 881**	**865 710**	**911 945**
	Gross domestic product: Income									
B.2g	Operating surplus, gross									
	Non-financial corporations									
	Public non-financial corporations	NRJT	5 986	6 844	7 143	8 902	8 815	7 249	7 754	7 678
	Private non-financial corporations	NRJK	108 489	118 761	135 868	146 226	162 704	174 906	178 804	183 283
	Financial corporations	NQNV	14 234	19 123	21 754	19 058	19 826	18 504	19 386	17 010
-P.119	Adjustment for financial services	-NSRV	–19 086	–19 569	–23 119	–23 215	–22 727	–22 741	–27 658	–29 468
	General government	NMXV	7 373	7 520	7 926	8 500	8 813	9 003	8 999	9 262
	Households and non-profit institutions serving households	QWLS	31 552	33 018	35 332	38 055	39 986	42 877	47 642	51 195
B.2g	Total operating surplus, gross	ABNF	148 548	165 697	184 904	197 526	217 417	229 798	234 927	238 960
B.3	Mixed income	QWLT	39 621	42 350	43 678	46 032	50 229	51 310	52 823	55 734
D.1	Compensation of employees	HAEA	347 546	356 595	369 146	386 035	403 887	429 967	466 080	495 793
D.2	Taxes on production and imports	NZGX	86 050	88 127	94 034	101 266	105 936	113 226	119 355	128 527
-D.3	*less* subsidies	-AAXJ	–6 989	–7 269	–7 695	–7 779	–8 564	–8 420	–7 475	–7 069
di	Statistical discrepancy between income components and GDP	RVFC	–	–	–	–	–	–	–	–
B.1*g	**Gross domestic product at market prices**	YBHA	**614 776**	**645 500**	**684 067**	**723 080**	**768 905**	**815 881**	**865 710**	**911 945**
	GROSS NATIONAL INCOME at market prices									
B.1*g	**Gross Domestic Product at market prices**	YBHA	**614 776**	**645 500**	**684 067**	**723 080**	**768 905**	**815 881**	**865 710**	**911 945**
D.1	Compensation of employees									
	receipts from the rest of the world (ROW)	KTMN	551	595	681	887	911	1 007	840	960
	less payments to the rest of the world (ROW)	-KTMO	–600	–560	–851	–1 183	–818	–924	–850	–759
D.1	Total	KTMP	–49	35	–170	–296	93	83	–10	201
	less Taxes on products paid to the ROW									
-D.21+D.31	*plus* Subsidies received from the ROW	-QZOZ	–4 319	–4 725	–3 349	–5 220	–3 116	–2 919	–3 651	–3 438
+D.29-D.39	Other subsidies on production	-IBJL	66	215	286	293	261	208	241	338
D.4	Property and entrepreneurial income									
	receipts from the rest of the world	HMBN	66 153	72 333	73 702	87 195	91 421	95 435	103 388	101 952
	less payments to the rest of the world	-HMBO	–65 976	–72 559	–70 184	–84 735	–90 958	–92 204	–91 058	–100 883
D.4	Total	HMBM	177	–226	3 518	2 460	463	3 231	12 330	1 069
B.5*g	**Gross National Income at market prices**	ABMX	**610 651**	**640 799**	**684 352**	**720 317**	**766 606**	**816 484**	**874 620**	**910 115**

1.2 UK gross domestic product and national income

Current prices

continued £ million

			2000	2001	2002	2003	2004	2005	2006
	GROSS DOMESTIC PRODUCT								
	Gross domestic product: Output								
B.1g	Gross value added, at basic prices								
P.1	Output of goods and services	NQAF	1 778 350	1 859 652	1 944 508	2 046 891	2 159 602	..	..
-P.2	*less* intermediate consumption	-NQAJ	–931 667	–970 589	–1 007 185	–1 053 384	–1 107 668	..	..
B.1g	**Total Gross Value Added**	ABML	**846 683**	**889 063**	**937 323**	**993 507**	**1 051 934**	**1 096 629**	**1 154 959**
D.211	Value added taxes (VAT) on products	QYRC	64 189	67 097	71 059	77 335	81 540	83 382	87 679
D.212,4	Other taxes on products	NSUI	54 086	52 845	53 945	54 813	58 102	59 076	62 752
-D.31	*less* subsidies on products	-NZHC	–6 027	–5 708	–6 534	–7 410	–7 280	–5 111	–5 768
B.1*g	**Gross Domestic Product at market prices**	YBHA	**958 931**	**1 003 297**	**1 055 793**	**1 118 245**	**1 184 296**	**1 233 976**	**1 299 622**
	Gross domestic product: Expenditure								
P.3	Final consumption expenditure								
P.41	Actual individual consumption								
P.3	Household final consumption expenditure	ABPB	600 826	632 496	664 562	697 160	732 531	760 869	794 768
P.3	Final consumption expenditure of NPISH	ABNV	23 169	24 720	25 968	27 185	28 953	31 585	33 313
P.31	Individual govt. final consumption expenditure	NNAQ	109 297	118 458	130 816	143 954	155 811	167 399	178 552
P.41	Total actual individual consumption	NQEO	733 292	775 674	821 346	868 299	917 295	959 853	1 006 633
P.32	Collective govt. final consumption expenditure	NQEP	72 554	76 045	81 648	88 745	94 897	101 502	108 260
P.3	Total final consumption expenditure	ABKW	805 846	851 719	902 994	957 044	1 012 192	1 061 355	1 114 893
P.3	Households and NPISH	NSSG	623 995	657 216	690 530	724 345	761 484	792 454	828 081
P.3	Central government	NMBJ	110 807	118 762	130 326	142 639	152 325	162 751	175 474
P.3	Local government	NMMT	71 044	75 741	82 138	90 060	98 383	106 150	111 338
P.5	Gross capital formation								
P.51	Gross fixed capital formation	NPQX	167 172	171 782	180 551	186 700	202 260	211 862	234 751
P.52	Changes in inventories	ABMP	5 271	6 189	2 909	3 983	4 856	4 071	3 735
P.53	Acquisitions less disposals of valuables	NPJO	3	396	214	–37	–37	–377	45
P.5	Total gross capital formation	NQFM	172 446	178 367	183 674	190 646	207 079	215 556	238 531
P.6	Exports of goods and services	KTMW	267 602	273 140	276 511	285 397	298 694	326 790	369 691
-P.7	*less* imports of goods and services	-KTMX	–286 963	–299 929	–307 386	–314 842	–333 669	–370 968	–424 128
B.11	External balance of goods and services	KTMY	–19 361	–26 789	–30 875	–29 445	–34 975	–44 178	–54 437
de	Statistical discrepancy between expenditure components and GDP	RVFD	–	–	–	–	–	1 243	635
B.1*g	**Gross Domestic Product at market prices**	YBHA	**958 931**	**1 003 297**	**1 055 793**	**1 118 245**	**1 184 296**	**1 233 976**	**1 299 622**
	Gross domestic product: Income								
B.2g	Operating surplus, gross								
	Non-financial corporations								
	Public non-financial corporations	NRJT	7 188	6 892	6 657	7 265	6 653	8 494	9 464
	Private non-financial corporations	NRJK	189 745	191 062	195 548	208 945	226 203	234 129	246 648
	Financial corporations	NQNV	13 555	13 242	33 614	41 419	47 324	39 697	45 710
-P.119	Adjustment for financial services	-NSRV	–33 465	–33 648	–41 136	–45 370	–50 165	–51 922	–57 566
	General government	NMXV	9 542	9 796	10 289	10 807	11 681	12 605	13 650
	Households and non-profit institutions serving households	QWLS	53 960	59 083	62 544	67 935	72 709	77 791	82 425
B.2g	Total operating surplus, gross	ABNF	240 525	246 427	267 516	291 001	314 405	320 794	340 331
B.3	Mixed income	QWLT	57 805	62 121	65 771	69 122	71 958	75 675	78 864
D.1	Compensation of employees	HAEA	532 179	564 194	587 396	616 893	648 717	686 805	721 287
D.2	Taxes on production and imports	NZGX	135 358	137 507	143 117	150 665	158 587	162 059	171 518
-D.3	*less* subsidies	-AAXJ	–6 936	–6 952	–8 007	–9 436	–9 371	–10 441	–11 827
di	Statistical discrepancy between income components and GDP	RVFC	–	–	–	–	–	–916	–551
B.1*g	**Gross domestic product at market prices**	YBHA	**958 931**	**1 003 297**	**1 055 793**	**1 118 245**	**1 184 296**	**1 233 976**	**1 299 622**
	GROSS NATIONAL INCOME at market prices								
B.1*g	**Gross Domestic Product at market prices**	YBHA	**958 931**	**1 003 297**	**1 055 793**	**1 118 245**	**1 184 296**	**1 233 976**	**1 299 622**
D.1	Compensation of employees								
	receipts from the rest of the world (ROW)	KTMN	1 032	1 087	1 121	1 116	1 171	974	1 047
	less payments to the rest of the world (ROW)	-KTMO	–882	–1 021	–1 054	–1 057	–1 100	–1 584	–1 785
D.1	Total	KTMP	150	66	67	59	71	–610	–738
-D.21+D.31	*less* Taxes on products paid to the ROW *plus* Subsidies received from the ROW	-QZOZ	–4 098	–3 920	–2 890	–2 596	–1 640	–4 260	–4 496
+D.29-D.39	Other subsidies on production	-IBJL	335	582	519	592	592	3 272	3 275
D.4	Property and entrepreneurial income								
	receipts from the rest of the world	HMBN	134 114	139 848	123 505	124 881	141 030	186 513	240 303
	less payments to the rest of the world	-HMBO	–129 724	–128 250	–100 129	–100 294	–114 505	–160 169	–221 010
D.4	Total	HMBM	4 390	11 598	23 376	24 587	26 525	26 344	19 293
B.5*g	**Gross National Income at market prices**	ABMX	**959 708**	**1 011 623**	**1 076 865**	**1 140 887**	**1 209 844**	**1 258 722**	**1 316 956**

1 These series are not available for the latest year.

1.3 UK gross domestic product

Chained volume measures (Reference year 2003)

£ million

			1992	1993	1994	1995	1996	1997	1998	1999
	GROSS DOMESTIC PRODUCT									
	Gross domestic product: expenditure approach									
P.3	Final consumption expenditure									
P.41	Actual individual consumption									
P.3	Household final consumption expenditure	ABPF	483 061	496 212	510 055	518 754	539 138	558 064	579 342	606 648
P.3	Final consumption expenditure of non-profit institutions serving households	ABNU	18 185	20 206	21 769	22 557	22 757	23 391	25 092	25 023
P.31	Individual government final consumption expenditure	NSZK	113 477	116 742	117 360	120 125	122 749	124 199	125 944	129 050
P.41	Total actual individual consumption	YBIO	612 886	630 933	647 225	659 279	682 820	704 229	729 353	760 172
P.32	Collective government final consumption expenditure	NSZL	78 687	74 399	75 666	75 551	74 582	72 383	72 925	76 926
P.3	Total final consumption expenditure	ABKX	691 097	705 126	722 676	734 635	757 269	776 609	802 340	837 119
P.5	Gross capital formation									
P.51	Gross fixed capital formation	NPQR	119 459	119 167	124 640	128 300	135 270	144 472	164 249	169 117
P.52	Changes in inventories	ABMQ	−2 599	−256	4 259	3 919	1 231	3 394	4 291	5 803
P.53	Acquisitions less disposals of valuables	NPJP	−26	−39	−1	−60	−75	−35	30	–
P.5	Total gross capital formation	NPQU	116 055	118 322	128 539	132 866	136 937	148 592	169 054	175 118
	Gross domestic final expenditure	YBIK	804 370	820 598	849 092	865 578	892 221	924 100	971 681	1 012 457
P.6	Exports of goods and services	KTMZ	157 387	164 330	179 521	196 507	213 902	231 494	238 344	247 289
	Gross final expenditure	ABME	954 073	977 618	1 022 897	1 058 750	1 104 754	1 155 838	1 209 699	1 259 336
-P.7	*less* imports of goods and services	-KTNB	−157 204	−162 367	−171 828	−181 413	−199 172	−218 613	−238 834	−257 809
de	Statistical discrepancy between expenditure components and GDP	GIXS	–	–	–	–	–	–	–	–
B.1*g	**Gross Domestic Product at market prices**	ABMI	**809 540**	**827 886**	**863 623**	**889 041**	**913 800**	**942 154**	**973 748**	**1 003 370**
B.11	*of which* External balance of goods and services	KTNC	183	1 963	7 693	15 094	14 730	12 881	−490	−10 520

1.3 UK gross domestic product

Chained volume measures (Reference year 2003)

continued £ million

			2000	2001	2002	2003	2004	2005	2006
	GROSS DOMESTIC PRODUCT								
	Gross domestic product: expenditure approach								
P.3	Final consumption expenditure								
P.41	Actual individual consumption								
P.3	Household final consumption expenditure	ABPF	633 662	653 326	676 833	697 160	721 434	732 005	746 030
P.3	Final consumption expenditure of non-profit institutions serving households	ABNU	27 177	27 155	27 130	27 185	27 327	28 167	29 944
P.31	Individual government final consumption expenditure	NSZK	131 426	134 867	139 546	143 954	148 294	150 996	153 262
P.41	Total actual individual consumption	YBIO	792 076	815 286	843 504	868 299	897 055	911 168	929 237
P.32	Collective government final consumption expenditure	NSZL	80 829	82 502	85 331	88 745	91 835	95 531	99 097
P.3	Total final consumption expenditure	ABKX	872 899	897 801	928 849	957 044	988 890	1 006 699	1 028 334
P.5	Gross capital formation								
P.51	Gross fixed capital formation	NPQR	173 710	178 203	184 701	186 700	197 655	200 654	216 667
P.52	Changes in inventories	ABMQ	4 648	5 577	2 289	3 982	4 597	3 611	3 758
P.53	Acquisitions less disposals of valuables	NPJP	–28	342	183	–37	–42	–354	66
P.5	Total gross capital formation	NPQU	178 660	184 462	187 374	190 646	202 210	203 911	220 491
	Gross domestic final expenditure	YBIK	1 051 600	1 082 333	1 116 239	1 147 690	1 191 099	1 210 610	1 248 825
P.6	Exports of goods and services	KTMZ	269 830	277 694	280 593	285 397	299 289	323 749	361 541
	Gross final expenditure	ABME	1 321 604	1 360 205	1 396 862	1 433 087	1 490 388	1 534 359	1 610 366
-P.7	*less* imports of goods and services	-KTNB	–281 081	–294 449	–308 706	–314 842	–335 703	–359 626	–401 614
de	Statistical discrepancy between expenditure components and GDP	GIXS	–	–	–	–	–	1 183	592
B.1*g	**Gross Domestic Product at market prices**	ABMI	**1 041 517**	**1 066 217**	**1 088 108**	**1 118 245**	**1 154 685**	**1 175 916**	**1 209 344**
B.11	*of which* External balance of goods and services	KTNC	–11 251	–16 755	–28 113	–29 445	–36 414	–35 877	–40 073

1.4 Indices of value, volume, prices and costs

Indices 2003=100

			1992	1993	1994	1995	1996	1997	1998	1999
	INDICES OF VALUE AT CURRENT PRICES									
	Gross measures, before deduction of fixed capital consumption									
	at current market prices									
B.1*g	Gross domestic product at current market prices ("money GDP")	YBEU	55.0	57.7	61.2	64.7	68.8	73.0	77.4	81.6
B.5*g	Gross national income at current market prices	YBEV	53.5	56.2	60.0	63.1	67.2	71.6	76.7	79.8
B.6*g	Gross national disposable income at current market prices	YBEW	53.8	56.5	60.2	63.4	67.5	71.8	76.8	80.0
	at current basic prices									
B.1g	Gross value added at current basic prices	YBEX	55.4	58.2	61.5	64.8	69.0	73.0	77.4	81.1
	CHAINED VOLUME INDICES ("real terms")									
	Gross measures, before deduction of fixed capital consumption at market prices									
B.1*g	Gross domestic product at market prices	YBEZ	72.4	74.0	77.2	79.5	81.7	84.3	87.1	89.7
	Categories of GDP expenditure									
P.3	Final consumption expenditure	YBFA	72.2	73.7	75.5	76.8	79.1	81.1	83.8	87.5
	by households and non-profit institutions serving households	YBFB	69.2	71.3	73.4	74.7	77.6	80.3	83.4	87.2
	by general government	YBFC	82.9	82.3	83.2	84.2	84.8	84.4	85.3	88.5
P.51	Gross fixed capital formation	YBFG	63.0	63.2	66.5	68.9	72.6	77.6	88.2	90.8
	Gross domestic final expenditure	YBFH	70.1	71.5	74.0	75.4	77.7	80.5	84.7	88.2
P.6	Exports of goods and services	YBFI	55.1	57.6	62.9	68.9	74.9	81.1	83.5	86.6
	of which, goods	YBFJ	58.1	60.3	66.3	72.8	78.4	84.9	85.8	88.6
	services	YBFK	48.9	51.9	55.7	60.3	67.8	73.3	79.2	83.2
	Gross final expenditure	YBFF	66.6	68.2	71.4	73.9	77.1	80.7	84.4	87.9
P.7	Imports of goods and services	YBFL	49.9	51.6	54.6	57.6	63.3	69.4	75.9	81.9
	of which, goods	YBFM	50.9	52.8	55.1	58.5	64.1	70.4	76.4	81.5
	services	YBFN	46.6	47.3	52.6	54.4	60.4	66.2	74.1	83.3
B.5*g	Gross national income at market prices	YBFO	69.7	71.2	74.5	75.7	77.9	81.7	85.7	87.4
B.6*g	Gross national disposable income at market prices	YBFP	70.1	71.7	74.8	75.9	78.3	81.9	85.8	87.6
	Adjustment to basic prices									
D.21-D.31	Taxes *less* subsidies on products	YBFQ	67.1	68.5	72.8	77.2	79.9	82.6	84.3	86.5
B.1g	Gross value added at basic prices	CGCE	73.1	74.8	77.8	79.8	82.0	84.5	87.5	90.2
	PRICE INDICES (IMPLIED DEFLATORS)[1]									
	Categories of GDP expenditure at market prices									
P.3	Final consumption expenditure	YBGA	75.3	77.6	79.3	81.7	84.4	86.4	88.7	90.7
	by households and non-profit institutions serving households	YBFS	77.5	80.1	81.8	84.6	87.4	89.6	91.8	93.4
	by general government	YBFT	68.2	69.8	71.4	72.9	75.3	76.7	78.8	82.4
P.51	Gross fixed capital formation	YBFU	88.3	88.1	89.9	94.4	96.1	95.5	94.8	95.4
	Total domestic expenditure	YBFV	77.4	79.4	81.1	83.9	86.5	88.1	89.8	91.6
P.6	Exports of goods and services	YBFW	91.6	99.7	100.7	103.9	105.3	101.1	97.4	97.0
	of which, goods	BQNK	99.8	109.0	109.6	113.4	114.7	108.9	102.7	99.6
	services	FKNW	76.6	82.5	84.4	86.4	88.0	87.3	88.5	91.1
	Total final expenditure	YBFY	80.3	83.4	85.0	87.9	90.2	90.7	91.3	92.7
P.7	Imports of goods and services	YBFZ	96.5	104.8	107.9	114.2	114.3	106.2	100.1	99.0
	of which, goods	BQNL	99.6	107.4	111.3	118.7	118.4	109.8	102.1	101.1
	services	FHMA	84.7	94.6	95.4	98.2	99.4	93.1	92.3	92.5
B.1*g	Gross domestic product at market prices	YBGB	75.9	78.0	79.2	81.3	84.1	86.6	88.9	90.9
	HOME COSTS PER UNIT OF OUTPUT[2]									
B.1*g	Total home costs (based on expenditure components of GDP)	YBGC	74.9	77.1	78.5	80.6	83.7	86.0	88.1	89.7
D.1	Compensation of employees	YBGD	77.8	78.1	77.5	78.7	80.1	82.7	86.8	89.6
B.2g,B.3g	Gross operating surplus and mixed income	YBGE	72.2	78.0	82.2	85.1	90.9	92.6	91.8	91.2

1 Implied deflators are derived by dividing the estimates for each component at current market prices by the corresponding chained volume estimate.
2 These index numbers show how employment and operating incomes relate to the implied deflator of GDP at market prices.

1.4 Indices of value, volume, prices and costs

continued

Indices 2003=100

			2000	2001	2002	2003	2004	2005	2006
	INDICES OF VALUE AT CURRENT PRICES								
	Gross measures, before deduction of fixed capital consumption								
	at current market prices								
B.1*g	Gross domestic product at current market prices ("money GDP")	YBEU	85.8	89.7	94.4	100.0	105.9	110.3	116.2
B.5*g	Gross national income at current market prices	YBEV	84.1	88.7	94.4	100.0	106.0	110.3	115.4
B.6*g	Gross national disposable income at current market prices	YBEW	84.2	89.0	94.5	100.0	105.9	110.1	115.3
	at current basic prices								
B.1g	Gross value added at current basic prices	YBEX	85.2	89.5	94.3	100.0	105.9	110.4	116.3
	CHAINED VOLUME INDICES ("real terms")								
	Gross measures, before deduction of fixed capital consumption at market prices								
B.1*g	Gross domestic product at market prices	YBEZ	93.1	95.3	97.3	100.0	103.3	105.2	108.1
	Categories of GDP expenditure								
P.3	Final consumption expenditure	YBFA	91.2	93.8	97.1	100.0	103.3	105.2	107.4
	by households and non-profit institutions serving households	YBFB	91.2	93.9	97.2	100.0	103.4	104.9	107.1
	by general government	YBFC	91.2	93.4	96.6	100.0	103.2	105.9	108.4
P.51	Gross fixed capital formation	YBFG	93.2	95.6	99.1	100.0	105.7	107.5	116.1
	Gross domestic final expenditure	YBFH	91.6	94.3	97.3	100.0	103.8	105.5	108.8
P.6	Exports of goods and services	YBFI	94.5	97.3	98.3	100.0	104.9	113.4	126.7
	of which, goods	YBFJ	99.3	101.5	100.3	100.0	101.5	111.0	128.2
	services	YBFK	85.1	89.1	94.5	100.0	111.4	118.3	123.6
	Gross final expenditure	YBFF	92.2	94.9	97.5	100.0	104.0	107.1	112.4
P.7	Imports of goods and services	YBFL	89.3	93.5	98.1	100.0	106.6	114.2	127.6
	of which, goods	YBFM	89.1	93.8	98.2	100.0	106.9	114.7	131.2
	services	YBFN	89.9	92.6	97.6	100.0	105.8	112.7	116.6
B.5*g	Gross national income at market prices	YBFO	90.7	93.4	97.1	100.0	103.5	104.5	106.3
B.6*g	Gross national disposable income at market prices	YBFP	90.7	93.7	97.1	100.0	103.4	104.3	106.2
	Adjustment to basic prices								
D.21-D.31	Taxes *less* subsidies on products	YBFQ	89.8	93.5	97.5	100.0	103.1	104.6	107.4
B.1g	Gross value added at basic prices	CGCE	93.6	95.6	97.3	100.0	103.3	105.2	108.2
	PRICE INDICES (IMPLIED DEFLATORS)[1]								
	Categories of GDP expenditure at market prices								
P.3	Final consumption expenditure	YBGA	92.3	94.9	97.2	100.0	102.4	105.4	108.4
	by households and non-profit institutions serving households	YBFS	94.4	96.6	98.1	100.0	101.7	104.2	106.7
	by general government	YBFT	85.7	89.5	94.5	100.0	104.4	109.1	113.7
P.51	Gross fixed capital formation	YBFU	96.0	96.2	97.6	100.0	102.5	105.6	108.3
	Total domestic expenditure	YBFV	93.0	95.2	97.4	100.0	102.4	105.5	108.4
P.6	Exports of goods and services	YBFW	99.2	98.4	98.5	100.0	99.8	100.9	102.3
	of which, goods	BQNK	100.5	98.9	98.8	100.0	99.8	101.3	101.5
	services	FKNW	96.5	97.2	98.1	100.0	99.7	100.3	103.8
	Total final expenditure	YBFY	94.3	95.8	97.6	100.0	101.9	104.5	107.0
P.7	Imports of goods and services	YBFZ	102.1	101.9	99.6	100.0	99.4	103.2	105.6
	of which, goods	BQNL	104.6	103.6	100.7	100.0	99.4	103.2	105.8
	services	FHMA	94.3	96.4	96.2	100.0	99.3	103.2	105.0
B.1*g	Gross domestic product at market prices	YBGB	92.1	94.1	97.0	100.0	102.6	104.9	107.5
	HOME COSTS PER UNIT OF OUTPUT[2]								
B.1*g	Total home costs (based on expenditure components of GDP)	YBGC	90.8	93.4	96.9	100.0	102.6	105.3	107.8
D.1	Compensation of employees	YBGD	92.6	95.9	97.9	100.0	101.8	105.9	108.1
B.2g,B.3g	Gross operating surplus and mixed income	YBGE	88.9	89.9	95.1	100.0	103.9	104.7	107.6

1 Implied deflators are derived by dividing the estimates for each component at current market prices by the corresponding chained volume estimate.
2 These index numbers show how employment and operating incomes relate to the implied deflator of GDP at market prices.

1.5 Population, employment and GDP per head

			1998	1999	2000	2001	2002	2003	2004	2005	2006
	POPULATION AND EMPLOYMENT (thousands)[1]										
POP	Home population[4]	DYAY	58 475	58 684	58 886	59 113	59 322	59 554	59 834	60 218	60 533
	Household population aged 16+										
ESE	Self-employed[2]	MGRQ	3 386	3 311	3 260	3 281	3 340	3 535	3 630	3 647	3 711
EEM	Employees[2]	MGRN	23 052	23 485	23 922	24 161	24 325	24 453	24 553	24 809	25 002
ETO	Total employment[2,3]	MGRZ	26 713	27 052	27 434	27 691	27 866	28 166	28 410	28 674	28 895
EUN	Unemployed[2]	MGSC	1 783	1 759	1 638	1 431	1 533	1 479	1 429	1 426	1 657
	All economically active[2]	MGSF	28 497	28 811	29 071	29 122	29 399	29 645	29 839	30 100	30 552
	Economically inactive[2]	MGSI	17 164	17 051	17 035	17 292	17 305	17 350	17 485	17 618	17 548
	Total[2]	MGSL	45 661	45 862	46 107	46 413	46 704	46 995	47 324	47 719	48 100
	GROSS DOMESTIC PRODUCT PER HEAD £										
	At current prices										
	Gross domestic product at market prices[4]	IHXT	14 720	15 448	16 187	16 865	17 679	18 643	19 663	20 492	21 469
	Chained volume measures										
	Gross domestic product at market prices[4]	IHXW	16 555	16 995	17 581	17 925	18 231	18 642	19 162	19 527	19 978
	Gross value added at basic prices[4]	YBGT	14 859	15 265	15 790	16 066	16 292	16 683	17 148	17 361	17 765

1 Components may not sum to totals due to rounding.
2 These seasonally adjusted data relate to spring (March to May) quarters in the Labour Force Survey, which does not include those resident in communal establishments except for those in student halls of residence and NHS accommodation.
3 Includes people on Government-supported training and employment programmes and unpaid family workers.
4 This data is consistent with the population estimates published on 26 June 2007. There is a discontinuity in this series between 2000 and 2001. For the latest year GAD population projections are used.

1.6.0 UK summary accounts
Total economy ESA95 sector S.1

£ million

			1998	1999	2000	2001	2002	2003	2004	2005	2006
0	**GOODS AND SERVICES ACCOUNT**										
	Resources										
P.1	Output										
P.11	Market output[1]	NQAG	1 358 770	1 424 441	1 503 686	1 564 408	1 625 677	1 698 999	1 786 979	..	..
P.12	Output for own final use[1]	NQAH	61 107	65 577	69 644	76 021	80 399	88 008	92 962	..	..
P.13	Other non-market output[1]	NQAI	177 246	191 394	205 020	219 223	238 432	259 884	279 661	..	..
P.1	Total output	NQAF	1 597 123	1 681 412	1 778 350	1 859 652	1 944 508	2 046 891	2 159 602	..	..
D.21	Taxes on products	NZGW	103 540	112 024	118 275	119 942	125 004	132 148	139 642	142 458	150 431
-D.31	*less* Subsidies on products	-NZHC	–6 424	–6 068	–6 027	–5 708	–6 534	–7 410	–7 280	–5 111	–5 768
P.7	Imports of goods and services	KTMX	239 175	255 236	286 963	299 929	307 386	314 842	333 669	370 968	424 128
Total	Total resources	NQBM	1 933 414	2 042 604	2 177 561	2 273 815	2 370 364	2 486 471	2 625 633	..	..
	Uses										
P.2	Intermediate consumption[1]	NQAJ	828 529	875 423	931 667	970 589	1 007 185	1 053 384	1 107 668	..	..
P.3	Final consumption expenditure										
P.31	By households	ABPB	534 153	567 994	600 826	632 496	664 562	697 160	732 531	760 869	794 768
P.31	By non-profit institutions serving households	ABNV	20 837	21 874	23 169	24 720	25 968	27 185	28 953	31 585	33 313
P.3	By government										
P.31	For individual consumption	NNAQ	94 783	102 742	109 297	118 458	130 816	143 954	155 811	167 399	178 552
P.32	For collective consumption	NQEP	61 626	66 778	72 554	76 045	81 648	88 745	94 897	101 502	108 260
P.3	Total by government	NMRK	156 409	169 520	181 851	194 503	212 464	232 699	250 708	268 901	286 812
P.3	Total final consumption expenditure[2]	ABKW	711 399	759 388	805 846	851 719	902 994	957 044	1 012 192	1 061 355	1 114 893
P.5	Gross capital formation										
P.51	Gross fixed capital formation	NPQX	155 997	161 722	167 172	171 782	180 551	186 700	202 260	211 862	234 751
P.52	Changes in inventories	ABMP	5 026	6 060	5 271	6 189	2 909	3 983	4 856	4 071	3 735
P.53	Acquisitions less disposals of valuables	NPJO	429	229	3	396	214	–37	–37	–377	45
P.5	Total gross capital formation	NQFM	161 452	168 011	172 446	178 367	183 674	190 646	207 079	215 556	238 531
P.6	Exports of goods and services	KTMW	232 034	239 782	267 602	273 140	276 511	285 397	298 694	326 790	369 691
de	Statistical discrepancy between expenditure components and GDP	RVFD	–	–	–	–	–	–	–	1 243	635
Total	Total uses[1]	NQBM	1 933 414	2 042 604	2 177 561	2 273 815	2 370 364	2 486 471	2 625 633	..	..

1 These series are not available for the latest two years
2 For the total economy, Total final consumption expenditure = P.4 Actual final consumption

1.6.1 UK summary accounts
Total economy ESA95 sector S.1

£ million

			1998	1999	2000	2001	2002	2003	2004
I	**PRODUCTION ACCOUNT**								
	Resources								
P.1	Output								
P.11	Market output	NQAG	1 358 770	1 424 441	1 503 686	1 564 408	1 625 677	1 698 999	1 786 979
P.12	Output for own final use	NQAH	61 107	65 577	69 644	76 021	80 399	88 008	92 962
P.13	Other non-market output	NQAI	177 246	191 394	205 020	219 223	238 432	259 884	279 661
P.1	Total output	NQAF	1 597 123	1 681 412	1 778 350	1 859 652	1 944 508	2 046 891	2 159 602
D.21	Taxes on products	NZGW	103 540	112 024	118 275	119 942	125 004	132 148	139 642
-D.31	*less* Subsidies on products	-NZHC	–6 424	–6 068	–6 027	–5 708	–6 534	–7 410	–7 280
Total	Total resources	NQBP	1 694 239	1 787 368	1 890 598	1 973 886	2 062 978	2 171 629	2 291 964
	Uses								
P.2	Intermediate consumption	NQAJ	828 529	875 423	931 667	970 589	1 007 185	1 053 384	1 107 668
B.1*g	**Gross Domestic Product**	YBHA	**865 710**	**911 945**	**958 931**	**1 003 297**	**1 055 793**	**1 118 245**	**1 184 296**
Total	Total uses	NQBP	1 694 239	1 787 368	1 890 598	1 973 886	2 062 978	2 171 629	2 291 964
B.1*g	**Gross Domestic Product**	YBHA	**865 710**	**911 945**	**958 931**	**1 003 297**	**1 055 793**	**1 118 245**	**1 184 296**
-K.1	*less* Fixed capital consumption	-NQAE	–95 051	–101 055	–106 372	–110 434	–116 007	–119 239	–128 427
B.1*n	Net domestic product	NHRK	770 659	810 890	852 559	892 863	939 786	999 006	1 055 869

1.6.2 UK summary accounts
Total economy ESA95 sector S.1

£ million

			1998	1999	2000	2001	2002	2003	2004
II	**DISTRIBUTION AND USE OF INCOME ACCOUNTS**								
II.1	**PRIMARY DISTRIBUTION OF INCOME ACCOUNT**								
II.1.1	**GENERATION OF INCOME ACCOUNT**								
	Resources								
B.1*g	**Total resources (Gross Domestic Product)**	YBHA	**865 710**	**911 945**	**958 931**	**1 003 297**	**1 055 793**	**1 118 245**	**1 184 296**
	Uses								
D.1	Compensation of employees								
D.11	Wages and salaries	NQAU	406 558	431 594	462 355	490 978	508 614	527 630	550 583
D.12	Employers' social contributions	NQAV	59 522	64 199	69 824	73 216	78 782	89 263	98 134
D.1	Total	HAEA	466 080	495 793	532 179	564 194	587 396	616 893	648 717
D.2	Taxes on production and imports, paid								
D.21	Taxes on products and imports	QZPQ	103 540	112 024	118 275	119 942	125 004	132 148	139 642
D.29	Production taxes other than on products	NMYD	15 815	16 503	17 083	17 565	18 113	18 517	18 945
D.2	Total taxes on production and imports	NZGX	119 355	128 527	135 358	137 507	143 117	150 665	158 587
-D.3	*less* Subsidies, received								
-D.31	Subsidies on products	-NZHC	–6 424	–6 068	–6 027	–5 708	–6 534	–7 410	–7 280
-D.39	Production subsidies other than on products	-LIUB	–1 051	–1 001	–909	–1 244	–1 473	–2 026	–2 091
-D.3	Total subsidies on production	-AAXJ	–7 475	–7 069	–6 936	–6 952	–8 007	–9 436	–9 371
B.2g	Operating surplus, gross	ABNF	234 927	238 960	240 525	246 427	267 516	291 001	314 405
B.3g	Mixed income, gross	QWLT	52 823	55 734	57 805	62 121	65 771	69 122	71 958
di	Statistical discrepancy between income components and GDP	RVFC	–	–	–	–	–	–	–
B.1*g	**Total uses (Gross Domestic Product)**	YBHA	**865 710**	**911 945**	**958 931**	**1 003 297**	**1 055 793**	**1 118 245**	**1 184 296**
-K.1	After deduction of fixed capital consumption:	-NQAE	–95 051	–101 055	–106 372	–110 434	–116 007	–119 239	–128 427
B.2n	Operating surplus, net	NQAR	150 014	149 694	147 227	150 223	166 939	187 150	205 782
B.3n	Mixed income, net	QWLV	42 685	43 945	44 731	47 891	50 341	53 734	52 154

1.6.3 UK summary accounts

Total economy ESA95 sector S.1

£ million

			1998	1999	2000	2001	2002	2003	2004	2005	2006
II.1.2	**ALLOCATION OF PRIMARY INCOME ACCOUNT**										
	Resources										
B.2g	Operating surplus, gross	ABNF	234 927	238 960	240 525	246 427	267 516	291 001	314 405	320 794	340 331
B.3g	Mixed income, gross	QWLT	52 823	55 734	57 805	62 121	65 771	69 122	71 958	75 675	78 864
D.1	Compensation of employees										
D.11	Wages and salaries	NQBI	406 548	431 795	462 505	491 044	508 681	527 689	550 654	578 300	605 320
D.12	Employers' social contributions	NQBJ	59 522	64 199	69 824	73 216	78 782	89 263	98 134	107 895	115 229
D.1	Total	NVCK	466 070	495 994	532 329	564 260	587 463	616 952	648 788	686 195	720 549
di	Statistical discrepancy between income components and GDP	RVFC	–	–	–	–	–	–	–	–916	–551
D.2	Taxes on production and imports, received										
D.21	Taxes on products										
D.211	Value added tax (VAT)	NZGF	52 313	57 701	59 985	63 522	68 251	74 595	79 751	81 383	85 512
D.212	Taxes and duties on imports excluding VAT	NMBU	–	–	–	–	–	–	–	–	–
D.2121	Import duties	NMXZ	–	–	–	–	–	–	–	–	–
D.2122	Taxes on imports excluding VAT and import duties	NMBT	–	–	–	–	–	–	–	–	–
D.214	Taxes on products excluding VAT and import duties	NMYB	44 881	48 442	51 956	50 745	52 001	52 858	55 932	56 815	60 423
D.21	Total taxes on products	NVCE	97 194	106 143	111 941	114 267	120 252	127 453	135 683	138 198	145 935
D.29	Other taxes on production	NMYD	15 815	16 503	17 083	17 565	18 113	18 517	18 945	19 601	21 087
D.2	Total taxes on production and imports, received	NMYE	113 009	122 646	129 024	131 832	138 365	145 970	154 628	157 799	167 022
-D.3	*less* Subsidies, paid										
-D.31	Subsidies on products	-NMYF	–3 729	–3 625	–3 791	–3 953	–4 672	–5 311	–4 961	–5 111	–5 768
-D.39	Other subsidies on production	-LIUF	–810	–663	–574	–662	–954	–1 434	–1 499	–2 058	–2 784
-D.3	Total subsidies	-NMRL	–4 539	–4 288	–4 365	–4 615	–5 626	–6 745	–6 460	–7 169	–8 552
D.4	Property income, received										
D.41	Interest	NHQY	262 625	229 774	279 119	270 982	226 462	226 432	265 062	326 994	406 289
D.42	Distributed income of corporations	NHQZ	106 435	112 390	128 676	145 607	133 637	161 002	163 859	172 703	179 354
D.43	Reinvested earnings on direct foreign investment	NHSK	14 071	21 392	25 178	27 220	32 209	21 456	32 430	42 236	52 372
D.44	Property income attributed to insurance policy holders	QYNF	56 785	56 727	56 427	56 505	55 417	55 460	55 053	64 400	68 981
D.45	Rent	NHRP	800	780	1 540	2 170	2 155	1 823	1 685	1 615	1 474
D.4	Total property income	NHRO	440 716	421 063	490 940	502 484	449 880	466 173	518 089	607 948	708 470
Total	Total resources	NQBR	1 303 006	1 330 109	1 446 258	1 502 509	1 503 369	1 582 473	1 701 408	1 840 326	2 006 133
	Uses										
D.4	Property income, paid										
D.41	Interest	NHQW	266 727	239 071	291 889	282 308	236 839	234 104	275 670	345 143	432 716
D.42	Distributed income of corporations	NHQX	101 352	117 510	124 878	149 605	127 211	141 527	148 739	159 242	162 009
D.43	Reinvested earnings on direct foreign investment	NHSJ	1 522	4 607	10 788	–992	3 647	7 429	9 320	10 107	23 073
D.44	Property income attributed to insurance policy holders	NQCG	57 985	58 026	57 455	57 795	56 652	56 703	56 150	65 497	69 905
D.45	Rent	NHRN	800	780	1 540	2 170	2 155	1 823	1 685	1 615	1 474
D.4	Total property income	NHRL	428 386	419 994	486 550	490 886	426 504	441 586	491 564	581 604	689 177
B.5*g	**Gross National Income (GNI)**	**ABMX**	**874 620**	**910 115**	**959 708**	**1 011 623**	**1 076 865**	**1 140 887**	**1 209 844**	**1 258 722**	**1 316 956**
Total	Total uses	NQBR	1 303 006	1 330 109	1 446 258	1 502 509	1 503 369	1 582 473	1 701 408	1 840 326	2 006 133
-K.1	After deduction of fixed capital consumption	-NQAE	–95 051	–101 055	–106 372	–110 434	–116 007	–119 239	–128 427	–131 093	–133 936
B.5*n	National income, net	NSRX	779 569	809 060	853 336	901 189	960 858	1 021 648	1 081 417	1 127 629	1 183 020

1.6.4 UK summary accounts

Total economy ESA95 sector S.1

£ million

			1998	1999	2000	2001	2002	2003	2004	2005	2006
II.2	**SECONDARY DISTRIBUTION OF INCOME ACCOUNT**										
	Resources										
B.5*g	**Gross National Income**	ABMX	**874 620**	**910 115**	**959 708**	**1 011 623**	**1 076 865**	**1 140 887**	**1 209 844**	**1 258 722**	**1 316 956**
D.5	Current taxes on income, wealth, etc.										
D.51	Taxes on income	NMZJ	123 683	129 553	140 002	147 264	142 842	144 234	154 717	172 619	193 017
D.59	Other current taxes	NVCQ	18 120	19 519	20 287	22 068	23 664	26 016	27 718	29 253	30 681
D.5	Total	NMZL	141 803	149 072	160 289	169 332	166 506	170 250	182 435	201 872	223 698
D.61	Social contributions										
D.611	Actual social contributions										
D.6111	Employers' actual social contributions	NQDA	48 138	52 529	57 288	60 296	64 805	77 571	87 347	95 997	103 557
D.6112	Employees' social contributions	NQDE	54 860	57 523	58 861	60 658	62 535	66 534	69 612	78 047	83 263
D.6113	Social contributions by self- and non-employed persons	NQDI	1 729	1 883	2 049	2 183	2 318	2 595	2 727	2 825	2 930
D.611	Total	NQCY	104 727	111 935	118 198	123 137	129 658	146 700	159 686	176 869	189 750
D.612	Imputed social contributions	NQDK	11 384	11 670	12 536	12 920	13 977	11 692	10 787	11 898	11 672
D.61	Total	NQCX	116 111	123 605	130 734	136 057	143 635	158 392	170 473	188 767	201 422
D.62	Social benefits other than social transfers in kind	QZQP	154 438	157 647	162 833	171 814	182 673	193 596	202 074	213 858	223 618
D.7	Other current transfers										
D.71	Net non-life insurance premiums	NQBY	25 059	22 613	25 235	25 477	26 631	24 625	25 867	31 661	31 957
D.72	Non-life insurance claims	NQDX	20 898	18 960	23 109	21 504	23 641	22 280	23 068	25 551	27 447
D.73	Current transfers within general government	NQDY	60 367	64 446	66 187	72 522	77 592	85 224	91 910	100 224	109 841
D.74	Current international cooperation from institutions of the EC	NQEA	1 384	3 176	2 084	4 568	3 112	3 570	3 604	3 668	3 594
D.75	Miscellaneous current transfers	QYNA	21 990	25 033	28 192	29 757	33 748	35 401	36 927	39 116	38 846
D.7	Total other current transfers	NQDU	129 698	134 228	144 807	153 828	164 724	171 100	181 376	200 220	211 685
Total	Total resources	NQBT	1 416 670	1 474 667	1 558 371	1 642 654	1 734 403	1 834 225	1 946 202	2 063 439	2 177 379
	Uses										
D.5	Current taxes on income, wealth etc.										
D.51	Taxes on income	NQCR	123 783	129 898	140 420	147 389	142 959	144 303	154 958	172 659	192 885
D.59	Other current taxes	NQCU	18 120	19 519	20 287	22 068	23 664	26 016	27 718	29 253	30 681
D.5	Total	NQCQ	141 903	149 417	160 707	169 457	166 623	170 319	182 676	201 912	223 566
D.61	Social contributions										
D.611	Actual social contributions										
D.6111	Employers' actual social contributions	NQDB	48 138	52 529	57 288	60 296	64 805	77 571	87 347	95 997	103 557
D.6112	Employees' actual social contributions	NQDF	54 761	57 434	58 806	60 599	62 458	66 490	69 576	78 033	83 209
D.6113	Social contributions by self- and non-employed persons	NQDJ	1 729	1 883	2 049	2 183	2 318	2 595	2 727	2 825	2 930
D.611	Total actual social contributions	NQCZ	104 628	111 846	118 143	123 078	129 581	146 656	159 650	176 855	189 696
D.612	Imputed social contributions	QZQQ	11 384	11 670	12 536	12 920	13 977	11 692	10 787	11 898	11 672
D.61	Total	NQBS	116 012	123 516	130 679	135 998	143 558	158 348	170 437	188 753	201 368
D.62	Social benefits other than social transfers in kind	NQDN	155 672	158 892	164 086	173 145	184 115	195 081	203 682	215 548	225 389
D.7	Other current transfers										
D.71	Net non-life insurance premiums	NQDW	20 898	18 960	23 109	21 504	23 641	22 280	23 068	25 551	27 447
D.72	Non-life insurance claims	NQBZ	25 059	22 613	25 235	25 477	26 631	24 625	25 867	31 661	31 957
D.73	Current transfers within general government	NNAF	60 367	64 446	66 187	72 522	77 592	85 224	91 910	100 224	109 841
D.74	Current international cooperation to institutions of the EC	NMDZ	1 705	1 667	2 418	2 434	2 573	2 720	3 180	3 300	3 583
D.75	Miscellaneous current transfers	NUHK	25 400	29 476	32 495	33 920	39 516	42 871	45 458	48 855	47 969
	Of which: GNP based fourth own resource	NMFH	3 920	4 632	4 379	3 858	5 335	6 772	7 549	8 732	8 521
D.7	Total other current transfers	NQDV	133 429	137 162	149 444	155 857	169 953	177 720	189 483	209 591	220 797
B.6*g	**Gross National Disposable Income**	NQCO	**869 654**	**905 680**	**953 455**	**1 008 197**	**1 070 154**	**1 132 757**	**1 199 924**	**1 247 635**	**1 306 259**
Total	Total uses	NQBT	1 416 670	1 474 667	1 558 371	1 642 654	1 734 403	1 834 225	1 946 202	2 063 439	2 177 379
-K.1	After deduction of fixed capital consumption	-NQAE	−95 051	−101 055	−106 372	−110 434	−116 007	−119 239	−128 427	−131 093	−133 936
B.6*n	Disposable income, net	NQCP	774 603	804 625	847 083	897 763	954 147	1 013 518	1 071 497	1 116 542	1 172 323

1.6.5 UK summary accounts

Total economy ESA95 sector S.1

£ million

			1998	1999	2000	2001	2002	2003	2004	2005	2006
II.3	**REDISTRIBUTION OF INCOME IN KIND ACCOUNT**										
	Resources										
B.6*g	**Gross National Disposable Income**	NQCO	**869 654**	**905 680**	**953 455**	**1 008 197**	**1 070 154**	**1 132 757**	**1 199 924**	**1 247 635**	**1 306 259**
D.63	Social transfers in kind										
D.631	Social benefits in kind										
D.6313	Social assistance benefits in kind	NRNC	–	–	–	–	–	–	–	–	–
D.632	Transfers of individual non-market goods and services	NRNE	115 620	124 616	132 466	143 178	156 784	171 139	184 764	198 984	211 865
D.63	Total social transfers in kind	NRNF	115 620	124 616	132 466	143 178	156 784	171 139	184 764	198 984	211 865
Total	Total resources	NQCB	985 274	1 030 296	1 085 921	1 151 375	1 226 938	1 303 896	1 384 688	1 446 619	1 518 124
	Uses										
D.63	Social transfers in kind										
D.631	Social benefits in kind										
D.6313	Social assistance benefits in kind	NRNI	–	–	–	–	–	–	–	–	–
D.632	Transfers of individual non-market goods and services	NRNK	115 620	124 616	132 466	143 178	156 784	171 139	184 764	198 984	211 865
D.63	Total social transfers in kind	NRNL	115 620	124 616	132 466	143 178	156 784	171 139	184 764	198 984	211 865
B.7g	Adjusted disposable income, gross	NRNM	869 654	905 680	953 455	1 008 197	1 070 154	1 132 757	1 199 924	1 247 635	1 306 259
Total	Total uses	NQCB	985 274	1 030 296	1 085 921	1 151 375	1 226 938	1 303 896	1 384 688	1 446 619	1 518 124

1.6.6 UK summary accounts

Total economy ESA95 sector S.1

£ million

			1998	1999	2000	2001	2002	2003	2004	2005	2006
II.4	**USE OF INCOME ACCOUNT**										
II.4.1	**USE OF DISPOSABLE INCOME ACCOUNT**										
	Resources										
B.6g	**Gross National Disposable Income**	NQCO	**869 654**	**905 680**	**953 455**	**1 008 197**	**1 070 154**	**1 132 757**	**1 199 924**	**1 247 635**	**1 306 259**
D.8	Adjustment for the change in net equity of households in pension funds	NVCI	14 044	14 016	14 164	16 041	17 783	21 377	25 108	31 210	35 720
Total	Total resources	NVCW	883 698	919 696	967 619	1 024 238	1 087 937	1 154 134	1 225 032	1 278 845	1 341 979
	Uses										
P.3	Final consumption expenditure										
P.31	Individual consumption expenditure	NQEO	649 773	692 610	733 292	775 674	821 346	868 299	917 295	959 853	1 006 633
P.32	Collective consumption expenditure	NQEP	61 626	66 778	72 554	76 045	81 648	88 745	94 897	101 502	108 260
P.3	Total	ABKW	711 399	759 388	805 846	851 719	902 994	957 044	1 012 192	1 061 355	1 114 893
D.8	Adjustment for the change in net equity of households in pension funds	NQEL	14 042	14 014	14 160	16 036	17 782	21 365	25 089	31 143	35 701
B.8g	**Gross Saving**	NQET	**158 257**	**146 294**	**147 613**	**156 483**	**167 161**	**175 725**	**187 751**	**186 347**	**191 385**
Total	Total uses	NVCW	883 698	919 696	967 619	1 024 238	1 087 937	1 154 134	1 225 032	1 278 845	1 341 979
-K.1	After deduction of fixed capital consumption	-NQAE	−95 051	−101 055	−106 372	−110 434	−116 007	−119 239	−128 427	−131 093	−133 936
B.8n	Saving, net	NQEJ	63 206	45 239	41 241	46 049	51 154	56 486	59 324	55 254	57 449
II.4.2	**USE OF ADJUSTED DISPOSABLE INCOME ACCOUNT**										
	Resources										
B.7g	Adjusted disposable income	NRNM	869 654	905 680	953 455	1 008 197	1 070 154	1 132 757	1 199 924	1 247 635	1 306 259
D.8	Adjustment for the change in net equity of households in pension funds	NVCI	14 044	14 016	14 164	16 041	17 783	21 377	25 108	31 210	35 720
Total	Total resources	NVCW	883 698	919 696	967 619	1 024 238	1 087 937	1 154 134	1 225 032	1 278 845	1 341 979
	Uses										
P.4	Actual final consumption										
P.41	Actual individual consumption	NQEO	649 773	692 610	733 292	775 674	821 346	868 299	917 295	959 853	1 006 633
P.42	Actual collective consumption	NRMZ	61 626	66 778	72 554	76 045	81 648	88 745	94 897	101 502	108 260
P.4	Total actual final consumption	NRMX	711 399	759 388	805 846	851 719	902 994	957 044	1 012 192	1 061 355	1 114 893
D.8	Adjustment for the change in net equity of households in pension funds	NQEL	14 042	14 014	14 160	16 036	17 782	21 365	25 089	31 143	35 701
B.8g	**Gross Saving**	NQET	**158 257**	**146 294**	**147 613**	**156 483**	**167 161**	**175 725**	**187 751**	**186 347**	**191 385**
Total	Total uses	NVCW	883 698	919 696	967 619	1 024 238	1 087 937	1 154 134	1 225 032	1 278 845	1 341 979

1.6.7 UK summary accounts

Total economy ESA95 sector S.1

£ million

			1998	1999	2000	2001	2002	2003	2004	2005	2006
III	**ACCUMULATION ACCOUNTS**										
III.1	**CAPITAL ACCOUNT**										
III.1.1	**CHANGE IN NET WORTH DUE TO SAVING & CAPITAL TRANSFERS**										
	Changes in liabilities and net worth										
B.8g	**Gross Saving**	NQET	**158 257**	**146 294**	**147 613**	**156 483**	**167 161**	**175 725**	**187 751**	**186 347**	**191 385**
D.9	Capital transfers receivable										
D.91	Capital taxes	NQEY	1 795	1 951	2 215	2 396	2 381	2 416	2 881	3 150	3 579
D.92	Investment grants	NQFB	8 344	8 935	9 667	11 645	13 679	17 614	17 766	22 008	21 196
D.99	Other capital transfers	NQFD	1 387	1 499	1 924	4 794	3 612	7 656	6 962	18 741	6 429
D.9	Total	NQEW	11 526	12 385	13 806	18 835	19 672	27 686	27 609	43 899	31 204
-D.9	*less* Capital transfers payable										
-D.91	Capital taxes	-NQCC	–1 795	–1 951	–2 215	–2 396	–2 381	–2 416	–2 881	–3 150	–3 579
-D.92	Investment grants	-NVDG	–8 113	–8 774	–8 821	–11 313	–13 646	–17 335	–17 045	–20 934	–21 000
-D.99	Other capital transfers	-NQCE	–1 081	–925	–1 091	–3 711	–2 581	–6 398	–5 301	–18 066	–5 590
-D.9	Total	-NQCF	–10 989	–11 650	–12 127	–17 420	–18 608	–26 149	–25 227	–42 150	–30 169
B.10.1g	Total change in liabilities and net worth	NQCT	158 794	147 029	149 292	157 898	168 225	177 262	190 133	188 096	192 420
	Changes in assets										
B.10.1g	Changes in net worth due to gross saving and capital transfers	NQCT	158 794	147 029	149 292	157 898	168 225	177 262	190 133	188 096	192 420
-K.1	After deduction of fixed capital consumption	-NQAE	–95 051	–101 055	–106 372	–110 434	–116 007	–119 239	–128 427	–131 093	–133 936
B.10.1n	Changes in net worth due to net saving and capital transfers	NQER	63 743	45 974	42 920	47 464	52 218	58 023	61 706	57 003	58 484
III.1.2	**ACQUISITION OF NON-FINANCIAL ASSETS ACCOUNT**										
	Changes in liabilities and net worth										
B.10.1n	Changes in net worth due to net saving and capital transfers	NQER	63 743	45 974	42 920	47 464	52 218	58 023	61 706	57 003	58 484
K.1	Consumption of fixed capital	NQAE	95 051	101 055	106 372	110 434	116 007	119 239	128 427	131 093	133 936
Total	Total change in liabilities and net worth	NQCT	158 794	147 029	149 292	157 898	168 225	177 262	190 133	188 096	192 420
	Changes in assets										
P.5	Gross capital formation										
P.51	Gross fixed capital formation	NPQX	155 997	161 722	167 172	171 782	180 551	186 700	202 260	211 862	234 751
P.52	Changes in inventories	ABMP	5 026	6 060	5 271	6 189	2 909	3 983	4 856	4 071	3 735
P.53	Acquisitions less disposals of valuables	NPJO	429	229	3	396	214	–37	–37	–377	45
P.5	Total	NQFM	161 452	168 011	172 446	178 367	183 674	190 646	207 079	215 556	238 531
K.2	Acquisitions less disposals of non-produced non-financial assets	NQFJ	48	–12	–24	98	132	71	319	258	205
de	Statistical discrepancy between expenditure components and GDP	RVFD	–	–	–	–	–	–	–	1 243	635
B.9	**Net lending(+) / net borrowing(-)**	NQFH	**–2 706**	**–20 970**	**–23 130**	**–20 567**	**–15 581**	**–13 455**	**–17 265**	**–28 961**	**–46 951**
Total	Total change in assets	NQCT	158 794	147 029	149 292	157 898	168 225	177 262	190 133	188 096	192 420

1.6.8 UK summary accounts

Total economy ESA95 sector S.1. Unconsolidated

£ million

			1998	1999	2000	2001	2002	2003	2004	2005	2006
III.2	**FINANCIAL ACCOUNT**										
F.A	**Net acquisition of financial assets**										
F.1	Monetary gold and special drawing rights (SDRs)	NQAD	915	–374	–956	–808	–240	–2	–37	–8	47
F.2	Currency and deposits										
F.21	Currency	NYPY	3 066	5 314	583	1 020	1 680	3 123	5 544	1 077	1 934
F.22	Transferable deposits										
F.221	Deposits with UK monetary financial institutions	NYQC	69 882	30 045	144 866	164 534	127 918	228 683	253 493	307 260	447 511
F.229	Deposits with rest of the world monetary financial institutions	NYQK	13 504	45 655	219 290	126 267	80 292	186 025	213 691	371 266	276 605
F.29	Other deposits	NYQM	–1 439	–1 572	4 998	–5 454	2 464	2 498	3 317	6 159	4 602
F.2	Total currency and deposits	NQAK	85 013	79 442	369 737	286 367	212 354	420 329	476 045	685 762	730 652
F.3	Securities other than shares										
F.331	Short term: money market instruments										
F.3311	Issued by UK central government	NYQQ	1 819	–814	–1 401	8 319	10 510	442	–974	–2 843	–2 415
F.3312	Issued by UK local government	NYQY	–6	–	–	–	–	–	–	–	–
F.3315	Issued by UK monetary financial institutions	NYRA	15 258	17 595	–14 324	3 756	6 639	–11 744	20	1 034	11 805
F.3316	Issued by other UK residents	NYRK	921	946	–1 330	–609	–1 969	2 142	–2 558	2 608	5 031
F.3319	Issued by the rest of the world	NYRM	2 206	13 931	–2 551	11 491	–6 132	12 223	–2 631	5 759	16 065
F.332	Medium (1 to 5 year) and long term (over 5 year) bonds										
F.3321	Issued by UK central government	NYRQ	–5 108	721	–12 399	–16 546	5 187	20 277	21 600	9 174	16 120
F.3322	Issued by UK local government	NYRW	6	–2	–12	–	47	18	–225	213	358
F.3325	Medium term bonds issued by UK MFIs[1]	NYRY	2 744	7 585	2 045	–480	2 463	11 387	11 063	15 105	14 499
F.3326	Other medium & long term bonds issued by UK residents	NYSE	20 920	36 454	67 533	48 506	24 811	37 606	32 497	34 422	44 800
F.3329	Long term bonds issued by the rest of the world	NYSG	27 898	–10 300	53 299	30 261	9 900	818	88 343	94 511	161 943
F.34	Financial derivatives	NYSI	3 038	–2 724	–1 570	–8 507	–1 433	5 136	7 682	–9 418	–7 869
F.3	Total securities other than shares	NQAL	69 696	63 392	89 290	76 191	50 023	78 305	154 817	150 565	260 337
F.4	Loans										
F.41	Short term loans										
F.411	Loans by UK monetary financial institutions, excluding loans secured on dwellings & financial leasing	NYSS	32 439	65 529	154 557	109 704	86 729	159 860	233 710	256 735	307 993
F.42	Long term loans										
F.421	Direct investment	NYTE	33 269	28 607	14 517	11 291	26 584	8 912	14 065	25 471	–6 367
F.422	Loans secured on dwellings	NYTK	25 315	37 900	42 206	54 323	83 644	101 994	99 281	89 942	109 691
F.423	Finance leasing	NYTS	404	337	374	438	979	1 444	1 656	1 594	1 657
F.424	Other long-term loans by UK residents	NYTU	3 002	25 485	25 226	13 349	6 389	11 001	12 240	40 026	47 692
F.4	Total loans	NQAN	94 429	157 858	236 880	189 105	204 325	283 211	360 952	413 768	460 666
F.5	Shares and other equity										
F.51	Shares and other equity, excluding mutual funds' shares										
F.514	Quoted UK shares	NYUG	–3 257	–8 988	104 947	6 615	15 119	11 752	21 658	–55 331	–9 392
F.515	Unquoted UK shares	NYUI	–2 539	–10 993	–19 292	–9 826	274	4 845	3 460	4 318	16 586
F.516	Other UK equity (including direct investment in property)	NYUK	–66	20	–24	73	32	105	–8	–1 249	–1 204
F.517	UK shares and bonds issued by other UK residents	NSQJ	–	–	–	–	–	–	–	–	–
F.519	Shares and other equity issued by the rest of the world	NYUQ	64 499	137 757	193 381	88 597	55 273	61 864	107 108	120 934	88 115
F.52	Mutual funds' shares										
F.521	UK mutual funds' shares	NYUY	10 974	14 716	14 059	9 333	6 251	8 208	3 461	8 251	15 106
F.529	Rest of the world mutual funds' shares	NYVA	–8	70	63	33	–8	41	536	1 810	811
F.5	Total shares and other equity	NQAP	69 603	132 582	293 134	94 825	76 941	86 815	136 215	78 733	110 022
F.6	Insurance technical reserves										
F.61	Net equity of households in life assurance and pension funds' reserves	NQAX	34 673	31 335	26 199	33 083	46 303	34 666	40 602	52 061	62 374
F.62	Prepayments of insurance premiums and reserves for outstanding claims	NQBD	–566	–999	524	–1 596	1 446	2 058	3 600	3 244	2 610
F.6	Total insurance technical reserves	NQAW	34 107	30 336	26 723	31 487	47 749	36 724	44 202	55 305	64 984
F.7	Other accounts receivable	NQBK	6 297	13 549	30 572	9 810	20 275	12 319	13 898	14 004	14 381
F.A	**Total net acquisition of financial assets**	NQBL	360 060	476 785	1 045 380	686 977	611 427	917 701	1 186 092	1 398 129	1 641 089

1 UK monetary financial institutions

1.6.8 UK summary accounts

Total economy ESA95 sector S.1. Unconsolidated

continued | £ million

			1998	1999	2000	2001	2002	2003	2004	2005	2006
III.2	**FINANCIAL ACCOUNT** continued										
F.L	**Net acquisition of financial liabilities**										
F.2	Currency and deposits										
F.21	Currency	NYPZ	3 135	5 422	674	966	1 712	3 174	5 631	1 127	1 899
F.22	Transferable deposits										
F.221	Deposits with UK monetary financial institutions	NYQD	121 986	42 505	344 048	289 104	217 744	398 030	562 029	586 972	780 241
F.29	Other deposits	NYQN	–1 135	–879	5 526	–5 632	2 440	2 730	2 440	6 102	5 076
F.2	Total currency and deposits	NQCK	123 986	47 048	350 248	284 438	221 896	403 934	570 100	594 201	787 216
F.3	Securities other than shares										
F.331	Short term: money market instruments										
F.3311	Issued by UK central government	NYQR	86	–404	–1 652	8 623	10 330	2 592	999	–3 902	–1 752
F.3312	Issued by UK local government	NYQZ	–6	–	–	–	–	–	–	–	–
F.3315	Issued by UK monetary financial institutions	NYRB	–1 159	31 134	23 941	22 836	25 599	–11 489	8 023	–3 490	53 189
F.3316	Issued by other UK residents	NYRL	3 350	2 729	1 370	–372	8 850	–2 181	–2 299	–102	1 560
F.332	Medium (1 to 5 year) and long term (over 5 year) bonds										
F.3321	Issued by UK central government	NYRR	–3 201	–4 560	–12 700	–17 219	1 555	31 474	34 219	39 846	41 021
F.3322	Issued by UK local government	NYRX	6	–2	–12	–	47	18	–225	213	358
F.3325	Medium term bonds issued by UK MFIs[1]	NYRZ	4 485	12 081	4 750	3 575	4 238	25 258	29 810	37 843	40 534
F.3326	Other medium & long term bonds issued by UK residents	NYSF	16 735	63 484	75 893	51 333	45 132	101 297	88 872	114 344	119 616
F.34	Financial derivatives	NYSJ	–5	–39	–67	–95	–274	–75	–175	–207	–110
F.3	Total securities other than shares	NQCM	20 291	104 423	91 523	68 681	95 477	146 894	159 224	184 545	254 416
F.4	Loans										
F.41	Short term loans										
F.411	Loans by UK monetary financial institutions, excluding loans secured on dwellings & financial leasing	NYST	31 471	48 609	97 057	61 612	69 542	89 051	121 692	121 516	188 617
F.419	Loans by rest of the world monetary financial institutions	NYTB	15 237	43 075	66 703	99 251	–18 389	76 913	95 932	228 075	120 775
F.42	Long term loans										
F.421	Direct investment	NYTF	36 312	30 111	41 688	31 172	50 445	12 927	18 739	47 588	–14 291
F.422	Loans secured on dwellings	NYTL	25 315	37 900	42 206	54 323	83 644	101 994	99 281	89 942	109 691
F.423	Finance leasing	NYTT	404	337	374	438	979	1 444	1 656	1 594	1 657
F.424	Other long-term loans by UK residents	NYTV	3 345	25 832	26 721	13 321	7 847	11 293	12 362	41 680	50 896
F.429	Other long-term loans by the rest of the world	NYTX	–254	–120	–293	17	–30	124	603	101	240
F.4	Total loans	NQCN	111 830	185 744	274 456	260 134	194 038	293 746	350 265	530 496	457 585
F.5	Shares and other equity										
F.51	Shares and other equity, excluding mutual funds' shares										
F.514	Quoted UK shares	NYUH	50 113	87 829	227 164	22 457	19 134	14 293	20 820	7 947	26 113
F.515	Unquoted UK shares	NYUJ	10 593	14 817	41 011	16 563	14 123	23 536	29 022	42 982	54 568
F.516	Other UK equity (including direct investment in property)	NYUL	632	833	1 605	864	780	500	615	–652	–737
F.517	UK shares and bonds issued by other UK residents	NSQK	–	–	–	–	–	–	–	–	–
F.52	Mutual funds' shares										
F.521	UK mutual funds' shares	NYUZ	10 976	14 719	14 102	9 338	6 259	8 212	3 489	8 300	15 156
F.5	Total shares and other equity	NQCS	72 314	118 198	283 882	49 222	40 296	46 541	53 946	58 577	95 100
F.6	Insurance technical reserves										
F.61	Net equity of households in life assurance and pension funds' reserves	NQCD	34 671	31 333	26 195	33 078	46 302	34 654	40 582	51 994	62 355
F.62	Prepayments of insurance premiums and reserves for outstanding claims	NQDD	–563	–1 601	1 466	–1 753	1 781	687	3 778	3 969	3 153
F.6	Total insurance technical reserves	NQCV	34 108	29 732	27 661	31 325	48 083	35 341	44 360	55 963	65 508
F.7	Other accounts payable	NQDG	7 453	13 056	30 214	10 680	18 839	11 752	13 838	15 258	14 069
F.L	**Total net acquisition of financial liabilities**	NQDH	369 982	498 201	1 057 984	704 480	618 629	938 208	1 191 733	1 439 040	1 673 894
B.9	**Net lending / borrowing**										
F.A	Total net acquisition of financial assets	NQBL	360 060	476 785	1 045 380	686 977	611 427	917 701	1 186 092	1 398 129	1 641 089
-F.L	*less* Total net acquisition of financial liabilities	-NQDH	–369 982	–498 201	–1 057 984	–704 480	–618 629	–938 208	–1 191 733	–1 439 040	–1 673 894
B.9f	Net lending (+) / net borrowing (-), from financial account	NQDL	–9 922	–21 416	–12 604	–17 503	–7 202	–20 507	–5 641	–40 911	–32 805
dB.9f	Statistical discrepancy between financial and non-financial accounts	NYVK	7 216	446	–10 526	–3 064	–8 379	7 052	–11 624	11 950	–14 146
B.9	**Net lending (+) / net borrowing (-), from capital account**	NQFH	**–2 706**	**–20 970**	**–23 130**	**–20 567**	**–15 581**	**–13 455**	**–17 265**	**–28 961**	**–46 951**

1 UK monetary financial institutions

1.6.9 UK summary accounts

Total economy ESA95 sector S.1. Unconsolidated

£ billion

			1998	1999	2000	2001	2002	2003	2004	2005	2006
IV.3	**FINANCIAL BALANCE SHEET** at end of period										
AN	**Non-financial assets**	CGJB	3 476.9	3 809.8	4 267.9	4 482.1	5 073.5	5 503.5	6 025.9	6 342.3	6 816.4
AF.A	**Financial assets**										
AF.1	Monetary gold and special drawing rights (SDRs)	NYVN	4.3	4.0	3.1	2.4	2.4	2.6	2.5	3.2	3.4
AF.2	Currency and deposits										
AF.21	Currency	NYVV	32.1	37.4	37.9	38.9	40.5	43.6	49.0	50.1	51.9
AF.22	Transferable deposits										
AF.221	Deposits with UK monetary financial institutions institutions	NYVZ	1 132.4	1 151.7	1 311.2	1 456.2	1 587.6	1 905.8	2 120.8	2 470.0	2 952.3
AF.229	Deposits with rest of the world monetary financial institutions	NYWH	885.4	907.0	1 138.8	1 240.6	1 297.3	1 474.0	1 643.6	2 079.3	2 193.0
AF.29	Other deposits	NYWJ	73.1	71.2	76.6	71.5	73.5	74.6	77.9	85.5	90.0
AF.2	Total currency and deposits	NYVT	2 122.9	2 167.2	2 564.5	2 807.1	2 999.0	3 498.0	3 891.4	4 684.8	5 287.3
AF.3	Securities other than shares										
AF.331	Short term: money market instruments										
AF.3311	Issued by UK central government	NYWP	4.5	4.1	2.6	11.1	21.2	22.1	21.0	18.4	15.8
AF.3312	Issued by UK local government	NYWX	–	–	–	–	–	–	–	–	–
AF.3315	Issued by UK monetary financial institutions	NYWZ	150.0	166.3	154.9	157.9	162.3	151.5	152.5	155.6	164.3
AF.3316	Issued by other UK residents	NYXJ	11.1	20.3	24.5	25.5	21.0	21.8	19.0	27.9	47.3
AF.3319	Issued by the rest of the world	NYXL	27.9	44.3	45.3	56.7	48.7	62.0	58.5	64.9	77.9
AF.332	Medium (1 to 5 year) and long term (over 5 year) bonds										
AF.3321	Issued by UK central government	NYXP	285.3	273.1	263.4	237.5	251.6	263.9	285.4	309.3	313.9
AF.3322	Issued by UK local government	NYXV	0.8	0.8	0.8	0.8	0.8	0.8	0.6	0.8	1.2
AF.3325	Medium term bonds issued by UK MFIs[1]	NYXX	24.5	33.0	36.2	35.1	37.4	53.3	63.8	80.0	91.0
AF.3326	Other medium & long term bonds issued by UK residents	NYYD	146.0	185.3	238.4	269.5	288.7	319.9	355.1	417.7	475.6
AF.3329	Long term bond issued by the rest of the world	NYYF	391.5	392.4	478.6	523.7	538.2	550.1	626.7	727.7	829.3
AF.34	Financial derivatives	NYYH	–	–0.4	–	0.7	0.2	–	0.2	0.6	0.7
AF.3	Total securities other than shares	NYWL	1 041.6	1 119.0	1 244.5	1 318.5	1 370.2	1 445.5	1 582.8	1 803.1	2 017.0
AF.4	Loans										
AF.41	Short term loans										
AF.411	Loans by UK monetary financial institutions, excluding loans secured on dwellings & financial leasing	NYYT	766.4	817.4	980.8	1 079.6	1 144.9	1 286.4	1 497.5	1 766.4	1 982.1
AF.42	Long term loans										
AF.421	Direct investment	NYZF	115.9	133.5	142.1	157.5	176.2	175.3	210.5	227.8	221.5
AF.422	Loans secured on dwellings	NYZL	455.9	492.9	535.1	590.2	669.4	772.9	875.9	965.4	1 077.1
AF.423	Finance leasing	NYZT	24.1	25.1	25.8	26.2	27.2	28.6	30.2	31.8	33.5
AF.424	Other long-term loans by UK residents	NYZV	120.4	137.7	138.9	146.9	147.7	162.2	181.0	185.2	209.6
AF.4	Total loans	NYYP	1 482.8	1 606.5	1 822.6	2 000.3	2 165.3	2 425.5	2 795.1	3 176.7	3 523.8
AF.5	Shares and other equity										
AF.51	Shares and other equity, excluding mutual funds' shares										
AF.514	Quoted UK shares	NZAJ	987.9	1 266.9	1 181.8	1 005.8	761.0	895.0	977.3	1 020.5	1 065.5
AF.515	Unquoted UK shares	NZAL	323.0	432.2	470.7	427.3	372.4	413.9	455.1	502.8	544.8
AF.516	Other UK equity (including direct investment in property)	NZAN	1.4	1.4	1.4	1.4	1.4	1.4	1.4	1.4	1.4
AF.517	UK shares and bonds issued by other UK residents	NSRC	–	–	–	–	–	–	–	–	–
AF.519	Shares and other equity issued by the rest of the world	NZAT	588.3	831.9	1 015.8	987.1	925.8	1 043.4	1 120.1	1 372.9	1 460.1
AF.52	Mutual funds' shares										
AF.521	UK mutual funds' shares	NZBB	216.6	297.4	302.9	267.0	214.9	265.2	302.7	383.5	450.7
AF.529	Rest of the world mutual fund share	NZBD	1.1	2.1	1.7	1.7	1.4	1.4	1.7	4.1	6.0
AF.5	Total shares and other equity	NYZZ	2 118.2	2 831.8	2 974.3	2 690.2	2 276.9	2 620.3	2 858.3	3 285.1	3 528.5
AF.6	Insurance technical reserves										
AF.61	Net equity of households in life assurance and pension funds' reserves	NZBH	1 393.2	1 631.3	1 599.0	1 531.3	1 384.1	1 509.2	1 603.2	1 894.3	2 070.8
AF.62	Prepayments of insurance premiums and reserves for outstanding claims	NZBN	45.8	44.8	52.0	48.4	50.1	53.3	56.8	57.0	59.6
AF.6	Total insurance technical reserves	NZBF	1 439.0	1 676.1	1 651.0	1 579.6	1 434.2	1 562.4	1 660.0	1 951.3	2 130.4
AF.7	Other accounts receivable	NZBP	232.4	234.8	269.4	274.7	290.3	319.2	334.8	354.9	369.8
AF.A	**Total financial assets**	NZBV	8 441.1	9 639.4	10 529.5	10 672.8	10 538.4	11 873.4	13 124.8	15 259.0	16 860.2

1 UK monetary financial institutions

1.6.9 UK summary accounts

Total economy ESA95 sector S.1. Unconsolidated

continued

£ billion

			1998	1999	2000	2001	2002	2003	2004	2005	2006
IV.3	**FINANCIAL BALANCE SHEET** continued at end of period										
AF.L	**Financial liabilities**										
AF.2	Currency and deposits										
AF.21	Currency	NYVW	32.6	38.0	38.6	39.5	41.1	44.2	49.8	50.9	52.8
AF.22	Transferable deposits										
AF.221	Deposits with UK monetary financial institutions	NYWA	2 171.2	2 183.4	2 575.8	2 829.2	3 027.1	3 510.9	3 976.2	4 669.8	5 323.1
AF.29	Other deposits	NYWK	73.7	72.5	78.4	73.1	75.2	76.5	78.9	86.4	91.4
AF.2	Total currency and deposits	NYVU	2 277.5	2 293.8	2 692.8	2 941.8	3 143.5	3 631.6	4 104.9	4 807.1	5 467.3
AF.3	Securities other than shares										
AF.331	Short term: money market instruments										
AF.3311	Issued by UK central government	NYWQ	4.8	4.2	2.6	11.2	21.4	24.0	25.0	21.1	19.4
AF.3312	Issued by UK local government	NYWY	–	–	–	–	–	–	–	–	–
AF.3315	Issued by UK monetary financial institutions	NYXA	204.3	233.5	265.8	291.0	302.6	282.1	283.2	291.7	327.7
AF.3316	Issued by other UK residents	NYXK	26.7	38.1	46.2	48.1	51.6	45.6	41.6	50.1	63.6
AF.332	Medium (1 to 5 year) and long term (over 5 year) bonds										
AF.3321	Issued by UK central government	NYXQ	359.3	334.0	325.8	297.4	308.0	330.0	369.2	420.0	449.3
AF.3322	Issued by UK local government	NYXW	0.8	0.8	0.8	0.8	0.8	0.8	0.6	0.8	1.2
AF.3325	Medium term bonds issued by UK MFIs[1]	NYXY	53.3	67.7	74.6	77.6	81.0	107.0	134.7	175.4	205.8
AF.3326	Other medium & long term bonds issued by UK residents	NYYE	270.2	330.4	409.6	458.1	517.6	615.5	715.4	882.8	1 000.6
AF.34	Financial derivatives	NYYI	–	–0.4	–0.1	0.3	–	–	0.1	0.2	0.7
AF.3	Total securities other than shares	NYWM	919.4	1 008.3	1 125.3	1 184.4	1 283.0	1 405.1	1 569.9	1 842.2	2 068.3
AF.4	Loans										
AF.41	Short term loans										
AF.411	Loans by UK monetary financial institutions, excluding loans secured on dwellings & financial leasing	NYYU	563.0	602.1	700.7	756.3	816.3	888.0	1 001.2	1 124.0	1 272.9
AF.419	Loans by rest of the world monetary financial institutions	NYZC	293.0	351.3	413.7	498.1	486.6	554.4	636.6	886.7	948.7
AF.42	Long term loans										
AF.421	Direct investment	NYZG	143.4	167.1	196.5	239.9	284.1	280.6	303.7	350.5	336.4
AF.422	Loans secured on dwellings	NYZM	455.9	492.9	535.1	590.2	669.4	772.9	875.9	965.4	1 077.1
AF.423	Finance leasing	NYZU	24.1	25.1	25.8	26.2	27.2	28.6	30.2	31.8	33.5
AF.424	Other long-term loans by UK residents	NYZW	110.1	127.5	130.3	138.1	140.4	155.1	173.7	177.9	203.6
AF.429	Other long-term loans by the rest of the world	NYZY	2.5	2.0	2.1	2.1	2.0	2.2	2.7	2.8	2.9
AF.4	Total loans	NYYQ	1 592.0	1 768.0	2 004.2	2 250.8	2 426.0	2 681.7	3 024.1	3 539.2	3 875.0
AF.5	Shares and other equity										
AF.51	Shares and other equity, excluding mutual funds' shares										
AF.514	Quoted UK shares	NZAK	1 372.0	1 751.1	1 754.3	1 494.3	1 146.8	1 359.8	1 486.1	1 644.5	1 804.5
AF.515	Unquoted UK shares	NZAM	488.6	636.8	728.1	712.6	608.9	669.3	729.9	851.3	955.4
AF.516	Other UK equity (including direct investment in property)	NZAO	12.2	13.1	14.9	15.5	17.3	17.3	19.2	19.7	21.6
AF.517	UK shares and bonds issued by other UK residents	NSRD	–	–	–	–	–	–	–	–	–
AF.52	Mutual funds' shares										
AF.521	UK mutual funds' shares	NZBC	217.9	299.0	304.5	268.2	215.8	266.3	303.9	385.0	452.4
AF.5	Total shares and other equity	NZAA	2 090.8	2 700.0	2 801.9	2 490.7	1 988.7	2 312.7	2 539.1	2 900.6	3 233.9
AF.6	Insurance technical reserves										
AF.61	Net equity of households in life assurance and pension funds' reserves	NZBI	1 393.4	1 631.5	1 599.2	1 531.5	1 384.3	1 509.4	1 603.4	1 894.5	2 071.1
AF.62	Prepayments of insurance premiums and reserves for outstanding claims	NZBO	60.8	58.9	62.8	59.0	62.8	63.5	67.2	71.2	74.4
AF.6	Total insurance technical reserves	NZBG	1 454.2	1 690.4	1 662.0	1 590.5	1 447.1	1 572.9	1 670.6	1 965.7	2 145.4
AF.7	Other accounts payable	NZBQ	223.9	233.2	267.2	273.0	286.4	313.5	327.1	347.7	362.2
AF.L	**Total financial liabilities**	NZBW	8 557.8	9 693.8	10 553.3	10 731.2	10 574.7	11 917.5	13 235.6	15 402.6	17 152.1
BF.90	**Net financial assets / liabilities**										
AF.A	Total financial assets	NZBV	8 441.1	9 639.4	10 529.5	10 672.8	10 538.4	11 873.4	13 124.8	15 259.0	16 860.2
-AF.L	*less* Total financial liabilities	-NZBW	–8 557.8	–9 693.8	–10 553.3	–10 731.2	–10 574.7	–11 917.5	–13 235.6	–15 402.6	–17 152.1
BF.90	**Net financial assets (+) / liabilities (-)**	NQFT	–116.7	–54.4	–23.9	–58.4	–36.3	–44.1	–110.9	–143.5	–291.9
	Net worth										
AN	Non-financial assets	CGJB	3 476.9	3 809.8	4 267.9	4 482.1	5 073.5	5 503.5	6 025.9	6 342.3	6 816.4
BF.90	Net financial assets (+) / liabilities (-)	NQFT	–116.7	–54.4	–23.9	–58.4	–36.3	–44.1	–110.9	–143.5	–291.9
B.90	**Net worth**	CGDA	3 360.2	3 755.4	4 244.1	4 423.7	5 037.2	5 459.4	5 915.0	6 198.7	6 524.5

1 UK monetary financial institutions

1.7A UK summary accounts 2003

Total economy: all sectors and the rest of the world

£ million

		RESOURCES							USES	TOTAL
		UK total economy	Non-financial corporations	Financial corporations	General government	Households & NPISH	Not sector -ised	Rest of the world	Goods & services	
		S.1	S.11	S.12	S.13	S.14+S.15	S.N	S.2		
	Current accounts									
I 0	**PRODUCTION / EXTERNAL ACCOUNT OF GOODS AND SERVICES**									
P.7	Imports of goods and services							314 842		314 842
P.6	Exports of goods and services								285 397	285 397
P.1	Output at basic prices	2 046 891	1 306 543	153 718	253 930	332 700				2 046 891
P.2	Intermediate consumption								1 053 384	1 053 384
D.21-D.31	Taxes *less* subsidies on products	124 738					124 738			124 738
II.1.1	**GENERATION OF INCOME**									
B.1g	**Gross domestic product, value added at market prices**	**1 118 245**	**634 224**	**77 815**	**132 432**	**194 406**	**79 368**			**1 118 245**
B.11	External balance of goods and services							29 445		29 445
II.1.2	**ALLOCATION OF PRIMARY INCOME**									
D.1	Compensation of employees	616 952				616 952		1 057		618 009
D.21-D.31	Taxes *less* subsidies on products	122 142			122 142			2 596		124 738
D.29-D.39	Other taxes *less* subsidies on production	16 491	15 603	1 419	–	–531		–592		16 491
B.2g	Operating surplus, gross	291 001	216 210	41 419	10 807	67 935	–45 370			291 001
B.3g	Mixed income, gross	69 122				69 122				69 122
di	Statistical discrepancy between income components and GDP	–					–			–
D.4	Property income	466 173	72 370	256 179	16 710	120 914		100 294		566 467
-P.119	Adjustment to property income for financial services (FISIM)			–45 370			45 370			
II.2	**SECONDARY DISTRIBUTION OF INCOME**									
B.5g	National income, balance of primary incomes, gross	1 140 887	147 816	32 157	139 787	821 127	–			1 140 887
D.5	Current taxes on income, wealth etc	170 250			170 250			444		170 694
D.61	Social contributions	158 392	4 229	65 164	88 494	505		–		158 392
D.62	Social benefits other than social transfers in kind	193 596				193 596		1 485		195 081
D.7	Other current transfers	171 100	6 595	25 342	89 652	49 511		15 713		186 813
II.3	**REDISTRIBUTION OF INCOME IN KIND**									
B.6g	Disposable income, gross	1 132 757	123 776	45 832	222 760	740 389	–			1 132 757
D.63	Social transfers in kind	171 139				171 139				171 139
II.4	**USE OF INCOME**									
B.7g	Adjusted disposable income, gross	1 132 757	123 776	45 832	78 806	884 343	–			1 132 757
B.6g	Disposable income, gross	1 132 757	123 776	45 832	222 760	740 389	–			1 132 757
P.4	Actual final consumption								957 044	957 044
P.3	Final consumption expenditure								957 044	957 044
D.8	Adjustment for change in households' net equity in pension funds	21 377				21 377		–12		21 365
	Accumulation accounts									
III.1.1	**CHANGE IN NET WORTH DUE TO SAVING AND CAPITAL TRANSFERS**									
B.8g	Saving, gross	175 725	123 776	24 467	–9 939	37 421	–			175 725
B.12	Current external balance							14 921		14 921
D.9	Capital transfers receivable	27 686	5 711	391	14 937	6 647		1 038		28 724
D.9	Capital transfers payable	–26 149	–705	–391	–21 699	–3 354		–2 575		–28 724
III.1.2	**ACQUISITION ON NON-FINANCIAL ASSETS**									
	Changes in liabilities and net worth									
B.10.1.g	Changes in net worth due to saving and capital transfers	177 262	128 782	24 467	–16 701	40 714	–	13 384		190 646
P.51	Gross fixed capital formation								186 700	186 700
-K.1	(Consumption of fixed capital)									
P.52	Changes in inventories								3 983	3 983
P.53	Acquisitions less disposals of valuables								–37	–37
K.2	Acquisitions less disposals of non-produced non-financial assets									
de	Statistical discrepancy between expenditure components and GDP								–	–
III.2	**FINANCIAL ACCOUNT**									
B.9	**Net lending(+) / net borrowing(-)**	–13 455	18 181	19 335	–36 284	–14 687	–	13 455		–
	Changes in liabilities									
F.2	Currency and deposits	403 934	–	400 452	3 482	–		186 055		589 989
F.3	Securities other than shares	146 894	17 747	94 936	34 084	127		18 252		165 146
F.4	Loans	293 746	57 519	112 675	–2 130	125 682		79 429		373 175
F.5	Shares and other equity	46 541	7 784	38 757		–		61 905		108 446
F.6	Insurance technical reserves	35 341		35 341						35 341
F.7	Other accounts payable	11 752	2 780	267	1 678	7 027		625		12 377

1.7A UK summary accounts 2003

continued

Total economy: all sectors and the rest of the world

£ million

		USES							RESOURCES	TOTAL
		UK total economy	Non-financial corporations	Financial corporations	General government	Households & NPISH	Not sector -ised	Rest of the world	Goods & services	
		S.1	S.11	S.12	S.13	S.14+S.15	S.N	S.2		
	Current accounts									
I 0	**PRODUCTION / EXTERNAL ACCOUNT OF GOODS AND SERVICES**									
P.7	Imports of goods and services								314 842	314 842
P.6	Exports of goods and services							285 397		285 397
P.1	Output at basic prices								2 046 891	2 046 891
P.2	Intermediate consumption	1 053 384	672 319	75 903	121 498	138 294	45 370			1 053 384
D.21-D.31	Taxes *less* subsidies on products								124 738	124 738
B.1g	**Gross domestic product, value added at market prices**	**1 118 245**	**634 224**	**77 815**	**132 432**	**194 406**	**79 368**			**1 118 245**
B.11	External balance of goods and services							29 445		29 445
II.1.1	**GENERATION OF INCOME**									
D.1	Compensation of employees	616 893	402 411	34 977	121 625	57 880		1 116		618 009
D.21-D.31	Taxes *less* subsidies on products	124 738					124 738			124 738
D.29-D.39	Other taxes *less* subsidies on production	16 491			16 491					16 491
B.2g	Operating surplus, gross	291 001	216 210	41 419	10 807	67 935	–45 370			291 001
B.3g	Mixed income, gross	69 122				69 122				69 122
di	Statistical discrepancy between income components and GDP	–					–			–
II.1.2	**ALLOCATION OF PRIMARY INCOME**									
D.4	Property income	441 586	140 764	220 071	26 955	53 796		124 881		566 467
-P.119	Adjustment to property income for financial services (FISIM)									
B.5g	National income, balance of primary incomes, gross	1 140 887	147 816	32 157	139 787	821 127	–			1 140 887
II.2	**SECONDARY DISTRIBUTION OF INCOME**									
D.5	Current taxes on income, wealth etc	170 319	23 702	7 514	842	138 261		375		170 694
D.61	Social contributions	158 348				158 348		44		158 392
D.62	Social benefits other than social transfers in kind	195 081	4 229	43 799	146 066	987				195 081
D.7	Other current transfers	177 720	6 933	25 518	118 515	26 754		9 093		186 813
B.6g	Disposable income, gross	1 132 757	123 776	45 832	222 760	740 389	–			1 132 757
II.3	**REDISTRIBUTION OF INCOME IN KIND**									
B.7g	Adjusted disposable income, gross	1 132 757	123 776	45 832	78 806	884 343	–			1 132 757
D.63	Social transfers in kind	171 139			143 954	27 185				171 139
II.4	**USE OF INCOME**									
B.6g	Disposable income, gross									
P.4	Actual final consumption	957 044			88 745	868 299				957 044
P.3	Final consumption expenditure	957 044			232 699	724 345				957 044
D.8	Adjustment for change in households' net equity in pension funds	21 365		21 365						21 365
B.8g	Saving, gross	175 725	123 776	24 467	–9 939	37 421	–			175 725
B.12	Current external balance							14 921		14 921
	Accumulation accounts									
III.1.1	**CHANGE IN NET WORTH DUE TO SAVING AND CAPITAL TRANSFERS**									
D.9	Capital transfers receivable									
D.9	Capital transfers payable									
B.10.1.g	Changes in net worth due to saving and capital transfers	177 262	128 782	24 467	–16 701	40 714	–	13 384		190 646
III.1.2	**ACQUISITION OF NON-FINANCIAL ASSETS**									
	Changes in assets									
P.51	Gross fixed capital formation	186 700	105 712	5 253	20 509	55 226				186 700
-K.1	(Consumption of fixed capital)	–119 239	–67 438	–4 091	–10 807	–36 903				–119 239
P.52	Changes in inventories	3 983	3 745	48	15	175				3 983
P.53	Acquisitions less disposals of valuables	–37	–97	–166	16	210				–37
K.2	Acquisitions less disposals of non-produced non-financial assets	71	1 241	–3	–957	–210		–71		–
de	Statistical discrepancy between expenditure components and GDP	–					–			–
B.9	**Net lending(+) / net borrowing(-)**	–13 455	18 181	19 335	–36 284	–14 687	–	13 455		–
III.2	**FINANCIAL ACCOUNT: changes in assets**									
F.1	Monetary gold and SDRs	–2			–2			2		
F.2	Currency and deposits	420 329	49 208	307 748	1 014	62 359		169 660		589 989
F.3	Securities other than shares	78 305	6 591	74 124	–2 794	384		86 841		165 146
F.4	Loans	283 211	5 535	272 946	–808	5 538		89 964		373 175
F.5	Shares and other equity	86 815	32 851	35 368	247	18 349		21 631		108 446
F.6	Insurance technical reserves	36 724	170	20	8	36 526		–1 383		35 341
F.7	Other accounts receivable	12 319	2 168	8 439	3 075	–1 363		58		12 377
dB.9f	Statistical discrepancy between non-financial and financial transactions	7 052	7 488	3 118	90	–3 644	–	–7 052		–

1.7B UK summary accounts 2004

Total economy: all sectors and the rest of the world

£ million

		RESOURCES							USES	TOTAL
		UK total economy	Non-financial corporations	Financial corporations	General government	Households & NPISH	Not sector -ised	Rest of the world	Goods & services	
		S.1	S.11	S.12	S.13	S.14+S.15	S.N	S.2		
	Current accounts									
I	**PRODUCTION / EXTERNAL**									
0	**ACCOUNT OF GOODS AND SERVICES**									
P.7	Imports of goods and services							333 669		333 669
P.6	Exports of goods and services								298 694	298 694
P.1	Output at basic prices	2 159 602	1 373 071	162 615	273 470	350 446				2 159 602
P.2	Intermediate consumption								1 107 668	1 107 668
D.21-D.31	Taxes *less* subsidies on products	132 362					132 362			132 362
II.1.1	**GENERATION OF INCOME**									
B.1g	**Gross domestic product, value added at market prices**	**1 184 296**	**668 344**	**86 062**	**142 458**	**205 235**	**82 197**			**1 184 296**
B.11	External balance of goods and services							34 975		34 975
II.1.2	**ALLOCATION OF PRIMARY INCOME**									
D.1	Compensation of employees	648 788				648 788		1 100		649 888
D.21-D.31	Taxes *less* subsidies on products	130 722			130 722			1 640		132 362
D.29-D.39	Other taxes *less* subsidies on production	17 446	17 426	1 455	–	–1 435		–592		16 854
B.2g	Operating surplus, gross	314 405	232 856	47 324	11 681	72 709	–50 165			314 405
B.3g	Mixed income, gross	71 958				71 958				71 958
di	Statistical discrepancy between income components and GDP	–					–			–
D.4	Property income	518 089	80 188	295 133	15 588	127 180		114 505		632 594
-P.119	Adjustment to property income for financial services (FISIM)			–50 165			50 165			
II.2	**SECONDARY DISTRIBUTION OF INCOME**									
B.5g	National income, balance of primary incomes, gross	1 209 844	163 746	39 977	148 387	857 734	–			1 209 844
D.5	Current taxes on income, wealth etc	182 435			182 435			615		183 050
D.61	Social contributions	170 473	3 864	69 707	96 407	495		–		170 473
D.62	Social benefits other than social transfers in kind	202 074				202 074		1 608		203 682
D.7	Other current transfers	181 376	6 619	26 570	96 409	51 778		17 704		199 080
II.3	**REDISTRIBUTION OF INCOME IN KIND**									
B.6g	Disposable income, gross	1 199 924	135 975	57 606	240 660	765 683	–			1 199 924
D.63	Social transfers in kind	184 764				184 764				184 764
II.4	**USE OF INCOME**									
B.7g	Adjusted disposable income, gross	1 199 924	135 975	57 606	84 849	921 494	–			1 199 924
B.6g	Disposable income, gross	1 199 924	135 975	57 606	240 660	765 683	–			1 199 924
P.4	Actual final consumption								1 012 192	1 012 192
P.3	Final consumption expenditure								1 012 192	1 012 192
D.8	Adjustment for change in households' net equity in pension funds	25 108				25 108		–19		25 089
	Accumulation accounts									
III.1.1	**CHANGE IN NET WORTH DUE TO SAVING AND CAPITAL TRANSFERS**									
B.8g	Saving, gross	187 751	135 975	32 517	–10 048	29 307	–			187 751
B.12	Current external balance							19 328		19 328
D.9	Capital transfers receivable	27 609	5 476	328	15 112	6 693		1 027		28 636
D.9	Capital transfers payable	–25 227	–528	–328	–20 647	–3 724		–3 409		–28 636
III.1.2	**ACQUISITION ON NON-FINANCIAL ASSETS**									
	Changes in liabilities and net worth									
B.10.1.g	Changes in net worth due to saving and capital transfers	190 133	140 923	32 517	–15 583	32 276	–	16 946		207 079
P.51	Gross fixed capital formation								202 260	202 260
-K.1	(Consumption of fixed capital)									
P.52	Changes in inventories								4 856	4 856
P.53	Acquisitions less disposals of valuables								–37	–37
K.2	Acquisitions less disposals of non-produced non-financial assets									
de	Statistical discrepancy between expenditure components and GDP								–	–
III.2	**FINANCIAL ACCOUNT**									
B.9	**Net lending(+) / net borrowing(-)**	–17 265	26 255	26 479	–37 758	–32 241	–	17 265		–
	Changes in liabilities									
F.2	Currency and deposits	570 100	–	567 507	2 593	–		213 737		783 837
F.3	Securities other than shares	159 224	5 523	118 645	34 993	63		93 569		252 793
F.4	Loans	350 265	77 226	133 312	9 002	130 725		125 961		476 226
F.5	Shares and other equity	53 946	16 201	37 745		–		107 644		161 590
F.6	Insurance technical reserves	44 360		44 360						44 360
F.7	Other accounts payable	13 838	2 433	8 353	–1 943	4 995		–103		13 735

1.7B UK summary accounts 2004

continued

Total economy: all sectors and the rest of the world

£ million

		USES							RESOURCES	TOTAL
		UK total economy	Non-financial corporations	Financial corporations	General government	Households & NPISH	Not sector -ised	Rest of the world	Goods & services	
		S.1	S.11	S.12	S.13	S.14+S.15	S.N	S.2		
	Current accounts									
I 0	**PRODUCTION / EXTERNAL ACCOUNT OF GOODS AND SERVICES**									
P.7	Imports of goods and services								333 669	333 669
P.6	Exports of goods and services							298 694		298 694
P.1	Output at basic prices								2 159 602	2 159 602
P.2	Intermediate consumption	1 107 668	704 727	76 553	131 012	145 211	50 165			1 107 668
D.21-D.31	Taxes *less* subsidies on products								132 362	132 362
B.1g	**Gross domestic product, value added at market prices**	**1 184 296**	**668 344**	**86 062**	**142 458**	**205 235**	**82 197**			**1 184 296**
B.11	External balance of goods and services							34 975		34 975
II.1.1	**GENERATION OF INCOME**									
D.1	Compensation of employees	648 717	419 561	37 283	130 777	61 096		1 171		649 888
D.21-D.31	Taxes *less* subsidies on products	132 362					132 362			132 362
D.29-D.39	Other taxes *less* subsidies on production	16 854			16 854					16 854
B.2g	Operating surplus, gross	314 405	232 856	47 324	11 681	72 709	–50 165			314 405
B.3g	Mixed income, gross	71 958				71 958				71 958
di	Statistical discrepancy between income components and GDP	–					–			–
II.1.2	**ALLOCATION OF PRIMARY INCOME**									
D.4	Property income	491 564	149 298	252 315	27 050	62 901		141 030		632 594
-P.119	Adjustment to property income for financial services (FISIM)									
B.5g	National income, balance of primary incomes, gross	1 209 844	163 746	39 977	148 387	857 734	–			1 209 844
II.2	**SECONDARY DISTRIBUTION OF INCOME**									
D.5	Current taxes on income, wealth etc	182 676	27 348	7 357	837	147 134		374		183 050
D.61	Social contributions	170 437				170 437		36		170 473
D.62	Social benefits other than social transfers in kind	203 682	3 864	44 618	154 216	984				203 682
D.7	Other current transfers	189 483	7 042	26 673	127 925	27 843		9 597		199 080
B.6g	Disposable income, gross	1 199 924	135 975	57 606	240 660	765 683	–			1 199 924
II.3	**REDISTRIBUTION OF INCOME IN KIND**									
B.7g	Adjusted disposable income, gross	1 199 924	135 975	57 606	84 849	921 494	–			1 199 924
D.63	Social transfers in kind	184 764			155 811	28 953				184 764
II.4	**USE OF INCOME**									
B.6g	Disposable income, gross									
P.4	Actual final consumption	1 012 192			94 897	917 295				1 012 192
P.3	Final consumption expenditure	1 012 192			250 708	761 484				1 012 192
D.8	Adjustment for change in households' net equity in pension funds	25 089		25 089						25 089
B.8g	Saving, gross	187 751	135 975	32 517	–10 048	29 307	–			187 751
B.12	Current external balance							19 328		19 328
	Accumulation accounts									
III.1.1	**CHANGE IN NET WORTH DUE TO SAVING AND CAPITAL TRANSFERS**									
D.9	Capital transfers receivable									
D.9	Capital transfers payable									
B.10.1.g	Changes in net worth due to saving and capital transfers	190 133	140 923	32 517	–15 583	32 276	–	16 946		207 079
III.1.2	**ACQUISITION OF NON-FINANCIAL ASSETS**									
	Changes in assets									
P.51	Gross fixed capital formation	202 260	108 509	6 169	23 206	64 376				202 260
-K.1	(Consumption of fixed capital)	–128 427	–69 979	–4 401	–11 681	–42 366				–128 427
P.52	Changes in inventories	4 856	4 586	48	20	202				4 856
P.53	Acquisitions less disposals of valuables	–37	–99	–173	20	215				–37
K.2	Acquisitions less disposals of non-produced non-financial assets	319	1 672	–6	–1 071	–276		–319		–
de	Statistical discrepancy between expenditure components and GDP	–					–			–
B.9	**Net lending(+) / net borrowing(-)**	–17 265	26 255	26 479	–37 758	–32 241	–	17 265		–
III.2	**FINANCIAL ACCOUNT: changes in assets**									
F.1	Monetary gold and SDRs	–37			–37			37		
F.2	Currency and deposits	476 045	68 775	341 881	14	65 375		307 792		783 837
F.3	Securities other than shares	154 817	816	153 089	1 778	–866		97 976		252 793
F.4	Loans	360 952	10 768	349 051	2 726	–1 593		115 274		476 226
F.5	Shares and other equity	136 215	44 339	90 782	–27	1 121		25 375		161 590
F.6	Insurance technical reserves	44 202	933	102	45	43 122		158		44 360
F.7	Other accounts receivable	13 898	–1 846	4 315	2 396	9 033		–163		13 735
dB.9f	Statistical discrepancy between non-financial and financial transactions	–11 624	3 853	–2 819	–8	–12 650	–	11 624		–

1.7C UK summary accounts 2005

Total economy: all sectors and the rest of the world

£ million

		RESOURCES							USES	TOTAL
		UK total economy	Non-financial corporations	Financial corporations	General government	Households & NPISH	Not sector -ised	Rest of the world	Goods & services	
		S.1	S.11	S.12	S.13	S.14+S.15	S.N	S.2		
	Current accounts									
I 0	**PRODUCTION / EXTERNAL ACCOUNT OF GOODS AND SERVICES**									
P.7	Imports of goods and services							370 968		370 968
P.6	Exports of goods and services								326 790	326 790
P.1	Output at basic prices	..	..	..	291 748	..				..
P.2	Intermediate consumption								..	..
D.21-D.31	Taxes *less* subsidies on products	137 347					137 347			137 347
II.1.1	**GENERATION OF INCOME**									
B.1g	**Gross domestic product, value added at market prices**	**1 233 976**	**..**	**80 407**	**152 479**	**..**	**84 509**			**1 233 976**
B.11	External balance of goods and services							44 178		44 178
II.1.2	**ALLOCATION OF PRIMARY INCOME**									
D.1	Compensation of employees	686 195				686 195		1 584		687 779
D.21-D.31	Taxes *less* subsidies on products	133 087			133 087			4 260		137 347
D.29-D.39	Other taxes *less* subsidies on production	17 543	18 051	1 482	–	–1 990		–3 272		14 271
B.2g	Operating surplus, gross	320 794	242 623	39 697	12 605	77 791	–51 922			320 794
B.3g	Mixed income, gross	75 675				75 675				75 675
di	Statistical discrepancy between income components and GDP	–916					–916			–916
D.4	Property income	607 948	95 746	355 033	10 282	146 887		160 169		768 117
-P.119	Adjustment to property income for financial services (FISIM)			–51 922			51 922			
II.2	**SECONDARY DISTRIBUTION OF INCOME**									
B.5g	National income, balance of primary incomes, gross	1 258 722	174 994	23 749	144 068	916 827	–916			1 258 722
D.5	Current taxes on income, wealth etc	201 872			201 872			584		202 456
D.61	Social contributions	188 767	3 612	80 106	104 549	500		–		188 767
D.62	Social benefits other than social transfers in kind	213 858				213 858		1 690		215 548
D.7	Other current transfers	200 220	7 248	32 464	104 847	55 661		22 796		223 016
II.3	**REDISTRIBUTION OF INCOME IN KIND**									
B.6g	Disposable income, gross	1 247 635	140 899	46 102	253 561	807 989	–916			1 247 635
D.63	Social transfers in kind	198 984				198 984				198 984
II.4	**USE OF INCOME**									
B.7g	Adjusted disposable income, gross	1 247 635	140 899	46 102	86 162	975 388	–916			1 247 635
B.6g	Disposable income, gross	1 247 635	140 899	46 102	253 561	807 989	–916			1 247 635
P.4	Actual final consumption								1 061 355	1 061 355
P.3	Final consumption expenditure								1 061 355	1 061 355
D.8	Adjustment for change in households' net equity in pension funds	31 210				31 210		–67		31 143
	Accumulation accounts									
III.1.1	**CHANGE IN NET WORTH DUE TO SAVING AND CAPITAL TRANSFERS**									
B.8g	Saving, gross	186 347	140 899	14 959	–15 340	46 745	–916			186 347
B.12	Current external balance							30 452		30 452
D.9	Capital transfers receivable	43 899	19 021	321	15 532	9 025		2 224		46 123
D.9	Capital transfers payable	–42 150	–1 257	–321	–36 508	–4 064		–3 973		–46 123
III.1.2	**ACQUISITION ON NON-FINANCIAL ASSETS**									
	Changes in liabilities and net worth									
B.10.1.g	Changes in net worth due to saving and capital transfers	188 096	158 663	14 959	–36 316	51 706	–916	28 703		216 799
P.51	Gross fixed capital formation								211 862	211 862
-K.1	(Consumption of fixed capital)									
P.52	Changes in inventories								4 071	4 071
P.53	Acquisitions less disposals of valuables								–377	–377
K.2	Acquisitions less disposals of non-produced non-financial assets									
de	Statistical discrepancy between expenditure components and GDP								1 243	1 243
III.2	**FINANCIAL ACCOUNT**									
B.9	**Net lending(+) / net borrowing(-)**	–28 961	21 233	8 168	–42 251	–13 952	–2 159	28 961		-
	Changes in liabilities									
F.2	Currency and deposits	594 201	–	588 529	5 672	–		371 280		965 481
F.3	Securities other than shares	184 545	12 166	136 278	36 157	–56		91 059		275 604
F.4	Loans	530 496	119 671	292 245	6 264	112 316		159 036		689 532
F.5	Shares and other equity	58 577	10 421	48 156		–		122 744		181 321
F.6	Insurance technical reserves	55 963		55 963						55 963
F.7	Other accounts payable	15 258	5 819	2 032	3 623	3 784		–1 096		14 162

1.7C UK summary accounts 2005

continued

Total economy: all sectors and the rest of the world

£ million

		USES							RESOURCES	TOTAL
		UK total economy	Non-financial corporations	Financial corporations	General government	Households & NPISH	Not sector -ised	Rest of the world	Goods & services	
		S.1	S.11	S.12	S.13	S.14+S.15	S.N	S.2		
	Current accounts									
I 0	**PRODUCTION / EXTERNAL ACCOUNT OF GOODS AND SERVICES**									
P.7	Imports of goods and services								370 968	370 968
P.6	Exports of goods and services							326 790		326 790
P.1	Output at basic prices								..	..
P.2	Intermediate consumption	..	..	..	140 817	..	51 922			..
D.21-D.31	Taxes *less* subsidies on products								137 347	137 347
B.1g	**Gross domestic product, value added at market prices**	**1 233 976**	**..**	**80 407**	**152 479**	**..**	**84 509**			**1 233 976**
B.11	External balance of goods and services							44 178		44 178
II.1.1	**GENERATION OF INCOME**									
D.1	Compensation of employees	686 805	443 406	39 228	139 874	64 297		974		687 779
D.21-D.31	Taxes *less* subsidies on products	137 347					137 347			137 347
D.29-D.39	Other taxes *less* subsidies on production	14 271			14 271					14 271
B.2g	Operating surplus, gross	320 794	242 623	39 697	12 605	77 791	–51 922			320 794
B.3g	Mixed income, gross	75 675				75 675				75 675
di	Statistical discrepancy between income components and GDP	–916					–916			–916
II.1.2	**ALLOCATION OF PRIMARY INCOME**									
D.4	Property income	581 604	163 375	319 059	29 449	69 721		186 513		768 117
-P.119	Adjustment to property income for financial services (FISIM)									
B.5g	National income, balance of primary incomes, gross	1 258 722	174 994	23 749	144 068	916 827	–916			1 258 722
II.2	**SECONDARY DISTRIBUTION OF INCOME**									
D.5	Current taxes on income, wealth etc	201 912	33 607	8 710	997	158 598		544		202 456
D.61	Social contributions	188 753				188 753		14		188 767
D.62	Social benefits other than social transfers in kind	215 548	3 612	48 963	161 979	994				215 548
D.7	Other current transfers	209 591	7 736	32 544	138 799	30 512		13 425		223 016
B.6g	Disposable income, gross	1 247 635	140 899	46 102	253 561	807 989	–916			1 247 635
II.3	**REDISTRIBUTION OF INCOME IN KIND**									
B.7g	Adjusted disposable income, gross	1 247 635	140 899	46 102	86 162	975 388	–916			1 247 635
D.63	Social transfers in kind	198 984			167 399	31 585				198 984
II.4	**USE OF INCOME**									
B.6g	Disposable income, gross									
P.4	Actual final consumption	1 061 355			101 502	959 853				1 061 355
P.3	Final consumption expenditure	1 061 355			268 901	792 454				1 061 355
D.8	Adjustment for change in households' net equity in pension funds	31 143		31 143						31 143
B.8g	Saving, gross	186 347	140 899	14 959	–15 340	46 745	–916			186 347
B.12	Current external balance							30 452		30 452
	Accumulation accounts									
III.1.1	**CHANGE IN NET WORTH DUE TO SAVING AND CAPITAL TRANSFERS**									
D.9	Capital transfers receivable									
D.9	Capital transfers payable									
B.10.1.g	Changes in net worth due to saving and capital transfers	188 096	158 663	14 959	–36 316	51 706	–916	28 703		216 799
III.1.2	**ACQUISITION OF NON-FINANCIAL ASSETS**									
	Changes in assets									
P.51	Gross fixed capital formation	211 862	131 525	7 043	7 130	66 164				211 862
-K.1	(Consumption of fixed capital)	–131 093	–71 335	–4 530	–12 605	–42 623				–131 093
P.52	Changes in inventories	4 071	4 292	48	–6	–263				4 071
P.53	Acquisitions less disposals of valuables	–377	–171	–299	16	77				–377
K.2	Acquisitions less disposals of non-produced non-financial assets	258	1 784	–1	–1 205	–320		–258		–
de	Statistical discrepancy between expenditure components and GDP	1 243					1 243			1 243
B.9	**Net lending(+) / net borrowing(-)**	–28 961	21 233	8 168	–42 251	–13 952	–2 159	28 961		–
III.2	**FINANCIAL ACCOUNT: changes in assets**									
F.1	Monetary gold and SDRs	–8			–8			8		
F.2	Currency and deposits	685 762	61 551	559 893	–1 195	65 513		279 719		965 481
F.3	Securities other than shares	150 565	–1 870	149 549	3 075	–189		125 039		275 604
F.4	Loans	413 768	36 118	370 162	5 097	2 391		275 764		689 532
F.5	Shares and other equity	78 733	69 604	38 019	–3 422	–25 468		102 588		181 321
F.6	Insurance technical reserves	55 305	965	107	44	54 189		658		55 963
F.7	Other accounts receivable	14 004	1 190	3 425	5 526	3 863		158		14 162
dB.9f	Statistical discrepancy between non-financial and financial transactions	11 950	1 752	10 216	348	1 793	–2 159	–11 950		–

1.7D UK summary accounts 2006

Total economy: all sectors and the rest of the world

£ million

		RESOURCES							USES	TOTAL
		UK total economy	Non-financial corporations	Financial corporations	General government	Households & NPISH	Not sector -ised	Rest of the world	Goods & services	
		S.1	S.11	S.12	S.13	S.14+S.15	S.N	S.2		
	Current accounts									
I	**PRODUCTION / EXTERNAL**									
0	**ACCOUNT OF GOODS AND SERVICES**									
P.7	Imports of goods and services							424 128		424 128
P.6	Exports of goods and services								369 691	369 691
P.1	Output at basic prices	..	..	..	..	..				..
P.2	Intermediate consumption								..	..
D.21-D.31	Taxes *less* subsidies on products	144 663					144 663			144 663
II.1.1	**GENERATION OF INCOME**									
B.1g	**Gross domestic product, value added at market prices**	**1 299 622**	**..**	**89 122**	**161 858**	**..**	**86 546**			**1 299 622**
B.11	External balance of goods and services							54 437		54 437
II.1.2	**ALLOCATION OF PRIMARY INCOME**									
D.1	Compensation of employees	720 549				720 549		1 785		722 334
D.21-D.31	Taxes *less* subsidies on products	140 167			140 167			4 496		144 663
D.29-D.39	Other taxes *less* subsidies on production	18 303	19 302	1 739	–	–2 738		–3 275		15 028
B.2g	Operating surplus, gross	340 331	256 112	45 710	13 650	82 425	–57 566			340 331
B.3g	Mixed income, gross	78 864				78 864				78 864
di	Statistical discrepancy between income components and GDP	–551					–551			–551
D.4	Property income	708 470	108 211	438 797	10 322	151 140		221 010		929 480
-P.119	Adjustment to property income for financial services (FISIM)			–57 566			57 566			
II.2	**SECONDARY DISTRIBUTION OF INCOME**									
B.5g	National income, balance of primary incomes, gross	1 316 956	183 799	22 377	152 021	959 310	–551			1 316 956
D.5	Current taxes on income, wealth etc	223 698			223 698			493		224 191
D.61	Social contributions	201 422	3 490	88 350	109 074	508		–		201 422
D.62	Social benefits other than social transfers in kind	223 618				223 618		1 771		225 389
D.7	Other current transfers	211 685	7 793	32 820	114 388	56 684		21 323		233 008
II.3	**REDISTRIBUTION OF INCOME IN KIND**									
B.6g	Disposable income, gross	1 306 259	146 101	42 553	281 955	836 201	–551			1 306 259
D.63	Social transfers in kind	211 865				211 865				211 865
II.4	**USE OF INCOME**									
B.7g	Adjusted disposable income, gross	1 306 259	146 101	42 553	103 403	1 014 753	–551			1 306 259
B.6g	Disposable income, gross	1 306 259	146 101	42 553	281 955	836 201	–551			1 306 259
P.4	Actual final consumption								1 114 893	1 114 893
P.3	Final consumption expenditure								1 114 893	1 114 893
D.8	Adjustment for change in households' net equity in pension funds	35 720				35 720		–19		35 701
	Accumulation accounts									
III.1.1	**CHANGE IN NET WORTH DUE TO SAVING AND CAPITAL TRANSFERS**									
B.8g	Saving, gross	191 385	146 101	6 852	–4 857	43 840	–551			191 385
B.12	Current external balance							47 781		47 781
D.9	Capital transfers receivable	31 204	7 970	446	14 480	8 308		2 358		33 562
D.9	Capital transfers payable	–30 169	–645	–446	–24 342	–4 736		–3 393		–33 562
III.1.2	**ACQUISITION ON NON-FINANCIAL ASSETS**									
	Changes in liabilities and net worth									
B.10.1.g	Changes in net worth due to saving and capital transfers	192 420	153 426	6 852	–14 719	47 412	–551	46 746		239 166
P.51	Gross fixed capital formation								234 751	234 751
-K.1	(Consumption of fixed capital)									
P.52	Changes in inventories								3 735	3 735
P.53	Acquisitions less disposals of valuables								45	45
K.2	Acquisitions less disposals of non-produced non-financial assets									
de	Statistical discrepancy between expenditure components and GDP								635	635
III.2	**FINANCIAL ACCOUNT**									
B.9	**Net lending(+) / net borrowing(-)**	–46 951	21 988	–966	–37 933	–28 854	–1 186	46 951		–
	Changes in liabilities									
F.2	Currency and deposits	787 216	–	781 839	5 377	–		276 708		1 063 924
F.3	Securities other than shares	254 416	11 699	202 021	39 627	1 069		170 249		424 665
F.4	Loans	457 585	126 915	201 403	1 416	127 851		109 805		567 390
F.5	Shares and other equity	95 100	11 615	83 485		–		88 926		184 026
F.6	Insurance technical reserves	65 508		65 508						65 508
F.7	Other accounts payable	14 069	3 513	4 586	4 414	1 556		369		14 438

1.7D UK summary accounts 2006

continued

Total economy: all sectors and the rest of the world

£ million

		USES							RESOURCES	TOTAL
		UK total economy	Non-financial corporations	Financial corporations	General government	Households & NPISH	Not sector -ised	Rest of the world	Goods & services	
		S.1	S.11	S.12	S.13	S.14+S.15	S.N	S.2		
	Current accounts									
I 0	**PRODUCTION / EXTERNAL ACCOUNT OF GOODS AND SERVICES**									
P.7	Imports of goods and services								424 128	424 128
P.6	Exports of goods and services							369 691		369 691
P.1	Output at basic prices								..	..
P.2	Intermediate consumption	..	..	..	..	..	57 566			..
D.21-D.31	Taxes *less* subsidies on products								144 663	144 663
B.1g	**Gross domestic product, value added at market prices**	**1 299 622**	**..**	**89 122**	**161 858**	**..**	**86 546**			**1 299 622**
B.11	External balance of goods and services							54 437		54 437
II.1.1	**GENERATION OF INCOME**									
D.1	Compensation of employees	721 287	463 742	..	..	68 111		1 047		722 334
D.21-D.31	Taxes *less* subsidies on products	144 663					144 663			144 663
D.29-D.39	Other taxes *less* subsidies on production	15 028			15 028					15 028
B.2g	Operating surplus, gross	340 331	256 112	45 710	13 650	82 425	–57 566			340 331
B.3g	Mixed income, gross	78 864				78 864				78 864
di	Statistical discrepancy between income components and GDP	–551					–551			–551
II.1.2	**ALLOCATION OF PRIMARY INCOME**									
D.4	Property income	689 177	180 524	404 564	30 421	73 668		240 303		929 480
-P.119	Adjustment to property income for financial services (FISIM)									
B.5g	National income, balance of primary incomes, gross	1 316 956	183 799	22 377	152 021	959 310	–551			1 316 956
II.2	**SECONDARY DISTRIBUTION OF INCOME**									
D.5	Current taxes on income, wealth etc	223 566	37 221	15 445	1 075	169 825		625		224 191
D.61	Social contributions	201 368				201 368		54		201 422
D.62	Social benefits other than social transfers in kind	225 389	3 490	52 649	168 246	1 004				225 389
D.7	Other current transfers	220 797	8 270	32 900	147 905	31 722		12 211		233 008
B.6g	Disposable income, gross	1 306 259	146 101	42 553	281 955	836 201	–551			1 306 259
II.3	**REDISTRIBUTION OF INCOME IN KIND**									
B.7g	Adjusted disposable income, gross	1 306 259	146 101	42 553	103 403	1 014 753	–551			1 306 259
D.63	Social transfers in kind	211 865			178 552	33 313				211 865
II.4	**USE OF INCOME**									
B.6g	Disposable income, gross									
P.4	Actual final consumption	1 114 893			108 260	1 006 633				1 114 893
P.3	Final consumption expenditure	1 114 893			286 812	828 081				1 114 893
D.8	Adjustment for change in households' net equity in pension funds	35 701		35 701						35 701
B.8g	Saving, gross	191 385	146 101	6 852	–4 857	43 840	–551			191 385
B.12	Current external balance							47 781		47 781
	Accumulation accounts									
III.1.1	**CHANGE IN NET WORTH DUE TO SAVING AND CAPITAL TRANSFERS**									
D.9	Capital transfers receivable									
D.9	Capital transfers payable									
B.10.1.g	Changes in net worth due to saving and capital transfers	192 420	153 426	6 852	–14 719	47 412	–551	46 746		239 166
III.1.2	**ACQUISITION OF NON-FINANCIAL ASSETS**									
	Changes in assets									
P.51	Gross fixed capital formation	234 751	126 224	7 919	24 147	76 461				234 751
-K.1	(Consumption of fixed capital)	–133 936	–72 737	–4 662	–13 650	–42 887				–133 936
P.52	Changes in inventories	3 735	3 803	48	–4	–112				3 735
P.53	Acquisitions less disposals of valuables	45	–90	–158	18	275				45
K.2	Acquisitions less disposals of non-produced non-financial assets	205	1 501	9	–947	–358		–205		–
de	Statistical discrepancy between expenditure components and GDP	635					635			635
B.9	**Net lending(+) / net borrowing(-)**	–46 951	21 988	–966	–37 933	–28 854	–1 186	46 951		–
III.2	**FINANCIAL ACCOUNT: changes in assets**									
F.1	Monetary gold and SDRs	47			47			–47		
F.2	Currency and deposits	730 652	63 708	585 037	6 781	75 126		333 272		1 063 924
F.3	Securities other than shares	260 337	7 489	258 735	2 168	–8 055		164 328		424 665
F.4	Loans	460 666	32 858	427 801	3 480	–3 473		106 724		567 390
F.5	Shares and other equity	110 022	72 610	61 867	–2 576	–21 879		74 004		184 026
F.6	Insurance technical reserves	64 984	766	84	35	64 099		524		65 508
F.7	Other accounts receivable	14 381	5 359	2 516	2 387	4 119		57		14 438
dB.9f	Statistical discrepancy between non-financial and financial transactions	–14 146	–7 060	1 836	579	–8 315	–1 186	14 146		–

1.7.1 UK summary accounts 2004

Total economy: all sectors and the rest of the world

£ million

		UK total economy S.1	Non-financial corporations S.11	Financial corporations S.12	Monetary financial institutions S.121+S.122	Other financial intermediaries & auxiliaries S.123+S.124	Insurance corporations & pension funds S.125
I	**PRODUCTION ACCOUNT**						
	Resources						
P.1	Output						
P.11	Market output*	1 786 979	1 361 125	160 157			
P.12	Output for own final use	92 962	11 946	2 458			
P.13	Other non-market output	279 661					
P.1	Total output	2 159 602	1 373 071	162 615			
D.21	Taxes on products	139 642					
-D.31	*less* Subsidies on products	–7 280					
Total	Total resources	2 291 964	1 373 071	162 615			
P.119	**of which* FISIM (financial intermediation services indirectly measured)	50 165		50 165			
	Uses						
P.2	Intermediate consumption	1 107 668	704 727	76 553			
B.1*g	**Gross Domestic Product**	**1 184 296**	**668 344**	**86 062**	**50 942**	**17 364**	**17 756**
Total	Total uses	2 291 964	1 373 071	162 615			
B.1*g	**Gross Domestic Product**	**1 184 296**	**668 344**	**86 062**	**50 942**	**17 364**	**17 756**
-K.1	*less* Fixed capital consumption	–128 427	–69 979	–4 401			
B.1*n	Net domestic product	1 055 869	598 365	81 661			

1.7.2 UK summary accounts 2004

Total economy: all sectors and the rest of the world

£ million

		UK total economy S.1	Non-financial corporations S.11	Financial corporations S.12	Monetary financial institutions S.121+S.122	Other financial intermediaries & auxiliaries S.123+S.124	Insurance corporations & pension funds S.125
II	**DISTRIBUTION AND USE OF INCOME ACCOUNTS**						
II.1	**PRIMARY DISTRIBUTION OF INCOME ACCOUNT**						
II.1.1	**GENERATION OF INCOME ACCOUNT**						
	Resources						
B.1*g	**Total resources (Gross Domestic Product)** external balance of goods & services	**1 184 296**	**668 344**	**86 062**	**50 942**	**17 364**	**17 756**
	Uses						
D.1	Compensation of employees						
D.11	Wages and salaries	550 583	357 937	31 811	15 360	9 980	6 471
D.12	Employers' social contributions	98 134	61 624	5 472	2 176	2 186	1 110
D.1	Total	648 717	419 561	37 283	17 536	12 166	7 581
D.2	Taxes on production and imports, paid						
D.21	Taxes on products and imports	139 642					
D.29	Production taxes other than on products	18 945	17 426	1 455	532	570	353
D.2	Total taxes on production and imports	158 587	17 426	1 455	532	570	353
-D.3	*less* Subsidies, received						
-D.31	Subsidies on products	–7 280					
-D.39	Production subsidies other than on products	–2 091	–1 499	–	–	–	–
-D.3	Total subsidies on production	–9 371	–1 499	–	–	–	–
B.2g	Operating surplus, gross	314 405	232 856	47 324	32 874	4 628	9 822
B.3g	Mixed income, gross	71 958					
di	Statistical discrepancy between income components and GDP	–					
B.1*g	**Total uses (Gross Domestic Product)**	**1 184 296**	**668 344**	**86 062**	**50 942**	**17 364**	**17 756**
-K.1	After deduction of fixed capital consumption	–128 427	–69 979	–4 401			
B.2n	Operating surplus, net	205 782	162 877	42 923			
B.3n	Mixed income, net	52 154					

1.7.1 UK summary accounts 2004

continued

Total economy: all sectors and the rest of the world

£ million

		General government	Central government	Local government	Households & NPISH	Not sector -ised	Taxes less subsidies	FISIM	Rest of the world
		S.13	S.1311	S.1313	S.14+S.15	S.N			S.2
I	**PRODUCTION ACCOUNT**								
	Resources								
P.1	Output								
P.11	Market output*	22 295	4 367	17 928	243 402				
P.12	Output for own final use	467	39	428	78 091				
P.13	Other non-market output	250 708	152 325	98 383	28 953				
P.1	Total output	273 470	156 731	116 739	350 446				
D.21	Taxes on products					139 642	139 642		
-D.31	*less* Subsidies on products					−7 280	−7 280		
Total	Total resources	273 470	156 731	116 739	350 446	132 362	132 362		
	**of which* FISIM (financial intermediation services indirectly measured)								
	Uses								
P.2	Intermediate consumption	131 012	79 853	51 159	145 211	50 165		50 165	
B.1*g	**Gross Domestic Product**	**142 458**	**76 878**	**65 580**	**205 235**	**82 197**	132 362	−50 165	
Total	Total uses	273 470	156 731	116 739	350 446	132 362	132 362		
B.1*g	**Gross Domestic Product**	**142 458**	**76 878**	**65 580**	**205 235**	**82 197**	132 362	−50 165	
-K.1	*less* Fixed capital consumption	−11 681	−6 224	−5 457	−42 366				
B.1*n	Net domestic product	130 777	70 654	60 123	162 869	82 197	132 362	−50 165	

1.7.2 UK summary accounts 2004

continued

Total economy: all sectors and the rest of the world

£ million

		General government	Central government	Local government	Households & NPISH	Not sector -ised	Taxes less subsidies	FISIM	Rest of the world
		S.13	S.1311	S.1313	S.14+S.15	S.N			S.2
II	**DISTRIBUTION AND USE OF INCOME ACCOUNTS**								
II.1	**PRIMARY DISTRIBUTION OF INCOME ACCOUNT**								
II.1.1	**GENERATION OF INCOME ACCOUNT**								
	Resources								
B.1*g	**Total Resources (Gross Domestic Product)**	**142 458**	**76 878**	**65 580**	**205 235**	**82 197**	132 362	−50 165	
	external balance of goods & services								34 975
	Uses								
D.1	Compensation of employees								
D.11	Wages and salaries	108 707	58 802	49 905	52 128				1 171
D.12	Employers' social contributions	22 070	11 852	10 218	8 968				
D.1	Total	130 777	70 654	60 123	61 096				1 171
D.2	Taxes on production and imports, paid								
D.21	Taxes on products and imports					139 642	139 642		–
D.29	Production taxes other than on products	–	–	–	64				
D.2	Total taxes on production and imports	–	–	–	64	139 642	139 642		–
-D.3	*less* Subsidies, received								
-D.31	Subsidies on products					−7 280	−7 280		
-D.39	Production subsidies other than on products	–	–	–	−592				
-D.3	Total subsidies on production	–	–	–	−592	−7 280	−7 280		
B.2g	Operating surplus, gross	11 681	6 224	5 457	72 709	−50 165		−50 165	
B.3g	Mixed income, gross				71 958				
di	Statistical discrepancy between income components and GDP					–			
B.1*g	**Total uses (Gross Domestic Product)**	**142 458**	**76 878**	**65 580**	**205 235**	**82 197**	132 362	−50 165	
-K.1	After deduction of fixed capital consumption	−11 681	−6 224	−5 457	−42 366				
B.2n	Operating surplus, net	–	–	–	50 147	−50 165		−50 165	
B.3n	Mixed income, net				52 154				

1.7.3 UK summary accounts 2005

Total economy: all sectors and the rest of the world

£ million

		UK total economy S.1	Non-financial corporations S.11	Financial corporations S.12	Monetary financial institutions S.121+S.122	Other financial intermediaries & auxiliaries S.123+S.124	Insurance corporations & pension funds S.125
II.1.2	**ALLOCATION OF PRIMARY INCOME ACCOUNT**						
	Resources						
B.2g	Operating surplus, gross	320 794	242 623	39 697	30 211	5 063	4 423
B.3g	Mixed income, gross	75 675					
D.1	Compensation of employees						
D.11	Wages and salaries	578 300					
D.12	Employers' social contributions	107 895					
D.1	Total	686 195					
di	Statistical discrepancy between income components and GDP	–916					
D.2	Taxes on production and imports, received						
D.21	Taxes on products						
D.211	Value added tax (VAT)	81 383					
D.212	Taxes and duties on imports excluding VAT	–					
D.2121	Import duties	–					
D.2122	Taxes on imports excluding VAT and import duties	–					
D.214	Taxes on products excluding VAT and import duties	56 815					
D.21	Total taxes on products	138 198					
D.29	Other taxes on production	19 601					
D.2	Total taxes on production and imports, received	157 799					
-D.3	*less* Subsidies, paid						
-D.31	Subsidies on products	–5 111					
-D.39	Other subsidies on production	–2 058					
-D.3	Total subsidies	–7 169					
D.4	Property income, received						
D.41	Interest	326 994	15 040	274 214	205 320	41 897	26 997
D.42	Distributed income of corporations	172 703	47 970	70 518	10 398	35 828	24 292
D.43	Reinvested earnings on direct foreign investment	42 236	32 032	10 204	4 927	2 170	3 107
D.44	Property income attributed to insurance policy holders	64 400	582	66	17	15	34
D.45	Rent	1 615	122	31	–	–	31
D.4	Total property income	607 948	95 746	355 033	220 662	79 910	54 461
-P.119	Adjustment to property income for financial services (FISIM)			–51 922	–43 912	–8 010	
Total	Total resources	1 840 326	338 369	342 808	206 961	76 963	58 884
	Uses						
D.4	Property income, paid						
D.41	Interest	345 143	49 725	196 472	150 274	44 242	1 956
D.42	Distributed income of corporations	159 242	107 215	52 027	21 426	26 971	3 630
D.43	Reinvested earnings on direct foreign investment	10 107	5 044	5 063	2 692	1 503	868
D.44	Property income attributed to insurance policy holders	65 497		65 497			65 497
D.45	Rent	1 615	1 391	–	–	–	–
D.4	Total property income	581 604	163 375	319 059	174 392	72 716	71 951
B.5*g	**Gross National Income (GNI)**	**1 258 722**	**174 994**	**23 749**	**32 569**	**4 247**	**–13 067**
Total	Total uses	1 840 326	338 369	342 808	206 961	76 963	58 884
-K.1	After deduction of fixed capital consumption	–131 093	–71 335	–4 530			
B.5*n	National income, net	1 127 629	103 659	19 219			

1.7.3 UK summary accounts 2005

continued

Total economy: all sectors and the rest of the world

£ million

		General government	Central government	Local government	Households & NPISH	Not sector -ised	Rest of the world
		S.13	S.1311	S.1313	S.14+S.15	S.N	S.2
II.1.2	**ALLOCATION OF PRIMARY INCOME ACCOUNT**						
	Resources						
B.2g	Operating surplus, gross	12 605	6 699	5 906	77 791	–51 922	
B.3g	Mixed income, gross				75 675		
D.1	Compensation of employees						
D.11	Wages and salaries				578 300		1 584
D.12	Employers' social contributions				107 895		
D.1	Total				686 195		1 584
di	Statistical discrepancy between income components and GDP					–916	
D.2	Taxes on production and imports, received						
D.21	Taxes on products						
D.211	Value added tax (VAT)	81 383	81 383				1 999
D.212	Taxes and duties on imports excluding VAT						
D.2121	Import duties	–	–				2 237
D.2122	Taxes on imports excluding VAT and import duties	–	–				–
D.214	Taxes on products excluding VAT and import duties	56 815	56 815				24
D.21	Total taxes on products	138 198	138 198				4 260
D.29	Other taxes on production	19 601	19 419	182			
D.2	Total taxes on production and imports, received	157 799	157 617	182			4 260
-D.3	*less* Subsidies, paid						
-D.31	Subsidies on products	–5 111	–3 419	–1 692			–
-D.39	Other subsidies on production	–2 058	–1 372	–686			–3 272
-D.3	Total subsidies	–7 169	–4 791	–2 378			–3 272
D.4	Property income, received						
D.41	Interest	6 318	5 265	1 053	31 422		111 771
D.42	Distributed income of corporations	2 585	2 164	421	51 630		37 194
D.43	Reinvested earnings on direct foreign investment						10 107
D.44	Property income attributed to insurance policy holders	27		27	63 725		1 097
D.45	Rent	1 352	1 352	–	110		
D.4	Total property income	10 282	8 781	1 501	146 887		160 169
-P.119	Adjustment to property income for financial services (FISIM)					51 922	
Total	Total resources	173 517	168 306	5 211	986 548	–916	
	Uses						
D.4	Property income, paid						
D.41	Interest	29 449	25 975	3 474	69 497		93 622
D.42	Distributed income of corporations						50 655
D.43	Reinvested earnings on direct foreign investment						42 236
D.44	Property income attributed to insurance policy holders						
D.45	Rent				224		
D.4	Total property income	29 449	25 975	3 474	69 721		186 513
B.5*g	**Gross National Income (GNI)**	**144 068**	**142 331**	**1 737**	**916 827**	**–916**	
Total	Total uses	173 517	168 306	5 211	986 548	–916	
-K.1	After deduction of fixed capital consumption	–12 605	–6 699	–5 906	–42 623		
B.5*n	National income, net	131 463	135 632	–4 169	874 204	–916	

1.7.4 UK summary accounts 2005

Total economy: all sectors and the rest of the world

£ million

		UK total economy S.1	Non-financial corporations S.11	Financial corporations S.12	Monetary financial institutions S.121+S.122	Other financial intermediaries & auxiliaries S.123+S.124	Insurance corporations & pension funds S.125
II.2	**SECONDARY DISTRIBUTION OF INCOME ACCOUNT**						
	Resources						
B.5*g	**Gross National Income**	**1 258 722**	**174 994**	**23 749**	**32 569**	**4 247**	**–13 067**
D.5	Current taxes on income, wealth etc.						
D.51	Taxes on income	172 619					
D.59	Other current taxes	29 253					
D.5	Total	201 872					
D.61	Social contributions						
D.611	Actual social contributions						
D.6111	Employers' actual social contributions	95 997		43 093			43 093
D.6112	Employees' social contributions	78 047		36 509	–	–	36 509
D.6113	Social contributions by self- and non-employed persons	2 825		–	–	–	–
D.611	Total	176 869		79 602	–		79 602
D.612	Imputed social contributions	11 898	3 612	504	239	165	100
D.61	Total	188 767	3 612	80 106	239	165	79 702
D.62	Social benefits other than social transfers in kind	213 858					
D.7	Other current transfers						
D.71	Net non-life insurance premiums	31 661		31 661			31 661
D.72	Non-life insurance claims	25 551	7 248	803	208	178	417
D.73	Current transfers within general government	100 224					
	Current international cooperation						
D.74	from institutions of the EC	3 668					
D.75	Miscellaneous current transfers	39 116	–	–	–	–	
D.7	Total, other current transfers	200 220	7 248	32 464	208	178	32 078
Total	Total resources	2 063 439	185 854	136 319	33 016	4 590	98 713
	Uses						
D.5	Current taxes on income, wealth etc.						
D.51	Taxes on income	172 659	33 607	8 710	3 943	–275	5 042
D.59	Other current taxes	29 253					
D.5	Total	201 912	33 607	8 710	3 943	–275	5 042
D.61	Social contributions						
D.611	Actual social contributions						
D.6111	Employers' actual social contributions	95 997					
D.6112	Employees' actual social contributions	78 033					
D.6113	Social contributions by self- and non-employed persons	2 825					
D.611	Total actual social contributions	176 855					
D.612	Imputed social contributions	11 898					
D.61	Total	188 753					
D.62	Social benefits other than social transfers in kind	215 548	3 612	48 963	239	165	48 559
D.7	Other current transfers						
D.71	Net non-life insurance premiums	25 551	7 248	803	208	178	417
D.72	Non-life insurance claims	31 661		31 661			31 661
D.73	Current transfers within general government	100 224					
	Current international cooperation						
D.74	to institutions of the EC	3 300					
D.75	Miscellaneous current transfers	48 855	488	80	56	24	–
	Of which: GNP based fourth own resource	8 732					
D.7	Total other current transfers	209 591	7 736	32 544	264	202	32 078
B.6*g	**Gross National Disposable Income**	**1 247 635**	**140 899**	**46 102**	**28 570**	**4 498**	**13 034**
Total	Total uses	2 063 439	185 854	136 319	33 016	4 590	98 713
-K.1	After deduction of fixed capital consumption	–131 093	–71 335	–4 530			
B.6*n	Disposable income, net	1 116 542	69 564	41 572			

1.7.4 UK summary accounts 2005

continued

Total economy: all sectors and the rest of the world

£ million

		General government	Central government	Local government	Households & NPISH	Not sector -ised	Rest of the world
		S.13	S.1311	S.1313	S.14+S.15	S.N	S.2
II.2	**SECONDARY DISTRIBUTION OF INCOME ACCOUNT**						
	Resources						
B.5*g	**Gross National Income**	**144 068**	**142 331**	**1 737**	**916 827**	**–916**	
D.5	Current taxes on income, wealth etc.						
D.51	Taxes on income	172 619	172 619				584
D.59	Other current taxes	29 253	8 137	21 116			
D.5	Total	201 872	180 756	21 116			584
D.61	Social contributions						
D.611	Actual social contributions						
D.6111	Employers' actual social contributions	52 904	52 904				
D.6112	Employees' social contributions	41 538	40 780	758			–
D.6113	Social contributions by self- and non-employed persons	2 825	2 825				
D.611	Total	97 267	96 509	758			–
D.612	Imputed social contributions	7 282	4 975	2 307	500		
D.61	Total	104 549	101 484	3 065	500		–
D.62	Social benefits other than social transfers in kind				213 858		1 690
D.7	Other current transfers						
D.71	Net non-life insurance premiums						16
D.72	Non-life insurance claims	328	–	328	17 172		6 126
D.73	Current transfers within general government	100 224	–	100 224			
	Current international cooperation						3 300
D.74	from institutions of the EC	3 668	3 668				
D.75	Miscellaneous current transfers	627	627		38 489		13 354
	Of which: GNP based fourth own resource						8 732
D.7	Total, other current transfers	104 847	4 295	100 552	55 661		22 796
Total	Total resources	555 336	428 866	126 470	1 186 846	–916	
	Uses						
D.5	Current taxes on income, wealth etc.						
D.51	Taxes on income				130 342		544
D.59	Other current taxes	997		997	28 256		
D.5	Total	997		997	158 598		544
D.61	Social contributions						
D.611	Actual social contributions						
D.6111	Employers' actual social contributions				95 997		
D.6112	Employees' social contributions				78 033		14
D.6113	Social contributions by self- and non-employed persons				2 825		
D.611	Total actual social contributions				176 855		14
D.612	Imputed social contributions				11 898		
D.61	Total				188 753		14
D.62	Social benefits other than social transfers in kind	161 979	143 708	18 271	994		900
D.7	Other current transfers						
D.71	Net non-life insurance premiums	328	–	328	17 172		6 126
D.72	Non-life insurance claims						16
D.73	Current transfers within general government	100 224	100 224	–			
	Current international cooperation						3 668
D.74	to institutions of the EC	3 300	3 300				
D.75	Miscellaneous current transfers	34 947	34 924	23	13 340		3 615
	Of which: GNP based fourth own resource	8 732	8 732				
D.7	Total other current transfers	138 799	138 448	351	30 512		13 425
B.6*g	**Gross National Disposable Income**	**253 561**	**146 710**	**106 851**	**807 989**	**–916**	
Total	Total uses	555 336	428 866	126 470	1 186 846	–916	
-K.1	After deduction of fixed capital consumption	–12 605	–6 699	–5 906	–42 623		
B.6*n	Disposable income, net	240 956	140 011	100 945	765 366	–916	

1.7.5 UK summary accounts 2005

Total economy: all sectors and the rest of the world

£ million

		UK total economy S.1	Non-financial corporations S.11	Financial corporations S.12	Monetary financial institutions S.121+S.122	Other financial intermediaries & auxiliaries S.123+S.124	Insurance corporations & pension funds S.125
II.3	**REDISTRIBUTION OF INCOME IN KIND ACCOUNT**						
	Resources						
B.6*g	**Gross National Disposable Income**	**1 247 635**	**140 899**	**46 102**	**28 570**	**4 498**	**13 034**
D.63	Social transfers in kind						
D.631	Social benefits in kind						
D.6313	Social assistance benefits in kind	–					
	Transfers of individual non-market goods						
D.632	and services	198 984					
D.63	Total social transfers in kind	198 984					
Total	Total resources	1 446 619	140 899	46 102	28 570	4 498	13 034
	Uses						
D.63	Social transfers in kind						
D.631	Social benefits in kind						
D.6313	Social assistance benefits in kind	–					
D.632	Transfers of individual non-market goods and services	198 984					
D.63	Total social transfers in kind	198 984					
B.7g	Adjusted disposable income, gross	1 247 635	140 899	46 102	28 570	4 498	13 034
Total	Total uses	1 446 619	140 899	46 102	28 570	4 498	13 034

1.7.5 UK summary accounts 2005

continued

Total economy: all sectors and the rest of the world

£ million

		General government	Central government	Local government	Households & NPISH	Not sector -ised	Rest of the world
		S.13	S.1311	S.1313	S.14+S.15	S.N	S.2
II.3	**REDISTRIBUTION OF INCOME IN KIND ACCOUNT**						
	Resources						
B.6*g	**Gross National Disposable Income**	**253 561**	**146 710**	**106 851**	**807 989**	**–916**	
D.63	Social transfers in kind						
D.631	Social benefits in kind						
D.6313	Social assistance benefits in kind				–		
D.632	Transfers of individual non-market goods and services				198 984		
D.63	Total social transfers in kind				198 984		
Total	Total resources	253 561	146 710	106 851	1 006 973	–916	
	Uses						
D.63	Social transfers in kind						
D.631	Social benefits in kind						
D.6313	Social assistance benefits in kind				–		
D.632	Transfers of individual non-market goods and services	167 399	97 295	70 104	31 585		
D.63	Total social transfers in kind	167 399	97 295	70 104	31 585		
B.7g	Adjusted disposable income, gross	86 162	49 415	36 747	975 388	–916	
Total	Total uses	253 561	146 710	106 851	1 006 973	–916	

1.7.6 UK summary accounts 2005

Total economy: all sectors and the rest of the world

£ million

		UK total economy	Non-financial corporations	Financial corporations	Monetary financial institutions	Other financial intermediaries & auxiliaries	Insurance corporations & pension funds
		S.1	S.11	S.12	S.121+S.122	S.123+S.124	S.125
II.4	**USE OF INCOME ACCOUNT**						
II.4.1	**USE OF DISPOSABLE INCOME ACCOUNT**						
	Resources						
B.6g	**Gross National Disposable Income**	**1 247 635**	**140 899**	**46 102**	**28 570**	**4 498**	**13 034**
	Adjustment for the change in net equity						
D.8	of households in pension funds	31 210					
Total	Total resources	1 278 845	140 899	46 102	28 570	4 498	13 034
	Uses						
P.3	Final consumption expenditure						
P.31	Individual consumption expenditure	959 853					
P.32	Collective consumption expenditure	101 502					
P.3	Total	1 061 355					
	Adjustment for the change in net equity						
D.8	of households in pension funds	31 143		31 143			31 143
B.8g	**Gross Saving**	**186 347**	**140 899**	**14 959**	**28 570**	**4 498**	**–18 109**
B.12	Current external balance						
Total	Total uses	1 278 845	140 899	46 102	28 570	4 498	13 034
-K.1	After deduction of fixed capital consumption	–131 093	–71 335	–4 530			
B.8n	Saving, net	55 254	69 564	10 429			
II.4.2	**USE OF ADJUSTED DISPOSABLE INCOME ACCOUNT**						
	Resources						
B.7g	Adjusted disposable income	1 247 635	140 899	46 102	28 570	4 498	13 034
	Adjustment for the change in net equity						
D.8	of households in pension funds	31 210					
Total	Total resources	1 278 845	140 899	46 102	28 570	4 498	13 034
	Uses						
P.4	Actual final consumption						
P.41	Actual individual consumption	959 853					
P.42	Actual collective consumption	101 502					
P.4	Total actual final consumption	1 061 355					
	Adjustment for the change in net equity						
D.8	of households in pension funds	31 143		31 143			
B.8g	**Gross Saving**	**186 347**	**140 899**	**14 959**	**28 570**	**4 498**	**–18 109**
Total	Total uses	1 278 845	140 899	46 102	28 570	4 498	13 034

1.7.6 UK summary accounts 2005

continued

Total economy: all sectors and the rest of the world

£ million

		General government	Central government	Local government	Households & NPISH	Not sector -ised	Rest of the world
		S.13	S.1311	S.1313	S.14+S.15	S.N	S.2
II.4	**USE OF INCOME ACCOUNT**						
II.4.1	**USE OF DISPOSABLE INCOME ACCOUNT**						
	Resources						
B.6g	**Gross National Disposable Income**	**253 561**	**146 710**	**106 851**	**807 989**	**–916**	
	Adjustment for the change in net equity						
D.8	of households in pension funds				31 210		–67
Total	Total resources	253 561	146 710	106 851	839 199	–916	
	Uses						
P.3	Final consumption expenditure						
P.31	Individual consumption expenditure	167 399	97 295	70 104	792 454		
P.32	Collective consumption expenditure	101 502	65 456	36 046			
P.3	Total	268 901	162 751	106 150	792 454		
	Adjustment for the change in net equity						
D.8	of households in pension funds						
B.8g	**Gross Saving**	**–15 340**	**–16 041**	**701**	**46 745**	**–916**	
B.12	Current external balance						30 452
Total	Total uses	253 561	146 710	106 851	839 199	–916	
-K.1	After deduction of fixed capital consumption	–12 605	–6 699	–5 906	–42 623		
B.8n	Saving, net	–27 945	–22 740	–5 205	4 122	–916	
II.4.2	**USE OF ADJUSTED DISPOSABLE INCOME ACCOUNT**						
	Resources						
B.7g	Adjusted disposable income	86 162	49 415	36 747	975 388	–916	
	Adjustment for the change in net equity						
D.8	of households in pension funds				31 210		–67
Total	Total resources	86 162	49 415	36 747	1 006 598	–916	
	Uses						
P.4	Actual final consumption						
P.41	Actual individual consumption				959 853		
P.42	Actual collective consumption	101 502	65 456	36 046			
P.4	Total actual final consumption	101 502	65 456	36 046	959 853		
	Adjustment for the change in net equity						
D.8	of households in pension funds						
B.8g	**Gross Saving**	**–15 340**	**–16 041**	**701**	**46 745**	**–916**	
Total	Total uses	86 162	49 415	36 747	1 006 598	–916	

1.7.7 UK summary accounts 2005

Total economy: all sectors and the rest of the world

£ million

		UK total economy S.1	Non-financial corporations S.11	Financial corporations S.12	Monetary financial institutions S.121+S.122	Other financial intermediaries & auxiliaries S.123+S.124	Insurance corporations & pension funds S.125
III	**ACCUMULATION ACCOUNTS**						
III.1	**CAPITAL ACCOUNT**						
III.1.1	**CHANGE IN NET WORTH DUE TO SAVING & CAPITAL TRANSFERS**						
	Changes in liabilities and net worth						
B.8g	**Gross Saving**	**186 347**	**140 899**	**14 959**	**28 570**	**4 498**	**–18 109**
B.12	Current external balance						
D.9	Capital transfers receivable						
D.91	Capital taxes	3 150					
D.92	Investment grants	22 008	7 218	–	–	–	–
D.99	Other capital transfers	18 741	11 803	321	–	–	321
D.9	Total	43 899	19 021	321	–	–	321
-D.9	*less* Capital transfers payable						
-D.91	Capital taxes	–3 150	–	–	–	–	–
-D.92	Investment grants	–20 934					
-D.99	Other capital transfers	–18 066	–1 257	–321	–	–	–321
-D.9	Total	–42 150	–1 257	–321	–	–	–321
B.10.1g	Total change in liabilities and net worth	188 096	158 663	14 959	28 570	4 498	–18 109
	Changes in assets						
B.10.1g	Changes in net worth due to gross saving and capital transfers	188 096	158 663	14 959	28 570	4 498	–18 109
-K.1	After deduction of fixed capital consumption	–131 093	–71 335	–4 530			
B.10.1n	Changes in net worth due to net saving and capital transfers	57 003	87 328	10 429			
III.1.2	**ACQUISITION OF NON-FINANCIAL ASSETS ACCOUNT**						
	Changes in liabilities and net worth						
B.10.1n	Changes in net worth due to net saving and capital transfers	57 003	87 328	10 429			
K.1	Consumption of fixed capital	131 093	71 335	4 530			
B.10.1g	Total change in liabilities and net worth	188 096	158 663	14 959	28 570	4 498	–18 109
	Changes in assets						
P.5	Gross capital formation						
P.51	Gross fixed capital formation	211 862	131 525	7 043	4 967	1 698	378
P.52	Changes in inventories	4 071	4 292	48	48	–	–
P.53	Acquisitions less disposals of valuables	–377	–171	–299	–	–	–299
P.5	Total	215 556	135 646	6 792	5 015	1 698	79
K.2	Acquisitions less disposals of non-produced non-financial assets	258	1 784	–1	–	20	–21
de	Statistical discrepancy between expenditure components and GDP	1 243					
B.9	**Net lending(+) / net borrowing(-)**	**–28 961**	**21 233**	**8 168**	**23 555**	**2 780**	**–18 167**
Total	Total change in assets	188 096	158 663	14 959	28 570	4 498	–18 109

1.7.7 UK summary accounts 2005

continued

Total economy: all sectors and the rest of the world

£ million

		General government	Central government	Local government	Households & NPISH	Not sector -ised	Rest of the world
		S.13	S.1311	S.1313	S.14+S.15	S.N	S.2
III	**ACCUMULATION ACCOUNTS**						
III.1	**CAPITAL ACCOUNT**						
III.1.1	**CHANGE IN NET WORTH DUE TO SAVING SAVING & CAPITAL TRANSFERS**						
	Changes in liabilities and net worth						
B.8g	**Gross Saving**	**–15 340**	**–16 041**	**701**	**46 745**	**–916**	
B.12	Current external balance						30 452
D.9	Capital transfers receivable						
D.91	Capital taxes	3 150	3 150				
D.92	Investment grants	8 512		8 512	6 278		408
D.99	Other capital transfers	3 870	2 443	1 427	2 747		1 816
D.9	Total	15 532	5 593	9 939	9 025		2 224
-D.9	*less* Capital transfers payable						
-D.91	Capital taxes				–3 150		
-D.92	Investment grants	–20 934	–19 364	–1 570			–1 482
-D.99	Other capital transfers	–15 574	–14 290	–1 284	–914		–2 491
-D.9	Total	–36 508	–33 654	–2 854	–4 064		–3 973
B.10.1g	Total change in liabilities and net worth	–36 316	–44 102	7 786	51 706	–916	28 703
	Changes in assets						
B.10.1g	Changes in net worth due to gross saving and capital transfers	–36 316	–44 102	7 786	51 706	–916	28 703
-K.1	After deduction of fixed capital consumption	–12 605	–6 699	–5 906	–42 623		
B.10.1n	Changes in net worth due to net saving and capital transfers	–48 921	–50 801	1 880	9 083	–916	
III.1.2	**ACQUISITION OF NON-FINANCIAL ASSETS ACCOUNT**						
	Changes in liabilities and net worth						
B.10.1n	Changes in net worth due to net saving and capital transfers	–48 921	–50 801	1 880	9 083	–916	
K.1	Consumption of fixed capital	12 605	6 699	5 906	42 623		
B.10.1g	Total change in liabilities and net worth	–36 316	–44 102	7 786	51 706	–916	28 703
	Changes in assets						
P.5	Gross capital formation						
P.51	Gross fixed capital formation	7 130	–6 386	13 516	66 164		
P.52	Changes in inventories	–6	–6	–	–263		
P.53	Acquisitions less disposals of valuables	16	16		77		
P.5	Total	7 140	–6 376	13 516	65 978		
K.2	Acquisitions less disposals of non-produced non-financial assets	–1 205	–303	–902	–320		–258
de	Statistical discrepancy between expenditure components and GDP					1 243	
B.9	**Net lending(+) / net borrowing(-)**	**–42 251**	**–37 423**	**–4 828**	**–13 952**	**–2 159**	28 961
Total	Total change in assets	–36 316	–44 102	7 786	51 706	–916	28 703

1.7.8 UK summary accounts 2006

Total economy: all sectors and the rest of the world. Unconsolidated

£ million

		UK total economy	Non-financial corporations	Financial corporations	Monetary financial institutions	Other financial intermediaries & auxiliaries	Insurance corporations & pension funds
		S.1	S.11	S.12	S.121+S.122	S.123+S.124	S.125
III.2	**FINANCIAL ACCOUNT**						
F.A	**Net acquisition of financial assets**						
F.1	Monetary gold and special drawing rights (SDRs)	47					
F.2	Currency and deposits						
F.21	Currency	1 934	238	–168	–168	–	
F.22	Transferable deposits						
F.221	Deposits with UK monetary financial institutions	447 511	27 050	349 724	231 978	112 440	5 306
F.229	Deposits with rest of the world monetary financial institutions	276 605	35 705	237 564	178 412	56 000	3 152
F.29	Other deposits	4 602	715	–2 083	–	–2 083	–
F.2	Total currency and deposits	730 652	63 708	585 037	410 222	166 357	8 458
F.3	Securities other than shares						
F.331	Short term: money market instruments						
F.3311	Issued by UK central government	–2 415	–26	–2 372	–3 746	1 150	224
F.3312	Issued by UK local authorities	–	–	–	–	–	
F.3315	Issued by UK monetary financial institutions	11 805	2 394	5 775	3 121	1 991	663
F.3316	Issued by other UK residents	5 031	2 237	949	2 239	–48	–1 242
F.3319	Issued by the rest of the world	16 065	5 359	9 343	5 058	4 290	–5
F.332	Medium (1 to 5 year) and long term (over 5 year) bonds						
F.3321	Issued by UK central government	16 120	–1 996	29 350	–4 583	14 281	19 652
F.3322	Issued by UK local authorities	358	–	269	–	–	269
F.3325	Medium term bonds issued by UK MFIs[1]	14 499	466	14 033	–58	3 565	10 526
F.3326	Other medium & long term bonds issued by UK residents	44 800	257	44 927	45 053	–4 368	4 242
F.3329	Long term bonds issued by the rest of the world	161 943	–1 201	163 910	100 963	41 427	21 520
F.34	Financial derivatives	–7 869	–1	–7 449	–7 449	–	
F.3	Total securities other than shares	260 337	7 489	258 735	140 598	62 288	55 849
F.4	Loans						
F.41	Short term loans						
F.411	Loans by UK monetary financial institutions, excluding loans secured on dwellings & financial leasing	307 993		307 993	307 993		
F.419	Loans by rest of the world monetary financial institutions						
F.42	Long term loans						
F.421	Direct investment	–6 367	–6 021	–346	–	240	–586
F.422	Loans secured on dwellings	109 691	–	109 645	46 430	63 435	–220
F.423	Finance leasing	1 657	991	666	–4	670	
F.424	Other long term loans	47 692	37 888	9 843	–478	5 134	5 187
F.429	Other long term loans by the rest of the world						
F.4	Total loans	460 666	32 858	427 801	353 941	69 479	4 381
F.5	Shares and other equity						
F.51	Shares and other equity, excluding mutual funds' shares						
F.514	Quoted UK shares	–9 392	19 896	–11 612	6 122	4 209	–21 943
F.515	Unquoted UK shares	16 586	9 873	19 803	21 099	–635	–661
F.516	Other UK equity (including direct investment in property)	–1 204					
F.517	UK shares and bonds issued by other UK residents	–	–	–	–	–	–
F.519	Shares and other equity issued by the rest of the world	88 115	42 824	42 679	34 106	–3 213	11 786
F.52	Mutual funds' shares						
F.521	UK mutual funds' shares	15 106	17	10 997	50	131	10 816
F.529	Rest of the world mutual funds' shares	811					
F.5	Total shares and other equity	110 022	72 610	61 867	61 377	492	–2
F.6	Insurance technical reserves						
F.61	Net equity of households in life assurance and pension funds' reserves	62 374					
F.62	Prepayments of insurance premiums and reserves for outstanding claims	2 610	766	84	–	40	44
F.6	Total insurance technical reserves	64 984	766	84	–	40	44
F.7	Other accounts receivable	14 381	5 359	2 516	–73	645	1 944
F.A	**Total net acquisition of financial assets**	1 641 089	182 790	1 336 040	966 065	299 301	70 674

1 UK monetary financial institutions

1.7.8 UK summary accounts 2006

continued

Total economy: all sectors and the rest of the world. Unconsolidated

£ million

		General government	Central government	Local government	Households & NPISH	Rest of the world
		S.13	S.1311	S.1313	S.14+S.15	S.2
III.2	**FINANCIAL ACCOUNT**					
F.A	**Net acquisition of financial assets**					
F.1	Monetary gold and special drawing rights (SDRs)	47	47			–47
F.2	Currency and deposits					
F.21	Currency				1 864	68
F.22	Transferable deposits					
F.221	Deposits with UK monetary financial institutions	7 634	2 246	5 388	63 103	332 730
F.229	Deposits with rest of the world monetary financial institutions	–671	–671		4 007	
F.29	Other deposits	–182	–1	–181	6 152	474
F.2	Total currency and deposits	6 781	1 574	5 207	75 126	333 272
F.3	Securities other than shares					
F.331	Short term: money market instruments					
F.3311	Issued by UK central government	–17		–17	–	663
F.3312	Issued by UK local authorities	–			–	
F.3315	Issued by UK monetary financial institutions	798	1 768	–970	2 838	41 384
F.3316	Issued by other UK residents	1 845	1 192	653	–	–3 471
F.3319	Issued by the rest of the world	1 363	1 363			
F.332	Medium (1 to 5 year) and long term (over 5 year) bonds					
F.3321	Issued by UK central government	72		72	–11 306	24 901
F.3322	Issued by UK local authorities				89	–
F.3325	Medium term bonds issued by UK MFIs[1]					26 035
F.3326	Other medium & long term bonds issued by UK residents	–620	–620	–	236	74 816
F.3329	Long term bonds issued by the rest of the world	–854	–854		88	
F.34	Financial derivatives	–419	–419		–	
F.3	Total securities other than shares	2 168	2 430	–262	–8 055	164 328
F.4	Loans					
F.41	Short term loans					
F.411	Loans by UK monetary financial institutions, excluding loans secured on dwellings & financial leasing					
F.419	Loans by rest of the world monetary financial institutions					120 775
F.42	Long term loans					
F.421	Direct investment					–14 291
F.422	Loans secured on dwellings	46	–	46		
F.423	Finance leasing					
F.424	Other long-term loans by UK residents	3 434	3 446	–12	–3 473	
F.429	Other long-term loans by the rest of the world					240
F.4	Total loans	3 480	3 446	34	–3 473	106 724
F.5	Shares and other equity					
F.51	Shares and other equity, excluding mutual funds' shares					
F.514	Quoted UK shares	240	32	208	–17 916	35 505
F.515	Unquoted UK shares	–2 431	–	–2 431	–10 659	37 982
F.516	Other UK equity (including direct investment in property)	–1 204	–1 204		–	467
F.517	UK shares and bonds issued by other UK residents	–	–	–	–	–
F.519	Shares and other equity issued by the rest of the world	819	819		1 793	
F.52	Mutual funds' shares					
F.521	UK mutual funds' shares				4 092	50
F.529	Rest of the world mutual funds' shares				811	
F.5	Total shares and other equity	–2 576	–353	–2 223	–21 879	74 004
F.6	Insurance technical reserves					
F.61	Net equity of households in life assurance and pension funds' reserves				62 374	–19
F.62	Prepayments of insurance premiums and reserves for outstanding claims	35		35	1 725	543
F.6	Total insurance technical reserves	35		35	64 099	524
F.7	Other accounts receivable	2 387	2 272	115	4 119	57
F.A	**Total net acquisition of financial assets**	12 322	9 416	2 906	109 937	678 862

1 UK monetary financial institutions

1.7.8 UK summary accounts 2006

continued

Total economy: all sectors and the rest of the world. Unconsolidated

£ million

		UK total economy	Non-financial corporations	Financial corporations	Monetary financial institutions	Other financial intermediaries & auxiliaries	Insurance corporations & pension funds
		S.1	S.11	S.12	S.121+S.122	S.123+S.124	S.125
III.2	**FINANCIAL ACCOUNT** continued						
F.L	**Net acquisition of financial liabilities**						
F.2	Currency and deposits						
F.21	Currency	1 899		1 745	1 745		
F.22	Transferable deposits						
F.221	Deposits with UK monetary financial institutions	780 241		780 241	780 241		
F.229	Deposits with rest of the world monetary financial institutions						
F.29	Other deposits	5 076	–	–147		–147	
F.2	Total currency and deposits	787 216	–	781 839	781 986	–147	
F.3	Securities other than shares						
F.331	Short term: money market instruments						
F.3311	Issued by UK central government	–1 752					
F.3312	Issued by UK local authorities	–					
F.3315	Issued by UK monetary financial institutions	53 189		53 189	53 189		
F.3316	Issued by other UK residents	1 560	436	455		455	
F.3319	Issued by the rest of the world						
F.332	Medium (1 to 5 year) and long term (over 5 year) bonds						
F.3321	Issued by UK central government	41 021					
F.3322	Issued by UK local authorities	358					
F.3325	Medium term bonds issued by UK MFIs[1]	40 534		40 534	40 534		
F.3326	Other medium & long term bonds issued by UK residents	119 616	11 263	107 953	–9 678	117 570	61
F.3329	Long term bonds issued by the rest of the world						
F.34	Financial derivatives	–110	–	–110	–110	–	
F.3	Total securities other than shares	254 416	11 699	202 021	83 935	118 025	61
F.4	Loans						
F.41	Short term loans						
F.411	Loans by UK monetary financial institutions, excluding loans secured on dwellings & financial leasing	188 617	55 603	119 304		119 022	282
F.419	Loans by rest of the world monetary financial institutions	120 775	77 207	38 393		31 685	6 708
F.42	Long term loans						
F.421	Direct investment	–14 291	–16 301	2 010	–7	534	1 483
F.422	Loans secured on dwellings	109 691	3 812				
F.423	Finance leasing	1 657	1 160	191	110	81	
F.424	Other long-term loans by UK residents	50 896	5 434	41 505		41 463	42
F.429	Other long-term loans by the rest of the world	240	–	–		–	
F.4	Total loans	457 585	126 915	201 403	103	192 785	8 515
F.5	Shares and other equity						
F.51	Shares and other equity, excluding mutual funds' shares						
F.514	Quoted UK shares	26 113	–3 456	29 569	2 881	16 399	10 289
F.515	Unquoted UK shares	54 568	15 808	38 760	2 303	34 484	1 973
F.516	Other UK equity (including direct investment in property)	–737	–737	–	–		
F.517	UK shares and bonds issued by other UK residents	–	–	–	–	–	
F.519	Shares and other equity issued by the rest of the world						
F.52	Mutual funds' shares						
F.521	UK mutual funds' shares	15 156		15 156		15 156	
F.529	Rest of the world mutual funds' shares						
F.5	Total shares and other equity	95 100	11 615	83 485	5 184	66 039	12 262
F.6	Insurance technical reserves						
F.61	Net equity of households in life assurance and pension funds' reserves	62 355		62 355			62 355
F.62	Prepayments of insurance premiums and reserves for outstanding claims	3 153		3 153			3 153
F.6	Total insurance technical reserves	65 508		65 508			65 508
F.7	Other accounts payable	14 069	3 513	4 586	621	17	3 948
F.L	**Total net acquisition of financial liabilities**	1 673 894	153 742	1 338 842	871 829	376 719	90 294
B.9	**Net lending / borrowing**						
F.A	Total net acquisition of financial assets	1 641 089	182 790	1 336 040	966 065	299 301	70 674
-F.L	*less* Total net acquisition of financial liabilities	–1 673 894	–153 742	–1 338 842	–871 829	–376 719	–90 294
B.9f	Net lending (+) / net borrowing (-), from financial account	–32 805	29 048	–2 802	94 236	–77 418	–19 620
dB.9f	Statistical discrepancy between financial & non-financial accounts	–14 146	–7 060	1 836	–66 960	65 917	2 879
B.9	**Net lending (+) / net borrowing (-), from capital account**	**–46 951**	**21 988**	**–966**	**27 276**	**–11 501**	**–16 741**

1.7.8 UK summary accounts 2006

continued

Total economy: all sectors and the rest of the world. Unconsolidated

£ million

		General government	Central government	Local government	Households & NPISH	Not sector -ised	Rest of the world
		S.13	S.1311	S.1313	S.14+S.15	S.N	S.2
III.2	**FINANCIAL ACCOUNT** continued						
F.L	**Net acquisition of financial liabilities**						
F.2	Currency and deposits						
F.21	Currency	154	154				103
F.22	Transferable deposits						
F.221	Deposits with UK monetary financial institutions						
F.229	Deposits with rest of the world monetary financial institutions						276 605
F.29	Other deposits	5 223	5 223				
F.2	Total currency and deposits	5 377	5 377				276 708
F.3	Securities other than shares						
F.331	Short term: money market instruments						
F.3311	Issued by UK central government	–1 752	–1 752				
F.3312	Issued by UK local authorities	–		–			
F.3315	Issued by UK monetary financial institutions						
F.3316	Issued by other UK residents				669		
F.3319	Issued by the rest of the world						16 065
F.332	Medium (1 to 5 year) and long term (over 5 year) bonds						
F.3321	Issued by UK central government	41 021	41 021				
F.3322	Issued by UK local authorities	358		358			
F.3325	Medium term bonds issued by UK MFIs[1]						
F.3326	Other medium & long term bonds issued by UK residents				400		
F.3329	Long term bonds issued by the rest of the world						161 943
F.34	Financial derivatives				–		–7 759
F.3	Total securities other than shares	39 627	39 269	358	1 069		170 249
F.4	Loans						
F.41	Short term loans						
F.411	Loans by UK monetary financial institutions, excluding loans secured on dwellings & financial leasing	–1 831	–2 997	1 166	15 541		119 376
F.419	Loans by rest of the world monetary financial institutions	–1	–	–1	5 176		
F.42	Long term loans						
F.421	Direct investment						–6 367
F.422	Loans secured on dwellings				105 879		
F.423	Finance leasing	306	303	3			–
F.424	Other long-term loans by UK residents	2 702	–7	2 709	1 255		–3 204
F.429	Other long-term loans by the rest of the world	240	7	233			
F.4	Total loans	1 416	–2 694	4 110	127 851		109 805
F.5	Shares and other equity						
F.51	Shares and other equity, excluding mutual funds' shares						
F.514	Quoted UK shares						
F.515	Unquoted UK shares						
F.516	Other UK equity (including direct investment in property)						
F.517	UK shares and bonds issued by other UK residents						
F.519	Shares and other equity issued by the rest of the world						88 115
F.52	Mutual funds' shares						
F.521	UK mutual funds' shares						
F.529	Rest of the world mutual funds' shares						811
F.5	Total shares and other equity						88 926
F.6	Insurance technical reserves						
F.61	Net equity of households in life assurance and pension funds' reserves						
F.62	Prepayments of insurance premiums and reserves for outstanding claims						
F.6	Total insurance technical reserves						
F.7	Other accounts payable	4 414	3 723	691	1 556		369
F.L	**Total net acquisition of financial liabilities**	50 834	45 675	5 159	130 476		646 057
B.9	**Net lending / borrowing**						
F.A	Total net acquisition of financial assets	12 322	9 416	2 906	109 937		678 862
-F.L	*less* Total net acquisition of financial liabilities	–50 834	–45 675	–5 159	–130 476		–646 057
B.9f	Net lending (+) / net borrowing (-), from financial account	–38 512	–36 259	–2 253	–20 539		32 805
dB.9f	Statistical discrepancy between financial & non-financial accounts	579	–185	764	–8 315	–1 186	14 146
B.9	**Net lending (+) / net borrowing (-), from capital account**	**–37 933**	**–36 444**	**–1 489**	**–28 854**	–1 186	46 951

1.7.9 UK summary accounts 2006

Total economy: all sectors and the rest of the world. Unconsolidated

£ billion

		UK total economy S.1	Non-financial corporations S.11	Financial corporations S.12	Monetary financial institutions S.121+S.122	Other financial intermediaries & auxiliaries S.123+S.124	Insurance corporations & pension funds S.125
IV.3	**FINANCIAL BALANCE SHEET** at end of period						
AF.A	**Financial assets**						
AF.1	Monetary gold and special drawing rights (SDRs)	3.4					
AF.2	Currency and deposits						
AF.21	Currency	51.9	4.5	10.1	10.0	0.1	
AF.22	Transferable deposits						
AF.221	Deposits with UK monetary financial institutions	2 952.3	254.5	1 829.6	1 280.2	482.8	66.5
AF.229	Deposits with rest of the world monetary financial institutions	2 193.0	295.4	1 850.2	1 285.1	545.0	20.2
AF.29	Other deposits	90.0	9.4	1.5	–	1.5	–
AF.2	Total currency and deposits	5 287.3	563.7	3 691.4	2 575.3	1 029.3	86.7
AF.3	Securities other than shares						
AF.331	Short term: money market instruments						
AF.3311	Issued by UK central government	15.8	–	15.7	12.1	2.9	0.7
AF.3312	Issued by UK local authorities	–	–	–	–	–	
AF.3315	Issued by UK monetary financial institutions	164.3	7.3	148.3	98.4	24.3	25.6
AF.3316	Issued by other UK residents	47.3	35.7	9.7	5.0	1.0	3.7
AF.3319	Issued by the rest of the world	77.9	17.4	57.4	42.8	11.1	3.5
AF.332	Medium (1 to 5 year) and long term (over 5 year) bonds						
AF.3321	Issued by UK central government	313.9	0.7	293.3	−7.7	58.0	243.0
AF.3322	Issued by UK local authorities	1.2	–	0.8	–	–	0.8
AF.3325	Medium term bonds issued by UK MFIs[1]	91.0	1.9	89.0	24.5	16.6	47.9
AF.3326	Other medium & long term bonds issued by UK residents	475.6	1.5	468.3	189.4	96.1	182.8
AF.3329	Long term bonds issued by the rest of the world	829.3	14.4	792.1	479.4	131.2	181.5
AF.34	Financial derivatives	0.7	–	–	–	–	
AF.3	Total securities other than shares	2 017.0	79.0	1 874.6	844.0	341.2	689.5
AF.4	Loans						
AF.41	Short term loans						
AF.411	Loans by UK monetary financial institutions, excluding loans secured on dwellings & financial leasing	1 982.1		1 982.1	1 982.1		
AF.419	Loans by rest of the world monetary financial institutions						
AF.42	Long term loans						
AF.421	Direct investment	221.5	191.8	29.7	–	21.2	8.5
AF.422	Loans secured on dwellings	1 077.1	–	1 075.6	795.5	279.4	0.8
AF.423	Finance leasing	33.5	6.4	27.1	2.6	24.5	
AF.424	Other long term loans	209.6	10.7	113.8	3.4	5.3	105.0
AF.429	Other long term loans by the rest of the world						
AF.4	Total loans	3 523.8	208.9	3 228.3	2 783.6	330.4	114.3
AF.5	Shares and other equity						
AF.51	Shares and other equity, excluding mutual funds' shares						
AF.514	Quoted UK shares	1 065.5	32.9	805.8	21.0	291.3	493.6
AF.515	Unquoted UK shares	544.8	61.1	393.9	153.0	235.1	5.7
AF.516	Other UK equity (including direct investment in property)	1.4					
AF.517	UK shares and bonds issued by other UK residents	–	–	–	–	–	–
AF.519	Shares and other equity issued by the rest of the world	1 460.1	594.5	783.0	163.3	221.2	398.4
AF.52	Mutual funds' shares						
AF.521	UK mutual funds' shares	450.7	0.6	299.2	1.7	4.7	292.8
AF.529	Rest of the world mutual funds' shares	6.0					
AF.5	Total shares and other equity	3 528.5	689.1	2 281.9	339.1	752.4	1 190.5
AF.6	Insurance technical reserves						
AF.61	Net equity of households in life assurance and pension funds' reserves	2 070.8					
AF.62	Prepayments of insurance premiums and reserves for outstanding claims	59.6	18.1	2.0		1.0	1.0
AF.6	Total insurance technical reserves	2 130.4	18.1	2.0		1.0	1.0
AF.7	Other accounts receivable	369.8	143.7	71.8	0.1	20.7	51.0
AF.A	**Total financial assets**	16 860.2	1 702.4	11 150.1	6 542.0	2 475.0	2 133.0

1 UK monetary financial institutions

1.7.9 UK summary accounts 2006

continued

Total economy: all sectors and the rest of the world. Unconsolidated

£ billion

		General government	Central government	Local government	Households & NPISH	Rest of the world
		S.13	S.1311	S.1313	S.14+S.15	S.2
IV.3	**FINANCIAL BALANCE SHEET** at end of period					
AF.A	**Financial assets**					
AF.1	Monetary gold and special drawing rights (SDRs)	3.4	3.4			
AF.2	Currency and deposits					
AF.21	Currency				37.4	1.5
AF.22	Transferable deposits					
AF.221	Deposits with UK monetary financial institutions	34.5	7.7	26.8	833.8	2 370.7
AF.229	Deposits with rest of the world monetary financial institutions	1.2	1.2		46.2	
AF.29	Other deposits	0.2	–	0.2	78.9	1.4
AF.2	Total currency and deposits	35.9	8.9	27.0	996.3	2 373.7
AF.3	Securities other than shares					
AF.331	Short term: money market instruments					
AF.3311	Issued by UK central government	0.1		0.1	–	3.5
AF.3312	Issued by UK local authorities	–			–	
AF.3315	Issued by UK monetary financial institutions	5.2	2.7	2.5	3.5	163.4
AF.3316	Issued by other UK residents	1.4	1.2	0.1	0.5	16.3
AF.3319	Issued by the rest of the world	3.0	3.0			
AF.332	Medium (1 to 5 year) and long term (over 5 year) bonds					
AF.3321	Issued by UK central government	0.2		0.2	19.6	135.5
AF.3322	Issued by UK local authorities	–	–		0.4	–
AF.3325	Medium term bonds issued by UK MFIs[1]					114.9
AF.3326	Other medium & long term bonds issued by UK residents	0.5	0.3	0.2	5.3	525.0
AF.3329	Long term bonds issued by the rest of the world	15.3	15.3		7.5	
AF.34	Financial derivatives	0.7	0.7		–	
AF.3	Total securities other than shares	26.5	23.3	3.2	36.8	958.5
AF.4	Loans					
AF.41	Short term loans					
AF.411	Loans by UK monetary financial institutions, excluding loans secured on dwellings & financial leasing					
AF.419	Loans by rest of the world monetary financial institutions					948.7
AF.42	Long term loans					
AF.421	Direct investment					336.4
AF.422	Loans secured on dwellings	1.4	0.1	1.3		
AF.423	Finance leasing					
AF.424	Other long-term loans by UK residents	77.9	77.7	0.2	7.3	
AF.429	Other long-term loans by the rest of the world					2.9
AF.4	Total loans	79.3	77.8	1.6	7.3	1 288.0
AF.5	Shares and other equity					
AF.51	Shares and other equity, excluding mutual funds' shares					
AF.514	Quoted UK shares	2.0	0.6	1.4	224.8	739.0
AF.515	Unquoted UK shares	1.2	0.8	0.4	88.7	410.6
AF.516	Other UK equity (including direct investment in property)				1.4	20.2
AF.517	UK shares and bonds issued by other UK residents	–	–	–	–	–
AF.519	Shares and other equity issued by the rest of the world	9.4	9.4		73.2	
AF.52	Mutual funds' shares					
AF.521	UK mutual funds' shares				150.9	1.7
AF.529	Rest of the world mutual funds' shares				6.0	
AF.5	Total shares and other equity	12.5	10.7	1.8	545.0	1 171.5
AF.6	Insurance technical reserves					
AF.61	Net equity of households in life assurance and pension funds' reserves				2 070.8	0.2
AF.62	Prepayments of insurance premiums and reserves for outstanding claims	0.8		0.8	38.7	14.8
AF.6	Total insurance technical reserves	0.8		0.8	2 109.6	15.0
AF.7	Other accounts receivable	49.2	47.8	1.4	105.1	1.9
AF.A	**Total financial assets**	207.7	171.8	35.8	3 800.1	5 808.5

1 UK monetary financial institutions

1.7.9 UK summary accounts 2006

continued

Total economy: all sectors and the rest of the world. Unconsolidated

£ billion

		UK total economy	Non-financial corporations	Financial corporations	Monetary financial institutions	Other financial intermediaries & auxiliaries	Insurance corporations & pension funds
		S.1	S.11	S.12	S.121+S.122	S.123+S.124	S.125
IV.3	**FINANCIAL BALANCE SHEET** continued at end of period						
AF.L	**Financial liabilities**						
AF.2	Currency and deposits						
AF.21	Currency	52.8		49.0	49.0		
AF.22	Transferable deposits						
AF.221	Deposits with UK monetary financial institutions	5 323.1		5 323.1	5 323.1		
AF.229	Deposits with rest of the world monetary financial institutions						
AF.29	Other deposits	91.4	–	1.6		1.6	
AF.2	Total currency and deposits	5 467.3	–	5 373.6	5 372.0	1.6	
AF.3	Securities other than shares						
AF.331	Short term: money market instruments						
AF.3311	Issued by UK central government	19.4					
AF.3312	Issued by UK local authorities	–					
AF.3315	Issued by UK monetary financial institutions	327.7		327.7	327.7		
AF.3316	Issued by other UK residents	63.6	21.7	41.8		41.8	
AF.3319	Issued by the rest of the world						
AF.332	Medium (1 to 5 year) and long term (over 5 year) bonds						
AF.3321	Issued by UK central government	449.3					
AF.3322	Issued by UK local authorities	1.2					
AF.3325	Medium term bonds issued by UK MFIs[1]	205.8		205.8	205.8		
AF.3326	Other medium & long term bonds issued by UK residents	1 000.6	361.2	636.3	110.6	525.4	0.3
AF.3329	Long term bonds issued by the rest of the world						
AF.34	Financial derivatives	0.7	–	0.7	0.7	–	
AF.3	Total securities other than shares	2 068.3	382.9	1 212.4	644.9	567.2	0.3
AF.4	Loans						
AF.41	Short term loans						
AF.411	Loans by UK monetary financial institutions, excluding loans secured on dwellings & financial leasing	1 272.9	398.2	656.2	–	643.7	12.5
AF.419	Loans by rest of the world monetary financial institutions	948.7	289.6	638.9		615.6	23.2
AF.42	Long term loans						
AF.421	Direct investment	336.4	284.2	52.1	1.3	39.7	11.1
AF.422	Loans secured on dwellings	1 077.1	3.8				
AF.423	Finance leasing	33.5	25.7	3.7	2.0	1.7	
AF.424	Other long-term loans by UK residents	203.6	89.1	36.8	–	36.3	0.5
AF.429	Other long-term loans by the rest of the world	2.9	0.4	0.5		0.5	
AF.4	Total loans	3 875.0	1 118.2	1 388.2	3.3	1 337.6	47.3
AF.5	Shares and other equity						
AF.51	Shares and other equity, excluding mutual funds' shares						
AF.514	Quoted UK shares	1 804.5	1 318.7	485.7	13.5	399.2	73.1
AF.515	Unquoted UK shares	955.4	580.7	374.7	126.8	235.9	12.0
AF.516	Other UK equity (including direct investment in property)	21.6	21.6				
AF.517	UK shares and bonds issued by other UK residents	–	–	–	–	–	–
AF.519	Shares and other equity issued by the rest of the world						
AF.52	Mutual funds' shares						
AF.521	UK mutual funds' shares	452.4		452.4		452.4	
AF.529	Rest of the world mutual funds' shares						
AF.5	Total shares and other equity	3 233.9	1 921.0	1 312.9	140.2	1 087.6	85.1
AF.6	Insurance technical reserves						
AF.61	Net equity of households in life assurance and pension funds' reserves	2 071.1		2 071.1			2 071.1
AF.62	Prepayments of insurance premiums and reserves for outstanding claims	74.4		74.4			74.4
AF.6	Total insurance technical reserves	2 145.4		2 145.4			2 145.4
AF.7	Other accounts payable	362.2	152.8	54.2	6.1	2.2	45.9
AF.L	**Total financial liabilities**	17 152.1	3 574.9	11 486.7	6 166.5	2 996.2	2 324.0
BF.90	**Net financial assets / liabilities**						
AF.A	Total financial assets	16 860.2	1 702.4	11 150.1	6 542.0	2 475.0	2 133.0
-AF.L	*less* Total financial liabilities	–17 152.1	–3 574.9	–11 486.7	–6 166.5	–2 996.2	–2 324.0
BF.90	**Net financial assets (+) / liabilities (-)**	–291.9	–1 872.5	–336.6	375.5	–521.2	–191.0

1 UK monetary financial institutions

1.7.9 UK summary accounts 2006

continued

Total economy: all sectors and the rest of the world. Unconsolidated

£ billion

		General government	Central government	Local government	Households & NPISH	Rest of the world
		S.13	S.1311	S.1313	S.14+S.15	S.2
IV.3	**FINANCIAL BALANCE SHEET** continued at end of period					
AF.L	**Financial liabilities**					
AF.2	Currency and deposits					
AF.21	Currency	3.8	3.8			0.7
AF.22	Transferable deposits					
AF.221	Deposits with UK monetary financial institutions					
AF.229	Deposits with rest of the world monetary financial institutions					2 193.0
AF.29	Other deposits	89.8	89.8			
AF.2	Total currency and deposits	93.6	93.6			2 193.7
AF.3	Securities other than shares					
AF.331	Short term: money market instruments					
AF.3311	Issued by UK central government	19.4	19.4			
AF.3312	Issued by UK local authorities	–		–		
AF.3315	Issued by UK monetary financial institutions					
AF.3316	Issued by other UK residents				0.1	
AF.3319	Issued by the rest of the world					77.9
AF.332	Medium (1 to 5 year) and long term (over 5 year) bonds					
AF.3321	Issued by UK central government	449.3	449.3			
AF.3322	Issued by UK local authorities	1.2		1.2		
AF.3325	Medium term bonds issued by UK MFIs[1]					
AF.3326	Other medium & long term bonds issued by UK residents				3.2	
AF.3329	Long term bonds issued by the rest of the world					829.3
AF.34	Financial derivatives				–	–
AF.3	Total securities other than shares	469.9	468.7	1.2	3.2	907.2
AF.4	Loans					
AF.41	Short term loans					
AF.411	Loans by UK monetary financial institutions, excluding loans secured on dwellings & financial leasing	34.1	25.0	9.1	184.4	709.2
AF.419	Loans by rest of the world monetary financial institutions	–	–	–	20.2	
AF.42	Long term loans					
AF.421	Direct investment					221.5
AF.422	Loans secured on dwellings				1 046.1	
AF.423	Finance leasing	4.1	4.0	0.1		–
AF.424	Other long-term loans by UK residents	50.7	0.1	50.6	26.9	6.1
AF.429	Other long-term loans by the rest of the world	2.1	–	2.1		
AF.4	Total loans	91.0	29.1	61.9	1 277.7	936.7
AF.5	Shares and other equity					
AF.51	Shares and other equity, excluding mutual funds' shares					
AF.514	Quoted UK shares					
AF.515	Unquoted UK shares					
AF.516	Other UK equity (including direct investment in property)					
AF.517	UK shares and bonds issued by other UK residents					
AF.519	Shares and other equity issued by the rest of the world					1 460.1
AF.52	Mutual funds' shares					
AF.521	UK mutual funds' shares					
AF.529	Rest of the world mutual funds' shares					6.0
AF.5	Total shares and other equity					1 466.1
AF.6	Insurance technical reserves					
AF.61	Net equity of households in life assurance and pension funds' reserves					
AF.62	Prepayments of insurance premiums and reserves for outstanding claims					
AF.6	Total insurance technical reserves					
AF.7	Other accounts payable	66.1	55.9	10.2	89.0	9.5
AF.L	**Total financial liabilities**	720.6	647.3	73.3	1 369.9	5 513.2
BF.90	**Net financial assets / liabilities**					
AF.A	Total financial assets	207.7	171.8	35.8	3 800.1	5 808.5
-AF.L	*less* Total financial liabilities	–720.6	–647.3	–73.3	–1 369.9	–5 513.2
BF.90	**Net financial assets (+) / liabilities (-)**	–512.9	–475.4	–37.5	2 430.2	295.3

1 UK monetary financial institutions

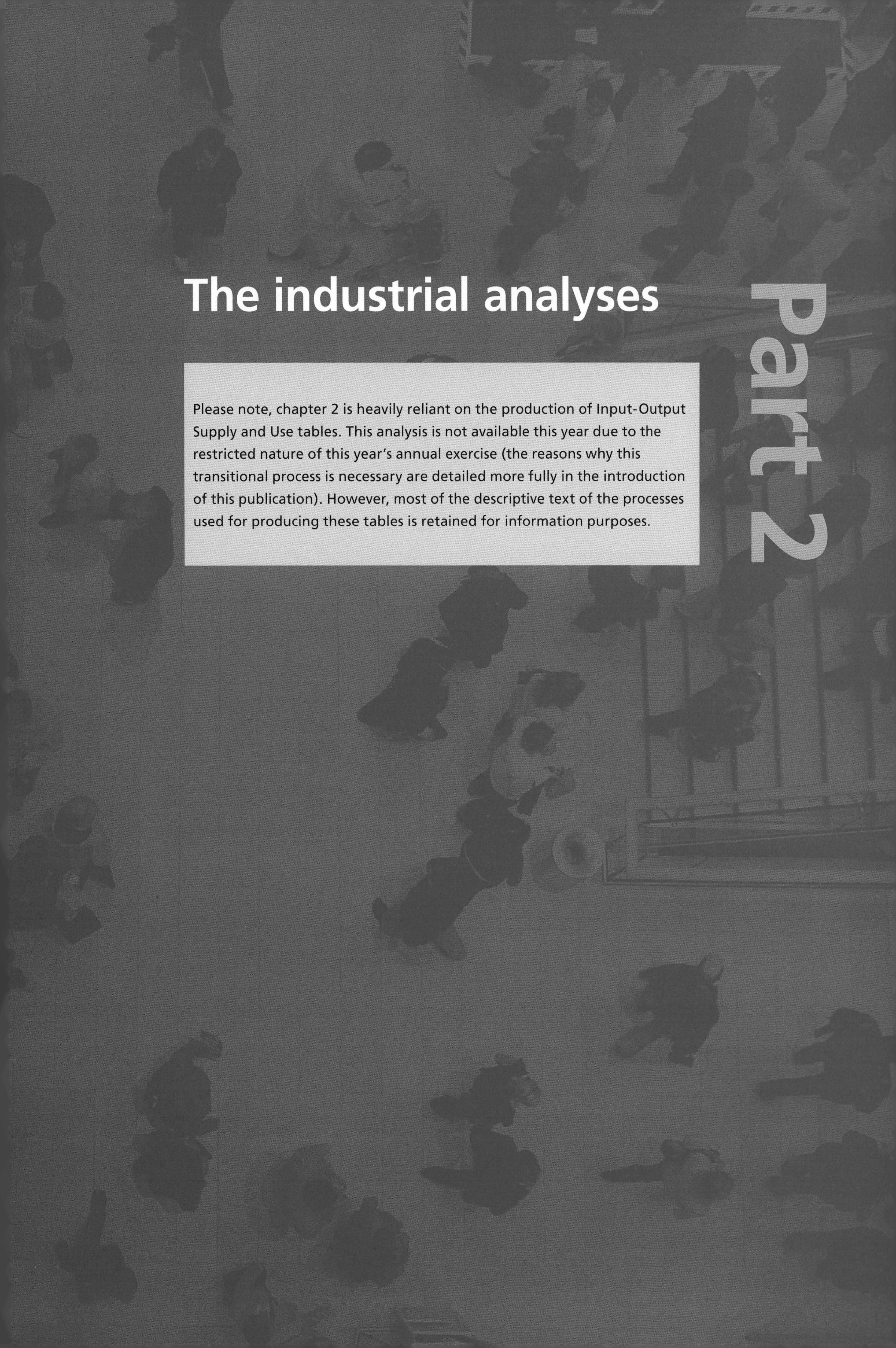

Part 2

The industrial analyses

Please note, chapter 2 is heavily reliant on the production of Input-Output Supply and Use tables. This analysis is not available this year due to the restricted nature of this year's annual exercise (the reasons why this transitional process is necessary are detailed more fully in the introduction of this publication). However, most of the descriptive text of the processes used for producing these tables is retained for information purposes.

Explanation of industrial analyses

Input-Output Supply and Use Tables

The annual estimates prepared for the *Blue Book* usually incorporate the results of annual inquiries which become available in the first part of the year, although estimates for the latest year are still based largely on quarterly information. As new data are collected it is likely that revisions will be necessary. The process of reassessing these estimates involves the preparation of Input-Output (I-O) Supply and Use Tables. This I-O approach amalgamates all the available information on inputs, outputs, gross value added, income and expenditure. Similarly the production of the consolidated sector and financial accounts requires the preparation of 'top-to-bottom' sector and sub-sector accounts to identify discrepancies in the estimates relating to each sector. The thorough and detailed nature of this estimation process is time consuming and so estimates for earlier years are not normally revisited unless there are strong reasons for doing so.

GDP and the balancing of the annual accounts

As discussed in Part 1, there are three different approaches to the estimation of current price GDP in the UK: the income approach, the expenditure approach and the production approach. In theory the three different approaches should produce the same result. However, the different approaches are based on different surveys and administrative data sources and each produces estimates which, like all statistical estimates, are subject to errors and omissions. A definitive GDP estimate can only emerge after a process of balancing and adjustment. ONS believes that the most reliable 'definitive' estimate of the current price level of GDP is that derived using the annual I-O Supply and Use Tables framework. Thus, for the years when I-O Supply and Use Tables are available, GDP is set at the level derived from that year's balance. For periods subsequent to the latest I-O Supply and Use Tables, the level of GDP is carried forward using movements in income, expenditure and production totals. (The annual balancing and compilation process is described in January 1997 edition of Economic Trends1 and this quarterly balancing process is described in Chapter 11 of *Concepts, Sources and Methods*[2].)

There are also various I-O based analyses published in the ONS *Economic Trends*, for example covering ICT and the oil and gas sector. See references for more details[3, 4, 12, 13, 14].

The Input-Output framework

The accounting framework shown in Figure 1 in the Introduction is mainly concerned with the composition and value of goods and services entering into final demand (for example, purchases by consumers) and the outputs and incomes generated in the production process. It does not display the inter-industry transactions which link these activities.

The UK I-O Supply and Use Tables, however, do include these intermediate transactions which form inputs into these processes, thus providing an extra dimension. The I-O analyses are constructed to show a balanced and complete picture of the flows of products in the economy and illustrate the relationships between producers and consumers of goods and services. On an annual basis I-O Supply and Use Tables are used to achieve consistency in the economic accounts' aggregates by linking the components of value added, inputs, outputs and final demand. As the income, production and expenditure measures of GDP can all be calculated from the I-O Supply and Use Tables, a single estimate of GDP can be derived by balancing the supply and demand for goods and services and reconciling them with the corresponding value added estimates.

Industrial analyses

The I-O process, which produces I-O Supply and Use Tables annually, has been speeded up considerably over the last few years and normally produce the first balance for a year around eighteen months after the end of that year.

Some background on the structure of the I-O Supply and Use Tables

The I-O Supply and Use Tables are based on a framework which incorporates estimates of industry inputs, outputs and value added. The tables consist of two matrices: the *Supply* matrix and the *Use* matrix, each of which breaks down and balances a number of different industries and products at purchasers' prices. Further details on the matrices are given in Chapter 13 of *Concepts, Sources and Methods*[2]. A full description of the present methodology is given in the *Input-Output Balances Methodological Guide*[6]. The following paragraphs summarise the methodology.

Supply table

At a very aggregate level the *Supply* table can be represented as follows:

	Output by industry	Imports of goods and services	Distributors' trading margins	Taxes *less* subsidies on products
Output by product				

The main part of the *Supply* table shows estimates of domestic industries' output (total sales adjusted for changes in inventories of work in progress and finished goods) compiled at basic prices. Basic prices value the goods leaving the factory gate but exclude any taxes on products and include any subsidies on products. However, for the balancing process, the estimates of supply of products are required at purchasers' prices, i.e. those actually paid by the purchasers to take delivery of the goods, excluding any deductible VAT. To convert the estimates of domestic output valued at basic prices to the total supply of products valued at purchasers' prices requires the addition of:

- the value of imports of goods and services;
- distributors' trading margins;
- taxes on products (e.g. VAT, excise duties, air

passenger tax, insurance premium tax etc);

less

- subsidies on products (e.g. agricultural and transport subsidies).

Use table

The *Use* table reveals the input structure of each industry in terms of combined domestic and imported goods and services. It also shows the product composition of final demand and, for each industry, the intermediate purchases adjusted for changes in inventories of materials and fuels. Consumption of products is represented in the rows of the balance while purchases by industries, and final demands, are represented in the columns. At a very aggregate level the Use table can be considered in three parts as shown below.

The body of the matrix, which represents consumption of products, is at purchasers' prices and so already includes the product-specific taxes and subsidies separately added in the *Supply* table.

The I-O balance is effectively achieved when:

For industries:

Inputs (from the *Use* table)

equals

Outputs (from the *Supply* table)

For products:

Supply (from the *Supply* table)

equals

Demand (from the *Use* table)

That is, when the data from the income, expenditure and production approaches used to fill the matrices all produce the same estimate of current price GDP at market prices. GDP at current market prices can be derived from the balances by taking the estimate of total gross value added at basic prices (from the Use table) and adding taxes on products and deducting subsidies on products (from the Supply table).

The balancing process

The balancing process is carried out over a number of months, and involves a central team and compilers who feed data directly into the process from surveys or through the economic accounts compilation process.

Initial estimates

Once the initial data estimates have been gathered, estimates of the components of supply and demand for products are prepared, together with the estimates of industry outputs and inputs and thus gross value added. The resulting production based estimates of current price gross value added are then

Industry consumption/final demand table

	Industry consumption	*Final demands*
Products consumed	Shows consumption by each industry to produce their own output (that is, intermediate consumption)	Shows final demand categories (for example households' expenditure) and the values of products going to these categories
Primary inputs	Shows the gross value added components of each industry, taxes less subsidies on production other than product specific taxes and subsidies, compensation of employees and gross operating surplus.	

compared with the expenditure and income measures, and the checks and analyses which follow extend the validation checks which will already have been carried out on the initial data estimates. The investigations which follow often lead to the revision and redelivery of data.

In parallel with this work alternative estimates of gross value added for each of the industries are prepared using income-based data.

The coherence of these initial estimates is then assessed by:

- comparisons of gross value added for each industry using the income and production-based approaches, and
- comparisons of the components of supply and demand for each type of product (which effectively compare the production and expenditure approaches).
- In addition a variety of time series (e.g. growth rates and the ratio of gross value added to total output) are compiled to aid the assessment.

At this stage the resulting income, production and expenditure aggregates will typically show different profiles over time.

Revised estimates

To obtain the revised estimates an iterative process begins, to reconcile:

- the income and production-based estimates of industry gross value added, and
- the supply and demand for each product.

These estimates are scrutinised, validated and checked for their plausibility and coherence across all industries and products. Consistency and coherence over time are also important and the impact of revisions to earlier years and the quality of the relative data sources are also taken into account. When necessary other sources (e.g. detailed National Statistics survey data and company reports and accounts) are used to inform the investigation of particular areas. Discussions follow between the Current Price I-O team and data compilers and any issues are resolved.

Final estimates

As final estimates are received from data compilers the steps of assessment, scrutiny, comparison and reconciliation continue. For the time series under consideration the quality of source data, revisions performance and any specific estimation problems are taken into account. Any changes to estimates are agreed and the inconsistencies between supply and demand, and between production and income-based gross value added, are progressively reduced. This process continues until convergence between the aggregate totals is achieved.

The single best estimate of GDP which emerges will reflect the relative merits of the production, income and expenditure estimates at the aggregate level. It will also have been assessed after consideration of the effect on current price and chained volume measure expenditure growth rates, the impact on the expenditure deflator and the relationship between the current price and chained volume measures of gross value added.

Once this GDP estimate has been fine-tuned and agreed by all concerned, the industry value added estimates and the gross value added weights are fixed after a full reconciliation of the income-based components with the production-based estimate. Product supply and demand will still differ at this stage, mainly reflecting the approximations in transforming source data to I-O group level. Further adjustments are made at this stage to address these imbalances; for example, distributors' trading margins and the allocation of other services provided by manufacturers. The *Use* matrix is then fully balanced by adjusting the intermediate purchases within the predetermined column and row totals.

This final step in the balancing process is to apply the r.A.s. method to the intermediate section of the *Use* matrix. This process will adjust the intermediate purchases in line with pre-determined row and column totals, resulting in a fully-balanced table. The term r.A.s. refers to an iterative mathematical process, where A is the coefficient form of the intermediate section of the Use matrix. A is premultiplied by a diagonal matrix, with the vector r of replacement factors forming the diagonal, and post-multiplied by a diagonal matrix with the substitution vector s forming the diagonal. A single iteration applies the above process for each row and then for each column. After each iteration the replacement factors are changed appropriately and the process is repeated until the desired balance has been achieved, that is supply being equal to demand for each product.

The end result is a full set of I-O Supply and Use Tables where, for each of the industries, inputs equal outputs, and for each of the product groups, supply equals demand.

Annual coherence adjustments in the *Blue Book* and the Input-Output Analyses

As described, the role of the I-O framework aims to present a fully consistent picture of the UK economy. In practice the data sources used in the National Accounts are subject to statistical error and complete coherence between measures of economic activity is not achieved without making specific adjustments..

An article in the October 1999 *Economic Trends*[7] describes the background to the adjustments and briefly shows how they are made. The balancing process is described in more detail in the *I-O Methodological Guide*[6]. The process of achieving coherence in the accounts by balancing I-O Supply and Use

Tables can most simply be explained as a series of different types of adjustment. The three main types of adjustment described in the *Economic Trends* article are:

- Conceptual and coverage adjustments
- Quality adjustments
- Coherence adjustments

The annual current price quality and coherence adjustments agreed for last year's 2006 *Blue Book* dataset and the 2006 *Input-Output Analyses* are shown in the table below:

Current price analyses

Table 2.3 presents GVA by industry at current prices for years up to and including 2004. Data for 2005 and 2006 are published in the experimental statistics area of the National Statistics website. Estimates of current price GVA data for 2004 and earlier are derived from balanced I-O Supply and Use Tables, drawing on survey data from the Annual Business Inquiry (ABI). The current price estimates for 2005 and 2006, which are based on short-term indicators, are less firm. Revisions to the early estimates of GVA over recent years indicate that this approach is not ideal. ONS is currently reviewing and improving the methods used to produce these later estimates, and while this programme is continuing these data will be withdrawn from the *Blue Book*. Instead, they will be published on the experimental area of the National Statistics website at: www.statistics.gov.uk/statbase/product.asp?vlnk=14490 The experimental 2005 and 2006 current price GVA includes estimates for private investment in own account computer software. However, in the absence of balanced I-O Supply and Use Tables this year these estimates have used a simplified approach, which does not involve detailed allocation of the production of the own-account software across industries. Current price GVA up to including 2004, as published in Blue Book 2006, does not reflect any estimates made for the production of own-account software.

Chained volume indices (2003=100) analyses (Table 2.4)

Table 2.4 shows chained volume estimates of gross value added at basic prices by industry. The basic methodology for these estimates can be found in the Government Statistical Service methodological publications **Gross Domestic Product: Output approach**[8,9]. A more detailed explanation is in **Concepts, Sources and Methods**[2].

The output approach provides the lead indicator of economic change in the short term. However in the longer term, it is required to follow the annual path indicated by the expenditure measure of real GDP (usually within 0.2 per cent of the average annual gross value added growth). To achieve this, balancing adjustments are sometimes applied to the output based gross value added estimates.

An examination of the chained volume gross value added and expenditure measures of GDP shows what are considered to be excessive differences in growth for a number of recent years. During 1995, 1996, 1997, 1998 and 1999 the output-based estimate increased significantly more than the expenditure measure. The output-based estimate grew more slowly than the expenditure measure in 2000 and 2003. To reduce these discrepancies, a number of balancing adjustments have been made to the chained volume gross value added annual growth rates.

Employment analyses (Table 2.5)

Table 2.5 breaks down employment data into six broad industry groupings. Employee jobs, the main component of the employment figures, uses an industry breakdown which is consistent with most

other parts of the National Accounts. This is because employee figures are obtained from surveys of businesses whose details are stored on National Statistics' Business Register. This is the same register which is used for all other business surveys collecting economic data.

The estimates of self-employment jobs come from the Labour Force Survey. This is a household survey which codes respondents according to their own view of the industry in which they work. Because of this, the industrial coding of the self employment jobs may not be consistent with the industrial codes for employees. Note that the data do not include UK armed forces or government supported trainees, which are the other components of the Workforce Jobs series.

Assigning adjustments: 2007 *Blue Book*

As the annual updating of the GDP accounts through the Input-Output Supply and Use framework did not take place in this year's Blue Book, the process of assigning balancing adjustments was not carried out.

Assigning adjustments: improvements for the 2006 *Blue Book*

For *Blue Book* 2006, there were significant improvements in the way that these balancing adjustments have been applied. For technical and other reasons, the adjustments are not at present made to the production industries for any years.

Apportioning between industries

Under the revisions policy in the 2005 *Blue Book*, revisions were only permitted for the predominantly 'government' components between 1996 and 2000. Consequently all adjustments to annual growth rates in these years were achieved via the following industries: public administration and defence; compulsory social security (section L), education (section M) and health and social work (section N). In some cases this restriction led to an inappropriate allocation across the components of gross value added.

The revisions policy for the 2006 *Blue Book* permitted revisions to all components between 1995 and 2006 quarter 1. This enabled a more appropriate allocation of the adjustments across industries. Adjustments were apportioned with reference to the relationship between the current price and chained volume measure (CVM) series for individual industries. In some instances, industries were adjusted more heavily to help reduce an apparent incoherence between the current price and CVM data. In general, however, there is a much more even allocation across the services industries.

This allocation led to changes in the balance of growth between the 'government' components and other industries.

Applying the adjustments

ONS has developed an automatic function for assigning the annual adjustments to gross value added. This is designed to be as faithful as possible to the quarterly paths whilst adjusting the overall annual growth rate of a group of series. The 2006 *Blue Book* was the first time that all adjustments to all industries were assigned using this system. Particularly in quarters between 1996 and 1998, this led to revisions to the quarterly path (see Humphries, 2006 and Marks, 2006). Details of these adjustments are given below. Using the automatic function produced some differences in the adjustments within the groupings shown. These differences were generally no greater than 0.2 per cent.

For 1995:

A downward adjustment of 0.6 per cent was applied to:

- insurance and pension funding, except compulsory social security, and activities auxiliary to financial intermediation (part of section J)

A downward adjustment of 0.7 per cent was applied to:

- distribution, hotels and catering; repairs (sections G and H)
- government and other services (sections L to P)

A downward adjustment of 0.8 per cent was applied to:

- real estate, renting and business activities (section K)

A downward adjustment of 0.9 per cent was applied to:

- transport storage and communication (section I)

The total effect of these adjustments was to reduce the 1994/1995 growth rate by 0.5 per cent.

For 1996:

A downward adjustment of 0.5 per cent was applied to:

- insurance and pension funding, except compulsory social security, and activities auxiliary to financial intermediation (part of section J)

A downward adjustment of 0.6 per cent was applied to:

- distribution, hotels and catering; repairs (sections G and H)
- land transport, water transport, air transport and supporting and auxiliary transport activities (part of section I)
- letting of dwellings, renting of machinery and equipment, computer and related activities, research and development and other business activities (part of section K)
- government and other services (sections L to Q)

A downward adjustment of 5 per cent was applied to:

- post and telecommunication (part of section I)

A downward adjustment of 3 per cent was applied to:

- real estate activities (part of section K)

The total effect of these adjustments was to reduce 1995/1996 growth rate by 0.6 per cent.

For 1997:

A downward adjustment of 0.4 was applied to:

- insurance and pension funding, except compulsory social security, and activities auxiliary to financial intermediation (part of section J)

A downward adjustment of 0.5 per cent was applied to:

- distribution, hotels and catering; repairs (sections G and H)
- transport storage and communication (section I)
- letting of dwellings, renting of machinery and equipment, computer and related activities, research and development and other business activities (part of section K)
- government and other services (sections L to P)

A downward adjustment of 7.0 per cent was applied to:

- real estate activities (part of section K)

The total effect of these adjustments was to reduce the 1996/1997 growth rate by 0.6 per cent.

1998:

A downward adjustment of 0.2 per cent was applied to:

- real estate, renting and business activities (section K)

A downward adjustment of 0.3 per cent was applied to:

- distribution, hotels and catering; repairs (sections G and H)
- transport storage and communication (section I)
- insurance and pension funding, except compulsory social security, and activities auxiliary to financial intermediation (part of section J)
- government and other services (sections L to P)

The total effect of these adjustments was to reduce the 1997/1998 growth rate by 0.2 per cent.

1999:

A downward adjustment of 0.1 per cent was applied to:

- real estate, renting and business activities (section K)

A downward adjustment of 0.2 per cent was applied to:

- distribution, hotels and catering (sections G and H)
- land transport, water transport and air transport (part of section I)
- business services (section K)
- government and other services (sections L to P)

A downward adjustment of 0.3 per cent was applied to:

- insurance and pension funding, except compulsory social security, and activities auxiliary to financial intermediation (part of section J)

A downward adjustment of 1.8 per cent was applied to:

- post and telecommunication (part of section I)

The total effect of these adjustments was to reduce the 1998/1999 growth rate by 0.2 per cent.

2000:

An upward adjustment of 0.3 per cent was applied to:

- insurance and pension funding, except compulsory social security, and activities auxiliary to financial intermediation (part of section J)

An upward adjustment of 0.4 per cent was applied to:

- distribution, hotels and catering; repairs (sections G and H)
- government and other services (sections L to P)

An upward adjustment of 0.5 per cent was applied to:

- transport storage and communication (section I)
- real estate, renting and business activities (section K)

The total effect of these adjustments was to increase the 1999/2000 growth rate by 0.3 per cent.

For 2001:

No annual balancing adjustments were applied.

For 2002:

No annual balancing adjustments were applied.

For 2003:

An upward adjustment of 0.5 per cent was applied to:

- distribution, hotels and catering; repairs (sections G and H)
- transport, storage and communication (section I)
- insurance and pension funding, except compulsory social security, and activities auxiliary to financial intermediation (part of section J)
- real estate, renting and business activities (section K)
- government and other services (sections L to P)

The total effect of these adjustments was to increase the 2002/2003 growth rate by 0.4 per cent.

References:

1 Mahajan S (1997) Balancing GDP: UK Annual Input-Output Balances. *Economic Trends* No. 519.

2 Office for National Statistics (1998) *National Accounts Concepts, Sources and Methods*, 1998 edition. The Stationery Office: London.

3 Mahajan S (2004) Information, Communications and Technology 1992-2001. *Economic Trends* No. 603, 54–62.

4 Mahajan S (2004) Oil and Gas Sector 1992-2001. *Economic Trends* No. 604, 47–63.

5 Office for National Statistics (2006) United Kingdom *Input-Output Analyses*, 2006 edition (Web only).

6 Office for National Statistics (1997) *Input-Output Balances Methodological Guide* 1997 edition.

7 Penneck S and Mahajan S (1999) Annual Coherence Adjustments in the National Accounts. *Economic Trends* No. 551, 27–32.

8 Government Statistical Service (1998) *Gross Domestic Product: Output methodological guide.*

9 Government Statistical Service (1998) *Gross Domestic Product: Output approach (Gross Value Added).* GSS Methodology Series No.15.

10 Humphries S (2006) Revisions planned for the 2006 annual Blue Book, Pink Book and Input-Output analyses. *Economic Trends* No. 629, 20–23.

11 Marks C (2006) Analysis of revisions to the early estimates of GDP. *Economic Trends* 632, 25–32.

12 Mahajan S (2004) Input-Output Analyses: Food sector, 1992-2002. *Economic Trends* No. 612, pp 41–54.

13 Mahajan S (2004) Input-Output Analyses: Creative sector, 1992-2002. *Economic Trends* No. 611, pp 30–42.

14 Mahajan S (2004) Input-Output and GDP revisions analyses: 1992-2002. *Economic Trends* No. 610, pp 74–110.

2.4 Gross value added at basic prices: by industry[1,2,3,4]

Chained volume indices

Indices 2003=100

		Weight per 1000[1] 2003		1998	1999	2000	2001	2002	2003	2004	2005	2006
A,B	**Agriculture, hunting, forestry and fishing**	10.2	GDQA	97.9	101.1	100.3	90.9	102.1	100.0	99.0	103.3	106.2
C,D,E	**Production**											
C	Mining and quarrying											
CA	Mining and quarrying of energy producing materials											
C10	Mining of coal	0.5	CKZP	149.5	132.5	113.1	112.6	105.9	100.0	85.8	67.2	64.2
C11	Extraction of mineral oil and natural gas	19.8	CKZO	112.4	117.7	113.6	107.3	105.9	100.0	91.6	82.0	74.7
CB	Other mining and quarrying	1.5	CKZQ	76.8	82.6	85.8	80.4	98.7	100.0	101.4	110.0	109.4
C	Total mining and quarrying	21.8	CKYX	110.2	114.8	111.1	105.0	105.4	100.0	92.1	83.7	76.9
D	Manufacturing											
DA	Food; beverages and tobacco	22.0	CKZA	97.6	97.5	96.7	98.0	100.0	100.0	101.6	102.5	102.1
DB	Textiles and textile products	4.4	CKZB	135.0	125.3	122.4	107.2	99.7	100.0	91.8	90.2	87.1
DC	Leather and leather products	0.5	CKZC	165.3	156.2	137.7	140.0	122.5	100.0	74.6	69.8	70.9
DD	Wood and wood products	2.7	CKZD	98.2	94.1	96.5	96.6	99.2	100.0	101.8	97.8	95.1
DE	Pulp, paper and paper products; publishing and printing	20.0	CKZE	100.9	101.1	101.5	101.3	101.4	100.0	99.1	94.0	91.7
DF	Coke, petroleum products and nuclear fuel	2.4	CKZF	118.9	107.2	112.9	106.9	108.3	100.0	105.8	110.1	105.3
DG	Chemicals, chemical products and man-made fibres	16.2	CKZG	85.8	88.9	93.6	99.3	99.1	100.0	103.4	103.5	106.6
DH	Rubber and plastic products	7.7	CKZH	107.4	107.0	107.0	103.2	99.2	100.0	98.5	95.1	98.4
DI	Other non-metallic mineral products	5.5	CKZI	93.0	92.8	95.6	96.0	94.5	100.0	105.8	105.4	107.0
DJ	Basic metals and fabricated metal products	15.0	CKZJ	103.9	101.4	103.5	101.4	102.4	100.0	103.1	102.4	103.6
DK	Machinery and equipment not elsewhere classified	12.2	CKZK	108.8	102.4	102.3	104.2	98.3	100.0	105.8	108.7	113.6
DL	Electrical and optical equipment	15.8	CKZL	101.0	111.5	128.2	118.7	102.6	100.0	101.8	97.3	98.0
DM	Transport equipment	16.0	CKZM	100.1	103.8	99.7	97.9	94.8	100.0	105.8	104.9	111.1
DN	Manufacturing not elsewhere classified	6.5	CKZN	98.7	101.6	100.4	99.9	100.5	100.0	99.3	100.2	100.7
D	Total manufacturing	147.0	CKYY	100.5	101.4	103.8	102.5	99.8	100.0	102.0	100.8	102.1
E	Electricity, gas and water supply	16.7	CKYZ	88.8	92.1	95.0	98.0	98.4	100.0	101.1	100.7	98.1
C,D,E	Total production	185.5	CKYW	100.5	101.9	103.8	102.3	100.3	100.0	100.8	98.8	98.8
F	**Construction**	60.7	GDQB	89.7	89.8	90.2	92.2	95.5	100.0	104.0	105.6	106.7
G-Q	**Service industries**											
G	Wholesale and retail trade (including motor trade); repair of motor vehicles, personal and household goods	122.4	GDQC	83.3	85.9	89.0	92.3	96.9	100.0	105.3	106.7	109.6
H	Hotels and restaurants	31.0	GDQD	84.6	88.3	89.4	91.3	94.4	100.0	104.5	105.6	112.1
I	Transport, storage and communication											
	Transport and storage	47.8	GDQF	87.2	90.5	95.6	97.7	99.2	100.0	103.4	108.4	113.6
	Communication	29.8	GDQG	61.2	73.4	88.8	96.0	96.5	100.0	101.2	104.6	106.8
I	Total	77.6	GDQH	76.2	83.4	92.9	97.0	98.2	100.0	102.5	106.9	111.0
J	Financial intermediation	79.0	GDQI	79.9	82.0	87.1	90.2	93.7	100.0	107.6	113.8	123.5
-P.119	Adjustment for financial services (FISIM)	–46.0	GDQJ	72.0	73.7	81.7	86.3	89.2	100.0	113.0	123.3	138.3
K	Real estate, renting and business activities											
	Letting of dwellings, including imputed rent of owner occupiers	79.1	GDQL	92.2	93.3	95.2	96.5	97.7	100.0	101.5	102.9	105.3
	Other real estate, renting and business activities	165.2	GDQK	74.4	80.6	87.6	92.9	94.7	100.0	107.7	114.8	122.8
K	Total	244.3	GDQM	79.8	84.5	89.9	94.0	95.7	100.0	105.7	111.0	117.1
L	Public administration and defence (PAD)[4]	52.1	GDQO	91.2	91.4	91.9	93.0	95.3	100.0	101.9	102.8	103.3
M	Education[4]	59.1	GDQP	94.4	95.7	96.9	97.6	99.3	100.0	100.4	101.5	101.8
N	Health and social work[4]	71.7	GDQQ	84.2	86.3	89.6	92.8	96.3	100.0	103.9	107.0	110.2
O,P,Q	Other social and personal services, private households with employees and extra-territorial organisations	52.6	GDQR	91.9	91.5	94.7	98.5	100.1	100.0	101.3	103.0	106.0
G-Q	Total service industries	743.6	GDQS	83.8	87.2	91.3	94.5	96.9	100.0	103.9	106.9	110.8
B.1g	**All industries**	1 000.0	CGCE	87.5	90.2	93.6	95.6	97.3	100.0	103.3	105.2	108.2

1 The weights shown are in proportion to total gross value added (GVA) in 2003 and are used to combine the industry output indices to calculate the totals for 2004 and 2005. For 2003 and earlier, totals are calculated using the equivalent weights for the previous year (e.g. totals for 2003 use 2002 weights). Weights may not sum to totals due to rounding.

2 As GVA is expressed in index number form, it is inappropriate to show as a statistical adjustment any divergence from the other measures of GDP. Such an adjustment does, however, exist implicitly.

3 See footnote 2 to Table 2.3.

4 The GVA for sections L, M and N in this table follows the SIC(2003) and differs from that used in Table 2.3, which is based on Input-Output groups. The administration costs of the NHS are included in PAD in this table but are included in Health and social work in Table 2.3. Central government expenditure on teachers is included in Education in this table.

2.5 Employment: by industry

Thousands

			1998	1999	2000	2001	2002	2003	2004	2005	2006
A,B	**Agriculture, hunting & forestry; fishing**										
	Self-employment jobs	YEKN	253	212	207	204	186	196	197	206	207
	Employee jobs	YEKO	322	318	321	279	256	228	226	239	227
	Total employed	YEKP	575	530	528	483	442	424	422	444	434
C-E	**Production industries, including energy**										
	Self-employment jobs	YEKQ	330	294	276	260	279	274	289	257	285
	Employee jobs	YEKR	4 405	4 256	4 153	4 009	3 797	3 594	3 413	3 255	3 157
	Total employed	YEKS	4 735	4 550	4 429	4 269	4 075	3 868	3 702	3 512	3 442
F	**Construction**										
	Self-employment jobs	YEKT	697	700	673	702	749	800	852	869	849
	Employee jobs	YEKU	1 098	1 110	1 183	1 176	1 147	1 145	1 169	1 206	1 288
	Total employed	YEKV	1 795	1 810	1 856	1 877	1 896	1 945	2 021	2 074	2 136
G-I	**Wholesale & retail trade (including motor trade); repair of motor vehicles, personal & household goods; hotels and restaurants; transport, storage & communication**										
	Self-emloyment jobs	YEKW	922	912	868	879	887	890	893	852	869
	Employee jobs	YEKX	7 292	7 433	7 586	7 773	7 866	7 914	7 971	8 049	8 038
	Total employed	YEKY	8 214	8 345	8 455	8 652	8 752	8 803	8 864	8 901	8 907
J-K	**Financial intermediation; real estate, renting & business activities**										
	Self-employment jobs	YEKZ	644	693	690	720	693	796	803	827	807
	Employee jobs	YELA	4 467	4 644	4 814	5 020	5 068	5 100	5 202	5 405	5 575
	Total employed	YELB	5 111	5 337	5 504	5 740	5 761	5 896	6 005	6 232	6 383
L-Q	**Other service activities** Public administration & defence, education, health and social work, other community, social & personal services, private households with employees										
	Self-employment jobs	YEJW	838	890	882	852	888	937	946	946	1 050
	Employee jobs	YEJX	7 146	7 330	7 601	7 728	7 948	8 166	8 377	8 594	8 750
	Total employed	YEJY	7 984	8 220	8 484	8 580	8 836	9 103	9 323	9 540	9 800
A-Q	**All industries**										
ESE	Self-employment jobs	BCAG	3 688	3 704	3 600	3 619	3 684	3 896	3 982	3 961	4 072
EEM	Employee jobs	BCAD	24 730	25 090	25 659	25 984	26 081	26 146	26 358	26 747	27 035
ETO	Total employed	YEJZ	28 418	28 794	29 259	29 603	29 765	30 042	30 340	30 708	31 108

1 Data sources are: Labour Force Survey for self-employed; employer surveys for employees. Figures as at June of each year.

Part 3

The sector accounts

The sector accounts at a glance

Net lending/borrowing

Net borrowing by general government decreased in 2006 to £37.9 billion compared to net borrowing of £42.3 billion in 2005. The net borrowing figures reflect continued high government expenditure growth with lower revenues. Private non-financial corporation sector was a net lender with £17.6 billion in 2006 and a net lender of £20.7 billion in 2005. This was driven by increased gross capital formation. Households and NPISH sector was a net borrower with £28.9 billion in 2006 compared to £14.0 billion in 2005. Financial corporations became net borrowers in 2006 at £1.0 billion, from net lending of £8.2 billion in 2005. This was driven by increased taxes on income and special payments to pension funds.

Net lending/borrowing, 2005

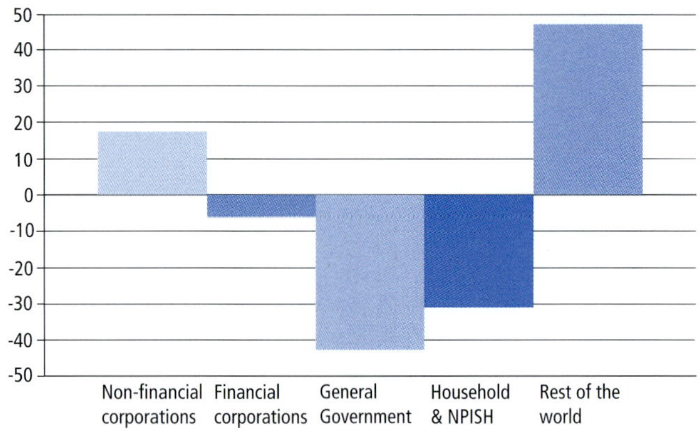

Net financial transactions

Net financial transactions by general government showed a deficit of £38.5 billion in 2006 and a £42.6 billion deficit in 2005. The deficit has mainly been funded by the net issuance of gilts by central government. The private non-financial corporations sector used its net lending to reduce their debt requirement, showing a surplus of £8.8 billion in 2006 compared to a deficit of £8.4 billion surplus in 2005. Households showed a deficit of £12.1 billion in 2006 compared to a surplus of £1.4 billion in 2005. This was driven by continued increases, in loans secured on dwellings. In 2006 financial corporations showed a net deficit of £2.8 billion, following on from a net deficit of £2.0 billion in 2005.

Financial balances by sector

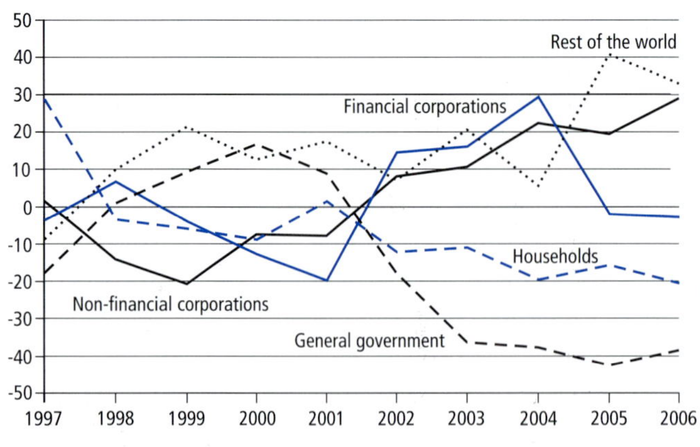

Gross trading profits of private non-financial corporations

Gross trading profit is the largest component of private non-financial corporations' gross operating surplus. Profits rose by 5.1 per cent between 2006 and 2005 compared with profits of 3.6 per cent between 2005 and 2004. This was due to stronger profits of non United Kingdom continental shelf companies.

Gross trading profits of private non-financial corporations

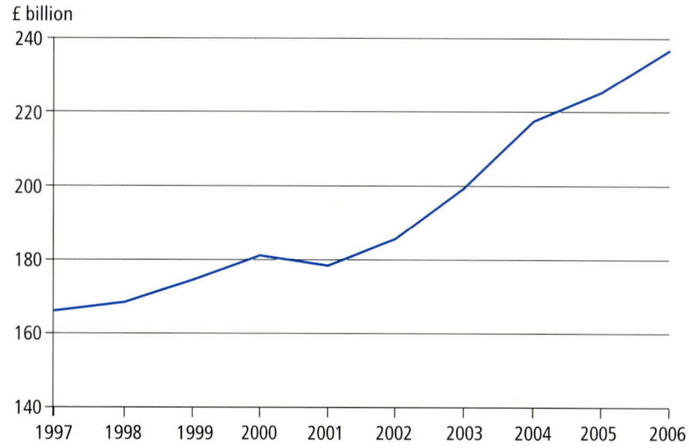

Real household disposable income

Real household disposable income (RHDI) is the amount of money in real terms the household sector has available for spending after taxes and other deductions. Between 2005 and 2006 RHDI increased by 1.1 per cent compared with an increase of 2.9 per cent between 2004 and 2005.

Annual changes in real household disposable income

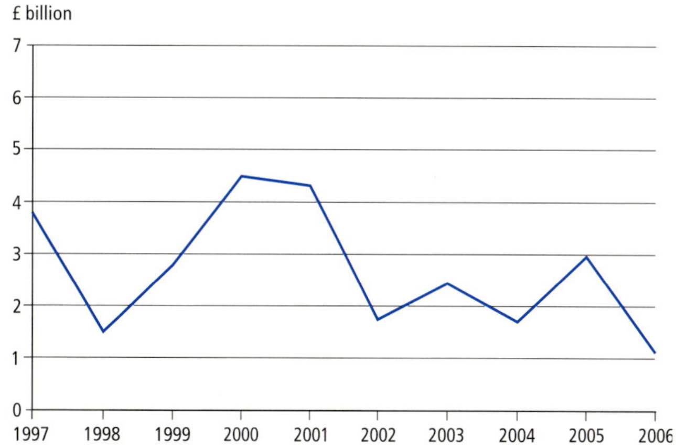

Household saving ratio

The household saving ratio reflects household gross savings as a percentage of their total available resources (the amount available to spend or save). Household resources rose by 3.9 per cent between 2006 and 2005. Household and NPISH final consumption expenditure rose by 4.5 per cent in the same period. As a consequence the household saving ratio fell from 5.6 per cent in 2005 to 5.0 per cent in 2006.

Household saving ratio

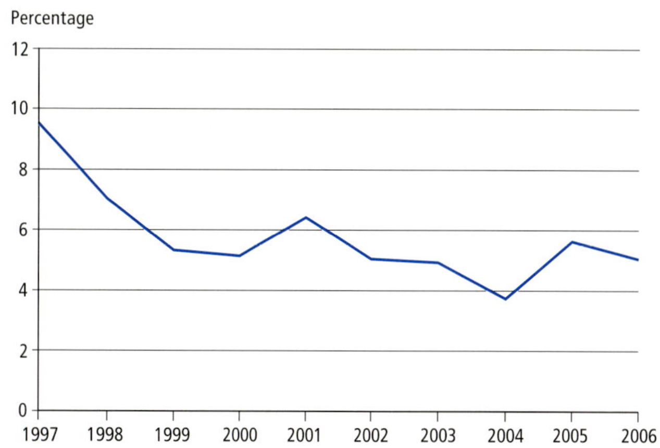

C The sector accounts: Key economic indicators

£ million

			1998	1999	2000	2001	2002	2003	2004	2005	2006
	Net lending/borrowing by:										
B.9	Non-financial corporations	EABO	–6 930	–13 157	–7 541	–10 509	6 529	18 181	26 255	21 233	21 988
B.9	Financial corporations	NHCQ	–5 086	–14 185	–27 457	–22 800	7 018	19 335	26 479	8 168	–966
B.9	General government	NNBK	545	10 484	16 073	9 804	–17 287	–36 284	–37 758	–42 251	–37 933
B.9	Households and NPISH's	NSSZ	8 765	–4 112	–4 205	2 938	–11 841	–14 687	–32 241	–13 952	–28 854
B.9	Rest of the world	NHRB	2 706	20 970	23 130	20 566	15 581	13 455	17 265	28 961	46 951
	Private non-financial corporations										
	Gross trading profits										
	Continental shelf profits	CAGJ	11 551	13 519	20 786	19 096	18 432	17 981	18 225	22 645	25 911
	Others	CAGK	156 732	160 743	160 153	159 134	167 068	181 339	199 272	202 699	210 817
	Rental of buildings	FCBW	9 767	10 821	11 747	12 394	12 904	13 891	14 864	15 404	16 005
	less Holding gains of inventories	-DLQZ	754	–1 800	–2 941	438	–2 856	–4 266	–6 158	–6 619	–6 085
B.2g	Gross operating surplus	NRJK	178 804	183 283	189 745	191 062	195 548	208 945	226 203	234 129	246 648
	Households and NPISH										
B.6g	Household gross disposable income	QWND	582 790	608 988	643 415	686 312	709 048	740 389	765 683	807 989	836 201
	Implied deflator of household and NPISH individual consumption expenditure index (2003=100)[1]	YBFS	91.8	93.4	94.4	96.6	98.1	100.0	101.7	104.2	106.7
	Real household disposable income:										
	Chained volume measures (Reference year 2003)	RVGK	634 508	652 060	681 249	710 531	722 823	740 389	752 890	775 074	783 584
	Index (2003=100)	OSXR	85.7	88.1	92.0	96.0	97.6	100.0	101.7	104.7	105.8
B.8g	Gross saving	NSSH	41 844	33 136	33 584	45 137	36 301	37 421	29 307	46 745	43 840
	Households total resources	NSSJ	691 617	725 746	766 876	820 811	857 647	905 720	946 602	1 006 598	1 050 473
	Saving ratio, per cent	RVGL	7.0	5.3	5.1	6.4	5.0	4.9	3.7	5.6	5.0

1 Rounded to one decimal place

The sector accounts

The sector accounts show the relationships between different sectors of the economy and different types of transactions. They summarise the transactions of particular groups of institutions in the economy, showing how income is distributed and redistributed, and how savings are used to add wealth through investment in physical or financial assets. This section introduces the tables in chapters 3 to 7 which deal with individual areas and subdivisions of the accounts. This introduction to the sector accounts has been divided into the following areas:

- The framework of the accounts
- The institutional sectors
- The types of transactions
- The sequence of accounts
- The statistical adjustment items
- Balance sheets

The framework of the accounts

The framework of national accounts detailed in Part 1 highlights the five main kinds of accounts; goods and services, production, distribution and use of income, capital, and financial. The production account records the activity of producing goods and services. The distribution and use of income accounts record how incomes are generated by production, distributed to institutional units with claims on the value added created by production, redistributed among institutional units, and eventually used by households, government units or non-profit institutions serving households for purposes of final consumption or saving. The capital account records the flows of non-financial assets acquired and disposed. The financial account shows how the net lending or borrowing on the capital account is financed by transactions in financial instruments.

The distribution and use of income accounts can be elaborated to form a consistent set of sector accounts. This is done in two dimensions, by sectors and types of transaction. A third dimension, related to capital and financial transactions is that of asset and liability levels, the national and sector balance sheets. The sectors and types of transaction are described below.

The institutional sectors

The system identifies two kinds of institutions: consuming units (mostly households); and production units (mainly corporations and non-profit institutions or government). Units can own goods and assets, incur liabilities and engage in economic activities and transactions with other units in their own right. All units within the country are put in one of the sectors. Also, the rest of the world is treated as a sector in respect of its dealings with the United Kingdom.

Non-financial corporations are those which exist to produce goods and non-financial services. They are, in the UK, mainly public limited companies, private companies and partnerships. They are mostly owned privately, but there are some public corporations, which are shown separately.

Financial corporations are those engaged primarily in financial activities, and are subdivided into monetary financial institutions, other financial intermediaries and financial auxiliaries, and insurance corporations and pension funds.

General government comprises central government and local government.

The Household sector contains all the resident people of the United Kingdom as receivers of income and consumers of products. It includes individuals such as prisoners as well as conventional family units. It also contains one person businesses where household and business accounts cannot be separated. This sector currently includes non-profit institutions serving households, which include productive units such as charities and universities.

The Rest of the world sector comprises those units that are not in the United Kingdom. The accounts for the rest of the world only record transactions between units in the rest of the world and units in the UK, and are equivalent to the balance of payments.

The tables in chapters 3 to 7 are based on the sector classification detailed above. More detailed definitions of these sectors are given in the appropriate chapters of the *UK National Accounts Concepts, Sources and Methods* and, in full detail, in the Business Monitor MA23 *Sector classification for the national accounts*, available from The Stationery Office.

The types of transactions

The other dimension is that of the types of transactions. These are divided into three types.

Transactions in products are related to goods and services, and include output, intermediate and final consumption, gross capital formation and exports and imports.

Distributive transactions transfer income or wealth between units of the economy, and include property income, taxes and subsidies, social contributions and benefits, and other current or capital transfers.

Financial transactions differ from distributive transactions in that they relate to transactions in financial claims by one unit on another, whereas distributive transactions are unrequited. The main categories in the classification of financial instruments are monetary gold and special drawing rights, currency and deposits, securities other than shares, loans, shares and other equity, insurance and pension funds reserves and other accounts receivable/payable.

The sequence of accounts

The transactions can be grouped broadly according to purpose in the production, distribution and use of income, capital or financial accounts. These are described briefly below:

Production account

The production account displays the transactions involved in the generation of income by the production of goods and services. This account is produced for the UK total economy (Table 1.6.1) and for the first four sectors (Tables 3.1.1, 4.1.1 etc.); the rest of the world does not have a production account. For each of the four sectors, the balancing item gross value added is shown as output less intermediate consumption. Gross value added at basic prices for each sector differs from gross domestic product for the UK total economy in that taxes *less* subsidies on products are not taken into the production accounts by sector but they are included within resources for the UK total economy. The sum of gross value added and taxes *less* subsidies on products for the UK economy is GDP at market prices.

Distribution and use of income account

The distribution and use of income accounts exist for all the main institutional sectors. To obtain the disposable income and savings of each sector we need to take account of transfers in and out of the sector. The accounts are not consolidated, so that in the whole economy account, transfers such as social contributions and benefits appear in both uses and resources.

These accounts describe the distribution and redistribution of income and its use in the form of final consumption. The distribution and use of income are analysed in four stages, each of which is presented as a separate account:

- The generation of income account
- The allocation of primary income account
- The secondary distribution of income account
- The use of disposable income account

Generation of income account

This is the first of the distribution and use of income accounts. It shows the sectors, sub-sectors and industries which are the source, rather than the destination, of income. It shows the derivation of the 'profit' arising from production, called the operating surplus (or mixed income in the case of unincorporated businesses in the households sector). The industry dimension is shown in Part 2, Table 2.1.

This account analyses the degree to which value added covers the compensation of employees (their wages and salaries etc.) and other taxes less subsidies on production. So it gives a figure for the operating surplus: the surplus (or deficit) on production activities before distributions such as interest, rent and income tax charges have been considered. Hence the operating surplus is the income which units obtain from their own use of the production facilities.

Note that taxes on production and imports are shown as a use by producing sectors in this account but not as a resource of government. This is because they do not relate to productive activity by government, and cannot therefore contribute to its operating surplus. They become a resource of government in the allocation of primary income account which follows.

Allocation of primary income account

This account shows the resident units and institutional sectors as recipients rather than producers of primary income. It demonstrates the extent to which operating surpluses are distributed (for example by dividends) to the owners of the enterprises. Also recorded in this account is the property income received by an owner of a financial asset in return for providing funds to, or putting a tangible non-produced asset at the disposal of, another unit. The receipt by government of taxes on production *less* subsidies is shown in resources.

The resources side of the allocation of primary income accounts includes the components of the income approach to measurement of gross domestic product and this is the starting point for the quarterly sector accounts. The accounts also include property income recorded as both resources for receipts and uses for payments.

The balance of this account is the gross balance of primary income (B.5g) for each sector, and if the gross balance of primary income is aggregated across all sectors of the UK economy the result is gross national income.

Secondary distribution of income account

This account describes how the balance of primary income for each institutional sector is allocated by redistribution; through transfers such as taxes on income, social contributions and benefits and other current transfers. It excludes social transfers in kind.

The balancing item of this account is gross disposable income (B.6g) which reflects current transactions and explicitly excludes capital transfers, real holding gains and losses, and the consequences of events such as natural disasters.

Use of disposable income account

This account illustrates how disposable income is split between final consumption expenditure and saving. In the system for recording economic accounts, only the government and the households and NPISH sectors have final consumption. In addition, for households and pension funds, there is an adjustment item in the account which reflects the way that transactions between households and pension funds are recorded. (This adjustment is D.8: Adjustment for the changes in the net equity of households in pension funds reserves.)

The balancing item for this account, and thus for this whole group of distribution and use of income accounts, is gross saving (B.8g).

Thus it is only in the case of non-financial corporations (public and private), that undistributed income and saving are equivalent.

Capital account

The capital account is presented in two parts.

The first part shows that saving (B.8g) – the balance between national disposable income and final consumption expenditure from the production and distribution and use of income accounts - is reduced or increased by the balance of capital transfers (D.9) to provide an amount available for financing investment (in both non-financial and financial assets).

Then in the second part, total investment in non-financial assets is the sum of gross fixed capital formation (P.51), changes in inventories (P.52), acquisitions less disposals of valuables (P.53) and acquisitions less disposals of non-financial non-produced assets (K.2). The balance on the capital account is known as net lending or borrowing. Conceptually this net lending or borrowing for all the domestic sectors represents net lending or borrowing to the rest of the world sector.

Thus, if investment is lower than the amount available for investment, the balance will be positive and is regarded as lending (if negative the balance is borrowing). Where the capital accounts relate to the individual institutional sectors, the net lending/borrowing of a particular sector represents the amounts available for lending or borrowing to other sectors. The value of net lending/borrowing is the same irrespective of whether the accounts are shown before or after deduction of fixed capital consumption (K.1), provided a consistent approach is adopted throughout. Financial account

The financial account elaborates the acquisition and disposal of financial assets and liabilities. Examples of financial assets include: bank deposits (which are assets of the depositors and liabilities of the banks), unit trust units (assets of the holders and liabilities of unit trusts) and Treasury Bills (assets of the holders and a liability of central government). The balance of all transactions in the financial account is net lending or borrowing.

The statistical adjustment items

Although in theory the net lending/borrowing from the financial account and the net lending/borrowing from the capital account for each sector should be equal, in practice they are not. This is because of the (sometimes substantial) errors and omissions in the accounts. The difference between the two balances is known as the statistical adjustment item.

Part of the balancing process for the economic accounts statistics for years before the latest one shown (that is, for years t-1 and earlier) involves assessing and modifying the component variables so that the estimates of net lending/borrowing made from the income and capital accounts, and from the financial accounts, are the same at the level of the whole economy, and reasonably close to each other at the sector level.

The sectoral statistical adjustment items are shown in Table D below. They provide a measure of the reliability of the accounts.

D Table D: Sector statistical adjustment

£ million

		1998	1999	2000	2001	2002	2003	2004	2005	2006
Households sector	NZDV	12 193	1 850	4 745	1 555	249	–3 644	–12 650	1 793	–8 315
Private non-financial corporations	NYPM	8 067	7 556	–516	–1 915	–1 234	7 598	3 961	2 050	–7 781
Financial corporations	NYOX	–11 885	–10 206	–14 650	–3 002	–7 608	3 118	–2 819	10 216	1 836
Public corporations	NYPI	–757	99	466	–699	–320	–110	–108	–298	721
Central government	NZDW	191	400	449	313	597	1 055	876	–582	–185
Local government	NYPC	–593	747	–1 020	684	–63	–965	–884	930	764
Rest of the world	NYPO	–7 216	–446	10 526	3 063	8 379	–7 052	11 624	–11 950	14 146
Total[1]	-RVFE	–	–	–	–	–	–	–	2 159	1 186

1 Equals, but opposite in sign to, the residual error observed between GDP measured by the income approach and GDP measured by the expenditure approach

Balance sheets

A financial balance sheet for each sector has been compiled using the same financial instrument classification as that used for financial transactions. The changes in the end period levels in the financial balance sheets do not equal the financial transactions because of holding gains or losses and reclassifications of units between sectors. Non-financial balance sheets for the ESA95 sectors are now included.

Further information

In addition to the articles and publications mentioned in Part 1, further information relating to the sector accounts and in particular the financial accounts can be found in the following articles and publications:

Office for National Statistics (2006) *Financial Statistics: Explanatory Handbook* 2007 edition. Palgrave Macmillan: Basingstoke.

Office for National Statistics *Financial Statistics*, monthly publication, Palgrave Macmillan: Basingstoke.

Turnbull P (Central Statistical Office) (1993) 'The UK Sector Accounts'. *Economic Trends*, No. 479, HMSO: London.

Bank of England (2002) Bank of England Statistical Abstract. Bank of England: London.

Articles relating to the Public Sector Finances

Golland J, Savage D, Pike T and Pike S (1999) 'Monthly Statistics on Public Sector Finances. A Methodological Guide'. GSS Methodology Series No. 12, Office for National Statistics: London.

Golland J, Louth N, Hill C (1998) 'New Format For Public Finances'. *Economic Trends*, No. 535, The Stationery Office: London.

Articles relating to monetary aggregates (M0, M4)

Bank of England (1994) 'The Determination of M0 and M4'. *Bank of England Quarterly Bulletin,* February 1994, pp 46-50.

Bank of England (1993) 'Divisia measures of money'. *Bank of England Quarterly Bulletin,* May 1993.

Chapter 3
Non-financial corporations

3.1.1 Non-financial corporations
ESA95 sector S.11

£ million

			1998	1999	2000	2001	2002	2003	2004
I	**PRODUCTION ACCOUNT**								
	Resources								
P.1	Output								
P.11	Market output	FAIN	1 066 664	1 114 874	1 177 211	1 213 638	1 243 635	1 294 414	1 361 125
P.12	Output for own final use	FAIO	8 203	8 714	9 448	10 293	10 727	12 129	11 946
P.1	Total resources	FAFA	1 074 867	1 123 588	1 186 659	1 223 931	1 254 362	1 306 543	1 373 071
	Uses								
P.2	Intermediate consumption	FAIQ	563 455	585 739	618 158	634 630	648 273	672 319	704 727
B.1g	**Gross Value Added**	FAIS	**511 412**	**537 849**	**568 501**	**589 301**	**606 089**	**634 224**	**668 344**
Total	Total uses	FAFA	1 074 867	1 123 588	1 186 659	1 223 931	1 254 362	1 306 543	1 373 071
B.1g	**Gross Value Added**	FAIS	**511 412**	**537 849**	**568 501**	**589 301**	**606 089**	**634 224**	**668 344**
-K.1	*less* Consumption of fixed capital	-DBGF	–57 625	–60 263	–62 465	–64 028	–65 775	–67 438	–69 979
B.1n	Value added, net	FAIT	453 787	477 586	506 036	525 273	540 314	566 786	598 365

3.1.2 Non-financial corporations
ESA95 sector S.11

£ million

			1998	1999	2000	2001	2002	2003	2004
II	**DISTRIBUTION AND USE OF INCOME ACCOUNTS**								
II.1	**PRIMARY DISTRIBUTION OF INCOME ACCOUNT**								
II.1.1	**GENERATION OF INCOME ACCOUNT** before deduction of fixed capital consumption								
	Resources								
B.1g	**Total resources (Gross Value Added)**	FAIS	**511 412**	**537 849**	**568 501**	**589 301**	**606 089**	**634 224**	**668 344**
	Uses								
D.1	Compensation of employees								
D.11	Wages and salaries	FAKT	275 828	293 542	313 703	330 912	340 164	347 038	357 937
D.12	Employers' social contributions	FAKU	35 569	39 117	42 631	44 927	47 995	55 373	61 624
D.1	Total	FCFV	311 397	332 659	356 334	375 839	388 159	402 411	419 561
D.2	Taxes on production and imports, paid								
D.29	Production taxes other than on products	EACJ	14 267	14 892	15 808	16 170	16 679	17 037	17 426
-D.3	*less* Subsidies, received								
-D.39	Production subsidies other than on products	-JQJV	–810	–663	–574	–662	–954	–1 434	–1 499
B.2g	Operating surplus, gross	NQBE	186 558	190 961	196 933	197 954	202 205	216 210	232 856
B.1g	**Total uses (Gross Value Added)**	FAIS	**511 412**	**537 849**	**568 501**	**589 301**	**606 089**	**634 224**	**668 344**
-K.1	After deduction of fixed capital consumption	-DBGF	–57 625	–60 263	–62 465	–64 028	–65 775	–67 438	–69 979
B.2n	Operating surplus, net	FAIR	128 933	130 698	134 468	133 926	136 430	148 772	162 877

3.1.3 Non-financial corporations
ESA95 sector S.11

£ million

			1998	1999	2000	2001	2002	2003	2004	2005	2006
II.1.2	**ALLOCATION OF PRIMARY INCOME ACCOUNT**										
	before deduction of fixed capital consumption										
	Resources										
B.2g	Operating surplus, gross	NQBE	186 558	190 961	196 933	197 954	202 205	216 210	232 856	242 623	256 112
D.4	Property income, received										
D.41	Interest	EABC	14 015	10 794	14 427	12 860	9 338	9 032	11 428	15 040	18 547
D.42	Distributed income of corporations	EABD	25 088	21 472	26 519	37 487	30 549	50 259	44 014	47 970	47 472
D.43	Reinvested earnings on direct foreign investment	WEYD	10 979	16 214	20 118	22 997	26 931	12 559	24 219	32 032	41 468
D.44	Attributed property income of insurance policy-holders	FAOF	463	338	290	335	304	400	405	582	604
D.45	Rent	FAOG	118	117	117	117	118	120	122	122	120
D.4	Total	FAKY	50 663	48 935	61 471	73 796	67 240	72 370	80 188	95 746	108 211
Total	Total resources	FBXJ	237 221	239 896	258 404	271 750	269 445	288 580	313 044	338 369	364 323
	Uses										
D.4	Property income, paid										
D.41	Interest	EABG	32 046	31 857	38 389	40 056	37 134	36 445	42 002	49 725	62 369
D.42	Distributed income of corporations	NVCS	79 645	88 395	86 521	105 807	90 162	98 761	99 106	107 215	100 237
D.43	Reinvested earnings on direct foreign investment	HDVB	3 117	2 776	7 348	1 699	1 614	3 955	6 729	5 044	16 668
D.45	Rent	FBXO	584	565	1 325	1 955	1 939	1 603	1 461	1 391	1 250
D.4	Total	FBXK	115 392	123 593	133 583	149 517	130 849	140 764	149 298	163 375	180 524
B.5g	**Balance of primary incomes, gross**	NQBG	**121 829**	**116 303**	**124 821**	**122 233**	**138 596**	**147 816**	**163 746**	**174 994**	**183 799**
Total	Total uses	FBXJ	237 221	239 896	258 404	271 750	269 445	288 580	313 044	338 369	364 323
-K.1	After deduction of fixed capital consumption	-DBGF	−57 625	−60 263	−62 465	−64 028	−65 775	−67 438	−69 979	−71 335	−72 737
B.5n	Balance of primary incomes, net	FBXQ	64 204	56 040	62 356	58 205	72 821	80 378	93 767	103 659	111 062

3.1.4 Non-financial corporations
ESA95 sector S.11

£ million

			1998	1999	2000	2001	2002	2003	2004	2005	2006
II.2	**SECONDARY DISTRIBUTION OF INCOME ACCOUNT**										
	Resources										
B.5g	**Balance of primary incomes, gross**	NQBG	**121 829**	**116 303**	**124 821**	**122 233**	**138 596**	**147 816**	**163 746**	**174 994**	**183 799**
D.61	Social contributions										
D.612	Imputed social contributions	NSTJ	3 454	3 845	4 175	4 357	4 575	4 229	3 864	3 612	3 490
D.7	Current transfers other than taxes, social contributions and benefits										
D.72	Non-life insurance claims	FCBP	4 849	4 151	5 923	5 000	5 452	6 471	6 591	7 248	7 793
D.75	Miscellaneous current transfers	CY8C	129	109	85	122	147	124	28	–	–
D.7	Total	NRJB	4 978	4 260	6 008	5 122	5 599	6 595	6 619	7 248	7 793
Total	Total resources	FCBR	130 261	124 408	135 004	131 712	148 770	158 640	174 229	185 854	195 082
	Uses										
D.5	Current taxes on income, wealth etc.										
D.51	Taxes on income	FCBS	27 256	22 948	24 497	23 177	24 038	23 702	27 348	33 607	37 221
D.62	Social benefits other than social transfers in kind	NSTJ	3 454	3 845	4 175	4 357	4 575	4 229	3 864	3 612	3 490
D.7	Current transfers other than taxes, social contributions and benefits										
D.71	Net non-life insurance premiums	FCBY	4 849	4 151	5 923	5 000	5 452	6 471	6 591	7 248	7 793
D.75	Miscellaneous current transfers	CY8B	626	709	553	506	480	462	451	488	477
D.7	Total, other current transfers	FCBX	5 475	4 860	6 476	5 506	5 932	6 933	7 042	7 736	8 270
B.6g	**Gross Disposable Income**	NRJD	**94 076**	**92 755**	**99 856**	**98 672**	**114 225**	**123 776**	**135 975**	**140 899**	**146 101**
Total	Total uses	FCBR	130 261	124 408	135 004	131 712	148 770	158 640	174 229	185 854	195 082
-K.1	After deduction of fixed capital consumption	-DBGF	−57 625	−60 263	−62 465	−64 028	−65 775	−67 438	−69 979	−71 335	−72 737
B.6n	Disposable income, net	FCCF	36 451	32 492	37 391	34 644	48 450	56 338	65 996	69 564	73 364

3.1.6 Non-financial corporations
ESA95 sector S.11

£ million

			1998	1999	2000	2001	2002	2003	2004	2005	2006
II.4.1	**USE OF DISPOSABLE INCOME ACCOUNT**										
	Resources										
B.6g	**Total resources (Gross Disposable Income)**	NRJD	**94 076**	**92 755**	**99 856**	**98 672**	**114 225**	**123 776**	**135 975**	**140 899**	**146 101**
	Uses										
B.8g	**Total uses (Gross Saving)**	NRJD	**94 076**	**92 755**	**99 856**	**98 672**	**114 225**	**123 776**	**135 975**	**140 899**	**146 101**
-K.1	After deduction of fixed capital consumption	-DBGF	–57 625	–60 263	–62 465	–64 028	–65 775	–67 438	–69 979	–71 335	–72 737
B.8n	Saving, net	FCCF	36 451	32 492	37 391	34 644	48 450	56 338	65 996	69 564	73 364

3.1.7 Non-financial corporations
ESA95 sector S.11

£ million

			1998	1999	2000	2001	2002	2003	2004	2005	2006
III	**ACCUMULATION ACCOUNTS**										
III.1	**CAPITAL ACCOUNT**										
III.1.1	**CHANGE IN NET WORTH DUE TO SAVING AND CAPITAL TRANSFERS**										
	Changes in liabilities and net worth										
B.8g	**Gross Saving**	NRJD	**94 076**	**92 755**	**99 856**	**98 672**	**114 225**	**123 776**	**135 975**	**140 899**	**146 101**
D.9	Capital transfers receivable										
D.92	Investment grants	FCCO	2 211	2 992	2 835	3 845	3 895	5 563	5 314	7 218	7 520
D.99	Other capital transfers	LNZN	186	150	142	915	184	148	162	11 803	450
D.9	Total	FCCQ	2 397	3 142	2 977	4 760	4 079	5 711	5 476	19 021	7 970
-D.9	*less* Capital transfers payable										
-D.91	Capital taxes	-QYKB	–	–	–	–	–	–	–	–	–
-D.99	Other capital transfers	-JRWI	–220	–265	–345	–473	–728	–705	–528	–1 257	–645
-D.9	Total	-JRWJ	–220	–265	–345	–473	–728	–705	–528	–1 257	–645
B.10.1g	Total change in liabilities and net worth	FCCY	96 253	95 632	102 488	102 959	117 576	128 782	140 923	158 663	153 426
	Changes in assets										
B.10.1g	Changes in net worth due to gross saving and capital transfers	FCCY	96 253	95 632	102 488	102 959	117 576	128 782	140 923	158 663	153 426
-K.1	After deduction of fixed capital consumption	-DBGF	–57 625	–60 263	–62 465	–64 028	–65 775	–67 438	–69 979	–71 335	–72 737
B.10.1n	Changes in net worth due to net saving and capital transfers	FCCV	38 628	35 369	40 023	38 931	51 801	61 344	70 944	87 328	80 689
III.1.2	**ACQUISITION OF NON-FINANCIAL ASSETS ACCOUNT**										
	Changes in liabilities and net worth										
B.10.1n	Changes in net worth due to net saving and capital transfers	FCCV	38 628	35 369	40 023	38 931	51 801	61 344	70 944	87 328	80 689
K.1	Consumption of fixed capital	DBGF	57 625	60 263	62 465	64 028	65 775	67 438	69 979	71 335	72 737
B.10.1g	Total change in liabilities and net worth	FCCY	96 253	95 632	102 488	102 959	117 576	128 782	140 923	158 663	153 426
	Changes in assets										
P.5	Gross capital formation										
P.51	Gross fixed capital formation	DBGP	97 405	101 701	103 951	106 310	107 012	105 712	108 509	131 525	126 224
P.52	Changes in inventories	DBGM	4 748	6 054	5 289	5 950	2 647	3 745	4 586	4 292	3 803
P.53	Acquisitions less disposals of valuables	NPOV	28	–17	–75	–	–43	–97	–99	–171	–90
P.5	Total gross capital formation	FCCZ	102 181	107 738	109 165	112 260	109 616	109 360	112 996	135 646	129 937
K.2	Acquisitions less disposals of non-produced non-financial assets	FCFY	1 002	1 051	864	1 208	1 431	1 241	1 672	1 784	1 501
B.9	**Net lending(+) / net borrowing(-)**	EABO	**–6 930**	**–13 157**	**–7 541**	**–10 509**	**6 529**	**18 181**	**26 255**	**21 233**	**21 988**
Total	Total change in assets	FCCY	96 253	95 632	102 488	102 959	117 576	128 782	140 923	158 663	153 426

3.1.8 Non-financial corporations

ESA95 sector S.11 Unconsolidated

£ million

			1998	1999	2000	2001	2002	2003	2004	2005	2006
III.2	**FINANCIAL ACCOUNT**										
F.A	**Net acquisition of financial assets**										
F.2	Currency and deposits										
F.21	Currency	NGIJ	184	378	308	277	10	338	–46	182	238
F.22	Transferable deposits										
F.2211	Sterling deposits with UK banks	NGIM	5 321	7 370	11 703	9 069	9 721	11 060	11 526	20 134	24 099
F.2212	Foreign currency deposits with UK banks	NGIN	–653	2 455	3 137	1 332	–273	3 868	2 558	2 643	2 652
F.2213	Sterling deposits with building societies	NGIO	–126	156	–134	301	–77	245	–313	–64	299
F.229	Deposits with rest of the world monetary financial institutions	NGIP	726	18 345	31 742	24 131	30 531	34 095	54 595	37 995	35 705
F.29	Other deposits	NGIQ	–2 536	–695	–251	–566	1 109	–398	455	661	715
F.2	Total currency and deposits	NGII	2 916	28 009	46 505	34 544	41 021	49 208	68 775	61 551	63 708
F.3	Securities other than shares										
F.331	Short term: money market instruments										
F.3311	Issued by UK central government	NGIT	8	144	–78	–100	–	2	–4	74	–26
F.3312	Issued by UK local government	NGIX	–	–	–	–	–	–	–	–	–
F.3315	Issued by UK monetary financial institutions	NGIY	2 542	–2 003	–81	234	230	601	86	–723	2 394
F.3316	Issued by other UK residents	NGJD	–1 486	–175	–2 797	136	–2 108	821	191	–1 604	2 237
F.3319	Issued by the rest of the world	NGJE	–956	722	1 110	1 912	1 110	3 798	615	1 661	5 359
F.332	Medium (1 to 5 year) and long term (over 5 year) bonds										
F.3321	Issued by UK central government	NGJG	1 363	–453	230	–579	148	–335	–92	–880	–1 996
F.3322	Issued by UK local government	NGJJ	–	–	–	–	–	–	–	–	–
F.3325	Medium term bonds issued by UK MFIs[1]	NGJK	46	54	–237	–333	42	167	–23	395	466
F.3326	Other medium & long term bonds issued by UK residents	NGJN	625	–1 347	1 141	1 784	559	–685	–403	–3 341	257
F.3329	Long term bonds issued by the rest of the world	NGJO	585	–934	1 792	1 759	–601	2 213	438	2 547	–1 201
F.34	Financial derivatives	NGJP	31	3	–92	–8	10	9	8	1	–1
F.3	Total securities other than shares	NGIR	2 758	–3 989	988	4 805	–610	6 591	816	–1 870	7 489
F.4	Loans										
F.42	Long term loans										
F.421	Direct investment	NGKB	32 996	28 144	13 030	8 935	21 891	9 678	9 259	21 452	–6 021
F.422	Loans secured on dwellings	NGKE	–2	–1	–1	–	–	–	–	–	–
F.423	Finance leasing	NGKI	243	603	665	116	221	720	947	1 043	991
F.424	Other long-term loans by UK residents	NGKJ	–2 122	–118	13 617	4 656	–27	–4 863	562	13 623	37 888
F.4	Total loans	NGJT	31 115	28 628	27 311	13 707	22 085	5 535	10 768	36 118	32 858
F.5	Shares and other equity										
F.51	Shares and other equity, excluding mutual funds' shares										
F.514	Quoted UK shares	NGKQ	23 986	24 186	87 591	10 041	17 519	7 356	14 882	13 531	19 896
F.515	Unquoted UK shares	NGKR	5 993	–9 292	–27 228	–471	3 345	6 100	3 028	15 947	9 873
F.517	UK shares and bonds issued by other UK residents	NSQC	–	–	–	–	–	–	–	–	–
F.519	Shares and other equity issued by the rest of the world	NGKV	48 497	112 093	166 680	36 002	49 469	19 394	26 420	40 109	42 824
F.52	Mutual funds' shares										
F.521	UK mutual funds' shares	NGKZ	1	1	14	2	3	1	9	17	17
F.5	Total shares and other equity	NGKL	78 477	126 988	227 057	45 574	70 336	32 851	44 339	69 604	72 610
F.6	Insurance technical reserves										
F.62	Prepayments of insurance premiums and reserves for outstanding claims	NGLE	–109	–291	344	–370	363	170	933	965	766
F.7	Other accounts receivable	NGLF	1 538	–2 224	25 027	–1 673	2 881	2 168	–1 846	1 190	5 359
F.A	**Total net acquisition of financial assets**	NRGP	116 695	177 121	327 232	96 587	136 076	96 523	123 785	167 558	182 790

1 UK monetary financial institutions

3.1.8 Non-financial corporations
ESA95 sector S.11 Unconsolidated

continued £ million

			1998	1999	2000	2001	2002	2003	2004	2005	2006
III.2	**FINANCIAL ACCOUNT** continued										
F.L	**Net acquisition of financial liabilities**										
F.2	Currency and deposits										
F.29	Other deposits	-A4VS	30	28	29	30	18	–	–	–	–
F.2	Total currency and deposits	-A4VR	30	28	29	30	18	–	–	–	–
F.3	Securities other than shares										
F.331	Short term: money market instruments										
F.3316	Issued by UK residents other than government or monetary financial institutions	NGMH	3 435	2 716	1 331	–426	8 543	–1 541	–2 999	–254	436
F.332	Medium (1 to 5 year) and long term (over 5 year) bonds										
F.3326	Other medium & long term bonds issued by UK residents or monetary financial institutions	NGMR	17 100	39 378	40 595	15 478	15 330	19 426	8 550	12 420	11 263
F.34	Financial derivatives	CY7W	–36	–42	–110	–184	–204	–138	–28	–	–
F.3	Total securities other than shares	NGLV	20 499	42 052	41 816	14 868	23 669	17 747	5 523	12 166	11 699
F.4	Loans										
F.41	Short term loans										
F.411	Loans by UK monetary financial institutions, excluding loans secured on dwellings & financial leasing	NGMZ	18 959	16 793	25 581	18 379	20 831	7 303	19 977	46 082	55 603
F.419	Loans by rest of the world monetary financial institutions	NGND	–58	9 383	3 136	30 752	14 693	34 807	41 488	9 157	77 207
F.42	Long term loans										
F.421	Direct investment	NGNF	36 102	27 029	40 792	17 919	43 802	10 162	14 072	53 298	–16 301
F.422	Loans secured by dwellings	G9JS	..	..	..	..	..	..	..	4 170	3 812
F.423	Finance leasing	NGNM	86	98	64	–52	290	636	988	944	1 160
F.424	Other long-term loans by UK residents	NGNN	939	2 040	–1 309	4 260	490	4 611	701	6 020	5 434
F.429	Other long-term loans by the rest of the world	NGNO	–5	–	–	–	–	–	–	–	–
F.4	Total loans	NGMX	56 023	55 343	68 264	71 258	80 106	57 519	77 226	119 671	126 915
F.5	Shares and other equity										
F.51	Shares and other equity, excluding mutual funds' shares										
F.514	Quoted UK shares	NGNU	45 680	85 600	209 418	9 234	16 508	–748	7 286	–4 608	–3 456
F.515	Unquoted UK shares	NGNV	6 014	5 805	12 818	4 795	4 622	8 023	8 292	15 681	15 808
F.516	Other UK equity (including direct investment in property)	NGNW	632	833	1 605	821	748	509	623	–652	–737
F.517	UK shares and bonds issued by other UK residents	NSQD	–	–	–	–	–	–	–	–	–
F.5	Total shares and other equity	NGNP	52 326	92 238	223 841	14 850	21 878	7 784	16 201	10 421	11 615
F.7	Other accounts payable	NGOJ	2 057	8 272	773	3 476	2 322	2 780	2 433	5 819	3 513
F.L	**Total net acquisition of financial liabilities**	NRGR	130 935	197 933	334 723	104 482	127 993	85 830	101 383	148 077	153 742
B.9	**Net lending / borrowing**										
F.A	Total net acquisition of financial assets	NRGP	116 695	177 121	327 232	96 587	136 076	96 523	123 785	167 558	182 790
-F.L	*less* Total net acquisition of financial liabilities	-NRGR	–130 935	–197 933	–334 723	–104 482	–127 993	–85 830	–101 383	–148 077	–153 742
B.9f	Net lending (+) / net borrowing (-), from financial account	NYNT	–14 240	–20 812	–7 491	–7 895	8 083	10 693	22 402	19 481	29 048
dB.9f	Statistical discrepancy	NYPF	7 310	7 655	–50	–2 614	–1 554	7 488	3 853	1 752	–7 060
B.9	**Net lending (+) / net borrowing (-), from capital account**	EABO	**–6 930**	**–13 157**	**–7 541**	**–10 509**	**6 529**	**18 181**	**26 255**	**21 233**	**21 988**

3.1.9 Non-financial corporations

ESA95 sector S.11 Unconsolidated

£ billion

			1998	1999	2000	2001	2002	2003	2004	2005	2006
IV.3	**FINANCIAL BALANCE SHEET** at end of period										
AN	**Non-financial assets**	CGES	1 130.0	1 173.7	1 278.1	1 263.1	1 311.2	1 337.4	1 387.4	1 487.9	1 506.6
AF.A	**Financial assets**										
AF.2	Currency and deposits										
AF.21	Currency	NNZG	2.9	3.3	3.6	3.8	3.8	4.1	4.1	4.3	4.5
AF.22	Transferable deposits										
AF.221	Deposits with UK monetary financial institutions	NNZI	132.9	143.1	160.3	171.9	178.1	191.5	205.6	230.9	254.5
AF.229	Deposits with rest of the world monetary financial institutions	NNZM	64.9	78.1	101.2	113.2	143.3	184.2	230.2	281.5	295.4
AF.29	Other deposits	NNZN	8.3	8.0	8.1	7.6	8.0	6.2	6.7	8.7	9.4
AF.2	Total currency and deposits	NNZF	209.1	232.5	273.3	296.4	333.2	386.0	446.5	525.3	563.7
AF.3	Securities other than shares										
AF.331	Short term: money market instruments										
AF.3311	Issued by UK central government	NNZQ	–	0.2	0.1	–	–	–	–	0.1	–
AF.3312	Issued by UK local government	NNZU	–	–	–	–	–	–	–	–	–
AF.3315	Issued by UK monetary financial institutions	NNZV	7.1	5.2	5.8	6.0	5.0	5.4	5.8	5.2	7.3
AF.3316	Issued by other UK residents	NOLO	6.3	13.6	16.4	18.6	13.9	13.8	13.6	18.3	35.7
AF.3319	Issued by the rest of the world	NOLP	1.2	1.9	3.0	4.9	6.0	9.8	10.4	12.0	17.4
AF.332	Medium (1 to 5 year) and long term (over 5 year) bonds										
AF.3321	Issued by UK central government	NOLR	4.2	3.8	4.0	3.4	3.5	3.2	3.1	2.7	0.7
AF.3322	Issued by UK local government	NOLU	–	–	–	–	–	–	–	–	–
AF.3325	Medium term bonds issued by UK MFIs[1]	NOLV	0.2	0.3	0.2	0.2	0.3	0.9	1.0	1.5	1.9
AF.3326	Other medium & long term bonds issued by UK residents	NOLY	3.5	1.9	2.5	4.1	6.1	5.2	5.1	1.5	1.5
AF.3329	Long term bonds issued by the rest of the world	NOLZ	6.3	7.2	28.4	28.8	29.3	30.0	28.2	14.8	14.4
AF.34	Financial derivatives	NOMA	–	–	–	–	–	–	–	–	–
AF.3	Total securities other than shares	NNZO	28.8	34.0	60.5	66.0	64.1	68.2	67.0	56.1	79.0
AF.4	Loans										
AF.42	Long term loans										
AF.421	Direct investment	NOMM	109.9	129.3	134.1	146.3	163.3	159.1	181.2	197.8	191.8
AF.422	Loans secured on dwellings	NOMP	–	–	–	–	–	–	–	–	–
AF.423	Finance leasing	NOMT	0.9	1.8	2.4	2.5	2.7	3.4	4.4	5.4	6.4
AF.424	Other long-term loans by UK residents	NOMU	12.5	12.9	12.0	12.3	12.3	12.3	12.3	11.9	10.7
AF.4	Total loans	NOME	123.4	144.0	148.5	161.1	178.3	174.8	197.9	215.1	208.9
AF.5	Shares and other equity										
AF.51	Shares and other equity, excluding mutual funds' shares										
AF.514	Quoted UK shares	NONB	18.5	38.8	26.4	14.8	8.8	9.4	9.2	19.3	32.9
AF.515	Unquoted UK shares	NONC	49.3	64.7	63.9	52.7	39.9	46.6	50.2	57.3	61.1
AF.517	UK shares and bonds issued by other UK residents	NSQW	–	–	–	–	–	–	–	–	–
AF.519	Shares and other equity issued by the rest of the world	NONG	214.0	340.7	507.4	495.2	522.3	565.7	548.2	614.7	594.5
AF.52	Mutual funds' shares										
AF.521	UK mutual funds' shares	NONK	0.4	0.6	0.5	0.4	0.3	0.3	0.4	0.5	0.6
AF.5	Total shares and other equity	NOMW	282.2	444.7	598.2	563.1	571.3	622.1	608.0	691.8	689.1
AF.6	Insurance technical reserves										
AF.62	Prepayments of insurance premiums and reserves for outstanding claims	NONP	11.8	10.7	14.7	12.5	12.8	15.7	16.6	17.3	18.1
AF.7	Other accounts receivable	NONQ	95.8	93.0	117.7	116.5	116.8	119.9	124.3	136.4	143.7
AF.A	**Total financial assets**	NNZB	751.1	959.0	1 212.9	1 215.5	1 276.5	1 386.7	1 460.4	1 642.1	1 702.4

1 UK monetary financial institutions

3.1.9 Non-financial corporations

ESA95 sector S.11 Unconsolidated

continued £ billion

			1998	1999	2000	2001	2002	2003	2004	2005	2006
IV.3	**FINANCIAL BALANCE SHEET** continued at end of period										
AF.L	**Financial liabilities**										
	Currency and deposits										
AF.29	Other deposits	NOOF	0.3	0.4	0.4	0.4	–	–	–	–	–
AF.2	Total currency and deposits	NONX	0.3	0.4	0.4	0.4	–	–	–	–	–
AF.3	Securities other than shares										
AF.331	Short term: money market instruments										
AF.3316	Issued by UK residents other than government or monetary financial institutions	NOOS	18.6	22.5	24.7	24.6	30.4	26.0	21.9	23.8	21.7
AF.332	Medium (1 to 5 year) and long term (over 5 year) bonds										
AF.3326	Other medium & long term bonds issued by UK residents or monetary financial institutions	NOPC	123.6	156.6	198.8	210.3	233.1	255.4	271.9	320.4	361.2
AF.34	Financial derivatives	NOPE	–	–	–	–	–	–	–	–	–
AF.3	Total securities other than shares	NOOG	142.2	179.1	223.5	234.9	263.4	281.4	293.8	344.2	382.9
AF.4	Loans										
AF.41	Short term loans										
AF.411	Loans by UK monetary financial institutions, excluding loans secured on dwellings & financial leasing	NOPK	205.5	222.1	250.5	268.3	285.8	286.7	300.8	347.9	398.2
AF.419	Loans by rest of the world monetary financial institutions	NOPO	72.7	88.4	99.9	121.1	139.6	170.5	208.5	223.5	289.6
AF.42	Long term loans										
AF.421	Direct investment	NOPQ	128.1	150.9	180.9	209.3	249.9	241.6	251.1	300.5	284.2
AF.422	Loans secured on dwellings	G9JO	..	..	..	..	..	..	..	27.1	30.9
AF.423	Finance leasing	NOPX	20.7	21.5	21.8	21.7	22.0	22.6	23.6	24.5	25.7
AF.424	Other long-term loans by UK residents	NOPY	36.3	48.8	50.4	55.4	56.0	72.5	83.9	77.3	89.1
AF.429	Other long-term loans by the rest of the world	NOPZ	0.4	0.4	0.4	0.3	0.4	0.4	0.4	0.4	0.4
AF.4	Total loans	NOPI	463.8	532.1	603.9	676.1	753.8	794.4	868.2	1 001.4	1 118.2
AF.5	Shares and other equity										
AF.51	Shares and other equity, excluding mutual funds' shares										
AF.514	Quoted UK shares	NOQF	1 059.5	1 394.4	1 375.5	1 134.7	873.0	1 022.0	1 112.5	1 235.4	1 318.7
AF.515	Unquoted UK shares	NOQG	356.3	462.5	490.1	455.6	353.0	393.2	428.1	514.0	580.7
AF.516	Other UK equity (including direct investment in property)	NOQH	12.2	13.1	14.9	15.5	17.3	17.3	19.2	19.7	21.6
AF.517	UK shares and bonds issued by other UK residents	NSQX	–	–	–	–	–	–	–	–	–
AF.5	Total shares and other equity	NOQA	1 428.0	1 869.9	1 880.5	1 605.9	1 243.3	1 432.5	1 559.8	1 769.1	1 921.0
AF.7	Other accounts payable	NOQU	130.6	135.9	139.9	141.4	141.4	143.7	146.6	150.6	152.8
AF.L	**Total financial liabilities**	NONT	2 164.9	2 717.4	2 848.3	2 658.7	2 401.9	2 652.0	2 868.4	3 265.3	3 574.9
BF.90	**Net financial assets / liabilities**										
AF.A	Total financial assets	NNZB	751.1	959.0	1 212.9	1 215.5	1 276.5	1 386.7	1 460.4	1 642.1	1 702.4
-AF.L	*less* Total financial liabilities	-NONT	–2 164.9	–2 717.4	–2 848.3	–2 658.7	–2 401.9	–2 652.0	–2 868.4	–3 265.3	–3 574.9
BF.90	**Net financial assets (+) / liabilities (-)**	NYOM	–1 413.8	–1 758.4	–1 635.4	–1 443.1	–1 125.4	–1 265.3	–1 408.0	–1 623.2	–1 872.5
	Net worth										
AN	Non-financial assets	CGES	1 130.0	1 173.7	1 278.1	1 263.1	1 311.2	1 337.4	1 387.4	1 487.9	1 506.6
BF.90	Net financial assets(+)/ liabilities(-)	NYOM	–1 413.8	–1 758.4	–1 635.4	–1 443.1	–1 125.4	–1 265.3	–1 408.0	–1 623.2	–1 872.5
B.90	**Net worth**	CGRV	–283.8	–584.8	–357.3	–180.1	185.8	72.0	–20.6	–135.2	–365.9

3.2.1 Public non-financial corporations[1]

ESA95 sector S.11001

£ million

			1998	1999	2000	2001	2002	2003	2004
I	**PRODUCTION ACCOUNT**								
	Resources								
P.1	Output								
P.11	Market output	FCZI	29 601	29 921	30 991	31 389	34 093	37 479	38 060
P.12	Output for own final use	GIRZ	216	189	183	164	224	205	117
P.1	Total resources	FCZG	29 817	30 110	31 174	31 553	34 317	37 684	38 177
	Uses								
P.2	Intermediate consumption	QZLQ	12 395	11 943	12 934	13 291	15 549	18 249	18 952
B.1g	**Gross Value Added**	FACW	**17 422**	**18 167**	**18 240**	**18 262**	**18 768**	**19 435**	**19 225**
Total	Total uses	FCZG	29 817	30 110	31 174	31 553	34 317	37 684	38 177
B.1g	**Gross Value Added**	FACW	**17 422**	**18 167**	**18 240**	**18 262**	**18 768**	**19 435**	**19 225**
-K.1	*less* Consumption of fixed capital	-NSRM	–3 341	–3 394	–3 470	–3 604	–3 900	–4 068	–4 077
B.1n	Value added, net	FACX	14 081	14 773	14 770	14 658	14 868	15 367	15 148

1 Public financial corporations are also included to avoid disclosure of commercial information

3.2.2 Public non-financial corporations[1]

ESA95 sector S.11001

£ million

			1998	1999	2000	2001	2002	2003	2004
II	**DISTRIBUTION AND USE OF INCOME ACCOUNTS**								
II.1	**PRIMARY DISTRIBUTION OF INCOME ACCOUNT**								
II.1.1	**GENERATION OF INCOME ACCOUNT** before deduction of fixed capital consumption								
	Resources								
B.1g	**Total resources (Gross Value Added)**	FACW	**17 422**	**18 167**	**18 240**	**18 262**	**18 768**	**19 435**	**19 225**
	Uses								
D.1	Compensation of employees								
D.11	Wages and salaries	FAIZ	8 812	9 296	9 689	9 949	10 523	10 513	10 758
D.12	Employers' social contributions	FAOH	1 555	1 639	1 710	1 758	1 859	1 855	1 898
D.1	Total	FDDI	10 367	10 935	11 399	11 707	12 382	12 368	12 656
D.2	Taxes on production and imports, paid								
D.29	Production taxes other than on products	FAOK	111	109	103	95	95	95	96
-D.3	*less* Subsidies, received								
-D.39	Production subsidies other than on products	-ARDD	–810	–555	–450	–432	–366	–293	–180
B.2g	Operating surplus, gross	NRJT	7 754	7 678	7 188	6 892	6 657	7 265	6 653
B.1g	**Total uses (Gross Value Added)**	FACW	**17 422**	**18 167**	**18 240**	**18 262**	**18 768**	**19 435**	**19 225**
-K.1	After deduction of fixed capital consumption	-NSRM	–3 341	–3 394	–3 470	–3 604	–3 900	–4 068	–4 077
B.2n	Operating surplus, net	FAOO	4 413	4 284	3 718	3 288	2 757	3 197	2 576

1 Public financial corporations are also included to avoid disclosure of commercial information

3.2.3 Public non-financial corporations[1]
ESA95 sector S.11001

£ million

			1998	1999	2000	2001	2002	2003	2004	2005	2006
II.1.2	**ALLOCATION OF PRIMARY INCOME ACCOUNT** before deduction of fixed capital consumption										
	Resources										
B.2g	Operating surplus, gross	NRJT	7 754	7 678	7 188	6 892	6 657	7 265	6 653	8 494	9 464
D.4	Property income, received										
D.41	Interest	CPBV	1 088	848	902	933	810	768	1 170	1 781	886
D.42	Distributed income of corporations	FACT	32	42	44	66	63	93	95	57	77
D.43	Property income reinvested earnings on foreign investments	WUHM	–	–	–	47	38	67	38	155	36
D.44	Property income attributed to insurance policy-holders	FAOT	–	–	–	–	–	–	–	–	–
D.4	Total	FAOP	1 120	890	946	1 046	911	928	1 303	1 993	999
Total	Total resources	FAOU	8 874	8 568	8 134	7 938	7 568	8 193	7 956	10 487	10 463
	Uses										
D.4	Property income, paid										
D.41	Interest	XAQZ	950	841	316	602	716	782	650	1 025	1 111
D.42	Distributed income of corporations	ZOYB	5 401	5 615	5 783	4 823	4 589	6 472	5 954	503	297
D.45	Rent	FAOZ	–	–	–	–	–	–	–	–	–
D.4	Total	FAOV	6 351	6 456	6 099	5 425	5 305	7 254	6 604	1 528	1 408
B.5g	**Balance of primary incomes, gross**	NRJX	**2 523**	**2 112**	**2 035**	**2 513**	**2 263**	**939**	**1 352**	**8 959**	**9 055**
Total	Total uses	FAOU	8 874	8 568	8 134	7 938	7 568	8 193	7 956	10 487	10 463
-K.1	After deduction of fixed capital consumption	-NSRM	–3 341	–3 394	–3 470	–3 604	–3 900	–4 068	–4 077	–4 282	–4 497
B.5n	Balance of primary incomes, net	FARX	–818	–1 282	–1 435	–1 091	–1 637	–3 129	–2 725	4 677	4 558

1 Public financial corporations are also included to avoid disclosure of commercial information

3.2.4 Public non-financial corporations[1]
ESA95 sector S.11001

£ million

			1998	1999	2000	2001	2002	2003	2004	2005	2006
II.2	**SECONDARY DISTRIBUTION OF INCOME ACCOUNT**										
	Resources										
B.5g	**Balance of primary incomes, gross**	NRJX	**2 523**	**2 112**	**2 035**	**2 513**	**2 263**	**939**	**1 352**	**8 959**	**9 055**
D.61	Social contributions										
D.612	Imputed social contributions	EWRS	124	121	108	128	138	131	128	132	132
D.7	Current transfers other than taxes, social contributions and benefits										
D.72	Net non-life insurance claims	FDDF	–	–	–	–	–	–	–	–	–
D.75	Miscellaneous current transfers	CY89	129	109	85	122	147	124	28	–	–
D.7	Total	FDEK	129	109	85	122	147	124	28	–	–
Total	Total resources	FDDH	2 776	2 342	2 228	2 763	2 548	1 194	1 508	9 091	9 187
	Uses										
D.5	Current taxes on income, wealth etc.										
D.51	Taxes on income	FCCS	379	340	218	90	61	94	61	122	353
D.62	Social benefits other than social transfers in kind	EWRS	124	121	108	128	138	131	128	132	132
D.7	Current transfers other than taxes, social contributions and benefits										
D.71	Net non-life insurance premiums	FDDM	–	–	–	–	–	–	–	–	–
D.75	Miscellaneous Current Transfers	CY87	182	140	140	95	58	28	5	–	–
D.7	Total	FDDL	182	140	140	95	58	28	5	–	–
B.6g	**Gross Disposable Income**	NRKD	**2 091**	**1 741**	**1 762**	**2 450**	**2 291**	**941**	**1 314**	**8 837**	**8 702**
Total	Total uses	FDDH	2 776	2 342	2 228	2 763	2 548	1 194	1 508	9 091	9 187
-K.1	After deduction of fixed capital consumption	-NSRM	–3 341	–3 394	–3 470	–3 604	–3 900	–4 068	–4 077	–4 282	–4 497
B.6n	Disposable income, net	FDDP	–1 250	–1 653	–1 708	–1 154	–1 609	–3 127	–2 763	4 555	4 205

1 Public financial corporations are also included to avoid disclosure of commercial information

3.2.6 Public non-financial corporations

ESA95 sector S.11001

£ million

			1998	1999	2000	2001	2002	2003	2004	2005	2006
II.4.1	**USE OF DISPOSABLE INCOME ACCOUNT**										
	Resources										
B.6g	**Total resources (Gross Disposable Income)**	NRKD	**2 091**	**1 741**	**1 762**	**2 450**	**2 291**	**941**	**1 314**	**8 837**	**8 702**
	Uses										
B.8g	**Total uses (Gross Saving)**	NRKD	**2 091**	**1 741**	**1 762**	**2 450**	**2 291**	**941**	**1 314**	**8 837**	**8 702**
-K.1	After deduction of fixed capital consumption	-NSRM	–3 341	–3 394	–3 470	–3 604	–3 900	–4 068	–4 077	–4 282	–4 497
B.8n	Saving, net	FDDP	–1 250	–1 653	–1 708	–1 154	–1 609	–3 127	–2 763	4 555	4 205

3.2.7 Public non-financial corporations[1]

ESA95 sector S.11001

£ million

			1998	1999	2000	2001	2002	2003	2004	2005	2006
III	**ACCUMULATION ACCOUNTS**										
III.1	**CAPITAL ACCOUNT**										
III.1.1	**CHANGE IN NET WORTH DUE TO SAVING AND CAPITAL TRANSFERS**										
	Changes in liabilities and net worth										
B.8g	**Gross Saving**	NRKD	**2 091**	**1 741**	**1 762**	**2 450**	**2 291**	**941**	**1 314**	**8 837**	**8 702**
D.9	Capital transfers receivable										
D.92	Investment grants	FDBV	1 121	1 583	1 329	797	764	504	400	1 791	1 486
D.99	Other capital transfers	NZGD	2	41	24	42	91	42	42	11 682	332
D.9	Total	FDBU	1 123	1 624	1 353	839	855	546	442	13 473	1 818
-D.9	*less* Capital transfers payable										
-D.99	Other capital transfers	-ZMLL	–27	–49	–55	–188	–236	–130	–109	–801	–122
B.10.1g	Total change in liabilities and net worth	FDEG	3 187	3 316	3 060	3 101	2 910	1 357	1 647	21 509	10 398
	Changes in assets										
B.10.1g	Changes in net worth due to gross saving and capital transfers	FDEG	3 187	3 316	3 060	3 101	2 910	1 357	1 647	21 509	10 398
-K.1	After deduction of fixed capital consumption	-NSRM	–3 341	–3 394	–3 470	–3 604	–3 900	–4 068	–4 077	–4 282	–4 497
B.10.1n	Changes in net worth due to net saving and capital transfers	FDED	–154	–78	–410	–503	–990	–2 711	–2 430	17 227	5 901
III.1.2	**ACQUISITION OF NON-FINANCIAL ASSETS ACCOUNT**										
	Changes in liabilities and net worth										
B.10.1n	Changes in net worth due to net saving and capital transfers	FDED	–154	–78	–410	–503	–990	–2 711	–2 430	17 227	5 901
K.1	Consumption of fixed capital	NSRM	3 341	3 394	3 470	3 604	3 900	4 068	4 077	4 282	4 497
B.10.1g	Total change in liabilities and net worth	FDEG	3 187	3 316	3 060	3 101	2 910	1 357	1 647	21 509	10 398
	Changes in assets										
P.5	Gross capital formation										
P.51	Gross fixed capital formation	FCCJ	3 299	2 712	2 354	3 183	3 830	1 857	1 260	20 576	5 564
P.52	Changes in inventories	DHHL	215	–120	–223	9	–30	11	20	–62	–47
P.5	Total	FDEH	3 514	2 592	2 131	3 192	3 800	1 868	1 280	20 514	5 517
K.2	Acquisitions less disposals of non-produced non-financial assets	FDEJ	–257	–2	13	70	176	282	346	428	512
B.9g	**Net lending (+) / net borrowing (-)**	CPCM	**–70**	**726**	**916**	**–161**	**–1 066**	**–793**	**21**	**567**	**4 369**
Total	Total change in assets	FDEG	3 187	3 316	3 060	3 101	2 910	1 357	1 647	21 509	10 398

1 Public financial corporations are also included to avoid disclosure of commercial information

3.2.8 Public non-financial corporations

ESA95 sector S.11001 Unconsolidated

£ million

			1998	1999	2000	2001	2002	2003	2004	2005	2006
III.2	**FINANCIAL ACCOUNT**										
F.A	**Net acquisition of financial assets**										
F.2	Currency and deposits										
F.21	Currency	NCXV	53	125	116	90	–143	141	–295	–16	23
F.22	Transferable deposits										
F.2211	Sterling deposits with UK banks	NCXY	1 133	1	584	754	–53	–403	–344	–243	961
F.2212	Foreign currency deposits with UK banks	NCXZ	–32	–	65	–2	–41	30	–4	33	1 200
F.2213	Sterling deposits with building societies	NCYA	–127	–10	–92	102	–73	–28	–2	34	–65
F.229	Deposits with rest of the world monetary financial institutions	NCYB	–	–	–	–	–30	3	–3	–	–
F.29	Other deposits	NCYC	–2 546	–466	–128	–842	477	–626	593	533	343
F.2	Total currency and deposits	NCXU	–1 519	–350	545	102	137	–883	–55	341	2 462
F.3	Securities other than shares										
F.331	Short term: money market instruments										
F.3311	Issued by UK central government	NCYF	–	140	–50	–90	–	–	–	–	–
F.3315	Issued by UK monetary financial institutions	NCYK	359	–	–	–	–	–	–	–	–
F.3316	Issued by other UK residents	NCYP	288	–191	–	–	223	104	–66	305	404
F.332	Medium (1 to 5 year) and long term (over 5 year) bonds										
F.3321	Issued by UK central government	NCYS	971	362	–183	–411	–67	–196	–50	–789	–1 972
F.3326	Other medium & long term bonds issued by UK residents	NCYZ	–	–	–	–	–	–	–	–	–
F.3329	Long term bonds issued by the rest of the world	NCZA	–	–	–	–	–	–	–	–	–
F.34	Financial derivatives	NSUH	31	3	–92	–8	10	9	8	1	–1
F.3	Total securities other than shares	NCYD	1 649	314	–325	–509	166	–83	–108	–483	–1 569
F.4	Loans										
F.42	Long term loans										
F.421	Direct investment loans	CFZI	–	–	–	115	120	–10	120	–	–
F.422	Loans secured on dwellings	NCZQ	–2	–1	–1	–	–	–	–	–	–
F.424	Other long-term loans by UK residents	NCZV	99	90	–171	–90	–489	–380	–421	–1 776	–2 740
F.4	Total loans	NCZF	97	89	–172	25	–369	–390	–301	–1 776	–2 740
F.5	Shares and other equity										
F.51	Shares and other equity, excluding mutual funds' shares										
F.514	Quoted UK shares	NEBC	71	30	16	13	23	24	24	–243	–
F.515	Unquoted UK shares	NEBD	–45	–	–	269	510	–2	–2	–	–1 248
F.517	UK shares and bonds issued by other UK residents	NSPN	–	–	–	–	–	–	–	–	–
F.519	Shares and other equity issued by the rest of the world	NEBH	75	290	570	97	158	–151	61	–7	–1 621
F.5	Total shares and other equity	NCZX	101	320	586	379	691	–129	83	–250	–2 869
F.6	Insurance technical reserves										
F.62	Prepayments of insurance premiums and reserves for outstanding claims	NEBQ	–	–	–	–	–	–	–	–	–
F.7	Other accounts receivable	NEBR	458	–481	–302	190	328	1 149	1 126	1 688	3 011
F.A	**Total net acquisition of financial assets**	NCXQ	786	–108	332	187	953	–336	745	–480	–1 705

3.2.8 Public non-financial corporations

ESA95 sector S.11001 Unconsolidated

continued | £ million

			1998	1999	2000	2001	2002	2003	2004	2005	2006
III.2	**FINANCIAL ACCOUNT** continued										
F.L	**Net acquisition of financial liabilities**										
F.2	Currency & deposits										
F.29	Other deposits	WUGZ	30	28	29	30	18	–	–	–	–
	Total currency & deposits	-A4FK	30	28	29	30	18	–	–	–	–
F.3	Securities other than shares										
F.332	Medium (1 to 5 year) and long term (over 5 year) bonds										
F.3326	Other medium & long term bonds issued by UK residents or monetary financial institutions	NEOF	–	–	160	–32	–1 541	–	–	856	–620
F.345	Financial derivatitives issued by UK residents	CY7U	–36	–42	–110	–184	–204	–138	–28	–	–
F.3	Total securities other than shares	NENJ	–36	–42	50	–216	–1 745	–138	–28	856	–620
F.4	Loans										
F.41	Short term loans										
F.411	Loans by UK monetary financial institutions, excluding loans secured on dwellings & financial leasing	NEON	123	–39	71	–145	305	–105	21	–300	118
F.42	Long term loans										
F.423	Finance leasing	NEPA	–20	41	228	–111	–57	206	472	536	685
F.424	Other long-term loans by UK residents	NEPB	–321	–687	–863	–290	3 019	406	283	–461	–355
F.429	Other long-term loans by the rest of the world	NEPC	–5	–	–	–	–	–	–	–	–
F.4	Total loans	NEOL	–223	–685	–564	–546	3 267	507	776	–225	448
F.5	Shares and other equity										
F.51	Shares and other equity, excluding mutual funds' shares										
F.515	Unquoted UK shares	NEPJ	–	–	–	–	–	–	–	–3 144	–2 431
F.516	Other UK equity (including direct investment in property)	NEPK	–	–	–	42	–	114	–	–1 249	–1 204
F.517	UK shares and bonds issued by other UK residents	NSPO	–	–	–	–	–	–	–	–	–
F.5	Total shares and other equity	NEPD	–	–	–	42	–	114	–	–4 393	–3 635
F.7	Other accounts payable	NEPX	328	–36	367	339	159	–136	–132	2 417	–1 546
F.L	**Total net acquisition of financial liabilities**	NEBU	99	–735	–118	–351	1 699	347	616	–1 345	–5 353
B.9	**Net lending / borrowing**										
F.A	Total net acquisition of financial assets	NCXQ	786	–108	332	187	953	–336	745	–480	–1 705
-F.L	*less* Total net acquisition of financial liabilities	-NEBU	–99	735	118	351	–1 699	–347	–616	1 345	5 353
B.9f	Net lending (+) / net borrowing (-), from financial account	NZEC	687	627	450	538	–746	–683	129	865	3 648
dB.9f	Statistical discrepancy	NYPI	–757	99	466	–699	–320	–110	–108	–298	721
B.9g	**Net lending (+) / net borrowing (-), from capital account**	CPCM	**–70**	**726**	**916**	**–161**	**–1 066**	**–793**	**21**	**567**	**4 369**

3.2.9 Public non-financial corporations

ESA95 sector S.11001 Unconsolidated

£ billion

			1998	1999	2000	2001	2002	2003	2004	2005	2006
IV.3	**FINANCIAL BALANCE SHEET** at end of period										
AN	**Non-financial assets**	CGGN	126.5	124.3	123.4	134.8	155.6	157.6	170.3	181.8	173.6
AF.A	**Financial assets**										
AF.2	Currency and deposits										
AF.21	Currency	NKDS	0.7	0.9	1.0	0.9	0.8	0.9	0.6	0.6	0.6
AF.22	Transferable deposits										
AF.221	Deposits with UK monetary financial institutions	NKDU	3.4	3.5	4.4	6.1	5.7	4.6	4.0	4.1	5.8
AF.229	Deposits with rest of the world monetary financial institutions	NKDY	–	–	–	–	–	–	–	–	–
AF.29	Other deposits	NKDZ	3.3	3.1	3.5	2.7	3.1	1.0	1.6	3.5	3.9
AF.2	Total currency and deposits	NKDR	7.4	7.5	8.9	9.7	9.6	6.5	6.3	8.2	10.3
AF.3	Securities other than shares										
AF.331	Short term: money market instruments										
AF.3311	Issued by UK central government	NKEC	–	0.1	0.1	–	–	–	–	–	–
AF.3315	Issued by UK monetary financial institutions	NKEH	0.4	0.4	0.4	0.4	0.4	0.4	0.4	0.4	0.4
AF.3316	Issued by other UK residents	NKEM	0.3	0.1	0.1	0.1	0.2	0.3	0.3	1.1	1.5
AF.332	Medium (1 to 5 year) and long term (over 5 year) bonds										
AF.3321	Issued by UK central government	NKEP	3.4	3.7	3.5	3.1	3.1	2.9	2.8	2.5	0.5
AF.3322	Issued by UK local government	NKES	–	–	–	–	–	–	–	–	–
AF.3326	Other medium & long term bonds issued by UK residents	NKEW	–	–	–	–	–	–	–	–	–
AF.3	Total securities other than shares	NKEA	4.0	4.4	4.1	3.6	3.7	3.6	3.5	4.0	2.4
AF.4	Loans										
AF.42	Long term loans										
AF.421	Direct investment loans	ZYBN	–	–	–	0.1	0.5	0.4	0.4	0.3	0.3
AF.422	Loans secured on dwellings	NKFN	–	–	–	–	–	–	–	–	–
AF.424	Other long-term loans by UK residents	NKFS	4.8	4.9	4.1	4.2	3.9	4.0	4.1	3.7	3.3
AF.4	Total loans	NKFC	4.8	4.9	4.1	4.3	4.4	4.5	4.5	4.0	3.6
AF.5	Shares and other equity										
AF.51	Shares and other equity, excluding mutual funds' shares										
AF.514	Quoted UK shares	NKFZ	0.1	0.2	0.2	0.2	0.2	0.2	0.2	–	–
AF.515	Unquoted UK shares	NKGA	0.3	0.3	0.3	0.3	0.3	0.3	0.3	0.3	0.3
AF.517	UK shares and bonds issued by other UK residents	NSOL	–	–	–	–	–	–	–	–	–
AF.519	Shares and other equity issued by the rest of the world	NKGE	0.9	1.2	1.8	0.8	1.0	1.1	1.3	1.6	1.0
AF.5	Total shares and other equity	NKFU	1.4	1.7	2.3	1.3	1.5	1.6	1.8	1.9	1.3
AF.6	Insurance technical reserves										
AF.62	Prepayments of insurance premiums and reserves for outstanding claims	NKGN	–	–	–	–	–	–	–	–	–
AF.7	Other accounts receivable	NKGO	5.3	4.9	5.4	5.6	6.4	7.5	8.7	10.5	13.0
AF.A	**Total financial assets**	NKFB	23.0	23.4	24.7	24.5	25.6	23.8	24.7	28.5	30.6

3.2.9 Public non-financial corporations

ESA95 sector S.11001 Unconsolidated

continued £ billion

			1998	1999	2000	2001	2002	2003	2004	2005	2006
IV.3	**FINANCIAL BALANCE SHEET** continued at end of period										
AF.L	**Financial liabilities**										
AF.2	Currency & deposits										
AF.29	Other deposits	NKHD	0.3	0.4	0.4	0.4	–	–	–	–	–
	Total currency & deposits	NKGV	0.3	0.4	0.4	0.4	–	–	–	–	–
AF.3	Securities other than shares										
AF.332	Medium (1 to 5 year) and long term (over 5 year) bonds										
AF.3326	Other medium & long term bonds issued by UK residents or monetary financial institutions	NKIA	1.0	1.1	0.4	0.4	0.9	1.3	1.0	5.9	5.3
AF.3	Total securities other than shares	NKHE	1.0	1.1	0.4	0.4	0.9	1.3	1.0	5.9	5.3
AF.4	Loans										
AF.41	Short term loans										
AF.411	Loans by UK monetary financial institutions, excluding loans secured on dwellings & financial leasing	NKII	0.4	0.3	0.4	0.2	0.6	0.5	0.5	1.4	0.6
AF.419	Loans by rest of the world monetary financial institutions	NKIM	–	–	–	–	–	–	–	–	–
AF.42	Long term loans										
AF.423	Finance leasing	NKIV	0.1	0.4	0.6	0.5	0.4	0.6	1.1	1.6	2.3
AF.424	Other long-term loans by UK residents	NKIW	5.4	4.4	3.2	2.4	11.3	3.3	2.5	3.2	2.8
AF.429	Other long-term loans by the rest of the world	NKIX	–	–	–	–	–	–	–	–	–
AF.4	Total loans	NKIG	5.9	5.2	4.2	3.1	12.3	4.3	4.0	6.2	5.7
AF.5	Shares and other equity										
AF.51	Shares and other equity, excluding mutual funds' shares										
AF.514	Quoted UK shares	C3O8	–	–	–	–	–	–	–	3.0	3.2
AF.515	Unquoted UK shares	NKJE	0.4	0.5	0.5	0.8	0.8	0.8	1.7	0.8	0.7
AF.517	UK shares and bonds issued by other UK residents	NSOM	–	–	–	–	–	–	–	–	–
AF.5	Total shares and other equity	NKIY	0.4	0.5	0.5	0.8	0.8	0.8	1.7	3.8	3.9
AF.7	Other accounts payable	NKJS	10.4	10.8	13.4	13.1	13.6	13.8	13.6	15.9	14.1
AF.L	**Total financial liabilities**	NKIF	18.1	18.0	19.0	17.7	27.7	20.2	20.3	31.8	29.0
BF.90	**Net financial assets / liabilities**										
AF.A	Total financial assets	NKFB	23.0	23.4	24.7	24.5	25.6	23.8	24.7	28.5	30.6
-AF.L	*less* Total financial liabilities	-NKIF	–18.1	–18.0	–19.0	–17.7	–27.7	–20.2	–20.3	–31.8	–29.0
BF.90	**Net financial assets (+) / liabilities (-)**	NYOP	4.9	5.4	5.8	6.8	–2.1	3.6	4.5	–3.3	1.6
	Net worth										
AN	Non-financial assets	CGGN	126.5	124.3	123.4	134.8	155.6	157.6	170.3	181.8	173.6
BF.90	Net financial assets (+) / liabilities (-)	NYOP	4.9	5.4	5.8	6.8	–2.1	3.6	4.5	–3.3	1.6
B.90	**Net worth**	CGRW	131.4	129.7	129.2	141.5	153.5	161.2	174.7	178.5	175.2

3.3.1 Private non-financial corporations

ESA95 sectors S.11002 National controlled and S.11003 Foreign controlled

£ million

			1998	1999	2000	2001	2002	2003	2004
I	**PRODUCTION ACCOUNT**								
	Resources								
P.1	Output								
P.11	Market output	FBXS	1 037 063	1 084 953	1 146 220	1 182 249	1 209 542	1 256 935	1 323 065
P.12	Output for own final use	FDCG	7 987	8 525	9 265	10 129	10 503	11 924	11 829
P.1	Total resources	FBXR	1 045 050	1 093 478	1 155 485	1 192 378	1 220 045	1 268 859	1 334 894
	Uses								
P.2	Intermediate consumption	FARP	551 060	573 796	605 224	621 339	632 724	654 070	685 775
B.1g	**Gross Value Added**	FARR	**493 990**	**519 682**	**550 261**	**571 039**	**587 321**	**614 789**	**649 119**
Total	Total uses	FBXR	1 045 050	1 093 478	1 155 485	1 192 378	1 220 045	1 268 859	1 334 894
B.1g	**Gross Value Added**	FARR	**493 990**	**519 682**	**550 261**	**571 039**	**587 321**	**614 789**	**649 119**
-K.1	*less* Consumption of fixed capital	-NSRK	–54 284	–56 869	–58 995	–60 424	–61 875	–63 370	–65 902
B.1n	Value added, net	FARS	439 706	462 813	491 266	510 615	525 446	551 419	583 217

3.3.2 Private non-financial corporations

ESA95 sectors S.11002 National controlled and S.11003 Foreign controlled

£ million

			1998	1999	2000	2001	2002	2003	2004
II	**DISTRIBUTION AND USE OF INCOME ACCOUNTS**								
II.1	**PRIMARY DISTRIBUTION OF INCOME ACCOUNT**								
II.1.1	**GENERATION OF INCOME ACCOUNT** before deduction of fixed capital consumption								
	Resources								
B.1g	**Total resources (Gross Value Added)**	FARR	**493 990**	**519 682**	**550 261**	**571 039**	**587 321**	**614 789**	**649 119**
	Uses								
D.1	Compensation of employees								
D.11	Wages and salaries	FAAX	267 016	284 246	304 014	320 963	329 641	336 525	347 179
D.12	Employers' social contributions	FABH	34 014	37 478	40 921	43 169	46 136	53 518	59 726
D.1	Total	FBDA	301 030	321 724	344 935	364 132	375 777	390 043	406 905
D.2	Taxes on production and imports, paid								
D.29	Production taxes other than on products	FACQ	14 156	14 783	15 705	16 075	16 584	16 942	17 330
-D.39	Production subsidies other than on products	-JQJW	–	–108	–124	–230	–588	–1 141	–1 319
B.2g	Operating surplus, gross	NRJK	178 804	183 283	189 745	191 062	195 548	208 945	226 203
B.1g	**Total uses (Gross Value Added)**	FARR	**493 990**	**519 682**	**550 261**	**571 039**	**587 321**	**614 789**	**649 119**
-K.1	After deduction of fixed capital consumption	-NSRK	–54 284	–56 869	–58 995	–60 424	–61 875	–63 370	–65 902
B.2n	Operating surplus, net	FACU	124 520	126 414	130 750	130 638	133 673	145 575	160 301

3.3.3 Private non-financial corporations

ESA95 sectors S.11002 National controlled and S.11003 Foreign controlled

£ million

			1998	1999	2000	2001	2002	2003	2004	2005	2006
II.1.2	**ALLOCATION OF PRIMARY INCOME ACCOUNT** before deduction of fixed capital consumption										
	Resources										
B.2g	Operating surplus, gross[1]	NRJK	178 804	183 283	189 745	191 062	195 548	208 945	226 203	234 129	246 648
D.4	Property income, received										
D.41	Interest	DSZR	12 927	9 946	13 525	11 927	8 528	8 264	10 258	13 259	17 661
D.42	Distributed income of corporations	DSZS	25 056	21 430	26 475	37 421	30 486	50 166	43 919	47 913	47 395
D.43	Reinvested earnings on direct foreign investment	HDVR	10 979	16 214	20 118	22 950	26 893	12 492	24 181	31 877	41 432
D.44	Property income attributed to insurance policy-holders	FCFP	463	338	290	335	304	400	405	582	604
D.45	Rent	FAOL	118	117	117	117	118	120	122	122	120
D.4	Total	FACV	49 543	48 045	60 525	72 750	66 329	71 442	78 885	93 753	107 212
Total	Total resources	FCFQ	228 347	231 328	250 270	263 812	261 877	280 387	305 088	327 882	353 860
	Uses										
D.4	Property income, paid										
D.41	Interest	DSZV	31 096	31 016	38 073	39 454	36 418	35 663	41 352	48 700	61 258
D.42	Distributed income of corporations	NVDC	74 244	82 780	80 738	100 984	85 573	92 289	93 152	106 712	99 940
	Of which: Dividend payments	NETZ	51 578	61 088	55 846	77 516	61 580	71 096	72 509	82 887	78 183
D.43	Reinvested earnings on direct foreign investment	HDVB	3 117	2 776	7 348	1 699	1 614	3 955	6 729	5 044	16 668
D.45	Rent	FCFU	584	565	1 325	1 955	1 939	1 603	1 461	1 391	1 250
D.4	Total	FCFR	109 041	117 137	127 484	144 092	125 544	133 510	142 694	161 847	179 116
B.5g	**Balance of primary incomes, gross**	NRJM	**119 306**	**114 191**	**122 786**	**119 720**	**136 333**	**146 877**	**162 394**	**166 035**	**174 744**
Total	Total uses	FCFQ	228 347	231 328	250 270	263 812	261 877	280 387	305 088	327 882	353 860
-K.1	After deduction of fixed capital consumption	-NSRK	–54 284	–56 869	–58 995	–60 424	–61 875	–63 370	–65 902	–67 053	–68 240
B.5n	Balance of primary incomes, net	FCFW	65 022	57 322	63 791	59 296	74 458	83 507	96 492	98 982	106 504

1 Companies gross trading profits and rental of buildings less holding gains of inventories, details of which are shown at Table C: The Sector Accounts Key Economic Indicators.

3.3.4 Private non-financial corporations

ESA95 sectors S.11002 National controlled and S.11003 Foreign controlled

£ million

			1998	1999	2000	2001	2002	2003	2004	2005	2006
II.2	**SECONDARY DISTRIBUTION OF INCOME ACCOUNT**										
	Resources										
B.5g	**Balance of primary incomes, gross**	NRJM	**119 306**	**114 191**	**122 786**	**119 720**	**136 333**	**146 877**	**162 394**	**166 035**	**174 744**
D.61	Social contributions										
D.612	Imputed social contributions	EWRT	3 330	3 724	4 067	4 229	4 437	4 098	3 736	3 480	3 358
D.7	Current transfers other than taxes, social contributions and benefits										
D.72	Net non-life insurance claims	FDBA	4 849	4 151	5 923	5 000	5 452	6 471	6 591	7 248	7 793
Total	Total resources	FDBC	127 485	122 066	132 776	128 949	146 222	157 446	172 721	176 763	185 895
	Uses										
D.5	Current taxes on income, wealth etc.										
D.51	Taxes on income	FCCP	26 877	22 608	24 279	23 087	23 977	23 608	27 287	33 485	36 868
D.62	Social benefits other than social transfers in kind	EWRT	3 330	3 724	4 067	4 229	4 437	4 098	3 736	3 480	3 358
D.7	Current transfers other than taxes, social contributions and benefits										
D.71	Net non-life insurance premiums	FDBH	4 849	4 151	5 923	5 000	5 452	6 471	6 591	7 248	7 793
D.75	Miscellaneous current transfers	CY88	444	569	413	411	422	434	446	488	477
D.7	Total	FCCN	5 293	4 720	6 336	5 411	5 874	6 905	7 037	7 736	8 270
B.6g	**Gross Disposable Income**	NRJQ	**91 985**	**91 014**	**98 094**	**96 222**	**111 934**	**122 835**	**134 661**	**132 062**	**137 399**
Total	Total uses	FDBC	127 485	122 066	132 776	128 949	146 222	157 446	172 721	176 763	185 895
-K.1	After deduction of fixed capital consumption	-NSRK	–54 284	–56 869	–58 995	–60 424	–61 875	–63 370	–65 902	–67 053	–68 240
B.6n	Disposable income, net	FDBK	37 701	34 145	39 099	35 798	50 059	59 465	68 759	65 009	69 159

3.3.6 Private non-financial corporations

ESA95 sectors S.11002 National controlled and S.11003 Foreign controlled

£ million

			1998	1999	2000	2001	2002	2003	2004	2005	2006
II.4.1	**USE OF DISPOSABLE INCOME ACCOUNT**										
	Resources										
B.6g	**Total resources (Gross Disposable Income)**	NRJQ	**91 985**	**91 014**	**98 094**	**96 222**	**111 934**	**122 835**	**134 661**	**132 062**	**137 399**
	Uses										
B.8g	**Total uses (Gross Saving)**	NRJQ	**91 985**	**91 014**	**98 094**	**96 222**	**111 934**	**122 835**	**134 661**	**132 062**	**137 399**
-K.1	After deduction of fixed capital consumption	-NSRK	–54 284	–56 869	–58 995	–60 424	–61 875	–63 370	–65 902	–67 053	–68 240
B.8n	Saving, net	FDBK	37 701	34 145	39 099	35 798	50 059	59 465	68 759	65 009	69 159

3.3.7 Private non-financial corporations

ESA95 sectors S.11002 National controlled and S.11003 Foreign controlled

£ million

			1998	1999	2000	2001	2002	2003	2004	2005	2006
III	**ACCUMULATION ACCOUNTS**										
III.1	**CAPITAL ACCOUNT**										
III.1.1	**CHANGE IN NET WORTH DUE TO SAVING AND CAPITAL TRANSFERS**										
	Changes in liabilities and net worth										
B.8g	**Gross Saving**	NRJQ	**91 985**	**91 014**	**98 094**	**96 222**	**111 934**	**122 835**	**134 661**	**132 062**	**137 399**
D.9	Capital transfers receivable										
D.92	Investment grants	AIBR	1 090	1 409	1 506	3 048	3 131	5 059	4 914	5 427	6 034
D.99	Other capital transfers	LNZM	184	109	118	873	93	106	120	121	118
-D.9	*less* Capital transfers payable										
-D.91	Capital taxes	-QYKB	–	–	–	–	–	–	–	–	–
-D.99	Other capital transfers	-CISB	–193	–216	–290	–285	–492	–575	–419	–456	–523
-D.9	Total	-FCFX	–193	–216	–290	–285	–492	–575	–419	–456	–523
B.10.1g	Total change in liabilities and net worth	NRMG	93 066	92 316	99 428	99 858	114 666	127 425	139 276	137 154	143 028
	Changes in assets										
B.10.1g	Changes in net worth due to gross saving and capital transfers	NRMG	93 066	92 316	99 428	99 858	114 666	127 425	139 276	137 154	143 028
-K.1	After deduction of fixed capital consumption	-NSRK	–54 284	–56 869	–58 995	–60 424	–61 875	–63 370	–65 902	–67 053	–68 240
B.10.1n	Changes in net worth due to net saving and capital transfers	FDCH	38 782	35 447	40 433	39 434	52 791	64 055	73 374	70 101	74 788
III.1.2	**ACQUISITION OF NON-FINANCIAL ASSETS ACCOUNT**										
	Changes in liabilities and net worth										
B.10.1n	Changes in net worth due to net saving and capital transfers	FDCH	38 782	35 447	40 433	39 434	52 791	64 055	73 374	70 101	74 788
K.1	Consumption of fixed capital	NSRK	54 284	56 869	58 995	60 424	61 875	63 370	65 902	67 053	68 240
B.10.1g	Total change in liabilities and net worth	NRMG	93 066	92 316	99 428	99 858	114 666	127 425	139 276	137 154	143 028
	Changes in assets										
P.5	Gross capital formation										
P.51	Gross fixed capital formation	FDBM	94 106	98 989	101 597	103 127	103 182	103 855	107 249	110 949	120 660
P.52	Changes in inventories	DLQX	4 533	6 174	5 512	5 941	2 677	3 734	4 566	4 354	3 850
P.53	Acquisitions less disposals of valuables	NPOV	28	–17	–75	–	–43	–97	–99	–171	–90
P.5	Total	FDCL	98 667	105 146	107 034	109 068	105 816	107 492	111 716	115 132	124 420
K.2	Acquisitions less disposals of non-produced non-financial assets	FDCN	1 259	1 053	851	1 138	1 255	959	1 326	1 356	989
B.9	**Net lending (+) / net borrowing (-)**	DTAL	**–6 860**	**–13 883**	**–8 457**	**–10 348**	**7 595**	**18 974**	**26 234**	**20 666**	**17 619**
Total	Total change in assets	NRMG	93 066	92 316	99 428	99 858	114 666	127 425	139 276	137 154	143 028

3.3.8 Private non-financial corporations

ESA95 sectors S.11002 National controlled and S.11003 Foreign controlled. Unconsolidated

£ million

			1998	1999	2000	2001	2002	2003	2004	2005	2006
III.2	**FINANCIAL ACCOUNT**										
F.A	**Net acquisition of financial assets**										
F.2	Currency and deposits										
F.21	Currency	NEQF	131	253	192	187	153	197	249	198	215
F.22	Transferable deposits										
F.2211	Sterling deposits with UK banks	NEQI	4 188	7 369	11 119	8 315	9 774	11 463	11 870	20 377	23 138
F.2212	Foreign currency deposits with UK banks	NEQJ	–621	2 455	3 072	1 334	–232	3 838	2 562	2 610	1 452
F.2213	Sterling deposits with building societies	NEQK	1	166	–42	199	–4	273	–311	–98	364
F.229	Deposits with rest of the world monetary financial institutions	NEQL	726	18 345	31 742	24 131	30 561	34 092	54 598	37 995	35 705
F.29	Other deposits	NEQM	10	–229	–123	276	632	228	–138	128	372
F.2	Total currency and deposits	NEQE	4 435	28 359	45 960	34 442	40 884	50 091	68 830	61 210	61 246
F.3	Securities other than shares										
F.331	Short term: money market instruments										
F.3311	Issued by UK central government	NEQP	8	4	–28	–10	–	2	–4	74	–26
F.3315	Issued by UK monetary financial institutions	NEQU	2 183	–2 003	–81	234	230	601	86	–723	2 394
F.3316	Issued by other UK residents	NEQZ	–1 774	16	–2 797	136	–2 331	717	257	–1 909	1 833
F.3319	Issued by the rest of the world	NERA	–956	722	1 110	1 912	1 110	3 798	615	1 661	5 359
F.332	Medium (1 to 5 year) and long term (over 5 year) bonds										
F.3321	Issued by UK central government	NERC	392	–815	413	–168	215	–139	–42	–91	–24
F.3325	Medium term bonds issued by UK MFIs[1]	NERG	46	54	–237	–333	42	167	–23	395	466
F.3326	Other medium & long term bonds issued by UK residents	NERJ	625	–1 347	1 141	1 784	559	–685	–403	–3 341	257
F.3329	Long term bonds issued by the rest of the world	NERK	585	–934	1 792	1 759	–601	2 213	438	2 547	–1 201
F.3	Total securities other than shares	NEQN	1 109	–4 303	1 313	5 314	–776	6 674	924	–1 387	9 058
F.4	Loans										
F.42	Long term loans										
F.4211	Outward direct investment	NERY	21 721	15 371	11 607	9 656	16 366	10 155	14 652	17 345	–9 253
F.4212	Inward direct investment	NERZ	11 275	12 773	1 423	–836	5 405	–467	–5 513	4 107	3 232
F.423	Finance leasing	F8Y9	243	603	665	116	221	720	947	1 043	991
F.424	Other long-term loans by UK residents	NESF	–2 221	–208	13 788	4 746	462	–4 483	983	15 399	40 628
F.4	Total loans	NERP	31 018	28 539	27 483	13 682	22 454	5 925	11 069	37 894	35 598
F.5	Shares and other equity										
F.51	Shares and other equity, excluding mutual funds' shares										
F.514	Quoted UK shares	NESM	23 915	24 156	87 575	10 028	17 496	7 332	14 858	13 774	19 896
F.515	Unquoted UK shares	NESN	6 038	–9 292	–27 228	–740	2 835	6 102	3 030	15 947	11 121
F.517	UK shares and bonds issued by other UK residents	NSPP	–	–	–	–	–	–	–	–	–
F.519	Shares and other equity issued by the rest of the world	NESR	48 422	111 803	166 110	35 905	49 311	19 545	26 359	40 116	44 445
F.52	Mutual funds' shares										
F.521	UK mutual funds' shares	NESV	1	1	14	2	3	1	9	17	17
F.5	Total shares and other equity	NESH	78 376	126 668	226 471	45 195	69 645	32 980	44 256	69 854	75 479
F.6	Insurance technical reserves										
F.62	Prepayments of insurance premiums and reserves for outstanding claims	NETA	–109	–291	344	–370	363	170	933	965	766
F.7	Other accounts receivable	NETB	1 080	–1 743	25 329	–1 863	2 553	1 019	–2 972	–498	2 348
F.A	**Total net acquisition of financial assets**	NEQA	115 909	177 229	326 900	96 400	135 123	96 859	123 040	168 038	184 495

1 UK monetary financial institutions

3.3.8 Private non-financial corporations

ESA95 sectors S.11002 National controlled and S.11003 Foreign controlled. Unconsolidated

continued £ million

			1998	1999	2000	2001	2002	2003	2004	2005	2006
III.2	**FINANCIAL ACCOUNT** continued										
F.L	**Net acquisition of financial liabilities**										
F.3	Securities other than shares										
F.331	Short term: money market instruments										
F.3316	Issued by UK residents other than government or monetary financial institutions	NEUD	3 435	2 716	1 331	–426	8 543	–1 541	–2 999	–254	436
F.332	Medium (1 to 5 year) and long term (over 5 year) bonds										
F.3326	Other medium & long term bonds issued by UK residents or monetary financial institutions	NEUN	17 100	39 378	40 435	15 510	16 871	19 426	8 550	11 564	11 883
F.3	Total securities other than shares	NETR	20 535	42 094	41 766	15 084	25 414	17 885	5 551	11 310	12 319
F.4	Loans										
F.41	Short term loans										
F.411	Loans by UK monetary financial institutions,										
	Sterling loans by UK banks	NEUW	8 968	9 067	21 912	15 786	22 369	11 773	19 445	36 225	48 265
	Foreign currency loans by UK banks	NEUX	8 734	6 145	1 996	903	–3 860	–5 516	639	9 232	4 231
	Sterling loans by building societies	NEUY	1 134	1 620	1 602	1 835	2 017	1 151	–128	925	2 989
F.419	Loans by rest of the world monetary financial institutions	NEUZ	–58	9 383	3 136	30 752	14 693	34 807	41 488	9 157	77 207
F.42	Long term loans										
F.4211	Outward direct investment	NEVC	10 483	9 978	30 178	13 746	38 989	12 030	8 439	27 320	–12 550
F.4212	Inward direct investment	NEVD	25 619	17 051	10 614	4 173	4 813	–1 868	5 633	25 978	–3 751
F.422	Loans secured on dwellings	G9JQ	..	..	..	..	..	..	..	4 170	3 812
F.423	Finance leasing	NEVI	106	57	–164	59	347	430	516	408	475
F.424	Other long-term loans by UK residents	NEVJ	1 260	2 727	–446	4 550	–2 529	4 205	418	6 481	5 789
F.429	Other long-term loans by the rest of the world	NEVK	–	–	–	–	–	–	–	–	–
F.4	Total loans	NEUT	56 246	56 028	68 828	71 804	76 839	57 012	76 450	119 896	126 467
F.5	Shares and other equity										
F.51	Shares and other equity, excluding mutual funds' shares										
F.514	Quoted UK shares	NEVQ	45 680	85 600	209 418	9 234	16 508	–748	7 286	–4 608	–3 456
F.515	Unquoted UK shares	NEVR	6 014	5 805	12 818	4 795	4 622	8 023	8 292	18 825	18 239
F.516	Other UK equity (including direct investment in property)	NEVS	632	833	1 605	779	748	395	623	597	467
F.517	UK shares and bonds issued by other UK residents	NSPQ	–	–	–	–	–	–	–	–	–
F.5	Total shares and other equity	NEVL	52 326	92 238	223 841	14 808	21 878	7 670	16 201	14 814	15 250
F.7	Other accounts payable	NEWF	1 729	8 308	406	3 137	2 163	2 916	2 565	3 402	5 059
F.L	**Total net acquisition of financial liabilities**	NETE	130 836	198 668	334 841	104 833	126 294	85 483	100 767	149 422	159 095
B.9	**Net lending / borrowing**										
F.A	Total net acquisition of financial assets	NEQA	115 909	177 229	326 900	96 400	135 123	96 859	123 040	168 038	184 495
-F.L	*less* Total net acquisition of financial liabilities	-NETE	–130 836	–198 668	–334 841	–104 833	–126 294	–85 483	–100 767	–149 422	–159 095
B.9f	Net lending (+) / net borrowing (-), from financial account	NYOA	–14 927	–21 439	–7 941	–8 433	8 829	11 376	22 273	18 616	25 400
dB.9f	Statistical discrepancy	NYPM	8 067	7 556	–516	–1 915	–1 234	7 598	3 961	2 050	–7 781
B.9	**Net lending (+) / net borrowing (-), from capital account**	DTAL	**–6 860**	**–13 883**	**–8 457**	**–10 348**	**7 595**	**18 974**	**26 234**	**20 666**	**17 619**

3.3.9 Private non-financial corporations

ESA95 sectors S.11002 National controlled and S.11003 Foreign controlled. Unconsolidated

£ billion

			1998	1999	2000	2001	2002	2003	2004	2005	2006
IV.3	**FINANCIAL BALANCE SHEET** at end of period										
AN	**Non-financial assets**	TMPL	1 003.5	1 049.4	1 154.7	1 128.3	1 155.6	1 179.8	1 217.2	1 306.1	1 333.1
AF.A	**Financial assets**										
AF.2	Currency and deposits										
AF.21	Currency	NKKA	2.2	2.4	2.7	2.8	3.0	3.2	3.4	3.6	3.8
AF.22	Transferable deposits										
AF.2211	Sterling deposits with UK banks	NKKD	109.6	117.6	129.6	136.8	146.4	158.8	171.4	192.6	215.3
AF.2212	Foreign currency deposits with UK banks	NKKE	17.4	19.5	24.1	24.6	23.5	25.4	27.8	31.9	30.7
AF.2213	Sterling deposits with building societies	NKKF	2.4	2.5	2.2	4.4	2.4	2.7	2.4	2.3	2.7
AF.229	Deposits with rest of the world monetary financial institutions	NKKG	64.9	78.1	101.2	113.2	143.3	184.2	230.2	281.5	295.4
AF.29	Other deposits	NKKH	5.1	4.8	4.6	4.9	4.9	5.1	5.1	5.2	5.6
AF.2	Total currency and deposits	NKJZ	201.7	225.0	264.4	286.7	323.6	379.5	440.2	517.1	553.4
AF.3	Securities other than shares										
AF.331	Short term: money market instruments										
AF.3311	Issued by UK central government	NKKK	–	–	–	–	–	–	–	0.1	–
AF.3315	Issued by UK monetary financial institutions	NKKP	6.8	4.8	5.4	5.6	4.6	5.0	5.4	4.8	6.9
AF.3316	Issued by other UK residents	NKKU	6.0	13.5	16.3	18.5	13.7	13.5	13.3	17.2	34.2
AF.3319	Issued by the rest of the world	NKKV	1.2	1.9	3.0	4.9	6.0	9.8	10.4	12.0	17.4
AF.332	Medium (1 to 5 year) and long term (over 5 year) bonds										
AF.3321	Issued by UK central government	NKKX	0.9	0.1	0.5	0.3	0.5	0.3	0.3	0.2	0.2
AF.3322	Issued by UK local government	NKLA	–	–	–	–	–	–	–	–	–
AF.3325	Medium term bonds issued by UK MFIs[1]	NKLB	0.2	0.3	0.2	0.2	0.3	0.9	1.0	1.5	1.9
AF.3326	Other medium & long term bonds issued by UK residents	NKLE	3.5	1.8	2.5	4.1	6.1	5.2	5.1	1.5	1.5
AF.3329	Long term bonds issued by the rest of the world	NKLF	6.3	7.2	28.4	28.8	29.3	30.0	28.2	14.8	14.4
AF.3	Total securities other than shares	NKKI	24.8	29.7	56.4	62.3	60.4	64.6	63.6	52.1	76.6
AF.4	Loans										
AF.42	Long term loans										
AF.4211	Outward direct investment	NKXH	73.0	78.2	85.9	97.5	110.5	110.7	125.2	136.7	127.5
AF.4212	Inward direct investment	NKXI	36.9	51.1	48.2	48.7	52.2	48.0	55.6	60.8	64.0
AF.423	Finance leasing	F8YG	0.9	1.8	2.4	2.5	2.7	3.4	4.4	5.4	6.4
AF.424	Other long-term loans by UK residents	NKXO	7.7	8.0	7.9	8.1	8.4	8.2	8.2	8.2	7.4
AF.4	Total loans	NKWY	118.5	139.0	144.5	156.8	173.9	170.3	193.4	211.1	205.3
AF.5	Shares and other equity										
AF.51	Shares and other equity, excluding mutual funds' shares										
AF.514	Quoted UK shares	NKXV	18.3	38.6	26.1	14.6	8.6	9.2	8.9	19.3	32.9
AF.515	Unquoted UK shares	NKXW	48.9	64.4	63.5	52.4	39.6	46.3	49.9	57.0	60.8
AF.517	UK shares and bonds issued by other UK residents	NSON	–	–	–	–	–	–	–	–	–
AF.519	Shares and other equity issued by the rest of the world	NKYA	213.1	339.4	505.6	494.4	521.3	564.6	546.9	613.2	593.5
AF.52	Mutual funds' shares										
AF.521	UK mutual funds' shares	NKYE	0.4	0.6	0.5	0.4	0.3	0.3	0.4	0.5	0.6
AF.5	Total shares and other equity	NKXQ	280.8	443.0	595.9	561.8	569.8	620.5	606.1	689.9	687.8
AF.6	Insurance technical reserves										
AF.62	Prepayments of insurance premiums and reserves for outstanding claims	NKYJ	11.8	10.7	14.7	12.5	12.8	15.7	16.6	17.3	18.1
AF.7	Other accounts receivable	NKYK	90.5	88.2	112.3	110.9	110.4	112.4	115.7	126.0	130.7
AF.A	**Total financial assets**	NKWX	728.1	935.6	1 188.2	1 191.0	1 250.8	1 362.9	1 435.6	1 613.6	1 671.8

1 UK monetary financial institutions

3.3.9 Private non-financial corporations

ESA95 sectors S.11002 National controlled and S.11003 Foreign controlled. Unconsolidated

continued

£ billion

			1998	1999	2000	2001	2002	2003	2004	2005	2006
IV.3	**FINANCIAL BALANCE SHEET** continued at end of period										
AF.L	**Financial liabilities**										
AF.3	Securities other than shares										
AF.331	Short term: money market instruments										
AF.3316	Issued by UK residents other than government or monetary financial institutions	NKZM	18.6	22.5	24.7	24.6	30.4	26.0	21.9	23.8	21.7
AF.332	Medium (1 to 5 year) and long term (over 5 year) bonds										
AF.3326	Other medium & long term bonds issued by UK residents or monetary financial institutions	NKZW	122.6	155.5	198.4	209.9	232.2	254.1	270.9	314.5	355.9
AF.3	Total securities other than shares	NKZA	141.2	178.0	223.1	234.5	262.5	280.2	292.8	338.3	377.5
AF.4	Loans										
AF.41	Short term loans										
AF.4111	Sterling deposits with UK banks	NLBF	166.5	176.2	198.6	214.1	235.4	242.9	257.9	291.5	338.8
AF.4112	Foreign currency deposits with UK banks	NLBG	36.3	41.8	45.9	46.5	41.0	33.3	32.5	43.3	44.1
AF.4113	Sterling deposits with building societies loans secured on dwellings & financial leasing	NLBH	2.3	3.8	5.6	7.4	8.9	10.0	9.9	11.8	14.8
AF.419	Loans by rest of the world monetary financial institutions	NLBI	72.7	88.4	99.9	121.1	139.6	170.5	208.5	223.5	289.6
AF.42	Long term loans										
AF.4211	Outward direct investment	NLBL	50.9	56.8	80.6	94.0	125.0	124.2	128.0	147.6	135.0
AF.4212	Inward direct investment	NLBM	77.2	94.2	100.4	115.3	124.9	117.4	123.1	152.9	149.2
AF.422	Loans secured on dwellings	G9JM	..	..	..	..	..	..	..	27.1	30.9
AF.423	Finance leasing	NLBR	20.6	21.0	21.1	21.2	21.5	22.0	22.5	22.9	23.4
AF.424	Other long-term loans by UK residents	NLBS	30.9	44.3	47.2	53.1	44.7	69.3	81.4	74.1	86.3
AF.429	Other long-term loans by the rest of the world	NLBT	0.4	0.4	0.4	0.3	0.4	0.4	0.4	0.4	0.4
AF.4	Total loans	NLBC	457.8	526.9	599.6	673.1	741.4	790.0	864.2	995.2	1 112.5
AF.5	Shares and other equity										
AF.51	Shares and other equity, excluding mutual funds' shares										
AF.514	Quoted UK shares	NLBZ	1 059.5	1 394.4	1 375.5	1 134.7	873.0	1 022.0	1 112.5	1 232.3	1 315.5
AF.515	Unquoted UK shares	NLCA	355.8	462.0	489.7	454.8	352.2	392.4	426.5	513.2	580.1
AF.516	Other UK equity (including direct investment in property)	NLCB	12.2	13.1	14.9	15.5	17.3	17.3	19.2	19.7	21.6
AF.517	UK shares and bonds issued by other UK residents	NSOO	–	–	–	–	–	–	–	–	–
AF.5	Total shares and other equity	NLBU	1 427.6	1 869.5	1 880.1	1 605.1	1 242.5	1 431.7	1 558.1	1 765.3	1 917.2
AF.7	Other accounts payable	NLCO	120.2	125.1	126.5	128.4	127.8	129.9	133.0	134.7	138.8
AF.L	**Total financial liabilities**	NLBB	2 146.8	2 699.4	2 829.3	2 640.9	2 374.2	2 631.8	2 848.1	3 233.4	3 545.9
BF.90	**Net financial assets / liabilities**										
AF.A	Total financial assets	NKWX	728.1	935.6	1 188.2	1 191.0	1 250.8	1 362.9	1 435.6	1 613.6	1 671.8
-AF.L	*less* Total financial liabilities	-NLBB	–2 146.8	–2 699.4	–2 829.3	–2 640.9	–2 374.2	–2 631.8	–2 848.1	–3 233.4	–3 545.9
BF.90	**Net financial assets (+) / liabilities (-)**	NYOT	–1 418.7	–1 763.8	–1 641.1	–1 449.9	–1 123.4	–1 268.9	–1 412.5	–1 619.9	–1 874.1
	Net worth										
AN	Non-financial assets	TMPL	1 003.5	1 049.4	1 154.7	1 128.3	1 155.6	1 179.8	1 217.2	1 306.1	1 333.1
BF.90	Net financial assets(+)/liabilities(-)	NYOT	–1 418.7	–1 763.8	–1 641.1	–1 449.9	–1 123.4	–1 268.9	–1 412.5	–1 619.9	–1 874.1
BF.90	**Net worth**	TMPN	–415.2	–714.5	–486.5	–321.6	32.3	–89.1	–195.3	–313.7	–541.0

Chapter 4
Financial corporations

4.1.1 Financial corporations
ESA95 sector S.12

£ million

			1998	1999	2000	2001	2002	2003	2004
I	**PRODUCTION ACCOUNT**								
	Resources								
P.1	Output								
P.11	Market output*	NHCV	103 773	110 137	115 804	123 609	141 665	151 159	160 157
P.12	Output for own final use	NHCW	1 592	1 766	2 008	2 106	2 388	2 559	2 458
P.1	Total resources	NHCT	105 365	111 903	117 812	125 715	144 053	153 718	162 615
P.119	**of which*, FISIM (financial intermediation services indirectly measured)	NSRV	27 658	29 468	33 465	33 648	41 136	45 370	50 165
	Uses								
P.2	Intermediate consumption	NHCX	57 932	65 304	71 550	78 329	75 936	75 903	76 553
B.1g	**Gross Value Added**	NHDB	**47 433**	**46 599**	**46 262**	**47 386**	**68 117**	**77 815**	**86 062**
Total	Total uses	NHCT	105 365	111 903	117 812	125 715	144 053	153 718	162 615
B.1g	**Gross Value Added**	NHDB	**47 433**	**46 599**	**46 262**	**47 386**	**68 117**	**77 815**	**86 062**
-K.1	*less* Consumption of fixed capital	-NHCE	–3 374	–3 554	–3 848	–3 701	–3 900	–4 091	–4 401
B.1n	Value added, net of fixed capital consumption	NHDC	44 059	43 045	42 414	43 685	64 217	73 724	81 661

4.1.2 Financial corporations
ESA95 sector S.12

£ million

			1998	1999	2000	2001	2002	2003	2004
II	**DISTRIBUTION AND USE OF INCOME ACCOUNTS**								
II.1	**PRIMARY DISTRIBUTION OF INCOME ACCOUNT**								
II.1.1	**GENERATION OF INCOME ACCOUNT**								
	Resources								
B.1g	**Total resources (Gross Value Added)**	NHDB	**47 433**	**46 599**	**46 262**	**47 386**	**68 117**	**77 815**	**86 062**
	Uses								
D.1	Compensation of employees								
D.11	Wages and salaries	NHCC	23 560	24 782	27 752	28 908	29 060	30 178	31 811
D.12	Employers' social contributions	NHCD	3 001	3 268	3 736	3 888	4 067	4 799	5 472
D.1	Total	NHCR	26 561	28 050	31 488	32 796	33 127	34 977	37 283
D.2	Taxes on production and imports, paid								
D.29	Production taxes other than on products	NHCS	1 486	1 539	1 219	1 348	1 376	1 419	1 455
-D.3	*less* Subsidies, received								
-D.39	Production subsidies other than on products	-NHCA	–	–	–	–	–	–	–
B.2g	Operating surplus, gross	NQNV	19 386	17 010	13 555	13 242	33 614	41 419	47 324
B.1g	**Total uses (Gross Value Added)**	NHDB	**47 433**	**46 599**	**46 262**	**47 386**	**68 117**	**77 815**	**86 062**
-K.1	After deduction of fixed capital consumption	-NHCE	–3 374	–3 554	–3 848	–3 701	–3 900	–4 091	–4 401
B.2n	Operating surplus, net	NHDA	16 012	13 456	9 707	9 541	29 714	37 328	42 923

4.1.3 Financial corporations

ESA95 sector S.12

£ million

			1998	1999	2000	2001	2002	2003	2004	2005	2006
II.1.2	**ALLOCATION OF PRIMARY INCOME ACCOUNT**										
	Resources										
B.2g	Operating surplus, gross	NQNV	19 386	17 010	13 555	13 242	33 614	41 419	47 324	39 697	45 710
D.4	Property income, received										
D.41	Interest	NHCK	210 831	187 498	229 113	223 967	189 622	189 381	221 112	274 214	347 701
D.42	Distributed income of corporations	NHCL	35 184	43 204	49 972	51 329	53 237	57 827	65 737	70 518	80 092
D.43	Reinvested earnings on direct foreign investment	NHEM	3 092	5 178	5 060	4 223	5 278	8 897	8 211	10 204	10 904
D.44	Attributed property income of insurance policy-holders	NHDG	32	53	35	37	34	44	42	66	68
D.45	Rent	NHDH	30	29	29	29	30	30	31	31	32
D.4	Total	NHDF	249 169	235 962	284 209	279 585	248 201	256 179	295 133	355 033	438 797
-P.119	Adjustment to property income for financial services (FISIM)	-NSRV	–27 658	–29 468	–33 465	–33 648	–41 136	–45 370	–50 165	–51 922	–57 566
Total	Total resources	NQNW	240 897	223 504	264 299	259 179	240 679	252 228	292 292	342 808	426 941
	Uses										
D.4	Property income, paid										
D.41	Interest	NHCM	148 601	129 081	169 986	162 146	122 729	117 128	143 941	196 472	266 482
D.42	Distributed income of corporations	NHCN	21 707	29 115	38 357	43 798	37 049	42 766	49 633	52 027	61 772
D.43	Reinvested earnings on direct foreign investment	NHEO	–1 595	1 831	3 440	–2 691	2 033	3 474	2 591	5 063	6 405
D.44	Attributed property income of insurance policy-holders	NQCG	57 985	58 026	57 455	57 795	56 652	56 703	56 150	65 497	69 905
D.45	Rent	NHDK	–	–	–	–	–	–	–	–	–
D.4	Total	NHDI	226 698	218 053	269 238	261 048	218 463	220 071	252 315	319 059	404 564
B.5g	**Balance of primary incomes, gross**	NQNY	**14 199**	**5 451**	**–4 939**	**–1 869**	**22 216**	**32 157**	**39 977**	**23 749**	**22 377**
Total	Total uses	NQNW	240 897	223 504	264 299	259 179	240 679	252 228	292 292	342 808	426 941
-K.1	After deduction of fixed capital consumption	-NHCE	–3 374	–3 554	–3 848	–3 701	–3 900	–4 091	–4 401	–4 530	–4 662
B.5n	Balance of primary incomes, net	NHDL	10 825	1 897	–8 787	–5 570	18 316	28 066	35 576	19 219	17 715

4.1.4 Financial corporations

ESA95 sector S.12

£ million

			1998	1999	2000	2001	2002	2003	2004	2005	2006
II.2	**SECONDARY DISTRIBUTION OF INCOME ACCOUNT**										
	Resources										
B.5g	**Balance of primary incomes, gross**	NQNY	**14 199**	**5 451**	**–4 939**	**–1 869**	**22 216**	**32 157**	**39 977**	**23 749**	**22 377**
D.61	Social contributions										
D.611	Actual social contributions										
D.6111	Employers' actual social contributions	NQOB	17 545	19 128	20 891	21 836	26 025	32 504	37 745	43 093	47 992
D.6112	Employees' social contributions	NQOC	29 626	30 878	31 568	31 933	32 967	32 158	31 462	36 509	39 850
D.6113	Social contributions by self-employed persons	NQOD	–	–	–	–	–	–	–	–	–
D.611	Total	NQOA	47 171	50 006	52 459	53 769	58 992	64 662	69 207	79 602	87 842
D.612	Imputed social contributions	NHDR	471	448	490	484	524	502	500	504	508
D.61	Total	NQNZ	47 642	50 454	52 949	54 253	59 516	65 164	69 707	80 106	88 350
D.7	Other current transfers										
D.71	Net non-life insurance premiums	NQOF	25 059	22 613	25 235	25 477	26 631	24 625	25 867	31 661	31 957
D.72	Non-life insurance claims	NHDN	326	637	633	544	612	689	698	803	863
D.75	Miscellaneous current transfers	NQOG	182	140	140	95	58	28	5	–	–
D.7	Total	NQOE	25 567	23 390	26 008	26 116	27 301	25 342	26 570	32 464	32 820
Total	Total resources	NQOH	87 408	79 295	74 018	78 500	109 033	122 663	136 254	136 319	143 547
	Uses										
D.5	Current taxes on income and wealth										
D.51	Taxes on income	NHDO	7 251	10 422	10 624	12 324	6 750	7 514	7 357	8 710	15 445
D.62	Social benefits other than social transfers in kind	NHDQ	33 600	36 440	38 800	38 220	41 733	43 799	44 618	48 963	52 649
D.7	Other current transfers										
D.71	Net non-life insurance premiums	NHDU	326	637	633	544	612	689	698	803	863
D.72	Non-life insurance claims	NQOI	25 059	22 613	25 235	25 477	26 631	24 625	25 867	31 661	31 957
D.75	Miscellaneous current transfers	NHEK	203	184	164	202	227	204	108	80	80
D.7	Total	NHDT	25 588	23 434	26 032	26 223	27 470	25 518	26 673	32 544	32 900
B.6g	**Gross Disposable Income**	NQOJ	**20 969**	**8 999**	**–1 438**	**1 733**	**33 080**	**45 832**	**57 606**	**46 102**	**42 553**
Total	Total uses	NQOH	87 408	79 295	74 018	78 500	109 033	122 663	136 254	136 319	143 547
-K.1	After deduction of fixed capital consumption	-NHCE	–3 374	–3 554	–3 848	–3 701	–3 900	–4 091	–4 401	–4 530	–4 662
B.6n	Disposable income, net	NHDV	17 595	5 445	–5 286	–1 968	29 180	41 741	53 205	41 572	37 891

4.1.6 Financial corporations
ESA95 sector S.12

£ million

			1998	1999	2000	2001	2002	2003	2004	2005	2006
II.4.1	**USE OF DISPOSABLE INCOME ACCOUNT**										
	Resources										
B.6g	**Total resources (Gross Disposable Income)**	NQOJ	**20 969**	**8 999**	**–1 438**	**1 733**	**33 080**	**45 832**	**57 606**	**46 102**	**42 553**
	Uses										
D.8	Adjustment for the change in net equity of households in pension funds	NQOK	14 042	14 014	14 160	16 036	17 782	21 365	25 089	31 143	35 701
B.8g	**Gross Saving**	NQOL	**6 927**	**–5 015**	**–15 598**	**–14 303**	**15 298**	**24 467**	**32 517**	**14 959**	**6 852**
B.6g	**Total uses (Gross Disposable Income)**	NQOJ	**20 969**	**8 999**	**–1 438**	**1 733**	**33 080**	**45 832**	**57 606**	**46 102**	**42 553**
-K.1	After deduction of fixed capital consumption	-NHCE	–3 374	–3 554	–3 848	–3 701	–3 900	–4 091	–4 401	–4 530	–4 662
B.8n	Saving, net	NQOM	3 553	–8 569	–19 446	–18 004	11 398	20 376	28 116	10 429	2 190

4.1.7 Financial corporations
ESA95 sector S.12

£ million

			1998	1999	2000	2001	2002	2003	2004	2005	2006
III	**ACCUMULATION ACCOUNTS**										
III.1	**CAPITAL ACCOUNT**										
III.1.1	**CHANGE IN NET WORTH DUE TO SAVING & CAPITAL TRANSFERS**										
	Changes in liabilities and net worth										
B.8g	**Gross Saving**	NQOL	**6 927**	**–5 015**	**–15 598**	**–14 303**	**15 298**	**24 467**	**32 517**	**14 959**	**6 852**
D.9	Capital transfers receivable										
D.92	Investment grants	NHEA	–	–	–	–	–	–	–	–	–
D.99	Other capital transfers	NHEB	–	–	–	412	412	391	328	321	446
D.9	Total	NHDZ	–	–	–	412	412	391	328	321	446
-D.9	*less* Capital transfers payable										
-D.91	Capital taxes	-NHBW	–	–	–	–	–	–	–	–	–
-D.99	Other capital transfers	-NHCB	–	–	–	–412	–412	–391	–328	–321	–446
-D.9	Total	-NHEC	–	–	–	–412	–412	–391	–328	–321	–446
B.10.1g	Total change in liabilities and net worth	NQON	6 927	–5 015	–15 598	–14 303	15 298	24 467	32 517	14 959	6 852
	Changes in assets										
B.10.1g	Changes in net worth due to gross saving and capital transfers	NQON	6 927	–5 015	–15 598	–14 303	15 298	24 467	32 517	14 959	6 852
-K.1	After deduction of fixed capital consumption	-NHCE	–3 374	–3 554	–3 848	–3 701	–3 900	–4 091	–4 401	–4 530	–4 662
B.10.1n	Changes in net worth due to net saving and capital transfers	NHEF	3 553	–8 569	–19 446	–18 004	11 398	20 376	28 116	10 429	2 190
III.1.2	**ACQUISITION OF NON-FINANCIAL ASSETS ACCOUNT**										
	Changes in liabilities and net worth										
B.10.1n	Changes in net worth due to net saving and capital transfers	NHEF	3 553	–8 569	–19 446	–18 004	11 398	20 376	28 116	10 429	2 190
K.1	Consumption of fixed capital	NHCE	3 374	3 554	3 848	3 701	3 900	4 091	4 401	4 530	4 662
Total	Total change in liabilities and net worth	NQON	6 927	–5 015	–15 598	–14 303	15 298	24 467	32 517	14 959	6 852
	Changes in assets										
P.5	Gross capital formation										
P.51	Gross fixed capital formation	NHCJ	11 934	9 188	11 976	8 482	8 323	5 253	6 169	7 043	7 919
P.52	Changes in inventories	NHCI	35	47	55	58	67	48	48	48	48
P.53	Acquisitions less disposals of valuables	NPQI	48	–28	–127	–	–74	–166	–173	–299	–158
P.5	Total	NHEG	12 017	9 207	11 904	8 540	8 316	5 135	6 044	6 792	7 809
K.2	Acquisitions less disposals of non-produced non-financial assets	NHEI	–4	–37	–45	–43	–36	–3	–6	–1	9
B.9	**Net lending(+) / net borrowing(-)**	NHCQ	**–5 086**	**–14 185**	**–27 457**	**–22 800**	**7 018**	**19 335**	**26 479**	**8 168**	**–966**
Total	Total change in assets	NQON	6 927	–5 015	–15 598	–14 303	15 298	24 467	32 517	14 959	6 852

4.1.8 Financial corporations

ESA95 sector S.12. Unconsolidated

£ million

			1998	1999	2000	2001	2002	2003	2004	2005	2006
III.2	**FINANCIAL ACCOUNT**										
F.A	**Net acquisition of financial assets**										
F.2	Currency and deposits										
F.21	Currency	NFCV	1 494	2 717	–1 419	–1 279	165	903	3 071	–1 104	–168
F.22	Transferable deposits										
F.221	Deposits with UK monetary financial institutions	NFCX	38 025	–7 839	83 632	121 699	76 155	157 642	181 362	226 460	349 724
F.229	Deposits with rest of the world monetary financial institutions	NFDB	12 208	21 900	185 654	98 650	47 078	150 267	156 062	333 146	237 564
F.29	Other deposits	NFDC	–10	–10	2 685	–1 570	1 263	–1 064	1 386	1 391	–2 083
F.2	Total currency and deposits	NFCU	51 717	16 768	270 552	217 500	124 661	307 748	341 881	559 893	585 037
F.3	Securities other than shares										
F.331	Short term: money market instruments										
F.3311	Issued by UK central government	NFDF	1 690	–1 145	–1 112	8 306	10 651	478	–911	–2 931	–2 372
F.3312	Issued by UK local government	NFDJ	–6	–	–	–	–	–	–	–	–
F.3315	Issued by UK monetary financial institutions	NFDK	12 195	18 323	–15 675	2 871	7 138	–12 099	–657	2 498	5 775
F.3316	Issued by other UK residents	NFDP	2 395	1 155	1 408	–1 112	–603	2 386	–2 759	4 252	949
F.3319	Issued by the rest of the world	NFDQ	2 223	13 546	–3 905	9 306	–5 666	9 412	–3 352	2 633	9 343
F.332	Medium (1 to 5 year) and long term (over 5 year) bonds										
F.3321	Issued by UK central government	NFDS	–5 022	–1 167	–12 173	–15 492	5 383	20 291	22 944	9 824	29 350
F.3322	Issued by UK local government	NFDV	–37	–36	60	–47	59	14	–92	139	269
F.3325	Medium term bonds issued by UK MFIs[1]	NFDW	2 698	7 531	2 282	–147	2 421	11 220	11 086	14 710	14 033
F.3326	Other medium & long term bonds issued by UK residents	NFDZ	20 313	38 152	66 213	46 095	24 056	38 252	32 717	36 474	44 927
F.3329	Long term bonds issued by the rest of the world	NFEA	27 343	–5 881	45 833	30 252	8 133	–1 093	86 266	91 506	163 910
F.34	Financial derivatives	NFEB	3 007	–2 727	–1 663	–8 601	–1 205	5 263	7 847	–9 556	–7 449
F.3	Total securities other than shares	NFDD	66 799	67 751	81 268	71 431	50 367	74 124	153 089	149 549	258 735
F.4	Loans										
F.41	Short term loans										
F.411	Loans by UK monetary financial institutions, excluding loans secured on dwellings & financial leasing	NFEH	32 439	65 529	154 557	109 704	86 729	159 860	233 710	256 735	307 993
F.42	Long term loans										
F.421	Direct investment	NFEN	273	463	1 487	2 356	4 693	–766	4 806	4 019	–346
F.422	Loans secured on dwellings	NFEQ	25 471	37 795	42 196	54 226	83 438	101 808	99 277	89 690	109 645
F.423	Finance leasing	NFEU	161	–266	–291	322	758	724	709	551	666
F.424	Other long term loans	NFEV	4 851	18 995	7 687	1 433	4 798	11 320	10 549	19 167	9 843
F.4	Total loans	NFEF	63 195	122 516	205 636	168 041	180 416	272 946	349 051	370 162	427 801
F.5	Shares and other equity										
F.51	Shares and other equity, excluding mutual funds' shares										
F.514	Quoted UK shares	NFFC	–1 344	–8 217	28 838	2 149	–6 936	–4 781	8 789	–50 065	–11 612
F.515	Unquoted UK shares	NFFD	–1 748	–1 670	13 925	–2 879	–1 881	542	5 345	5 163	19 803
F.517	UK shares and bonds issued by other UK residents	NSPS	–	–	–	–	–	–	–	–	–
F.519	Shares and other equity issued by the rest of the world	NFFH	15 548	24 451	26 872	50 913	5 074	38 706	76 257	71 077	42 679
F.52	Mutual funds' shares										
F.521	UK mutual funds' shares	NFFL	2 426	5 629	7 261	1 914	3 370	901	391	11 844	10 997
F.5	Total shares and other equity	NFEX	14 882	20 193	76 896	52 097	–373	35 368	90 782	38 019	61 867
F.6	Insurance technical reserves										
F.62	Prepayments of insurance premiums and reserves for outstanding claims	NFFQ	–7	–46	36	–41	42	20	102	107	84
F.7	Other accounts receivable	NFFR	4 393	3 215	–2 457	9 050	15 697	8 439	4 315	3 425	2 516
F.A	**Total net acquisition of financial assets**	NFCQ	200 979	230 397	631 931	518 078	370 810	698 645	939 220	1 121 155	1 336 040

1 UK monetary financial institutions

4.1.8 Financial corporations

ESA95 sector S.12. Unconsolidated

continued | £ million

			1998	1999	2000	2001	2002	2003	2004	2005	2006
III.2	**FINANCIAL ACCOUNT** continued										
F.L	**Net acquisition of financial liabilities**										
F.2	Currency and deposits										
F.21	Currency	NFFZ	2 967	5 231	448	738	1 532	2 958	5 460	945	1 745
F.22	Transferable deposits										
F.221	Deposits with UK monetary financial institutions	NFGB	121 986	42 505	344 048	289 104	217 744	398 030	562 029	586 972	780 241
F.29	Other deposits	NFGG	–	–	2 919	–2 578	476	–536	18	612	–147
F.2	Total currency and deposits	NFFY	124 953	47 736	347 415	287 264	219 752	400 452	567 507	588 529	781 839
F.3	Securities other than shares										
F.331	Short term: money market instruments										
F.3315	Issued by UK monetary financial institutions	NFGO	–1 159	31 134	23 941	22 836	25 599	–11 489	8 023	–3 490	53 189
F.3316	Issued by other non-government UK residents	NFGT	–93	31	–16	–	267	–567	704	239	455
F.332	Medium (1 to 5 year) and long term (over 5 year) bonds										
F.3325	Medium term bonds issued by UK MFIs[1]	NFHA	4 485	12 081	4 750	3 575	4 238	25 258	29 810	37 843	40 534
F.3326	Other medium & long term bonds issued by UK residents	NFHD	–595	24 106	35 298	35 807	29 802	81 671	80 255	101 893	107 953
F.34	Financial derivatives	NFHF	31	3	43	89	–70	63	–147	–207	–110
F.3	Total securities other than shares	NFGH	2 669	67 355	64 016	62 307	59 836	94 936	118 645	136 278	202 021
F.4	Loans										
F.41	Short term loans										
F.411	Loans by UK monetary financial institutions, excluding loans secured on dwellings & financial leasing	NFHL	–451	14 243	55 753	31 959	26 935	64 075	71 085	54 992	119 304
F.419	Loans by rest of the world monetary financial institutions	NFHP	14 895	33 049	63 159	66 681	–34 545	40 025	51 644	217 948	38 393
F.42	Long term loans										
F.421	Direct investment	NFHR	210	3 082	896	13 253	6 643	2 765	4 667	–5 710	2 010
F.423	Finance leasing	NFHY	55	–323	–127	263	411	294	193	143	191
F.424	Other long-term loans by UK residents	NFHZ	–4 089	8 818	18 319	9 197	3 474	5 558	5 713	24 843	41 505
F.429	Other long-term loans by the rest of the world	NFIA	–115	46	–30	6	–21	–42	10	29	–
F.4	Total loans	NFHJ	10 505	58 915	137 970	121 359	2 897	112 675	133 312	292 245	201 403
F.5	Shares and other equity										
F.51	Shares and other equity, excluding mutual funds' shares										
F.514	Quoted UK shares	NFIG	4 433	2 229	17 746	13 223	2 626	15 041	13 534	12 555	29 569
F.515	Unquoted UK shares	NFIH	4 579	9 012	28 193	11 768	9 501	15 513	20 730	27 301	38 760
F.516	Other UK equity (including direct investment in property)	NFII	–	–	–	43	32	–9	–8	–	–
F.517	UK shares and bonds issued by other UK residents	NSPT	–	–	–	–	–	–	–	–	–
F.52	Mutual funds' shares										
F.521	UK mutual funds' shares	NFIP	10 976	14 719	14 102	9 338	6 259	8 212	3 489	8 300	15 156
F.5	Total shares and other equity	NFIB	19 988	25 960	60 041	34 372	18 418	38 757	37 745	48 156	83 485
F.6	Insurance technical reserves										
F.61	Net equity of households in life assurance and pension funds' reserves	NFIR	34 671	31 333	26 195	33 078	46 302	34 654	40 582	51 994	62 355
F.62	Prepayments of insurance premiums and reserves for outstanding claims	NFIU	–563	–1 601	1 466	–1 753	1 781	687	3 778	3 969	3 153
F.6	Total insurance technical reserves	NPWS	34 108	29 732	27 661	31 325	48 083	35 341	44 360	55 963	65 508
F.7	Other accounts payable	NFIV	1 957	4 678	7 635	1 249	7 198	267	8 353	2 032	4 586
F.L	**Total net acquisition of financial liabilities**	NFFU	194 180	234 376	644 738	537 876	356 184	682 428	909 922	1 123 203	1 338 842
B.9	**Net lending / borrowing**										
F.A	Total net acquisition of financial assets	NFCQ	200 979	230 397	631 931	518 078	370 810	698 645	939 220	1 121 155	1 336 040
-F.L	*less* Total net acquisition of financial liabilities	-NFFU	–194 180	–234 376	–644 738	–537 876	–356 184	–682 428	–909 922	–1 123 203	–1 338 842
B.9f	Net lending (+) / net borrowing (-), from financial account	NYNL	6 799	–3 979	–12 807	–19 798	14 626	16 217	29 298	–2 048	–2 802
dB.9f	Statistical discrepancy	NYOX	–11 885	–10 206	–14 650	–3 002	–7 608	3 118	–2 819	10 216	1 836
B.9	**Net lending (+) / net borrowing (-), from capital account**	NHCQ	**–5 086**	**–14 185**	**–27 457**	**–22 800**	**7 018**	**19 335**	**26 479**	**8 168**	**–966**

1 UK monetary financial institutions

4.1.9 Financial corporations

ESA95 sector S.12. Unconsolidated

£ billion

			1998	1999	2000	2001	2002	2003	2004	2005	2006
IV.3	**FINANCIAL BALANCE SHEET** at end of period										
AN	**Non-financial assets**	CGDB	102.4	114.0	118.0	121.4	122.0	128.5	137.1	152.3	154.2
AF.A	**Financial assets**										
AF.2	Currency and deposits										
AF.21	Currency	NLJE	7.2	9.9	8.5	7.2	7.4	8.3	11.3	10.2	10.1
AF.22	Transferable deposits										
AF.221	Deposits with UK monetary financial institutions	NLJG	525.0	506.4	600.2	701.3	784.5	1 033.6	1 176.7	1 442.7	1 829.6
AF.229	Deposits with rest of the world monetary financial institutions	NLJK	793.7	794.4	1 003.1	1 090.2	1 114.3	1 247.5	1 368.9	1 752.1	1 850.2
AF.29	Other deposits	NLJL	0.1	0.1	2.8	1.2	1.9	0.8	2.2	3.6	1.5
AF.2	Total currency and deposits	NLJD	1 326.0	1 310.8	1 614.5	1 799.8	1 908.0	2 290.1	2 559.2	3 208.7	3 691.4
AF.3	Securities other than shares										
AF.331	Short term: money market instruments										
AF.3311	Issued by UK central government	NLJO	4.2	3.5	2.2	10.7	21.0	21.9	20.9	18.2	15.7
AF.3312	Issued by UK local government	NLJS	–	–	–	–	–	–	–	–	–
AF.3315	Issued by UK monetary financial institutions	NLJT	138.4	155.6	141.4	145.2	151.1	140.0	139.8	144.1	148.3
AF.3316	Issued by other UK residents	NLJY	4.4	6.3	7.4	6.0	5.3	7.3	4.8	8.9	9.7
AF.3319	Issued by the rest of the world	NLJZ	24.7	40.6	40.0	49.1	41.6	52.1	47.8	51.1	57.4
AF.332	Medium (1 to 5 year) and long term (over 5 year) bonds										
AF.3321	Issued by UK central government	NLKB	247.3	235.6	226.1	203.0	216.6	228.0	253.3	279.1	293.3
AF.3322	Issued by UK local government	NLKE	0.6	0.6	0.5	0.6	0.5	0.5	0.4	0.4	0.8
AF.3325	Medium term bonds issued by UK MFIs[1]	NLKF	24.3	32.6	36.0	34.9	37.1	52.4	62.8	78.5	89.0
AF.3326	Other medium & long term bonds issued by UK residents	NLKI	138.3	179.3	231.7	261.0	278.0	309.9	345.0	409.9	468.3
AF.3329	Long term bonds issued by the rest of the world	NLKJ	367.3	370.6	426.0	472.9	484.4	496.2	573.8	687.8	792.1
AF.34	Financial derivatives	NLKK	–	–	–	–	–	–	–	–	–
AF.3	Total securities other than shares	NLJM	949.5	1 024.7	1 111.3	1 183.4	1 235.7	1 308.2	1 448.6	1 678.2	1 874.6
AF.4	Loans										
AF.41	Short term loans										
AF.411	Loans by UK monetary financial institutions, excluding loans secured on dwellings & financial leasing	NLKQ	766.4	817.4	980.8	1 079.6	1 144.9	1 286.4	1 497.5	1 766.4	1 982.1
AF.42	Long term loans										
AF.421	Direct investment	NLKW	6.0	4.2	7.9	11.2	12.8	16.2	29.2	30.0	29.7
AF.422	Loans secured on dwellings	NLKZ	455.4	492.2	534.4	589.5	668.5	771.8	874.7	964.1	1 075.6
AF.423	Finance leasing	NLLD	23.2	23.3	23.4	23.7	24.5	25.2	25.9	26.4	27.1
AF.424	Other long term loans	NLLE	40.6	55.4	54.1	58.6	60.0	75.0	91.9	91.8	113.8
AF.4	Total loans	NLKO	1 291.6	1 392.6	1 600.6	1 762.6	1 910.7	2 174.6	2 519.3	2 878.7	3 228.3
AF.5	Shares and other equity										
AF.51	Shares and other equity, excluding mutual funds' shares										
AF.514	Quoted UK shares	NLLL	734.7	905.1	836.0	763.6	568.7	680.9	743.1	760.6	805.8
AF.515	Unquoted UK shares	NLLM	86.9	118.1	180.0	219.2	238.5	266.8	305.0	333.8	393.9
AF.517	UK shares and bonds issued by other UK residents	NSQL	–	–	–	–	–	–	–	–	–
AF.519	Shares and other equity issued by the rest of the world	NLLQ	350.9	464.6	481.3	464.8	376.4	441.7	526.1	685.1	783.0
AF.52	Mutual funds' shares										
AF.521	UK mutual funds' shares	NLLU	116.6	145.6	150.5	130.5	106.3	146.0	164.1	243.3	299.2
AF.5	Total shares and other equity	NLLG	1 289.0	1 633.4	1 647.8	1 578.1	1 289.9	1 535.4	1 738.3	2 022.8	2 281.9
AF.6	Insurance technical reserves										
AF.62	Prepayments of insurance premiums and reserves for outstanding claims	NLLZ	0.8	1.7	1.6	1.4	1.4	1.7	1.8	1.9	2.0
AF.7	Other accounts receivable	NLMA	26.0	26.7	29.0	31.2	49.5	66.1	67.4	70.3	71.8
AF.A	**Total financial assets**	NLIZ	4 882.8	5 389.8	6 004.9	6 356.5	6 395.2	7 376.2	8 334.6	9 860.6	11 150.1

1 UK monetary financial institutions

4.1.9 Financial corporations

ESA95 sector S.12. Unconsolidated

continued £ billion

			1998	1999	2000	2001	2002	2003	2004	2005	2006
IV.3	**FINANCIAL BALANCE SHEET** continued at end of period										
AF.L	**Financial liabilities**										
AF.2	Currency and deposits										
AF.21	Currency	NLMI	29.9	35.1	35.6	36.3	37.9	40.8	46.3	47.2	49.0
AF.22	Transferable deposits										
AF.221	Deposits with UK monetary financial institutions	NLMK	2 171.2	2 183.4	2 575.8	2 829.2	3 027.1	3 510.9	3 976.2	4 669.8	5 323.1
AF.29	Other deposits	NLMP	–	–	2.9	0.3	0.8	0.3	0.3	1.8	1.6
AF.2	Total currency and deposits	NLMH	2 201.2	2 218.5	2 614.3	2 865.8	3 065.8	3 552.0	4 022.7	4 718.8	5 373.6
AF.3	Securities other than shares										
AF.331	Short term: money market instruments										
AF.3315	Issued by UK monetary financial institutions	NLMX	204.3	233.5	265.8	291.0	302.6	282.1	283.2	291.7	327.7
AF.3316	Issued by other non-government UK residents	NLNC	8.1	15.6	21.4	23.3	21.1	19.4	19.6	26.2	41.8
AF.332	Medium (1 to 5 year) and long term (over 5 year) bonds										
AF.3325	Medium term bonds issued by UK MFIs[1]	NLNJ	53.3	67.7	74.6	77.6	81.0	107.0	134.7	175.4	205.8
AF.3326	Other medium & long term bonds issued by UK residents	NLNM	144.3	171.0	208.1	245.0	281.7	357.1	440.4	559.2	636.3
AF.34	Financial derivatives	NLNO	–	–0.4	–0.1	0.3	–	–	0.1	0.2	0.7
AF.3	Total securities other than shares	NLMQ	410.1	487.4	569.8	637.3	686.4	765.7	878.1	1 052.8	1 212.4
AF.4	Loans										
AF.41	Short term loans										
AF.411	Loans by UK monetary financial institutions, excluding loans secured on dwellings & financial leasing	NLNU	248.6	254.8	306.9	335.2	359.8	424.5	498.8	562.0	656.2
AF.419	Loans by rest of the world monetary financial institutions	NLNY	214.9	256.7	306.8	368.8	337.1	372.0	413.7	647.5	638.9
AF.42	Long term loans										
AF.421	Direct investment	NLOA	15.3	16.2	15.6	30.6	34.1	39.0	52.7	50.0	52.1
AF.423	Finance leasing	NLOH	2.6	2.3	2.2	2.5	2.9	3.2	3.4	3.5	3.7
AF.424	Other long-term loans by UK residents	NLOI	11.6	14.0	13.8	14.4	15.1	16.2	20.2	26.7	36.8
AF.429	Other long-term loans by the rest of the world	NLOJ	0.7	0.5	0.5	0.5	0.5	0.5	0.5	0.5	0.5
AF.4	Total loans	NLNS	493.8	544.4	645.7	751.9	749.5	855.4	989.3	1 290.1	1 388.2
AF.5	Shares and other equity										
AF.51	Shares and other equity, excluding mutual funds' shares										
AF.514	Quoted UK shares	NLOP	312.5	356.7	378.8	359.6	273.8	337.8	373.6	409.2	485.7
AF.515	Unquoted UK shares	NLOQ	132.4	174.3	238.0	257.0	255.8	276.1	301.8	337.3	374.7
AF.517	UK shares and bonds issued by other UK residents	NSQM	–	–	–	–	–	–	–	–	–
AF.52	Mutual funds' shares										
AF.521	UK mutual funds' shares	NLOY	217.9	299.0	304.5	268.2	215.8	266.3	303.9	385.0	452.4
AF.5	Total shares and other equity	NLOK	662.7	830.1	921.3	884.8	745.4	880.1	979.3	1 131.5	1 312.9
AF.6	Insurance technical reserves										
AF.61	Net equity of households in life assurance and pension funds' reserves	NLPA	1 393.4	1 631.5	1 599.2	1 531.5	1 384.3	1 509.4	1 603.4	1 894.5	2 071.1
AF.62	Prepayments of insurance premiums and reserves for outstanding claims	NLPD	60.8	58.9	62.8	59.0	62.8	63.5	67.2	71.2	74.4
AF.6	Total insurance technical reserves	NPYI	1 454.2	1 690.4	1 662.0	1 590.5	1 447.1	1 572.9	1 670.6	1 965.7	2 145.4
AF.7	Other accounts payable	NLPE	18.5	23.0	28.8	31.6	33.8	41.9	48.9	50.5	54.2
AF.L	**Total financial liabilities**	NLMD	5 240.4	5 793.9	6 441.9	6 761.9	6 728.0	7 668.1	8 589.0	10 209.4	11 486.7
BF.90	**Net financial assets / liabilities**										
AF.A	Total financial assets	NLIZ	4 882.8	5 389.8	6 004.9	6 356.5	6 395.2	7 376.2	8 334.6	9 860.6	11 150.1
-AF.L	*less* Total financial liabilities	-NLMD	–5 240.4	–5 793.9	–6 441.9	–6 761.9	–6 728.0	–7 668.1	–8 589.0	–10 209.4	–11 486.7
BF.90	**Net financial assets (+) / liabilities (-)**	NYOE	–357.5	–404.0	–437.0	–405.4	–332.8	–291.8	–254.4	–348.8	–336.6
	Net worth										
AN	Non-financial assets	CGDB	102.4	114.0	118.0	121.4	122.0	128.5	137.1	152.3	154.2
BF.90	Net financial assets (+) / liabilities (-)	NYOE	–357.5	–404.0	–437.0	–405.4	–332.8	–291.8	–254.4	–348.8	–336.6
BF.90	**Net worth**	CGRU	–255.1	–290.0	–319.0	–284.0	–210.8	–163.3	–117.2	–196.5	–182.4

1 UK monetary financial institutions

4.2.2 Monetary financial institutions
ESA95 sectors S.121 Central bank & S.122 Other monetary financial institutions

£ million

			1998	1999	2000	2001	2002	2003	2004
II	**DISTRIBUTION AND USE OF INCOME ACCOUNTS**								
II.1	**PRIMARY DISTRIBUTION OF INCOME ACCOUNT**								
II.1.1	**GENERATION OF INCOME ACCOUNT** before deduction of fixed capital consumption								
	Resources								
B.1g	**Total resources (Gross Value Added)**	NHJN	**34 787**	**27 624**	**28 875**	**37 165**	**39 957**	**42 818**	**50 942**
	Uses								
D.1	Compensation of employees								
D.11	Wages and salaries	NHDJ	10 442	10 995	12 629	13 036	12 750	13 821	15 360
D.12	Employers' social contributions	NHDM	1 167	1 255	1 447	1 519	1 576	1 755	2 176
D.1	Total	NHFL	11 609	12 250	14 076	14 555	14 326	15 576	17 536
D.2	Taxes on production and imports, paid								
D.29	Production taxes other than on products	NHJE	781	832	480	496	512	522	532
-D.3	*less* Subsidies, received								
-D.39	Production subsidies other than on products	-NHET	–	–	–	–	–	–	–
B.2g	Operating surplus, gross	NHBX	22 397	14 542	14 319	22 114	25 119	26 720	32 874
B.1g	**Total uses (Gross Value Added)**	NHJN	**34 787**	**27 624**	**28 875**	**37 165**	**39 957**	**42 818**	**50 942**

4.2.3 Monetary financial institutions

ESA95 sectors S.121 Central bank & S.122 Other monetary financial institutions

£ million

			1998	1999	2000	2001	2002	2003	2004	2005	2006
II.1.2	**ALLOCATION OF PRIMARY INCOME ACCOUNT**										
	Resources										
B.2g	Operating surplus, gross	NHBX	22 397	14 542	14 319	22 114	25 119	26 720	32 874	30 211	35 209
D.4	Property income, received										
D.41	Interest	NHFE	162 342	143 820	177 704	172 882	144 213	141 299	163 254	205 320	264 280
D.42	Distributed income of corporations	NHFF	2 015	4 597	7 570	7 222	6 626	8 041	10 850	10 398	11 473
D.43	Reinvested earnings on direct foreign investment	NHKY	747	1 439	1 669	2 423	2 411	3 321	4 130	4 927	5 938
D.44	Property income attributed to insurance policy-holders	NHJS	8	14	8	9	8	11	11	17	18
D.45	Rent	NHJT	–	–	–	–	–	–	–	–	–
D.4	Total	NHJR	165 112	149 870	186 951	182 536	153 258	152 672	178 245	220 662	281 709
-P.119	Adjustment to property income for financial services (FISIM)	-QTFB	–35 419	–31 039	–31 472	–39 614	–40 561	–40 177	–43 773	–43 912	–48 067
Total	Total resources	NRKH	152 090	133 373	169 798	165 036	137 816	139 215	167 346	206 961	268 851
	Uses										
D.4	Property income, paid										
D.41	Interest	NHFG	121 099	104 410	136 320	127 989	94 619	88 990	108 986	150 274	205 086
D.42	Distributed income of corporations	NHFH	4 791	12 917	18 580	14 126	13 399	18 384	23 295	21 426	24 681
D.43	Reinvested earnings on direct foreign investment	NHLB	–320	986	1 911	997	1 215	1 948	481	2 692	1 487
D.45	Rent	NHJW	–	–	–	–	–	–	–	–	–
D.4	Total	NHJU	125 570	118 313	156 811	143 112	109 233	109 322	132 762	174 392	231 254
B.5g	**Balance of primary incomes, gross**	NRKI	**26 520**	**15 060**	**12 987**	**21 924**	**28 583**	**29 893**	**34 584**	**32 569**	**37 597**
Total	Total uses	NRKH	152 090	133 373	169 798	165 036	137 816	139 215	167 346	206 961	268 851

4.2.4 Monetary financial institutions

ESA95 sectors S.121 Central bank & S.122 Other monetary financial institutions

£ million

			1998	1999	2000	2001	2002	2003	2004	2005	2006
II.2	**SECONDARY DISTRIBUTION OF INCOME ACCOUNT**										
	Resources										
B.5g	**Balance of primary incomes, gross**	NRKI	**26 520**	**15 060**	**12 987**	**21 924**	**28 583**	**29 893**	**34 584**	**32 569**	**37 597**
D.61	Social contributions										
D.612	Imputed social contributions	NHKD	183	172	190	188	204	189	197	239	253
D.7	Other current transfers										
D.72	Non-life insurance claims	NHJZ	75	160	152	142	160	172	180	208	224
D.75	Miscellaneous current transfers	CY8D	182	140	140	95	58	28	5	–	–
D.7	Total	NRKN	257	300	292	237	218	200	185	208	224
Total	Total resources	NRKP	26 960	15 532	13 469	22 349	29 005	30 282	34 966	33 016	38 074
	Uses										
D.5	Current taxes on income, wealth etc.										
D.51	Taxes on income	NHKA	2 780	4 436	4 151	4 601	4 054	4 131	4 534	3 943	5 259
D.62	Social benefits other than social transfers in kind	NHKC	183	172	190	188	204	189	197	239	253
D.7	Other current transfers										
D.71	Net non-life insurance premiums	NHKG	75	160	152	142	160	172	180	208	224
D.75	Miscellaneous current transfers	NHKW	181	161	140	178	203	180	84	56	56
D.7	Total	NHKF	256	321	292	320	363	352	264	264	280
B.6g	**Gross Disposable Income**	NRKQ	**23 741**	**10 603**	**8 836**	**17 240**	**24 384**	**25 610**	**29 971**	**28 570**	**32 282**
Total	Total uses	NRKP	26 960	15 532	13 469	22 349	29 005	30 282	34 966	33 016	38 074

4.2.6 Monetary financial institutions

ESA95 sectors S.121 Central bank & S.122 Other monetary financial institutions

£ million

			1998	1999	2000	2001	2002	2003	2004	2005	2006
II.4.1	**USE OF DISPOSABLE INCOME ACCOUNT**										
	Resources										
B.6g	**Total resources (Gross Disposable Income)**	NRKQ	**23 741**	**10 603**	**8 836**	**17 240**	**24 384**	**25 610**	**29 971**	**28 570**	**32 282**
	Uses										
B.8g	**Total uses (Gross Saving)**	NRKT	**23 741**	**10 603**	**8 836**	**17 240**	**24 384**	**25 610**	**29 971**	**28 570**	**32 282**

4.2.7 Monetary financial institutions

ESA95 sectors S.121 Central bank & S.122 Other monetary financial institutions

£ million

			1998	1999	2000	2001	2002	2003	2004	2005	2006
III	**ACCUMULATION ACCOUNTS**										
III.1	**CAPITAL ACCOUNT**										
III.1.1	**CHANGE IN NET WORTH DUE TO SAVING & CAPITAL TRANSFERS ACCOUNT**										
	Changes in liabilities and net worth										
B.8g	**Gross Saving**	NRKT	**23 741**	**10 603**	**8 836**	**17 240**	**24 384**	**25 610**	**29 971**	**28 570**	**32 282**
D.9	Capital transfers receivable										
D.92	Investment grants	NHKM	–	–	–	–	–	–	–	–	–
D.99	Other capital transfers	NHKN	–	–	–	–	–	–	–	–	–
D.9	Total	NHKL	–	–	–	–	–	–	–	–	–
-D.9	*less* Capital transfers payable										
-D.91	Capital taxes	-NHEQ	–	–	–	–	–	–	–	–	..
-D.99	Other capital transfers	-NHEV	–	–	–	–	–	–	–	–	–
-D.9	Total	-NHKP	–	–	–	–	–	–	–	–	–
B.10.1g	Total change in liabilities and net worth	NRMH	23 741	10 603	8 836	17 240	24 384	25 610	29 971	28 570	32 282
	Changes in assets										
B.10.1g	Changes in net worth due to saving and capital transfers before deduction of fixed capital consumption	NRMH	23 741	10 603	8 836	17 240	24 384	25 610	29 971	28 570	32 282
III.1.2	**ACQUISITION OF NON-FINANCIAL ASSETS ACCOUNT**										
B.10.1g	**Total changes in liabilities and net worth due to saving & capital transfers**	NRMH	23 741	10 603	8 836	17 240	24 384	25 610	29 971	28 570	32 282
	Changes in assets										
P.5	Gross capital formation										
P.51	Gross fixed capital formation	NHFD	4 508	3 553	3 961	4 127	5 008	4 555	4 169	4 967	4 958
P.52	Changes in inventories	NHFC	35	47	55	58	67	48	48	48	48
P.53	Acquisitions less disposals of valuables	NHKT	–	–	–	–	–	–	–	–	–
P.5	Total	NHKS	4 543	3 600	4 016	4 185	5 075	4 603	4 217	5 015	5 006
K.2	Acquisitions less disposals of non-produced non-financial assets	NHKU	–	–	–	–	–	–	–	–	–
B.9	**Net lending (+) / net borrowing (-)**	NHFK	**19 198**	**7 003**	**4 820**	**13 055**	**19 309**	**21 007**	**25 754**	**23 555**	**27 276**
B.10.1g	Total change in assets	NRMH	23 741	10 603	8 836	17 240	24 384	25 610	29 971	28 570	32 282

4.2.8 Monetary financial institutions

ESA95 sectors S.121 Central bank & S.122 Other monetary financial institutions. Unconsolidated

£ million

			1998	1999	2000	2001	2002	2003	2004	2005	2006
III.2	**FINANCIAL ACCOUNT**										
F.A	**Net acquisition of financial assets**										
F.2	Currency and deposits										
F.21	Currency	NGCB	1 494	2 717	–1 419	–1 279	165	903	3 071	–1 104	–168
F.22	Transferable deposits										
F.221	Deposits with UK MFIs[1]	NGCD	21 793	3 013	39 114	83 111	74 857	128 497	132 249	129 571	231 978
F.229	Deposits with rest of the world monetary financial institutions	NGCH	18 587	–29 232	131 854	36 128	53 582	87 554	105 554	157 215	178 412
F.29	Other deposits	NGCI	–10	–10	–6	–3	–2	–1	–6	–	–
F.2	Total currency and deposits	NGCA	41 864	–23 512	169 543	117 957	128 602	216 953	240 868	285 682	410 222
F.3	Securities other than shares										
F.331	Short term: money market instruments										
F.3311	Issued by UK central government	NGCL	1 124	35	–1 222	6 859	10 798	–1 655	–2 362	–304	–3 746
F.3312	Issued by UK local government	NGCP	–	–	–	–	–	–	–	–	–
F.3315	Issued by UK MFIs[1]	NGCQ	3 631	10 743	–19 114	6 124	330	–14 166	1 811	3 729	3 121
F.3316	Issued by other UK residents	NGCV	164	63	847	–536	–225	2 139	–1 166	909	2 239
F.3319	Issued by the rest of the world	NGCW	4 153	9 724	345	7 372	–3 981	7 431	–4 619	2 143	5 058
F.332	Medium (1 to 5 year) and long term (over 5 year) bonds										
F.3321	Issued by UK central government	NGCY	–7 954	–6 472	–6 954	–4 787	–4 803	–5 029	5 122	–1 312	–4 583
F.3322	Issued by UK local government	NGDB	–	–	–	–	–	–	–	–	–
F.3325	Medium term bonds issued by UK MFIs[1]	NGDC	1 644	5 071	3 976	–1 282	–860	2 590	2 525	1 640	–58
F.3326	Other medium & long term bonds issued by UK residents	NGDF	1 303	6 917	18 503	9 222	–1 753	8 419	12 244	26 009	45 053
F.3329	Long term bonds issued by the rest of the world	NGDG	44 509	11 842	36 532	39 224	3 768	–14 511	58 779	62 415	100 963
F.34	Financial derivatives	NGDH	3 007	–2 727	–1 663	–8 601	–1 205	5 263	7 847	–9 556	–7 449
F.3	Total securities other than shares	NGCJ	51 581	35 196	31 250	53 595	2 069	–9 519	80 181	85 673	140 598
F.4	Loans										
F.41	Short term loans										
F.411	Loans by UK MFIs[1], excluding loans secured on dwellings & financial leasing	NGDN	32 439	65 529	154 557	109 704	86 729	159 860	233 710	256 735	307 993
F.42	Long term loans										
F.421	Direct investment	NGDT	–115	–	–	–	–52	–4	–	–	–
F.422	Loans secured on dwellings	NGDW	22 962	32 143	28 420	37 927	59 962	66 529	60 004	46 295	46 430
F.423	Finance leasing	NGEA	34	37	–40	1	8	–21	–13	–14	–4
F.424	Other long term loans	LNPM	–7	–355	–1 476	187	–1 017	113	231	–106	–478
F.4	Total loans	NGDL	55 313	97 354	181 461	147 819	145 630	226 477	293 932	302 910	353 941
F.5	Shares and other equity										
F.51	Shares and other equity, excluding mutual funds' shares										
F.514	Quoted UK shares	NGEI	472	208	619	39	–752	654	5 598	4 967	6 122
F.515	Unquoted UK shares	NGEJ	988	1 943	8 931	759	347	2 564	8 434	4 208	21 099
F.517	UK shares and bonds issued by other UK residents	NSQA	–	–	–	–	–	–	–	–	–
F.519	Shares and other equity issued by the rest of the world	NGEN	5 487	1 405	10 513	2 237	–9 268	22 544	46 981	46 341	34 106
F.52	Mutual funds' shares										
F.521	UK mutual funds' shares	NGER	2	3	43	5	8	4	28	49	50
F.5	Total shares and other equity	NGED	6 949	3 559	20 106	3 040	–9 665	25 766	61 041	55 565	61 377
F.7	Other accounts receivable	NGEX	22	–85	37	–29	–180	–143	–99	16	–73
F.A	**Total net acquisition of financial assets**	NGBW	155 729	112 512	402 397	322 382	266 456	459 534	675 923	729 846	966 065

1 UK monetary financial institutions

4.2.8 Monetary financial institutions

ESA95 sectors S.121 Central bank & S.122 Other monetary financial institutions. Unconsolidated

continued | £ million

			1998	1999	2000	2001	2002	2003	2004	2005	2006
III.2	**FINANCIAL ACCOUNT** continued										
F.L	**Net acquisition of financial liabilities**										
F.2	Currency and deposits										
F.21	Currency	NGFF	2 967	5 231	448	738	1 532	2 958	5 460	945	1 745
F.22	Transferable deposits										
F.221	Deposits with UK MFIs[1]	NGFH	121 986	42 505	344 048	289 104	217 744	398 030	562 029	586 972	780 241
F.2	Total currency and deposits	NGFE	124 953	47 736	344 496	289 842	219 276	400 988	567 489	587 917	781 986
F.3	Securities other than shares										
F.331	Short term: money market instruments										
F.3315	Issued by UK MFIs[1]	NGFU	−1 159	31 134	23 941	22 836	25 599	−11 489	8 023	−3 490	53 189
F.332	Medium (1 to 5 year) and long term (over 5 year) bonds										
F.3325	Medium term bonds issued by UK MFIs[1]	NGGG	4 485	12 081	4 750	3 575	4 238	25 258	29 810	37 843	40 534
F.3326	Other medium & long term bonds issued by UK residents	NGGJ	−3 394	5 818	11 006	10 068	8 801	26 069	7 934	16 894	−9 678
F.34	Financial derivatives	NGGL	31	3	43	89	−70	63	−147	−207	−110
F.3	Total securities other than shares	NGFN	−37	49 036	39 740	36 568	38 568	39 901	45 620	51 040	83 935
F.4	Loans										
F.42	Long term loans										
F.421	Direct investment	NGGX	−31	9	223	165	−92	171	137	27	−7
F.423	Finance leasing	NGHE	20	−168	−61	135	275	190	98	72	110
F.4	Total loans	NGGP	−11	−159	162	300	183	361	235	99	103
F.5	Shares and other equity										
F.51	Shares and other equity, excluding mutual funds' shares										
F.514	Quoted UK shares	NGHM	−1 868	−519	2 410	2 723	2 041	2 979	3 183	3 266	2 881
F.515	Unquoted UK shares	NGHN	−266	1 111	10 862	1 634	1 756	2 755	1 274	3 508	2 303
F.516	Other UK equity (including direct investment in property)	NGHO	–	–	–	43	32	−9	−8	–	–
F.517	UK shares and bonds issued by other UK residents	NSQB	–	–	–	–	–	–	–	–	–
F.5	Total shares and other equity	NGHH	−2 134	592	13 272	4 400	3 829	5 725	4 449	6 774	5 184
F.7	Other accounts payable	NGIB	487	−283	1 449	−2 376	−571	221	1 038	1 011	621
F.L	**Total net acquisition of financial liabilities**	NGFA	123 258	96 922	399 119	328 734	261 285	447 196	618 831	646 841	871 829
B.9	**Net lending / borrowing**										
F.A	Total net acquisition of financial assets	NGBW	155 729	112 512	402 397	322 382	266 456	459 534	675 923	729 846	966 065
-F.L	*less* Total net acquisition of financial liabilities	-NGFA	−123 258	−96 922	−399 119	−328 734	−261 285	−447 196	−618 831	−646 841	−871 829
B.9f	Net lending (+) / net borrowing (-), from financial account	NYNS	32 471	15 590	3 278	−6 352	5 171	12 338	57 092	83 005	94 236
dB.9f	Statistical discrepancy	NYPE	−13 273	−8 587	1 542	19 407	14 138	8 669	−31 338	−59 450	−66 960
B.9	**Net lending (+) / net borrowing (-), from capital account**	NHFK	**19 198**	**7 003**	**4 820**	**13 055**	**19 309**	**21 007**	**25 754**	**23 555**	**27 276**

1 UK monetary financial institutions

4.2.9 Monetary financial institutions

ESA95 sectors S.121 Central bank & S.122 Other monetary financial institutions. Unconsolidated

£ billion

			1998	1999	2000	2001	2002	2003	2004	2005	2006
IV.3	**FINANCIAL BALANCE SHEET** at end of period										
AF.A	**Financial assets**										
AF.2	Currency and deposits										
AF.21	Currency	NNSY	7.1	9.9	8.4	7.1	7.3	8.2	11.3	10.2	10.0
AF.22	Transferable deposits										
AF.221	Deposits with UK MFIs[1]	NNTA	308.5	305.8	352.3	414.3	504.9	732.0	829.8	999.0	1 280.2
AF.229	Deposits with rest of the world monetary financial institutions	NNTE	666.5	622.4	773.7	803.2	841.1	919.5	1 005.2	1 197.6	1 285.1
AF.29	Other deposits	NNTF	0.1	0.1	0.1	–	–	–	–	–	–
AF.2	Total currency and deposits	NNSX	982.3	938.1	1 134.4	1 224.7	1 353.3	1 659.7	1 846.4	2 206.8	2 575.3
AF.3	Securities other than shares										
AF.331	Short term: money market instruments										
AF.3311	Issued by UK central government	NNTI	3.0	2.8	1.6	8.5	19.3	18.4	16.1	15.8	12.1
AF.3312	Issued by UK local government	NNTM	–	–	–	–	–	–	–	–	–
AF.3315	Issued by UK MFIs[1]	NNTN	104.6	114.5	97.0	103.6	102.5	89.8	90.9	96.1	98.4
AF.3316	Issued by other UK residents	NNTS	0.7	0.7	1.9	1.4	1.1	3.2	1.9	2.9	5.0
AF.3319	Issued by the rest of the world	NNTT	21.6	31.7	34.9	42.1	34.6	42.8	37.2	39.8	42.8
AF.332	Medium (1 to 5 year) and long term (over 5 year) bonds										
AF.3321	Issued by UK central government	NNTV	21.8	15.8	8.6	3.7	−1.0	−6.3	−1.4	−2.8	−7.7
AF.3322	Issued by UK local government	NNTY	–	–	–	–	–	–	–	–	–
AF.3325	Medium term bonds issued by UK MFIs[1]	NNTZ	11.7	16.6	20.7	18.8	18.5	21.1	23.4	25.2	24.5
AF.3326	Other medium & long term bonds issued by UK residents	NNUC	48.8	61.8	71.2	71.8	51.0	66.0	90.1	133.7	189.4
AF.3329	Long term bonds issued by the rest of the world	NNUD	227.8	243.1	288.7	323.4	336.3	327.3	359.7	415.2	479.4
AF.34	Financial derivatives	NNUE	–	–	–	–	–	–	–	–	–
AF.3	Total securities other than shares	NNTG	440.0	487.1	524.6	573.3	562.2	562.2	618.0	726.0	844.0
AF.4	Loans										
AF.41	Short term loans										
AF.411	Loans by UK MFIs[1], excluding loans secured on dwellings & financial leasing	NNUK	766.4	817.4	980.8	1 079.6	1 144.9	1 286.4	1 497.5	1 766.4	1 982.1
AF.42	Long term loans										
AF.421	Direct investment	NNUQ	–	–	–	0.3	–	–	–	–	–
AF.422	Loans secured on dwellings	NNUT	426.9	458.5	493.3	532.1	591.2	653.4	703.2	749.0	795.5
AF.423	Finance leasing	NNUX	2.3	2.7	2.7	2.7	2.7	2.7	2.6	2.6	2.6
AF.424	Other long term loans	LNPN	6.0	6.0	4.8	5.1	3.8	3.7	4.2	4.3	3.4
AF.4	Total loans	NNUI	1 201.6	1 284.6	1 481.6	1 619.7	1 742.6	1 946.1	2 207.5	2 522.4	2 783.6
AF.5	Shares and other equity										
AF.51	Shares and other equity, excluding mutual funds' shares										
AF.514	Quoted UK shares	NNVF	6.9	8.2	11.6	12.6	2.5	8.5	7.4	15.1	21.0
AF.515	Unquoted UK shares	NNVG	28.7	38.3	60.4	66.1	70.7	89.4	108.8	113.8	153.0
AF.517	UK shares and bonds issued by other UK residents	NSQU	–	–	–	–	–	–	–	–	–
AF.519	Shares and other equity issued by the rest of the world	NNVK	22.9	21.1	38.0	35.9	26.4	44.2	87.4	127.6	163.3
AF.52	Mutual funds' shares										
AF.521	UK mutual funds' shares	NNVO	1.3	1.7	1.6	1.3	0.9	1.0	1.2	1.5	1.7
AF.5	Total shares and other equity	NNVA	59.7	69.3	111.7	115.8	100.4	143.2	204.8	258.1	339.1
AF.7	Other accounts receivable	NNVU	0.9	1.0	1.0	1.0	0.8	0.6	0.5	0.2	0.1
AF.A	**Total financial assets**	NNST	2 684.5	2 780.1	3 253.4	3 534.4	3 759.3	4 311.8	4 877.2	5 713.5	6 542.0

1 UK monetary financial institutions

4.2.9 Monetary financial institutions

ESA95 sectors S.121 Central bank & S.122 Other monetary financial institutions. Unconsolidated

continued £ billion

			1998	1999	2000	2001	2002	2003	2004	2005	2006
IV.3	**FINANCIAL BALANCE SHEET** continued at end of period										
AF.L	**Financial liabilities**										
AF.2	Currency and deposits										
AF.21	Currency	NNWC	29.9	35.1	35.6	36.3	37.9	40.8	46.3	47.2	49.0
AF.22	Transferable deposits										
AF.221	Deposits with UK MFIs[1]	NNWE	2 171.2	2 183.4	2 575.8	2 829.2	3 027.1	3 510.9	3 976.2	4 669.8	5 323.1
AF.2	Total currency and deposits	NNWB	2 201.2	2 218.5	2 611.4	2 865.5	3 065.0	3 551.7	4 022.4	4 717.0	5 372.0
AF.3	Securities other than shares										
AF.331	Short term: money market instruments										
AF.3315	Issued by UK MFIs[1]	NNWR	204.3	233.5	265.8	291.0	302.6	282.1	283.2	291.7	327.7
AF.332	Medium (1 to 5 year) and long term (over 5 year) bonds										
AF.3325	Medium term bonds issued by UK MFIs[1]	NNXD	53.3	67.7	74.6	77.6	81.0	107.0	134.7	175.4	205.8
AF.3326	Other medium & long term bonds issued by UK residents	NNXG	52.5	55.3	69.2	79.3	92.2	113.2	95.4	107.3	110.6
AF.34	Financial derivatives	NNXI	–	–0.4	–0.1	0.3	–	–	0.1	0.2	0.7
AF.3	Total securities other than shares	NNWK	310.2	356.1	409.5	448.2	475.8	502.4	513.5	574.7	644.9
AF.4	Loans										
AF.41	Short term loans										
AF.411	Loans by UK MFIs[1], excluding loans secured on dwellings & financial leasing	NNXO	–	–	–	–	–	–	–	–	–
AF.42	Long term loans										
AF.421	Direct investment	NNXU	4.1	2.7	0.6	0.9	0.9	1.2	1.3	1.3	1.3
AF.423	Finance leasing	NNYB	1.3	1.1	1.1	1.2	1.5	1.7	1.8	1.9	2.0
AF.424	Other long-term loans by UK residents	NNYC	–	–	–	–	–	–	–	–	–
AF.4	Total loans	NNXM	5.4	3.9	1.7	2.2	2.4	2.9	3.1	3.2	3.3
AF.5	Shares and other equity										
AF.51	Shares and other equity, excluding mutual funds' shares										
AF.514	Quoted UK shares	NNYJ	84.6	63.4	39.1	28.3	19.4	20.8	14.0	11.3	13.5
AF.515	Unquoted UK shares	NNYK	39.5	58.4	94.2	104.5	109.1	108.0	119.8	124.5	126.8
AF.517	UK shares and bonds issued by other UK residents	NSQV	–	–	–	–	–	–	–	–	–
AF.5	Total shares and other equity	NNYE	124.0	121.8	133.4	132.7	128.5	128.8	133.8	135.7	140.2
AF.7	Other accounts payable	NNYY	4.4	3.9	4.8	4.4	3.8	4.0	4.9	5.7	6.1
AF.L	**Total financial liabilities**	NNVX	2 645.2	2 704.1	3 160.7	3 453.0	3 675.5	4 189.8	4 677.7	5 436.3	6 166.5
BF.90	**Net financial assets / liabilities**										
AF.A	Total financial assets	NNST	2 684.5	2 780.1	3 253.4	3 534.4	3 759.3	4 311.8	4 877.2	5 713.5	6 542.0
-AF.L	*less* Total financial liabilities	-NNVX	–2 645.2	–2 704.1	–3 160.7	–3 453.0	–3 675.5	–4 189.8	–4 677.7	–5 436.3	–6 166.5
BF.90	**Net financial assets (+) / liabilities (-)**	NYOL	39.3	76.0	92.6	81.4	83.8	122.0	199.5	277.1	375.5

1 UK monetary financial institutions

4.3.2 Other financial intermediaries and financial auxiliaries

ESA95 sectors S.123 Other financial intermediaries & S.124 Financial auxiliaries

£ million

			1998	1999	2000	2001	2002	2003	2004
II	**DISTRIBUTION AND USE OF INCOME ACCOUNTS**								
II.1	**PRIMARY DISTRIBUTION OF INCOME ACCOUNT**								
II.1.1	**GENERATION OF INCOME ACCOUNT** before deduction of fixed capital consumption								
	Resources								
B.1g	**Total resources (Gross Value Added)**	NHMH	**1 946**	**6 132**	**7 196**	**54**	**10 405**	**14 393**	**17 364**
	Uses								
D.1	Compensation of employees								
D.11	Wages and salaries	NHED	7 377	7 797	8 432	8 965	9 373	9 181	9 980
D.12	Employers' social contributions	NHEE	1 103	1 221	1 390	1 439	1 520	1 880	2 186
D.1	Total	NHLX	8 480	9 018	9 822	10 404	10 893	11 061	12 166
D.2	Taxes on production and imports, paid								
D.29	Production taxes other than on products	NHLY	475	456	429	528	527	551	570
-D.3	*less* Subsidies, received								
-D.39	Production subsidies other than on products	-NHLF	–	–	–	–	–	–	–
B.2g	Operating surplus, gross	NHBY	–7 009	–3 342	–3 055	–10 878	–1 015	2 781	4 628
B.1g	**Total uses (Gross Value Added)**	NHMH	**1 946**	**6 132**	**7 196**	**54**	**10 405**	**14 393**	**17 364**

4.3.3 Other financial intermediaries and financial auxiliaries

ESA95 sectors S.123 Other financial intermediaries & S.124 Financial auxiliaries

£ million

			1998	1999	2000	2001	2002	2003	2004	2005	2006
II.1.2	**ALLOCATION OF PRIMARY INCOME ACCOUNT**										
	Resources										
B.2g	Operating surplus, gross	NHBY	–7 009	–3 342	–3 055	–10 878	–1 015	2 781	4 628	5 063	1 868
D.4	Property income, received										
D.41	Interest	NHLQ	22 949	20 834	25 763	27 301	22 307	23 354	30 451	41 897	55 821
D.42	Distributed income of corporations	NHLR	6 516	13 526	23 267	20 878	24 771	29 121	33 612	35 828	41 065
D.43	Reinvested earnings on direct foreign investment	NHNS	1 810	2 763	2 849	2 699	2 942	4 004	1 382	2 170	2 529
D.44	Property income attributed to insurance policy-holders	NHMM	8	11	8	9	8	9	9	15	15
D.45	Rent	NHMN	–	–	–	–	–	–	–	–	–
D.4	Total	NHML	31 283	37 134	51 887	50 887	50 028	56 488	65 454	79 910	99 430
-P.119	Adjustment to property income for financial services (FISIM)	-QTFD	7 761	1 571	–1 993	5 966	–575	–5 193	–6 392	–8 010	–9 499
Total	Total resources	NRKX	32 035	35 363	46 839	45 975	48 438	54 076	63 690	76 963	91 799
	Uses										
D.4	Property income										
D.41	Interest	NHLS	26 514	23 783	32 453	33 030	26 936	27 083	33 415	44 242	59 253
D.42	Distributed income of corporations	NHLT	12 190	13 028	15 528	25 626	21 007	21 426	22 304	26 971	32 545
D.43	Reinvested earnings on direct foreign investment	NHNU	–1 570	767	1 485	–2 568	873	991	1 190	1 503	3 145
D.45	Rent	NHMQ	–	–	–	–	–	–	–	–	–
D.4	Total	NHMO	37 134	37 578	49 466	56 088	48 816	49 500	56 909	72 716	94 943
B.5g	**Balance of primary incomes, gross**	NRKZ	**–5 099**	**–2 215**	**–2 627**	**–10 113**	**–378**	**4 576**	**6 781**	**4 247**	**–3 144**
Total	Total uses	NRKX	32 035	35 363	46 839	45 975	48 438	54 076	63 690	76 963	91 799

4.3.4 Other financial intermediaries and financial auxiliaries

ESA95 sectors S.123 Other financial intermediaries & S.124 Financial auxiliaries

£ million

			1998	1999	2000	2001	2002	2003	2004	2005	2006
II.2	**SECONDARY DISTRIBUTION OF INCOME ACCOUNT**										
	Resources										
B.5g	**Balance of primary incomes, gross**	NRKZ	**–5 099**	**–2 215**	**–2 627**	**–10 113**	**–378**	**4 576**	**6 781**	**4 247**	**–3 144**
D.61	Social contributions										
D.612	Imputed social contributions	NHMX	174	166	182	180	195	193	201	165	166
D.7	Other current transfers										
D.72	Non-life insurance claims	NHMT	75	136	127	118	133	148	155	178	192
D.75	Miscellaneous current transfers	NRLD	–	–	–	–	–	–	–	–	–
D.7	Total	NRLE	75	136	127	118	133	148	155	178	192
Total	Total resources	NRLF	–4 850	–1 913	–2 318	–9 815	–50	4 917	7 137	4 590	–2 786
	Uses										
D.5	Current taxes on income, wealth etc.										
D.51	Taxes on income	NHMU	1 174	3 299	4 859	9 100	4 772	1 659	–765	–275	6 483
D.62	Social benefits other than social transfers in kind	NHMW	174	166	182	180	195	193	201	165	166
D.7	Other current transfers										
D.71	Net non-life insurance premiums	NHNA	75	136	127	118	133	148	155	178	192
D.75	Miscellaneous current transfers	NHNQ	22	23	24	24	24	24	24	24	24
D.7	Total	NHMZ	97	159	151	142	157	172	179	202	216
B.6g	**Gross Disposable Income**	NRLG	**–6 295**	**–5 537**	**–7 510**	**–19 237**	**–5 174**	**2 893**	**7 522**	**4 498**	**–9 651**
Total	Total uses	NRLF	–4 850	–1 913	–2 318	–9 815	–50	4 917	7 137	4 590	–2 786

4.3.6 Other financial intermediaries and financial auxiliaries

ESA95 sectors S.123 Other financial intermediaries & S.124 Financial auxiliaries

£ million

			1998	1999	2000	2001	2002	2003	2004	2005	2006
II.4.1	**USE OF DISPOSABLE INCOME ACCOUNT**										
	Resources										
B.6g	**Total resources (Gross Disposable Income)**	NRLG	**–6 295**	**–5 537**	**–7 510**	**–19 237**	**–5 174**	**2 893**	**7 522**	**4 498**	**–9 651**
	Uses										
B.8g	**Total uses (Gross Saving)**	NRLJ	**–6 295**	**–5 537**	**–7 510**	**–19 237**	**–5 174**	**2 893**	**7 522**	**4 498**	**–9 651**

4.3.7 Other financial intermediaries and financial auxiliaries

ESA95 sectors S.123 Other financial intermediaries & S.124 Financial auxiliaries

£ million

			1998	1999	2000	2001	2002	2003	2004	2005	2006
III	**ACCUMULATION ACCOUNTS**										
III.1	**CAPITAL ACCOUNT**										
III.1.1	**CHANGE IN NET WORTH DUE TO SAVING & CAPITAL TRANSFERS ACCOUNT**										
	Changes in liabilities and net worth										
B.8g	**Gross Saving**	NRLJ	**–6 295**	**–5 537**	**–7 510**	**–19 237**	**–5 174**	**2 893**	**7 522**	**4 498**	**–9 651**
D.9	Capital transfers receivable										
D.92	Investment grants	NHNG	–	–	–	–	–	–	–	–	–
D.99	Other capital transfers	NHNH	–	–	–	–	–	–	–	–	–
D.9	Total	NHNF	–	–	–	–	–	–	–	–	–
-D.9	*less* Capital transfers payable										
-D.91	Capital taxes	-NRXX	–	–	–	–	–	–	–	–	–
-D.99	Other capital transfers	-NHLH	–	–	–	–	–	–	–	–	..
-D.9	Total	-NHNI	–	–	–	–	–	–	–	–	–
B.10.1g	Total change in liabilities and net worth	NRMI	–6 295	–5 537	–7 510	–19 237	–5 174	2 893	7 522	4 498	–9 651
	Changes in assets										
B.10.1g	Change in net worth due to saving and capital transfers before deduction of fixed capital consumption	NRMI	–6 295	–5 537	–7 510	–19 237	–5 174	2 893	7 522	4 498	–9 651
III.1.2	**ACQUISITION OF NON-FINANCIAL ASSETS ACCOUNT**										
B.10.1g	**Total changes in liabilities and net worth due to saving and capital transfers**	NRMI	–6 295	–5 537	–7 510	–19 237	–5 174	2 893	7 522	4 498	–9 651
	Changes in assets										
P.5	Gross capital formation										
P.51	Gross fixed capital formation	NHLP	2 315	2 298	2 310	1 546	1 379	1 162	1 640	1 698	1 827
P.52	Changes in inventories	NHLO	–	–	–	–	–	–	–	–	–
P.53	Acquisitions less disposals of valuables	NHNN	–	–	–	–	–	–	–	–	–
P.5	Total	NHNM	2 315	2 298	2 310	1 546	1 379	1 162	1 640	1 698	1 827
K.2	Acquisitions less disposals of non-produced non-financial assets	NHNO	33	–	–	–	6	11	18	20	23
B.9	**Net lending (+) / net borrowing (-)**	NHLW	**–8 643**	**–7 835**	**–9 820**	**–20 783**	**–6 559**	**1 720**	**5 864**	**2 780**	**–11 501**
Total	Total change in assets	NRMI	–6 295	–5 537	–7 510	–19 237	–5 174	2 893	7 522	4 498	–9 651

4.3.8 Other financial intermediaries and financial auxiliaries

ESA95 sectors S.123 and S.124 Unconsolidated

£ million

			1998	1999	2000	2001	2002	2003	2004	2005	2006
III.2	**FINANCIAL ACCOUNT**										
F.A	**Net acquisition of financial assets**										
F.2	Currency and deposits										
F.21	Currency	NFJD	–	–	–	–	–	–	–	–	–
F.22	Transferable deposits										
F.2211	Sterling deposits with UK banks	NFJG	12 738	–11 801	17 215	11 739	6 497	3 838	25 432	71 174	71 031
F.2212	Foreign currency deposits with UK banks	NFJH	–1 345	2 615	20 593	28 198	–2 991	26 533	16 500	29 709	41 256
F.2213	Sterling deposits with UK building societies	NFJI	300	454	141	326	102	1 298	177	255	153
F.229	Deposits with rest of the world monetary financial institutions	NFJJ	–6 271	49 820	51 040	61 164	–8 606	57 873	45 842	172 891	56 000
F.29	Other deposits	NFJK	–	–	2 691	–1 567	1 265	–1 063	1 392	1 391	–2 083
F.2	Total currency and deposits	NFJC	5 422	41 088	91 680	99 860	–3 733	88 479	89 343	275 420	166 357
F.3	Securities other than shares										
F.331	Short term: money market instruments										
F.3311	Issued by UK central government	NFJN	281	–650	–59	1 071	–413	2 492	1 075	–2 090	1 150
F.3312	Issued by UK local government	NFJR	–6	–	–	–	–	–	–	–	–
F.3315	Issued by UK monetary financial institutions	NFJS	7 848	6 431	2 651	–6 807	4 125	–1 035	–4 474	472	1 991
F.3316	Issued by other UK residents	NFJX	1 316	191	486	–1 037	–429	118	341	–102	–48
F.3319	Issued by the rest of the world	NFJY	–372	3 579	–4 144	2 093	–2 018	1 911	665	–929	4 290
F.332	Medium (1 to 5 year) and long term (over 5 year) bonds										
F.3321	Issued by UK central government	NFKA	3 039	2 229	9 854	–5 382	4 934	2 031	238	3 000	14 281
F.3322	Issued by UK local government	NFKD	25	16	28	22	39	9	8	–	–
F.3325	Medium term bonds issued by UK MFIs[1]	NFKE	298	604	–422	576	839	2 191	2 189	3 312	3 565
F.3326	Other medium & long term bonds issued by UK residents	NFKH	4 899	12 475	15 573	11 126	4 064	15 705	8 636	9 623	–4 368
F.3329	Long term bonds issued by the rest of the world	NFKI	–32 320	–27 709	–1 307	–18 168	–464	12 422	23 431	22 850	41 427
F.34	Financial derivatives	NFKJ	–	–	–	–	–	–	–	–	–
F.3	Total securities other than shares	NFJL	–14 992	–2 834	22 660	–16 506	10 677	35 844	32 109	36 136	62 288
F.4	Loans										
F.42	Long term loans										
F.421	Direct investment	NFKV	322	493	253	1 142	3 705	–2 731	3 255	2 411	240
F.422	Loans secured on dwellings	NFKY	2 395	6 298	13 608	16 256	23 641	35 070	39 239	43 823	63 435
F.423	Finance leasing	NFLC	127	–303	–251	321	750	745	722	565	670
F.424	Other long-term loans by UK residents	NFLD	2 479	3 070	5	2 776	4 253	4 978	2 550	9 997	5 134
F.4	Total loans	NFKN	5 323	9 558	13 615	20 495	32 349	38 062	45 766	56 796	69 479
F.5	Shares and other equity										
F.51	Shares and other equity, excluding mutual funds' shares										
F.514	Quoted UK shares	NFLK	7 421	4 594	11 328	26 271	9 361	14 356	22 156	–8 929	4 209
F.515	Unquoted UK shares	NFLL	–2 973	–3 270	9 711	–2 047	–1 338	–579	–2 529	1 842	–635
F.517	UK shares and bonds issued by other UK residents	NSPJ	–	–	–	–	–	–	–	–	–
F.519	Shares and other equity issued by the rest of the world	NFLP	6 314	20 549	32 127	30 906	–5 177	13 651	13 185	–6 681	–3 213
F.52	Mutual funds' shares										
F.521	UK mutual funds' shares	NFLT	–6	29	118	–12	41	16	76	143	131
F.5	Total shares and other equity	NFLF	10 756	21 902	53 284	55 118	2 887	27 444	32 888	–13 625	492
F.6	Insurance technical reserves										
F.62	Prepayments of insurance premiums and reserves for outstanding claims	NFLY	–4	–22	15	–20	20	10	48	52	40
F.7	Other accounts receivable	NFLZ	638	706	657	393	618	605	644	643	645
F.A	**Total net acquisition of financial assets**	NFIY	7 143	70 398	181 911	159 340	42 818	190 444	200 798	355 422	299 301

1 UK monetary financial institutions

4.3.8 Other financial intermediaries and financial auxiliaries

ESA95 sectors S.123 and S.124 Unconsolidated

continued £ million

			1998	1999	2000	2001	2002	2003	2004	2005	2006
III.2	**FINANCIAL ACCOUNT** continued										
F.L	**Net acquisition of financial liabilities**										
F.2	Currency and deposits	NFMG	–	–	2 919	–2 578	476	–536	18	612	–147
F.3	Securities other than shares										
F.331	Short term: money market instruments										
F.3316	Issued by UK residents other than monetary financial institutions and government	NFNB	–93	31	–16	–	267	–567	704	239	455
F.332	Medium (1 to 5 year) and long term (over 5 year) bonds										
F.3326	Other medium & long term bonds issued by UK residents institutions and government	NFNL	2 349	17 162	24 073	23 255	20 662	53 255	70 726	83 767	117 570
F.34	Financial derivatives	NFNN	–	–	–	–	–	–	–	–	–
F.3	Total securities other than shares	NFMP	2 256	17 193	24 057	23 255	20 929	52 688	71 430	84 006	118 025
F.4	Loans										
F.41	Short term loans										
F.4111	Sterling loans by UK banks	NFNU	21 479	13 389	21 300	4 045	9 292	17 059	28 823	32 242	48 228
F.4112	Foreign currency loans by the UK banks	NFNV	–22 841	–3 626	30 936	27 031	17 208	41 429	33 334	18 057	62 328
F.4113	Sterling loans by building societies	NFNW	1 890	1 944	2 216	1 598	1 892	4 937	3 832	6 683	8 466
F.419	Loans by rest of the world monetary financial institutions	NFNX	14 637	31 058	64 327	64 513	–37 164	38 226	49 247	216 607	31 685
F.42	Long term loans										
F.421	Direct investment	NFNZ	909	1 283	601	11 060	6 554	2 200	3 973	–6 990	534
F.423	Finance leasing	NFOG	35	–155	–66	128	136	104	95	71	81
F.424	Other long-term loans by UK residents	NFOH	–3 309	4 184	18 442	7 582	2 042	1 114	5 869	21 771	41 463
F.429	Other long-term loans by the rest of the world	NFOI	–115	46	–30	6	–21	–42	10	29	–
F.4	Total loans	NFNR	12 685	48 123	137 726	115 963	–61	105 027	125 183	288 470	192 785
F.5	Shares and other equity										
F.51	Shares and other equity, excluding mutual funds' shares										
F.514	Quoted UK shares	NFOO	6 274	2 355	6 750	10 451	–556	10 829	8 417	8 423	16 399
F.515	Unquoted UK shares	NFOP	4 485	7 823	17 287	11 253	6 772	12 223	18 536	23 082	34 484
F.517	UK shares and bonds issued by other UK residents	NSPK	–	–	–	–	–	–	–	–	–
F.52	Mutual funds' shares										
F.521	UK mutual funds' shares	NFOX	10 976	14 719	14 102	9 338	6 259	8 212	3 489	8 300	15 156
F.5	Total shares and other equity	NFOJ	21 735	24 897	38 139	31 042	12 475	31 264	30 442	39 805	66 039
F.7	Other accounts payable	NFPD	–191	33	22	–2	500	–614	–169	153	17
F.L	**Total net acquisition of financial liabilities**	NFMC	36 485	90 246	202 863	167 680	34 319	187 829	226 904	413 046	376 719
B.9	**Net lending / borrowing**										
F.A	Total net acquisition of financial assets	NFIY	7 143	70 398	181 911	159 340	42 818	190 444	200 798	355 422	299 301
-F.L	*less* Total net acquisition of financial liabilities	-NFMC	–36 485	–90 246	–202 863	–167 680	–34 319	–187 829	–226 904	–413 046	–376 719
B.9f	Net lending (+) / net borrowing (-), from financial account	NYNM	–29 342	–19 848	–20 952	–8 340	8 499	2 615	–26 106	–57 624	–77 418
dB.9f	Statistical discrepancy	NYOY	20 699	12 013	11 132	–12 443	–15 058	–895	31 970	60 404	65 917
B.9	**Net lending (+) / net borrowing (-), from capital account**	NHLW	**–8 643**	**–7 835**	**–9 820**	**–20 783**	**–6 559**	**1 720**	**5 864**	**2 780**	**–11 501**

4.3.9 Other financial intermediaries and financial auxiliaries

ESA95 sectors S.123 and S.124 Unconsolidated

£ billion

			1998	1999	2000	2001	2002	2003	2004	2005	2006
IV.3	**FINANCIAL BALANCE SHEET** at end of period										
AF.A	**Financial assets**										
AF.2	Currency and deposits										
AF.21	Currency	NLPM	0.1	0.1	0.1	0.1	0.1	0.1	0.1	0.1	0.1
AF.22	Transferable deposits										
AF.2211	Sterling deposits with UK banks	NLPP	86.6	75.2	94.4	106.6	112.2	110.8	133.4	202.7	272.9
AF.2212	Foreign currency deposits with UK banks	NLPQ	66.5	64.1	87.6	115.9	105.2	129.8	145.3	176.9	206.8
AF.2213	Sterling deposits with UK building societies	NLPR	1.1	1.4	0.8	1.1	1.2	2.5	2.7	2.9	3.1
AF.229	Deposits with rest of the world monetary financial institutions	NLPS	123.0	167.0	223.1	279.7	264.0	315.8	348.1	534.7	545.0
AF.29	Other deposits	NLPT	–	–	2.7	1.1	1.8	0.8	2.2	3.5	1.5
AF.2	Total currency and deposits	NLPL	277.2	307.7	408.7	504.6	484.5	559.8	631.7	920.8	1 029.3
AF.3	Securities other than shares										
AF.331	Short term: money market instruments										
AF.3311	Issued by UK central government	NLPW	–	–	–	1.7	0.9	3.1	4.2	1.9	2.9
AF.3312	Issued by UK local government	NLQA	–	–	–	–	–	–	–	–	–
AF.3315	Issued by UK monetary financial institutions	NLQB	20.5	26.6	29.2	22.8	27.1	25.6	22.3	23.1	24.3
AF.3316	Issued by other UK residents	NLQG	2.0	2.9	2.7	1.4	0.9	0.7	1.3	1.1	1.0
AF.3319	Issued by the rest of the world	NLQH	1.9	7.5	3.8	6.0	5.6	7.8	8.5	7.8	11.1
AF.332	Medium (1 to 5 year) and long term (over 5 year) bonds										
AF.3321	Issued by UK central government	NLQJ	16.6	18.1	27.1	24.2	29.8	33.3	31.1	46.9	58.0
AF.3322	Issued by UK local government	NLQM	–	–	–	–	–	–	–	–	–
AF.3325	Medium term bonds issued by UK MFIs[1]	NLQN	3.4	4.6	3.8	4.3	5.0	8.2	10.2	13.8	16.6
AF.3326	Other medium & long term bonds issued by UK residents	NLQQ	18.9	29.3	40.2	51.6	56.0	69.7	79.5	89.9	96.1
AF.3329	Long term bonds issued by the rest of the world	NLQR	72.8	51.7	52.1	43.3	38.8	50.3	71.8	104.3	131.2
AF.34	Financial derivatives	NLQS	–	–	–	–	–	–	–	–	–
AF.3	Total securities other than shares	NLPU	136.2	140.8	159.0	155.3	164.0	198.7	228.9	288.7	341.2
AF.4	Loans										
AF.42	Long term loans										
AF.421	Direct investment	NLRE	1.7	2.1	2.2	3.5	7.1	11.3	22.3	20.9	21.2
AF.422	Loans secured on dwellings	NLRH	26.7	32.6	39.8	56.1	76.1	117.1	170.1	214.1	279.4
AF.423	Finance leasing	NLRL	20.9	20.6	20.7	21.0	21.8	22.5	23.2	23.8	24.5
AF.424	Other long-term loans by UK residents	NLRM	8.8	6.4	7.6	4.9	4.8	6.3	3.0	1.3	5.3
AF.4	Total loans	NLQW	58.2	61.7	70.3	85.6	109.8	157.2	218.7	260.0	330.4
AF.5	Shares and other equity										
AF.51	Shares and other equity, excluding mutual funds' shares										
AF.514	Quoted UK shares	NLRT	109.5	166.6	146.2	201.7	166.2	222.8	259.9	258.0	291.3
AF.515	Unquoted UK shares	NLRU	53.6	74.1	112.9	145.9	160.0	170.6	191.7	214.7	235.1
AF.517	UK shares and bonds issued by other UK residents	NSOH	–	–	–	–	–	–	–	–	–
AF.519	Shares and other equity issued by the rest of the world	NLRY	122.7	159.6	184.4	173.1	142.7	169.9	183.2	206.0	221.2
AF.52	Mutual funds' shares										
AF.521	UK mutual funds' shares	NLSC	3.6	4.7	4.4	3.4	2.4	2.9	3.2	4.2	4.7
AF.5	Total shares and other equity	NLRO	289.5	405.0	447.9	524.2	471.3	566.3	638.1	682.9	752.4
AF.6	Insurance technical reserves										
AF.62	Prepayments of insurance premiums and reserves for outstanding claims	NLSH	0.4	0.8	0.7	0.6	0.7	0.8	0.9	0.9	1.0
AF.7	Other accounts receivable	NLSI	8.5	9.8	10.9	11.8	13.2	14.8	17.3	20.0	20.7
AF.A	**Total financial assets**	NLPH	770.0	925.8	1 097.5	1 282.1	1 243.5	1 497.7	1 735.7	2 173.3	2 475.0

1 UK monetary financial institutions

4.3.9 Other financial intermediaries and financial auxiliaries

ESA95 sectors S.123 and S.124 Unconsolidated

continued £ billion

			1998	1999	2000	2001	2002	2003	2004	2005	2006
IV.3	**FINANCIAL BALANCE SHEET** continued at end of period										
AF.L	**Financial liabilities**										
AF.2	Currency and deposits	NLSP	–	–	2.9	0.3	0.8	0.3	0.3	1.8	1.6
AF.3	Securities other than shares										
AF.331	Short term: money market instruments										
AF.3316	Issued by UK residents other than monetary financial institutions and government	NLTK	8.1	15.6	21.4	23.3	21.1	19.4	19.6	26.2	41.8
AF.332	Medium (1 to 5 year) and long term (over 5 year) bonds										
AF.3326	Other medium & long term bonds issued by UK residents institutions and government	NLTU	91.7	115.7	138.2	165.2	189.4	243.6	344.4	451.6	525.4
AF.34	Financial derivatives	NLTW	–	–	–	–	–	–	–	–	–
AF.3	Total securities other than shares	NLSY	99.8	131.3	159.6	188.5	210.5	263.1	364.1	477.8	567.2
AF.4	Loans										
AF.41	Short term loans										
AF.4111	Sterling loans by UK banks	NLUD	141.8	155.1	166.7	167.9	174.4	194.8	236.7	267.0	316.9
AF.4112	Foreign currency loans by UK banks	NLUE	89.2	80.9	121.1	147.6	165.6	204.2	228.1	256.2	294.0
AF.4113	Sterling loans by UK building societies	NLUF	10.8	9.4	8.4	9.8	11.3	16.4	19.8	26.5	32.8
AF.419	Loans by rest of the world monetary financial institutions	NLUG	209.1	248.6	299.4	359.9	325.4	358.7	398.2	630.3	615.6
AF.42	Long term loans										
AF.421	Direct investment	NLUI	5.1	6.6	8.1	20.0	25.6	29.9	42.9	39.1	39.7
AF.423	Finance leasing	NLUP	1.3	1.2	1.1	1.3	1.4	1.5	1.6	1.7	1.7
AF.424	Other long-term loans by UK residents	NLUQ	10.9	13.5	13.3	13.9	14.6	15.8	19.7	26.2	36.3
AF.429	Other long-term loans by the rest of the world	NLUR	0.7	0.5	0.5	0.5	0.5	0.5	0.5	0.5	0.5
AF.4	Total loans	NLUA	468.9	515.8	618.6	720.8	718.7	821.7	947.4	1 247.4	1 337.6
AF.5	Shares and other equity										
AF.51	Shares and other equity, excluding mutual funds' shares										
AF.514	Quoted UK shares	NLUX	155.5	220.5	270.7	275.0	220.8	279.3	311.7	341.0	399.2
AF.515	Unquoted UK shares	NLUY	86.6	106.2	133.9	142.5	135.0	154.5	172.2	202.8	235.9
AF.517	UK shares and bonds issued by other UK residents	NSOI	–	–	–	–	–	–	–	–	–
AF.52	Mutual funds' shares										
AF.521	UK mutual funds' shares	NLVG	217.9	299.0	304.5	268.2	215.8	266.3	303.9	385.0	452.4
AF.5	Total shares and other equity	NLUS	459.9	625.8	709.1	685.7	571.6	700.0	787.9	928.8	1 087.6
AF.7	Other accounts payable	NLVM	0.9	0.9	0.9	0.7	1.8	2.3	2.2	2.1	2.2
AF.L	**Total financial liabilities**	NLSL	1 029.5	1 273.8	1 491.1	1 596.1	1 503.4	1 787.3	2 101.9	2 657.8	2 996.2
BF.90	**Net financial assets / liabilities**										
AF.A	Total financial assets	NLPH	770.0	925.8	1 097.5	1 282.1	1 243.5	1 497.7	1 735.7	2 173.3	2 475.0
-AF.L	*less* Total financial liabilities	-NLSL	–1 029.5	–1 273.8	–1 491.1	–1 596.1	–1 503.4	–1 787.3	–2 101.9	–2 657.8	–2 996.2
BF.90	**Net financial assets (+) / liabilities (-)**	NYOF	–259.5	–348.0	–393.6	–314.0	–259.9	–289.7	–366.1	–484.5	–521.2

4.4.2 Insurance corporations and pension funds
ESA95 sector S.125

£ million

			1998	1999	2000	2001	2002	2003	2004
II	**DISTRIBUTION AND USE OF INCOME ACCOUNTS**								
II.1	**PRIMARY DISTRIBUTION OF INCOME ACCOUNT**								
II.1.1	**GENERATION OF INCOME ACCOUNT**								
	Resources								
B.1g	**Total resources (Gross Value Added)**	NRHH	**10 700**	**12 843**	**10 191**	**10 167**	**17 755**	**20 604**	**17 756**
	Uses								
D.1	Compensation of employees								
D.11	Wages and salaries	NHEJ	5 741	5 990	6 691	6 907	6 937	7 176	6 471
D.12	Employers' social contributions	NHEL	731	792	899	930	971	1 164	1 110
D.1	Total	NSCV	6 472	6 782	7 590	7 837	7 908	8 340	7 581
D.2	Taxes on production and imports, paid								
D.29	Production taxes other than on products	NHOS	230	251	310	324	337	346	353
-D.3	*less* Subsidies, received								
-D.39	Production subsidies other than on products	-NHNZ	–	–	–	–	–	–	–
B.2g	Operating surplus, gross	NHBZ	3 998	5 810	2 291	2 006	9 510	11 918	9 822
B.1g	**Total uses (Gross Value Added)**	NRHH	**10 700**	**12 843**	**10 191**	**10 167**	**17 755**	**20 604**	**17 756**

4.4.3 Insurance corporations and pension funds
ESA95 sector S.125

continued £ million

			1998	1999	2000	2001	2002	2003	2004	2005	2006
II.1.2	**ALLOCATION OF PRIMARY INCOME ACCOUNT**										
	Resources										
B.2g	Operating surplus, gross	NHBZ	3 998	5 810	2 291	2 006	9 510	11 918	9 822	4 423	8 633
D.4	Property income, received										
D.41	Interest	NHOK	25 540	22 844	25 646	23 784	23 102	24 728	27 407	26 997	27 600
D.42	Distributed income of corporations	NHOL	26 653	25 081	19 135	23 229	21 840	20 665	21 275	24 292	27 554
D.43	Reinvested earnings on direct foreign investment	NHQM	535	976	542	–899	–75	1 572	2 699	3 107	2 437
D.44	Property income attributed to insurance policy-holders	NHPG	16	28	19	19	18	24	22	34	35
D.45	Rent	NHPH	30	29	29	29	30	30	31	31	32
D.4	Total	NHPF	52 774	48 958	45 371	46 162	44 915	47 019	51 434	54 461	57 658
Total	Total resources	NRMN	56 772	54 768	47 662	48 168	54 425	58 937	61 256	58 884	66 291
	Uses										
D.4	Property income										
D.41	Interest	NHOM	988	888	1 213	1 127	1 174	1 055	1 540	1 956	2 143
D.42	Distributed income of corporations	NHON	4 726	3 170	4 249	4 046	2 643	2 956	4 034	3 630	4 546
D.43	Reinvested earnings on direct foreign investment	NHQO	295	78	44	–1 120	–55	535	920	868	1 773
D.44	Property income attributed to insurance policy-holders	NQCG	57 985	58 026	57 455	57 795	56 652	56 703	56 150	65 497	69 905
D.45	Rent	NHPK	–	–	–	–	–	–	–	–	–
D.4	Total	NHPI	63 994	62 162	62 961	61 848	60 414	61 249	62 644	71 951	78 367
B.5g	**Balance of primary incomes, gross**	NRMO	**–7 222**	**–7 394**	**–15 299**	**–13 680**	**–5 989**	**–2 312**	**–1 388**	**–13 067**	**–12 076**
Total	Total uses	NRMN	56 772	54 768	47 662	48 168	54 425	58 937	61 256	58 884	66 291

4.4.4 Insurance corporations and pension funds

ESA95 sector S.125

£ million

			1998	1999	2000	2001	2002	2003	2004	2005	2006
II.2	**SECONDARY DISTRIBUTION OF INCOME ACCOUNT**										
	Resources										
B.5g	**Balance of primary incomes, gross**	NRMO	**–7 222**	**–7 394**	**–15 299**	**–13 680**	**–5 989**	**–2 312**	**–1 388**	**–13 067**	**–12 076**
D.61	Social contributions										
D.611	Actual social contributions										
D.6111	Employers' actual contributions	NSAR	17 545	19 128	20 891	21 836	26 025	32 504	37 745	43 093	47 992
D.6112	Employees social contributions	NSAS	29 626	30 878	31 568	31 933	32 967	32 158	31 462	36 509	39 850
D.6113	Social contributions by the self-employed	NSAT	–	–	–	–	–	–	–	–	–
D.611	Total	NSCN	47 171	50 006	52 459	53 769	58 992	64 662	69 207	79 602	87 842
D.612	Imputed social contributions	NHPR	114	110	118	116	125	120	102	100	89
D.61	Total	NRMP	47 285	50 116	52 577	53 885	59 117	64 782	69 309	79 702	87 931
D.7	Other current transfers										
D.71	Net non-life insurance premiums	NSCT	25 059	22 613	25 235	25 477	26 631	24 625	25 867	31 661	31 957
D.72	Non-life insurance claims	NHPN	176	341	354	284	319	369	363	417	447
D.7	Total	NRMR	25 235	22 954	25 589	25 761	26 950	24 994	26 230	32 078	32 404
Total	Total resources	NRMS	65 298	65 676	62 867	65 966	80 078	87 464	94 151	98 713	108 259
	Uses										
D.5	Current taxes on income, wealth, etc.										
D.51	Taxes on income	NHPO	3 297	2 687	1 614	–1 377	–2 076	1 724	3 588	5 042	3 703
D.62	Social benefits other than social transfers in kind										
D.622	Private funded social benefits	SBDW	33 129	35 992	38 310	37 736	41 209	43 297	44 118	48 459	52 141
D.623	Unfunded employee social benefits	NHPR	114	110	118	116	125	120	102	100	89
D.62	Total	NHPQ	33 243	36 102	38 428	37 852	41 334	43 417	44 220	48 559	52 230
D.7	Other current transfers										
D.71	Net non-life insurance premiums	NHPU	176	341	354	284	319	369	363	417	447
D.72	Non-life insurance claims	NSCS	25 059	22 613	25 235	25 477	26 631	24 625	25 867	31 661	31 957
D.75	Miscellaneous current transfers	NHQK	–	–	–	–	–	–	–	–	–
D.7	Total	NHPT	25 235	22 954	25 589	25 761	26 950	24 994	26 230	32 078	32 404
B.6g	**Gross Disposable Income**	NRMT	**3 523**	**3 933**	**–2 764**	**3 730**	**13 870**	**17 329**	**20 113**	**13 034**	**19 922**
Total	Total uses	NRMS	65 298	65 676	62 867	65 966	80 078	87 464	94 151	98 713	108 259

4.4.6 Insurance corporations and pension funds

ESA95 sector S.125

£ million

			1998	1999	2000	2001	2002	2003	2004	2005	2006
II.4.1	**USE OF DISPOSABLE INCOME ACCOUNT**										
	Resources										
B.6g	**Total resources (Gross Disposable Income)**	NRMT	**3 523**	**3 933**	**–2 764**	**3 730**	**13 870**	**17 329**	**20 113**	**13 034**	**19 922**
	Uses										
D.8	Adjustment for the change in net equity of households in pension funds	NRYH	14 042	14 014	14 160	16 036	17 782	21 365	25 089	31 143	35 701
B.8g	**Gross Saving**	NRMV	**–10 519**	**–10 081**	**–16 924**	**–12 306**	**–3 912**	**–4 036**	**–4 976**	**–18 109**	**–15 779**
B.6g	**Total uses (Gross Disposable Income)**	NRMT	**3 523**	**3 933**	**–2 764**	**3 730**	**13 870**	**17 329**	**20 113**	**13 034**	**19 922**

4.4.7 Insurance corporations and pension funds

ESA95 sector S.125

£ million

			1998	1999	2000	2001	2002	2003	2004	2005	2006
III	**ACCUMULATION ACCOUNTS**										
III.1	**CAPITAL ACCOUNT**										
III.1.1	**CHANGE IN NET WORTH DUE TO SAVING & CAPITAL TRANSFERS**										
	Changes in liabilities and net worth										
B.8g	**Gross Saving**	NRMV	**–10 519**	**–10 081**	**–16 924**	**–12 306**	**–3 912**	**–4 036**	**–4 976**	**–18 109**	**–15 779**
D.9	Capital transfers receivable										
D.92	Investment grants	NHQA	–	–	–	–	–	–	–	–	–
D.99	Other capital transfers	NHQB	–	–	–	412	412	391	328	321	446
D.9	Total	NHPZ	–	–	–	412	412	391	328	321	446
-D.9	*less* Capital transfers payable										
-D.91	Capital taxes	-NHNW	–	–	–	–	–	–	–	–	–
-D.99	Other capital transfers	-NHOB	–	–	–	–412	–412	–391	–328	–321	–446
-D.9	Total	-NHQD	–	–	–	–412	–412	–391	–328	–321	–446
B.10.1g	Total change in liabilities and net worth	NRYI	–10 519	–10 081	–16 924	–12 306	–3 912	–4 036	–4 976	–18 109	–15 779
	Changes in assets										
B.10.1g	Change in net worth due to saving and capital transfers before deduction of fixed capital consumption	NRYI	–10 519	–10 081	–16 924	–12 306	–3 912	–4 036	–4 976	–18 109	–15 779
III.1.2	**ACQUISITION OF NON-FINANCIAL ASSETS ACCOUNT**										
B.10.1g	**Total changes in liabilities and net worth due to saving and capital transfers**	NRYI	–10 519	–10 081	–16 924	–12 306	–3 912	–4 036	–4 976	–18 109	–15 779
	Changes in assets										
P.5	Gross capital formation										
P.51	Gross fixed capital formation	NHOJ	5 111	3 337	5 705	2 809	1 936	–464	360	378	1 134
P.52	Changes in inventories	NHOI	–	–	–	–	–	–	–	–	–
P.53	Acquisitions less disposals of valuables	NHQH	48	–28	–127	–	–74	–166	–173	–299	–158
P.5	Total	NHQG	5 159	3 309	5 578	2 809	1 862	–630	187	79	976
K.2	Acquisitions less disposals of non-produced non-financial assets	NHQI	–37	–37	–45	–43	–42	–14	–24	–21	–14
B.9	**Net lending (+) / net borrowing (-)**	NHOQ	**–15 641**	**–13 353**	**–22 457**	**–15 072**	**–5 732**	**–3 392**	**–5 139**	**–18 167**	**–16 741**
Total	Total change in assets	NRYI	–10 519	–10 081	–16 924	–12 306	–3 912	–4 036	–4 976	–18 109	–15 779

4.4.8 Insurance corporations and pension funds

ESA95 sector S.125. Unconsolidated

£ million

			1998	1999	2000	2001	2002	2003	2004	2005	2006
III.2	**FINANCIAL ACCOUNT**										
F.A	**Net acquisition of financial assets**										
F.2	Currency and deposits										
F.22	Transferable deposits										
F.2211	Sterling deposits with UK banks	NBSK	4 851	−3 274	6 645	−2 059	−2 667	−2 258	6 677	−4 196	4 853
F.2213	Sterling deposits with UK building societies	NBSM	−312	1 154	−76	384	357	−266	327	−53	453
F.229	Deposits with rest of the world monetary financial institutions	NBSN	−108	1 312	2 760	1 358	2 102	4 840	4 666	3 040	3 152
F.29	Other deposits	NBSO	–	–	–	–	–	–	–	–	–
F.2	Total currency and deposits	NBSG	4 431	−808	9 329	−317	−208	2 316	11 670	−1 209	8 458
F.3	Securities other than shares										
F.331	Short term: money market instruments										
F.3311	Issued by UK central government	NBSR	285	−530	169	376	266	−359	376	−537	224
F.3315	Issued by UK monetary financial institutions	NBSW	716	1 149	788	3 554	2 683	3 102	2 006	−1 703	663
F.3316	Issued by other UK residents	NBTB	915	901	75	461	51	129	−1 934	3 445	−1 242
F.3319	Issued by the rest of the world	NBTC	−1 558	243	−106	−159	333	70	602	1 419	−5
F.332	Medium (1 to 5 year) and long term (over 5 year) bonds										
F.3321	Issued by UK central government	NBTE	−107	3 076	−15 073	−5 323	5 252	23 289	17 584	8 136	19 652
F.3322	Issued by UK local government	NBTH	−62	−52	32	−69	20	5	−100	139	269
F.33251	Medium term bonds issued by UK banks	NBTJ	619	1 443	−1 261	738	1 329	5 191	5 451	8 310	10 591
F.33252	Medium term bonds issued by UK building societies	NBTK	137	413	−11	−179	1 113	1 248	921	1 448	−65
F.3326	Other medium & long term bonds issued by UK residents	NBTL	14 111	18 760	32 137	25 747	21 745	14 128	11 837	842	4 242
F.3329	Long term bonds issued by the rest of the world	NBTM	15 154	9 986	10 608	9 196	4 829	996	4 056	6 241	21 520
F.3	Total securities other than shares	NBSP	30 210	35 389	27 358	34 342	37 621	47 799	40 799	27 740	55 849
F.4	Loans										
F.42	Long term loans										
F.421	Direct investment	NBTZ	66	−30	1 234	1 214	1 040	1 969	1 551	1 608	−586
F.422	Loans secured on dwellings	NBUC	114	−646	168	43	−165	209	34	−428	−220
F.424	Other long-term loans by UK residents	NBUH	2 379	16 280	9 158	−1 530	1 562	6 229	7 768	9 276	5 187
F.4	Total loans	NBTR	2 559	15 604	10 560	−273	2 437	8 407	9 353	10 456	4 381
F.5	Shares and other equity										
F.51	Shares and other equity, excluding mutual funds' shares										
F.514	Quoted UK shares	NBUO	−9 237	−13 019	16 891	−24 161	−15 545	−19 791	−18 965	−46 103	−21 943
F.515	Unquoted UK shares	NBUP	237	−343	−4 717	−1 591	−890	−1 443	−560	−887	−661
F.517	UK shares and bonds issued by other UK residents	NSPC	–	–	–	–	–	–	–	–	–
F.519	Shares and other equity issued by the rest of the world	NBUT	3 747	2 497	−15 768	17 770	19 519	2 511	16 091	31 417	11 786
F.52	Mutual funds' shares										
F.521	UK mutual funds' shares	NBUX	2 430	5 597	7 100	1 921	3 321	881	287	11 652	10 816
F.5	Total shares and other equity	NBUJ	−2 823	−5 268	3 506	−6 061	6 405	−17 842	−3 147	−3 921	−2
F.6	Insurance technical reserves										
F.62	Prepayments of insurance premiums and reserves for outstanding claims	NBVC	−3	−24	21	−21	22	10	54	55	44
F.7	Other accounts receivable	NBVD	3 733	2 594	−3 151	8 686	15 259	7 977	3 770	2 766	1 944
F.A	**Total net acquisition of financial assets**	NBSC	38 107	47 487	47 623	36 356	61 536	48 667	62 499	35 887	70 674

4.4.8 Insurance corporations and pension funds

ESA95 sector S.125. Unconsolidated

continued £ million

			1998	1999	2000	2001	2002	2003	2004	2005	2006
III.2	**FINANCIAL ACCOUNT** continued										
F.L	**Net acquisition of financial liabilities**										
F.3	Securities other than shares										
F.332	Medium (1 to 5 year) and long term (over 5 year) bonds										
F.3326	Other medium & long term bonds issued by UK residents institutions and government	NBWP	450	1 126	219	2 484	339	2 347	1 595	1 232	61
F.3	Total securities other than shares	NBVT	450	1 126	219	2 484	339	2 347	1 595	1 232	61
F.4	Loans										
F.41	Short term loans										
F.411	Loans by UK monetary financial institutions, excluding loans secured on dwellings & financial leasing	NBWX	–979	2 536	1 301	–715	–1 457	650	5 096	–1 990	282
F.419	Loans by rest of the world monetary financial institutions	NBXB	258	1 991	–1 168	2 168	2 619	1 799	2 397	1 341	6 708
F.42	Long term loans										
F.421	Direct investment	NBXD	–668	1 790	72	2 028	181	394	557	1 253	1 483
F.424	Other long-term loans by UK residents	NBXL	–780	4 634	–123	1 615	1 432	4 444	–156	3 072	42
F.4	Total loans	NBWV	–2 169	10 951	82	5 096	2 775	7 287	7 894	3 676	8 515
F.5	Shares and other equity										
F.51	Shares and other equity, excluding mutual funds' shares										
F.514	Quoted UK shares	NBXS	27	393	8 586	49	1 141	1 233	1 934	866	10 289
F.515	Unquoted UK shares	NBXT	360	78	44	–1 119	973	535	920	711	1 973
F.5	Total shares and other equity	NBXN	387	471	8 630	–1 070	2 114	1 768	2 854	1 577	12 262
F.6	Insurance technical reserves										
F.61	Net equity of households in life assurance and pension funds' reserves	NBYD	34 671	31 333	26 195	33 078	46 302	34 654	40 582	51 994	62 355
F.62	Prepayments of insurance premiums and reserves for outstanding claims	NBYG	–563	–1 601	1 466	–1 753	1 781	687	3 778	3 969	3 153
F.6	Total insurance technical reserves	NPWC	34 108	29 732	27 661	31 325	48 083	35 341	44 360	55 963	65 508
F.7	Other accounts payable	NBYH	1 661	4 928	6 164	3 627	7 269	660	7 484	868	3 948
F.L	**Total net acquisition of financial liabilities**	NBVG	34 437	47 208	42 756	41 462	60 580	47 403	64 187	63 316	90 294
B.9	**Net lending / borrowing**										
F.A	Total net acquisition of financial assets	NBSC	38 107	47 487	47 623	36 356	61 536	48 667	62 499	35 887	70 674
-F.L	*less* Total net acquisition of financial liabilities	-NBVG	–34 437	–47 208	–42 756	–41 462	–60 580	–47 403	–64 187	–63 316	–90 294
B.9f	Net lending (+) / net borrowing (-), from financial account	NYNN	3 670	279	4 867	–5 106	956	1 264	–1 688	–27 429	–19 620
dB.9f	Statistical discrepancy	NYPB	–19 311	–13 632	–27 324	–9 966	–6 688	–4 656	–3 451	9 262	2 879
B.9	**Net lending (+) / net borrowing (-), from capital account**	NHOQ	**–15 641**	**–13 353**	**–22 457**	**–15 072**	**–5 732**	**–3 392**	**–5 139**	**–18 167**	**–16 741**

4.4.9 Insurance corporations and pension funds

ESA95 sector S.125. Unconsolidated

£ billion

			1998	1999	2000	2001	2002	2003	2004	2005	2006
IV.3	**FINANCIAL BALANCE SHEET** at end of period										
AF.A	**Financial assets**										
AF.2	Currency and deposits										
AF.22	Transferable deposits										
AF.2211	Sterling deposits with UK banks	NIYH	59.0	55.7	62.3	60.3	57.6	55.3	62.0	57.8	62.7
AF.2213	Sterling deposits with UK building societies	NIYJ	3.4	4.3	2.7	3.0	3.4	3.1	3.5	3.4	3.9
AF.229	Deposits with rest of the world monetary financial institutions	NIYK	4.2	5.0	6.3	7.3	9.3	12.1	15.7	19.8	20.2
AF.29	Other deposits	NIYL	–	–	–	–	–	–	–	–	–
AF.2	Total currency and deposits	NIYD	66.5	65.0	71.3	70.6	70.2	70.6	81.1	81.1	86.7
AF.3	Securities other than shares										
AF.331	Short term: money market instruments										
AF.3311	Issued by UK central government	NIYO	1.1	0.6	0.6	0.6	0.8	0.5	0.6	0.4	0.7
AF.3315	Issued by UK monetary financial institutions	NIYT	13.3	14.5	15.3	18.8	21.5	24.6	26.6	24.9	25.6
AF.3316	Issued by other UK residents	NIYY	1.8	2.7	2.8	3.2	3.3	3.4	1.5	4.9	3.7
AF.3319	Issued by the rest of the world	NIYZ	1.1	1.4	1.3	1.1	1.4	1.5	2.1	3.5	3.5
AF.332	Medium (1 to 5 year) and long term (over 5 year) bonds										
AF.3321	Issued by UK central government	NIZB	208.9	201.6	190.3	175.0	187.9	201.0	223.6	235.0	243.0
AF.3322	Issued by UK local government	NIZE	0.6	0.6	0.5	0.5	0.5	0.4	0.3	0.4	0.8
AF.3325	Medium term bonds issued by UK MFIs[1]	NIZF	9.1	11.5	11.4	11.8	13.7	23.1	29.1	39.5	47.9
AF.3326	Other medium & long term bonds issued by UK residents	NIZI	70.7	88.2	120.3	137.6	171.1	174.2	175.4	186.4	182.8
AF.3329	Long term bonds issued by the rest of the world	NIZJ	66.7	75.8	85.3	106.2	109.3	118.6	142.3	168.3	181.5
AF.3	Total securities other than shares	NIYM	373.3	396.7	427.7	454.9	509.4	547.4	601.6	663.5	689.5
AF.4	Loans										
AF.42	Long term loans										
AF.421	Direct investment	NIZW	4.2	2.1	5.7	7.4	5.7	4.8	6.9	9.1	8.5
AF.422	Loans secured on dwellings	NIZZ	1.8	1.1	1.3	1.3	1.2	1.4	1.4	1.0	0.8
AF.424	Other long-term loans by UK residents	NJAE	25.8	43.0	41.7	48.6	51.4	65.1	84.7	86.3	105.0
AF.4	Total loans	NIZO	31.8	46.2	48.7	57.3	58.3	71.3	93.0	96.4	114.3
AF.5	Shares and other equity										
AF.51	Shares and other equity, excluding mutual funds' shares										
AF.514	Quoted UK shares	NJAL	618.2	730.4	678.3	549.3	400.1	449.6	475.8	487.5	493.6
AF.515	Unquoted UK shares	NJAM	4.5	5.6	6.7	7.2	7.7	6.7	4.5	5.2	5.7
AF.517	UK shares and bonds issued by other UK residents	NSOC	–	–	–	–	–	–	–	–	–
AF.519	Shares and other equity issued by the rest of the world	NJAQ	205.3	283.9	258.8	255.7	207.3	227.6	255.4	351.5	398.4
AF.52	Mutual funds' shares										
AF.521	UK mutual funds' shares	NJAU	111.7	139.2	144.5	125.8	103.1	142.0	159.8	237.6	292.8
AF.5	Total shares and other equity	NJAG	939.8	1 159.2	1 088.3	938.1	718.2	825.9	895.5	1 081.8	1 190.5
AF.6	Insurance technical reserves										
AF.62	Prepayments of insurance premiums and reserves for outstanding claims	NJAZ	0.4	0.9	0.9	0.7	0.8	0.9	0.9	1.0	1.0
AF.7	Other accounts receivable	NJBA	16.5	16.0	17.2	18.4	35.5	50.7	49.5	50.2	51.0
AF.A	**Total financial assets**	NIZN	1 428.3	1 684.0	1 654.0	1 540.0	1 392.4	1 566.8	1 721.7	1 973.8	2 133.0

1 UK monetary financial institutions

4.4.9 Insurance corporations and pension funds

ESA95 sector S.125. Unconsolidated

continued £ billion

			1998	1999	2000	2001	2002	2003	2004	2005	2006
IV.3	**FINANCIAL BALANCE SHEET** continued at end of period										
AF.L	**Financial liabilities**										
AF.3	Securities other than shares										
AF.332	Medium (1 to 5 year) and long term (over 5 year) bonds										
AF.3326	Other medium & long term bonds issued by UK residents institutions and government	NJCM	0.1	0.1	0.7	0.5	0.1	0.3	0.6	0.3	0.3
AF.3	Total securities other than shares	NJBQ	0.1	0.1	0.7	0.5	0.1	0.3	0.6	0.3	0.3
AF.4	Loans										
AF.41	Short term loans										
AF.411	Loans by UK monetary financial institutions, excluding loans secured on dwellings & financial leasing	NJCU	6.8	9.4	10.7	10.0	8.5	9.1	14.2	12.3	12.5
AF.419	Loans by Rest of World monetary financial institutions	C657	5.8	8.0	7.3	8.9	11.7	13.4	15.5	17.2	23.2
AF.42	Long term loans										
AF.421	Direct investment	NJDA	6.1	6.8	6.9	9.6	7.6	7.9	8.5	9.6	11.1
AF.424	Other long-term loans by UK residents	NJDI	0.7	0.5	0.5	0.5	0.5	0.5	0.5	0.5	0.5
AF.4	Total loans	NJCS	19.4	24.7	25.4	28.9	28.3	30.8	38.7	39.6	47.3
AF.5	Shares and other equity										
AF.51	Shares and other equity, excluding mutual funds' shares										
AF.514	Quoted UK shares	NJDP	72.5	72.8	69.0	56.3	33.6	37.7	47.9	56.9	73.1
AF.515	Unquoted UK shares	NJDQ	6.3	9.6	9.8	10.0	11.7	13.6	9.8	10.1	12.0
AF.517	UK shares and bonds issued by other UK residents	NSOD	–	–	–	–	–	–	–	–	–
AF.5	Total shares and other equity	NJDK	78.8	82.5	78.8	66.4	45.3	51.3	57.7	67.0	85.1
AF.6	Insurance technical reserves										
AF.61	Net equity of households in life assurance and pension funds' reserves	NJEA	1 393.4	1 631.5	1 599.2	1 531.5	1 384.3	1 509.4	1 603.4	1 894.5	2 071.1
AF.62	Prepayments of insurance premiums and reserves for outstanding claims	NJED	60.8	58.9	62.8	59.0	62.8	63.5	67.2	71.2	74.4
AF.6	Total insurance technical reserves	NPXS	1 454.2	1 690.4	1 662.0	1 590.5	1 447.1	1 572.9	1 670.6	1 965.7	2 145.4
AF.7	Other accounts payable	NJEE	13.2	18.2	23.1	26.5	28.2	35.6	41.8	42.8	45.9
AF.L	**Total financial liabilities**	NJCR	1 565.7	1 816.0	1 790.0	1 712.8	1 549.0	1 690.9	1 809.4	2 115.3	2 324.0
BF.90	**Net financial assets / liabilities**										
AF.A	Total financial assets	NIZN	1 428.3	1 684.0	1 654.0	1 540.0	1 392.4	1 566.8	1 721.7	1 973.8	2 133.0
-AF.L	*less* Total financial liabilities	-NJCR	–1 565.7	–1 816.0	–1 790.0	–1 712.8	–1 549.0	–1 690.9	–1 809.4	–2 115.3	–2 324.0
BF.90	**Net financial assets (+) / liabilities (-)**	NYOI	–137.3	–132.0	–136.0	–172.8	–156.6	–124.1	–87.8	–141.5	–191.0

4.5 Financial derivatives: Gross positions of UK banks, securities dealers and other institutions by counterparty

£ million

	MFIs[1]		Other Financial[2]		Other UK[3]		Rest of World		
	Sterling	Other currencies	Sterling	Other currencies	Sterling	Other currencies	Sterling	Other currencies	Total
2001									
FINANCIAL BALANCE SHEET									
Assets									
UK banks[4]	29 077	112 464	11 899	65 799	5 126	4 247	43 496	480 990	753 098
Securities dealers[5]	5 535	29 861	2 559	5 208	1 302	1 021	13 194	51 901	110 581
Total	34 612	142 325	14 458	71 007	6 428	5 268	56 690	532 891	863 679
Liabilities									
UK banks[4]	26 870	114 279	16 376	64 844	4 120	4 463	43 811	485 773	760 536
Securities dealers[5]	6 899	27 845	4 384	6 673	723	215	13 588	50 204	110 531
Total	33 769	142 124	20 760	71 517	4 843	4 678	57 399	535 977	871 067

	UK	Rest of World	Total
2001			
FINANCIAL BALANCE SHEET			
Assets			
Insurance[6]	6 809	994	7 803
Pension Funds[7]	3 050	753	3 803
Insurance and Pension Funds Total	9 859	1 747	11 606
Other Financial Intermediaries[8]	1 703	220	1 923
Total	11 562	1 967	13 529
Liabilities			
Insurance[6]	2 077	203	2 280
Pension Funds[7]	722	738	1 460
Insurance and Pension Funds Total	2 799	941	3 740
Other Financial Intermediaries[8]	1 822	8	1 830
Total	4 621	949	5 570

KEY:

Source: ONS, Bank of England and Financial Services Authority

These data are not included in the aggregates shown in the main tables.

1 MFIs = Monetary financial institutions covers banks and building societies.
2 Other Financial = Other financial institutions and insurance corporations and pension funds.
3 Other UK = Government, private and public non-financial corporations and households.
4 UK banks = Collected by the Bank of England.
5 Securities dealers = Collected by ONS.
6 Insurance = Includes both general and long-term insurance, and are collected by ONS.
7 Pension Funds = Relates to self administered pension funds only, and are collected by ONS.
8 Other Financial Intermediaries = This does not include securities dealers (see above), includes unit trusts, investment trusts, OEICS, finance leasing, credit grantors and factoring companies all collected by ONS. This also includes Building Societies data collected by the Financial Services Authority.

Further information about the data on financial derivatives collected by ONS, including transactions, can be obtained from an article in the May 2005 edition of Economic Trends.

4.5 Financial derivatives: Gross positions of UK banks, securities dealers and other institutions by counterparty

continued | £ million

	MFIs[1]		Other Financial[2]		Other UK[3]		Rest of World		
	Sterling	Other currencies	Sterling	Other currencies	Sterling	Other currencies	Sterling	Other currencies	Total
2002									
FINANCIAL BALANCE SHEET									
Assets									
UK banks[4]	46 219	187 463	19 391	83 408	8 131	3 645	56 656	626 158	1 031 071
Securities dealers[5]	5 849	20 716	6 272	43 187	1 139	2 436	16 214	70 901	166 714
Total	52 068	208 179	25 663	126 595	9 270	6 081	72 870	697 059	1 197 785
Liabilities									
UK banks[4]	41 139	192 769	20 830	82 738	4 500	7 013	57 118	631 538	1 037 645
Securities dealers[5]	7 551	21 701	9 382	41 798	1 003	1 782	17 188	73 745	174 150
Total	48 690	214 470	30 212	124 536	5 503	8 795	74 306	705 283	1 211 795

	UK	Rest of World	Total
2002			
FINANCIAL BALANCE SHEET			
Assets			
Insurance[6]	5 491	791	6 282
Pension Funds[7]	1 775	696	2 471
Insurance and Pension Funds Total	7 266	1 487	8 753
Other Financial Intermediaries[8]	2 035	359	2 394
Total	9 301	1 846	11 147
Liabilities			
Insurance[6]	20	531	551
Pension Funds[7]	1 282	392	1 674
Insurance and Pension Funds Total	1 302	923	2 225
Other Financial Intermediaries[8]	1 296	69	1 365
Total	2 598	992	3 590

KEY:

Source: ONS, Bank of England and Financial Services Authority

These data are not included in the aggregates shown in the main tables.

1 MFIs = Monetary financial institutions covers banks and building societies.
2 Other Financial = Other financial institutions and insurance corporations and pension funds.
3 Other UK = Government, private and public non-financial corporations and households.
4 UK banks = Collected by the Bank of England.
5 Securities dealers = Collected by ONS.
6 Insurance = Includes both general and long-term insurance, and are collected by ONS.
7 Pension Funds = Relates to self administered pension funds only, and are collected by ONS.
8 Other Financial Intermediaries = This does not include securities dealers (see above), includes unit trusts, investment trusts, OEICS, finance leasing, credit grantors and factoring companies all collected by ONS. This also includes Building Societies data collected by the Financial Services Authority.

Further information about the data on financial derivatives collected by ONS, including transactions, can be obtained from an article in the May 2005 edition of Economic Trends.

4.5 Financial derivatives: Gross positions of UK banks, securities dealers and other institutions by counterparty

continued £ million

	MFIs[1]		Other Financial[2]		Other UK[3]		Rest of World		
	Sterling	Other currencies	Sterling	Other currencies	Sterling	Other currencies	Sterling	Other currencies	Total
2003									
FINANCIAL BALANCE SHEET									
Assets									
UK banks[4]	40 068	155 012	21 256	101 044	9 185	4 983	44 141	579 275	954 964
Securities dealers[5]	6 201	19 410	9 367	17 133	511	474	10 640	144 041	207 777
Total	46 269	174 422	30 623	118 177	9 696	5 457	54 781	723 316	1 162 741
Liabilities									
UK banks[4]	28 991	164 651	20 418	100 278	6 023	7 812	32 391	600 008	960 572
Securities dealers[5]	8 048	23 431	13 619	18 402	540	244	13 971	149 960	228 215
Total	37 039	188 082	34 037	118 680	6 563	8 056	46 362	749 968	1 188 787

	UK	Rest of World	Total
2003			
FINANCIAL BALANCE SHEET			
Assets			
Insurance[6]	4 445	204	4 649
Pension Funds[7]	3 089	561	3 650
Insurance and Pension Funds Total	7 534	765	8 299
Other Financial Intermediaries[8]	5 253	572	5 825
Total	12 787	1 337	14 124
Liabilities			
Insurance[6]	877	215	1 092
Pension Funds[7]	1 817	437	2 254
Insurance and Pension Funds Total	2 694	652	3 346
Other Financial Intermediaries[8]	2 838	700	3 538
Total	5 532	1 352	6 884

KEY:

Source: ONS, Bank of England and Financial Services Authority

These data are not included in the aggregates shown in the main tables.

1 MFIs = Monetary financial institutions covers banks and building societies.
2 Other Financial = Other financial institutions and insurance corporations and pension funds.
3 Other UK = Government, private and public non-financial corporations and households.
4 UK banks = Collected by the Bank of England.
5 Securities dealers = Collected by ONS.
6 Insurance = Includes both general and long-term insurance, and are collected by ONS.
7 Pension Funds = Relates to self administered pension funds only, and are collected by ONS.
8 Other Financial Intermediaries = This does not include securities dealers (see above), includes unit trusts, investment trusts, OEICS, finance leasing, credit grantors and factoring companies all collected by ONS. This also includes Building Societies data collected by the Financial Services Authority.

Further information about the data on financial derivatives collected by ONS, including transactions, can be obtained from an article in the May 2005 edition of Economic Trends.

4.5 Financial derivatives: Gross positions of UK banks, securities dealers and other institutions by counterparty

continued £ million

	MFIs[1]		Other Financial[2]		Other UK[3]		Rest of World		
	Sterling	Other currencies	Sterling	Other currencies	Sterling	Other currencies	Sterling	Other currencies	Total
2004									
FINANCIAL BALANCE SHEET									
Assets									
UK banks[4]	37 727	207 204	35 908	154 678	10 803	4 755	46 078	663 302	1 160 455
Securities dealers[5]	11 669	54 662	7 350	13 764	507	347	11 485	104 670	204 454
Total	49 396	261 866	43 258	168 442	11 310	5 102	57 563	767 972	1 364 909
Liabilities									
UK banks[4]	27 833	223 191	34 316	152 452	6 506	7 695	36 268	678 753	1 167 014
Securities dealers[5]	17 958	61 129	8 642	11 592	712	517	14 034	112 155	226 739
Total	45 791	284 320	42 958	164 044	7 218	8 212	50 302	790 908	1 393 753

	UK	Rest of World	Total
2004			
FINANCIAL BALANCE SHEET			
Assets			
Insurance[6]	3 862	3	3 865
Pension Funds[7]	10 235	2 962	13 197
Insurance and Pension Funds Total	14 097	2 965	17 062
Other Financial Intermediaries[8]	3 490	408	3 898
Total	17 587	3 373	20 960
Liabilities			
Insurance[6]	692	141	833
Pension Funds[7]	7 873	3 082	10 955
Insurance and Pension Funds Total	8 565	3 223	11 788
Other Financial Intermediaries[8]	2 641	137	2 778
Total	11 206	3 360	14 566

KEY:

Source: ONS, Bank of England and Financial Services Authority

These data are not included in the aggregates shown in the main tables.

1 MFIs = Monetary financial institutions covers banks and building societies.
2 Other Financial = Other financial institutions and insurance corporations and pension funds.
3 Other UK = Government, private and public non-financial corporations and households.
4 UK banks = Collected by the Bank of England.
5 Securities dealers = Collected by ONS.
6 Insurance = Includes both general and long-term insurance, and are collected by ONS.
7 Pension Funds = Relates to self administered pension funds only, and are collected by ONS.
8 Other Financial Intermediaries = This does not include securities dealers (see above), includes unit trusts, investment trusts, OEICS, finance leasing, credit grantors and factoring companies all collected by ONS. This also includes Building Societies data collected by the Financial Services Authority.

Further information about the data on financial derivatives collected by ONS, including transactions, can be obtained from an article in the May 2005 edition of Economic Trends.

4.5 Financial derivatives: Gross positions of UK banks, securities dealers and other institutions by counterparty

continued £ million

	MFIs[1]		Other Financial[2]		Other UK[3]		Rest of World		
	Sterling	Other currencies	Sterling	Other currencies	Sterling	Other currencies	Sterling	Other currencies	Total
2005									
FINANCIAL BALANCE SHEET									
Assets									
UK banks[4]	51 702	262 038	36 522	195 784	14 750	7 762	51 327	768 752	1 388 637
Securities dealers[5]	11 869	102 410	6 509	20 674	1 048	1 168	15 002	186 531	345 211
Total	63 571	364 448	43 031	216 458	15 798	8 930	66 329	955 283	1 733 848
Liabilities									
UK banks[4]	59 243	272 352	30 422	193 338	10 667	8 666	66 286	764 817	1 405 791
Securities dealers[5]	24 491	119 426	12 739	18 797	1 368	11 487	18 190	183 147	389 645
Total	83 734	391 778	43 161	212 135	12 035	20 153	84 476	947 964	1 795 436

	UK	Rest of World	Total
2005			
FINANCIAL BALANCE SHEET			
Assets			
Insurance[6]	5 830	–47	5 783
Pension Funds[7]	22 157	2 668	24 825
Insurance and Pension Funds Total	27 987	2 621	30 608
Other Financial Intermediaries[8]	6 141	538	6 679
Total	34 128	3 159	37 287
Liabilities			
Insurance[6]	773	12	785
Pension Funds[7]	16 818	2 785	19 603
Insurance and Pension Funds Total	17 591	2 797	20 388
Other Financial Intermediaries[8]	3 815	111	3 926
Total	21 406	2 908	24 314

Source: ONS, Bank of England and Financial Services Authority

KEY:

These data are not included in the aggregates shown in the main tables.

1 MFIs = Monetary financial institutions covers banks and building societies.
2 Other Financial = Other financial institutions and insurance corporations and pension funds.
3 Other UK = Government, private and public non-financial corporations and households.
4 UK banks = Collected by the Bank of England.
5 Securities dealers = Collected by ONS.
6 Insurance = Includes both general and long-term insurance, and are collected by ONS.
7 Pension Funds = Relates to self administered pension funds only, and are collected by ONS.
8 Other Financial Intermediaries = This does not include securities dealers (see above), includes unit trusts, investment trusts, OEICS, finance leasing, credit grantors and factoring companies all collected by ONS. This also includes Building Societies data collected by the Financial Services Authority.

Further information about the data on financial derivatives collected by ONS, including transactions, can be obtained from an article in the May 2005 edition of Economic Trends.

4.5 Financial derivatives: Gross positions of UK banks, securities dealers and other institutions by counterparty

continued — £ million

	MFIs[1]		Other Financial[2]		Other UK[3]		Rest of World		
	Sterling	Other currencies	Sterling	Other currencies	Sterling	Other currencies	Sterling	Other currencies	Total
2006									
FINANCIAL BALANCE SHEET									
Assets									
UK banks[4]	65 931	281 076	44 398	197 161	18 263	5 570	62 865	790 853	1 466 117
Securities dealers[5]	16 415	45 918	19 134	33 419	2 630	2 111	28 596	234 529	382 752
Total	82 346	326 994	63 532	230 580	20 893	7 681	91 461	1 025 382	1 848 869
Liabilities									
UK banks[4]	61 786	299 782	30 659	194 813	11 620	8 840	62 364	828 112	1 497 976
Securities dealers[5]	23 552	85 572	13 407	28 463	1 676	2 884	23 625	234 353	413 532
Total	85 338	385 354	44 066	223 276	13 296	11 724	85 989	1 062 465	1 911 508

	UK	Rest of World	Total
2006			
FINANCIAL BALANCE SHEET			
Assets			
Insurance[6]	..	..	..
Pension Funds[7]	..	..	..
Insurance and Pension Funds Total	..	..	..
Other Financial Intermediaries[8]	..	..	..
Total	..	..	..
Liabilities			
Insurance[6]	..	..	..
Pension Funds[7]	..	..	..
Insurance and Pension Funds Total	..	..	..
Other Financial Intermediaries[8]	..	..	..
Total	..	..	..

KEY:

Source: ONS, Bank of England and Financial Services Authority

These data are not included in the aggregates shown in the main tables.

1 MFIs = Monetary financial institutions covers banks and building societies.
2 Other Financial = Other financial institutions and insurance corporations and pension funds.
3 Other UK = Government, private and public non-financial corporations and households.
4 UK banks = Collected by the Bank of England.
5 Securities dealers = Collected by ONS.
6 Insurance = Includes both general and long-term insurance, and are collected by ONS.
7 Pension Funds = Relates to self administered pension funds only, and are collected by ONS.
8 Other Financial Intermediaries = This does not include securities dealers (see above), includes unit trusts, investment trusts, OEICS, finance leasing, credit grantors and factoring companies all collected by ONS. This also includes Building Societies data collected by the Financial Services Authority.

Further information about the data on financial derivatives collected by ONS, including transactions, can be obtained from an article in the May 2005 edition of Economic Trends.

Gross Positions for Insurance, Pension Funds and Other Financial Intermediaries are collected annually, 2005 data currently not available.

Chapter 5
General government

5.1.1 General government
ESA95 sector S.13 Unconsolidated

£ million

			1998	1999	2000	2001	2002	2003	2004
I	**PRODUCTION ACCOUNT**								
	Resources								
P.1	Output								
P.11	Market output	NMXJ	12 303	13 568	14 930	17 438	19 464	20 780	22 295
P.12	Output for own final use	NMXK	413	448	430	407	428	451	467
P.13	Other non-market output	NMYK	156 409	169 520	181 851	194 503	212 464	232 699	250 708
P.1	Total resources	NMXL	169 125	183 536	197 211	212 348	232 356	253 930	273 470
	Uses								
P.2	Intermediate consumption	NMXM	74 651	84 555	92 133	99 151	110 715	121 498	131 012
B.1g	**Gross Value Added**	NMXN	**94 474**	**98 981**	**105 078**	**113 197**	**121 641**	**132 432**	**142 458**
Total	Total uses	NMXL	169 125	183 536	197 211	212 348	232 356	253 930	273 470
B.1g	**Gross Value Added**	NMXN	**94 474**	**98 981**	**105 078**	**113 197**	**121 641**	**132 432**	**142 458**
K.1	*less* Consumption of fixed capital	-NMXO	–8 999	–9 262	–9 542	–9 796	–10 289	–10 807	–11 681
B.1n	Value added, net of fixed capital consumption	NMXP	85 475	89 719	95 536	103 401	111 352	121 625	130 777

5.1.2 General government
ESA95 sector S.13 Unconsolidated

£ million

			1998	1999	2000	2001	2002	2003	2004
II	**DISTRIBUTION AND USE OF INCOME ACCOUNTS**								
II.1	**PRIMARY DISTRIBUTION OF INCOME ACCOUNT**								
II.1.1	**GENERATION OF INCOME ACCOUNT**								
	Resources								
B.1g	**Total resources (Gross Value Added)**	NMXN	**94 474**	**98 981**	**105 078**	**113 197**	**121 641**	**132 432**	**142 458**
	Uses								
D.1	Compensation of employees								
D.11	Wages and salaries	NMXQ	69 342	73 190	77 871	85 183	91 355	100 475	108 707
D.12	Employers' social contributions	NMXR	16 133	16 529	17 665	18 218	19 997	21 150	22 070
D.1	Total	NMXS	85 475	89 719	95 536	103 401	111 352	121 625	130 777
D.2	Taxes on production and imports, paid								
D.29	Production taxes other than on products	NMXT	–	–	–	–	–	–	–
D.3	*less* Subsidies, received								
D.39	Production subsidies other than on products	-NMXU	–	–	–	–	–	–	–
B.2g	Operating surplus, gross	NMXV	8 999	9 262	9 542	9 796	10 289	10 807	11 681
B.1g	**Total uses (Gross Value Added)**	NMXN	**94 474**	**98 981**	**105 078**	**113 197**	**121 641**	**132 432**	**142 458**
K.1	After deduction of fixed capital consumption	-NMXO	–8 999	–9 262	–9 542	–9 796	–10 289	–10 807	–11 681
B.2n	Operating surplus, net	NMXW	–	–	–	–	–	–	–

5.1.3 General government
ESA95 sector S.13 Unconsolidated

£ million

			1998	1999	2000	2001	2002	2003	2004	2005	2006
II.1.2	**ALLOCATION OF PRIMARY INCOME ACCOUNT**										
	Resources										
B.2g	Operating surplus, gross	NMXV	8 999	9 262	9 542	9 796	10 289	10 807	11 681	12 605	13 650
D.2	Taxes on production and imports, received										
D.21	Taxes on products										
D.211	Value added tax (VAT)	NZGF	52 313	57 701	59 985	63 522	68 251	74 595	79 751	81 383	85 512
D.212	Taxes and duties on imports excluding VAT										
D.2121	Import duties	NMXZ	–	–	–	–	–	–	–	–	–
D.2122	Taxes on imports excluding VAT and import duties	NMBT	–	–	–	–	–	–	–	–	–
D.214	Taxes on products excluding VAT and import duties	NMYB	44 881	48 442	51 956	50 745	52 001	52 858	55 932	56 815	60 423
D.21	Total taxes on products	NVCC	97 194	106 143	111 941	114 267	120 252	127 453	135 683	138 198	145 935
D.29	Other taxes on production	NMYD	15 815	16 503	17 083	17 565	18 113	18 517	18 945	19 601	21 087
D.2	Total taxes on production and imports, received	NMYE	113 009	122 646	129 024	131 832	138 365	145 970	154 628	157 799	167 022
-D.3	*less* Subsidies, paid										
-D.31	Subsidies on products	-NMYF	–3 729	–3 625	–3 791	–3 953	–4 672	–5 311	–4 961	–5 111	–5 768
-D.39	Other subsidies on production	-LIUF	–810	–663	–574	–662	–954	–1 434	–1 499	–2 058	–2 784
-D.3	Total	-NMRL	–4 539	–4 288	–4 365	–4 615	–5 626	–6 745	–6 460	–7 169	–8 552
D.4	Property income, received										
D.41	Total Interest	NMYL	7 912	7 335	7 340	7 332	6 624	7 053	6 280	6 318	6 912
D.42	Distributed income of corporations	NMYM	7 514	7 303	7 777	6 910	6 156	8 073	7 869	2 585	2 173
D.44	Property income attributed to insurance policy holders	NMYO	48	33	54	24	22	19	17	27	27
D.45	Rent from sectors other than general government	NMYR	547	529	1 289	1 919	1 901	1 565	1 422	1 352	1 210
D.4	Total	NMYU	16 021	15 200	16 460	16 185	14 703	16 710	15 588	10 282	10 322
Total	Total resources	NMYV	133 490	142 820	150 661	153 198	157 731	166 742	175 437	173 517	182 442
	Uses										
D.4	Property income, paid										
D.41	Total interest	NRKB	34 861	30 699	30 639	27 965	25 463	26 955	27 050	29 449	30 421
D.4	Total	NMYY	34 861	30 699	30 639	27 965	25 463	26 955	27 050	29 449	30 421
B.5g	**Balance of primary incomes, gross**	NMZH	**98 629**	**112 121**	**120 022**	**125 233**	**132 268**	**139 787**	**148 387**	**144 068**	**152 021**
Total	Total uses	NMYV	133 490	142 820	150 661	153 198	157 731	166 742	175 437	173 517	182 442
K.1	After deduction of fixed capital consumption	-NMXO	–8 999	–9 262	–9 542	–9 796	–10 289	–10 807	–11 681	–12 605	–13 650
B.5n	Balance of primary incomes,net	NMZI	89 630	102 859	110 480	115 437	121 979	128 980	136 706	131 463	138 371

5.1.4 General government

ESA95 sector S.13 Unconsolidated

£ million

			1998	1999	2000	2001	2002	2003	2004	2005	2006
II.2	**SECONDARY DISTRIBUTION OF INCOME ACCOUNT**										
	Resources										
B.5g	Balance of primary incomes, gross	NMZH	98 629	112 121	120 022	125 233	132 268	139 787	148 387	144 068	152 021
D.5	Current taxes on income, wealth, etc.										
D.51	Taxes on income	NMZJ	123 683	129 553	140 002	147 264	142 842	144 234	154 717	172 619	193 017
D.59	Other current taxes	NVCM	18 120	19 519	20 287	22 068	23 664	26 016	27 718	29 253	30 681
D.5	Total	NMZL	141 803	149 072	160 289	169 332	166 506	170 250	182 435	201 872	223 698
D.61	Social contributions										
D.611	Actual social contributions										
D.6111	Employers' actual social contributions	NMZM	30 593	33 401	36 397	38 460	38 780	45 067	49 602	52 904	55 565
D.6112	Employees' social contributions	NMZN	25 234	26 645	27 293	28 725	29 568	34 376	38 150	41 538	43 413
D.6113	Social contributions by self- and non-employed persons	NMZO	1 729	1 883	2 049	2 183	2 318	2 595	2 727	2 825	2 930
D.611	Total	NMZP	57 556	61 929	65 739	69 368	70 666	82 038	90 479	97 267	101 908
D.612	Imputed social contributions	NMZQ	6 981	6 927	7 395	7 577	8 348	6 456	5 928	7 282	7 166
D.61	Total	NMZR	64 537	68 856	73 134	76 945	79 014	88 494	96 407	104 549	109 074
D.7	Other current transfers										
D.72	Non-life insurance claims	NMZS	499	410	403	353	400	296	285	328	351
D.73	Current transfers within general government	NMZT	60 367	64 446	66 187	72 522	77 592	85 224	91 910	100 224	109 841
D.74	Current international cooperation	NMZU	1 384	3 176	2 084	4 568	3 112	3 570	3 604	3 668	3 594
	Miscellaneous current transfers										
D.75	from sectors other than general government	NMZX	498	392	447	460	502	562	610	627	602
D.7	Other current transfers	NNAA	62 748	68 424	69 121	77 903	81 606	89 652	96 409	104 847	114 388
Total	Total resources	NNAB	367 717	398 473	422 566	449 413	459 394	488 183	523 638	555 336	599 181
	Uses										
D.59	Other current taxes	EBFQ	830	861	860	902	876	842	837	997	1 075
D.62	Social benefits other than social transfers in kind	NNAD	117 668	117 685	120 163	129 591	136 801	146 066	154 216	161 979	168 246
D.7	Other current transfers										
D.71	Net non-life insurance premiums	NNAE	499	410	403	353	400	296	285	328	351
D.73	Current transfers within general government	NNAF	60 367	64 446	66 187	72 522	77 592	85 224	91 910	100 224	109 841
D.74	Current international cooperation	NNAG	1 705	1 667	2 418	2 434	2 573	2 720	3 180	3 300	3 583
	Miscellaneous current transfers										
D.75	to sectors other than general government	NNAI	14 829	18 466	20 913	22 131	27 351	30 275	32 550	34 947	34 130
	Of which: GNP based fourth own resource	NMFH	3 920	4 632	4 379	3 858	5 335	6 772	7 549	8 732	8 521
D.7	Other current transfers	NNAN	77 400	84 989	89 921	97 440	107 916	118 515	127 925	138 799	147 905
B.6g	**Gross Disposable Income**	NNAO	**171 819**	**194 938**	**211 622**	**221 480**	**213 801**	**222 760**	**240 660**	**253 561**	**281 955**
Total	Total uses	NNAB	367 717	398 473	422 566	449 413	459 394	488 183	523 638	555 336	599 181
K.1	After deduction of fixed capital consumption	-NMXO	–8 999	–9 262	–9 542	–9 796	–10 289	–10 807	–11 681	–12 605	–13 650
B.6n	Disposable income, net	NNAP	162 820	185 676	202 080	211 684	203 512	211 953	228 979	240 956	268 305

5.1.5 General government

ESA95 sector S.13 Unconsolidated

£ million

			1998	1999	2000	2001	2002	2003	2004	2005	2006
II.3	**REDISTRIBUTION OF INCOME IN KIND ACCOUNT**										
	Resources										
B.6g	**Total resources (Gross Disposable Income)**	NNAO	**171 819**	**194 938**	**211 622**	**221 480**	**213 801**	**222 760**	**240 660**	**253 561**	**281 955**
	Uses										
D.63	Social transfers in kind										
D.632	Transfers of individual non-market goods and services	NSZE	94 783	102 742	109 297	118 458	130 816	143 954	155 811	167 399	178 552
B.7g	Adjusted disposable income, gross	NSZI	77 036	92 196	102 325	103 022	82 985	78 806	84 849	86 162	103 403
B.6g	**Total uses (Gross Disposable Income)**	NNAO	**171 819**	**194 938**	**211 622**	**221 480**	**213 801**	**222 760**	**240 660**	**253 561**	**281 955**

5.1.6 General government

ESA95 sector S.13 Unconsolidated

£ million

			1998	1999	2000	2001	2002	2003	2004	2005	2006
II.4	**USE OF INCOME ACCOUNT**										
II.4.1	**USE OF DISPOSABLE INCOME ACCOUNT**										
	Resources										
B.6g	**Total resources (Gross Disposable Income)**	NNAO	**171 819**	**194 938**	**211 622**	**221 480**	**213 801**	**222 760**	**240 660**	**253 561**	**281 955**
	Uses										
P.3	Final consumption expenditure										
P.31	Individual consumption expenditure	NNAQ	94 783	102 742	109 297	118 458	130 816	143 954	155 811	167 399	178 552
P.32	Collective consumption expenditure	NQEP	61 626	66 778	72 554	76 045	81 648	88 745	94 897	101 502	108 260
P.3	Total	NMRK	156 409	169 520	181 851	194 503	212 464	232 699	250 708	268 901	286 812
B.8g	**Gross Saving**	NNAU	**15 410**	**25 418**	**29 771**	**26 977**	**1 337**	**–9 939**	**–10 048**	**–15 340**	**–4 857**
B.6g	**Total uses (Gross Disposable Income)**	NNAO	**171 819**	**194 938**	**211 622**	**221 480**	**213 801**	**222 760**	**240 660**	**253 561**	**281 955**
-K.1	After deduction of fixed capital consumption	-NMXO	–8 999	–9 262	–9 542	–9 796	–10 289	–10 807	–11 681	–12 605	–13 650
B.8n	Saving, net	NNAV	6 411	16 156	20 229	17 181	–8 952	–20 746	–21 729	–27 945	–18 507
II.4.2	**USE OF ADJUSTED DISPOSABLE INCOME ACCOUNT**										
	Resources										
B.7g	Total resources, adjusted disposable income, gross	NSZI	77 036	92 196	102 325	103 022	82 985	78 806	84 849	86 162	103 403
	Uses										
P.4	Actual final consumption										
P.42	Actual collective consumption	NRMZ	61 626	66 778	72 554	76 045	81 648	88 745	94 897	101 502	108 260
B.8g	**Gross Saving**	NNAU	**15 410**	**25 418**	**29 771**	**26 977**	**1 337**	**–9 939**	**–10 048**	**–15 340**	**–4 857**
Total	Total uses	NSZI	77 036	92 196	102 325	103 022	82 985	78 806	84 849	86 162	103 403

5.1.7 General government

ESA95 sector S.13 Unconsolidated

£ million

			1998	1999	2000	2001	2002	2003	2004	2005	2006
III	**ACCUMULATION ACCOUNTS**										
III.1	**CAPITAL ACCOUNT**										
III.1.1	**CHANGE IN NET WORTH DUE TO SAVING & CAPITAL TRANSFERS**										
	Changes in liabilities and net worth										
B.8g	**Gross Saving**	NNAU	**15 410**	**25 418**	**29 771**	**26 977**	**1 337**	**–9 939**	**–10 048**	**–15 340**	**–4 857**
D.9	Capital transfers receivable										
D.91	Capital taxes from sectors other than general government	NMGI	1 795	1 951	2 215	2 396	2 381	2 416	2 881	3 150	3 579
D.92	Investment grants	NSZF	2 656	3 298	4 105	4 652	6 328	7 360	8 565	8 512	8 360
D.99	Other capital transfers	NNAX	191	205	411	828	1 147	5 161	3 666	3 870	2 541
D.9	Total capital transfers receivable	NNAY	4 642	5 454	6 731	7 876	9 856	14 937	15 112	15 532	14 480
-D.9	*less* Capital transfers payable										
-D.92	Investment grants	-NNAW	–8 113	–8 774	–8 821	–11 313	–13 646	–17 335	–17 045	–20 934	–21 000
-D.99	Other capital transfers	-NNBB	–330	–161	–285	–1 114	–447	–4 364	–3 602	–15 574	–3 342
-D.9	Total capital transfers payable	-NNBC	–8 443	–8 935	–9 106	–12 427	–14 093	–21 699	–20 647	–36 508	–24 342
B.10.1g	Total change in liabilities and net worth	NMWG	11 609	21 937	27 396	22 426	–2 900	–16 701	–15 583	–36 316	–14 719
	Changes in assets										
B.10.1g	Changes in net worth due to gross saving and capital transfers	NMWG	11 609	21 937	27 396	22 426	–2 900	–16 701	–15 583	–36 316	–14 719
K.1	After deduction of fixed capital consumption	-NMXO	–8 999	–9 262	–9 542	–9 796	–10 289	–10 807	–11 681	–12 605	–13 650
B.10.1n	Changes in net worth due to net saving and capital transfers	NNBD	2 610	12 675	17 854	12 630	–13 189	–27 508	–27 264	–48 921	–28 369
III.1.2	**ACQUISITION OF NON-FINANCIAL ASSETS ACCOUNT**										
	Changes in liabilities and net worth										
B.10.1n	Changes in net worth due to net saving and capital transfers	NNBD	2 610	12 675	17 854	12 630	–13 189	–27 508	–27 264	–48 921	–28 369
K.1	Consumption of fixed capital	NMXO	8 999	9 262	9 542	9 796	10 289	10 807	11 681	12 605	13 650
B.10.1g	Total change in liabilities and net worth	NMWG	11 609	21 937	27 396	22 426	–2 900	–16 701	–15 583	–36 316	–14 719
	Changes in assets										
P.5	Gross capital formation										
P.51	Gross fixed capital formation	NNBF	11 910	12 599	12 227	13 533	15 452	20 509	23 206	7 130	24 147
P.52	Changes in inventories	NNBG	107	–268	–140	–18	–	15	20	–6	–4
P.53	Acquisitions less disposals of valuables	NPOZ	14	10	12	22	22	16	20	16	18
P.5	Total	NNBI	12 031	12 341	12 099	13 537	15 474	20 540	23 246	7 140	24 161
K.2	Acquisitions less disposals of non-produced non-financial assets	NNBJ	–967	–888	–776	–915	–1 087	–957	–1 071	–1 205	–947
B.9g	**Net lending(+) / net borrowing(-)**	NNBK	**545**	**10 484**	**16 073**	**9 804**	**–17 287**	**–36 284**	**–37 758**	**–42 251**	**–37 933**
Total	Total change in assets	NMWG	11 609	21 937	27 396	22 426	–2 900	–16 701	–15 583	–36 316	–14 719

5.1.8 General government

ESA95 sector S.13 Unconsolidated

£ million

			1998	1999	2000	2001	2002	2003	2004	2005	2006
III.2	**FINANCIAL ACCOUNT**										
F.A	**Net acquisition of financial assets**										
F.1	Monetary gold and special drawing rights (SDRs)	NWXM	915	–374	–956	–808	–240	–2	–37	–8	47
F.2	Currency and deposits										
F.22	Transferable deposits with monetary financial institutions										
F.221	UK institutions	NFPN	289	–144	15 799	–9 098	–3 479	2 476	1 488	334	7 634
F.229	Rest of the world institutions	NFPR	–1 804	3 177	–840	–261	–299	–916	–1 407	–1 516	–671
F.29	Other deposits	NFPS	–	–	3 009	–2 637	644	–546	–67	–13	–182
F.2	Total currency and deposits	NFPK	–1 515	3 033	17 968	–11 996	–3 134	1 014	14	–1 195	6 781
F.3	Securities other than shares										
F.331	Short term: money market instruments										
F.3311	Issued by UK central government	NFPV	106	204	–218	119	–141	–38	–59	14	–17
F.3312	Issued by UK local government	NFPZ	–	–	–	–	–	–	–	–	–
F.3315	Issued by UK monetary financial institutions	NFQA	232	565	1 850	–1 305	–233	–75	440	54	798
F.3316	Issued by other UK residents	NFQF	58	–34	59	366	741	–1 067	10	–41	1 845
F.3319	Issued by the rest of the world	NFQG	939	–337	244	273	–1 576	–987	106	1 465	1 363
F.332	Medium (1 to 5 year) and long term (over 5 year) bonds										
F.3321	Issued by UK central government	NFQI	95	–17	–195	191	–264	–101	–97	5	72
F.3326	Other medium & long term bonds issued by UK residents	NFQP	–	–387	11	–49	–17	–	–	1 071	–620
F.3329	Long term bonds issued by the rest of the world	NFQQ	–214	–3 105	5 418	–1 838	2 280	–390	1 551	370	–854
F.34	Financial derivatives	NFQR	–	–	185	102	–238	–136	–173	137	–419
F.3	Total securities other than shares	NFPT	1 216	–3 111	7 354	–2 141	552	–2 794	1 778	3 075	2 168
F.4	Loans										
F.42	Long term loans										
F.422	Loans secured on dwellings	NFRG	–154	106	11	97	206	186	4	252	46
F.424	Other long-term loans by UK residents	NFRL	730	2 803	3 736	3 771	–314	–994	2 722	4 845	3 434
F.429	Other long-term loans by the rest of the world	NATS	–	–	–	–	–	–	–	–	–
F.4	Total loans	NFQV	576	2 909	3 747	3 868	–108	–808	2 726	5 097	3 480
F.5	Shares and other equity										
F.51	Shares and other equity, excluding mutual funds' shares										
F.514	Quoted UK shares	NFRS	51	–316	54	–54	–218	45	–117	312	240
F.515	Unquoted UK shares	NFRT	–40	–	–	–811	–	–29	–	–3 144	–2 431
F.516	Other UK equity (including direct investment in property)	NFRU	–	–	–	85	32	105	–8	–1 249	–1 204
F.517	UK shares and bonds issued by other UK residents	NSPW	–	–	–	–	–	–	–	–	–
F.519	Shares and other equity issued by the rest of the world	NFRX	67	91	53	56	90	126	98	659	819
F.5	Total shares and other equity	NFRN	78	–225	107	–724	–96	247	–27	–3 422	–2 576
F.6	Insurance technical reserves										
F.62	Prepayments of insurance premiums and reserves for outstanding claims	NFSG	–11	–30	24	–26	27	8	45	44	35
F.7	Other accounts receivable	NFSH	–2 371	7 804	1 301	717	–1 488	3 075	2 396	5 526	2 387
F.A	**Total net acquisition of financial assets**	NFPG	–1 112	10 006	29 545	–11 110	–4 487	740	6 895	9 117	12 322

5.1.8 General government
ESA95 sector S.13 Unconsolidated

continued £ million

			1998	1999	2000	2001	2002	2003	2004	2005	2006
III.2	**FINANCIAL ACCOUNT** continued										
F.L	**Net acquisition of financial liabilities**										
F.2	Currency and deposits										
F.21	Currency	NFSP	168	191	226	228	180	216	171	182	154
F.29	Non-transferable deposits	NFSW	–1 165	–907	2 578	–3 084	1 946	3 266	2 422	5 490	5 223
F.2	Total currency and deposits	NFSO	–997	–716	2 804	–2 856	2 126	3 482	2 593	5 672	5 377
F.3	Securities other than shares										
F.331	Short term: money market instruments										
F.3311	Issued by UK central government	NFSZ	86	–404	–1 652	8 623	10 330	2 592	999	–3 902	–1 752
F.3312	Issued by UK local government	NFTD	–6	–	–	–	–	–	–	–	–
F.332	Medium (1 to 5 year) and long term (over 5 year) bonds										
F.3321	Issued by UK central government	NFTM	–3 201	–4 560	–12 700	–17 219	1 555	31 474	34 219	39 846	41 021
F.3322	Issued by UK local government	NFTP	6	–2	–12	–	47	18	–225	213	358
F.3	Total securities other than shares	NFSX	–3 115	–4 966	–14 364	–8 596	11 932	34 084	34 993	36 157	39 627
F.4	Loans										
F.41	Short term loans										
F.411	Loans by UK monetary financial institutions, excluding loans secured on dwellings & financial leasing	NFUB	530	5 270	–337	–6 615	1 731	1 109	7 434	3 084	–1 831
F.419	Loans by rest of the world monetary financial institutions	NFUF	–44	–45	–39	–36	–14	–7	–6	–3	–1
F.42	Long term loans										
F.423	Finance leasing	NFUO	263	562	437	227	278	514	475	507	306
F.424	Other long-term loans by UK residents	NFUP	807	1 870	1 419	–212	–1 727	–3 912	506	2 604	2 702
F.429	Other long-term loans by the rest of the world	NFUQ	–134	–166	–263	11	–9	166	593	72	240
F.4	Total loans	NFTZ	1 422	7 491	1 217	–6 625	259	–2 130	9 002	6 264	1 416
F.7	Other accounts payable	NFVL	631	–1 140	23 244	–1 840	–983	1 678	–1 943	3 623	4 414
F.L	**Total net acquisition of financial liabilities**	NFSK	–2 059	669	12 901	–19 917	13 334	37 114	44 645	51 716	50 834
B.9	**Net lending / borrowing**										
F.A	Total net acquisition of financial assets	NFPG	–1 112	10 006	29 545	–11 110	–4 487	740	6 895	9 117	12 322
-F.L	*less* Total net acquisition of financial liabilities	-NFSK	2 059	–669	–12 901	19 917	–13 334	–37 114	–44 645	–51 716	–50 834
B.9f	Net lending (+) / net borrowing (-), from financial account	NYNO	947	9 337	16 644	8 807	–17 821	–36 374	–37 750	–42 599	–38 512
dB.9f	Statistical discrepancy	NYOZ	–402	1 147	–571	997	534	90	–8	348	579
B.9g	**Net lending (+) / net borrowing (-), from capital account**	NNBK	**545**	**10 484**	**16 073**	**9 804**	**–17 287**	**–36 284**	**–37 758**	**–42 251**	**–37 933**

5.1.9 General government
ESA95 sector S.13 Unconsolidated

£ billion

			1998	1999	2000	2001	2002	2003	2004	2005	2006
IV.3	**FINANCIAL BALANCE SHEET** at end of period										
AN	**Non-financial assets**	CGIX	369.3	385.3	440.7	490.3	505.3	545.9	601.0	657.2	687.1
AF.A	**Financial assets**										
AF.1	Monetary gold and special drawing rights (SDRs)	NIFC	4.3	4.0	3.1	2.4	2.4	2.6	2.5	3.2	3.4
AF.2	Currency and deposits										
AF.22	Transferable deposits										
AF.221	Deposits with UK monetary financial institutions	NLVW	14.8	14.5	32.2	23.1	20.3	23.9	26.8	27.1	34.5
AF.229	Deposits with rest of the world monetary financial institutions	NLWA	6.1	8.7	6.6	6.3	5.9	4.9	3.3	2.0	1.2
AF.29	Other deposits	NLWB	–	–	3.0	0.3	1.0	0.4	0.4	0.4	0.2
AF.2	Total currency and deposits	NLUT	20.9	23.2	41.8	29.7	27.1	29.2	30.5	29.4	35.9
AF.3	Securities other than shares										
AF.331	Short term: money market instruments										
AF.3311	Issued by UK central government	NLWE	0.2	0.5	0.2	0.4	0.2	0.2	0.1	0.1	0.1
AF.3312	Issued by UK local government	NLWI	–	–	–	–	–	–	–	–	–
AF.3315	Issued by UK monetary financial institutions	NLWJ	2.4	3.0	5.4	4.0	3.9	3.9	4.4	4.5	5.2
AF.3316	Issued by other UK residents	NLWO	0.1	0.1	0.2	0.5	1.3	0.2	0.2	0.3	1.4
AF.3319	Issued by the rest of the world	NLWP	2.1	1.8	2.3	2.6	1.2	0.2	0.3	1.7	3.0
AF.332	Medium (1 to 5 year) and long term (over 5 year) bonds										
AF.3321	Issued by UK central government	NLWR	0.8	0.7	0.5	0.7	0.4	0.3	0.2	0.2	0.2
AF.3322	Issued by UK local government	NLWU	–	–	–	–	–	–	–	–	–
AF.3326	Other medium & long term bonds issued by UK residents	NLWY	0.6	0.2	0.1	0.1	0.1	0.1	0.1	1.1	0.5
AF.3329	Long term bonds issued by the rest of the world	NLWZ	10.9	7.6	16.7	14.4	16.8	16.2	17.1	17.5	15.3
AF.34	Financial derivatives	NLXA	–	–0.4	–	0.7	0.2	–	0.2	0.6	0.7
AF.3	Total securities other than shares	NLWC	17.2	13.5	25.3	23.4	24.0	20.9	22.5	26.0	26.5
AF.4	Loans										
AF.42	Long term loans										
AF.422	Loans secured on dwellings	NLXP	0.5	0.6	0.6	0.7	0.9	1.1	1.1	1.4	1.4
AF.424	Other long-term loans by UK residents	NLXU	60.5	62.8	66.1	69.2	68.6	68.1	69.8	74.4	77.9
AF.4	Total loans	NLXE	61.1	63.4	66.8	69.9	69.6	69.2	70.9	75.8	79.3
AF.5	Shares and other equity										
AF.51	Shares and other equity, excluding mutual funds' shares										
AF.514	Quoted UK shares	NLYB	1.0	2.5	1.4	1.2	1.0	1.2	1.2	1.5	2.0
AF.515	Unquoted UK shares	NLYC	0.5	0.5	0.5	1.3	1.3	1.3	2.1	1.2	1.2
AF.517	UK shares and bonds issued by other UK residents	NSQP	–	–	–	–	–	–	–	–	–
AF.519	Shares and other equity issued by the rest of the world	NLYG	1.7	1.8	1.9	1.9	2.0	2.1	2.2	8.8	9.4
AF.5	Total shares and other equity	NLXW	3.2	4.8	3.8	4.4	4.3	4.7	5.5	11.5	12.5
AF.6	Insurance technical reserves										
AF.62	Prepayments of insurance premiums and reserves for outstanding claims	NLYP	1.2	1.1	1.0	0.9	0.9	0.8	0.8	0.8	0.8
AF.7	Other accounts receivable	NLYQ	39.5	38.8	39.9	40.6	39.4	43.2	45.0	46.5	49.2
AF.A	**Total financial assets**	NPUP	147.3	148.8	181.7	171.3	167.7	170.6	177.7	193.3	207.7

5.1.9 General government
ESA95 sector S.13 Unconsolidated

continued £ billion

			1998	1999	2000	2001	2002	2003	2004	2005	2006
IV.3	**FINANCIAL BALANCE SHEET** continued at end of period										
AF.L	**Financial liabilities**										
AF.2	Currency and deposits										
AF.21	Currency	NLYY	2.6	2.8	3.0	3.2	3.3	3.4	3.5	3.7	3.8
AF.29	Non-transferable deposits	NLZF	73.4	72.0	75.1	72.4	74.4	76.2	78.6	84.7	89.8
AF.2	Total currency and deposits	NLYX	76.0	74.9	78.1	75.6	77.7	79.6	82.2	88.3	93.6
AF.3	Securities other than shares										
AF.331	Short term: money market instruments										
AF.3311	Issued by UK central government	NLZI	4.8	4.2	2.6	11.2	21.4	24.0	25.0	21.1	19.4
AF.3312	Issued by UK local government	NLZM	–	–	–	–	–	–	–	–	–
AF.332	Medium (1 to 5 year) and long term (over 5 year) bonds										
AF.3321	Issued by UK central government	NLZV	359.3	334.0	325.8	297.4	308.0	330.0	369.2	420.0	449.3
AF.3322	Issued by UK local government	NLZY	0.8	0.8	0.8	0.8	0.8	0.8	0.6	0.8	1.2
AF.3	Total securities other than shares	NLZG	364.8	339.0	329.1	309.3	330.2	354.8	394.8	441.9	469.9
AF.4	Loans										
AF.41	Short term loans										
AF.411	Loans by UK monetary financial institutions, excluding loans secured on dwellings & financial leasing	NNKY	16.6	22.0	26.0	20.2	22.8	25.0	32.5	35.7	34.1
AF.419	Loans by rest of the world monetary financial institutions	NNLC	0.2	0.2	0.1	–	–	–	–	–	–
AF.42	Long term loans										
AF.423	Finance leasing	NNLL	0.8	1.3	1.8	2.0	2.3	2.8	3.3	3.8	4.1
AF.424	Other long-term loans by UK residents	NNLM	47.8	49.1	50.1	50.1	48.3	44.5	45.6	48.0	50.7
AF.429	Other long-term loans by the rest of the world	NNLN	1.4	1.2	1.3	1.3	1.2	1.3	1.9	1.9	2.1
AF.4	Total loans	NNKW	66.7	73.9	79.2	73.6	74.7	73.7	83.2	89.3	91.0
AF.7	Other accounts payable	NNMI	19.8	19.1	42.0	41.6	39.1	42.3	46.0	58.9	66.1
AF.L	**Total financial liabilities**	NPVQ	527.3	506.9	528.4	500.0	521.7	550.5	606.3	678.5	720.6
AF.A	Total financial assets	NPUP	147.3	148.8	181.7	171.3	167.7	170.6	177.7	193.3	207.7
-AF.L	*less* Total financial liabilities	-NPVQ	–527.3	–506.9	–528.4	–500.0	–521.7	–550.5	–606.3	–678.5	–720.6
BF.90	**Net financial assets (+) / liabilities (-)**	NYOG	–380.0	–358.0	–346.7	–328.7	–353.9	–379.9	–428.6	–485.2	–512.9
	Net worth										
AN	Non-financial assets	CGIX	369.3	385.3	440.7	490.3	505.3	545.9	601.0	657.2	687.1
BF.90	Net financial assets (+) / liabilities (-)	NYOG	–380.0	–358.0	–346.7	–328.7	–353.9	–379.9	–428.6	–485.2	–512.9
BF.90	**Net worth**	CGRX	–10.8	27.3	94.0	161.6	151.4	166.0	172.4	172.0	174.2

5.2.1 Central government
ESA95 sector S.1311

£ million

			1998	1999	2000	2001	2002	2003	2004
I	**PRODUCTION ACCOUNT**								
	Resources								
P.1	Output								
P.11	Market output	NMIW	2 511	2 606	2 535	3 075	3 480	3 514	4 367
P.12	Output for own final use	QYJV	151	134	86	44	42	44	39
P.13	Other non-market output	NMBJ	97 145	103 580	110 807	118 762	130 326	142 639	152 325
P.1	Total resources	NMAE	99 807	106 320	113 428	121 881	133 848	146 197	156 731
	Uses								
P.2	Intermediate consumption	NMAF	48 138	53 850	58 055	61 643	68 868	74 364	79 853
B.1g	**Gross Value Added**	NMBR	**51 669**	**52 470**	**55 373**	**60 238**	**64 980**	**71 833**	**76 878**
Total	Total uses	NMAE	99 807	106 320	113 428	121 881	133 848	146 197	156 731
B.1g	**Gross Value Added**	NMBR	**51 669**	**52 470**	**55 373**	**60 238**	**64 980**	**71 833**	**76 878**
-K.1	*less* Consumption of fixed capital	-NSRN	–5 333	–5 396	–5 495	–5 483	–5 636	–5 902	–6 224
B.1n	Value added, net of fixed capital consumption	NMAH	46 336	47 074	49 878	54 755	59 344	65 931	70 654

5.2.2 Central government
ESA95 sector S.1311

£ million

			1998	1999	2000	2001	2002	2003	2004
II	**DISTRIBUTION AND USE OF INCOME ACCOUNTS**								
II.1	**PRIMARY DISTRIBUTION OF INCOME ACCOUNT**								
II.1.1	**GENERATION OF INCOME ACCOUNT**								
	Resources								
B.1g	**Total resources (Gross Value Added)**	NMBR	**51 669**	**52 470**	**55 373**	**60 238**	**64 980**	**71 833**	**76 878**
	Uses								
D.1	Compensation of employees								
D.11	Wages and salaries	NMAI	37 655	38 346	40 437	45 292	48 648	54 514	58 802
D.12	Employers' social contributions	NMAL	8 681	8 728	9 441	9 463	10 696	11 417	11 852
D.1	Total	NMBG	46 336	47 074	49 878	54 755	59 344	65 931	70 654
D.2	Taxes on production and imports, paid								
D.29	Production taxes other than on products	NMAN	–	–	–	–	–	–	–
-D.3	*less* Subsidies, received								
-D.39	Production subsidies other than on products	-NMAO	–	–	–	–	–	–	–
B.2g	Operating surplus, gross	NRLN	5 333	5 396	5 495	5 483	5 636	5 902	6 224
B.1g	**Total uses (Gross Value Added)**	NMBR	**51 669**	**52 470**	**55 373**	**60 238**	**64 980**	**71 833**	**76 878**
-K.1	After deduction of fixed capital consumption	-NSRN	–5 333	–5 396	–5 495	–5 483	–5 636	–5 902	–6 224
B.2n	Operating surplus, net	NMAP	–	–	–	–	–	–	–

5.2.3 Central government
ESA95 sector S.1311

£ million

			1998	1999	2000	2001	2002	2003	2004	2005	2006
II.1.2	**ALLOCATION OF PRIMARY INCOME ACCOUNT**										
	Resources										
B.2g	Operating surplus, gross	NRLN	5 333	5 396	5 495	5 483	5 636	5 902	6 224	6 699	7 224
D.2	Taxes on production and imports, received										
D.21	Taxes on products										
D.211	Value added tax (VAT)	NZGF	52 313	57 701	59 985	63 522	68 251	74 595	79 751	81 383	85 512
D.212	Taxes and duties on imports excluding VAT										
D.2121	Import duties	NMXZ	–	–	–	–	–	–	–	–	–
D.2122	Taxes on imports excluding VAT and import duties	NMBT	–	–	–	–	–	–	–	–	–
D.214	Taxes on products excluding VAT and import duties	NMYB	44 881	48 442	51 956	50 745	52 001	52 858	55 932	56 815	60 423
D.21	Total taxes on products	NMYC	97 194	106 143	111 941	114 267	120 252	127 453	135 683	138 198	145 935
D.29	Other taxes on production	NMBX	15 687	16 361	16 934	17 408	17 940	18 329	18 741	19 419	20 885
D.2	Total taxes on production and imports, received	NMBY	112 881	122 504	128 875	131 675	138 192	145 782	154 424	157 617	166 820
-D.3	*less* Subsidies, paid										
-D.31	Subsidies on products	-NMCB	–2 913	–2 976	–3 083	–3 096	–3 634	–4 030	–3 376	–3 419	–4 027
-D.39	Other subsidies on production	-NMCC	–809	–647	–553	–653	–937	–1 416	–1 476	–1 372	–1 415
-D.3	Total	-NMCD	–3 722	–3 623	–3 636	–3 749	–4 571	–5 446	–4 852	–4 791	–5 442
D.4	Property income										
D.41	Total Interest	NMCE	6 796	6 490	6 359	6 477	5 854	6 321	5 309	5 265	5 732
D.42	Distributed income of corporations	NMCH	2 486	2 045	2 358	2 392	1 789	1 773	2 040	2 164	1 866
D.45	Rent from sectors other than general government	NMCK	547	529	1 289	1 919	1 901	1 565	1 422	1 352	1 210
D.4	Total	NMCL	9 829	9 064	10 006	10 788	9 544	9 659	8 771	8 781	8 808
Total	Total resources	NMCM	124 321	133 341	140 740	144 197	148 801	155 897	164 567	168 306	177 410
	Uses										
D.4	Property income										
D.41	Total Interest	RVFK	30 312	26 274	26 398	23 672	21 440	22 430	23 268	25 975	26 753
D.4	Total property income	NUHA	30 312	26 274	26 398	23 672	21 440	22 430	23 268	25 975	26 753
B.5g	**Balance of primary incomes, gross**	NRLP	**94 009**	**107 067**	**114 342**	**120 525**	**127 361**	**133 467**	**141 299**	**142 331**	**150 657**
Total	Total uses	NMCM	124 321	133 341	140 740	144 197	148 801	155 897	164 567	168 306	177 410
-K.1	After deduction of fixed capital consumption	-NSRN	–5 333	–5 396	–5 495	–5 483	–5 636	–5 902	–6 224	–6 699	–7 224
B.5n	Balance of primary incomes, net	NMCT	88 676	101 671	108 847	115 042	121 725	127 565	135 075	135 632	143 433

5.2.4 Central government
ESA95 sector S.1311

£ million

			1998	1999	2000	2001	2002	2003	2004	2005	2006
II.2	**SECONDARY DISTRIBUTION OF INCOME ACCOUNT**										
	Resources										
B.5g	**Balance of primary incomes, gross**	NRLP	**94 009**	**107 067**	**114 342**	**120 525**	**127 361**	**133 467**	**141 299**	**142 331**	**150 657**
D.5	Current taxes on income, wealth, etc.										
D.51	Taxes on income	NMCU	123 683	129 553	140 002	147 264	142 842	144 234	154 717	172 619	193 017
D.59	Other current taxes	NMCV	6 372	6 753	6 369	6 920	7 133	7 534	7 757	8 137	8 493
D.5	Total	NMCP	130 055	136 306	146 371	154 184	149 975	151 768	162 474	180 756	201 510
D.61	Social contributions										
D.611	Actual social contributions										
D.6111	Employers' actual social contributions	NMCY	30 593	33 401	36 397	38 460	38 780	45 067	49 602	52 904	55 565
D.6112	Employees' social contributions	NMDB	24 683	26 062	26 715	28 116	28 931	33 717	37 447	40 780	42 616
D.6113	Social contributions by self- and non-employed persons	NMDE	1 729	1 883	2 049	2 183	2 318	2 595	2 727	2 825	2 930
D.611	Total	NMCX	57 005	61 346	65 161	68 759	70 029	81 379	89 776	96 509	101 111
D.612	Imputed social contributions	QYJS	5 328	5 213	5 538	5 620	6 282	4 311	3 709	4 975	4 743
D.61	Total	NMCW	62 333	66 559	70 699	74 379	76 311	85 690	93 485	101 484	105 854
D.7	Other current transfers										
D.72	Non-life insurance claims	NMDJ	–	–	–	–	–	–	–	–	–
D.73	Current transfers within general government	NMDK	–	–	–	–	–	–	–	–	–
D.74	Current international cooperation	NQEA	1 384	3 176	2 084	4 568	3 112	3 570	3 604	3 668	3 594
	Miscellaneous current transfers										
D.75	from sectors other than general government	NMEZ	498	392	447	460	502	562	610	627	602
D.7	Other current transfers	NMDI	1 882	3 568	2 531	5 028	3 614	4 132	4 214	4 295	4 196
Total	Total resources	NMDN	288 279	313 500	333 943	354 116	357 261	375 057	401 472	428 866	462 217
	Uses										
D.62	Social benefits other than social transfers in kind	NMDR	102 217	102 867	105 672	114 509	120 938	129 606	136 977	143 708	148 882
D.7	Other current transfers										
D.71	Net non-life insurance premiums	NMDX	–	–	–	–	–	–	–	–	–
D.73	Current transfers within general government	QYJR	60 367	64 446	66 187	72 522	77 592	85 224	91 910	100 224	109 841
D.74	Current international cooperation	NMDZ	1 705	1 667	2 418	2 434	2 573	2 720	3 180	3 300	3 583
D.75	Miscellaneous current transfers										
	to sectors other than general government										
	GNP based fourth own resource	NMFH	3 920	4 632	4 379	3 858	5 335	6 772	7 549	8 732	8 521
	Grants to higher education institutions	CJTH	4 718	4 378	4 532	4 819	5 357	5 896	6 661	7 238	6 729
	Grants to further education colleges	CJTG	3 661	3 217	3 354	4 294	5 169	5 833	6 324	7 428	7 313
	Other grants to non profit institutions	GDXH	2 513	6 214	8 616	9 137	11 467	11 750	11 991	11 526	11 542
D.75	Total	NMFC	14 812	18 441	20 881	22 108	27 328	30 251	32 525	34 924	34 105
D.7	Other current transfers	NMDW	76 884	84 554	89 486	97 064	107 493	118 195	127 615	138 448	147 529
B.6g	**Gross Disposable Income**	NRLR	**109 178**	**126 079**	**138 785**	**142 543**	**128 830**	**127 256**	**136 880**	**146 710**	**165 806**
Total	Total uses	NMDN	288 279	313 500	333 943	354 116	357 261	375 057	401 472	428 866	462 217
-K.1	After deduction of fixed capital consumption	-NSRN	–5 333	–5 396	–5 495	–5 483	–5 636	–5 902	–6 224	–6 699	–7 224
B.6n	Disposable income, net	NMEB	103 845	120 683	133 290	137 060	123 194	121 354	130 656	140 011	158 582

5.2.4S Central government Social contributions and benefits

ESA95 sector S.1311

£ million

			1998	1999	2000	2001	2002	2003	2004	2005	2006
Part	**SECONDARY DISTRIBUTION OF INCOME** (further detail of certain items)										
	Resources										
D.61	Social contributions										
	National Insurance Contributions (NICs)										
D.611	Actual social contributions										
D.61111	Employers' NICs	CEAN	28 731	31 286	34 028	35 706	35 735	39 890	43 586	46 741	48 624
D.61121	Employees' NICs	GCSE	22 528	23 573	24 175	25 236	25 357	29 055	32 396	34 742	36 415
D.61131	Self- and non-employed persons' NICs	NMDE	1 729	1 883	2 049	2 183	2 318	2 595	2 727	2 825	2 930
D.61	Total national insurance contributions	AIIH	52 988	56 742	60 252	63 125	63 410	71 540	78 709	84 308	87 969
	Pension schemes[1]										
D.611	Actual social contributions										
D.61112	Employers' contributions	GCMP	1 862	2 115	2 369	2 754	3 045	5 177	6 016	6 163	6 941
D.61122	Employees' contributions	CX3X	2 155	2 489	2 540	2 880	3 574	4 662	5 051	6 038	6 201
D.612	Imputed social contributions	QYJS	5 328	5 213	5 538	5 620	6 282	4 311	3 709	4 975	4 743
D.61	Total pension schemes	FAD5	9 345	9 817	10 447	11 254	12 901	14 150	14 776	17 176	17 885
D.61	Total social contributions	NMCW	62 333	66 559	70 699	74 379	76 311	85 690	93 485	101 484	105 854
	Uses										
D.62	Social benefits										
D.621	Social security benefits in cash										
	National insurance fund										
	Retirement pensions	CSDG	35 435	37 319	38 686	41 323	43 967	46 098	48 498	50 949	53 201
	Widows' and guardians' allowances	CSDH	979	970	984	1 080	1 096	1 027	939	883	822
	Unemployment benefit	CSDI	–	–1	–1	–	–2	–	–	–3	–
	Jobseeker's allowance	CJTJ	500	473	436	454	512	519	453	487	476
	Sickness benefit	CSDJ	–	–	–	–	–	–	–	–	–
	Invalidity benefit	CSDK	–	–	–	–	–	–	–	–	–
	Incapacity benefit	CUNL	7 320	6 925	6 705	6 736	6 754	6 792	6 777	6 644	6 692
	Maternity benefit	CSDL	39	40	42	55	66	107	147	162	173
	Death grant	CSDM	–	–	–	–	–	–	–	–	–
	Statutory sick pay	CSDQ	28	29	28	25	19	58	75	78	80
	Statutory maternity pay	GTKZ	543	580	610	663	711	1 130	1 336	1 249	1 316
	Payment in lieu of benefits foregone	GTKV	–	–	–	–	–	–	–	–	–
	Total national insurance fund benefits	ACHH	44 844	46 335	47 490	50 336	53 123	55 731	58 225	60 449	62 760
	Redundancy fund benefit	GTKN	106	137	167	198	278	245	169	274	200
	Maternity fund benefit	GTKO	–	–	–	–	–	–	–	–	–
	Social fund benefit	GTLQ	356	1 087	1 753	1 885	1 910	2 135	2 240	2 232	2 274
	Benefits paid to overseas residents	FJVZ	1 091	1 123	1 161	1 239	1 338	1 404	1 527	1 583	1 676
D.621	Total social security benefits in cash	QYRJ	46 397	48 682	50 571	53 658	56 649	59 515	62 161	64 538	66 910
D.623	Total unfunded social benefits	QYJT	11 547	11 647	12 439	13 027	14 744	15 602	15 799	17 345	18 867
D.624	Social assistance benefits in cash										
	War pensions and allowances	CSDD	1 260	1 255	1 214	1 200	1 173	1 108	1 136	1 034	995
	Income support	CSDE	11 778	12 068	12 830	13 901	14 400	14 986	16 124	15 626	15 935
	Income tax credits and reliefs	RYCQ	2 172	1 863	4 532	5 586	6 344	8 805	11 329	12 418	13 767
	Child Benefit	EKY3	9 709	10 366	8 631	8 728	8 906	9 281	9 526	9 627	10 113
	Non-contributory job seekers' allowance	EKY4	3 086	2 900	2 529	2 175	2 112	2 098	1 841	1 904	2 005
	Care allowances	EKY5	2 656	2 790	2 911	4 579	5 174	5 379	5 661	6 069	6 458
	Disability benefits	EKY6	5 203	5 544	5 919	7 016	7 716	8 249	8 795	9 261	9 835
	Other benefits	EKY7	8 338	5 692	4 039	4 586	3 670	4 535	4 557	5 838	3 949
	Benefits paid to overseas residents	RNNF	71	60	57	53	50	48	48	48	48
D.624	Total social assistance benefits in cash	NZGO	44 273	42 538	42 662	47 824	49 545	54 489	59 017	61 825	63 105
D.62	Total social benefits	NMDR	102 217	102 867	105 672	114 509	120 938	129 606	136 977	143 708	148 882

1 Mainly civil service, armed forces', teachers' and NHS pension schemes

5.2.5 Central government
ESA95 sector S.1311

£ million

			1998	1999	2000	2001	2002	2003	2004	2005	2006
II.3	**REDISTRIBUTION OF INCOME IN KIND ACCOUNT**										
	Resources										
B.6g	**Total resources (Gross Disposable Income)**	NRLR	**109 178**	**126 079**	**138 785**	**142 543**	**128 830**	**127 256**	**136 880**	**146 710**	**165 806**
	Uses										
D.63	Social transfers in kind										
D.631	Social benefits in kind										
D.632	Transfers of individual non-market goods and services	NMED	56 117	59 909	63 042	68 211	75 408	83 215	90 682	97 295	105 137
B.7g	Adjusted disposable income, gross	NSVS	53 061	66 170	75 743	74 332	53 422	44 041	46 198	49 415	60 669
B.6g	**Total uses (Gross Disposable Income)**	NRLR	**109 178**	**126 079**	**138 785**	**142 543**	**128 830**	**127 256**	**136 880**	**146 710**	**165 806**

5.2.6 Central government
ESA95 sector S.1311

£ million

			1998	1999	2000	2001	2002	2003	2004	2005	2006
II.4	**USE OF INCOME ACCOUNT**										
II.4.1	**USE OF DISPOSABLE INCOME ACCOUNT**										
	Resources										
B.6g	**Total resources (Gross Disposable Income)**	NRLR	**109 178**	**126 079**	**138 785**	**142 543**	**128 830**	**127 256**	**136 880**	**146 710**	**165 806**
	Uses										
P.3	Final consumption expenditure										
P.31	Individual consumption expenditure	NMED	56 117	59 909	63 042	68 211	75 408	83 215	90 682	97 295	105 137
P.32	Collective consumption expenditure	NMEE	41 028	43 671	47 765	50 551	54 918	59 424	61 643	65 456	70 337
P.3	Total	NMBJ	97 145	103 580	110 807	118 762	130 326	142 639	152 325	162 751	175 474
B.8g	**Gross Saving**	NRLS	**12 033**	**22 499**	**27 978**	**23 781**	**–1 496**	**–15 383**	**–15 445**	**–16 041**	**–9 668**
B.6g	**Total uses (Gross Disposable Income)**	NRLR	**109 178**	**126 079**	**138 785**	**142 543**	**128 830**	**127 256**	**136 880**	**146 710**	**165 806**
-K.1	After deduction of fixed capital consumption	-NSRN	–5 333	–5 396	–5 495	–5 483	–5 636	–5 902	–6 224	–6 699	–7 224
B.8n	Saving, net	NMEG	6 700	17 103	22 483	18 298	–7 132	–21 285	–21 669	–22 740	–16 892
II.4.2	**USE OF ADJUSTED DISPOSABLE INCOME ACCOUNT**										
	Resources										
B.7g	Total resources, adjusted disposable income, gross	NSVS	53 061	66 170	75 743	74 332	53 422	44 041	46 198	49 415	60 669
	Uses										
P.4	Actual final consumption										
P.42	Actual collective consumption	NMEE	41 028	43 671	47 765	50 551	54 918	59 424	61 643	65 456	70 337
B.8g	**Gross Saving**	NRLS	**12 033**	**22 499**	**27 978**	**23 781**	**–1 496**	**–15 383**	**–15 445**	**–16 041**	**–9 668**
Total	Total uses	NSVS	53 061	66 170	75 743	74 332	53 422	44 041	46 198	49 415	60 669

5.2.7 Central government

ESA95 sector S.1311

£ million

			1998	1999	2000	2001	2002	2003	2004	2005	2006
III	**ACCUMULATION ACCOUNTS**										
III.1	**CAPITAL ACCOUNT**										
III.1.1	**CHANGE IN NET WORTH DUE TO SAVINGS AND CAPITAL TRANSFERS**										
	Changes in liabilities and net worth										
B.8g	**Gross Saving**	NRLS	**12 033**	**22 499**	**27 978**	**23 781**	**–1 496**	**–15 383**	**–15 445**	**–16 041**	**–9 668**
D.9	Capital transfers receivable										
D.91	Capital taxes										
	from sectors other than general government	NMGI	1 795	1 951	2 215	2 396	2 381	2 416	2 881	3 150	3 579
D.92	Investment grants	GCMT	–	–	–	–	–	–	–	–	–
D.99	Other capital transfers	NMEK	–	–	–	412	412	391	1 470	2 443	1 454
D.9	Total capital transfers receivable	NMEH	1 795	1 951	2 215	2 808	2 793	2 807	4 351	5 593	5 033
-D.9	*less* Capital transfers payable										
-D.92	Investment grants	-NMEN	–6 831	–7 618	–7 821	–10 396	–12 807	–16 170	–15 542	–19 364	–19 454
-D.99	Other capital transfers	-NMEO	–330	–161	–285	–1 114	–442	–4 359	–2 455	–14 290	–2 491
-D.9	Total capital transfers payable	-NMEL	–7 161	–7 779	–8 106	–11 510	–13 249	–20 529	–17 997	–33 654	–21 945
B.10.1g	Total change in liabilities and net worth	NMEP	6 667	16 671	22 087	15 079	–11 952	–33 105	–29 091	–44 102	–26 580
	Changes in assets										
B.10.1g	Changes in net worth due to gross saving and capital transfers	NMEP	6 667	16 671	22 087	15 079	–11 952	–33 105	–29 091	–44 102	–26 580
-K.1	After deduction of fixed capital consumption	-NSRN	–5 333	–5 396	–5 495	–5 483	–5 636	–5 902	–6 224	–6 699	–7 224
B.10.1n	Changes in net worth due to net saving and capital transfers	NMEQ	1 334	11 275	16 592	9 596	–17 588	–39 007	–35 315	–50 801	–33 804
III.1.2	**ACQUISITION OF NON-FINANCIAL ASSETS ACCOUNT**										
	Changes in liabilities and net worth										
B.10.1n	Changes in net worth due to saving and capital transfers	NMEQ	1 334	11 275	16 592	9 596	–17 588	–39 007	–35 315	–50 801	–33 804
K.1	Consumption of fixed capital	NSRN	5 333	5 396	5 495	5 483	5 636	5 902	6 224	6 699	7 224
B.10.1g	Total changes in liabilities and net worth	NMEP	6 667	16 671	22 087	15 079	–11 952	–33 105	–29 091	–44 102	–26 580
	Changes in assets										
P.5	Gross capital formation										
P.51	Gross fixed capital formation	NMES	6 007	6 356	5 675	5 964	7 506	6 372	8 315	–6 386	9 850
P.52	Changes in inventories	NMFE	107	–268	–140	–18	–	15	20	–6	–4
P.53	Acquisitions less disposals of valuables	NPPD	14	10	12	22	22	16	20	16	18
P.5	Total	NMER	6 128	6 098	5 547	5 968	7 528	6 403	8 355	–6 376	9 864
K.2	Acquisitions less disposals of non-produced non-financial assets	NMFG	–314	–173	–187	–196	–327	–157	–214	–303	–
B.9g	**Net lending(+) / net borrowing(-)**	NMFJ	**853**	**10 746**	**16 727**	**9 307**	**–19 153**	**–39 351**	**–37 232**	**–37 423**	**–36 444**
Total	Total change in assets	NMEP	6 667	16 671	22 087	15 079	–11 952	–33 105	–29 091	–44 102	–26 580

5.2.8 Central government
ESA95 sector S.1311 Unconsolidated

£ million

			1998	1999	2000	2001	2002	2003	2004	2005	2006
III.2	**FINANCIAL ACCOUNT**										
F.A	**Net acquisition of financial assets**										
F.1	Monetary gold and special drawing rights (SDRs)	NWXM	915	−374	−956	−808	−240	−2	−37	−8	47
F.2	Currency and deposits										
F.22	Transferable deposits										
F.2211	Sterling deposits with UK banks	NAUB	−314	−78	15 063	−8 521	−4 516	1 200	−1 506	538	1 656
F.2212	Foreign currency deposits with UK banks	NARV	−20	12	120	−1 270	−356	−41	−947	−329	542
F.2213	Sterling deposits with UK building societies	NARW	−2	−4	11	5	63	4	−35	47	48
F.229	Deposits with rest of the world monetary financial institutions	NARX	−1 804	3 177	−840	−261	−299	−916	−1 407	−1 516	−671
F.29	Other deposits national savings & tax	RYWO	–	–	2 919	−2 578	376	−681	–	–	−1
F.2	Total currency and deposits	NARQ	−2 140	3 107	17 273	−12 625	−4 732	−434	−3 895	−1 260	1 574
F.3	Securities other than shares										
F.331	Short term: money market instruments										
F.3315	Issued by UK MFI's	NSUN	–	–	1 435	−1 285	−720	−99	751	213	1 768
F.3316	Issued by other UK residents	NSRI	–	–	–	325	730	−1 029	–	–	1 192
F.3319	Issued by the rest of the world	NASM	939	−337	244	273	−1 576	−987	106	1 465	1 363
F.332	Medium (1 to 5 year) and long term (over 5 year) bonds										
F.3326	Other medium & long term bonds issued by UK residents	NASV	–	−387	11	−49	−17	–	–	856	−620
F.3329	Long term bonds issued by the rest of the world	NASW	−214	−3 105	5 418	−1 838	2 280	−390	1 551	370	−854
F.34	Financial derivatives	-CFZG	–	–	185	102	−238	−136	−173	137	−419
F.3	Total securities other than shares	NARZ	725	−3 829	7 293	−2 472	459	−2 641	2 235	3 041	2 430
F.4	Loans										
F.42	Long term loans										
F.422	Loans secured on dwellings	NATM	−1	−1	−1	–	–	–	–	–	–
F.424	Other long-term loans by UK residents	NATR	679	2 786	3 767	3 847	−231	−976	2 749	4 643	3 446
F.429	Other long-term loans by the rest of the world	NATS	–	–	–	–	–	–	–	–	–
F.4	Total loans	NATB	678	2 785	3 766	3 847	−231	−976	2 749	4 643	3 446
F.5	Shares and other equity										
F.51	Shares and other equity, excluding mutual funds' shares										
F.514	Quoted UK shares	NATY	−21	−12	−103	–	–	–	–	295	32
F.515	Unquoted UK shares	NATZ	–	–	–	−518	–	−29	–	−550	–
F.516	Other UK equity (including direct investment in property)	NAUA	–	–	–	85	32	105	−8	−1 249	−1 204
F.517	UK shares and bonds issued by other UK residents	NSOX	–	–	–	–	–	–	–	–	–
F.519	Shares and other equity issued by the rest of the world	NAUD	67	91	53	56	90	126	98	659	819
F.5	Total shares and other equity	NATT	46	79	−50	−377	122	202	90	−845	−353
F.7	Other accounts receivable	NAUN	−2 050	7 998	1 356	1 141	−365	2 794	2 394	5 325	2 272
F.A	**Total net acquisition of financial assets**	NARM	−1 826	9 766	28 682	−11 294	−4 987	−1 057	3 536	10 896	9 416

5.2.8 Central government
ESA95 sector S.1311 Unconsolidated

continued £ million

			1998	1999	2000	2001	2002	2003	2004	2005	2006
III.2	**FINANCIAL ACCOUNT** continued										
F.L	**Net acquisition of financial liabilities**										
F.2	Currency and deposits										
F.21	Currency	NAUV	168	191	226	228	180	216	171	182	154
F.29	Non-transferable deposits	NAVC	−1 165	−907	2 578	−3 084	1 946	3 266	2 422	5 490	5 223
F.2	Total currency and deposits	NAUU	−997	−716	2 804	−2 856	2 126	3 482	2 593	5 672	5 377
F.3	Securities other than shares										
F.331	Short term: money market instruments										
F.3311	Issued by UK central government	NAVF	86	−404	−1 652	8 623	10 330	2 592	999	−3 902	−1 752
F.332	Medium (1 to 5 year) and long term (over 5 year) bonds										
F.33211	British government securities	NAVT	−3 250	−4 504	−12 684	−11 568	4 701	29 748	34 205	39 829	41 006
F.33212	Other central government bonds	NAVU	49	−56	−16	−5 651	−3 146	1 726	14	17	15
F.3	Total securities other than shares	NAVD	−3 115	−4 964	−14 352	−8 596	11 885	34 066	35 218	35 944	39 269
F.4	Loans										
F.41	Short term loans										
F.411	Loans by UK monetary financial institutions, excluding loans secured on dwellings & financial leasing	NAWH	1 066	6 087	−55	−6 615	915	−53	5 878	2 336	−2 997
F.419	Loans by rest of the world monetary financial institutions	NAWL	−2	−1	–	−2	−1	–	–	–	–
F.42	Long term loans										
F.423	Finance leasing	NAWU	263	562	437	227	260	499	451	502	303
F.424	Other long-term loans by UK residents	NAWV	−51	−38	−25	−23	−18	−19	−14	−12	−7
F.429	Other long-term loans by the rest of the world	NAWW	−91	−105	−114	−45	−48	−45	−46	−65	7
F.4	Total loans	NAWF	1 185	6 505	243	−6 458	1 108	382	6 269	2 761	−2 694
F.7	Other accounts payable	NAXR	439	−1 405	23 709	−2 378	−356	1 419	−2 436	3 360	3 723
F.L	**Total net acquisition of financial liabilities**	NAUQ	−2 488	−580	12 404	−20 288	14 763	39 349	41 644	47 737	45 675
B.9	**Net lending / borrowing**										
F.A	Total net acquisition of financial assets	NARM	−1 826	9 766	28 682	−11 294	−4 987	−1 057	3 536	10 896	9 416
-F.L	*less* Total net acquisition of financial liabilities	-NAUQ	2 488	580	−12 404	20 288	−14 763	−39 349	−41 644	−47 737	−45 675
B.9f	Net lending (+) / net borrowing (-), from financial account	NZDX	662	10 346	16 278	8 994	−19 750	−40 406	−38 108	−36 841	−36 259
dB.9f	Statistical discrepancy	NZDW	191	400	449	313	597	1 055	876	−582	−185
B.9g	**Net lending (+) / net borrowing (-), from capital account**	NMFJ	**853**	**10 746**	**16 727**	**9 307**	**−19 153**	**−39 351**	**−37 232**	**−37 423**	**−36 444**

5.2.9 Central government

ESA95 sector S.1311 Unconsolidated

£ billion

			1998	1999	2000	2001	2002	2003	2004	2005	2006
IV.3	**FINANCIAL BALANCE SHEET** at end of period										
AN	**Non-financial assets**	CGIY	156.8	157.4	182.6	189.0	197.8	211.8	221.4	250.8	269.1
AF.A	**Financial assets**										
AF.1	Monetary gold and special drawing rights (SDRs)	NIFC	4.3	4.0	3.1	2.4	2.4	2.6	2.5	3.2	3.4
AF.2	Currency and deposits										
AF.22	Transferable deposits										
AF.221	Deposits with UK monetary financial institutions	NIFI	1.9	1.8	18.9	9.1	4.6	6.8	5.5	5.6	7.7
AF.229	Deposits with rest of the world monetary financial institutions	NIFM	6.1	8.7	6.6	6.3	5.9	4.9	3.3	2.0	1.2
AF.29	Other deposits	NIFN	–	–	2.9	0.3	0.7	–	–	–	–
AF.2	Total currency and deposits	NIFF	8.0	10.6	28.5	15.8	11.2	11.7	8.8	7.6	8.9
AF.3	Securities other than shares										
AF.331	Short term: money market instruments										
AF.3315	Issued by UK MFI's	NSUO	–	–	2.0	0.8	0.1	–	0.8	1.0	2.7
AF.3316	Issued by other UK residents	NSRH	–	–	–	0.3	1.1	–	–	–	1.2
AF.3319	Issued by the rest of the world	NIGB	2.1	1.8	2.3	2.6	1.2	0.2	0.3	1.7	3.0
AF.332	Medium (1 to 5 year) and long term (over 5 year) bonds										
AF.3322	Issued by UK local government	NIGG	–	–	–	–	–	–	–	–	–
AF.3326	Other medium & long term bonds issued by UK residents	NIGK	0.6	0.2	0.1	0.1	0.1	0.1	0.1	0.9	0.3
AF.3329	Long term bonds issued by the rest of the world	NIGL	10.9	7.6	16.7	14.4	16.8	16.2	17.1	17.5	15.3
AF.34	Financial derivatives	ZYBQ	–	–0.4	–	0.7	0.2	–	0.2	0.6	0.7
AF.3	Total securities other than shares	NIFO	13.6	9.3	21.1	18.9	19.4	16.4	18.4	21.8	23.3
AF.4	Loans										
AF.42	Long term loans										
AF.422	Loans secured on dwellings	NIHB	0.1	0.1	0.1	0.1	0.1	0.1	0.1	0.1	0.1
AF.424	Other long-term loans by UK residents	NIHG	60.3	62.5	65.8	68.9	68.4	67.9	69.6	74.2	77.7
AF.4	Total loans	NIGQ	60.3	62.6	65.9	69.0	68.4	68.0	69.7	74.3	77.8
AF.5	Shares and other equity										
AF.51	Shares and other equity, excluding mutual funds' shares										
AF.514	Quoted UK shares	NIHN	0.2	0.2	0.1	–	–	–	–	0.3	0.6
AF.515	Unquoted UK shares	NIHO	0.1	0.1	0.1	0.9	0.9	0.9	1.7	0.8	0.8
AF.517	UK shares and bonds issued by other UK residents	NSNX	–	–	–	–	–	–	–	–	–
AF.519	Shares and other equity issued by the rest of the world	NIHS	1.7	1.8	1.9	1.9	2.0	2.1	2.2	8.8	9.4
AF.5	Total shares and other equity	NIHI	2.0	2.2	2.1	2.8	2.9	3.1	3.9	9.9	10.7
AF.7	Other accounts receivable	NIIC	37.2	37.0	38.3	39.4	39.0	42.4	44.7	45.2	47.8
AF.A	**Total financial assets**	NIGP	125.4	125.6	158.9	148.3	143.3	144.1	147.9	161.9	171.8

5.2.9 Central government

ESA95 sector S.1311 Unconsolidated

continued £ billion

			1998	1999	2000	2001	2002	2003	2004	2005	2006
IV.3	**FINANCIAL BALANCE SHEET** continued at end of period										
AF.L	**Financial liabilities**										
AF.2	Currency and deposits										
AF.21	Currency	NIIK	2.6	2.8	3.0	3.2	3.3	3.4	3.5	3.7	3.8
AF.29	Non-transferable deposits	NIIR	73.4	72.0	75.1	72.4	74.4	76.2	78.6	84.7	89.8
AF.2	Total currency and deposits	NIIJ	76.0	74.9	78.1	75.6	77.7	79.6	82.2	88.3	93.6
AF.3	Securities other than shares										
AF.331	Short term: money market instruments										
AF.33111	Sterling Treasury bills	NIIV	2.4	4.2	2.6	11.2	21.4	24.0	25.0	21.1	19.4
AF.33112	ECU Treasury bills	NIIW	2.4	–	–	–	–	–	–	–	–
AF.332	Medium (1 to 5 year) and long term (over 5 year) bonds										
AF.33211	British government securities	NIJI	349.0	324.3	315.5	292.9	306.1	327.1	366.4	417.0	446.5
AF.33212	Other central government bonds	NIJJ	10.3	9.7	10.3	4.5	1.8	2.9	2.8	3.0	2.9
AF.3	Total securities other than shares	NIIS	364.1	338.2	328.4	308.6	329.4	354.0	394.2	441.1	468.7
AF.4	Loans										
AF.41	Short term loans										
AF.411	Loans by UK monetary financial institutions, excluding loans secured on dwellings & financial leasing	NIJW	13.5	19.6	24.3	18.2	20.0	20.8	26.3	28.1	25.0
AF.419	Loans by rest of the world monetary financial institutions	NIKA	–	–	–	–	–	–	–	–	–
AF.42	Long term loans										
AF.423	Finance leasing	NIKJ	0.8	1.3	1.8	2.0	2.3	2.8	3.2	3.7	4.0
AF.424	Other long-term loans by UK residents	NIKK	0.2	0.2	–	–	–	0.1	0.1	0.1	0.1
AF.429	Other long-term loans by the rest of the world	NIKL	0.4	0.4	0.5	0.5	0.4	0.2	0.1	0.1	–
AF.4	Total loans	NIJU	14.9	21.5	26.6	20.7	22.6	23.8	29.8	31.9	29.1
AF.7	Other accounts payable	NILG	10.5	9.6	32.9	31.8	30.0	32.8	36.4	49.3	55.9
AF.L	**Total financial liabilities**	NIJT	465.4	444.2	465.9	436.7	459.6	490.3	542.6	610.6	647.3
BF.90	**Net financial assets / liabilities**										
AF.A	Total financial assets	NIGP	125.4	125.6	158.9	148.3	143.3	144.1	147.9	161.9	171.8
-AF.L	*less* Total financial liabilities	-NIJT	–465.4	–444.2	–465.9	–436.7	–459.6	–490.3	–542.6	–610.6	–647.3
BF.90	**Net financial assets (+) / liabilities (-)**	NZDZ	–340.0	–318.6	–307.1	–288.4	–316.3	–346.3	–394.6	–448.7	–475.4
	Net worth										
AN	Non-financial assets	CGIY	156.8	157.4	182.6	189.0	197.8	211.8	221.4	250.8	269.1
BF.90	Net financial assets (+) / liabilities (-)	NZDZ	–340.0	–318.6	–307.1	–288.4	–316.3	–346.3	–394.6	–448.7	–475.4
BF.90	**Net worth**	CGRY	–183.2	–161.3	–124.5	–99.4	–118.5	–134.4	–173.2	–197.9	–206.3

5.3.1 Local government
ESA95 sector S.1313

£ million

			1998	1999	2000	2001	2002	2003	2004
I	**PRODUCTION ACCOUNT**								
	Resources								
P.1	Output								
P.11	Market output	NMIX	9 792	10 962	12 395	14 363	15 984	17 266	17 928
P.12	Output for own final use	QYJW	262	314	344	363	386	407	428
P.13	Other non-market output	NMMT	59 264	65 940	71 044	75 741	82 138	90 060	98 383
P.1	Total resources	NMIZ	69 318	77 216	83 783	90 467	98 508	107 733	116 739
	Uses								
P.2	Intermediate consumption	NMJA	26 513	30 705	34 078	37 508	41 847	47 134	51 159
B.1g	**Gross Value Added**	NMJB	**42 805**	**46 511**	**49 705**	**52 959**	**56 661**	**60 599**	**65 580**
Total	Total uses	NMIZ	69 318	77 216	83 783	90 467	98 508	107 733	116 739
B.1g	**Gross Value Added**	NMJB	**42 805**	**46 511**	**49 705**	**52 959**	**56 661**	**60 599**	**65 580**
-K.1	*less* Consumption of fixed capital	-NSRO	–3 666	–3 866	–4 047	–4 313	–4 653	–4 905	–5 457
B.1n	Value added, net of fixed capital consumption	NMJD	39 139	42 645	45 658	48 646	52 008	55 694	60 123

5.3.2 Local government
ESA95 sector S.1313

£ million

			1998	1999	2000	2001	2002	2003	2004
II	**DISTRIBUTION AND USE OF INCOME ACCOUNTS**								
II.1	**PRIMARY DISTRIBUTION OF INCOME ACCOUNT**								
II.1.1	**GENERATION OF INCOME ACCOUNT**								
	Resources								
B.1g	**Total resources (Gross Value Added)**	NMJB	**42 805**	**46 511**	**49 705**	**52 959**	**56 661**	**60 599**	**65 580**
	Uses								
D.1	Compensation of employees								
D.11	Wages and salaries	NMJF	31 687	34 844	37 434	39 891	42 707	45 961	49 905
D.12	Employers' social contributions	NMJG	7 452	7 801	8 224	8 755	9 301	9 733	10 218
D.1	Total	NMJE	39 139	42 645	45 658	48 646	52 008	55 694	60 123
D.2	Taxes on production and imports, paid								
D.29	Production taxes other than on products	NMHY	–	–	–	–	–	–	–
-D.3	*less* Subsidies, received								
-D.39	Production subsidies other than on products	-NMJL	–	–	–	–	–	–	–
B.2g	Operating surplus, gross	NRLT	3 666	3 866	4 047	4 313	4 653	4 905	5 457
B.1g	**Total uses (Gross Valued Added)**	NMJB	**42 805**	**46 511**	**49 705**	**52 959**	**56 661**	**60 599**	**65 580**
-K.1	After deduction of fixed capital consumption	-NSRO	–3 666	–3 866	–4 047	–4 313	–4 653	–4 905	–5 457
B.2n	Operating surplus, net	NMJM	–	–	–	–	–	–	–

5.3.3 Local government
ESA95 sector S.1313

£ million

			1998	1999	2000	2001	2002	2003	2004	2005	2006
II.1.2	**ALLOCATION OF PRIMARY INCOME ACCOUNT**										
	Resources										
B.2g	Operating surplus, gross	NRLT	3 666	3 866	4 047	4 313	4 653	4 905	5 457	5 906	6 426
D.2	Taxes on production and imports, received										
D.29	Taxes on production other than on products	NMYH	128	142	149	157	173	188	204	182	202
-D.3	*less* Subsidies, paid										
-D.31	Subsidies on products	-LIUA	–816	–649	–708	–857	–1 038	–1 281	–1 585	–1 692	–1 741
-D.39	Other subsidies on production	-LIUC	–1	–16	–21	–9	–17	–18	–23	–686	–1 369
D.4	Property income										
D.41	Total interest	NMKB	1 116	845	981	855	770	732	971	1 053	1 180
D.42	Distributed income of corporations	FDDA	5 028	5 258	5 419	4 518	4 367	6 300	5 829	421	307
D.44	Property income attributed to insurance policy holders	NMKK	48	33	54	24	22	19	17	27	27
D.45	Rent										
	from sectors other than general government	NMKM	–	–	–	–	–	–	–	–	–
D.4	Total property income	NMJZ	6 192	6 136	6 454	5 397	5 159	7 051	6 817	1 501	1 514
Total	Total resources	NMKN	9 169	9 479	9 921	9 001	8 930	10 845	10 870	5 211	5 032
	Uses										
D.4	Property income										
D.41	Total interest	NCBW	4 549	4 425	4 241	4 293	4 023	4 525	3 782	3 474	3 668
D.4	Total property income	NUHI	4 549	4 425	4 241	4 293	4 023	4 525	3 782	3 474	3 668
B.5g	**Balance of primary incomes, gross**	NRLU	**4 620**	**5 054**	**5 680**	**4 708**	**4 907**	**6 320**	**7 088**	**1 737**	**1 364**
Total	Total uses	NMKN	9 169	9 479	9 921	9 001	8 930	10 845	10 870	5 211	5 032
-K.1	After deduction of fixed capital consumption	-NSRO	–3 666	–3 866	–4 047	–4 313	–4 653	–4 905	–5 457	–5 906	–6 426
B.5n	Balance of primary incomes, net	NMKZ	954	1 188	1 633	395	254	1 415	1 631	–4 169	–5 062

5.3.4 Local government
ESA95 sector S.1313

£ million

			1998	1999	2000	2001	2002	2003	2004	2005	2006
II.2	**SECONDARY DISTRIBUTION OF INCOME ACCOUNT**										
	Resources										
B.5g	**Balance of primary incomes, gross**	NRLU	**4 620**	**5 054**	**5 680**	**4 708**	**4 907**	**6 320**	**7 088**	**1 737**	**1 364**
D.5	Current taxes on income, wealth etc.										
D.59	Current taxes other than on income	NMIS	11 748	12 766	13 918	15 148	16 531	18 482	19 961	21 116	22 188
D.61	Social contributions										
D.611	Actual social contributions										
D.6112	Employees' social contributions	NMWM	551	583	578	609	637	659	703	758	797
D.612	Imputed social contributions	GCMN	1 653	1 714	1 857	1 957	2 066	2 145	2 219	2 307	2 423
D.61	Total	NSMM	2 204	2 297	2 435	2 566	2 703	2 804	2 922	3 065	3 220
D.7	Other current transfers										
D.72	Non-life insurance claims	NMLR	499	410	403	353	400	296	285	328	351
D.73	Current transfers within general government	QYJR	60 367	64 446	66 187	72 522	77 592	85 224	91 910	100 224	109 841
D.7	Other current transfers	NMLO	60 866	64 856	66 590	72 875	77 992	85 520	92 195	100 552	110 192
Total	Total resources	NMLX	79 438	84 973	88 623	95 297	102 133	113 126	122 166	126 470	136 964
	Uses										
D.59	Other current taxes	EBFS	830	861	860	902	876	842	837	997	1 075
D.62	Social benefits other than social transfers in kind	NSMN	15 451	14 818	14 491	15 082	15 863	16 460	17 239	18 271	19 364
D.7	Other current transfers										
D.71	Net non-life insurance premiums	NMMI	499	410	403	353	400	296	285	328	351
D.73	Current transfers within general government	NMDK	–	–	–	–	–	–	–	–	–
D.75	Miscellaneous current transfers	EBFE	17	25	32	23	23	24	25	23	25
D.7	Other current transfers	NMMF	516	435	435	376	423	320	310	351	376
B.6g	**Gross Disposable Income**	NRLW	**62 641**	**68 859**	**72 837**	**78 937**	**84 971**	**95 504**	**103 780**	**106 851**	**116 149**
Total	Total uses	NMLX	79 438	84 973	88 623	95 297	102 133	113 126	122 166	126 470	136 964
-K.1	After deduction of fixed capital consumption	-NSRO	–3 666	–3 866	–4 047	–4 313	–4 653	–4 905	–5 457	–5 906	–6 426
B.6n	Disposable income, net	NMMQ	58 975	64 993	68 790	74 624	80 318	90 599	98 323	100 945	109 723

5.3.4S Local government Social contributions and benefits

ESA95 sector S.1313

£ million

			1998	1999	2000	2001	2002	2003	2004	2005	2006
Part	**SECONDARY DISTRIBUTION OF INCOME** (further detail of certain items)										
	Resources										
D.61	Social contributions										
	Unfunded pension schemes[1]										
D.611	Actual social contributions										
D.61122	Employees' voluntary contributions	NMWM	551	583	578	609	637	659	703	758	797
D.612	Imputed social contributions										
D.612	Employers' contributions	GCMN	1 653	1 714	1 857	1 957	2 066	2 145	2 219	2 307	2 423
D.61	Total social contributions	NSMM	2 204	2 297	2 435	2 566	2 703	2 804	2 922	3 065	3 220
	Uses										
D.62	Social benefits										
D.623	Unfunded employee social benefits										
	Unfunded pensions paid[1]	NMWK	1 749	1 863	1 975	2 083	2 192	2 317	2 446	2 585	2 736
	Other unfunded employee benefits	EWRN	455	434	460	483	511	487	476	480	484
D.623	Total unfunded social benefits	GCMO	2 204	2 297	2 435	2 566	2 703	2 804	2 922	3 065	3 220
D.624	Social assistance benefits in cash										
	Student grants	GCSI	2 143	1 407	848	996	1 082	1 208	1 341	1 449	1 645
	Rent rebates	CTML	5 372	5 350	5 284	5 277	5 232	5 120	5 159	5 247	5 407
	Rent allowances	GCSR	5 696	5 752	5 921	6 241	6 846	7 328	7 817	8 510	9 092
	Total other transfers	ZXHZ	36	12	3	2	–	–	–	–	–
D.624	Total social assistance benefits in cash	ADAL	13 247	12 521	12 056	12 516	13 160	13 656	14 317	15 206	16 144
D.62	Total social benefits	NSMN	15 451	14 818	14 491	15 082	15 863	16 460	17 239	18 271	19 364

1 Mainly police and firefighters' schemes

5.3.5 Local government

ESA95 sector S.1313

£ million

			1998	1999	2000	2001	2002	2003	2004	2005	2006
II.3	**REDISTRIBUTION OF INCOME IN KIND ACCOUNT**										
	Resources										
B.6g	**Total resources (Gross Disposable Income)**	NRLW	**62 641**	**68 859**	**72 837**	**78 937**	**84 971**	**95 504**	**103 780**	**106 851**	**116 149**
	Uses										
D.63	Social transfers in kind										
D.631	Social benefits in kind										
D.632	Transfers of individual non-market goods and services	NMMU	38 666	42 833	46 255	50 247	55 408	60 739	65 129	70 104	73 415
B.7g	Adjusted disposable income, gross	NSXL	23 975	26 026	26 582	28 690	29 563	34 765	38 651	36 747	42 734
B.6g	**Total uses (Gross Disposable Income)**	NRLW	**62 641**	**68 859**	**72 837**	**78 937**	**84 971**	**95 504**	**103 780**	**106 851**	**116 149**

5.3.6 Local government

ESA95 sector S.1313

£ million

			1998	1999	2000	2001	2002	2003	2004	2005	2006
II.4	**USE OF INCOME ACCOUNT**										
II.4.1	**USE OF DISPOSABLE INCOME ACCOUNT**										
	Resources										
B.6g	**Total resources (Gross Disposable Income)**	NRLW	**62 641**	**68 859**	**72 837**	**78 937**	**84 971**	**95 504**	**103 780**	**106 851**	**116 149**
	Uses										
P.3	Final consumption expenditure										
P.31	Individual consumption expenditure	NMMU	38 666	42 833	46 255	50 247	55 408	60 739	65 129	70 104	73 415
P.32	Collective consumption expenditure	NMMV	20 598	23 107	24 789	25 494	26 730	29 321	33 254	36 046	37 923
P.3	Total	NMMT	59 264	65 940	71 044	75 741	82 138	90 060	98 383	106 150	111 338
B.8g	**Gross Saving**	NRLX	**3 377**	**2 919**	**1 793**	**3 196**	**2 833**	**5 444**	**5 397**	**701**	**4 811**
B.6g	**Total uses (Gross Disposable Income)**	NRLW	**62 641**	**68 859**	**72 837**	**78 937**	**84 971**	**95 504**	**103 780**	**106 851**	**116 149**
-K.1	After deduction of fixed capital consumption	-NSRO	−3 666	−3 866	−4 047	−4 313	−4 653	−4 905	−5 457	−5 906	−6 426
B.8n	Saving, net	NMMX	−289	−947	−2 254	−1 117	−1 820	539	−60	−5 205	−1 615
II.4.2	**USE OF ADJUSTED DISPOSABLE INCOME ACCOUNT**										
	Resources										
B.7g	Total resources, adjusted disposable income, gross	NSXL	23 975	26 026	26 582	28 690	29 563	34 765	38 651	36 747	42 734
	Uses										
P.4	Actual final consumption										
P.42	Actual collective consumption	NMMV	20 598	23 107	24 789	25 494	26 730	29 321	33 254	36 046	37 923
B.8g	**Gross Saving**	NRLX	**3 377**	**2 919**	**1 793**	**3 196**	**2 833**	**5 444**	**5 397**	**701**	**4 811**
Total	Total uses	NSXL	23 975	26 026	26 582	28 690	29 563	34 765	38 651	36 747	42 734

5.3.7 Local government

ESA95 sector S.1313

£ million

			1998	1999	2000	2001	2002	2003	2004	2005	2006
III	**ACCUMULATION ACCOUNTS**										
III.1	**CAPITAL ACCOUNT**										
III.1.1	**CHANGE IN NET WORTH DUE TO SAVINGS AND CAPITAL TRANSFERS**										
	Changes in liabilities and net worth										
B.8g	**Gross Saving**	NRLX	**3 377**	**2 919**	**1 793**	**3 196**	**2 833**	**5 444**	**5 397**	**701**	**4 811**
D.9	Capital transfers receivable										
D.92	Investment grants	NMNE	2 656	3 298	4 105	4 652	6 328	7 360	8 565	8 512	8 360
D.99	Other capital transfers	NMNH	191	205	411	416	735	4 770	2 196	1 427	1 087
D.9	Total capital transfers receivable	NMMY	2 847	3 503	4 516	5 068	7 063	12 130	10 761	9 939	9 447
-D.9	*less* Capital transfers payable										
-D.92	Investment grants	-NMNR	–1 282	–1 156	–1 000	–917	–839	–1 165	–1 503	–1 570	–1 546
-D.99	Other capital transfers	-NMNU	–	–	–	–	–5	–5	–1 147	–1 284	–851
-D.9	Total capital transfers payable	-NMNL	–1 282	–1 156	–1 000	–917	–844	–1 170	–2 650	–2 854	–2 397
B.10.1g	Total change in liabilities and net worth	NRMJ	4 942	5 266	5 309	7 347	9 052	16 404	13 508	7 786	11 861
	Changes in assets										
B.10.1g	Changes in net worth due to gross saving and capital transfers	NRMJ	4 942	5 266	5 309	7 347	9 052	16 404	13 508	7 786	11 861
-K.1	After deduction of fixed capital consumption	-NSRO	–3 666	–3 866	–4 047	–4 313	–4 653	–4 905	–5 457	–5 906	–6 426
B.10.1n	Changes in net worth due to net saving and capital transfers	NMNX	1 276	1 400	1 262	3 034	4 399	11 499	8 051	1 880	5 435
III.1.2	**ACQUISITION OF NON-FINANCIAL ASSETS ACCOUNT**										
	Changes in liabilities and net worth										
B.10.1n	Changes in net worth due to saving and capital transfers	NMNX	1 276	1 400	1 262	3 034	4 399	11 499	8 051	1 880	5 435
K.1	Consumption of fixed capital	NSRO	3 666	3 866	4 047	4 313	4 653	4 905	5 457	5 906	6 426
B.10.1g	Total changes in liabilities and net worth	NRMJ	4 942	5 266	5 309	7 347	9 052	16 404	13 508	7 786	11 861
	Changes in assets										
P.5	Gross capital formation										
P.51	Gross fixed capital formation	NMOA	5 903	6 243	6 552	7 569	7 946	14 137	14 891	13 516	14 297
P.52	Changes in inventories	NMOB	–	–	–	–	–	–	–	–	–
P.5	Total	NMNZ	5 903	6 243	6 552	7 569	7 946	14 137	14 891	13 516	14 297
K.2	Acquisitions less disposals of non-produced non-financial assets	NMOD	–653	–715	–589	–719	–760	–800	–857	–902	–947
B.9g	**Net lending(+) / net borrowing(-)**	NMOE	**–308**	**–262**	**–654**	**497**	**1 866**	**3 067**	**–526**	**–4 828**	**–1 489**
Total	Total change in assets	NRMJ	4 942	5 266	5 309	7 347	9 052	16 404	13 508	7 786	11 861

5.3.8 Local government
ESA95 sector S.1313 Unconsolidated

£ million

			1998	1999	2000	2001	2002	2003	2004	2005	2006
III.2	**FINANCIAL ACCOUNT**										
F.A	**Net acquisition of financial assets**										
F.2	Currency and deposits										
F.22	Transferable deposits										
F.2211	Sterling deposits with UK banks	NBYS	–90	–728	207	256	894	234	2 863	275	3 776
F.2212	Foreign currency deposits with UK banks	NBYT	20	–25	14	–7	–1	–9	1	28	–20
F.2213	Sterling deposits with building societies	NBYU	695	679	384	439	437	1 088	1 112	–225	1 632
F.29	Other deposits	NBYW	–	–	90	–59	268	135	–67	–13	–181
F.2	Total currency and deposits	NBYO	625	–74	695	629	1 598	1 448	3 909	65	5 207
F.3	Securities other than shares										
F.331	Short term: money market instruments										
F.3311	Issued by UK central government	NBYZ	106	204	–218	119	–141	–38	–59	14	–17
F.3315	Issued by UK monetary financial institutions	NBZE	232	565	415	–20	487	24	–311	–159	–970
F.3316	Issued by other UK residents	NBZJ	58	–34	59	41	11	–38	10	–41	653
F.332	Medium (1 to 5 year) and long term (over 5 year) bonds										
F.3321	Issued by UK central government	NBZM	95	–17	–195	191	–264	–101	–97	5	72
F.3326	Issued by other UK residents	E55E	–	–	–	–	–	–	–	215	–
F.3	Total securities other than shares	NBYX	491	718	61	331	93	–153	–457	34	–262
F.4	Loans										
F.42	Long term loans										
F.422	Loans secured on dwellings	NCAK	–153	107	12	97	206	186	4	252	46
F.424	Other long-term loans by UK residents	NCAP	51	17	–31	–76	–83	–18	–27	202	–12
F.4	Total loans	NBZZ	–102	124	–19	21	123	168	–23	454	34
F.5	Shares and other equity										
F.51	Shares and other equity, excluding mutual funds' shares										
F.514	Quoted UK shares	NCAW	72	–304	157	–54	–218	45	–117	17	208
F.515	Unquoted UK shares	NCAX	–40	–	–	–293	–	–	–	–2 594	–2 431
F.517	UK shares and bonds issued by other UK residents	NSPE	–	–	–	–	–	–	–	–	–
F.5	Total shares and other equity	NCAR	32	–304	157	–347	–218	45	–117	–2 577	–2 223
F.6	Insurance technical reserves										
F.62	Prepayments of insurance premiums and reserves for outstanding claims	NCBK	–11	–30	24	–26	27	8	45	44	35
F.7	Other accounts receivable	NCBL	–321	–194	–55	–424	–1 123	281	2	201	115
F.A	**Total net acquisition of financial assets**	NBYK	714	240	863	184	500	1 797	3 359	–1 779	2 906

5.3.8 Local government
ESA95 sector S.1313 Unconsolidated

continued £ million

			1998	1999	2000	2001	2002	2003	2004	2005	2006
III.2	**FINANCIAL ACCOUNT** continued										
F.L	**Net acquisition of financial liabilities**										
F.3	Securities other than shares										
F.331	Short term: money market instruments										
F.3312	Issued by UK local government	NCCH	–6	–	–	–	–	–	–	–	–
F.332	Medium (1 to 5 year) and long term (over 5 year) bonds										
F.3322	Issued by UK local authorities	NCCT	6	–2	–12	–	47	18	–225	213	358
F.3	Total securities other than shares	NCCB	–	–2	–12	–	47	18	–225	213	358
F.4	Loans										
F.41	Short term loans										
F.411	Loans by UK monetary financial institutions, excluding loans secured on dwellings & financial leasing	NCDF	–536	–817	–282	–	816	1 162	1 556	748	1 166
F.419	Loans by rest of the world monetary financial institutions	NCDJ	–42	–44	–39	–34	–13	–7	–6	–3	–1
F.42	Long term loans										
F.423	Finance leasing	NCDS	–	–	–	–	18	15	24	5	3
F.424	Other long-term loans by UK residents	NCDT	858	1 908	1 444	–189	–1 709	–3 893	520	2 616	2 709
F.429	Other long-term loans by the rest of the world	NCDU	–43	–61	–149	56	39	211	639	137	233
F.4	Total loans	NCDD	237	986	974	–167	–849	–2 512	2 733	3 503	4 110
F.7	Other accounts payable	NCEP	192	265	–465	538	–627	259	493	263	691
F.L	**Total net acquisition of financial liabilities**	NCBO	429	1 249	497	371	–1 429	–2 235	3 001	3 979	5 159
B.9	**Net lending / borrowing**										
F.A	Total net acquisition of financial assets	NBYK	714	240	863	184	500	1 797	3 359	–1 779	2 906
-F.L	*less* Total net acquisition of financial liabilities	-NCBO	–429	–1 249	–497	–371	1 429	2 235	–3 001	–3 979	–5 159
B.9f	Net lending (+) / net borrowing (-), from financial account	NYNQ	285	–1 009	366	–187	1 929	4 032	358	–5 758	–2 253
dB.9f	Statistical discrepancy	NYPC	–593	747	–1 020	684	–63	–965	–884	930	764
B.9g	**Net lending (+) / net borrowing (-), from capital account**	NMOE	**–308**	**–262**	**–654**	**497**	**1 866**	**3 067**	**–526**	**–4 828**	**–1 489**

5.3.9 Local government

ESA95 sector S.1313 Unconsolidated

£ billion

			1998	1999	2000	2001	2002	2003	2004	2005	2006
IV.3	**FINANCIAL BALANCE SHEET** at end of period										
AN	**Non-financial assets**	CGIZ	212.5	228.0	258.1	301.3	307.5	334.1	379.6	406.4	418.0
AF.A	**Financial assets**										
AF.2	Currency and deposits										
AF.22	Transferable deposits										
AF.2211	Sterling deposits with UK banks	NJEP	8.7	8.3	8.7	8.9	10.2	10.6	13.6	13.9	17.6
AF.2212	Foreign currency deposits with UK banks	NJEQ	–	–	–	–	–	–	–	–	–
AF.2213	Sterling deposits with UK building societies	NJER	4.1	4.4	4.6	5.0	5.4	6.5	7.7	7.6	9.2
AF.29	Other deposits	NJET	–	–	0.1	–	0.3	0.4	0.4	0.4	0.2
AF.2	Total currency and deposits	NJEL	12.9	12.7	13.4	14.0	15.9	17.6	21.7	21.9	27.0
AF.3	Securities other than shares										
AF.331	Short term: money market instruments										
AF.3311	Issued by UK central government	NJEW	0.2	0.5	0.2	0.4	0.2	0.2	0.1	0.1	0.1
AF.3315	Issued by UK monetary financial institutions	NJFB	2.4	3.0	3.4	3.3	3.8	3.9	3.6	3.5	2.5
AF.3316	Issued by other UK residents	NJFG	0.1	0.1	0.2	0.2	0.2	0.2	0.1	0.3	0.1
AF.332	Medium (1 to 5 year) and long term (over 5 year) bonds										
AF.3321	Issued by UK central government	NJFJ	0.8	0.7	0.5	0.7	0.4	0.3	0.2	0.2	0.2
AF.3326	Issued by other UK residents	E55D	–	–	–	–	–	–	–	0.2	0.2
AF.3	Total securities other than shares	NJEU	3.6	4.2	4.3	4.5	4.7	4.5	4.1	4.3	3.2
AF.4	Loans										
AF.42	Long term loans										
AF.422	Loans secured on dwellings	NJGH	0.4	0.5	0.5	0.6	0.8	1.0	1.0	1.3	1.3
AF.424	Other long-term loans by UK residents	NJGM	0.3	0.3	0.3	0.3	0.3	0.3	0.3	0.3	0.2
AF.4	Total loans	NJFW	0.7	0.8	0.8	0.9	1.1	1.3	1.3	1.5	1.6
AF.5	Shares and other equity										
AF.51	Shares and other equity, excluding mutual funds' shares										
AF.514	Quoted UK shares	NJGT	0.8	2.2	1.4	1.1	1.0	1.2	1.2	1.2	1.4
AF.515	Unquoted UK shares	NJGU	0.4	0.4	0.4	0.4	0.4	0.4	0.4	0.4	0.4
AF.517	UK shares and bonds issued by other UK residents	NSOE	–	–	–	–	–	–	–	–	–
AF.5	Total shares and other equity	NJGO	1.2	2.6	1.8	1.5	1.4	1.6	1.6	1.6	1.8
AF.6	Insurance technical reserves										
AF.62	Prepayments of insurance premiums and reserves for outstanding claims	NJHH	1.2	1.1	1.0	0.9	0.9	0.8	0.8	0.8	0.8
AF.7	Other accounts receivable	NJHI	2.3	1.8	1.6	1.3	0.3	0.8	0.3	1.3	1.4
AF.A	**Total financial assets**	NJFV	21.8	23.3	22.8	23.1	24.4	26.6	29.8	31.4	35.8

5.3.9 Local government

ESA95 sector S.1313 Unconsolidated

continued £ billion

			1998	1999	2000	2001	2002	2003	2004	2005	2006
IV.3	**FINANCIAL BALANCE SHEET** continued at end of period										
AF.L	**Financial liabilities**										
AF.3	Securities other than shares										
AF.331	Short term: money market instruments										
AF.3312	Issued by UK local government	NJIE	–	–	–	–	–	–	–	–	–
AF.332	Medium (1 to 5 year) and long term (over 5 year) bonds										
AF.3322	Issued by UK local government	NJIQ	0.8	0.8	0.8	0.8	0.8	0.8	0.6	0.8	1.2
AF.3	Total securities other than shares	NJHY	0.8	0.8	0.8	0.8	0.8	0.8	0.6	0.8	1.2
AF.4	Loans										
AF.41	Short term loans										
AF.411	Loans by UK monetary financial institutions, excluding loans secured on dwellings & financial leasing	NJJC	3.1	2.4	1.7	1.9	2.9	4.3	6.2	7.6	9.1
AF.419	Loans by rest of the world monetary financial institutions	NJJG	0.2	0.2	0.1	–	–	–	–	–	–
AF.42	Long term loans										
AF.423	Finance leasing	NJJP	–	–	–	–	–	–	0.1	0.1	0.1
AF.424	Other long-term loans by UK residents	NJJQ	47.6	48.9	50.1	50.1	48.4	44.5	45.5	47.9	50.6
AF.429	Other long-term loans by the rest of the world	NJJR	0.9	0.9	0.7	0.8	0.8	1.1	1.7	1.9	2.1
AF.4	Total loans	NJJA	51.8	52.4	52.6	52.9	52.1	49.9	53.5	57.5	61.9
AF.7	Other accounts payable	NJKM	9.3	9.5	9.0	9.7	9.1	9.5	9.6	9.5	10.2
AF.L	**Total financial liabilities**	NJIZ	61.9	62.7	62.4	63.3	62.0	60.2	63.7	67.8	73.3
BF.90	**Net financial assets / liabilities**										
AF.A	Total financial assets	NJFV	21.8	23.3	22.8	23.1	24.4	26.6	29.8	31.4	35.8
-AF.L	*less* Total financial liabilities	-NJIZ	–61.9	–62.7	–62.4	–63.3	–62.0	–60.2	–63.7	–67.8	–73.3
BF.90	**Net financial assets (+) / liabilities (-)**	NYOJ	–40.0	–39.4	–39.6	–40.3	–37.6	–33.7	–33.9	–36.5	–37.5
	Net worth										
AN	Non-financial assets	CGIZ	212.5	228.0	258.1	301.3	307.5	334.1	379.6	406.4	418.0
BF.90	Net financial assets (+) / liabilities (-)	NYOJ	–40.0	–39.4	–39.6	–40.3	–37.6	–33.7	–33.9	–36.5	–37.5
BF.90	**Net worth**	CGRZ	172.5	188.6	218.5	261.1	269.9	300.4	345.6	370.0	380.5

Chapter 6

Households and non-profit institutions serving households (NPISH)

6.1.1 Households and non-profit institutions serving households
ESA95 sectors S.14 and S.15

£ million

			1998	1999	2000	2001	2002	2003	2004
I	**PRODUCTION ACCOUNT**								
	Resources								
P.1	Output								
P.11	Market output	QWLF	176 030	185 862	195 741	209 723	220 913	232 646	243 402
P.12	Output for own final use	QWLG	50 899	54 649	57 758	63 215	66 856	72 869	78 091
P.13	Other non-market output	QWLH	20 837	21 874	23 169	24 720	25 968	27 185	28 953
P.1	Total resources	QWLI	247 766	262 385	276 668	297 658	313 737	332 700	350 446
	Uses								
P.2	Intermediate consumption	QWLJ	104 833	110 357	116 361	124 831	131 125	138 294	145 211
B.1g	**Gross Value Added**	QWLK	**142 933**	**152 028**	**160 307**	**172 827**	**182 612**	**194 406**	**205 235**
Total	Total uses	QWLI	247 766	262 385	276 668	297 658	313 737	332 700	350 446
B.1g	**Gross Value Added**	QWLK	**142 933**	**152 028**	**160 307**	**172 827**	**182 612**	**194 406**	**205 235**
-K.1	*less* Consumption of fixed capital	-QWLL	–25 053	–27 976	–30 517	–32 909	–36 043	–36 903	–42 366
B.1n	Value added, net	QWLM	117 880	124 052	129 790	139 918	146 569	157 503	162 869

6.1.2 Households and non-profit institutions serving households
ESA95 sectors S.14 and S.15

£ million

			1998	1999	2000	2001	2002	2003	2004
II	**DISTRIBUTION AND USE OF INCOME ACCOUNTS**								
II.1	**PRIMARY DISTRIBUTION OF INCOME ACCOUNT**								
II.1.1	**GENERATION OF INCOME ACCOUNT** before deduction of fixed capital consumption								
	Resources								
B.1g	**Total resources (Gross Value Added)**	QWLK	**142 933**	**152 028**	**160 307**	**172 827**	**182 612**	**194 406**	**205 235**
	Uses								
D.1	Compensation of employees								
D.11	Wages and salaries	QWLN	37 828	40 080	43 029	45 975	48 035	49 939	52 128
D.12	Employers' social contributions	QWLO	4 819	5 285	5 792	6 183	6 723	7 941	8 968
D.1	Total	QWLP	42 647	45 365	48 821	52 158	54 758	57 880	61 096
D.2	Taxes on production and imports, paid								
D.29	Production taxes other than on products	QWLQ	62	72	56	47	58	61	64
-D.3	*less* Subsidies received								
-D.39	Production subsidies other than on products	-QWLR	–241	–338	–335	–582	–519	–592	–592
B.2g	Operating surplus, gross	QWLS	47 642	51 195	53 960	59 083	62 544	67 935	72 709
B.3g	Mixed income, gross	QWLT	52 823	55 734	57 805	62 121	65 771	69 122	71 958
B.1g	**Total uses (Gross Value Added)**	QWLK	**142 933**	**152 028**	**160 307**	**172 827**	**182 612**	**194 406**	**205 235**
-K.1	After deduction of fixed capital consumption	-QWLL	–25 053	–27 976	–30 517	–32 909	–36 043	–36 903	–42 366
B.2n	Operating surplus, net	QWLU	32 727	35 008	36 517	40 404	41 931	46 420	50 147
B.3n	Mixed income, net	QWLV	42 685	43 945	44 731	47 891	50 341	53 734	52 154

6.1.3 Households and non-profit institutions serving households

ESA95 sectors S.14 and S.15

£ million

			1998	1999	2000	2001	2002	2003	2004	2005	2006
II.1.2	**ALLOCATION OF PRIMARY INCOME ACCOUNT** before deduction of fixed capital consumption										
	Resources										
B.2g	Operating surplus, gross	QWLS	47 642	51 195	53 960	59 083	62 544	67 935	72 709	77 791	82 425
B.3g	Mixed income, gross	QWLT	52 823	55 734	57 805	62 121	65 771	69 122	71 958	75 675	78 864
D.1	Compensation of employees										
D.11	Wages and salaries	QWLW	406 548	431 795	462 505	491 044	508 681	527 689	550 654	578 300	605 320
D.12	Employers' social contributions	QWLX	59 522	64 199	69 824	73 216	78 782	89 263	98 134	107 895	115 229
D.1	Total	QWLY	466 070	495 994	532 329	564 260	587 463	616 952	648 788	686 195	720 549
D.4	Property income, received										
D.41	Interest	QWLZ	29 867	24 147	28 239	26 823	20 878	20 966	26 242	31 422	33 129
D.42	Distributed income of corporations	QWMA	38 649	40 411	44 408	49 881	43 695	44 843	46 239	51 630	49 617
D.44	Attributed property income of insurance policy holders	QWMC	56 242	56 303	56 048	56 109	55 057	54 997	54 589	63 725	68 282
D.45	Rent	QWMD	105	105	105	105	106	108	110	110	112
D.4	Total	QWME	124 863	120 966	128 800	132 918	119 736	120 914	127 180	146 887	151 140
Total	Total resources	QWMF	691 398	723 889	772 894	818 382	835 514	874 923	920 635	986 548	1 032 978
	Uses										
D.4	Property income, paid										
D.41	Interest	QWMG	51 219	47 434	52 875	52 141	51 513	53 576	62 677	69 497	73 444
D.45	Rent	QWMH	216	215	215	215	216	220	224	224	224
D.4	Total	QWMI	51 435	47 649	53 090	52 356	51 729	53 796	62 901	69 721	73 668
B.5g	**Balance of primary incomes, gross**	QWMJ	**639 963**	**676 240**	**719 804**	**766 026**	**783 785**	**821 127**	**857 734**	**916 827**	**959 310**
Total	Total uses	QWMF	691 398	723 889	772 894	818 382	835 514	874 923	920 635	986 548	1 032 978
-K.1	After deduction of fixed capital consumption	-QWLL	–25 053	–27 976	–30 517	–32 909	–36 043	–36 903	–42 366	–42 623	–42 887
B.5n	Balance of primary incomes, net	QWMK	614 910	648 264	689 287	733 117	747 742	784 224	815 368	874 204	916 423

6.1.4 Households and non-profit institutions serving households

ESA95 sectors S.14 and S.15

£ million

			1998	1999	2000	2001	2002	2003	2004	2005	2006
II.2	**SECONDARY DISTRIBUTION OF INCOME ACCOUNT**										
	Resources										
B.5g	**Balance of primary incomes, gross**	QWMJ	**639 963**	**676 240**	**719 804**	**766 026**	**783 785**	**821 127**	**857 734**	**916 827**	**959 310**
D.612	Imputed social contributions	RVFH	478	450	476	502	530	505	495	500	508
D.62	Social benefits other than social transfers in kind	QWML	154 438	157 647	162 833	171 814	182 673	193 596	202 074	213 858	223 618
D.7	Other current transfers										
D.72	Non-life insurance claims	QWMM	15 224	13 762	16 150	15 607	17 177	14 824	15 494	17 172	18 440
D.75	Miscellaneous current transfers	QWMN	21 181	24 392	27 520	29 080	33 041	34 687	36 284	38 489	38 244
D.7	Total	QWMO	36 405	38 154	43 670	44 687	50 218	49 511	51 778	55 661	56 684
	Total resources	QWMP	831 284	872 491	926 783	983 029	1 017 206	1 064 739	1 112 081	1 186 846	1 240 120
	Uses										
D.5	Current taxes on income, wealth, etc										
D.51	Taxes on income	QWMQ	89 276	96 528	105 299	111 888	112 171	113 087	120 253	130 342	140 219
D.59	Other current taxes	NVCO	17 290	18 658	19 427	21 166	22 788	25 174	26 881	28 256	29 606
D.5	Total	QWMS	106 566	115 186	124 726	133 054	134 959	138 261	147 134	158 598	169 825
D.61	Social contributions										
D.611	Actual social contributions										
D.6111	Employers' actual social contributions	QWMT	48 138	52 529	57 288	60 296	64 805	77 571	87 347	95 997	103 557
D.6112	Employees' social contributions	QWMU	54 761	57 434	58 806	60 599	62 458	66 490	69 576	78 033	83 209
D.6113	Social contributions by self- and non-employed	QWMV	1 729	1 883	2 049	2 183	2 318	2 595	2 727	2 825	2 930
D.611	Total	QWMW	104 628	111 846	118 143	123 078	129 581	146 656	159 650	176 855	189 696
D.612	Imputed social contributions	QWMX	11 384	11 670	12 536	12 920	13 977	11 692	10 787	11 898	11 672
D.61	Total	QWMY	116 012	123 516	130 679	135 998	143 558	158 348	170 437	188 753	201 368
D.62	Social benefits other than social transfers in kind	QWMZ	950	922	948	977	1 006	987	984	994	1 004
D.7	Other current transfers										
D.71	Net non-life insurance premiums	QWNA	15 224	13 762	16 150	15 607	17 177	14 824	15 494	17 172	18 440
D.75	Miscellaneous current transfers	QWNB	9 742	10 117	10 865	11 081	11 458	11 930	12 349	13 340	13 282
D.7	Total	QWNC	24 966	23 879	27 015	26 688	28 635	26 754	27 843	30 512	31 722
B.6g	**Gross Disposable Income**[1]	QWND	**582 790**	**608 988**	**643 415**	**686 312**	**709 048**	**740 389**	**765 683**	**807 989**	**836 201**
	Total uses	QWMP	831 284	872 491	926 783	983 029	1 017 206	1 064 739	1 112 081	1 186 846	1 240 120
-K.1	After deduction of fixed capital consumption	-QWLL	–25 053	–27 976	–30 517	–32 909	–36 043	–36 903	–42 366	–42 623	–42 887
B.6n	Disposable income, net	QWNE	557 737	581 012	612 898	653 403	673 005	703 486	723 317	765 366	793 314

1 Gross household disposable income revalued by the implied households and NPISH's final consumption expenditure deflator is as follows:

6.1.4S Households and non-profit institutions serving households
Social benefits and contributions

ESA95 sectors S.14 and S.15

£ million

Part			1998	1999	2000	2001	2002	2003	2004	2005	2006
	SECONDARY DISTRIBUTION OF INCOME (further detail of certain items)										
	Benefits										
	Resources										
D.62	Social benefits										
D.621	Social security benefits in cash										
	National insurance fund benefits[1]	ACHH	44 844	46 335	47 490	50 336	53 123	55 731	58 225	60 449	62 760
	Redundancy fund benefit	GTKN	106	137	167	198	278	245	169	274	200
	Social fund benefit	GTLQ	356	1 087	1 753	1 885	1 910	2 135	2 240	2 232	2 274
	Maternity fund benefits	GTKO	–	–	–	–	–	–	–	–	–
D.621	Total social security benefits in cash	HAYQ	45 306	47 559	49 410	52 419	55 311	58 111	60 634	62 955	65 234
D.622	Private funded social benefits										
	Funded social benefits	D3N3	32 505	35 428	37 817	37 106	40 224	42 121	42 816	47 000	50 636
	Employee benefits from employers' liability insurance	NRXD	552	502	458	591	930	1 143	1 269	1 400	1 458
D.622	Total private funded social benefits	HAYR	33 057	35 930	38 275	37 697	41 155	43 264	44 085	48 400	52 094
D.623	Unfunded employee social benefits										
	Unfunded central government pensions paid[2]	E8AF	11 192	11 295	12 076	12 645	14 345	15 221	15 427	16 969	18 487
	Unfunded local government pensions paid[3]	NMWK	1 749	1 863	1 975	2 083	2 192	2 317	2 446	2 585	2 736
	Other unfunded employee benefits[4]	EWRM	5 213	5 529	5 964	6 208	6 539	6 104	5 707	5 472	5 370
D.623	Total unfunded social benefits	RVFF	18 154	18 687	20 015	20 936	23 076	23 642	23 580	25 026	26 593
D.624	Social assistance benefits in cash										
	Received from central government	LNJT	44 202	42 478	42 605	47 771	49 495	54 441	58 969	61 777	63 057
	Received from local government	ADAL	13 247	12 521	12 056	12 516	13 160	13 656	14 317	15 206	16 144
	Received from NPISHs	HABJ	472	472	472	475	476	482	489	494	496
D.624	Total social assistance benefits in cash	HAYU	57 921	55 471	55 133	60 762	63 131	68 579	73 775	77 477	79 697
D.62	Total social benefits	QWML	154 438	157 647	162 833	171 814	182 673	193 596	202 074	213 858	223 618
	Uses										
D.62	Social benefits	QWMZ	950	922	948	977	1 006	987	984	994	1 004
	Contributions										
	Resources										
D.612	Imputed social contributions	RVFH	478	450	476	502	530	505	495	500	508
	Uses										
D.61	Social Contributions										
D.611	Actual social contributions										
D.6111	Employers' actual social contributions										
	National Insurance contributions	CEAN	28 731	31 286	34 028	35 706	35 735	39 890	43 586	46 741	48 624
	Notionally funded pension schemes	GCMP	1 862	2 115	2 369	2 754	3 045	5 177	6 016	6 163	6 941
	Funded pension schemes	RIUO	17 545	19 128	20 891	21 836	26 025	32 504	37 745	43 093	47 992
D.6111	Total employers' actual social contributions	QWMT	48 138	52 529	57 288	60 296	64 805	77 571	87 347	95 997	103 557
D.6112	Employees' actual social contributions										
	National Insurance contributions	GCSE	22 528	23 573	24 175	25 236	25 357	29 055	32 396	34 742	36 415
	Unfunded central government pension schemes	E8AA	2 126	2 460	2 516	2 855	3 550	4 639	5 029	6 016	6 175
	Unfunded local government pension schemes	NMWM	551	583	578	609	637	659	703	758	797
	Funded pension schemes	GCRR	29 556	30 818	31 537	31 899	32 914	32 137	31 448	36 517	39 822
D.6112	Total employees' actual social contributions	QWMU	54 761	57 434	58 806	60 599	62 458	66 490	69 576	78 033	83 209
D.6113	Social contributions by self and non-employed	QWMV	1 729	1 883	2 049	2 183	2 318	2 595	2 727	2 825	2 930
D.611	Total actual social contributions	QWMW	104 628	111 846	118 143	123 078	129 581	146 656	159 650	176 855	189 696
D.612	Imputed social contributions										
	Employers imputed contributions to unfunded central government pension schemes	E8AC	4 973	4 861	5 175	5 238	5 883	3 930	3 337	4 599	4 363
	Employers imputed contributions to unfunded local government pension schemes	NMWL	1 198	1 280	1 397	1 474	1 555	1 658	1 743	1 827	1 939
	Other imputed unfunded employers' contributions	EWRM	5 213	5 529	5 964	6 208	6 539	6 104	5 707	5 472	5 370
D.612	Total imputed social contributions	QWMX	11 384	11 670	12 536	12 920	13 977	11 692	10 787	11 898	11 672
D.61	Total social contributions	QWMY	116 012	123 516	130 679	135 998	143 558	158 348	170 437	188 753	201 368

1 For a more detailed analysis see table 5.2.4S
2 Mainly civil service, armed forces', teachers' and NHS staff
3 Mainly police and fire fighters
4 Such as payments whilst absent from work due to illness

6.1.5 Households and non-profit institutions serving households

ESA95 sectors S.14 and S.15

£ million

			1998	1999	2000	2001	2002	2003	2004	2005	2006
II.3	REDISTRIBUTION OF INCOME IN KIND ACCOUNT										
	Resources										
B.6g	**Gross Disposable Income**	QWND	**582 790**	**608 988**	**643 415**	**686 312**	**709 048**	**740 389**	**765 683**	**807 989**	**836 201**
D.63	Social transfers in kind										
D.631	Social benefits in kind										
D.6313	Social assistance benefits in kind	QWNH	–	–	–	–	–	–	–	–	–
D.632	Transfers of individual non-market goods and services	NSSA	115 620	124 616	132 466	143 178	156 784	171 139	184 764	198 984	211 865
D.63	Total social transfers in kind	NSSB	115 620	124 616	132 466	143 178	156 784	171 139	184 764	198 984	211 865
Total	Total resources	NSSC	698 410	733 604	775 881	829 490	865 832	911 528	950 447	1 006 973	1 048 066
	Uses										
D.63	Social transfers in kind										
D.631	Social benefits in kind										
D.6313	Social assistance benefits in kind	HAEJ	–	–	–	–	–	–	–	–	–
D.632	Transfers of individual non-market goods and services	HABK	20 837	21 874	23 169	24 720	25 968	27 185	28 953	31 585	33 313
D.63	Total social transfers in kind	HAEK	20 837	21 874	23 169	24 720	25 968	27 185	28 953	31 585	33 313
B.7g	Adjusted disposable income, gross	NSSD	677 573	711 730	752 712	804 770	839 864	884 343	921 494	975 388	1 014 753
Total	Total uses	NSSC	698 410	733 604	775 881	829 490	865 832	911 528	950 447	1 006 973	1 048 066

6.1.6 Households and non-profit institutions serving households

ESA95 sectors S.14 and S.15

£ million

			1998	1999	2000	2001	2002	2003	2004	2005	2006
II.4	USE OF INCOME ACCOUNT										
II.4.1	USE OF DISPOSABLE INCOME ACCOUNT										
	Resources										
B.6g	**Gross Disposable Income**	QWND	**582 790**	**608 988**	**643 415**	**686 312**	**709 048**	**740 389**	**765 683**	**807 989**	**836 201**
D.8	Adjustment for the change in net equity of households in pension funds	NSSE	14 044	14 016	14 164	16 041	17 783	21 377	25 108	31 210	35 720
Total	Total resources	NSSF	596 834	623 004	657 579	702 353	726 831	761 766	790 791	839 199	871 921
	Uses										
P.3	Final consumption expenditure										
P.31	Individual consumption expenditure	NSSG	554 990	589 868	623 995	657 216	690 530	724 345	761 484	792 454	828 081
B.8g	**Gross Saving**	NSSH	**41 844**	**33 136**	**33 584**	**45 137**	**36 301**	**37 421**	**29 307**	**46 745**	**43 840**
Total	Total uses	NSSF	596 834	623 004	657 579	702 353	726 831	761 766	790 791	839 199	871 921
-K.1	After deduction of fixed capital consumption	-QWLL	–25 053	–27 976	–30 517	–32 909	–36 043	–36 903	–42 366	–42 623	–42 887
B.8n	Saving, net	NSSI	16 791	5 160	3 067	12 228	258	518	–13 059	4 122	953
II.4.2	USE OF ADJUSTED DISPOSABLE INCOME ACCOUNT										
	Resources										
B.7g	Adjusted disposable income, gross	NSSD	677 573	711 730	752 712	804 770	839 864	884 343	921 494	975 388	1 014 753
D.8	Adjustment for the change in net equity of households in pension funds	NSSE	14 044	14 016	14 164	16 041	17 783	21 377	25 108	31 210	35 720
Total	Total resources	NSSJ	691 617	725 746	766 876	820 811	857 647	905 720	946 602	1 006 598	1 050 473
	Uses										
P.4	Actual final consumption										
P.41	Actual individual consumption	NQEO	649 773	692 610	733 292	775 674	821 346	868 299	917 295	959 853	1 006 633
B.8g	**Gross Saving**[1]	NSSH	**41 844**	**33 136**	**33 584**	**45 137**	**36 301**	**37 421**	**29 307**	**46 745**	**43 840**
Total	Total uses	NSSJ	691 617	725 746	766 876	820 811	857 647	905 720	946 602	1 006 598	1 050 473

1 Households' saving as a percentage of total available households' resources is as follows:

		1997	1998	1999	2000	2001	2002	2003	2004	2005
Households' saving ratio (per cent)	RVGL	9.5	7.0	5.3	5.1	6.4	5.0	4.9	3.7	4.8

6.1.7 Households and non-profit institutions serving households

ESA95 sectors S.14 and S.15

£ million

			1998	1999	2000	2001	2002	2003	2004	2005	2006
III	**ACCUMULATION ACCOUNTS**										
III.1	**CAPITAL ACCOUNT**										
III.1.1	**CHANGE IN NET WORTH DUE TO SAVING & CAPITAL TRANSFERS ACCOUNT**										
	Changes in liabilities and net worth										
B.8g	**Gross Saving**	NSSH	**41 844**	**33 136**	**33 584**	**45 137**	**36 301**	**37 421**	**29 307**	**46 745**	**43 840**
D.9	Capital transfers receivable										
D.92	Investment grants	NSSL	3 477	2 645	2 727	3 148	3 456	4 691	3 887	6 278	5 316
D.99	Other capital transfers	NSSM	1 010	1 144	1 371	2 639	1 869	1 956	2 806	2 747	2 992
D.9	Total	NSSN	4 487	3 789	4 098	5 787	5 325	6 647	6 693	9 025	8 308
-D.9	*less* Capital transfers payable										
-D.91	Capital taxes	-NSSO	–1 795	–1 951	–2 215	–2 396	–2 381	–2 416	–2 881	–3 150	–3 579
-D.99	Other capital transfers	-NSSQ	–531	–499	–461	–1 712	–994	–938	–843	–914	–1 157
-D.9	Total	-NSSR	–2 326	–2 450	–2 676	–4 108	–3 375	–3 354	–3 724	–4 064	–4 736
B.10.1g	Total change in liabilities and net worth	NSSS	44 005	34 475	35 006	46 816	38 251	40 714	32 276	51 706	47 412
	Changes in assets										
B.10.1g	Changes in net worth due to gross saving and capital transfers	NSSS	44 005	34 475	35 006	46 816	38 251	40 714	32 276	51 706	47 412
-K.1	After deduction of fixed capital consumption	-QWLL	–25 053	–27 976	–30 517	–32 909	–36 043	–36 903	–42 366	–42 623	–42 887
B.10.1n	Changes in net worth due to saving and capital transfers	NSST	18 952	6 499	4 489	13 907	2 208	3 811	–10 090	9 083	4 525
III.1.2	**ACQUISITION OF NON-FINANCIAL ASSETS ACCOUNT**										
	Changes in liabilities and net worth										
B.10.1n	Changes in net worth due to saving and capital transfers	NSST	18 952	6 499	4 489	13 907	2 208	3 811	–10 090	9 083	4 525
K.1	Consumption of fixed capital	QWLL	25 053	27 976	30 517	32 909	36 043	36 903	42 366	42 623	42 887
B.10.1g	Total change in liabilities and net worth	NSSS	44 005	34 475	35 006	46 816	38 251	40 714	32 276	51 706	47 412
	Changes in assets										
P.5	Gross capital formation										
P.51	Gross fixed capital formation	NSSU	34 748	38 234	39 018	43 457	49 764	55 226	64 376	66 164	76 461
P.52	Changes in inventories	NSSV	136	227	67	199	195	175	202	–263	–112
P.53	Acquisitions less disposals of valuables	NSSW	339	264	193	374	309	210	215	77	275
P.5	Total gross capital formation	NSSX	35 223	38 725	39 278	44 030	50 268	55 611	64 793	65 978	76 624
K.2	Acquisitions less disposals of non-produced non-financial assets	NSSY	17	–138	–67	–152	–176	–210	–276	–320	–358
B.9	**Net lending (+) / net borrowing (-)**	NSSZ	**8 765**	**–4 112**	**–4 205**	**2 938**	**–11 841**	**–14 687**	**–32 241**	**–13 952**	**–28 854**
Total	Total change in assets	NSSS	44 005	34 475	35 006	46 816	38 251	40 714	32 276	51 706	47 412

6.1.8 Households and non-profit institutions serving households

ESA95 sectors S.14 and S.15 Unconsolidated

£ million

			1998	1999	2000	2001	2002	2003	2004	2005	2006
III.2	**FINANCIAL ACCOUNT**										
F.A	**Net acquisition of financial assets**										
F.2	Currency and deposits										
F.21	Currency	NFVT	1 388	2 219	1 694	2 022	1 505	1 882	2 519	1 999	1 864
F.22	Transferable deposits										
F.2211	Sterling deposits with UK banks	NFVW	16 915	16 386	18 488	27 236	33 885	42 573	43 413	43 545	48 063
F.2212	Foreign currency deposits with UK banks	NFVX	–400	455	724	199	–344	2 376	603	99	812
F.2213	Sterling deposits with UK building societies	NFVY	10 511	11 206	11 517	13 796	12 330	8 443	12 856	14 109	14 228
F.229	Deposits with rest of the world monetary financial institutions	NFVZ	2 374	2 233	2 734	3 747	2 982	2 579	4 441	1 641	4 007
F.29	Other deposits	NFWA	1 107	–867	–445	–681	–552	4 506	1 543	4 120	6 152
F.2	Total currency and deposits	NFVS	31 895	31 632	34 712	46 319	49 806	62 359	65 375	65 513	75 126
F.3	Securities other than shares										
F.331	Short term: money market instruments										
F.3311	Issued by UK central government	NFWD	15	–17	7	–6	–	–	–	–	–
F.3312	Issued by UK local authorities	NFWH	–	–	–	–	–	–	–	–	–
F.3315	Issued by UK monetary financial institutions	NFWI	289	710	–418	1 956	–496	–171	151	–795	2 838
F.3316	Issued by other UK residents	NFWN	–46	–	–	1	1	2	–	1	–
F.332	Medium (1 to 5 year) and long term (over 5 year) bonds										
F.3321	Issued by UK central government	NFWQ	–1 544	2 358	–261	–666	–80	422	–1 155	225	–11 306
F.3322	Issued by UK local authorities	NFWT	43	34	–72	47	–12	4	–133	74	89
F.3326	Other medium & long term bonds issued by UK residents	NFWX	–18	36	168	676	213	39	183	218	236
F.3329	Long term bonds issued by the rest of the world	NFWY	184	–380	256	88	88	88	88	88	88
F.34	Financial derivatives	NFWZ	–	–	–	–	–	–	–	–	–
F.3	Total securities other than shares	NFWB	–1 077	2 741	–320	2 096	–286	384	–866	–189	–8 055
F.4	Loans										
F.42	Long term loans										
F.424	Other long-term loans by UK residents	NFXT	–457	3 805	186	3 489	1 932	5 538	–1 593	2 391	–3 473
F.4	Total loans	NFXD	–457	3 805	186	3 489	1 932	5 538	–1 593	2 391	–3 473
F.5	Shares and other equity										
F.51	Shares and other equity, excluding mutual funds' shares										
F.514	Quoted UK shares	NFYA	–25 950	–24 641	–11 536	–5 521	4 754	9 132	–1 896	–19 109	–17 916
F.515	Unquoted UK shares	NFYB	–6 744	–31	–5 989	–5 665	–1 190	–1 768	–4 913	–13 648	–10 659
F.516	Other UK equity (including direct investment in property)	NFYC	–66	20	–24	–12	–	–	–	–	–
F.517	UK shares and bonds issued by other UK residents	NSPY	–	–	–	–	–	–	–	–	–
F.519	Shares and other equity issued by the rest of the world	NFYF	387	1 122	–224	1 626	640	3 638	4 333	9 089	1 793
F.52	Mutual funds' shares										
F.521	UK mutual funds' shares	NFYJ	8 547	9 086	6 784	7 417	2 878	7 306	3 061	–3 610	4 092
F.529	Rest of the world mutual funds' shares	NFYK	–8	70	63	33	–8	41	536	1 810	811
F.5	Total shares and other equity	NFXV	–23 834	–14 374	–10 926	–2 122	7 074	18 349	1 121	–25 468	–21 879
F.6	Insurance technical reserves										
F.61	Net equity of households in life assurance and pension funds' reserves	NFYL	34 673	31 335	26 199	33 083	46 303	34 666	40 602	52 061	62 374
F.62	Prepayments of insurance premiums and reserves for outstanding claims	NFYO	–439	–632	120	–1 159	1 014	1 860	2 520	2 128	1 725
F.6	Total insurance technical reserves	NPWX	34 234	30 703	26 319	31 924	47 317	36 526	43 122	54 189	64 099
F.7	Other accounts receivable	NFYP	2 737	4 754	6 701	1 716	3 185	–1 363	9 033	3 863	4 119
F.A	**Total net acquisition of financial assets**	NFVO	43 498	59 261	56 672	83 422	109 028	121 793	116 192	100 299	109 937

6.1.8 Households and non-profit institutions serving households

ESA95 sectors S.14 and S.15 Unconsolidated

continued £ million

			1998	1999	2000	2001	2002	2003	2004	2005	2006
III.2	**FINANCIAL ACCOUNT** continued										
F.L	**Net acquisition of financial liabilities**										
F.3	Securities other than shares										
F.331	Short term: money market instruments										
F.3316	Issued by UK residents other than monetary financial institutions and general government	NFZR	8	−18	55	54	40	−73	−4	−87	669
F.332	Medium (1 to 5 year) and long term (over 5 year) bonds										
F.3326	Other medium & long term bonds issued by UK residents institutions and general government	NGAB	230	–	–	48	–	200	67	31	400
F.34	Financial derivatives	NGAD	–	–	–	–	–	–	–	–	–
F.3	Total securities other than shares	NFZF	238	−18	55	102	40	127	63	−56	1 069
F.4	Loans										
F.41	Short term loans										
F.4111	Sterling loans by UK banks	NGAK	12 350	12 470	15 868	17 449	19 949	16 496	22 991	16 888	15 555
F.4112	Foreign currency loans by UK banks	NGAL	−53	–	–	–	–	–	–	–	–
F.4113	Sterling loans by UK building societies	NGAM	136	−167	192	440	96	68	205	470	−14
F.419	Loans by rest of the world monetary financial institutions	NGAN	444	688	447	1 854	1 477	2 088	2 806	973	5 176
F.42	Long term loans										
F.4221	Loans secured on dwellings by banks	NGAT	15 119	21 492	19 482	31 094	48 928	47 579	42 844	29 931	28 056
F.4222	Loans secured on dwellings by building societies	NGAU	7 843	10 651	8 938	6 833	11 034	18 950	17 160	12 093	15 255
F.4229	Loans secured on dwellings by others	NGAV	2 353	5 757	13 786	16 396	23 682	35 465	39 277	43 748	62 568
F.424	Other long-term loans by UK residents	NGAX	5 688	13 104	8 292	76	5 610	5 036	5 442	8 213	1 255
F.4	Total loans	NGAH	43 880	63 995	67 005	74 142	110 776	125 682	130 725	112 316	127 851
F.7	Other accounts payable	NGBT	2 808	1 246	−1 438	7 795	10 302	7 027	4 995	3 784	1 556
F.L	**Total net acquisition of financial liabilities**	NFYS	46 926	65 223	65 622	82 039	121 118	132 836	135 783	116 044	130 476
B.9	**Net lending / borrowing**										
F.A	Total net acquisition of financial assets	NFVO	43 498	59 261	56 672	83 422	109 028	121 793	116 192	100 299	109 937
-F.L	*less* Total net acquisition of financial liabilities	-NFYS	−46 926	−65 223	−65 622	−82 039	−121 118	−132 836	−135 783	−116 044	−130 476
B.9f	Net lending (+) / net borrowing (-), from financial account	NZDY	−3 428	−5 962	−8 950	1 383	−12 090	−11 043	−19 591	−15 745	−20 539
dB.9f	Statistical discrepancy	NZDV	12 193	1 850	4 745	1 555	249	−3 644	−12 650	1 793	−8 315
B.9	**Net lending (+) / net borrowing (-), from capital account**	NSSZ	**8 765**	**−4 112**	**−4 205**	**2 938**	**−11 841**	**−14 687**	**−32 241**	**−13 952**	**−28 854**

6.1.9 Households and non-profit institutions serving households

ESA95 sectors S.14 and S.15 Unconsolidated

£ billion

			1998	1999	2000	2001	2002	2003	2004	2005	2006
IV.3	**FINANCIAL BALANCE SHEET** at end of period										
AN.2	**Non-financial assets**	CGCZ	1 875.2	2 136.8	2 431.1	2 607.3	3 135.0	3 491.7	3 900.3	4 044.8	4 468.4
AF.A	**Financial assets**										
AF.2	Currency and deposits										
AF.21	Currency	NNMQ	21.9	24.1	25.8	27.9	29.3	31.2	33.6	35.6	37.4
AF.22	Transferable deposits										
AF.2211	Sterling deposits with UK banks	NNMT	351.3	373.4	405.4	432.8	466.0	508.4	552.2	591.1	640.8
AF.2212	Foreign currency deposits with UK banks	NNMU	2.9	3.0	3.9	4.1	3.7	5.0	3.1	3.4	3.9
AF.2213	Sterling deposits with UK building societies	NNMV	105.5	111.2	109.2	123.0	135.0	143.5	156.3	174.8	189.1
AF.229	Deposits with rest of the world monetary financial institutions	NNMW	20.6	25.7	27.9	30.9	33.8	37.4	41.2	43.7	46.2
AF.29	Other deposits	NNMX	64.7	63.1	62.7	62.4	62.7	67.2	68.7	72.8	78.9
AF.2	Total currency and deposits	NNMP	566.9	600.6	634.9	681.1	730.7	792.6	855.2	921.4	996.3
AF.3	Securities other than shares										
AF.331	Short term: money market instruments										
AF.3311	Issued by UK central government	NNNA	–	–	–	–	–	–	–	–	–
AF.3312	Issued by UK local authorities	NNNE	–	–	–	–	–	–	–	–	–
AF.3315	Issued by UK monetary financial institutions	NNNF	2.0	2.5	2.2	2.6	2.3	2.3	2.5	1.8	3.5
AF.3316	Issued by other UK residents	NNNK	0.2	0.2	0.5	0.4	0.5	0.5	0.5	0.4	0.5
AF.332	Medium (1 to 5 year) and long term (over 5 year) bonds										
AF.3321	Issued by UK central government	NNNN	33.0	33.0	32.8	30.4	31.0	32.4	28.8	27.3	19.6
AF.3322	Issued by UK local authorities	NNNQ	0.2	0.2	0.2	0.2	0.3	0.4	0.3	0.4	0.4
AF.3326	Other medium & long term bonds issued by UK residents	NNNU	3.6	3.9	4.1	4.3	4.5	4.7	4.9	5.1	5.3
AF.3329	Long term bonds issued by the rest of the world	NNNV	7.1	6.9	7.5	7.6	7.8	7.7	7.7	7.7	7.5
AF.34	Financial derivatives	NNNW	–	–	–	–	–	–	–	–	–
AF.3	Total securities other than shares	NNMY	46.1	46.8	47.4	45.7	46.5	48.1	44.7	42.7	36.8
AF.4	Loans										
AF.42	Long term loans										
AF.424	Other long-term loans by UK residents	NNOQ	6.8	6.6	6.7	6.8	6.7	6.8	7.0	7.0	7.3
AF.4	Total loans	NNOA	6.8	6.6	6.7	6.8	6.7	6.8	7.0	7.0	7.3
AF.5	Shares and other equity										
AF.51	Shares and other equity, excluding mutual funds' shares										
AF.514	Quoted UK shares	NNOX	233.8	320.5	318.0	226.2	182.5	203.5	223.9	239.1	224.8
AF.515	Unquoted UK shares	NNOY	186.4	248.8	226.3	154.0	92.7	99.2	97.8	110.6	88.7
AF.516	Other UK equity (including direct investment in property)	NNOZ	1.4	1.4	1.4	1.4	1.4	1.4	1.4	1.4	1.4
AF.517	UK shares and bonds issued by other UK residents	NSQR	–	–	–	–	–	–	–	–	–
AF.519	Shares and other equity issued by the rest of the world	NNPC	21.6	24.8	25.2	25.2	25.1	33.8	43.6	64.2	73.2
AF.52	Mutual funds' shares										
AF.521	UK mutual funds' shares	NNPG	99.6	151.2	151.8	136.1	108.3	118.9	138.2	139.7	150.9
AF.529	Rest of the world mutual funds' shares	NNPH	1.1	2.1	1.7	1.7	1.4	1.4	1.7	4.1	6.0
AF.5	Total shares and other equity	NNOS	543.8	748.9	724.5	544.6	411.4	458.1	506.5	559.0	545.0
AF.6	Insurance technical reserves										
AF.61	Net equity of households in life assurance and pension funds' reserves	NNPI	1 393.2	1 631.3	1 599.0	1 531.3	1 384.1	1 509.2	1 603.2	1 894.3	2 070.8
AF.62	Prepayments of insurance premiums and reserves for outstanding claims	NNPL	32.0	31.4	34.8	33.7	34.9	35.1	37.6	37.0	38.7
AF.6	Total insurance technical reserves	NPYL	1 425.2	1 662.7	1 633.7	1 564.9	1 419.0	1 544.3	1 640.8	1 931.3	2 109.6
AF.7	Other accounts receivable	NNPM	71.2	76.1	82.8	86.3	84.7	90.0	98.0	101.6	105.1
AF.A	**Total financial assets**	NNML	2 659.9	3 141.7	3 130.0	2 929.4	2 699.0	2 939.9	3 152.1	3 563.0	3 800.1

6.1.9 Households and non-profit institutions serving households

ESA95 sectors S.14 and S.15 Unconsolidated

£ billion

			1998	1999	2000	2001	2002	2003	2004	2005	2006
IV.3	**FINANCIAL BALANCE SHEET** continued at end of period										
AF.L	**Financial liabilities**										
AF.3	Securities other than shares										
AF.331	Short term: money market instruments										
AF.3316	Issued by other UK residents	NNQO	–	–	0.1	0.1	0.2	0.1	0.1	0.1	0.1
AF.332	Medium (1 to 5 year) and long term (over 5 year) bonds										
AF.3326	Other medium & long term bonds issued by UK residents	NNQY	2.3	2.7	2.8	2.8	2.8	3.0	3.1	3.1	3.2
AF.34	Financial derivatives	NNRA	–	–	–	–	–	–	–	–	–
AF.3	Total securities other than shares	NNQC	2.3	2.8	2.9	3.0	3.0	3.1	3.2	3.3	3.2
AF.4	Loans										
AF.41	Short term loans										
AF.411	Loans by UK monetary financial institutions, excluding loans secured on dwellings & financial leasing	NNRG	92.3	103.2	117.4	132.7	147.9	151.7	169.0	178.4	184.4
AF.419	Loans by rest of the world monetary financial institutions	NNRK	5.1	6.0	7.0	8.2	9.9	11.8	14.4	15.7	20.2
AF.42	Long term loans										
AF.4221	Loans secured on dwellings by banks	NNRQ	320.6	345.0	386.3	418.6	467.6	511.0	543.1	558.6	586.6
AF.4222	Loans secured on dwellings by building societies	NNRR	106.3	113.5	107.0	113.4	123.6	142.3	160.1	167.0	182.4
AF.4229	Loans secured on dwellings by others	NNRS	29.0	34.3	41.7	58.2	78.2	119.6	172.7	212.7	277.1
AF.424	Other long-term loans by UK residents	NNRU	14.5	15.6	16.0	18.1	20.9	21.8	24.1	25.9	26.9
AF.4	Total loans	NNRE	567.8	617.7	675.4	749.2	848.0	958.2	1 083.3	1 158.3	1 277.7
AF.7	Other accounts payable	NNSQ	55.1	55.2	56.5	58.5	72.1	85.6	85.5	87.8	89.0
AF.L	**Total financial liabilities**	NNPP	625.1	675.6	734.8	810.7	923.1	1 046.9	1 172.0	1 249.4	1 369.9
BF.90	**Net financial assets / liabilities**										
AF.A	Total financial assets	NNML	2 659.9	3 141.7	3 130.0	2 929.4	2 699.0	2 939.9	3 152.1	3 563.0	3 800.1
-AF.L	*less* Total financial liabilities	-NNPP	–625.1	–675.6	–734.8	–810.7	–923.1	–1 046.9	–1 172.0	–1 249.4	–1 369.9
BF.90	**Net financial assets (+) / liabilities (-)**	NZEA	2 034.7	2 466.1	2 395.2	2 118.7	1 775.8	1 892.9	1 980.1	2 313.6	2 430.2
	Total net worth										
AN	Non-financial assets	CGCZ	1 875.2	2 136.8	2 431.1	2 607.3	3 135.0	3 491.7	3 900.3	4 044.8	4 468.4
BF.90	Net financial assets (+) / liabilities (-)	NZEA	2 034.7	2 466.1	2 395.2	2 118.7	1 775.8	1 892.9	1 980.1	2 313.6	2 430.2
BF.90	**Net worth**	CGRC	3 909.9	4 602.9	4 826.3	4 726.1	4 910.8	5 384.6	5 880.5	6 358.4	6 898.6

6.2 Households final consumption expenditure: classified by purpose
At current market prices

£ million

			1998	1999	2000	2001	2002	2003	2004	2005	2006
P.31	**FINAL CONSUMPTION EXPENDITURE OF HOUSEHOLDS**										
	Durable goods										
05.	Furnishings, household equipment and routine maintenance of the house	LLIJ	15 873	16 566	18 006	19 275	20 470	21 595	22 363	22 535	23 188
06.	Health	LLIK	1 717	1 881	1 997	2 109	2 411	2 604	2 727	2 710	3 101
07.	Transport	LLIL	30 851	31 888	33 291	35 864	36 574	38 016	38 792	38 319	38 646
08.	Communication	LLIM	440	512	601	636	644	810	859	958	937
09.	Recreation and culture	LLIN	12 953	14 262	14 878	15 970	16 471	17 752	19 373	19 593	20 285
12.	Miscellaneous goods and services	LLIO	3 320	3 398	3 403	3 750	4 204	4 284	4 539	4 357	4 566
D	Total durable goods	UTIA	65 154	68 507	72 176	77 604	80 774	85 061	88 653	88 472	90 723
	Semi-durable goods										
03.	Clothing and footwear	LLJL	31 249	32 661	34 759	36 092	38 351	40 389	42 006	43 170	45 301
05.	Furnishings, household equipment and routine maintenance of the house	LLJM	9 751	10 577	11 677	12 400	13 361	13 932	14 462	13 641	14 273
07.	Transport	LLJN	2 925	3 018	2 772	2 783	3 112	3 423	3 381	3 537	3 784
09.	Recreation and culture	LLJO	17 292	19 049	20 405	21 606	23 910	26 009	28 228	28 692	29 831
12.	Miscellaneous goods and services	LLJP	1 816	1 926	2 018	2 427	2 886	3 356	3 754	3 432	3 305
SD	Total semi-durable goods	UTIQ	63 033	67 231	71 631	75 308	81 620	87 109	91 831	92 472	96 494
	Non-durable goods										
01.	Food & drink	ABZV	55 162	57 040	58 628	59 804	61 310	63 174	65 521	67 539	70 908
02.	Alcohol & tobacco	ADFL	22 459	24 458	24 617	25 158	25 966	27 297	27 713	28 073	28 538
04.	Housing, water, electricity, gas and other fuels	LLIX	22 094	21 800	22 265	23 076	23 444	24 241	27 011	28 441	32 875
05.	Furnishings, household equipment and routine maintenance of the house	LLIY	2 505	2 657	2 786	2 972	3 169	3 338	3 391	3 456	3 679
06.	Health	LLIZ	2 975	3 111	3 268	3 613	3 855	3 938	4 023	3 815	3 937
07.	Transport	LLJA	16 615	18 210	19 987	19 391	19 129	20 072	21 873	23 689	23 858
09.	Recreation and culture	LLJB	12 136	12 665	12 959	13 107	13 392	13 507	13 650	13 831	14 081
12.	Miscellaneous goods and services	LLJC	8 727	9 121	9 463	9 884	11 272	12 602	13 486	14 108	14 338
ND	Total non-durable goods	UTII	142 673	149 062	153 973	157 005	161 537	168 169	176 668	182 952	192 214
	Total goods	UTIE	270 860	284 800	297 780	309 917	323 931	340 339	357 152	363 896	379 431
	Services										
03.	Clothing and footwear	LLJD	698	714	720	730	741	766	786	843	913
04.	Housing, water, electricity, gas and other fuels	LLJE	76 020	81 393	85 785	92 829	97 794	104 810	111 029	118 484	125 928
05.	Furnishings, household equipment and routine maintenance of the house	LLJF	2 873	3 046	3 206	3 327	3 448	3 601	3 813	4 013	4 166
06.	Health	LLJG	3 614	3 783	3 943	4 254	4 512	4 793	5 182	5 577	5 689
07.	Transport	LLJH	32 115	34 121	37 002	38 397	41 332	43 058	45 167	47 393	50 083
08.	Communication	LLJI	10 462	11 493	12 755	13 521	14 031	14 844	15 589	15 814	16 081
09.	Recreation and culture	LLJJ	20 865	21 505	21 912	22 769	25 349	27 118	29 806	32 003	33 544
10.	Education	ADIE	7 814	8 943	9 534	9 409	9 381	9 610	9 990	10 409	10 998
11.	Restaurants and hotels	ADIF	61 807	64 387	68 557	71 620	76 426	78 902	83 595	88 934	91 962
12.	Miscellaneous goods and services	LLJK	44 656	48 431	52 691	56 199	57 054	57 161	58 381	61 454	64 014
S	Total services	UTIM	260 924	277 816	296 105	313 055	330 068	344 663	363 338	384 924	403 378
0.	**Final consumption expenditure in the UK by resident and non-resident households (domestic concept)**	ABQI	531 784	562 616	593 885	622 972	653 999	685 002	720 490	748 820	782 809
P.33	Final consumption expenditure outside the UK by UK resident households	ABTA	16 913	19 690	21 654	22 907	24 435	26 314	27 739	29 209	30 564
-P.34	*Less* Final consumption expenditure in the UK by households resident in the rest of the world	CDFD	−14 544	−14 312	−14 713	−13 383	−13 872	−14 156	−15 698	−17 160	−18 605
P.31	**Final consumption expenditure by UK resident households in the UK and abroad (national concept)**	ABPB	534 153	567 994	600 826	632 496	664 562	697 160	732 531	760 869	794 768

Additional detail is published in *Consumer Trends* and table A7 of *UK Economic Accounts*, available from the ONS website (www.statistics.gov.uk/consumertrends).

6.3 Households final consumption expenditure: classified by purpose Chained volume measures (reference year 2003)

£ million

			1998	1999	2000	2001	2002	2003	2004	2005	2006
P.31	**FINAL CONSUMPTION EXPENDITURE OF HOUSEHOLDS**										
	Durable goods										
05.	Furnishings, household equipment and routine maintenance of the house	LLME	16 112	16 764	18 442	19 542	20 603	21 595	22 030	21 892	22 226
06.	Health	LLMF	2 749	2 585	2 455	2 337	2 421	2 604	2 612	2 562	2 947
07.	Transport	LLMG	27 974	29 455	31 680	35 100	36 057	38 016	39 107	39 571	40 365
08.	Communication	LLMH	322	428	536	582	640	810	883	1 082	1 136
09.	Recreation and culture	LLMI	7 644	9 657	11 243	13 344	14 911	17 752	21 381	24 909	28 961
12.	Miscellaneous goods and services	LLMJ	3 632	3 656	3 618	3 932	4 360	4 284	4 445	4 227	4 170
D	Total durable goods	UTIC	56 607	61 603	67 366	74 551	78 825	85 061	90 458	94 243	99 805
	Semi-durable goods										
03.	Clothing and footwear	LLNG	25 971	27 921	30 969	33 712	37 727	40 389	43 327	45 637	48 374
05.	Furnishings, household equipment and routine maintenance of the house	LLNH	9 321	10 177	11 473	12 221	13 215	13 932	14 426	13 862	14 617
07.	Transport	LLNI	3 089	3 136	2 856	2 880	3 172	3 423	3 313	3 369	3 484
09.	Recreation and culture	LLNJ	15 150	17 229	19 175	20 339	23 040	26 009	29 115	30 179	31 895
12.	Miscellaneous goods and services	LLNK	1 814	1 932	2 053	2 438	2 920	3 356	3 771	3 354	3 180
SD	Total semi-durable goods	UTIS	55 217	60 277	66 478	71 563	80 058	87 109	93 952	96 401	101 550
	Non-durable goods										
01.	Food & drink	ADIP	58 058	59 904	61 944	61 048	62 143	63 174	65 181	66 231	67 953
02.	Alcohol & tobacco	ADIS	26 829	27 623	26 704	26 497	26 884	27 297	27 444	27 325	26 910
04.	Housing, water, electricity, gas and other fuels	LLMS	22 897	22 594	23 189	23 958	23 881	24 241	25 723	24 743	24 513
05.	Furnishings, household equipment and routine maintenance of the house	LLMT	2 401	2 492	2 666	2 878	3 101	3 338	3 519	3 582	3 685
06.	Health	LLMU	3 242	3 314	3 397	3 686	3 895	3 938	4 043	3 830	3 945
07.	Transport	LLMV	19 538	19 691	19 114	19 550	19 825	20 072	20 731	20 719	19 822
09.	Recreation and culture	LLMW	13 410	13 713	13 657	13 537	13 681	13 507	13 463	13 571	13 477
12.	Miscellaneous goods and services	LLMX	8 456	8 669	9 248	9 586	11 124	12 602	13 631	14 399	15 136
ND	Total non-durable goods	UTIK	154 422	157 573	159 677	160 597	164 482	168 169	173 735	174 400	175 441
	Total goods	UTIG	263 426	277 468	292 390	306 198	323 179	340 339	358 145	365 044	376 796
	Services										
03.	Clothing and footwear	LLMY	834	819	805	790	775	766	760	773	800
04.	Housing, water, electricity, gas and other fuels	LLMZ	100 061	101 184	102 168	102 778	104 106	104 810	105 767	107 013	109 007
05.	Furnishings, household equipment and routine maintenance of the house	LLNA	3 834	3 874	3 821	3 718	3 646	3 601	3 602	3 595	3 568
06.	Health	LLNB	4 595	4 531	4 612	4 683	4 665	4 793	4 954	5 244	5 158
07.	Transport	LLNC	39 140	41 413	43 153	40 971	42 611	43 058	43 459	43 657	44 314
08.	Communication	LLND	9 341	10 527	12 167	13 877	14 158	14 844	15 478	16 038	16 308
09.	Recreation and culture	LLNE	24 555	24 795	25 101	25 960	26 216	27 118	28 930	29 935	29 889
10.	Education	ADMJ	10 530	11 394	11 489	10 692	10 091	9 610	9 541	9 476	9 481
11.	Restaurants and hotels	ADMK	73 811	74 191	76 252	76 434	78 303	78 902	81 796	83 893	83 592
12.	Miscellaneous goods and services	LLNF	51 249	53 735	55 696	57 368	57 336	57 161	56 232	55 739	55 654
S	Total services	UTIO	316 510	325 416	334 699	337 218	341 883	344 663	350 519	355 363	357 771
0.	**Final consumption expenditure in the UK by resident and non-resident households (domestic concept)**	ABQJ	576 994	600 627	625 437	642 595	664 790	685 002	708 664	720 407	734 567
P.33	Final consumption expenditure outside the UK by UK resident households	ABTC	18 787	21 899	24 189	24 897	26 376	26 314	28 068	27 750	28 418
-P.34	*Less* Final consumption expenditure in the UK by households resident in the rest of the world	CCHX	−16 713	−16 031	−16 038	−14 164	−14 292	−14 156	−15 298	−16 152	−16 955
P.3	**Final consumption expenditure by UK resident households in the UK and abroad (national concept)**	ABPF	579 342	606 648	633 662	653 326	676 833	697 160	721 434	732 005	746 030

Additional detail is published in *Consumer Trends* and table A7 of *UK Economic Accounts*, available from the ONS website (www.statistics.gov.uk/consumertrends).

6.4 Individual consumption expenditure at current market prices by households, non-profit institutions serving households and general government

Classified by function (COICOP/COPNI/COFOG)[1]

£ million

			1998	1999	2000	2001	2002	2003	2004	2005	2006
P.31	**FINAL CONSUMPTION EXPENDITURE OF HOUSEHOLDS**										
01.	**Food and non-alcoholic beverages**	ABZV	55 162	57 040	58 628	59 804	61 310	63 174	65 521	67 539	70 908
01.1	Food	ABZW	49 104	50 685	51 905	52 742	53 984	55 507	57 357	59 366	61 796
01.2	Non-alcoholic beverages	ADFK	6 058	6 355	6 723	7 062	7 326	7 667	8 164	8 173	9 112
02.	**Alcoholic beverages and tobacco**	ADFL	22 459	24 458	24 617	25 158	25 966	27 297	27 713	28 073	28 538
02.1	Alcoholic beverages	ADFM	9 096	10 166	10 395	10 700	11 344	12 027	12 213	12 344	12 411
02.2	Tobacco	ADFN	13 363	14 292	14 222	14 458	14 622	15 270	15 500	15 729	16 127
03.	**Clothing and footwear**	ADFP	31 947	33 375	35 479	36 822	39 092	41 155	42 792	44 013	46 214
03.1	Clothing	ADFQ	27 508	28 932	31 048	32 103	33 927	35 689	37 112	38 351	40 475
03.2	Footwear	ADFR	4 439	4 443	4 431	4 719	5 165	5 466	5 680	5 662	5 739
04.	**Housing, water, electricity, gas and other fuels**	ADFS	98 114	103 193	108 050	115 905	121 238	129 051	138 040	146 925	158 803
04.1	Actual rentals for housing	ADFT	21 155	22 584	23 595	25 302	25 828	27 610	28 784	30 286	32 497
04.2	Imputed rentals for housing	ADFU	47 689	51 401	54 378	59 581	63 279	68 458	73 160	78 502	82 744
04.3	Maintenance and repair of the dwelling	ADFV	9 960	10 234	10 512	11 340	12 306	12 615	13 379	13 440	13 911
04.4	Water supply and miscellaneous dwelling services	ADFW	4 961	5 201	5 033	5 059	5 222	5 438	5 698	6 389	6 952
04.5	Electricity, gas and other fuels	ADFX	14 349	13 773	14 532	14 623	14 603	14 930	17 019	18 308	22 699
05.	**Furnishings, household equipment and routine maintenance of the house**	ADFY	31 002	32 846	35 675	37 974	40 448	42 466	44 029	43 645	45 306
05.1	Furniture, furnishings, carpets and other floor coverings	ADFZ	11 667	12 437	13 758	14 362	15 591	16 789	17 645	17 616	18 354
05.2	Household textiles	ADGG	3 676	3 972	4 465	4 636	5 086	5 452	5 680	5 326	5 405
05.3	Household appliances	ADGL	5 080	5 038	5 156	5 758	5 715	5 578	5 563	5 560	5 799
05.4	Glassware, tableware and household utensils	ADGM	3 410	3 722	4 231	4 609	4 710	4 701	4 635	4 591	4 767
05.5	Tools and equipment for house and garden	ADGN	2 332	2 586	2 722	2 977	3 355	3 589	3 919	3 670	3 677
05.6	Goods and services for routine household maintenance	ADGO	4 837	5 091	5 343	5 632	5 991	6 357	6 587	6 882	7 304
06.	**Health**	ADGP	8 306	8 775	9 208	9 976	10 778	11 335	11 932	12 102	12 727
06.1	Medical products, appliances and equipment	ADGQ	4 692	4 992	5 265	5 722	6 266	6 542	6 750	6 525	7 038
06.2	Out-patient services	ADGR	2 010	2 107	2 178	2 344	2 422	2 553	2 752	3 007	2 997
06.3	Hospital services	ADGS	1 604	1 676	1 765	1 910	2 090	2 240	2 430	2 570	2 692
07.	**Transport**	ADGT	82 506	87 237	93 052	96 435	100 147	104 569	109 213	112 938	116 371
07.1	Purchase of vehicles	ADGU	30 851	31 888	33 291	35 864	36 574	38 016	38 792	38 319	38 646
07.2	Operation of personal transport equipment	ADGV	32 045	34 450	37 059	37 028	38 816	40 507	42 915	45 683	47 248
07.3	Transport services	ADGW	19 610	20 899	22 702	23 543	24 757	26 046	27 506	28 936	30 477
08.	**Communication**	ADGX	10 902	12 005	13 356	14 157	14 675	15 654	16 448	16 772	17 018
08.1	Postal services	CDEF	919	899	873	870	878	890	892	926	895
08.2	Telephone & telefax equipment	ADWO	440	512	601	636	644	810	859	958	937
08.3	Telephone & telefax services	ADWP	9 543	10 594	11 882	12 651	13 153	13 954	14 697	14 888	15 186
09.	**Recreation and culture**	ADGY	63 246	67 481	70 154	73 452	79 122	84 386	91 057	94 119	97 741
09.1	Audio-visual, photographic and information processing equipment	ADGZ	15 132	16 312	17 034	17 580	18 051	19 408	21 820	21 586	21 742
09.2	Other major durables for recreation and culture	ADHL	3 089	3 582	3 944	4 325	4 672	5 126	5 428	5 737	6 262
09.3	Other recreational items and equipment; flowers, garden and pets	ADHZ	16 237	17 655	18 636	20 216	22 475	23 894	25 041	25 605	26 972
09.4	Recreational and cultural services	ADIA	19 255	19 876	20 272	21 034	23 555	25 278	27 772	29 888	31 298
09.5	Newspapers, books and stationery	ADIC	9 533	10 056	10 268	10 297	10 369	10 680	10 996	11 303	11 467
09.6	Package holidays[2]	ADID	–	–	–	–	–	–	–	–	–
10.	**Education**										
10.	Education services	ADIE	7 814	8 943	9 534	9 409	9 381	9 610	9 990	10 409	10 998
11.	**Restaurants and hotels**	ADIF	61 807	64 387	68 557	71 620	76 426	78 902	83 595	88 934	91 962
11.1	Catering services	ADIG	52 671	55 164	59 019	62 449	66 701	68 839	72 837	77 046	78 819
11.2	Accommodation services	ADIH	9 136	9 223	9 538	9 171	9 725	10 063	10 758	11 888	13 143
12.	**Miscellaneous goods and services**	ADII	58 519	62 876	67 575	72 260	75 416	77 403	80 160	83 351	86 223
12.1	Personal care	ADIJ	12 574	13 229	13 883	14 626	16 444	18 181	19 558	20 328	20 580
12.3	Personal effects n.e.c.	ADIK	4 490	4 673	4 748	5 455	6 140	6 462	6 866	6 581	6 847
12.4	Social protection	ADIL	8 332	8 446	8 643	8 963	9 219	9 501	9 821	10 124	10 279
12.5	Insurance	ADIM	17 911	20 257	22 238	25 423	25 456	24 373	23 178	24 393	24 778
12.6	Financial services n.e.c.	ADIN	8 742	10 009	11 974	11 708	11 982	12 529	14 208	15 166	16 956
12.7	Other services n.e.c.	ADIO	6 470	6 262	6 089	6 085	6 175	6 357	6 529	6 759	6 783
0.	**Final consumption expenditure in the UK by resident and non-resident households (domestic concept)**	ABQI	531 784	562 616	593 885	622 972	653 999	685 002	720 490	748 820	782 809
P.33	Final consumption expenditure outside the UK by UK resident households	ABTA	16 913	19 690	21 654	22 907	24 435	26 314	27 739	29 209	30 564
-P.34	*less* Final consumption expenditure in the UK by households resident in the rest of the world	CDFD	−14 544	−14 312	−14 713	−13 383	−13 872	−14 156	−15 698	−17 160	−18 605
P.31	**Final consumption expenditure by UK resident households in the UK and abroad (national concept)**	ABPB	534 153	567 994	600 826	632 496	664 562	697 160	732 531	760 869	794 768

6.4 Individual consumption expenditure at current market prices by households, non-profit institutions serving households and general government

continued

Classified by function (COICOP/COPNI/COFOG)[1]

£ million

		1998	1999	2000	2001	2002	2003	2004	2005	2006
P.31 CONSUMPTION EXPENDITURE OF UK RESIDENT HOUSEHOLDS										
P.31 Final consumption expenditure of UK resident households in the UK and abroad	ABPB	534 153	567 994	600 826	632 496	664 562	697 160	732 531	760 869	794 768
13. **FINAL INDIVIDUAL CONSUMPTION EXPENDITURE OF NPISH**										
P.31 Final individual consumption expenditure of NPISH	ABNV	20 837	21 874	23 169	24 720	25 968	27 185	28 953	31 585	33 313
14. **FINAL INDIVIDUAL CONSUMPTION EXPENDITURE OF OF GENERAL GOVERNMENT**										
14.1 Health	QYOT	45 836	50 254	53 236	58 032	63 388	69 888	76 855	82 864	90 159
14.2 Recreation and culture	QYSU	5 642	6 104	6 240	6 665	7 404	7 800	8 141	8 522	8 809
14.3 Education	QYSE	27 874	29 570	31 682	34 174	37 533	40 423	43 000	46 386	48 949
14.4 Social protection	QYSP	15 431	16 814	18 139	19 587	22 491	25 843	27 815	29 627	30 635
14.5 Housing	QYXO	–	–	–	–	–	–	–	–	–
P.31 Final individual consumption expenditure of general government	NNAQ	94 783	102 742	109 297	118 458	130 816	143 954	155 811	167 399	178 552
P.31 Total, individual consumption expenditure/ P.41 actual individual consumption	NQEO	649 773	692 610	733 292	775 674	821 346	868 299	917 295	959 853	1 006 633

1 "Purpose" or "function" classifications are designed to indicate the "socio-economic objectives" that institutional units aim to achieve through various kinds of outlays. COICOP is the Classification of Individual Consumption by Purpose and applies to households. COPNI is the Classification of the Purposes of Non-profit Institutions Serving Households and COFOG the Classification of the Functions of Government. The introduction of ESA95 coincides with the redefinition of these classifications and data will be available on a consistent basis for all European Union member states.

2 Package holidays data are dispersed between components (transport etc)

6.5 Individual consumption expenditure by households, NPISH and general government
Chained volume measures (reference year 2003)

Classified by function (COICOP/COPNI/COFOG)[1]

£ million

			1998	1999	2000	2001	2002	2003	2004	2005	2006
P.31	**FINAL CONSUMPTION EXPENDITURE OF HOUSEHOLDS**										
01.	**Food and non-alcoholic beverages**	ADIP	58 058	59 904	61 944	61 048	62 143	63 174	65 181	66 231	67 953
01.1	Food	ADIQ	52 174	53 697	55 255	53 992	54 835	55 507	56 946	57 997	59 107
01.2	Non-alcoholic beverages	ADIR	5 945	6 260	6 725	7 063	7 312	7 667	8 235	8 234	8 846
02.	**Alcoholic beverages and tobacco**	ADIS	26 829	27 623	26 704	26 497	26 884	27 297	27 444	27 325	26 910
02.1	Alcoholic beverages	ADIT	9 290	10 309	10 476	10 831	11 516	12 027	12 369	12 590	12 462
02.2	Tobacco	ADIU	17 988	17 541	16 341	15 716	15 380	15 270	15 075	14 735	14 448
03.	**Clothing and footwear**	ADIW	26 736	28 689	31 744	34 485	38 499	41 155	44 087	46 410	49 174
03.1	Clothing	ADIX	22 562	24 424	27 394	29 827	33 315	35 689	38 407	40 606	43 204
03.2	Footwear	ADIY	4 264	4 324	4 360	4 660	5 185	5 466	5 680	5 804	5 970
04.	**Housing, water, electricity, gas and other fuels**	ADIZ	122 959	123 662	125 299	126 749	127 979	129 051	131 490	131 756	133 520
04.1	Actual rentals for housing	ADJA	27 333	27 366	27 345	27 418	27 084	27 610	27 555	27 782	28 817
04.2	Imputed rentals for housing	ADJB	63 624	64 980	65 704	66 495	67 872	68 458	69 617	70 651	71 233
04.3	Maintenance and repair of the dwelling	ADJC	11 784	11 791	11 675	12 139	12 702	12 615	13 007	12 683	12 728
04.4	Water supply and miscellaneous dwelling services	ADJD	5 218	5 228	5 386	5 379	5 424	5 438	5 412	5 522	5 627
04.5	Electricity, gas and other fuels	ADJE	14 877	14 363	15 149	15 277	14 891	14 930	15 899	15 118	15 115
05.	**Furnishings, household equipment and routine maintenance of the house**	ADJF	31 443	33 130	36 305	38 310	40 552	42 466	43 577	42 931	44 096
05.1	Furniture, furnishings, carpets and other floor coverings	ADJG	12 452	13 120	14 514	14 860	15 896	16 789	17 206	16 715	17 019
05.2	Household textiles	ADJH	3 448	3 743	4 361	4 534	5 043	5 452	5 604	5 375	5 573
05.3	Household appliances	ADJI	4 613	4 648	4 922	5 549	5 566	5 578	5 649	5 735	6 153
05.4	Glassware, tableware and household utensils	ADJJ	3 383	3 699	4 266	4 655	4 717	4 701	4 620	4 674	4 861
05.5	Tools and equipment for house and garden	ADJK	2 167	2 435	2 590	2 856	3 238	3 589	3 972	3 796	3 726
05.6	Goods and services for routine household maintenance	ADJL	5 468	5 556	5 708	5 859	6 092	6 357	6 526	6 636	6 764
06.	**Health**	ADJM	10 472	10 362	10 421	10 697	10 980	11 335	11 609	11 636	12 050
06.1	Medical products, appliances and equipment	ADJN	5 885	5 839	5 819	6 020	6 315	6 542	6 655	6 392	6 892
06.2	Out-patient services	ADJO	2 624	2 556	2 528	2 560	2 492	2 553	2 685	2 903	2 781
06.3	Hospital services	ADJP	1 974	1 976	2 082	2 122	2 173	2 240	2 269	2 341	2 377
07.	**Transport**	ADJQ	89 008	92 969	96 209	98 485	101 621	104 569	106 610	107 316	107 985
07.1	Purchase of vehicles	ADJR	27 974	29 455	31 680	35 100	36 057	38 016	39 107	39 571	40 365
07.2	Operation of personal transport equipment	ADJS	39 196	39 617	39 124	39 225	40 668	40 507	40 578	40 225	39 431
07.3	Transport services	ADJT	22 700	24 661	25 913	24 214	24 965	26 046	26 925	27 520	28 189
08.	**Communication**	ADJU	9 644	10 948	12 698	14 452	14 796	15 654	16 361	17 120	17 444
08.1	Postal services	CCGZ	980	960	916	901	906	890	866	941	995
08.2	Telephone & telefax equipment	ADQF	322	428	536	582	640	810	883	1 082	1 136
08.3	Telephone & telefax services	ADQG	8 416	9 604	11 264	12 978	13 254	13 954	14 612	15 097	15 313
09.	**Recreation and culture**	ADJV	57 871	63 601	68 038	72 552	77 597	84 386	92 889	98 594	104 222
09.1	Audio-visual, photographic and information processing equipment	ADJW	9 019	11 178	13 022	14 690	16 301	19 408	24 316	27 665	31 289
09.2	Other major durables for recreation and culture	ADJX	3 330	3 798	4 182	4 560	4 817	5 126	5 261	5 489	5 972
09.3	Other recreational items and equipment; flowers, gardens and pets	ADJY	14 621	16 190	17 455	18 980	21 642	23 894	25 585	26 490	28 354
09.4	Recreational and cultural services	ADJZ	22 533	22 827	23 206	24 049	24 333	25 278	26 993	28 012	27 928
09.5	Newspapers, books and stationery	ADKM	10 998	11 242	11 181	10 910	10 756	10 680	10 734	10 938	10 679
09.6	Package holidays[2]	ADMI	–	–	–	–	–	–	–	–	–
10.	**Education**										
10.	Education services	ADMJ	10 530	11 394	11 489	10 692	10 091	9 610	9 541	9 476	9 481
11.	**Restaurants and Hotels**	ADMK	73 811	74 191	76 252	76 434	78 303	78 902	81 796	83 893	83 592
11.1	Catering services	ADML	62 710	63 354	65 644	66 815	68 462	68 839	71 244	72 812	71 919
11.2	Accommodation services	ADMM	11 123	10 851	10 610	9 620	9 843	10 063	10 552	11 081	11 673
12.	**Miscellaneous goods and services**	ADMN	65 059	67 867	70 524	73 239	75 715	77 403	78 079	77 719	78 140
12.1	Personal care	ADMO	13 192	13 497	14 251	14 719	16 526	18 181	19 482	20 113	20 671
12.3	Personal effects n.e.c.	ADMP	4 741	4 871	4 922	5 607	6 289	6 462	6 791	6 428	6 398
12.4	Social protection	ADMQ	11 178	10 778	10 357	10 058	9 760	9 501	9 306	9 033	8 633
12.5	Insurance	ADMR	20 780	22 511	23 526	25 453	24 880	24 373	22 776	22 399	21 992
12.6	Financial services n.e.c.	ADMS	7 776	8 966	10 421	10 694	11 733	12 529	13 678	13 815	14 805
12.7	Other services n.e.c.	ADMT	8 524	7 937	7 336	6 827	6 536	6 357	6 046	5 931	5 641
0.	**Final consumption expenditure in the UK by resident and non-resident households (domestic concept)**	ABQJ	576 994	600 627	625 437	642 595	664 790	685 002	708 664	720 407	734 567
P.33	Final consumption expenditure outside the UK by UK resident households	ABTC	18 787	21 899	24 189	24 897	26 376	26 314	28 068	27 750	28 418
-P.34	*less* Final consumption expenditure in the UK by households resident in the rest of the world	CCHX	–16 713	–16 031	–16 038	–14 164	–14 292	–14 156	–15 298	–16 152	–16 955
P.31	**Final consumption expenditure by UK resident households in the UK and abroad (national concept)**	ABPF	579 342	606 648	633 662	653 326	676 833	697 160	721 434	732 005	746 030

6.5 Individual consumption expenditure by households, NPISH and general government Chained volume measures (reference year 2003)

continued

Classified by function (COICOP/COPNI/COFOG)[1]

£ million

		1998	1999	2000	2001	2002	2003	2004	2005	2006
P.31 CONSUMPTION EXPENDITURE OF UK RESIDENT HOUSEHOLDS										
P.31 Final consumption expenditure of UK resident households in the UK and abroad	ABPF	579 342	606 648	633 662	653 326	676 833	697 160	721 434	732 005	746 030
13. FINAL INDIVIDUAL CONSUMPTION EXPENDITURE OF NPISH										
P.31 Final individual consumption expenditure of NPISH	ABNU	25 092	25 023	27 177	27 155	27 130	27 185	27 327	28 167	29 944
14. FINAL INDIVIDUAL CONSUMPTION EXPENDITURE OF GENERAL GOVERNMENT										
14.1 Health	EMOA	58 615	60 466	62 289	64 952	67 350	69 888	72 785	75 058	76 832
14.2 Recreation and culture	QYXK	5 876	6 340	6 361	6 611	7 162	7 800	7 872	8 263	8 350
14.3 Education	EMOB	38 499	39 122	39 504	39 743	40 210	40 423	40 826	40 977	40 757
14.4 Social protection	QYXM	23 369	23 359	23 454	23 645	24 864	25 843	26 811	26 698	27 323
14.5 Housing	QYXN	–	–	–	–	–	–	–	–	–
P.31 Final individual consumption expenditure of general government	NSZK	125 944	129 050	131 426	134 867	139 546	143 954	148 294	150 996	153 262
P.31 Total, individual consumption expenditure/ P.41 actual individual consumption	YBIO	729 353	760 172	792 076	815 286	843 504	868 299	897 055	911 168	929 237

1 "Purpose" or "function" classifications are designed to indicate the "socio-economic objectives" that institutional units aim to achieve through various kinds of outlays. COICOP is the Classification of Individual Consumption by Purpose and applies to households. COPNI is the Classification of the Purposes of Non-profit Institutions Serving Households and COFOG the Classification of the Functions of Government. The introduction of ESA95 coincides with the redefinition of these classifications and data will be available on a consistent basis for all European Union member states.

2 Package holidays data are dispersed between components (transport etc)

Chapter 7

Rest of the world

7.1.0 Rest of the world

ESA95 sector S.

£ million

			1998	1999	2000	2001	2002	2003	2004	2005	2006
V.I	**EXTERNAL ACCOUNT OF GOODS AND SERVICES**										
	Resources										
P.7	Imports of goods and services										
P.71	Imports of goods	LQBL	185 869	195 217	220 912	230 305	234 229	236 927	251 770	280 397	328 736
P.72	Imports of services	KTMR	53 306	60 019	66 051	69 624	73 157	77 915	81 899	90 571	95 392
P.7	Total resources, total imports	KTMX	239 175	255 236	286 963	299 929	307 386	314 842	333 669	370 968	424 128
	Uses										
P.6	Exports of goods and services										
P.61	Exports of goods	LQAD	164 056	166 166	187 936	189 093	186 524	188 320	190 877	211 608	245 105
P.62	Exports of services	KTMQ	67 978	73 616	79 666	84 047	89 987	97 077	107 817	115 182	124 586
P.6	Total exports	KTMW	232 034	239 782	267 602	273 140	276 511	285 397	298 694	326 790	369 691
B.11	**External balance of goods and services**	-KTMY	**7 141**	**15 454**	**19 361**	**26 789**	**30 875**	**29 445**	**34 975**	**44 178**	**54 437**
P.7	Total uses	KTMX	239 175	255 236	286 963	299 929	307 386	314 842	333 669	370 968	424 128

7.1.2 Rest of the world

ESA95 sector S.2

£ million

			1998	1999	2000	2001	2002	2003	2004	2005	2006
V.II	**EXTERNAL ACCOUNT OF PRIMARY INCOMES AND CURRENT TRANSFERS**										
	Resources										
B.11	**External balance of goods and services**	-KTMY	**7 141**	**15 454**	**19 361**	**26 789**	**30 875**	**29 445**	**34 975**	**44 178**	**54 437**
D.1	Compensation of employees										
D.11	Wages and salaries	KTMO	850	759	882	1 021	1 054	1 057	1 100	1 584	1 785
D.2	Taxes on production and imports, received										
D.21	Taxes on products										
D.211	Value added type taxes (VAT)	FJKM	4 228	3 811	4 204	3 575	2 808	2 740	1 789	1 999	2 167
D.212	Taxes and duties on imports excluding VAT										
D.2121	Import duties	FJWE	2 076	2 024	2 086	2 069	1 919	1 937	2 145	2 237	2 329
D.2122	Taxes on imports excluding VAT and duties	FJWF	–	–	–	–	–	–	–	–	–
D.214	Taxes on products excluding VAT and import duties	FJWG	42	46	44	31	25	18	25	24	–
D.2	Total taxes on production and imports, received	FJWB	6 346	5 881	6 334	5 675	4 752	4 695	3 959	4 260	4 496
-D.3	*less* Subsidies, paid										
-D.31	Subsidies on products	-FJWJ	–2 695	–2 443	–2 236	–1 755	–1 862	–2 099	–2 319	–	–
-D.39	Other subsidies on production	-NHQR	–241	–338	–335	–582	–519	–592	–592	–3 272	–3 275
-D.3	Total	-FJWI	–2 936	–2 781	–2 571	–2 337	–2 381	–2 691	–2 911	–3 272	–3 275
D.4	Property income, received										
D.41	Interest	QYNG	73 736	71 747	94 566	96 696	73 127	68 108	76 282	111 771	160 316
D.42	Distributed income of corporations	QYNH	14 600	23 230	23 342	31 256	22 120	23 514	27 806	37 194	36 697
D.43	Reinvested earnings on direct foreign investment	QYNI	1 522	4 607	10 788	–992	3 647	7 429	9 320	10 107	23 073
D.44	Property income attributed to insurance policy-holders	NHRM	1 200	1 299	1 028	1 290	1 235	1 243	1 097	1 097	924
D.4	Total	HMBO	91 058	100 883	129 724	128 250	100 129	100 294	114 505	160 169	221 010
D.5	Current taxes on income, wealth etc										
D.51	Taxes on income	FJWM	454	682	775	523	644	444	615	584	493
D.61	Social contributions										
D.611	Actual social contributions										
D.6112	Employees' social contributions	FJWQ	–	–	–	–	–	–	–	–	–
D.62	Social benefits other than social transfers in kind										
D.621	Social security benefits in cash	FJVZ	1 091	1 123	1 161	1 239	1 338	1 404	1 527	1 583	1 676
D.622	Private funded social benefits	QZEM	72	62	35	39	54	33	33	59	47
D.624	Social assistance benefits in cash	RNNF	71	60	57	53	50	48	48	48	48
D.62	Total	FJKO	1 234	1 245	1 253	1 331	1 442	1 485	1 608	1 690	1 771
D.7	Other current transfers										
D.71	Net non-life insurance premiums	FJKS	7	10	18	25	19	19	47	16	27
D.72	Non-life insurance claims	NHRR	4 168	3 663	2 144	3 998	3 009	2 364	2 846	6 126	4 537
D.74	Current international cooperation	FJWT	1 705	1 667	2 418	2 434	2 573	2 720	3 180	3 300	3 583
D.75	Miscellaneous current transfers	FJWU	6 826	7 607	7 615	7 222	8 878	10 610	11 631	13 354	13 176
	of which GNP based fourth own resource	NMFH	3 920	4 632	4 379	3 858	5 335	6 772	7 549	8 732	8 521
D.7	Total	FJWR	12 706	12 947	12 195	13 679	14 479	15 713	17 704	22 796	21 323
D.8	Adjustment for the change in net equity of households in pension funds	QZEP	–2	–2	–4	–5	–1	–12	–19	–67	–19
Total	Total resources	NSUK	116 851	135 068	167 949	174 926	150 993	150 430	171 536	231 922	302 021

7.1.2 Rest of the world

ESA95 sector S.2

continued £ million

			1998	1999	2000	2001	2002	2003	2004	2005	2006
V.II	**EXTERNAL ACCOUNT OF PRIMARY INCOMES AND CURRENT TRANSFERS continued**										
	Uses										
D.1	Compensation of employees										
D.11	Wages and salaries	KTMN	840	960	1 032	1 087	1 121	1 116	1 171	974	1 047
D.2	Taxes on production and imports, paid										
D.21	Taxes on products										
D.212	Taxes and duties on imports excluding VAT										
D.2121	Import duties	FJVQ	–	–	–	–	–	–	–	–	–
D.2122	Taxes on imports excluding VAT and duties	FJVR	–	–	–	–	–	–	–	–	–
D.214	Taxes on products excluding VAT and import duties	FJVS	–	–	–	–	–	–	–	–	–
D.21	Total taxes on products	FJVN	–	–	–	–	–	–	–	–	–
D.2	Total taxes on production and imports, paid	FJVM	–	–	–	–	–	–	–	–	–
D.4	Property income, paid										
D.41	Interest	QYNJ	69 634	62 450	81 796	85 370	62 750	60 436	65 674	93 622	133 889
D.42	Distributed income of corporations	QYNK	19 683	18 110	27 140	27 258	28 546	42 989	42 926	50 655	54 042
D.43	Reinvested earnings on direct foreign investment	QYNL	14 071	21 392	25 178	27 220	32 209	21 456	32 430	42 236	52 372
D.44	Property income attributed to insurance policy-holders										
D.4	Total	HMBN	103 388	101 952	134 114	139 848	123 505	124 881	141 030	186 513	240 303
D.5	Current taxes on income, wealth etc										
D.51	Taxes on income	NHRS	354	337	357	398	527	375	374	544	625
D.61	Social contributions										
D.6112	Employee's social contributions	FKAA	99	89	55	59	77	44	36	14	54
D.7	Other current transfers										
D.71	Net non-life insurance premiums	NHRX	4 168	3 663	2 144	3 998	3 009	2 364	2 846	6 126	4 537
D.72	Non-life insurance claims	FJTT	7	10	18	25	19	19	47	16	27
D.74	Current international cooperation	FJWA	1 384	3 176	2 084	4 568	3 112	3 570	3 604	3 668	3 594
D.75	Miscellaneous current transfers	NHSI	3 416	3 164	3 312	3 059	3 110	3 140	3 100	3 615	4 053
D.7	Total	NHRW	8 975	10 013	7 558	11 650	9 250	9 093	9 597	13 425	12 211
B.12	**Current external balance**	-HBOG	**3 195**	**21 717**	**24 833**	**21 884**	**16 513**	**14 921**	**19 328**	**30 452**	**47 781**
Total	Total uses	NSUK	116 851	135 068	167 949	174 926	150 993	150 430	171 536	231 922	302 021

7.1.7 Rest of the world

ESA95 sector S.2

£ million

			1998	1999	2000	2001	2002	2003	2004	2005	2006
V.III	**ACCUMULATION ACCOUNTS**										
V.III.1	**CAPITAL ACCOUNT**										
	Changes in liabilities and net worth										
B.12	**Current external balance**	-HBOG	**3 195**	**21 717**	**24 833**	**21 884**	**16 513**	**14 921**	**19 328**	**30 452**	**47 781**
D.9	Capital transfers receivable										
D.92	Investment grants	NHSA	182	171	225	237	263	345	390	408	472
D.99	Other capital transfers	NHSB	704	570	538	1 506	833	693	637	1 816	1 886
D.9	Total	NHRZ	886	741	763	1 743	1 096	1 038	1 027	2 224	2 358
-D.9	*less* Capital transfers payable										
-D.92	Investment grants	-NHQQ	–413	–332	–1 071	–569	–296	–624	–1 111	–1 482	–668
-D.99	Other capital transfers	-NHQS	–1 010	–1 144	–1 371	–2 589	–1 864	–1 951	–2 298	–2 491	–2 725
-D.9	Total	-NHSC	–1 423	–1 476	–2 442	–3 158	–2 160	–2 575	–3 409	–3 973	–3 393
B.10.1	Total, change in net worth due to saving (current external balance)and capital transfers	NHSD	2 658	20 982	23 154	20 469	15 449	13 384	16 946	28 703	46 746
	Changes in assets										
K.2	Acquisitions less disposals of non-produced non-financial assets	NHSG	–48	12	24	–97	–132	–71	–319	–258	–205
B.9	**Net lending(+)/net borrowing(-)**	NHRB	**2 706**	**20 970**	**23 130**	**20 566**	**15 581**	**13 455**	**17 265**	**28 961**	**46 951**
Total	Total change in assets	NHSD	2 658	20 982	23 154	20 469	15 449	13 384	16 946	28 703	46 746

7.1.8 Rest of the world
ESA95 sector S.2 Unconsolidated

£ million

			1998	1999	2000	2001	2002	2003	2004	2005	2006
III.2	**FINANCIAL ACCOUNT**										
F.A	**Net acquisition of financial assets**										
F.1	Monetary gold and special drawing rights	NEWJ	–915	374	956	808	240	2	37	8	–47
F.2	Currency and deposits										
F.21	Currency	NEWN	109	85	75	–57	86	81	133	64	68
F.22	Transferable deposits										
F.2211	Sterling deposits with UK banks	NWXP	13 800	23 179	32 508	16 381	11 181	22 785	26 660	45 822	56 984
F.2212	Foreign currency deposits with UK banks	NFAS	37 421	–11 261	166 107	107 666	78 337	146 075	281 571	232 594	275 125
F.2213	Sterling deposits with UK building societies	NEWS	883	542	567	523	308	487	305	1 296	621
F.29	Other deposits	NEWU	304	693	528	–178	–24	232	–877	–57	474
F.2	Total currency and deposits	NEWM	52 517	13 238	199 785	124 335	89 888	169 660	307 792	279 719	333 272
F.3	Securities other than shares										
F.331	Short term: money market instruments										
F.3311	Issued by UK central government	NEWX	–1 733	410	–251	304	–180	2 150	1 973	–1 059	663
F.3315	Issued by UK monetary financial institutions	NEXC	–16 417	13 539	38 265	19 080	18 960	255	8 003	–4 524	41 384
F.3316	Issued by other UK residents	NEXH	2 429	1 783	2 700	237	10 819	–4 323	259	–2 710	–3 471
F.332	Medium (1 to 5 year) and long term (over 5 year) bonds										
F.3321	Issued by UK central government	NEXK	1 907	–5 281	–301	–673	–3 632	11 197	12 619	30 672	24 901
F.3322	Issued by UK local authorities	NEXN	–	–	–	–	–	–	–	–	–
F.33251	Medium term bonds issued by UK banks	NEXP	1 881	4 244	891	3 425	1 706	12 117	16 525	19 240	26 148
F.33252	Medium term bonds issued by building societies	NEXQ	–140	252	1 814	630	69	1 754	2 222	3 498	–113
F.3326	Other medium & long term bonds issued by UK residents	NEXR	–4 185	27 030	8 360	2 827	20 321	63 691	56 375	79 922	74 816
F.3	Total securities other than shares	NEWV	–16 258	41 977	51 478	25 830	48 063	86 841	97 976	125 039	164 328
F.4	Loans										
F.41	Short term loans										
F.4191	Loans by rest of the world monetary financial institutions	NEYD	–9 305	20 622	19 279	43 984	24 909	43 056	80 824	38 411	113 660
F.4192	Other Short-term loans by Rest of the World	ZMDZ	24 542	22 453	47 424	55 267	–43 298	33 857	15 108	189 664	7 115
F.42	Long term loans										
F.4211	Outward direct investment	NEYG	10 220	13 068	29 481	13 467	39 286	12 453	17 965	29 218	–12 775
F.4212	Inward direct investment	NEYH	26 092	17 043	12 207	17 705	11 159	474	774	18 370	–1 516
F.429	Other long-term loans by the rest of the world	QYLT	–254	–120	–293	17	–30	124	603	101	240
F.4	Total loans	NEXX	51 295	73 066	108 098	130 440	32 026	89 964	115 274	275 764	106 724
F.5	Shares and other equity										
F.51	Shares and other equity, excluding mutual funds' shares										
F.514	Quoted UK shares	NEYU	53 370	96 817	122 217	15 842	4 015	2 541	–838	63 278	35 505
F.515	Unquoted UK shares	NEYV	13 132	25 810	60 303	26 389	13 849	18 691	25 562	38 664	37 982
F.516	Other UK equity (including direct investment in property)	NEYW	698	813	1 629	791	748	395	623	597	467
F.517	UK shares and bonds issued by other UK residents	NSPR	–	–	–	–	–	–	–	–	–
F.52	Mutual funds' shares										
F.521	UK mutual funds' shares	NEZD	2	3	43	5	8	4	28	49	50
F.5	Total shares and other equity	NEYP	67 202	123 443	184 192	43 027	18 620	21 631	25 375	102 588	74 004
F.6	Insurance technical reserves										
F.61	Net equity of households in life assurance and pension funds' reserves	NEZF	–2	–2	–4	–5	–1	–12	–20	–67	–19
F.62	Prepayments of insurance premiums and reserves for outstanding claims	NEZI	3	–602	942	–157	335	–1 371	178	725	543
F.6	Total insurance technical reserves	NPWP	1	–604	938	–162	334	–1 383	158	658	524
F.7	Other accounts receivable	NEZJ	65	–135	–90	526	–613	58	–163	158	57
F.A	**Total net acquisition of financial assets**	NEWI	153 907	251 359	545 357	324 804	188 558	366 773	546 449	783 934	678 862

7.1.8 Rest of the world
ESA95 sector S.2 Unconsolidated

continued — £ million

			1998	1999	2000	2001	2002	2003	2004	2005	2006
III.2	**FINANCIAL ACCOUNT** continued										
F.L	**Net acquisition of financial liabilities**										
F.2	Currency and deposits										
F.21	Currency	NEZR	40	−23	−16	−3	54	30	46	14	103
F.22	Transferable deposits										
F.229	Deposits with rest of the world monetary financial institutions[1]	NEZX	13 504	45 655	219 290	126 267	80 292	186 025	213 691	371 266	276 605
F.2	Total currency and deposits	NEZQ	13 544	45 632	219 274	126 264	80 346	186 055	213 737	371 280	276 708
F.3	Securities other than shares										
F.331	Short term: money market instruments										
F.3319	Issued by the rest of the world[1]	NFAM	2 206	13 931	−2 551	11 491	−6 132	12 223	−2 631	5 759	16 065
F.332	Medium (1 to 5 year) and long term (over 5 year) bonds										
F.3329	Long term bonds issued by the rest of the world	NFAW	27 898	−10 300	53 299	30 261	9 900	818	88 343	94 511	161 943
F.34	Financial derivatives	NSUL	3 043	−2 685	−1 503	−8 412	−1 159	5 211	7 857	−9 211	−7 759
F.3	Total securities other than shares	NEZZ	33 147	946	49 245	33 340	2 609	18 252	93 569	91 059	170 249
F.4	Loans										
F.41	Short term loans										
F.4111	Sterling loans by UK banks	NFBE	−613	2 621	1 869	4 863	4 768	360	6 871	20 209	22 120
F.4112	Foreign currency loans by UK banks	NFBF	1 581	14 299	55 631	43 228	12 416	70 447	105 144	115 008	97 257
F.4113	Sterling loans by UK building societies	NFBG	–	–	–	1	3	2	3	2	−1
F.42	Long term loans										
F.4211	Outward direct investment	NFBK	22 214	15 323	11 750	10 225	16 530	11 961	19 602	18 137	−10 663
F.4212	Inward direct investment	NFBL	11 055	13 284	2 767	1 066	10 054	−3 049	−5 537	7 334	4 296
F.423	Finance leasing	NFBQ	–	–	–	–	–	–	–	–	–
F.424	Other long-term loans by UK residents	NSRT	−343	−347	−1 495	28	−1 458	−292	−122	−1 654	−3 204
F.4	Total loans	NFBB	33 894	45 180	70 522	59 411	42 313	79 429	125 961	159 036	109 805
F.5	Shares and other equity										
F.51	Shares and other equity, excluding mutual funds' shares										
F.519	Shares and other equity issued by the rest of the world	NFCD	64 499	137 757	193 381	88 597	55 273	61 864	107 108	120 934	88 115
F.52	Mutual funds' shares										
F.529	Rest of the world mutual funds' shares	NFCI	−8	70	63	33	−8	41	536	1 810	811
F.5	Total shares and other equity	NFBT	64 491	137 827	193 444	88 630	55 265	61 905	107 644	122 744	88 926
F.7	Other accounts payable	NFCN	−1 091	358	268	−344	823	625	−103	−1 096	369
F.L	**Total net acquisition of financial liabilities**	NEZM	143 985	229 943	532 753	307 301	181 356	346 266	540 808	743 023	646 057
B.9	**Net lending / borrowing**										
F.A	Total net acquisition of financial assets	NEWI	153 907	251 359	545 357	324 804	188 558	366 773	546 449	783 934	678 862
-F.L	*less* Total net acquisition of financial liabilities	-NEZM	−143 985	−229 943	−532 753	−307 301	−181 356	−346 266	−540 808	−743 023	−646 057
B.9f	Net lending (+) / net borrowing (-), from financial account	NYOD	9 922	21 416	12 604	17 503	7 202	20 507	5 641	40 911	32 805
dB.9f	Statistical discrepancy	NYPO	−7 216	−446	10 526	3 063	8 379	−7 052	11 624	−11 950	14 146
B.9	**Net lending (+) / net borrowing (-), from capital account**	NHRB	**2 706**	**20 970**	**23 130**	**20 566**	**15 581**	**13 455**	**17 265**	**28 961**	**46 951**

1 There is a discontinuity in this series between 1995 and 1996 because an instrument breakdown of offical reserves is not available prior to 1996

7.1.9 Rest of the world

ESA95 sector S.2 Unconsolidated

£ billion

			1998	1999	2000	2001	2002	2003	2004	2005	2006
IV.3	**FINANCIAL BALANCE SHEET**										
	at end of period										
AF.A	**Financial assets**										
AF.2	Currency and deposits										
AF.21	Currency	NLCW	1.0	1.1	1.1	1.1	1.2	1.3	1.4	1.5	1.5
AF.22	Transferable deposits										
AF.2211	Sterling deposits with UK banks	NLCZ	147.2	167.5	200.4	215.9	228.0	251.7	279.6	331.3	389.0
AF.2212	Foreign curency deposits with UK banks	NLDA	886.7	859.0	1 060.0	1 152.5	1 206.6	1 347.9	1 570.0	1 861.5	1 974.2
AF.2213	Sterling deposits with UK building societies	NLDB	4.9	5.2	4.1	4.6	4.9	5.4	5.7	6.9	7.6
AF.29	Other deposits	NLDD	0.6	1.3	1.8	1.7	1.6	1.9	1.0	0.9	1.4
AF.2	Total currency and deposits	NLCV	1 040.4	1 034.1	1 267.5	1 375.8	1 442.3	1 608.2	1 857.8	2 202.1	2 373.7
AF.3	Securities other than shares										
AF.331	Short term: money market instruments										
AF.3311	Issued by UK central government	NLDG	0.3	0.1	–	0.1	0.2	1.9	4.0	2.7	3.5
AF.3315	Issued by UK monetary financial institutions	NLDL	54.4	67.2	111.0	133.1	140.3	130.6	130.7	136.1	163.4
AF.3316	Issued by other UK residents	NLDQ	15.6	17.8	21.7	22.5	30.6	23.7	22.6	22.2	16.3
AF.332	Medium (1 to 5 year) and long term (over 5 year) bonds										
AF.3321	Issued by UK central government	NLDT	73.9	60.9	62.4	59.9	56.4	66.1	83.8	110.7	135.5
AF.3322	Issued by UK local authorities	NLDW	–	–	–	–	–	–	–	–	–
AF.33251	Medium term bonds issued by UK banks	NLDY	27.7	33.5	35.8	39.2	40.4	49.5	64.5	85.6	105.0
AF.33252	Medium term bonds issued by UK building societies	NLDZ	1.1	1.2	2.6	3.3	3.2	4.2	6.4	9.9	9.9
AF.3326	Other medium & long term bonds issued by UK residents	NLEA	124.2	145.1	171.3	188.6	228.8	295.7	360.3	465.0	525.0
AF.3	Total securities other than shares	NLDE	297.3	326.0	404.8	446.6	499.9	571.8	672.3	832.2	958.5
AF.4	Loans										
AF.41	Short term loans										
AF.4191	Loans by rest of the world monetary financial institutions	NLEM	134.9	161.6	192.9	224.1	254.2	291.6	365.3	414.9	503.8
AF.4192	Other short-term loans by rest of the World	ZMEA	158.1	189.8	220.8	274.0	232.4	262.8	271.3	471.8	444.9
AF.42	Long term loans										
AF.4211	Outward direct investment	NLEP	56.9	64.4	84.3	97.4	128.4	127.7	151.2	172.1	159.5
AF.4212	Inward direct investment	NLEQ	86.5	102.8	112.2	142.5	155.6	152.9	152.5	178.4	176.9
AF.429	Other long-term loans by the rest of the world	NLEX	2.5	2.0	2.1	2.1	2.0	2.2	2.7	2.8	2.9
AF.4	Total loans	NLEG	438.9	520.5	612.3	740.0	772.7	837.2	943.1	1 240.0	1 288.0
AF.5	Shares and other equity										
AF.51	Shares and other equity, excluding mutual funds' shares										
AF.514	Quoted UK shares	NLFD	384.1	484.2	572.5	488.5	385.8	464.9	508.7	624.1	739.0
AF.515	Unquoted UK shares	NLFE	165.6	204.6	257.4	285.3	236.5	255.4	274.9	348.5	410.6
AF.516	Other UK equity (including direct investment in property)	NLFF	10.9	11.7	13.5	14.1	15.9	15.9	17.8	18.4	20.2
AF.517	UK shares and bonds issued by other UK residents	NSOP	–	–	–	–	–	–	–	–	–
AF.52	Mutual funds' shares										
AF.521	UK mutual funds' shares	NLFM	1.3	1.7	1.6	1.3	0.9	1.0	1.2	1.5	1.7
AF.5	Total shares and other equity	NLEY	561.9	702.2	845.0	789.2	639.0	737.2	802.6	992.4	1 171.5
AF.6	Insurance technical reserves										
AF.61	Net equity of households in life assurance and pension funds' reserves	NLFO	0.2	0.2	0.2	0.2	0.2	0.2	0.2	0.2	0.2
AF.62	Prepayments of insurance premiums and reserves for outstanding claims	NLFR	15.0	14.1	10.8	10.7	12.6	10.2	10.4	14.2	14.8
AF.6	Total insurance technical reserves	NPYF	15.2	14.3	11.0	10.9	12.9	10.4	10.6	14.4	15.0
AF.7	Other accounts receivable	NLFS	4.0	2.2	2.1	2.7	2.0	1.9	1.7	2.0	1.9
AF.A	**Total financial assets**	NLEF	2 357.7	2 599.2	3 142.8	3 365.2	3 368.8	3 766.7	4 288.1	5 283.2	5 808.5

7.1.9 Rest of the world

ESA95 sector S.2 Unconsolidated

continued £ billion

			1998	1999	2000	2001	2002	2003	2004	2005	2006
IV.3	**FINANCIAL BALANCE SHEET** continued at end of period										
AF.L	**Financial liabilities**										
AF.2	Currency and deposits										
AF.21	Currency	NLGA	0.5	0.5	0.5	0.5	0.5	0.6	0.6	0.6	0.7
AF.22	Transferable deposits										
AF.229	Deposits with rest of the world monetary financial institutions[1]	NLGG	885.4	907.0	1 138.8	1 240.6	1 297.3	1 474.0	1 643.6	2 079.3	2 193.0
AF.2	Total currency and deposits	NLFZ	885.9	907.4	1 139.2	1 241.1	1 297.8	1 474.5	1 644.3	2 079.9	2 193.7
AF.3	Securities other than shares										
AF.331	Short term: money market instruments										
AF.3319	Issued by the rest of the world[1]	NLGV	27.9	44.3	45.3	56.7	48.7	62.0	58.5	64.9	77.9
AF.332	Medium (1 to 5 year) and long term (over 5 year) bonds										
AF.3329	Long term bonds issued by the rest of the world	NLHF	391.5	392.4	478.6	523.7	538.2	550.1	626.7	727.7	829.3
AF.34	Financial Derivatives	NLEC	–	–	0.1	0.4	0.2	–	0.1	0.4	–
AF.3	Total securities other than shares	NLGI	419.4	436.6	524.0	580.7	587.1	612.1	685.3	793.0	907.2
AF.4	Loans										
AF.41	Short term loans										
AF.4111	Sterling loans by UK banks	NLHN	23.4	26.1	27.6	32.3	37.6	40.2	47.4	66.9	87.8
AF.4112	Foreign currency loans by UK banks	NLHO	180.1	189.1	252.5	290.9	291.0	358.3	448.9	575.6	621.3
AF.4113	Sterling loans by UK building societies	NLHP	–	–	–	–	–	–	–	–	–
AF.42	Long term loans										
AF.4211	Outward direct investment	NLHT	76.5	81.6	88.6	101.2	114.5	116.3	145.2	157.3	146.7
AF.4212	Inward direct investment	NLHU	39.4	51.9	53.4	56.3	61.6	59.0	65.3	70.5	74.8
AF.423	Finance leasing	NLHZ	–	–	–	–	–	–	–	–	–
AF.424	Other long-term loans by UK residents	NROS	10.3	10.2	8.6	8.8	7.3	7.2	7.3	7.3	6.1
AF.4	Total loans	NLHK	329.6	359.0	430.7	489.6	512.0	580.9	714.1	877.5	936.7
AF.5	Shares and other equity										
AF.51	Shares and other equity, excluding mutual funds' shares										
AF.519	Shares and other equity issued by the rest of the world	NLIM	588.3	831.9	1 015.8	987.1	925.8	1 043.4	1 120.1	1 372.9	1 460.1
AF.52	Mutual funds' shares										
AF.529	Rest of the world mutual funds' shares	NLIR	1.1	2.1	1.7	1.7	1.4	1.4	1.7	4.1	6.0
AF.5	Total shares and other equity	NLIC	589.3	834.0	1 017.5	988.7	927.2	1 044.8	1 121.8	1 377.0	1 466.1
AF.7	Other accounts payable	NLIW	12.5	3.7	4.4	4.4	5.9	7.7	9.4	9.1	9.5
AF.L	**Total financial liabilities**	NLHJ	2 236.7	2 540.8	3 115.9	3 304.4	3 330.1	3 720.0	4 174.8	5 136.5	5 513.2
BF.90	**Net financial assets / liabilities**										
AF.A	Total financial assets	NLEF	2 357.7	2 599.2	3 142.8	3 365.2	3 368.8	3 766.7	4 288.1	5 283.2	5 808.5
-AF.L	*less* Total financial liabilities	-NLHJ	-2 236.7	-2 540.8	-3 115.9	-3 304.4	-3 330.1	-3 720.0	-4 174.8	-5 136.5	-5 513.2
BF.90	**Net financial assets (+) / liabilities (-)**	NLFK	120.9	58.4	26.9	60.8	38.7	46.7	113.3	146.7	295.3

1 There is a discontinuity in this series between 1995 and 1996 because an instrument breakdown of official reserves is not available prior to 1996

Part 4

Other analyses and derived statistics

Chapter 8

Percentage distributions and growth rates

8.1 Composition of UK gross domestic product at market prices By category of expenditure[1]

Current prices

Percentage

		1998	1999	2000	2001	2002	2003	2004	2005	2006
	Gross domestic product: expenditure approach									
P.3	Final consumption expenditure									
P.41	Actual individual consumption									
P.3	Household final consumption expenditure	61.7	62.3	62.7	63.0	62.9	62.3	61.9	61.7	61.2
P.3	Final consumption expenditure of NPISH	2.4	2.4	2.4	2.5	2.5	2.4	2.4	2.6	2.6
P.31	Individual government final consumption expenditure	10.9	11.3	11.4	11.8	12.4	12.9	13.2	13.6	13.7
P.41	Total actual individual consumption	75.1	75.9	76.5	77.3	77.8	77.6	77.5	77.8	77.5
P.32	Collective government final consumption expenditure	7.1	7.3	7.6	7.6	7.7	7.9	8.0	8.2	8.3
P.3	Total final consumption expenditure	82.2	83.3	84.0	84.9	85.5	85.6	85.5	86.0	85.8
P.3	Households and NPISH	64.1	64.7	65.1	65.5	65.4	64.8	64.3	64.2	63.7
P.3	Central government	11.2	11.4	11.6	11.8	12.3	12.8	12.9	13.2	13.5
P.3	Local government	6.8	7.2	7.4	7.5	7.8	8.1	8.3	8.6	8.6
P.5	Gross capital formation									
P.51	Gross fixed capital formation	18.0	17.7	17.4	17.1	17.1	16.7	17.1	17.2	18.1
P.52	Changes in inventories	0.6	0.7	0.5	0.6	0.3	0.4	0.4	0.3	0.3
P.53	Acquisitions less disposals of valuables	–	–	–	–	–	–	–	–	–
P.5	Total gross capital formation	18.6	18.4	18.0	17.8	17.4	17.0	17.5	17.5	18.4
P.6	Exports of goods and services	26.8	26.3	27.9	27.2	26.2	25.5	25.2	26.5	28.4
-P.7	*less* imports of goods and services	–27.6	–28.0	–29.9	–29.9	–29.1	–28.2	–28.2	–30.1	–32.6
B.11	External balance of goods and services	–0.8	–1.7	–2.0	–2.7	–2.9	–2.6	–3.0	–3.6	–4.2
de	Statistical discrepancy between expenditure components and GDP	–	–	–	–	–	–	–	0.1	–
B.1*g	Gross domestic product at market prices	100.0	100.0	100.0	100.0	100.0	100.0	100.0	100.0	100.0

1 Based on table 1.2

8.2 Composition of UK gross domestic product at market prices By category of income[1,2]

Current prices

Percentage

		1998	1999	2000	2001	2002	2003	2004	2005	2006
B.2g	Total gross operating surplus									
	Public non-financial corporations	0.9	0.8	0.7	0.7	0.6	0.6	0.6	0.7	0.7
	Private non-financial corporations	20.7	20.1	19.8	19.0	18.5	18.7	19.1	19.0	19.0
	Financial corporations	2.2	1.9	1.4	1.3	3.2	3.7	4.0	3.2	3.5
-P.119	FISIM	–3.2	–3.2	–3.5	–3.4	–3.9	–4.1	–4.2	–4.2	–4.4
	Central government	0.6	0.6	0.6	0.5	0.5	0.5	0.5	0.5	0.6
	Local government	0.4	0.4	0.4	0.4	0.4	0.4	0.5	0.5	0.5
	Households and NPISH	5.5	5.6	5.6	5.9	5.9	6.1	6.1	6.3	6.3
B.2g	Total gross operating surplus	27.1	26.2	25.1	24.6	25.3	26.0	26.5	26.0	26.2
B.3	Mixed income	6.1	6.1	6.0	6.2	6.2	6.2	6.1	6.1	6.1
D.1	Compensation of employees	53.8	54.4	55.5	56.2	55.6	55.2	54.8	55.7	55.5
D.2	Taxes on production and imports[2]	13.8	14.1	14.1	13.7	13.6	13.5	13.4	13.1	13.2
-D.3	Subsidies on products	–0.9	–0.8	–0.7	–0.7	–0.8	–0.8	–0.8	–0.8	–0.9
di	Statistical discrepancy between income components and GDP	–	–	–	–	–	–	–	–0.1	–
B.1*g	Gross domestic product	100.0	100.0	100.0	100.0	100.0	100.0	100.0	100.0	100.0

1 Based on table 1.2
2 Includes taxes on products

8.4 Annual increases in categories of expenditure (chained volume measures)

Percentage increases over previous year

		1998	1999	2000	2001	2002	2003	2004	2005	2006
P.3	Household final consumption expenditure	3.8	4.7	4.5	3.1	3.6	3.0	3.5	1.5	1.9
P.3	NPISH final consumption expenditure	7.3	–0.3	8.6	–0.1	–0.1	0.2	0.5	3.1	6.3
P.3	General government final consumption	1.1	3.7	3.1	2.4	3.5	3.5	3.2	2.7	2.4
P.5	Gross fixed capital formation:									
	Private sector	13.2	4.0	4.2	1.6	4.0	1.9	8.2	3.6	11.3
	Public non-financial corporations	–4.9	–17.8	–13.2	35.2	20.3	–51.5	–32.1	1 533.0	–73.0
	General government	13.6	5.8	–3.0	10.7	14.2	32.7	13.2	–69.3	238.7
	Total	13.7	3.0	2.7	2.6	3.6	1.1	5.9	1.5	8.0
P.6	Exports of goods and services	3.0	3.8	9.1	2.9	1.0	1.7	4.9	8.2	11.7
P.7	Imports of goods and services	9.2	7.9	9.0	4.8	4.8	2.0	6.6	7.1	11.7
B.1*g	Gross domestic product at market prices	3.4	3.0	3.8	2.4	2.1	2.8	3.3	1.8	2.8

8.5 Aggregates related to gross national income[1]

Percentages increases over previous year

		1998	1999	2000	2001	2002	2003	2004	2005	2006
D.2	Taxes on production and imports[2]	13.6	14.1	14.1	13.6	13.3	13.2	13.1	12.9	13.0
D.5	Current taxes on income wealth etc	16.2	16.4	16.7	16.7	15.5	14.9	15.1	16.0	17.0
D.61	Compulsory social contributions[3]	6.1	6.2	6.3	6.2	5.9	6.3	6.5	6.7	6.7
D.91	Capital taxes	0.2	0.2	0.2	0.2	0.2	0.2	0.2	0.3	0.3
	Paid to central government	34.0	34.9	35.2	34.7	32.9	32.6	32.9	33.8	34.9
	Paid to local government	1.4	1.4	1.5	1.5	1.6	1.6	1.7	1.7	1.7
	Paid to institutions of the European Union	0.7	0.6	0.7	0.6	0.4	0.4	0.3	0.3	0.3
	Total taxes	36.1	37.0	37.3	36.8	34.9	34.6	34.9	35.9	37.0
D.3	Subsidies	0.9	0.8	0.7	0.7	0.7	0.8	0.8	0.8	0.9

1 Based on tables 1.2, 11.1 and 7.1.8.
2 Including National Insurance surcharge.
3 Including employers', employees', self employed and non-employed persons contributions

8.6 Rates of change of gross domestic product at current market prices ('money GDP')

Percentage change, at annual rate

Initial year	Terminal year 1965	1966	1967	1968	1969	1970	1971	1972	1973	1974	1975	1976	1977	1978	1979	1980	1981	1982	1983	1984	1985
1964	8.0	7.2	6.6	7.0	7.2	7.6	8.2	8.6	9.3	9.7	11.1	11.7	12.1	12.3	12.6	12.9	12.7	12.5	12.3	12.1	12.0
1965		6.4	6.0	6.7	7.0	7.6	8.2	8.7	9.5	9.9	11.5	12.1	12.4	12.6	13.0	13.2	13.0	12.8	12.6	12.3	12.2
1966			5.5	6.9	7.2	7.8	8.6	9.1	10.0	10.4	12.0	12.6	13.0	13.2	13.5	13.7	13.5	13.2	13.0	12.6	12.5
1967				8.3	8.0	8.6	9.4	9.9	10.7	11.1	12.9	13.5	13.7	13.9	14.2	14.4	14.0	13.7	13.5	13.1	12.9
1968					7.7	8.8	9.7	10.3	11.2	11.5	13.5	14.1	14.4	14.5	14.7	14.9	14.5	14.1	13.8	13.4	13.1
1969						9.9	10.7	11.1	12.1	12.3	14.5	15.1	15.2	15.2	15.5	15.6	15.1	14.6	14.3	13.8	13.5
1970							11.5	11.7	12.8	12.9	15.5	15.9	16.0	15.9	16.1	16.2	15.6	15.1	14.6	14.1	13.7
1971								12.0	13.5	13.4	16.5	16.9	16.8	16.6	16.7	16.7	16.0	15.4	14.9	14.2	13.9
1972									15.0	14.1	18.1	18.1	17.8	17.3	17.4	17.3	16.4	15.7	15.1	14.4	14.0
1973										13.2	19.6	19.1	18.4	17.8	17.8	17.6	16.6	15.8	15.1	14.4	14.0
1974											26.3	22.2	20.2	19.0	18.7	18.4	17.1	16.1	15.4	14.5	14.0
1975												18.3	17.3	16.6	16.9	16.9	15.6	14.7	14.0	13.3	12.9
1976													16.3	15.8	16.4	16.5	15.1	14.2	13.5	12.6	12.3
1977														15.3	16.4	16.6	14.8	13.7	13.0	12.1	11.8
1978															17.6	17.2	14.7	13.4	12.5	11.6	11.3
1979																16.9	13.2	12.0	11.3	10.5	10.3
1980																	9.7	9.6	9.5	8.9	9.0
1981																		9.5	9.4	8.6	8.8
1982																			9.3	8.2	8.6
1983																				7.1	8.3
1984																					9.4

Initial year	Terminal year 1986	1987	1988	1989	1990	1991	1992	1993	1994	1995	1996	1997	1998	1999	2000	2001	2002	2003	2004	2005	2006
1964	11.7	11.7	11.7	11.6	11.5	11.2	11.0	10.8	10.6	10.5	10.3	10.2	10.1	9.9	9.8	9.7	9.5	9.4	9.4	9.2	9.1
1965	11.9	11.9	11.9	11.8	11.6	11.4	11.1	10.9	10.7	10.5	10.4	10.3	10.1	10.0	9.8	9.7	9.6	9.5	9.4	9.3	9.2
1966	12.2	12.1	12.1	12.0	11.9	11.6	11.3	11.0	10.9	10.7	10.5	10.4	10.3	10.1	10.0	9.8	9.7	9.6	9.5	9.3	9.2
1967	12.6	12.5	12.4	12.3	12.1	11.8	11.5	11.3	11.1	10.9	10.7	10.6	10.4	10.2	10.1	9.9	9.8	9.7	9.6	9.4	9.3
1968	12.8	12.7	12.6	12.5	12.3	12.0	11.7	11.4	11.2	11.0	10.8	10.6	10.5	10.3	10.1	10.0	9.8	9.7	9.6	9.5	9.3
1969	13.1	13.0	12.9	12.8	12.5	12.2	11.8	11.5	11.3	11.1	10.9	10.7	10.6	10.4	10.2	10.0	9.9	9.8	9.7	9.5	9.4
1970	13.3	13.2	13.1	12.9	12.7	12.3	11.9	11.6	11.4	11.1	11.0	10.8	10.6	10.4	10.2	10.1	9.9	9.8	9.7	9.5	9.4
1971	13.5	13.3	13.2	13.0	12.7	12.3	11.9	11.6	11.4	11.1	10.9	10.7	10.6	10.4	10.2	10.0	9.8	9.7	9.6	9.4	9.3
1972	13.6	13.4	13.2	13.0	12.8	12.4	11.9	11.6	11.3	11.1	10.9	10.7	10.5	10.3	10.1	9.9	9.8	9.6	9.5	9.4	9.2
1973	13.5	13.2	13.1	12.9	12.7	12.2	11.8	11.4	11.2	10.9	10.7	10.5	10.3	10.1	10.0	9.8	9.6	9.5	9.4	9.2	9.1
1974	13.5	13.2	13.1	12.9	12.6	12.2	11.7	11.3	11.1	10.8	10.6	10.4	10.2	10.0	9.8	9.6	9.5	9.3	9.2	9.1	8.9
1975	12.4	12.2	12.2	12.0	11.8	11.3	10.9	10.6	10.3	10.1	9.9	9.7	9.6	9.4	9.2	9.0	8.9	8.8	8.7	8.5	8.4
1976	11.8	11.7	11.7	11.5	11.3	10.9	10.5	10.1	9.9	9.7	9.5	9.3	9.2	9.0	8.9	8.7	8.5	8.4	8.4	8.2	8.1
1977	11.3	11.2	11.3	11.1	10.9	10.5	10.1	9.8	9.5	9.3	9.2	9.0	8.9	8.7	8.5	8.4	8.2	8.2	8.1	7.9	7.8
1978	10.8	10.8	10.9	10.8	10.6	10.1	9.7	9.4	9.2	9.0	8.8	8.7	8.5	8.4	8.2	8.1	8.0	7.9	7.8	7.7	7.6
1979	9.9	9.9	10.1	10.1	10.0	9.5	9.1	8.8	8.6	8.5	8.3	8.2	8.1	8.0	7.8	7.7	7.6	7.5	7.4	7.3	7.2
1980	8.8	9.0	9.3	9.4	9.3	8.9	8.5	8.2	8.1	7.9	7.8	7.7	7.6	7.5	7.4	7.2	7.2	7.1	7.1	6.9	6.9
1981	8.6	8.9	9.3	9.3	9.2	8.8	8.4	8.1	7.9	7.8	7.7	7.6	7.5	7.4	7.3	7.1	7.0	7.0	6.9	6.8	6.8
1982	8.3	8.7	9.2	9.3	9.2	8.8	8.3	8.0	7.8	7.7	7.6	7.5	7.4	7.3	7.1	7.0	6.9	6.9	6.8	6.7	6.6
1983	8.0	8.6	9.2	9.3	9.2	8.7	8.2	7.9	7.7	7.5	7.4	7.3	7.3	7.1	7.0	6.9	6.8	6.7	6.7	6.6	6.5
1984	8.4	9.1	9.7	9.8	9.5	8.9	8.3	7.9	7.7	7.6	7.5	7.3	7.3	7.1	7.0	6.9	6.8	6.7	6.7	6.6	6.5
1985	7.5	8.9	9.8	9.8	9.6	8.8	8.1	7.8	7.6	7.4	7.3	7.2	7.1	7.0	6.8	6.7	6.6	6.6	6.5	6.4	6.4
1986		10.4	11.0	10.6	10.1	9.1	8.3	7.8	7.6	7.4	7.3	7.1	7.1	6.9	6.8	6.7	6.6	6.5	6.5	6.4	6.3
1987			11.7	10.8	10.0	8.8	7.8	7.4	7.2	7.0	6.9	6.8	6.8	6.6	6.5	6.4	6.3	6.3	6.3	6.1	6.1
1988				9.8	9.2	7.8	6.9	6.5	6.4	6.3	6.3	6.3	6.3	6.2	6.1	6.0	5.9	5.9	5.9	5.8	5.8
1989					8.5	6.8	5.9	5.7	5.8	5.7	5.8	5.9	5.9	5.8	5.8	5.7	5.6	5.7	5.7	5.6	5.6
1990						5.1	4.7	4.8	5.1	5.2	5.4	5.5	5.6	5.5	5.5	5.4	5.4	5.5	5.5	5.4	5.4
1991							4.2	4.6	5.1	5.2	5.4	5.6	5.6	5.6	5.6	5.5	5.4	5.5	5.5	5.4	5.4
1992								5.0	5.5	5.6	5.8	5.8	5.9	5.8	5.7	5.6	5.6	5.6	5.6	5.5	5.5
1993									6.0	5.8	6.0	6.0	6.0	5.9	5.8	5.7	5.6	5.6	5.7	5.5	5.5
1994										5.7	6.0	6.0	6.1	5.9	5.8	5.6	5.6	5.6	5.6	5.5	5.5
1995											6.3	6.2	6.2	6.0	5.8	5.6	5.6	5.6	5.6	5.5	5.5
1996												6.1	6.1	5.9	5.7	5.5	5.4	5.5	5.5	5.4	5.4
1997													6.1	5.7	5.5	5.3	5.3	5.4	5.5	5.3	5.3
1998														5.3	5.2	5.0	5.1	5.3	5.4	5.2	5.2
1999															5.2	4.9	5.0	5.2	5.4	5.2	5.2
2000																4.6	4.9	5.3	5.4	5.2	5.2
2001																	5.2	5.6	5.7	5.3	5.3
2002																		5.9	5.9	5.3	5.3
2003																			5.9	5.0	5.1
2004																				4.2	4.8
2005																					5.3

8.7 Rates of change of gross domestic product (chained volume measures)

Percentage change, at annual rate

Initial year	Terminal year 1965	1966	1967	1968	1969	1970	1971	1972	1973	1974	1975	1976	1977	1978	1979	1980	1981	1982	1983	1984	1985
1964	2.2	2.1	2.2	2.7	2.6	2.5	2.4	2.6	3.1	2.6	2.3	2.4	2.4	2.4	2.4	2.2	1.9	1.9	2.0	2.0	2.1
1965		1.9	2.2	2.9	2.7	2.6	2.5	2.6	3.2	2.7	2.3	2.4	2.4	2.4	2.5	2.1	1.9	1.9	2.0	2.0	2.1
1966			2.5	3.3	2.9	2.7	2.6	2.8	3.4	2.8	2.4	2.4	2.4	2.5	2.5	2.2	1.9	1.9	2.0	2.0	2.1
1967				4.2	3.1	2.8	2.6	2.8	3.5	2.8	2.4	2.4	2.4	2.5	2.5	2.1	1.9	1.9	2.0	2.0	2.1
1968					2.1	2.2	2.1	2.5	3.4	2.6	2.1	2.2	2.2	2.3	2.3	2.0	1.7	1.7	1.8	1.9	2.0
1969						2.2	2.1	2.6	3.7	2.7	2.1	2.2	2.2	2.3	2.4	2.0	1.7	1.7	1.8	1.9	2.0
1970							2.0	2.8	4.2	2.8	2.1	2.2	2.2	2.3	2.4	1.9	1.6	1.6	1.8	1.8	2.0
1971								3.6	5.3	3.1	2.1	2.2	2.3	2.4	2.4	1.9	1.6	1.6	1.8	1.8	1.9
1972									7.1	2.8	1.6	1.9	2.0	2.2	2.3	1.7	1.4	1.4	1.6	1.7	1.8
1973										-1.4	-1.0	0.2	0.7	1.2	1.5	1.0	0.7	0.8	1.1	1.2	1.4
1974											-0.6	1.0	1.5	1.9	2.1	1.4	0.9	1.1	1.3	1.5	1.6
1975												2.6	2.5	2.8	2.7	1.8	1.2	1.3	1.6	1.7	1.9
1976													2.4	2.8	2.8	1.5	0.9	1.1	1.4	1.6	1.8
1977														3.2	3.0	1.3	0.6	0.8	1.3	1.5	1.7
1978															2.7	0.3	-0.3	0.2	0.9	1.2	1.5
1979																-2.1	-1.8	-0.6	0.4	0.9	1.3
1980																	-1.5	0.2	1.3	1.6	2.0
1981																		1.9	2.7	2.7	2.9
1982																			3.5	3.0	3.2
1983																				2.6	3.0
1984																					3.5

Initial year	Terminal year 1986	1987	1988	1989	1990	1991	1992	1993	1994	1995	1996	1997	1998	1999	2000	2001	2002	2003	2004	2005	2006
1964	2.2	2.3	2.4	2.4	2.3	2.2	2.1	2.1	2.2	2.2	2.2	2.3	2.3	2.3	2.4	2.4	2.4	2.4	2.4	2.4	2.4
1965	2.2	2.3	2.4	2.4	2.3	2.2	2.1	2.1	2.2	2.2	2.2	2.3	2.3	2.3	2.4	2.4	2.4	2.4	2.4	2.4	2.4
1966	2.2	2.3	2.4	2.4	2.4	2.2	2.1	2.1	2.2	2.2	2.3	2.3	2.3	2.3	2.4	2.4	2.4	2.4	2.4	2.4	2.4
1967	2.2	2.3	2.4	2.4	2.4	2.2	2.1	2.1	2.2	2.2	2.2	2.3	2.3	2.3	2.4	2.4	2.4	2.4	2.4	2.4	2.4
1968	2.1	2.2	2.4	2.3	2.3	2.1	2.0	2.0	2.1	2.2	2.2	2.2	2.3	2.3	2.3	2.3	2.3	2.3	2.4	2.3	2.4
1969	2.1	2.2	2.4	2.4	2.3	2.1	2.0	2.0	2.1	2.2	2.2	2.2	2.3	2.3	2.3	2.3	2.3	2.3	2.4	2.3	2.4
1970	2.1	2.2	2.4	2.4	2.3	2.1	2.0	2.0	2.1	2.2	2.2	2.2	2.3	2.3	2.3	2.3	2.3	2.3	2.4	2.4	2.4
1971	2.1	2.2	2.4	2.4	2.3	2.1	2.0	2.0	2.1	2.2	2.2	2.2	2.3	2.3	2.3	2.3	2.3	2.3	2.4	2.4	2.4
1972	2.0	2.1	2.3	2.3	2.2	2.0	1.9	2.0	2.1	2.1	2.1	2.2	2.2	2.2	2.3	2.3	2.3	2.3	2.3	2.3	2.3
1973	1.6	1.8	2.0	2.0	1.9	1.8	1.7	1.7	1.8	1.9	1.9	2.0	2.0	2.1	2.1	2.1	2.1	2.2	2.2	2.2	2.2
1974	1.8	2.0	2.3	2.3	2.2	1.9	1.9	1.9	2.0	2.0	2.1	2.1	2.2	2.2	2.3	2.3	2.3	2.3	2.3	2.3	2.3
1975	2.1	2.3	2.5	2.5	2.3	2.1	2.0	2.0	2.1	2.2	2.2	2.2	2.3	2.3	2.4	2.4	2.4	2.4	2.4	2.4	2.4
1976	2.0	2.2	2.5	2.4	2.3	2.1	2.0	2.0	2.1	2.1	2.2	2.2	2.3	2.3	2.4	2.4	2.4	2.4	2.4	2.4	2.4
1977	2.0	2.2	2.5	2.5	2.3	2.1	1.9	1.9	2.1	2.1	2.2	2.2	2.3	2.3	2.4	2.4	2.4	2.4	2.4	2.4	2.4
1978	1.8	2.1	2.4	2.4	2.2	2.0	1.8	1.9	2.0	2.1	2.1	2.2	2.2	2.3	2.3	2.3	2.3	2.3	2.4	2.4	2.4
1979	1.7	2.0	2.4	2.3	2.2	1.9	1.8	1.8	2.0	2.0	2.1	2.1	2.2	2.2	2.3	2.3	2.3	2.3	2.4	2.3	2.4
1980	2.3	2.6	2.9	2.9	2.6	2.3	2.1	2.1	2.3	2.3	2.3	2.4	2.4	2.5	2.5	2.5	2.5	2.5	2.6	2.5	2.5
1981	3.1	3.3	3.6	3.4	3.1	2.7	2.4	2.4	2.6	2.6	2.6	2.6	2.7	2.7	2.8	2.7	2.7	2.7	2.7	2.7	2.7
1982	3.4	3.6	3.9	3.6	3.3	2.7	2.5	2.5	2.6	2.6	2.6	2.7	2.7	2.7	2.8	2.8	2.7	2.7	2.8	2.7	2.7
1983	3.4	3.7	3.9	3.6	3.2	2.6	2.4	2.4	2.5	2.6	2.6	2.6	2.7	2.7	2.8	2.7	2.7	2.7	2.7	2.7	2.7
1984	3.8	4.0	4.3	3.9	3.3	2.6	2.3	2.3	2.5	2.6	2.6	2.6	2.7	2.7	2.8	2.7	2.7	2.7	2.7	2.7	2.7
1985	4.0	4.3	4.5	3.9	3.3	2.5	2.2	2.2	2.4	2.5	2.5	2.5	2.6	2.6	2.7	2.7	2.7	2.7	2.7	2.7	2.7
1986		4.6	4.8	3.9	3.1	2.2	1.9	1.9	2.2	2.3	2.4	2.4	2.5	2.5	2.6	2.6	2.6	2.6	2.6	2.6	2.6
1987			5.0	3.6	2.6	1.6	1.3	1.5	1.9	2.0	2.1	2.2	2.3	2.4	2.5	2.5	2.4	2.5	2.5	2.5	2.5
1988				2.2	1.5	0.5	0.4	0.8	1.4	1.6	1.8	1.9	2.0	2.1	2.3	2.3	2.3	2.3	2.4	2.3	2.4
1989					0.8	-0.3	-0.1	0.5	1.2	1.5	1.7	1.9	2.0	2.1	2.3	2.3	2.3	2.3	2.4	2.3	2.4
1990						-1.4	-0.6	0.4	1.3	1.7	1.8	2.0	2.2	2.3	2.4	2.4	2.4	2.4	2.5	2.4	2.5
1991							0.2	1.2	2.3	2.4	2.5	2.6	2.7	2.7	2.9	2.8	2.7	2.7	2.8	2.7	2.7
1992								2.3	3.3	3.2	3.1	3.1	3.1	3.1	3.2	3.1	3.0	3.0	3.0	2.9	2.9
1993									4.3	3.6	3.3	3.3	3.3	3.3	3.3	3.2	3.1	3.1	3.1	3.0	3.0
1994										2.9	2.9	2.9	3.0	3.0	3.2	3.1	2.9	2.9	2.9	2.8	2.8
1995											2.8	2.9	3.1	3.1	3.2	3.1	2.9	2.9	2.9	2.8	2.8
1996												3.1	3.2	3.2	3.3	3.1	3.0	2.9	3.0	2.8	2.8
1997													3.4	3.2	3.4	3.1	2.9	2.9	2.9	2.8	2.8
1998														3.0	3.4	3.1	2.8	2.8	2.9	2.7	2.7
1999															3.8	3.1	2.7	2.7	2.8	2.7	2.7
2000																2.4	2.2	2.4	2.6	2.5	2.5
2001																	2.1	2.4	2.7	2.5	2.6
2002																		2.8	3.0	2.6	2.7
2003																			3.3	2.5	2.6
2004																				1.8	2.3
2005																					2.8

8.8 Rates of change of GDP at market prices (current prices) Per capita

Percentage change, at annual rate

Initial year	Terminal year 1986	1987	1988	1989	1990	1991	1992	1993	1994	1995	1996	1997	1998	1999	2000	2001	2002	2003	2004	2005	2006
1985	7.2	8.5	9.5	9.5	9.2	8.5	7.8	7.4	7.2	7.0	7.0	6.8	6.8	6.6	6.5	6.4	6.3	6.2	6.2	6.1	6.0
1986		9.8	10.6	10.2	9.7	8.7	7.9	7.4	7.2	7.0	6.9	6.8	6.7	6.6	6.5	6.3	6.2	6.2	6.1	6.0	6.0
1987			11.4	10.4	9.7	8.4	7.5	7.1	6.9	6.7	6.6	6.5	6.5	6.3	6.2	6.1	6.0	5.9	5.9	5.8	5.8
1988				9.5	8.8	7.4	6.6	6.2	6.1	6.0	6.0	6.0	6.0	5.9	5.8	5.7	5.6	5.6	5.6	5.5	5.5
1989					8.1	6.4	5.6	5.4	5.5	5.5	5.5	5.6	5.6	5.5	5.5	5.4	5.3	5.3	5.3	5.3	5.2
1990						4.8	4.4	4.5	4.8	4.9	5.1	5.2	5.3	5.2	5.2	5.1	5.1	5.1	5.1	5.1	5.1
1991							4.0	4.4	4.8	5.0	5.2	5.3	5.3	5.3	5.2	5.1	5.1	5.1	5.2	5.1	5.1
1992								4.8	5.2	5.3	5.5	5.5	5.6	5.5	5.4	5.3	5.2	5.2	5.3	5.2	5.2
1993									5.7	5.5	5.7	5.7	5.7	5.6	5.5	5.3	5.3	5.3	5.3	5.2	5.2
1994										5.4	5.7	5.7	5.8	5.6	5.5	5.3	5.2	5.2	5.3	5.2	5.1
1995											6.1	5.9	5.9	5.6	5.5	5.3	5.2	5.2	5.3	5.1	5.1
1996												5.7	5.8	5.5	5.3	5.1	5.0	5.1	5.2	5.0	5.0
1997													5.8	5.4	5.2	4.9	4.9	5.0	5.1	5.0	4.9
1998														4.9	4.9	4.6	4.7	4.8	4.9	4.8	4.8
1999															4.8	4.5	4.6	4.8	4.9	4.8	4.8
2000																4.2	4.5	4.8	5.0	4.8	4.8
2001																	4.8	5.1	5.2	5.0	4.9
2002																		5.5	5.5	5.0	5.0
2003																			5.5	4.8	4.8
2004																				4.2	4.5
2005																					4.8

8.9 Rates of change of GDP at market prices (chained volume measures) Per capita

Percentage change, at annual rate

Initial year	Terminal year 1986	1987	1988	1989	1990	1991	1992	1993	1994	1995	1996	1997	1998	1999	2000	2001	2002	2003	2004	2005	2006
1985	3.7	4.0	4.3	3.7	3.0	2.2	1.9	1.9	2.1	2.2	2.2	2.3	2.3	2.3	2.4	2.4	2.4	2.3	2.4	2.3	2.3
1986		4.3	4.5	3.6	2.8	1.9	1.6	1.6	1.9	2.0	2.1	2.1	2.2	2.2	2.3	2.3	2.3	2.3	2.3	2.3	2.3
1987			4.8	3.3	2.3	1.3	1.0	1.2	1.6	1.7	1.8	1.9	2.0	2.1	2.2	2.2	2.1	2.1	2.2	2.2	2.2
1988				1.9	1.1	0.2	0.1	0.5	1.1	1.3	1.5	1.6	1.7	1.8	2.0	2.0	1.9	2.0	2.0	2.0	2.0
1989					0.4	-0.6	-0.4	0.2	0.9	1.2	1.4	1.6	1.7	1.8	2.0	2.0	2.0	2.0	2.0	2.0	2.0
1990						-1.7	-0.9	0.1	1.1	1.4	1.6	1.7	1.9	2.0	2.1	2.1	2.1	2.1	2.1	2.1	2.1
1991							-0.0	1.0	2.0	2.2	2.2	2.3	2.4	2.5	2.6	2.5	2.4	2.4	2.4	2.4	2.4
1992								2.1	3.0	2.9	2.8	2.8	2.8	2.8	2.9	2.8	2.7	2.6	2.7	2.6	2.6
1993									4.0	3.3	3.1	3.0	3.0	2.9	3.0	2.9	2.8	2.7	2.7	2.6	2.6
1994										2.6	2.6	2.6	2.7	2.7	2.8	2.7	2.6	2.6	2.6	2.5	2.5
1995											2.5	2.6	2.8	2.7	2.9	2.7	2.6	2.5	2.6	2.5	2.5
1996												2.8	2.9	2.8	3.0	2.8	2.6	2.6	2.6	2.5	2.5
1997													3.1	2.9	3.1	2.8	2.6	2.5	2.6	2.5	2.5
1998														2.7	3.1	2.7	2.4	2.4	2.5	2.4	2.4
1999															3.4	2.7	2.4	2.3	2.4	2.3	2.3
2000																2.0	1.8	2.0	2.2	2.1	2.2
2001																	1.7	2.0	2.2	2.2	2.2
2002																		2.3	2.5	2.3	2.3
2003																			2.8	2.3	2.3
2004																				1.9	2.1
2005																					2.3

8.10 Rates of change of household disposable income (chained volume measures) Total

Percentage change, at annual rate

Initial year \ Terminal year	1965	1966	1967	1968	1969	1970	1971	1972	1973	1974	1975	1976	1977	1978	1979	1980	1981	1982	1983	1984	1985
1964	1.9	2.1	1.9	1.9	1.7	2.0	1.9	2.7	3.1	2.7	2.5	2.3	2.0	2.3	2.6	2.5	2.3	2.2	2.2	2.2	2.3
1965		2.3	1.9	1.9	1.7	2.1	1.9	2.8	3.2	2.8	2.6	2.3	2.0	2.4	2.6	2.5	2.4	2.2	2.2	2.3	2.3
1966			1.5	1.7	1.4	2.0	1.8	2.9	3.4	2.8	2.6	2.3	1.9	2.4	2.6	2.6	2.4	2.2	2.2	2.3	2.3
1967				1.9	1.4	2.2	1.9	3.2	3.7	3.0	2.8	2.4	2.0	2.4	2.7	2.6	2.4	2.2	2.2	2.3	2.4
1968					0.9	2.3	2.0	3.5	4.1	3.2	2.9	2.5	2.0	2.5	2.8	2.7	2.5	2.3	2.2	2.3	2.4
1969						3.7	2.5	4.4	4.8	3.7	3.2	2.7	2.1	2.7	3.0	2.9	2.6	2.4	2.3	2.4	2.5
1970							1.2	4.7	5.2	3.7	3.1	2.5	1.9	2.5	2.9	2.8	2.5	2.2	2.2	2.3	2.4
1971								8.3	7.3	4.5	3.6	2.8	2.0	2.7	3.1	3.0	2.6	2.3	2.3	2.4	2.5
1972									6.3	2.7	2.1	1.5	0.8	1.8	2.4	2.3	2.0	1.8	1.8	1.9	2.1
1973										-0.8	0.1	-0.1	-0.6	1.0	1.8	1.8	1.5	1.3	1.3	1.6	1.7
1974											1.0	0.3	-0.5	1.4	2.3	2.2	1.8	1.5	1.6	1.8	1.9
1975												-0.4	-1.2	1.6	2.6	2.4	1.9	1.6	1.7	1.9	2.0
1976													-2.0	2.5	3.6	3.1	2.4	1.9	2.0	2.2	2.3
1977														7.3	6.6	4.9	3.6	2.8	2.6	2.8	2.9
1978															5.9	3.8	2.3	1.7	1.7	2.1	2.3
1979																1.7	0.6	0.3	0.7	1.3	1.7
1980																	-0.5	-0.4	0.4	1.2	1.7
1981																		-0.3	0.8	1.8	2.2
1982																			2.0	2.9	3.1
1983																				3.7	3.6
1984																					3.4

Initial year \ Terminal year	1986	1987	1988	1989	1990	1991	1992	1993	1994	1995	1996	1997	1998	1999	2000	2001	2002	2003	2004	2005	2006
1964	2.4	2.4	2.6	2.7	2.7	2.7	2.7	2.7	2.6	2.6	2.6	2.6	2.6	2.6	2.7	2.7	2.7	2.7	2.7	2.7	2.6
1965	2.4	2.5	2.6	2.7	2.7	2.7	2.7	2.7	2.6	2.6	2.6	2.7	2.6	2.6	2.7	2.7	2.7	2.7	2.7	2.7	2.6
1966	2.4	2.5	2.6	2.7	2.7	2.7	2.7	2.7	2.7	2.7	2.6	2.7	2.6	2.7	2.7	2.7	2.7	2.7	2.7	2.7	2.7
1967	2.5	2.5	2.7	2.8	2.8	2.7	2.8	2.7	2.7	2.7	2.7	2.7	2.7	2.7	2.7	2.8	2.8	2.7	2.7	2.7	2.7
1968	2.5	2.6	2.7	2.8	2.8	2.8	2.8	2.8	2.7	2.7	2.7	2.8	2.7	2.7	2.8	2.8	2.8	2.8	2.7	2.7	2.7
1969	2.6	2.6	2.8	2.9	2.9	2.9	2.9	2.9	2.8	2.8	2.8	2.8	2.8	2.8	2.8	2.9	2.8	2.8	2.8	2.8	2.8
1970	2.5	2.6	2.7	2.8	2.9	2.8	2.8	2.8	2.8	2.8	2.7	2.8	2.7	2.7	2.8	2.8	2.8	2.8	2.8	2.8	2.7
1971	2.6	2.7	2.8	2.9	3.0	2.9	2.9	2.9	2.8	2.8	2.8	2.8	2.8	2.8	2.9	2.9	2.9	2.8	2.8	2.8	2.8
1972	2.2	2.3	2.5	2.6	2.7	2.6	2.6	2.6	2.6	2.6	2.6	2.6	2.6	2.6	2.7	2.7	2.7	2.7	2.6	2.7	2.6
1973	1.9	2.0	2.3	2.4	2.5	2.4	2.5	2.5	2.4	2.4	2.4	2.5	2.4	2.5	2.5	2.6	2.6	2.6	2.5	2.5	2.5
1974	2.1	2.2	2.5	2.6	2.7	2.6	2.6	2.6	2.6	2.6	2.6	2.6	2.6	2.6	2.7	2.7	2.7	2.7	2.6	2.7	2.6
1975	2.2	2.4	2.6	2.7	2.8	2.7	2.7	2.7	2.7	2.7	2.7	2.7	2.7	2.7	2.7	2.8	2.7	2.7	2.7	2.7	2.7
1976	2.5	2.6	2.8	3.0	3.0	2.9	2.9	2.9	2.8	2.8	2.8	2.9	2.8	2.8	2.9	2.9	2.9	2.9	2.8	2.8	2.8
1977	3.0	3.1	3.3	3.4	3.4	3.3	3.3	3.2	3.1	3.1	3.1	3.1	3.0	3.0	3.1	3.1	3.1	3.0	3.0	3.0	2.9
1978	2.5	2.6	2.9	3.1	3.1	3.0	3.0	3.0	2.9	2.9	2.8	2.9	2.8	2.8	2.9	2.9	2.9	2.9	2.8	2.8	2.8
1979	2.0	2.2	2.6	2.8	2.8	2.8	2.8	2.8	2.7	2.7	2.7	2.7	2.7	2.7	2.7	2.8	2.8	2.8	2.7	2.7	2.7
1980	2.1	2.3	2.7	2.9	3.0	2.9	2.9	2.9	2.8	2.7	2.7	2.8	2.7	2.7	2.8	2.9	2.8	2.8	2.8	2.8	2.7
1981	2.6	2.8	3.1	3.3	3.3	3.2	3.2	3.1	3.0	3.0	2.9	3.0	2.9	2.9	3.0	3.0	3.0	3.0	2.9	2.9	2.8
1982	3.3	3.4	3.7	3.9	3.8	3.6	3.5	3.5	3.3	3.2	3.2	3.2	3.1	3.1	3.2	3.2	3.1	3.1	3.1	3.0	3.0
1983	3.8	3.7	4.1	4.2	4.1	3.8	3.7	3.6	3.4	3.3	3.3	3.3	3.2	3.2	3.2	3.3	3.2	3.2	3.1	3.1	3.0
1984	3.8	3.7	4.2	4.3	4.1	3.8	3.7	3.6	3.4	3.3	3.2	3.3	3.1	3.1	3.2	3.3	3.2	3.1	3.1	3.1	3.0
1985	4.1	3.9	4.4	4.5	4.3	3.9	3.8	3.6	3.4	3.3	3.2	3.3	3.1	3.1	3.2	3.3	3.2	3.1	3.0	3.0	3.0
1986		3.7	4.6	4.6	4.3	3.8	3.7	3.5	3.3	3.2	3.1	3.2	3.0	3.0	3.1	3.2	3.1	3.1	3.0	3.0	2.9
1987			5.5	5.1	4.5	3.9	3.7	3.5	3.2	3.1	3.1	3.1	3.0	3.0	3.1	3.2	3.1	3.0	2.9	2.9	2.8
1988				4.7	4.0	3.4	3.2	3.1	2.8	2.8	2.8	2.9	2.7	2.7	2.9	3.0	2.9	2.9	2.8	2.8	2.7
1989					3.4	2.7	2.8	2.7	2.5	2.5	2.5	2.6	2.5	2.5	2.7	2.8	2.8	2.7	2.7	2.7	2.6
1990						2.0	2.5	2.5	2.3	2.3	2.3	2.5	2.4	2.4	2.6	2.8	2.7	2.7	2.6	2.6	2.5
1991							2.9	2.8	2.3	2.4	2.4	2.6	2.5	2.5	2.7	2.9	2.8	2.7	2.7	2.7	2.6
1992								2.6	2.0	2.2	2.3	2.6	2.4	2.4	2.7	2.9	2.8	2.7	2.6	2.7	2.6
1993									1.5	2.0	2.2	2.6	2.3	2.4	2.7	2.9	2.8	2.7	2.6	2.7	2.5
1994										2.6	2.5	2.9	2.6	2.6	2.9	3.1	2.9	2.9	2.8	2.8	2.6
1995											2.4	3.1	2.5	2.6	3.0	3.2	3.0	2.9	2.8	2.8	2.6
1996												3.8	2.6	2.7	3.1	3.4	3.1	3.0	2.8	2.8	2.7
1997													1.5	2.1	2.9	3.3	2.9	2.9	2.7	2.7	2.5
1998														2.8	3.6	3.8	3.3	3.1	2.9	2.9	2.7
1999															4.5	4.4	3.5	3.2	2.9	2.9	2.7
2000																4.3	3.0	2.8	2.5	2.6	2.4
2001																	1.7	2.1	1.9	2.2	2.0
2002																		2.4	2.1	2.4	2.0
2003																			1.7	2.3	1.9
2004																				2.9	2.0
2005																					1.1

8.11 Rates of change of household disposable income (chained volume measures) (Per capita)

Percentage change, at annual rate

Initial year	1966	1967	1968	1969	1970	1971	1972	1973	1974	1975	1976	1977	1978	1979	1980	1981	1982	1983	1984	1985	1986
	Terminal year																				
1965	1.8	1.4	1.4	1.1	1.6	1.4	2.4	2.8	2.4	2.3	2.0	1.7	2.1	2.4	2.3	2.1	2.0	2.0	2.1	2.1	2.2
1966		0.9	1.2	0.9	1.5	1.4	2.4	3.0	2.5	2.3	2.0	1.7	2.1	2.4	2.3	2.1	2.0	2.0	2.1	2.1	2.2
1967			1.4	0.9	1.8	1.5	2.8	3.3	2.7	2.5	2.2	1.7	2.2	2.5	2.4	2.2	2.1	2.1	2.2	2.2	2.3
1968				0.5	1.9	1.5	3.1	3.7	2.9	2.6	2.3	1.8	2.3	2.6	2.5	2.3	2.1	2.1	2.2	2.3	2.3
1969					3.4	2.0	4.0	4.5	3.4	3.0	2.5	1.9	2.5	2.8	2.7	2.5	2.2	2.2	2.3	2.4	2.5
1970						0.7	4.3	4.9	3.4	2.9	2.4	1.7	2.4	2.8	2.7	2.4	2.1	2.1	2.2	2.3	2.4
1971							8.0	7.0	4.3	3.5	2.7	1.9	2.7	3.1	2.9	2.5	2.3	2.3	2.4	2.4	2.5
1972								6.0	2.5	2.0	1.4	0.7	1.8	2.4	2.3	1.9	1.7	1.8	1.9	2.0	2.1
1973									-0.8	0.1	-0.1	-0.5	1.0	1.8	1.7	1.4	1.3	1.3	1.5	1.7	1.8
1974										1.0	0.3	-0.5	1.4	2.3	2.2	1.8	1.5	1.6	1.8	1.9	2.1
1975											-0.4	-1.2	1.6	2.6	2.4	1.9	1.6	1.6	1.9	2.0	2.2
1976												-2.0	2.6	3.6	3.1	2.4	1.9	1.9	2.1	2.2	2.4
1977													7.4	6.6	4.9	3.5	2.7	2.6	2.7	2.8	2.9
1978														5.8	3.6	2.2	1.6	1.7	2.0	2.2	2.4
1979															1.5	0.5	0.2	0.7	1.3	1.6	1.9
1980																-0.5	-0.4	0.4	1.2	1.6	2.0
1981																	-0.2	0.9	1.8	2.1	2.5
1982																		2.0	2.8	2.9	3.1
1983																			3.6	3.4	3.5
1984																				3.1	3.5
1985																					3.9

Initial year	1987	1988	1989	1990	1991	1992	1993	1994	1995	1996	1997	1998	1999	2000	2001	2002	2003	2004	2005	2006
	Terminal year																			
1965	2.3	2.4	2.5	2.5	2.5	2.5	2.5	2.4	2.4	2.4	2.4	2.4	2.4	2.5	2.5	2.5	2.5	2.4	2.4	2.4
1966	2.3	2.4	2.5	2.5	2.5	2.5	2.5	2.4	2.4	2.4	2.5	2.4	2.4	2.5	2.5	2.5	2.5	2.4	2.4	2.4
1967	2.4	2.5	2.6	2.6	2.6	2.6	2.6	2.5	2.5	2.5	2.5	2.5	2.5	2.5	2.6	2.5	2.5	2.5	2.5	2.4
1968	2.4	2.5	2.6	2.7	2.6	2.6	2.6	2.5	2.5	2.5	2.6	2.5	2.5	2.6	2.6	2.6	2.5	2.5	2.5	2.5
1969	2.5	2.7	2.7	2.8	2.7	2.7	2.7	2.6	2.6	2.6	2.6	2.6	2.6	2.6	2.7	2.6	2.6	2.6	2.6	2.5
1970	2.5	2.6	2.7	2.7	2.7	2.7	2.7	2.6	2.6	2.6	2.6	2.6	2.6	2.6	2.6	2.6	2.6	2.5	2.5	2.5
1971	2.6	2.7	2.8	2.8	2.8	2.8	2.8	2.7	2.7	2.6	2.7	2.6	2.6	2.7	2.7	2.7	2.6	2.6	2.6	2.5
1972	2.2	2.4	2.5	2.6	2.5	2.5	2.5	2.4	2.4	2.4	2.5	2.4	2.4	2.5	2.5	2.5	2.5	2.4	2.4	2.4
1973	2.0	2.2	2.3	2.4	2.3	2.3	2.3	2.3	2.3	2.3	2.3	2.3	2.3	2.4	2.4	2.4	2.4	2.3	2.3	2.3
1974	2.2	2.4	2.5	2.6	2.5	2.5	2.5	2.4	2.4	2.4	2.5	2.4	2.4	2.5	2.5	2.5	2.5	2.4	2.4	2.4
1975	2.3	2.5	2.6	2.7	2.6	2.6	2.6	2.5	2.5	2.5	2.5	2.5	2.5	2.5	2.6	2.5	2.5	2.5	2.5	2.4
1976	2.5	2.7	2.9	2.9	2.8	2.8	2.8	2.7	2.7	2.6	2.7	2.6	2.6	2.7	2.7	2.7	2.6	2.6	2.6	2.5
1977	3.0	3.2	3.3	3.3	3.1	3.1	3.1	3.0	2.9	2.9	2.9	2.8	2.8	2.9	2.9	2.8	2.8	2.8	2.7	2.7
1978	2.5	2.8	2.9	2.9	2.8	2.8	2.8	2.7	2.7	2.6	2.7	2.6	2.6	2.7	2.7	2.7	2.6	2.6	2.6	2.5
1979	2.1	2.4	2.6	2.7	2.6	2.6	2.6	2.5	2.5	2.5	2.5	2.4	2.4	2.5	2.6	2.5	2.5	2.5	2.5	2.4
1980	2.2	2.6	2.8	2.8	2.7	2.7	2.7	2.6	2.5	2.5	2.6	2.5	2.5	2.6	2.6	2.6	2.6	2.5	2.5	2.4
1981	2.6	3.0	3.2	3.2	3.0	3.0	2.9	2.8	2.8	2.7	2.8	2.7	2.7	2.7	2.8	2.7	2.7	2.6	2.6	2.5
1982	3.2	3.6	3.7	3.6	3.4	3.3	3.2	3.1	3.0	2.9	3.0	2.9	2.8	2.9	3.0	2.9	2.8	2.8	2.7	2.7
1983	3.5	3.9	4.0	3.8	3.6	3.5	3.3	3.2	3.1	3.0	3.0	2.9	2.9	3.0	3.0	2.9	2.9	2.8	2.8	2.7
1984	3.5	3.9	4.0	3.9	3.6	3.4	3.3	3.1	3.0	3.0	3.0	2.9	2.8	2.9	3.0	2.9	2.8	2.8	2.7	2.6
1985	3.7	4.2	4.3	4.0	3.6	3.5	3.3	3.1	3.0	2.9	3.0	2.9	2.8	2.9	3.0	2.9	2.8	2.7	2.7	2.6
1986	3.5	4.4	4.4	4.1	3.6	3.4	3.3	3.0	2.9	2.9	2.9	2.8	2.7	2.8	2.9	2.8	2.8	2.7	2.7	2.6
1987		5.3	4.8	4.3	3.6	3.4	3.2	2.9	2.9	2.8	2.9	2.7	2.7	2.8	2.9	2.8	2.7	2.6	2.6	2.5
1988			4.4	3.7	3.0	2.9	2.8	2.6	2.5	2.5	2.6	2.5	2.4	2.6	2.7	2.6	2.6	2.5	2.5	2.4
1989				3.1	2.4	2.5	2.4	2.2	2.2	2.2	2.4	2.2	2.3	2.4	2.5	2.5	2.4	2.3	2.3	2.2
1990					1.7	2.1	2.2	2.0	2.0	2.1	2.3	2.1	2.2	2.4	2.5	2.4	2.4	2.3	2.3	2.2
1991						2.6	2.5	2.1	2.1	2.1	2.4	2.2	2.2	2.4	2.6	2.5	2.4	2.3	2.3	2.2
1992							2.4	1.8	2.0	2.0	2.3	2.1	2.2	2.4	2.6	2.5	2.4	2.3	2.3	2.2
1993								1.2	1.8	1.9	2.3	2.1	2.1	2.4	2.6	2.5	2.4	2.3	2.3	2.2
1994									2.3	2.2	2.6	2.3	2.3	2.6	2.8	2.6	2.5	2.4	2.4	2.2
1995										2.1	2.8	2.3	2.3	2.7	2.9	2.7	2.6	2.4	2.4	2.2
1996											3.5	2.4	2.4	2.8	3.0	2.7	2.6	2.5	2.4	2.3
1997												1.2	1.8	2.6	2.9	2.6	2.5	2.3	2.3	2.1
1998													2.4	3.3	3.5	2.9	2.8	2.5	2.5	2.2
1999														4.1	4.0	3.1	2.8	2.5	2.5	2.2
2000															3.9	2.6	2.4	2.1	2.2	1.9
2001																1.4	1.7	1.5	1.7	1.5
2002																	2.0	1.6	1.8	1.5
2003																		1.2	1.8	1.4
2004																			2.3	1.4
2005																				0.6

Chapter 9

Fixed capital formation supplementary tables

9.1 Gross fixed capital formation at current purchasers' prices
Analysis by type of asset and sector

£ million

			1998	1999	2000	2001	2002	2003	2004	2005	2006
	Dwellings, excluding land										
	Public non-financial corporations	DEER	1 632	1 529	1 421	2 387	2 837	3 509	3 235	3 574	4 132
	Private non-financial corporations	DLWG	271	279	303	324	374	414	502	552	656
	Financial corporations	DFIX	–	–	–	–	–	–	–	–	–
	Central government	DFIZ	273	250	369	334	207	149	137	71	6
	Local government	DKQC	–	–	–	–	–	–	–	–	–
	Households and NPISH	DLWK	23 046	23 642	25 301	26 761	31 081	34 390	40 425	43 846	50 835
	Total	DFDK	25 222	25 700	27 394	29 806	34 499	38 462	44 299	48 043	55 629
	Other buildings and structures										
	Public non-financial corporations	DEES	1 608	1 692	1 775	1 854	2 304	2 236	1 493	2 111	1 819
	Private non-financial corporations	DLWN	24 094	26 594	27 124	27 936	29 123	30 643	32 309	34 281	38 017
	Financial corporations	GGBT	2 819	2 509	2 176	2 017	2 007	2 089	1 602	2 479	2 296
	Central government	DLWP	4 220	3 990	3 390	3 610	4 717	5 663	6 072	7 712	8 677
	Local government	DJYS	5 082	5 424	6 044	6 738	6 961	9 030	9 794	11 172	12 527
	Households and NPISH	DLWR	2 451	2 725	2 666	2 777	2 450	2 634	3 083	2 815	3 116
	Total	DLWS	40 274	42 934	43 175	44 932	47 562	52 295	54 353	60 570	66 452
	Transport equipment										
	Public non-financial corporations	DEEP	179	155	178	171	110	126	193	334	235
	Private non-financial corporations	DLWU	13 315	12 348	11 701	12 721	14 376	13 575	12 322	12 722	13 541
	Financial corporations	GGBR	810	591	334	159	178	109	396	163	111
	Central government	DLWW	481	384	353	355	372	505	638	221	59
	Local government	DKPN	211	225	187	233	195	253	373	389	372
	Households and NPISH	DLWY	1 117	980	824	1 017	1 083	1 024	1 017	1 145	1 179
	Total	DLWZ	16 113	14 683	13 577	14 656	16 314	15 592	14 939	14 974	15 497
	Other machinery and equipment and cultivated assets										
	Public non-financial corporations	DEEQ	437	617	600	628	787	1 037	1 042	16 478	1 192
	Private non-financial corporations	DLXD	48 840	50 297	52 829	50 058	45 145	42 881	44 258	44 613	47 178
	Financial corporations	DLXE	3 904	3 275	3 723	3 550	3 846	2 945	3 186	3 649	3 971
	Central government	DLXF	1 214	1 702	1 346	1 566	2 040	2 058	2 213	–13 828	1 195
	Local government	DLXG	372	394	353	673	827	1 118	1 439	1 390	1 385
	Households and NPISH	DLXH	4 148	4 385	4 684	4 454	4 507	4 402	4 915	4 661	5 020
	Total	DLXI	58 915	60 670	63 535	60 929	57 152	54 441	57 053	56 963	59 941
	Intangible fixed assets										
	Public non-financial corporations	DLXJ	605	625	551	397	556	623	737	754	769
	Private non-financial corporations	DLXK	6 642	6 965	7 429	8 151	8 939	9 886	10 142	10 401	11 310
	Financial corporations	DLXL	1 634	1 814	2 064	2 165	2 455	2 630	2 534	2 552	2 650
	Central government	DLXM	194	173	108	55	52	56	49	37	201
	Local government	DLXN	193	223	259	279	306	328	351	267	314
	Households and NPISH	DLXO	193	223	259	279	306	327	351	376	401
	Total	DLXP	9 461	10 023	10 670	11 326	12 614	13 850	14 164	14 387	15 645
	Costs associated with the transfer of ownership of non-produced assets										
	Public non-financial corporations	DLXQ	–1 162	–1 906	–2 171	–2 254	–2 764	–5 674	–5 440	–2 675	–2 583
	Private non-financial corporations	DLXR	944	2 506	2 211	3 937	5 225	6 456	7 716	8 380	9 958
	Financial corporations	DLXS	2 767	999	3 679	591	–163	–2 520	–1 549	–1 800	–1 109
	Central government	DLXT	–375	–143	109	44	118	–2 059	–794	–599	–288
	Local government	DLXU	45	–23	–291	–354	–343	3 408	2 934	298	–301
	Households and NPISH	DLXV	3 793	6 279	5 284	8 169	10 337	12 449	14 585	13 321	15 910
	Total	DFBH	6 012	7 712	8 821	10 133	12 410	12 060	17 452	16 925	21 587
P.51	**Gross fixed capital formation**										
S.11001	Public non-financial corporations	FCCJ	3 299	2 712	2 354	3 183	3 830	1 857	1 260	20 576	5 564
S.11002	Private non-financial corporations	FDBM	94 106	98 989	101 597	103 127	103 182	103 855	107 249	110 949	120 660
S.12	Financial corporations	NHCJ	11 934	9 188	11 976	8 482	8 323	5 253	6 169	7 043	7 919
S.1311	Central government	NMES	6 007	6 356	5 675	5 964	7 506	6 372	8 315	–6 386	9 850
S.1313	Local government	NMOA	5 903	6 243	6 552	7 569	7 946	14 137	14 891	13 516	14 297
S.14+S.15	Households and NPISH	NSSU	34 748	38 234	39 018	43 457	49 764	55 226	64 376	66 164	76 461
S.1, P.51	Total gross fixed capital formation	NPQX	155 997	161 722	167 172	171 782	180 551	186 700	202 260	211 862	234 751

1 Components may not sum to totals due to rounding.

9.2 Gross fixed capital formation at current purchasers' prices Analysis by broad sector and type of asset

Total economy

£ million

			1998	1999	2000	2001	2002	2003	2004	2005	2006
	Private sector										
	New dwellings, excluding land	DFDF	23 317	23 921	25 604	27 085	31 455	34 804	40 927	44 398	51 491
	Other buildings and structures	EQBU	29 364	31 828	31 966	32 730	33 580	35 366	36 994	39 575	43 429
	Transport equipment	EQBV	15 242	13 919	12 859	13 897	15 637	14 708	13 735	14 030	14 831
	Other machinery and equipment and cultivated assets	EQBW	56 892	57 957	61 236	58 062	53 498	50 228	52 359	52 923	56 169
	Intangible fixed assets	EQBX	8 469	9 002	9 752	10 595	11 700	12 843	13 027	13 329	14 361
	Costs associated with the transfer of ownership of non-produced assets	EQBY	7 504	9 784	11 174	12 697	15 399	16 385	20 752	19 901	24 759
P.51	Total	EQBZ	140 788	146 411	152 591	155 066	161 269	164 334	177 794	184 156	205 040
S.11001	**Public non-financial corporations**										
	New dwellings, excluding land	DEER	1 632	1 529	1 421	2 387	2 837	3 509	3 235	3 574	4 132
	Other buildings and structures	DEES	1 608	1 692	1 775	1 854	2 304	2 236	1 493	2 111	1 819
	Transport equipment	DEEP	179	155	178	171	110	126	193	334	235
	Other machinery and equipment and cultivated assets	DEEQ	437	617	600	628	787	1 037	1 042	16 478	1 192
	Intangible fixed assets	DLXJ	605	625	551	397	556	623	737	754	769
	Costs associated with the transfer of ownership of non-produced assets	DLXQ	–1 162	–1 906	–2 171	–2 254	–2 764	–5 674	–5 440	–2 675	–2 583
P.51	Total	FCCJ	3 299	2 712	2 354	3 183	3 830	1 857	1 260	20 576	5 564
S.13	**General government**										
	New dwellings, excluding land	DFHW	273	250	369	334	207	149	137	71	6
	Other buildings and structures	EQCH	9 302	9 414	9 434	10 348	11 678	14 693	15 866	18 884	21 204
	Transport equipment	EQCI	692	609	540	588	567	758	1 011	610	431
	Other machinery and equipment and cultivated assets	EQCJ	1 586	2 096	1 699	2 239	2 867	3 176	3 652	–12 438	2 580
	Intangible fixed assets	EQCK	387	396	367	334	358	384	400	304	515
	Costs associated with the transfer of ownership of non-produced assets	EQCL	–330	–166	–182	–310	–225	1 349	2 140	–301	–589
P.51	Total	NNBF	11 910	12 599	12 227	13 533	15 452	20 509	23 206	7 130	24 147
P.51	Total gross fixed capital formation	NPQX	155 997	161 722	167 172	171 782	180 551	186 700	202 260	211 862	234 751

1 Components may not sum to totals due to rounding.

9.3 Gross fixed capital formation at current purchasers' prices Analysis by type of asset

Total economy

£ million

			1998	1999	2000	2001	2002	2003	2004	2005	2006
	Tangible fixed assets										
	New dwellings, excluding land	DFDK	25 222	25 700	27 394	29 806	34 499	38 462	44 299	48 043	55 629
	Other buildings and structures	DLWS	40 274	42 934	43 175	44 932	47 562	52 295	54 353	60 570	66 452
	Transport equipment	DLWZ	16 113	14 683	13 577	14 656	16 314	15 592	14 939	14 974	15 497
	Other machinery and equipment and cultivated assets	DLXI	58 915	60 670	63 535	60 929	57 152	54 441	57 053	56 963	59 941
	Total	EQCQ	140 524	143 987	147 681	150 323	155 527	160 790	170 644	180 550	197 519
	Intangible fixed assets	DLXP	9 461	10 023	10 670	11 326	12 614	13 850	14 164	14 387	15 645
	Costs associated with the transfer of ownership of non-produced assets	DFBH	6 012	7 712	8 821	10 133	12 410	12 060	17 452	16 925	21 587
P.51	Total gross fixed capital formation	NPQX	155 997	161 722	167 172	171 782	180 551	186 700	202 260	211 862	234 751

1 Components may not sum to totals due to rounding.

9.4 Gross fixed capital formation[1] Chained volume measures (reference year 2003)

Total economy: Analysis by broad sector and type of asset

£ million

			1998	1999	2000	2001	2002	2003	2004	2005	2006
	Private sector										
	New dwellings, excluding land	DFDP	31 971	30 928	31 041	31 318	33 748	34 804	38 245	38 845	41 796
	Other buildings and structures	EQCU	32 821	33 931	33 206	33 251	33 406	35 366	35 786	38 155	41 754
	Transport equipment	EQCV	15 334	13 778	12 713	13 863	15 708	14 708	13 704	13 831	14 446
	Other machinery and equipment and cultivated assets	EQCW	46 556	49 522	53 869	54 140	52 405	50 228	53 997	54 572	59 100
	Intangible fixed assets	EQCX	9 846	10 185	10 702	11 228	11 680	12 843	13 043	13 072	13 916
	Costs associated with the transfer of ownership of non-produced assets	EQCY	15 614	16 821	16 293	16 173	17 369	16 385	19 616	16 773	18 547
P.51	Total	EQCZ	151 162	154 580	158 347	160 569	164 304	164 334	174 391	175 248	189 559
S.11001	**Public non-financial corporations**										
	New dwellings, excluding land	DEEW	1 974	1 747	1 552	2 521	2 898	3 509	3 161	3 423	3 890
	Other buildings and structures	DEEX	1 852	1 890	1 939	1 961	2 342	2 236	1 426	1 928	1 568
	Transport equipment	DEEU	193	164	186	180	114	126	193	326	230
	Other machinery and equipment and cultivated assets	DEEV	332	504	516	588	765	1 037	1 063	16 173	1 230
	Intangible fixed assets	EQDE	672	684	586	415	572	623	716	711	710
	Costs associated with the transfer of ownership of non-produced assets	EQDF	–2 284	–3 141	–3 093	–2 825	–3 092	–5 674	–5 561	–2 813	–2 018
P.51	Total	EQDG	2 030	1 796	1 695	2 424	3 019	1 857	998	19 748	5 610
S.13	**General government**										
	New dwellings, excluding land	DFID	333	286	404	354	213	149	135	69	6
	Other buildings and structures	EQDI	10 936	10 792	10 513	11 107	12 115	14 693	14 877	16 506	17 283
	Transport equipment	EQDJ	773	676	606	672	586	758	809	751	809
	Other machinery and equipment and cultivated assets	EQDK	1 115	1 632	1 424	2 063	2 801	3 176	3 757	–11 906	3 189
	Intangible fixed assets	EQDL	245	241	219	196	211	384	698	294	495
	Costs associated with the transfer of ownership of non-produced assets	EQDM	32 408	–1 728	–542	–548	–261	1 349	1 991	–56	–282
P.51	Total	EQDN	12 218	13 059	12 665	13 980	15 740	20 509	22 266	5 658	21 498
P.51	Total gross fixed capital formation	NPQR	164 249	169 117	173 710	178 203	184 701	186 700	197 655	200 654	216 667

1 For the years before 2003, totals differ from the sum of their components.
2 Components may not sum to totals due to rounding.

9.5 Gross fixed capital formation[1] Chained volume measures (reference year 2003)

Total economy: Analysis by type of asset

£ million

			1998	1999	2000	2001	2002	2003	2004	2005	2006
	Tangible fixed assets										
	New dwellings, excluding land	DFDV	34 201	32 863	32 888	34 172	36 839	38 462	41 541	42 337	45 692
	Other buildings and structures	EQDP	45 712	46 738	45 780	46 413	47 913	52 295	52 089	56 589	60 605
	Transport equipment	DLWJ	16 279	14 602	13 489	14 698	16 414	15 592	14 706	14 908	15 485
	Other machinery and equipment and cultivated assets	DLWM	47 942	51 667	55 774	56 780	55 971	54 441	58 817	58 839	63 519
	Total	EQDS	142 732	145 621	148 509	152 571	157 257	160 790	167 152	172 672	185 300
	Intangible fixed assets	EQDT	10 742	11 079	11 445	11 742	12 371	13 850	14 457	14 077	15 120
	Costs associated with the transfer of ownership of non-produced assets	DFDW	12 098	13 088	12 810	12 960	14 097	12 060	16 046	13 904	16 247
P.51	Total gross fixed capital formation	NPQR	164 249	169 117	173 710	178 203	184 701	186 700	197 655	200 654	216 667

1 For the years before 2003, totals differ from the sum of their components.
2 Components may not sum to totals due to rounding.

Chapter 10
Non-financial balance sheets

The non-financial balance sheets show the market value of non-financial assets in the UK and as such are a measure of the wealth of the UK.

When financial assets are added to the value of the non-financial assets, the result, the net worth of the UK, is estimated at £6,525 billion in 2006 – an increase of £326 billion on the previous year. The non-financial balance sheets figures also show that the most valuable asset continues to be housing with a total value of £3,915 billion in 2006 – up 10 per cent on the previous year and equivalent to 60 per cent of the nation's total wealth. The housing stock belonging to the household and non-profit organisations sector was worth £3,696 billion, up 11 per cent on the previous year.

Non-financial assets include both tangible and intangible assets. Tangible assets consist of property, plant & machinery, agricultural assets, vehicles and also include certain types of farming stocks (mainly dairy cattle and orchards) and military equipment whose use is not solely destructive. Intangible assets consist of the value of computer software, patents, mineral exploration and artistic originals.

Data sources include:

- Other government departments and agencies
- Annual reports of public corporations and major businesses
- Industry publications
- Chartered Institute of Public Finance and Accountancy report on Local Authority Assets

Where non-financial asset market valuations are not readily available, the UK net capital stocks data modelled in the PIM within ONS is used as a proxy.

For Central Government, data are taken from returns made by government departments to HM Treasury. Central Government assets also include the value of the electro-magnetic spectrum. The spectrum is treated as a tangible non-produced asset and the payments made by mobile phone companies as rent.

Local authority housing is shown in the public corporations sector. This is because government-owned market activities are always treated as being carried out by public corporations, either in their own right or via quasi-corporations.

This publication contains upward revisions in private non-financial and financial corporations' data reflecting improved methodology for the measurement of private sector own-account computer software investment. Other revisions in the data are due to improvements in the Non-Financial Balance Sheets system, started in 2005 which were continued during the year, as well as increased use of direct data for some previously estimated public sector aggregates.

10.1 National balance sheet
Sector totals: summary of net worth

£ billion at end year

			1998	1999	2000	2001	2002	2003	2004	2005	2006
	Non-financial corporations[2]										
S.11001	Public[4]	CGRW	131.4	129.7	129.2	141.5	153.5	161.2	174.7	178.5	175.2
S.11002	Private[2]	TMPN	–415.2	–714.5	–486.5	–321.6	32.3	–89.1	–195.3	–313.7	–541.0
S.11	Total	CGRV	–283.8	–584.8	–357.3	–180.1	185.8	72.0	–20.6	–135.2	–365.9
S.12	Financial corporations	CGRU	–255.1	–290.0	–319.0	–284.0	–210.8	–163.3	–117.2	–196.5	–182.4
	General government[4]										
S.1311	Central government	CGRY	–183.2	–161.3	–124.5	–99.4	–118.5	–134.4	–173.2	–197.9	–206.3
S.1313	Local government	CGRZ	172.5	188.6	218.5	261.1	269.9	300.4	345.6	370.0	380.5
S.13	Total	CGRX	–10.8	27.3	94.0	161.6	151.4	166.0	172.4	172.0	174.2
S.14+S.15	Households and NPISH[3]	CGRC	3 909.9	4 602.9	4 826.3	4 726.1	4 910.8	5 384.6	5 880.5	6 358.4	6 898.6
S.1	Total net worth	CGDA	3 360.2	3 755.4	4 244.1	4 423.7	5 037.2	5 459.4	5 915.0	6 198.7	6 524.5

1 See footnotes in tables 10.2-10.11 for changes to allocations of assets between sectors.
2 Including quasi-corporations.
3 Non-profit institutions serving households
4 Public sector (General government plus public non-financial corporations) is as follows:-

		1997	1998	1999	2000	2001	2002	2003	2004	2005
Public sector	CGTY	119.9	118.3	154.7	221.1	300.5	301.7	324.0	345.2	338.8

10.2 National balance sheet
Asset totals

£ billion at end year

		1998	1999	2000	2001	2002	2003	2004	2005	2006
Non-financial assets										
Tangible assets:										
Residential buildings	CGLK	1 633.8	1 848.9	2 106.5	2 267.8	2 737.1	3 054.9	3 427.0	3 555.0	3 915.3
Agricultural assets	CGMP	50.5	53.3	54.0	53.2	53.8	54.7	54.8	54.6	54.2
Commercial, industrial and other buildings	CGMU	478.0	509.8	599.2	562.5	588.8	592.2	625.7	738.0	740.9
Civil engineering works	CGQZ	476.3	496.1	520.7	573.3	583.9	620.1	662.7	703.0	723.4
Plant and machinery	CGRA	344.1	352.0	363.0	368.3	366.9	371.8	373.3	378.3	389.8
Vehicles, including ships, aircraft, etc	CGRB	111.7	110.2	114.3	122.0	134.7	146.6	151.4	153.3	161.1
Stocks and work in progress	CGRD	159.4	167.2	174.9	174.7	180.4	184.8	198.1	204.6	215.7
Spectrum[2]	ZLDX	–	–	21.9	21.9	21.9	21.9	21.9	21.9	21.9
Total tangible assets	CGRE	3 253.7	3 537.6	3 954.5	4 143.7	4 667.6	5 047.1	5 514.9	5 808.7	6 222.3
Intangible assets:										
Non-marketable tenancy rights	CGRF	190.2	237.4	276.7	300.1	365.3	413.5	466.1	486.9	545.1
Other intangible assets	CGRG	33.0	34.9	36.7	38.4	40.5	42.9	44.9	46.6	48.9
Total intangible assets	CGRH	223.2	272.3	313.4	338.5	405.9	456.4	511.0	533.5	594.1
Total non-financial assets	CGJB	3 476.9	3 809.8	4 267.9	4 482.1	5 073.5	5 503.5	6 025.9	6 342.3	6 816.4
Total net financial assets/liabilities	NQFT	–116.7	–54.4	–23.9	–58.4	–36.3	–44.1	–110.9	–143.5	–291.9
Total net worth[1]	CGDA	3 360.2	3 755.4	4 244.1	4 423.7	5 037.2	5 459.4	5 915.0	6 198.7	6 524.5

1 Net worth was previously defined as *net wealth.*
2 Following the grant of licences to mobile phone companies, the electro-magnetic spectrum is included as an asset for the first time in 2000.

10.3 Non-financial corporations

£ billion at end year

		1998	1999	2000	2001	2002	2003	2004	2005	2006
Non-financial assets										
Tangible assets:										
Residential buildings[2]	CGUT	124.6	125.8	134.6	147.5	164.8	182.0	200.9	214.2	212.8
of which Local Authority housing	CGWM	77.0	69.7	71.0	79.6	86.5	96.3	107.9	118.1	107.2
Agricultural assets	CGUU	4.0	4.0	4.0	3.9	4.1	4.2	4.2	4.2	4.1
Commercial, industrial and other buildings	CGUV	228.2	244.0	322.5	276.0	291.1	274.4	284.3	349.8	337.0
Civil engineering works	CGUW	255.3	260.7	255.3	265.6	269.6	280.5	284.2	295.0	302.8
Plant and machinery	CGUX	304.4	310.8	319.9	325.0	323.4	324.2	326.4	330.9	337.5
Vehicles, including ships, aircraft, etc	CGUY	42.0	47.6	52.1	54.4	60.8	68.7	69.5	67.6	73.0
Stocks and work in progress	CGUZ	143.4	151.3	159.0	158.8	164.0	168.0	181.0	188.0	199.1
Total tangible assets	CGVA	1 101.8	1 144.1	1 247.4	1 231.2	1 277.7	1 302.1	1 350.6	1 449.7	1 466.4
Intangible non-financial assets										
Non-marketable tenancy rights	CGVB	–	–	–	–	–	–	–	–	–
Other intangible assets	CGVC	28.2	29.5	30.7	31.9	33.5	35.3	36.8	38.3	40.2
Total intangible assets	CGVE	28.2	29.5	30.7	31.9	33.5	35.3	36.8	38.3	40.2
Total non-financial assets	CGES	1 130.0	1 173.7	1 278.1	1 263.1	1 311.2	1 337.4	1 387.4	1 487.9	1 506.6
Total net financial assets/liabilities	NYOM	–1 413.8	–1 758.4	–1 635.4	–1 443.1	–1 125.4	–1 265.3	–1 408.0	–1 623.2	–1 872.5
Total net worth[1]	CGRV	–283.8	–584.8	–357.3	–180.1	185.8	72.0	–20.6	–135.2	–365.9

1 Net worth was previously defined as *net wealth*.
2 Residential buildings in this table now include both council housing and housing association properties. The latter were formally included in table 10.10 (Non-profit institutions serving households).

10.4 Public non-financial corporations

£ billion at end year

		1998	1999	2000	2001	2002	2003	2004	2005	2006
Non-financial assets										
Tangible assets:										
Residential buildings[2]	CGVF	80.5	73.6	74.9	83.9	91.0	101.1	111.9	122.3	111.8
of which Local authority housing	CGWM	77.0	69.7	71.0	79.6	86.5	96.3	107.9	118.1	107.2
Agricultural assets	CGVG	1.2	1.0	0.9	0.9	0.9	0.9	0.9	0.9	0.9
Commercial, industrial and other buildings	CGVH	21.2	25.6	21.8	20.3	25.5	23.7	25.2	26.3	26.5
Civil engineering works	CGVI	8.1	8.6	10.4	14.3	20.0	13.4	12.7	12.1	13.4
Plant and machinery	CGVJ	5.2	5.1	4.9	4.8	7.4	7.7	8.3	8.3	8.5
Vehicles, including ships, aircraft, etc	CGVK	1.8	1.7	1.6	1.7	1.6	1.4	1.5	2.0	2.2
Stocks and work in progress	CGVL	5.3	5.3	5.2	5.2	5.1	5.1	5.2	5.3	5.2
Total tangible assets	CGVM	123.5	120.9	119.7	131.0	151.6	153.4	165.8	177.0	168.5
Intangible non-financial assets										
Non-marketable tenancy rights	CGVN	–	–	–	–	–	–	–	–	–
Other intangible assets	CGVO	3.0	3.4	3.7	3.8	4.0	4.2	4.5	4.8	5.0
Total intangible assets	CGVP	3.0	3.4	3.7	3.8	4.0	4.2	4.5	4.8	5.0
Total non-financial assets	CGGN	126.5	124.3	123.4	134.8	155.6	157.6	170.3	181.8	173.6
Total net financial assets/liabilities	NYOP	4.9	5.4	5.8	6.8	–2.1	3.6	4.5	–3.3	1.6
Total net worth[1]	CGRW	131.4	129.7	129.2	141.5	153.5	161.2	174.7	178.5	175.2

1 Net worth was previously defined as *net wealth*.
2 Residential buildings in this table now include council housing.

10.5 Private non-financial corporations

£ billion at end year

		1998	1999	2000	2001	2002	2003	2004	2005	2006
Non-financial assets										
Tangible assets:										
Residential buildings[2]	TMPB	44.1	52.2	59.6	63.6	73.8	80.8	89.0	92.0	101.0
Agricultural assets	TMPC	2.7	3.0	3.1	3.1	3.1	3.3	3.3	3.3	3.2
Commercial, industrial and other buildings	TMPD	206.9	218.4	300.7	255.7	265.6	250.8	259.1	323.5	310.5
Civil engineering works	TMPE	247.1	252.1	245.0	251.3	249.5	267.1	271.5	282.9	289.5
Plant and machinery	TMPF	299.1	305.7	315.0	320.2	316.1	316.5	318.1	322.7	329.0
Vehicles, including ships, aircraft, etc	TMPO	40.2	45.9	50.5	52.8	59.2	67.3	67.9	65.5	70.8
Stocks and work in progress	TMPG	138.0	146.0	153.9	153.6	158.9	162.9	175.8	182.7	193.9
Total tangible assets	TMPH	978.3	1 023.2	1 127.7	1 100.2	1 126.1	1 148.7	1 184.8	1 272.6	1 297.9
Intangible non-financial assets										
Non-marketable tenancy rights	TMPI	–	–	–	–	–	–	–	–	–
Other intangible assets	TMPJ	25.2	26.1	27.0	28.1	29.5	31.1	32.3	33.5	35.2
Total intangible assets	TMPK	25.2	26.1	27.0	28.1	29.5	31.1	32.3	33.5	35.2
Total non-financial assets	TMPL	1 003.5	1 049.4	1 154.7	1 128.3	1 155.6	1 179.8	1 217.2	1 306.1	1 333.1
Total net financial assets/liabilities	NYOT	–1 418.7	–1 763.8	–1 641.1	–1 449.9	–1 123.4	–1 268.9	–1 412.5	–1 619.9	–1 874.1
Total net worth[1]	TMPN	–415.2	–714.5	–486.5	–321.6	32.3	–89.1	–195.3	–313.7	–541.0

1 Net worth was previously defined as *net wealth*.
2 Residential buildings now include Housing Association properties. These were formally included in table 10.10 (Non profit institutions serving households).

10.6 Financial corporations

£ billion at end year

		1998	1999	2000	2001	2002	2003	2004	2005	2006
Non-financial assets										
Tangible assets:										
Residential buildings	CGUD	1.1	1.0	0.8	0.6	0.7	0.5	0.4	0.9	1.4
Agricultural assets	CGUE	0.8	0.9	0.9	0.9	0.9	0.9	0.9	0.9	0.9
Commercial, industrial and other buildings	CGUF	84.5	95.9	98.7	102.9	103.0	109.2	117.4	131.1	131.9
Civil engineering works	CGUG	–	–	–	–	–	–	–	–	–
Plant and machinery	CGUH	9.8	10.9	11.7	11.1	11.3	11.5	11.8	12.0	12.4
Vehicles, including ships, aircraft, etc	CGUI	2.7	1.3	1.4	0.9	0.7	0.5	0.4	0.9	0.9
Stocks and work in progress	CGUO	–	–	–	–	–	–	–	–	–
Total tangible assets	CGUP	98.9	110.0	113.5	116.4	116.5	122.6	130.9	145.9	147.5
Intangible non-financial assets										
Non-marketable tenancy rights	CGUQ	–	–	–	–	–	–	–	–	–
Other intangible assets	CGUR	3.5	4.0	4.5	5.0	5.4	5.9	6.2	6.5	6.7
Total intangible assets	CGUS	3.5	4.0	4.5	5.0	5.4	5.9	6.2	6.5	6.7
Total non-financial assets	CGDB	102.4	114.0	118.0	121.4	122.0	128.5	137.1	152.3	154.2
Total net financial assets/liabilities	NYOE	–357.5	–404.0	–437.0	–405.4	–332.8	–291.8	–254.4	–348.8	–336.6
Total net worth[1]	CGRU	–255.1	–290.0	–319.0	–284.0	–210.8	–163.3	–117.2	–196.5	–182.4

1 Net worth was previously defined as *net wealth*.

10.7 General government

£ billion at end year

		1998	1999	2000	2001	2002	2003	2004	2005	2006
Non-financial assets										
Tangible assets:										
Residential buildings[2]	CGVQ	3.2	3.2	3.2	3.2	3.5	3.3	4.3	3.8	4.8
Agricultural assets	CGVR	1.9	2.0	2.1	2.1	2.1	2.2	2.2	2.1	2.1
Commercial, industrial and other buildings	CGVS	123.7	126.2	131.0	137.2	146.0	157.9	174.2	200.5	212.8
Civil engineering works	CGVT	219.5	233.9	263.2	305.6	312.2	337.5	376.5	406.1	418.6
Plant and machinery	CGVU	15.8	15.2	14.9	15.0	14.2	17.6	16.4	16.2	20.0
Vehicles, including ships, aircraft, etc	CGVV	3.9	3.6	3.3	4.3	4.4	4.3	4.4	5.5	5.6
Stocks and work in progress	CGVW	0.6	0.3	0.2	0.1	0.1	0.2	0.2	0.2	0.2
Spectrum[3]	ZLDB	–	–	21.9	21.9	21.9	21.9	21.9	21.9	21.9
Total tangible assets	CGVX	368.5	384.4	439.8	489.4	504.4	544.9	600.0	656.2	686.1
Intangible non-financial assets										
Non-marketable tenancy rights	CGVY	–	–	–	–	–	–	–	–	–
Other intangible assets	CGVZ	0.8	0.9	0.9	0.9	0.9	0.9	1.0	1.0	1.0
Total intangible assets	CGWA	0.8	0.9	0.9	0.9	0.9	0.9	1.0	1.0	1.0
Total non-financial assets	CGIX	369.3	385.3	440.7	490.3	505.3	545.9	601.0	657.2	687.1
Total net financial assets/liabilities	NYOG	–380.0	–358.0	–346.7	–328.7	–353.9	–379.9	–428.6	–485.2	–512.9
Total net worth[1]	CGRX	–10.8	27.3	94.0	161.6	151.4	166.0	172.4	172.0	174.2

1 Net worth was previously defined as *net wealth*.
2 Council housing has now been transferred from General Government to the Public non-financial corporations sector.
3 Following the grant of licences to mobile phone companies, the electro-magnetic spectrum is included as an asset for the first time in 2000.

10.8 Central government[1]

£ billion at end year

		1998	1999	2000	2001	2002	2003	2004	2005	2006
Non-financial assets										
Tangible assets:										
Residential buildings	CGWB	3.2	3.2	3.2	3.2	3.5	3.3	4.3	3.8	4.8
Agricultural assets	CGWC	0.1	0.1	0.1	0.1	0.1	0.1	0.1	0.1	0.1
Commercial, industrial and other buildings	CGWD	49.9	48.8	49.5	52.1	56.7	63.0	69.1	87.9	92.9
Civil engineering works	CGWE	87.3	89.6	92.8	95.9	100.1	105.2	109.9	121.1	130.2
Plant and machinery	CGWF	12.0	11.8	11.7	11.6	11.4	14.3	12.2	11.4	14.5
Vehicles, including ships, aircraft, etc	CGWG	3.4	3.1	2.8	3.7	3.6	3.6	3.6	4.3	4.4
Stocks and work in progress	CGWH	0.6	0.3	0.2	0.1	0.1	0.2	0.2	0.2	0.2
Spectrum[3]	ZLDA	–	–	21.9	21.9	21.9	21.9	21.9	21.9	21.9
Total tangible assets	CGWI	156.4	156.9	182.2	188.7	197.6	211.6	221.3	250.6	269.0
Intangible non-financial assets										
Non-marketable tenancy rights	CGWJ	–	–	–	–	–	–	–	–	–
Other intangible assets	CGWK	0.4	0.4	0.4	0.3	0.2	0.2	0.2	0.1	0.1
Total intangible assets	CGWL	0.4	0.4	0.4	0.3	0.2	0.2	0.2	0.1	0.1
Total non-financial assets	CGIY	156.8	157.4	182.6	189.0	197.8	211.8	221.4	250.8	269.1
Total net financial assets/liabilities	NZDZ	–340.0	–318.6	–307.1	–288.4	–316.3	–346.3	–394.6	–448.7	–475.4
Total net worth[2]	CGRY	–183.2	–161.3	–124.5	–99.4	–118.5	–134.4	–173.2	–197.9	–206.3

1 UK national accounts classification excludes fighting equipment from tangible assets.
2 Net worth was previously defined as *net wealth*.
3 Following the grant of licences to mobile phone companies, the electro-magnetic spectrum is included as an asset for the first time in 2000.

10.9 Local government

£ billion at end year

		1998	1999	2000	2001	2002	2003	2004	2005	2006
Non-financial assets										
Tangible assets:										
Local Authority housing[2]	ZLCS	–	–	–	–	–	–	–	–	–
Agricultural assets	CGWN	1.8	1.9	2.0	2.0	2.0	2.1	2.1	2.0	2.0
Commercial, industrial and other buildings	CGWO	73.8	77.4	81.5	85.1	89.3	94.9	105.1	112.5	119.9
Civil engineering works	CGWP	132.2	144.3	170.4	209.7	212.0	232.3	266.6	285.0	288.4
Plant and machinery	CGWQ	3.8	3.4	3.2	3.4	2.8	3.4	4.2	4.9	5.5
Vehicles, including ships, aircraft, etc	CGWR	0.5	0.5	0.5	0.6	0.7	0.7	0.8	1.1	1.3
Stocks and work in progress	CGWS	–	–	–	–	–	–	–	–	–
Total tangible assets	CGWT	212.1	227.5	257.6	300.7	306.8	333.3	378.8	405.6	417.1
Intangible non-financial assets										
Non-marketable tenancy rights	CGWU	–	–	–	–	–	–	–	–	–
Other intangible assets	CGWV	0.4	0.5	0.5	0.6	0.7	0.8	0.8	0.9	0.9
Total intangible assets	CGWW	0.4	0.5	0.5	0.6	0.7	0.8	0.8	0.9	0.9
Total non-financial assets	CGIZ	212.5	228.0	258.1	301.3	307.5	334.1	379.6	406.4	418.0
Total net financial assets/liabilities	NYOJ	–40.0	–39.4	–39.6	–40.3	–37.6	–33.7	–33.9	–36.5	–37.5
Total net worth[1]	CGRZ	172.5	188.6	218.5	261.1	269.9	300.4	345.6	370.0	380.5

1 Net worth was previously defined as *net wealth*.
2 The value of council housing is now shown in table 10.4 (Public non- financial corporations).

10.10 Households & non-profit institutions serving households (NPISH)

£ billion at end year

		1998	1999	2000	2001	2002	2003	2004	2005	2006
Non-financial assets										
Tangible assets:										
Residential buildings[2]	CGRI	1 504.9	1 718.9	1 967.9	2 116.5	2 568.1	2 869.0	3 221.3	3 336.2	3 696.3
Agricultural assets	CGRJ	43.8	46.4	47.0	46.3	46.8	47.4	47.5	47.3	47.1
Commercial, industrial and other buildings	CGRK	41.6	43.7	47.0	46.4	48.8	50.7	49.7	56.6	59.1
Civil engineering works	CGRL	1.6	1.6	2.2	2.2	2.2	2.1	2.0	2.0	2.0
Plant and machinery	CGRM	14.1	15.1	16.4	17.1	18.0	18.5	18.8	19.2	20.0
Vehicles, including ships, aircraft, etc	CGRN	63.1	57.6	57.5	62.4	68.8	73.1	77.1	79.3	81.5
Stocks and work in progress	CGRO	15.4	15.6	15.8	15.8	16.2	16.7	16.9	16.4	16.4
Total tangible assets	CGRP	1 684.6	1 899.0	2 153.8	2 306.6	2 768.9	3 077.5	3 433.4	3 557.0	3 922.3
Intangible non-financial assets										
Non-marketable tenancy rights	CGRQ	190.2	237.4	276.7	300.1	365.3	413.5	466.1	486.9	545.1
Other intangible assets	CGRS	0.4	0.5	0.6	0.6	0.7	0.8	0.8	0.9	0.9
Total intangible assets	CGRT	190.6	237.8	277.2	300.7	366.0	414.2	466.9	487.8	546.1
Total non-financial assets	CGCZ	1 875.2	2 136.8	2 431.1	2 607.3	3 135.0	3 491.7	3 900.3	4 044.8	4 468.4
Total net financial assets/liabilities	NZEA	2 034.7	2 466.1	2 395.2	2 118.7	1 775.8	1 892.9	1 980.1	2 313.6	2 430.2
Total net worth[1]	CGRC	3 909.9	4 602.9	4 826.3	4 726.1	4 910.8	5 384.6	5 880.5	6 358.4	6 898.6

1 Net worth was previously defined as *net wealth*.
2 Figures for Housing association properties are now included in table 10.5 (Private non-financial corporations).

10.11 Public sector

£ billion at end year

		1998	1999	2000	2001	2002	2003	2004	2005	2006
Non-financial assets										
Tangible assets:										
Residential buildings	CGWX	83.7	76.8	78.1	87.1	94.5	104.4	116.3	126.0	116.6
Agricultural assets	CGWY	3.1	3.1	3.0	2.9	3.0	3.1	3.1	3.1	3.0
Commercial, industrial and other buildings	CGWZ	144.9	151.8	152.8	157.5	171.5	181.6	199.4	226.7	239.3
Civil engineering works	CGXA	227.6	242.5	273.6	319.9	332.2	350.9	389.2	418.1	432.0
Plant and machinery	CGXB	21.0	20.3	19.9	19.8	21.6	25.4	24.6	24.5	28.5
Vehicles, including ships, aircraft, etc	CGXC	5.6	5.3	4.9	5.9	6.0	5.7	5.9	7.5	7.9
Stocks and work in progress	CGXD	5.9	5.6	5.3	5.3	5.3	5.2	5.4	5.4	5.4
Spectrum[2]	ZLDC	–	–	21.9	21.9	21.9	21.9	21.9	21.9	21.9
Total tangible assets	CGXE	492.0	505.3	559.5	620.4	656.0	698.3	765.8	833.3	854.6
Intangible non-financial assets										
Non-marketable tenancy rights	CGXF	–	–	–	–	–	–	–	–	–
Other intangible assets	CGXG	3.9	4.3	4.6	4.7	4.9	5.1	5.5	5.8	6.1
Total intangible assets	CGXH	3.9	4.3	4.6	4.7	4.9	5.1	5.5	5.8	6.1
Total non-financial assets	CGJA	495.8	509.7	564.2	625.1	660.9	703.4	771.3	839.0	860.7
Total net financial assets/liabilities	CGSA	–375.1	–352.6	–340.9	–321.9	–356.0	–376.3	–424.1	–488.5	–511.3
Total net worth[1]	CGTY	120.7	157.0	223.2	303.2	304.9	327.1	347.1	350.5	349.4

1 Net worth was previously defined as *net wealth*.
2 Following the grant of licences to mobile phone companies, the electro-magnetic spectrum is included as an asset for the first time in 2000.

Chapter 11

Public sector supplementary tables

Introduction

The National Accounts are traditionally updated with long-period revisions once a year, and then published in the *Blue Book*. The 2007 edition has been restricted in the revisions taken on as a result of an ONS decision to divert resources elsewhere. The process of revision can be complex, particularly if the time series being revised forms part of GDP.

The Government's fiscal policy rules rely on statistical measures based on the National Accounts framework. The speed with which revisions could be taken on in the National Accounts was proving deficient for the purposes of fiscal policy, which is based on an economic cycle and requires up to date information over the entire cycle. This led to a separate revisions policy for the *Public Sector Finances*, which takes through revisions immediately with the National Accounts catching up with these revisions when it can. In normal circumstances this would be in the next *Blue Book*.

The version of Chapter 11 published here is consistent with the National Accounts, but this is not the most up to date version. Alternative versions, on both calendar and financial year basis, have been published in the July *Public Sector Finances* consistent with that dataset.

Table 11.3 has been withdrawn from the *Blue Book*. This showed key fiscal aggregates, and thus it would be confusing and misleading to publish an alternative incorrect version of these in the *Blue Book*. The main part of this table is already published once a quarter and the other series will be updated once a year in the *Public Sector Finances*.

Table 11.2 (functional breakdown of General Government) has been withdrawn from this year's *Blue Book*. It will be published later in the year alongside the *Public Sector Finances*.

Taxes payable by UK residents (Table 11.1)

This table is consistent with the National Accounts. A more up to date version consistent with the latest Public Sector Finance data, incorporating revisions, is available in the July *Public Sector Finances* release.

This table shows the taxes and national insurance contributions payable to central government, local government, and to the institutions of the European Union.

Taxes on production are included in GDP at market prices. Taxes on products are taxes levied on the sale of goods and services. Other taxes on production include taxes levied on inputs to production (for example, non-domestic rates by businesses) and some compulsory unrequited levies that producers have to pay.

Taxes on income and wealth include income tax and corporation tax. Also included are some charges payable by households (for example, local government taxes and motor vehicle duty), which are classified as taxes on production when payable by businesses. The totals are measured gross of any tax credits and reliefs recorded as expenditure in the National Accounts, such as working families and child tax credit.

ESA95 has a category called compulsory social contributions. In the UK accounts this category includes all national insurance contributions. Details of total social contributions and benefits are shown in Tables 5.2.4S and 5.3.4S of Chapter 5.

Some UK taxes are recorded as the resources of the European Union. These include taxes on imports and an amount calculated as the hypothetical yield from VAT at a standard rate on a harmonised base across the EU.

Reconciliation of financial transactions and balance sheets (Tables 11.4–11.6)

Tables 11.4, 11.5 and 11.6 reconcile financial transactions with movements in financial balance sheets for the general government sector and the central and local government sub-sectors. The lines K.12, K.11 and K.10 show movements in financial balance sheets not attributable to financial transactions. K.12 changes in classification and structure include the reclassification of a body from one sector to another and changes in the balance sheet in connection with privatisation. K.11 nominal holding gains/losses consists of changes in balance sheets due to changes in prices. This includes price changes due to the effect of exchange rate movements on the value of financial assets denominated in foreign currencies and changes in market prices of other marketable financial instruments. K.10 Other volume changes includes exceptional losses of currency or securities and writing-off or writing-down of bad debt by creditors (but not debt forgiveness). K.10 also includes statistical discrepancies between financial transactions and balance sheets; ONS is taking steps to improve the quality of balance sheet data to remove these discrepancies from the accounts.

Table 11.7

This table is consistent with the National Accounts. A more up to date version consistent with the latest Public Sector Finance data, incorporating revisions, is available in the July *Public Sector Finances* release.

11.1 Taxes paid by UK residents to general government and the European Union

Total economy sector S.1

£ million

Part			1998	1999	2000	2001	2002	2003	2004	2005	2006
	GENERATION OF INCOME										
	Uses										
D.2	Taxes on production and imports										
D.21	Taxes on products and imports										
D.211	Value added tax (VAT)										
	Paid to central government	NZGF	52 313	57 701	59 985	63 522	68 251	74 595	79 751	81 383	85 512
	Paid to the European Union	FJKM	4 228	3 811	4 204	3 575	2 808	2 740	1 789	1 999	2 167
D.211	Total	QYRC	56 541	61 512	64 189	67 097	71 059	77 335	81 540	83 382	87 679
D.212	Taxes and duties on imports excluding VAT										
D.2121	Paid to CG: import duties[1]	NMXZ	–	–	–	–	–	–	–	–	–
D.2121	Paid to EU: import duties	FJWE	2 076	2 024	2 086	2 069	1 919	1 937	2 145	2 237	2 329
D.212	Total	QYRB	2 076	2 024	2 086	2 069	1 919	1 937	2 145	2 237	2 329
D.214	Taxes on products excluding VAT and import duties										
	Paid to central government										
	Customs & excise revenue										
	Beer	GTAM	2 718	2 792	2 813	2 888	2 934	3 035	3 111	3 072	3 065
	Wines, cider, perry & spirits	GTAN	3 183	3 595	3 751	4 025	4 333	4 491	4 761	4 802	4 779
	Tobacco	GTAO	7 590	7 693	7 666	7 638	7 947	8 079	8 097	8 021	8 089
	Hydrocarbon oils	GTAP	20 996	22 391	23 041	22 046	22 070	22 476	23 412	23 346	23 448
	Car tax	GTAT	–	–	–	–	–	–	–	–	–
	Betting, gaming & lottery	CJQY	1 538	1 521	1 522	1 406	997	933	872	864	958
	Air passenger duty	CWAA	823	884	940	824	814	781	856	896	963
	Insurance premium tax	CWAD	1 245	1 423	1 707	1 861	2 138	2 294	2 359	2 343	2 328
	Landfill tax	BKOF	333	430	461	502	541	607	672	733	808
	Other	ACDN	–	–	–	–	–	–	–	–	–
	Fossil fuel levy	CIQY	181	104	56	86	32	–	–	–	–
	Gas levy	GTAZ	32	–	–	–	–	–	–	–	–
	Stamp duties	GTBC	4 451	6 000	8 367	7 344	7 431	7 256	8 884	9 910	13 118
	Levies on exports (Third country trade)	CUDF	–	–	–	–	–	–	–	–	–
	Camelot payments to National Lottery Distribution Fund	LIYH	1 693	1 574	1 590	1 480	1 452	1 293	1 342	1 349	1 440
	Purchase Tax	EBDB	–	–	–	–	–	–	–	–	–
	Hydro-benefit	LITN	32	35	42	46	44	44	40	10	–
	Aggregates levy	MDUQ	–	–	–	–	213	340	328	327	325
	Milk super levy	DFT3	–	–	–	14	35	56	69	19	1
	Climate change levy	LSNT	–	–	–	585	825	828	756	747	711
	Channel 4 funding formula	EG9G	66	–	–	–	–	–	–	–	–
	Renewable energy obligations	EP89	–	–	–	–	195	345	373	376	390
	Other taxes and levies	GCSP	–	–	–	–	–	–	–	–	–
	Total paid to central government	NMYB	44 881	48 442	51 956	50 745	52 001	52 858	55 932	56 815	60 423
	Paid to the European Union										
	Sugar levy	GTBA	42	46	44	31	25	18	25	24	–
	European Coal & Steel Community levy	GTBB	–	–	–	–	–	–	–	–	–
	Total paid to the European Union	FJWG	42	46	44	31	25	18	25	24	–
D.214	Total taxes on products excluding VAT & import duties	QYRA	44 923	48 488	52 000	50 776	52 026	52 876	55 957	56 839	60 423
D.21	Total taxes on products and imports	NZGW	103 540	112 024	118 275	119 942	125 004	132 148	139 642	142 458	150 431
D.29	Production taxes other than on products										
	Paid to central government										
	Consumer Credit Act fees	CUDB	187	157	119	205	190	208	220	197	363
	National non-domestic rates	CUKY	13 643	14 208	14 954	15 979	16 604	16 891	17 264	17 945	19 204
	Northern Ireland non-domestic rates	NSEZ	129	126	128	133	134	139	144	155	164
	Levies paid to CG levy-funded bodies	LITK	159	226	217	215	195	193	214	235	218
	Selective employment tax	CSAH	–	–	–	–	–	–	–	–	–
	National insurance surcharge	GTAY	–	–	–	–	–	–	–	–	–
	London regional transport levy	GTBE	–	–	–	–	–	–	–	–	–
	IBA levy	GTAL	–	–	–	–	–	–	–	–	–
	Motor vehicle duties paid by businesses	EKED	1 509	1 565	1 415	778	724	797	808	809	865
	Regulator fees	GCSQ	60	79	101	98	93	101	91	78	71
	Tithe Act payments[2]	EBDD	–	–	–	–	–	–	–	–	–
	Total	NMBX	15 687	16 361	16 934	17 408	17 940	18 329	18 741	19 419	20 885
	Paid to local government										
	Non-domestic rates[3]	NMYH	128	142	149	157	173	188	204	182	202
D.29	Total production taxes other than on products	NMYD	15 815	16 503	17 083	17 565	18 113	18 517	18 945	19 601	21 087
D.2	Total taxes on production and imports, paid										
	Paid to central government	NMBY	112 881	122 504	128 875	131 675	138 192	145 782	154 424	157 617	166 820
	Paid to local government	NMYH	128	142	149	157	173	188	204	182	202
	Paid to the European Union	FJWB	6 346	5 881	6 334	5 675	4 752	4 695	3 959	4 260	4 496
D.2	Total	NZGX	119 355	128 527	135 358	137 507	143 117	150 665	158 587	162 059	171 518

1 These taxes existed before the UK's entry into the EEC in 1973
2 These taxes existed before 1969
3 From 190/1991 onwards thse series only contain rates paid in Northern Ireland

11.1 Taxes paid by UK residents to general government and the European Union

Total economy sector S.1

continued | £ million

			1998	1999	2000	2001	2002	2003	2004	2005	2006
Part	**SECONDARY DISTRIBUTION OF INCOME**										
	Uses										
D.5	Current taxes on income, wealth etc										
D.51	Taxes on income										
	Paid to central government										
	Household income taxes	DRWH	88 074	94 713	103 129	108 506	109 358	111 559	117 954	128 240	137 617
	Corporation tax	ACCD	31 232	32 924	33 003	33 520	28 866	28 489	31 104	37 808	47 123
	Petroleum revenue tax	DBHA	662	472	1 540	1 526	946	1 146	1 166	1 799	2 543
	Windfall tax	EYNK	2 614	–	–	–	–	–	–	–	–
	Other taxes on income	BMNX	1 101	1 444	2 330	3 712	3 672	3 040	4 493	4 772	5 734
D.51	Total	NMCU	123 683	129 553	140 002	147 264	142 842	144 234	154 717	172 619	193 017
D.59	Other current taxes										
	Paid to central government										
	Motor vehicle duty paid by households	CDDZ	3 122	3 308	3 191	3 324	3 570	3 923	3 955	3 953	4 145
	Northern Ireland domestic rates	NSFA	115	115	112	107	106	101	96	85	76
	Licences	NSNP	8	8	4	–	–	–	–	–	–
	National non-domestic rates paid by non-market sectors[1]	BMNY	960	994	1 000	1 047	1 029	996	996	1 165	1 254
	Passport fees	E8A6	27	77	107	140	148	185	220	279	322
	Television licence fee	DH7A	2 140	2 251	1 955	2 302	2 280	2 329	2 490	2 655	2 696
	Total	NMCV	6 372	6 753	6 369	6 920	7 133	7 534	7 757	8 137	8 493
	Paid to local government										
	Domestic rates[2]	NMHK	62	67	73	80	83	91	98	147	155
	Community charge	NMHL	–	–	–	–	–	–	–	–	–
	Council tax	NMHM	11 686	12 699	13 845	15 068	16 448	18 391	19 863	20 969	22 033
	Total	NMIS	11 748	12 766	13 918	15 148	16 531	18 482	19 961	21 116	22 188
D.59	Total	NVCM	18 120	19 519	20 287	22 068	23 664	26 016	27 718	29 253	30 681
D.5	Total current taxes on income, wealth etc										
	Paid to central government	NMCP	130 055	136 306	146 371	154 184	149 975	151 768	162 474	180 756	201 510
	Paid to local government	NMIS	11 748	12 766	13 918	15 148	16 531	18 482	19 961	21 116	22 188
D.5	Total	NMZL	141 803	149 072	160 289	169 332	166 506	170 250	182 435	201 872	223 698
D.61	Social contributions										
D.611	Actual social contributions										
	Paid to central government										
	(National Insurance Contributions)										
D.61111	Employers' compulsory contributions	CEAN	28 731	31 286	34 028	35 706	35 735	39 890	43 586	46 741	48 624
D.61121	Employees' compulsory contributions	GCSE	22 528	23 573	24 175	25 236	25 357	29 055	32 396	34 742	36 415
D.61131	Self- and non-employed persons' compulsory contributions	NMDE	1 729	1 883	2 049	2 183	2 318	2 595	2 727	2 825	2 930
D.611	Total	AIIH	52 988	56 742	60 252	63 125	63 410	71 540	78 709	84 308	87 969
Part	**CAPITAL ACCOUNT**										
	Changes in liabilities and net worth										
D.91	Other capital taxes										
	Paid to central government										
	Inheritance tax	ACCH	1 781	1 941	2 203	2 374	2 359	2 400	2 861	3 134	3 507
	Tax on other capital transfers	LSON	14	10	12	22	22	16	20	16	18
	On equal pay capital transfers	C625	–	–	–	–	–	–	–	–	54
	Development land tax and other[3]	GCSV	–	–	–	–	–	–	–	–	–
D.91	Total	NMGI	1 795	1 951	2 215	2 396	2 381	2 416	2 881	3 150	3 579
	TOTAL TAXES AND COMPULSORY SOCIAL CONTRIBUTIONS										
	Paid to central government	GCSS	297 719	317 503	337 713	351 380	353 958	371 506	398 488	425 831	459 878
	Paid to local government	GCST	11 876	12 908	14 067	15 305	16 704	18 670	20 165	21 298	22 390
	Paid to the European Union	FJWB	6 346	5 881	6 334	5 675	4 752	4 695	3 959	4 260	4 496
	Total	GCSU	315 941	336 292	358 114	372 360	375 414	394 871	422 612	451 389	486 764

1 Up until 1995/96 these payments are included in national non-domestic rates under production taxes other than on products

2 From 1990/1991 onwards these series only contain rates paid in Northern Ireland

3 Development Land Tax, Betterment Levy and special taxes, charges and contributions

11.4 General government: reconciliation of financial balance sheets and transactions

ESA95 sector S.13 Unconsolidated

£ million

			2000	2001	2002	2003	2004	2005	2006
	Assets								
	Financial assets at beginning of period (balance sheet)		148 838	181 704	171 338	167 727	170 618	177 672	193 270
F.A	Net acquisition of financial assets (transactions)	NFPG	29 545	–11 110	–4 487	740	6 895	9 117	12 322
K.12	Changes in classifications and structure	MDQJ	3 522	709	441	324	401	429	396
K.11	Nominal holding gains /losses	YEPT	4 528	437	658	653	1 085	2 002	–201
K.10	Other volume changes	YEPS	–4 729	–402	–223	1 174	–1 327	4 050	1 885
AF.A	Financial assets at end of period (balance sheet)	NPUP	181 704	171 338	167 727	170 618	177 672	193 270	207 672
	Liabilities								
	Financial liabilities at beginning of period (balance sheet)		506 862	528 393	500 021	521 669	550 522	606 254	678 456
F.L	Net acquisition of financial liabilities (transactions)	NFSK	12 901	–19 917	13 334	37 114	44 645	51 716	50 834
K.11	Nominal holding gains / losses	YEPW	9 099	–10 819	8 111	–7 963	5 056	10 318	–11 830
K.10	Other volume changes	YEPV	–469	2 364	203	–298	6 031	10 168	3 109
AF.L	Financial liabilities at end of period (balance sheet)	NPVQ	528 393	500 021	521 669	550 522	606 254	678 456	720 569
	Net								
	Net financial balance sheet at beginning of period		–358 024	–346 689	–328 683	–353 942	–379 904	–428 582	–485 186
B.9f	Net acquisition of financial assets and liabilities (transactions)	NYNO	16 644	8 807	–17 821	–36 374	–37 750	–42 599	–38 512
K.12	Changes in classifications and structure	MDQJ	3 522	709	441	324	401	429	396
K.11	Nominal holding gains / losses	YEPZ	–4 571	11 256	–7 453	8 616	–3 971	–8 316	11 629
K.10	Other volume changes	YEPY	–4 260	–2 766	–426	1 472	–7 358	–6 118	–1 224
BF.90	Net financial balance sheet at end of period	NYOG	–346 689	–328 683	–353 942	–379 904	–428 582	–485 186	–512 897

11.5 Central government: reconciliation of financial balance sheets and transactions

ESA95 sector S.1311 Unconsolidated

£ million

			2000	2001	2002	2003	2004	2005	2006
	Assets								
	Financial assets at beginning of period (balance sheet)		125 573	158 883	148 263	143 340	144 060	147 913	161 920
F.A	Net acquisition of financial assets (transactions)	NARM	28 682	–11 294	–4 987	–1 057	3 536	10 896	9 416
K.12	Changes in classifications and structure	YEQA	–	–	–	–	–	–	–
K.11	Nominal holding gains /losses	YENX	4 527	438	657	653	1 085	2 002	–198
K.10	Other volume changes	YENW	101	236	–593	1 124	–768	1 109	702
AF.A	Financial assets at end of period (balance sheet)	NIGP	158 883	148 263	143 340	144 060	147 913	161 920	171 840
	Liabilities								
	Financial liabilities at beginning of period (balance sheet)		444 198	465 945	436 689	459 645	490 311	542 557	610 644
F.L	Net acquisition of financial liabilities (transactions)	NAUQ	12 404	–20 288	14 763	39 349	41 644	47 737	45 675
K.11	Nominal holding gains / losses	YEON	9 166	–10 818	8 110	–7 961	5 056	10 320	–11 829
K.10	Other volume changes	YEOM	177	1 850	83	–722	5 546	10 030	2 777
AF.L	Financial liabilities at end of period (balance sheet)	NIJT	465 945	436 689	459 645	490 311	542 557	610 644	647 267
	Net								
	Net financial balance sheet at beginning of period		–318 625	–307 062	–288 426	–316 305	–346 251	–394 644	–448 724
B.9f	Net acquisition of financial assets and liabilities (transactions)	NZDX	16 278	8 994	–19 750	–40 406	–38 108	–36 841	–36 259
K.12	Changes in classifications and structure	YEQA	–	–	–	–	–	–	–
K.11	Nominal holding gains / losses	YEOR	–4 639	11 256	–7 453	8 614	–3 971	–8 318	11 631
K.10	Other volume changes	YEOQ	–76	–1 614	–676	1 846	–6 314	–8 921	–2 075
BF.90	Net financial balance sheet at end of period	NZDZ	–307 062	–288 426	–316 305	–346 251	–394 644	–448 724	–475 427

11.6 Local government: reconciliation of financial balance sheets and transactions

ESA95 sector S.1313 Unconsolidated

£ million

			2000	2001	2002	2003	2004	2005	2006
	Assets								
	Financial assets at beginning of period (balance sheet)		23 265	22 821	23 075	24 387	26 558	29 759	31 350
F.A	Net acquisition of financial assets (transactions)	NBYK	863	184	500	1 797	3 359	–1 779	2 906
K.12	Changes in classifications and structure	MDQI	3 522	709	441	324	401	429	396
K.11	Nominal holding gains /losses	YEOT	1	–1	1	–	–	–	–3
K.10	Other volume changes	YEPD	–4 830	–638	370	50	–559	2 941	1 183
AF.A	Financial assets at end of period (balance sheet)	NJFV	22 821	23 075	24 387	26 558	29 759	31 350	35 832
	Liabilities								
	Financial liabilities at beginning of period (balance sheet)		62 664	62 448	63 332	62 024	60 211	63 697	67 812
F.L	Net acquisition of financial liabilities (transactions)	NCBO	497	371	–1 429	–2 235	3 001	3 979	5 159
K.11	Nominal holding gains / losses	YEPO	–67	–1	1	–2	–	–2	–1
K.10	Other volume changes	YEPN	–646	514	120	424	485	138	332
AF.L	Financial liabilities at end of period (balance sheet)	NJIZ	62 448	63 332	62 024	60 211	63 697	67 812	73 302
	Net								
	Net financial balance sheet at beginning of period		–39 399	–39 627	–40 257	–37 637	–33 653	–33 938	–36 462
B.9f	Net acquisition of financial assets and liabilities (transactions)	NYNQ	366	–187	1 929	4 032	358	–5 758	–2 253
K.12	Changes in classifications and structure	MDQI	3 522	709	441	324	401	429	396
K.11	Nominal holding gains / losses	YEPQ	68	–	–	2	–	2	–2
K.10	Other volume changes	YEPP	–4 184	–1 152	250	–374	–1 044	2 803	851
BF.90	Net financial balance sheet at end of period	NYOJ	–39 627	–40 257	–37 637	–33 653	–33 938	–36 462	–37 470

11.7 Housing operating account[1]

£ million

			1998	1999	2000	2001	2002	2003	2004	2005	2006
	Resources										
P.11	Market output	CTMQ	10 144	9 754	9 431	9 335	9 167	8 896	8 382	9 002	9 754
	of which:										
	paid by tenants	CTMK	3 305	3 178	3 073	2 932	2 789	2 534	2 141	2 000	1 894
	rent rebates	CTML	5 372	5 350	5 284	5 277	5 232	5 120	5 159	5 247	5 407
	rent on other properties	CTMM	216	230	224	227	228	225	228	224	229
	subsidies:										
	Central government	CTMN	744	491	379	304	236	234	113	140	157
	Local authorities	CTMO	1	16	21	9	17	18	23	30	37
	Imputed	GNM2	–	–	–	–	–	–	–	656	1 332
	other income	CTMP	506	489	450	586	665	765	718	705	698
	Uses[2]										
	Supervision and management	CTMR	2 218	2 241	2 243	2 297	2 349	2 373	2 487	2 592	2 709
	Repairs	CTMS	2 771	2 678	2 615	2 505	2 431	2 329	2 233	2 263	2 313
	Other current expenditure	CTMT	242	339	334	321	288	263	247	307	418
B.2g	Operating surplus, gross	ADAE	4 913	4 496	4 239	4 212	4 099	3 931	3 415	3 840	4 314

1 Part of the public corporations account
2 Includes compensation of employees (D.1), intermediate consumption (P2) and taxes on production (D.29)

Chapter 12

Statistics for European Union purposes

The European Union uses National Accounts data for a number of administrative and economic purposes. Gross National Product (GNP), calculated in accordance with the European System of Accounts 1979 (ESA79), has been used in setting a ceiling on the EU budget and calculating part of Member States' contributions to the budget.

However, from 2002, the calculation reflects the move to the new European System of Accounts 1995 (ESA95) and the progression to Gross National Income (GNI) from GNP.[1] ESA95 is the basis on which most UK statistical information is now supplied to the EU.

ESA95 differs from the ESA79 in a number of ways, for example, the recording of interest payments, and the treatment of software in gross fixed capital formation and roads and bridges in the consumption of fixed capital formation.[2]

Data supplied for EU budgetary purposes

The GNP/GNI measure[3] is one component in the calculation of Member States' contributions to the EU Budget.

GNP data up to and including 2001 have been frozen, or 'closed' in the calculation of UK contributions. In future, revisions will only be made due to methodological improvements to the transition mechanism (see note 2).

The years 2002 onwards remain 'open' years, reflecting any revisions to National Accounts. From 2002, UK contributions are calculated under the ESA95 framework as shown in Table 1.2.

UK transactions with the institutions of the EU

Table 12.1 shows the UK contribution to the budget under the four categories of revenue raising ('own resources'), and payments flowing into the UK in the form of EU expenditure and the UK budgetary rebate. UK GNP/GNI forms the basis of the 'Fourth Resource' contributions.

Data to monitor government deficit and debt

The convergence criteria for Economic and Monetary Union (EMU) are set out in the 1992 Treaty on European Union (The Maastricht Treaty).[4] The Treaty, plus the Stability and Growth Pact, requires Member States to avoid excessive government deficits defined as general government net borrowing and gross debt as a percentage of GDP. Member States report their planned and actual deficits, and the levels of their debt, to the European Commission. Data to monitor excessive deficits are supplied in accordance with EU legislation.[5]

The Treaty does not determine what constitutes 'excessive'. This is agreed by the Economic and Finance Council (ECOFIN). However, a Protocol to the Treaty does provide a reference value of 3 per cent of GDP for net borrowing and 60 per cent of GDP for gross debt.

The United Kingdom submitted the estimates in the following table to the European Commission in March 2007.

	2003	2004	2005	2006
General government deficit				
net borrowing (£bn)	34.9	36.7	37.4	35.4
as a percentage of GDP[6]	13.1	3.1	3.0	2.7
General government debt				
debt at nominal value (£bn)[7]	438.9	483.4	527.1	571.8
as a percentage of GDP[6]	38.8	40.3	42.2	43.5

References

1 The harmonisation of gross national income at market prices (GNI regulation) was adopted in July 2003 under Council Regulation (EC) No. 1287/2003.

2 Commission Decision 97/178 set down a transition mechanism for deriving ESA79 GNP figures from ESA95 for the purposes of the EC budget. The mechanism was extended following Commission Decision 98/501 and the July 2001 meeting of the GNP Committee.

3 Council Directive 89/130/EEC.

4 Treaty on European Union (Luxembourg, Office for Official Publications of the European Communities, 1992).

5 Council Regulation (EC) No. 3605/93.

6 Uses FISIM-adjusted version of GDP.

7 At end year.

12.1 UK official transactions with institutions of the EU

UK transactions with ESA95 sector S.212

£ million

			1997	1998	1999	2000	2001	2002	2003	2004	2005
	UK resources										
P.62	Exports of services										
	UK charge for collecting duties and levies(net)[1,2]	QWUE	240	212	208	217	525	487	489	544	561
D.31	Subsidies on products, paid (negative resources)										
	Agricultural guarantee fund	EBGL	3 063	2 935	2 781	2 571	2 336	2 381	2 691	2 909	3 216
	European Coal & Steel Community grants	FJKP	5	1	–	–	1	–	–	2	–
D.75	Social assistance										
	European Social Fund	HDIZ	615	783	434	659	370	412	427	433	900
D.74	Current international co-operation										
	Fontainebleau abatement[2]	FKKL	1 733	1 377	3 171	2 084	4 560	3 099	3 560	3 592	3 655
	Grants to research councils and miscellaneous[2]	GCSD	6	7	5	–	8	13	10	12	–
D.92	Capital transfers, payable										
	Agricultural guidance fund	FJXL	57	56	47	82	26	–	2	49	80
	European regional development fund	HBZA	812	357	285	989	543	296	622	1 062	1 393
D.99	Agricultural compensation scheme payments[5]	EBGO	178	43	–	–	322	–	–	–	–
	Total identified UK resources	GCSL	6 709	5 771	6 931	6 602	8 691	6 688	7 801	8 603	9 805
	UK uses										
D.21	Taxes on products										
	EU traditional own resources										
D.212	Import duties	FJWD	2 291	2 076	2 024	2 086	2 069	1 919	1 937	2 145	2 220
D.214	Sugar levy	GTBA	91	42	46	44	31	25	18	25	24
D.214	European Coal & Steel Community levy	GTBB	–	–	–	–	–	–	–	–	–
	Third own resource contribution										
D.211	VAT contribution	HCML	3 646	3 758	3 920	4 104	3 624	2 720	2 775	1 764	1 980
D.211	Adjustment to VAT contribution	FSVL	–249	470	–109	100	–49	88	–35	25	19
D.75	Miscellaneous current transfers										
	Fourth own resource contribution[3]										
	GNP fourth resource	HCSO	2 655	3 516	4 403	4 243	3 859	5 259	6 622	7 565	8 597
	GNP adjustment	HCSM	–197	404	229	136	–1	76	150	–16	135
	Total GNP based fourth own resource	NMFH	2 458	3 920	4 632	4 379	3 858	5 335	6 772	7 549	8 732
D.74	Other current transfers										
	JET contributions and miscellaneous[3]	GVEG	31	–1	11	6	24	10	18	–3	106
	Inter-government agreements[3]	HCBW	–	–	–	–	–	–	–	–	–
	EU non-budget (miscellaneous)[3]	HRTM	–	–	–	–	–	–	–	–	–
	Total identified UK uses	GCSM	8 268	10 265	10 524	10 719	9 557	10 097	11 485	11 505	13 081
	Balance, UK net contribution to the EU[4]	BLZS	–1 559	–4 494	–3 593	–4 117	–866	–3 409	–3 684	–2 902	–3 276

1 Before 1989 this is netted off the VAT contribution but cannot be identfified separately.
2 UK central government resources.
3 UK central government uses.
4 As defined in pre-ESA95 Blue Books.
5 Before 1999 these have been included in Agricultural guarantee fund payments (series EBGL).

Part 5

UK Environmental Accounts

Chapter 13

The UK Environmental Accounts at a glance

Oil and gas reserves

At the end of 2005, UK oil reserves were valued at £84 billion while gas reserves were estimated to be worth £64 billion.

The value of the UK's recoverable oil and gas reserves mainly depends upon the estimated physical amounts remaining, the current rate of extraction and the assumed future price per unit of oil or gas, net of the cost of extraction. Since 1994, the estimated physical stock of reserves has fallen as a result of extraction, but the value of the reserves has generally risen, with increases in the price of oil being particularly significant. Since 2002, there has also been an increase in gas prices.

Value of oil and gas reserves, 1994–2005

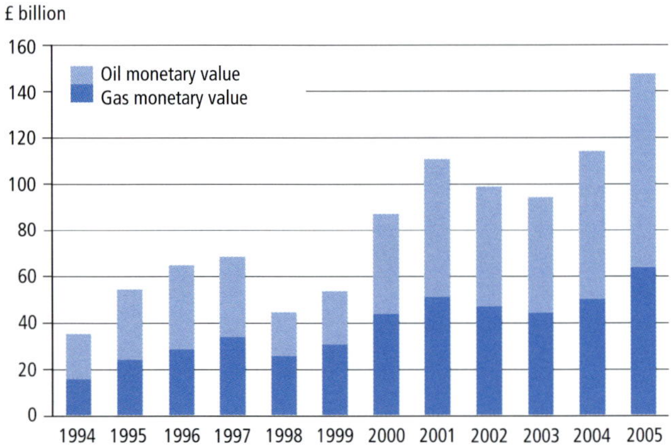

Source: ONS

Atmospheric emissions

On a national accounts basis, UK non-domestic greenhouse gas and acid rain precursor emissions fell between 1990 and 2005, by 13.4 per cent and 52.9 per cent respectively. In contrast, emissions of greenhouse gases from the domestic sector have risen by 10.0 per cent over the same period.

The electricity, gas and water supply industry is the biggest contributor of Greenhouse Gas emissions accounting for 25.7 per cent of the total. The next largest contributor was the domestic sector, which was responsible for 21.3 per cent of Greenhouse Gas emissions. The transport and communications industry was the largest contributor of acid rain precursor emissions (31.3 per cent), followed by the electricity, gas and water supply industry (19.9 per cent).

There were substantial improvements in emissions intensity, as measured by the ratio of greenhouse gas emissions per unit of output, in most sectors of the economy between 1990 and 2005. Overall, the emissions intensity of the non-domestic sector fell 10.4 per cent between 2004 and 2005, following a 12.3 per cent increase in output, compared with a 0.6 per cent increase in emissions from the non-domestic sector over the same period.

The largest fall in emissions intensity is in the commerce and public administration sector where emissions per unit of output fell by 17.4 per cent between 2004 and 2005 and have fallen by over half since 1990.

Atmospheric emissions of greenhouse gases and acid precursors, percentage change, 1990–2005

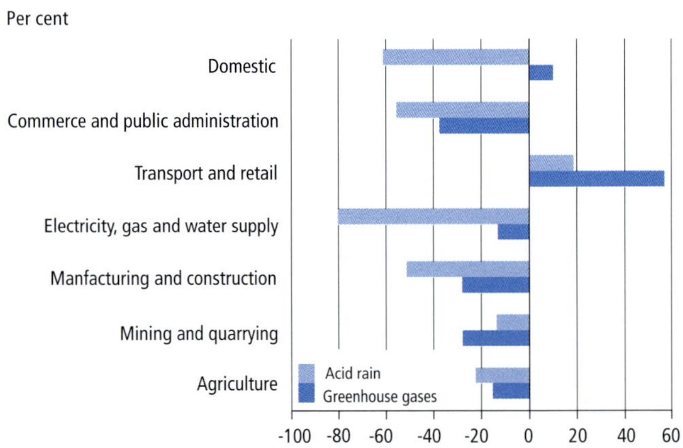

Source: ONS

Greenhouse gas emissions per unit of output, (Gross value added CVM), 1990–2005

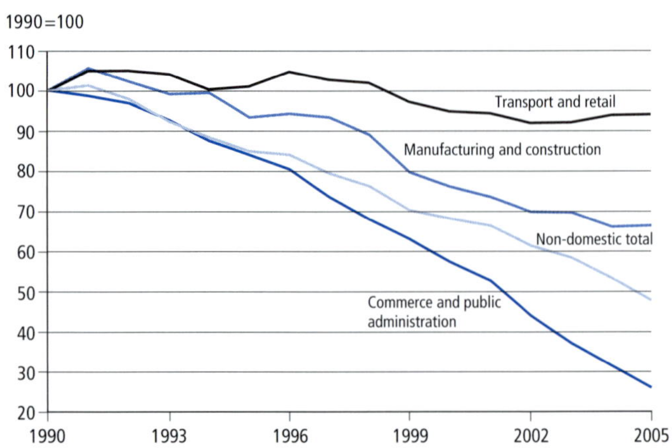

Source: ONS

Energy use

In 2005, direct use of energy including electricity in the non-domestic sector was 10.6 per cent higher than its 1990 level. During the same period Gross Domestic Product (GDP) increased 43.6 per cent in real terms. As a result, energy intensity (energy consumed per unit of output) has decreased by 22.9 per cent between 1990 and 2005. Energy derived from renewable sources amounted to 1.9 per cent compared to 0.9 per cent in 1990.

Non-domestic energy consumption and output (Gross Domestic Product, CVM), 1990–2005

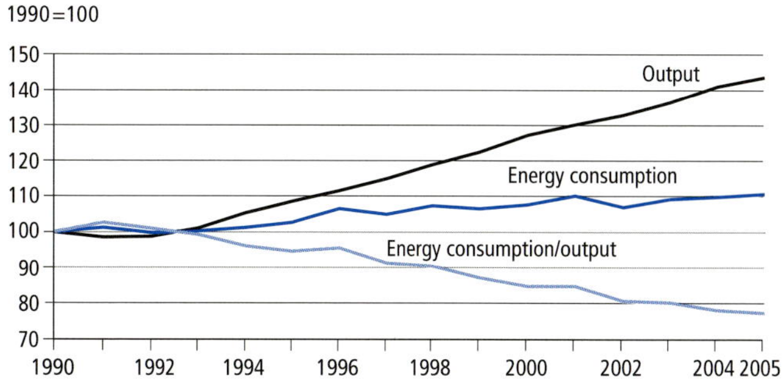

Source: ONS

Material flow accounting

Current data indicate that material use is falling in relation to the level of economic activity in the UK and support evidence that domestic material use and economic growth have decoupled since 1990. However, the mass of material imported has generally risen over the same period suggesting that some of the environmental impacts associated with consumption are being transferred abroad.

Material flows in the UK

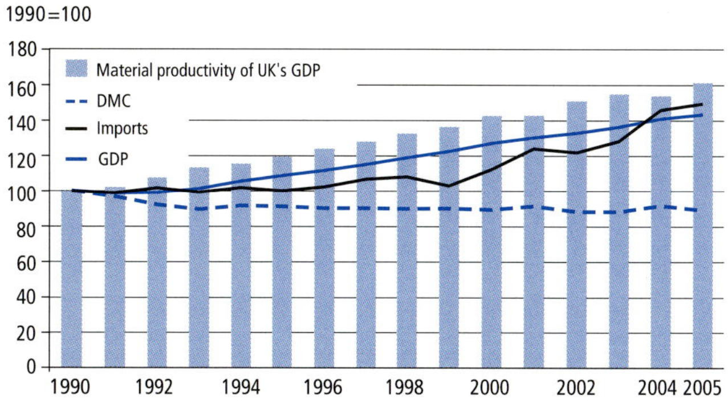

Source: ONS

Environmental taxes

In 2006, environmental tax receipts amounted to £35.4 billion. By far the largest contributor to environmental taxes is duty on hydrocarbon oils such as petrol and diesel, which accounted for 66.3 per cent of the total in 2006.

Table 13.8 contains a breakdown of these taxes by 13 industries for 2004. This shows that UK households pay £18.6 billion in environmental taxes, over half of all environmental taxes and almost three times the next highest contributor, the transport and communications industry.

Government receipts from environmental taxes, 1993–2006

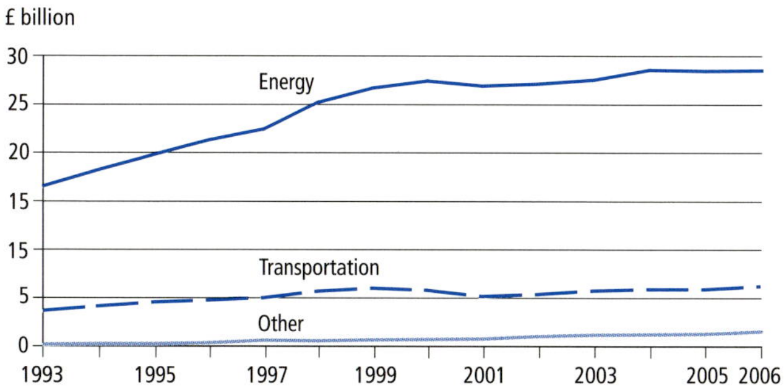

Source: ONS

Environmental protection expenditure

In 2004, public sector expenditure is estimated at £5.9 billion with £3.5 billion spent on waste management and a further £0.7 billion on nature conservation, but only £0.3 billion directly on waste water management. Measures to protect air quality and the climate amounted to a further £0.3 billion.

Environmental protection expenditure data by industry for 2004, published by the Department for Environment, Food and Rural Affairs (Defra), is also included in this chapter.

Public sector environmental protection expenditure, 2001–2004

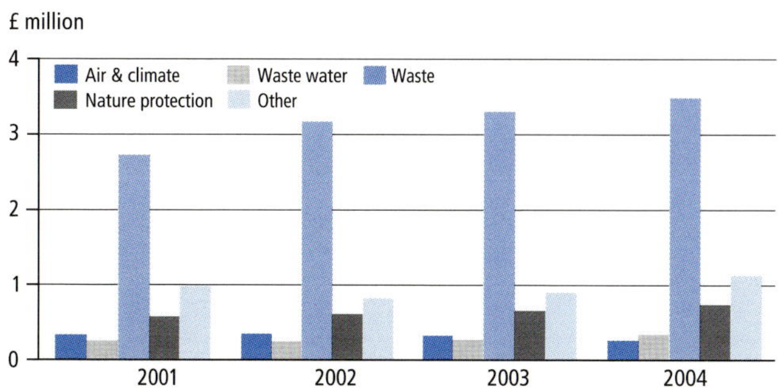

Source: ONS

UK Environmental Accounts

Environmental accounts are "satellite accounts" to the main National Accounts. Satellite accounts are extensions to the National Accounts, which facilitate analysis of the wider impact of economic change. Environmental accounts provide information on the environmental impact of economic activity (in particular on the emissions of pollutants) and on the importance of natural resources to the economy. Environmental accounts use similar concepts and classifications of industries to those employed in the National Accounts, and they reflect the recommended European Union and United Nations frameworks for developing such accounts.

The accounts are used to inform sustainable development policy, to model impacts of fiscal or monetary measures and to evaluate the environmental performance of different industrial sectors.

Most data are provided in units of physical measurement (volume or mass), although where appropriate some accounts are shown in monetary units.

This chapter includes information previously published in the Spring 2007 edition of *Environmental Accounts*[1]. It updates information on environmental taxes and the value of oil and gas reserves. More detailed information on each of these accounts is available in *UK Environmental Accounts* on the national statistics website.

www.nationalstatistics.gov.uk/statbase/Product.asp?vlnk=3698

The diagram below shows how the areas covered by environmental accounts relate to the economy as described by the National Accounts.

Environment and economy interactions

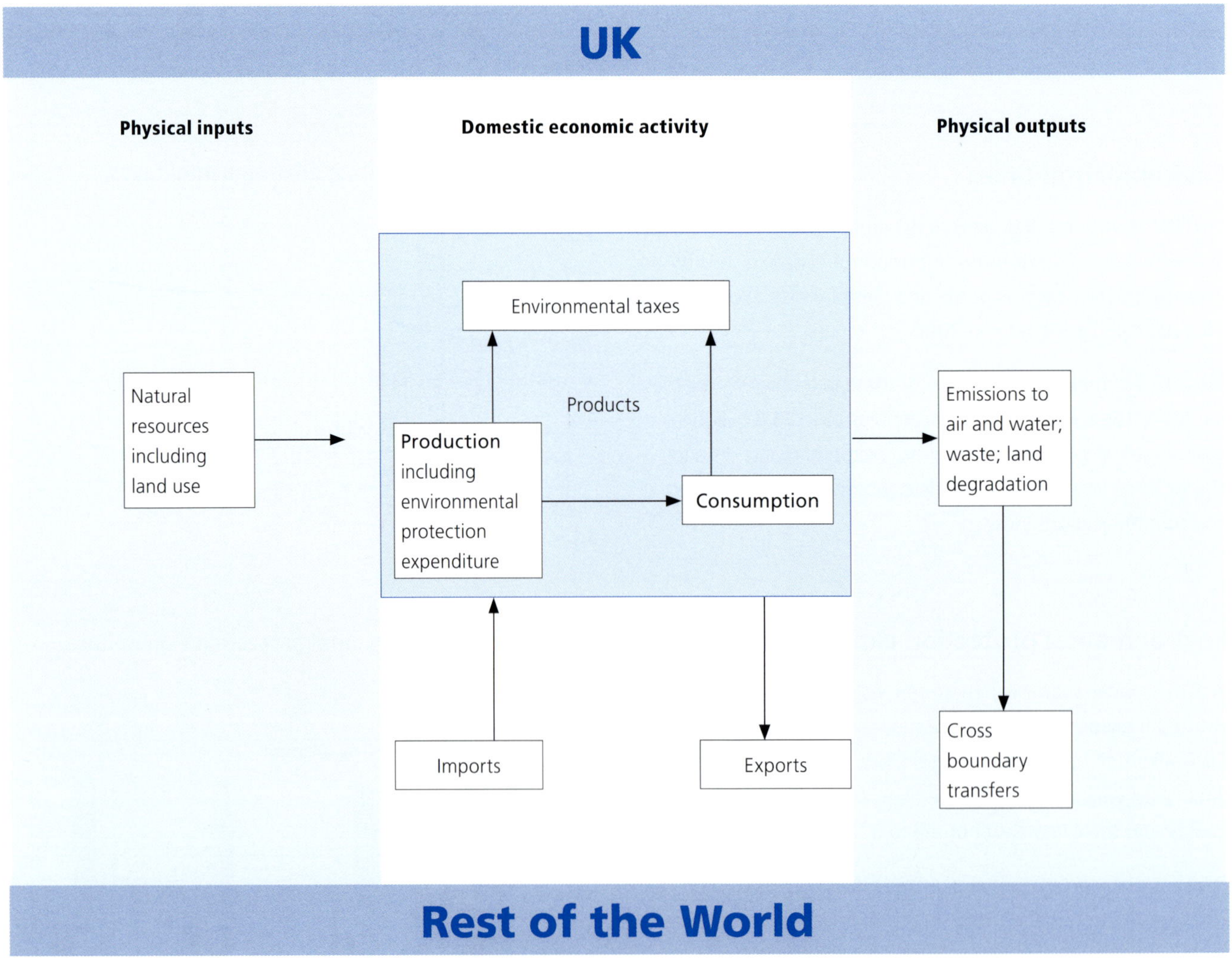

Oil and gas reserves (Tables 13.1 and 13.2)

Definition of oil and gas

Oil reserves include both oil and the liquids and liquefied products obtained from gas fields, gas-condensate fields and from the associated gas in oil fields. Gas reserves are the quantity of gas expected to be available for sale from dry gas fields, gas-condensate fields and oil fields with associated gas. Gas which is expected to be flared or used offshore is not included.

Table 13.1 gives estimates of the level of recoverable oil and gas reserves in the United Kingdom, published on the Department for Business Enterprise & Regulatory Reform (BERR (formerly Department for Trade and Industry)) oil and gas website[2].

Reserves are classified into the following categories: reserves, potential additional reserves and undiscovered resources. Undiscovered resources relate to those resources as yet undiscovered but potentially recoverable in mapped leads. Potential additional reserves are defined as discovered reserves that are not currently technically or economically producible. Reserves are classified as discovered, remaining reserves which are recoverable and commercial. These can be subdivided into proven, probable or possible depending on confidence level. **Proven reserves** are known reserves which, on the available evidence, are virtually certain to be technically and economically producible, i.e. having a better than 90 per cent chance of being produced. **Probable reserves** are known reserves which are not yet proven but which are estimated to have a better than 50 per cent chance of being technically and economically producible. **Possible reserves** are those reserves which, at present, cannot be regarded as 'probable', but are estimated to have a significant but less than 50 per cent chance of being technically and economically producible.

Simulation models using Monte Carlo techniques have been used each year by the BERR to assess the likely existence and size of **undiscovered oil and gas fields** on the UK Continental Shelf (UKCS). The assessments are presented as ranges, but the limits of the ranges should not be regarded as maxima or minima. Estimates of the volume of undiscovered reserves have fluctuated considerably in recent years as new areas of UKCS have been subjected to statistical analysis and older areas have been re-assessed.

The lower ends of the ranges of total reserves shown in the table are sums of estimated remaining proven reserves and the lower end of the range of undiscovered reserves for the end of that year. The upper ends of the ranges of total reserves are sums of estimated proven, possible and probable reserves, plus the upper end of the range of undiscovered reserves, for the end of that year.

The expected level of reserves is calculated as the sum of proven and probable reserves and the lower bound estimate of the range of undiscovered reserves. **Other volume changes** are calculated as the difference between the expected level of reserves at the start of the year, less extraction in that year, and the estimated level of reserves at the start of the following year.

Life expectancy is calculated as the expected level of reserves at the end of the year divided by the current level of annual extraction. This calculation gives an indication of the theoretical number of years for which extraction could be sustained at current levels. In practice, towards the end of that period, the rate of extraction is likely to decrease as individual oil and gas fields are exhausted, so the period of extraction will be longer than that implied by the life expectancy calculation.

Monetary valuation of oil and gas reserves

Expressing UK oil and gas reserves in monetary terms allows these subsoil assets to be compared with other economic entities. This provides a means for the commercial depletion of subsoil assets to be set against national income. Results are presented in Table 13.2 in the form of a balance sheet.

Since observed market values for transactions in the assets *in situ* are not widely available, the **present value method** is used to put a monetary value on the physical stocks of assets. This is an indirect valuation method measuring the current value of the asset's future streams of income by discounting the expected future rent, often referred to as the **economic rent** or **resource rent.** The method relies on information about the size of resource rent, the number of years for which the rent is to be received and the social discount rate to be applied.

The **resource rent** is the net income from extraction defined as total revenue from sales less all costs incurred in the extraction process that is, operating costs, depreciation of capital and allowances for decommissioning costs and the return on capital. The rate of return on capital is estimated to be 8 per cent in real terms, in line with Eurostat recommendations[3],
but it is worth noting that the resulting valuations are very sensitive to variations in this estimate. Future resource rents can then be calculated using the assumption that the future unit resource rents (that is, the resource rent per unit of fuel extracted) is constant in real terms and equal to the average of the last three years' unit rents. The estimated values are also very sensitive to this assumption.

In the calculation, it is assumed that the amounts extracted decrease as the reserves are gradually exhausted. The time span until the complete exhaustion of the reserves is the period over which resource rents are discounted, using a social discount rate of 4 per cent, again in line with Eurostat recommendations[2].

Using these assumptions it is possible to calculate a present value of the stocks of oil and gas reserves at the start and end of each year. The accumulation account then breaks down the change between the start-of-year balance and the end-of-year balance. While physical stocks may change only as a result of extraction and other volume changes such as reassessments, monetary stocks can change for a number of other reasons.

Extraction is equal to the total resource rent for the year, effectively reducing the present value of the stocks by that amount.

Revaluation due to time passing takes account of the fact that, as we move forward in time, the period over which the future rents are discounted is one year less, thereby reducing the effect of discounting future incomes.

Other volume changes are reassessments which change the estimated physical stock of recoverable reserves.

The **change in the extraction path** sets out in monetary terms the addition or subtraction to the present value arising from a change in the amounts assumed to be extracted each year.

The **change in unit rent** gives the change in the future stream of income resulting from a change in the estimated unit resource rent.

Energy consumption (Table 13.3)

Table 13.3 gives estimates of total energy used by each sector and the proportion of total energy used from renewable resources. Detailed estimates of consumption of different fuel types by each sub-sector are given on the National Statistics website.

www.nationalstatistics.gov.uk/statbase/Product.asp?vlnk=3698

Unit of measurement

The unit of measurement is tonne of oil equivalent (toe), which enables different fuels to be compared and aggregated. It should be regarded as a measure of energy content rather than a physical quantity. Standard conversion factors for each type of fuel are given in the *Digest of UK Energy Statistics* (DUKES)[4].

Consumption of carbon fuels, energy used in transformation processes and losses in distribution

The consumption of carbon fuels, and the related consumption of energy, can be analysed from a number of different perspectives. In terms of atmospheric emissions, it may be helpful to identify which sectors are actually consuming the carbon fuels that give rise to emissions. From this perspective, fuels used by the electricity generation sector are attributed entirely to that sector, even though some of the energy is transformed into electricity and used by other sectors. This analysis is shown in Part 1 of Table 13.3 and is consistent with that used in the atmospheric emissions accounts (see Tables 13.4 and 13.5). Hence the estimated carbon fuel consumption by each sector shown in Part 1 of Table 13.3 can be directly related to the estimated emissions of air pollutants by those sectors.

In terms of energy consumption, it is possible to attribute energy used during the process of transformation into electricity, and the energy lost in distributing electricity to end users, either **directly** to the electricity generation sector, or **indirectly** to the consumers of energy. Parts 2 and 3 of Table 13.3 consider energy consumption from both points of view. Part 2 allocates the consumption of energy directly to the immediate consumer of the energy, while Part 3 allocates these "electricity overheads" of the major power producers to the user of the electricity. For this purpose, the consumption of electrical energy produced by autogenerators, either for their own use or supplied directly to other consumers, has been ignored.

Renewable energy sources

Renewable energy is defined to include solar power, energy from wind, wave and tide, hydroelectricity, and energy from wood, straw and sewage gas. Landfill gas and municipal solid waste combustion have also been included with renewable energy for the purposes of defining energy sources in the context of sustainable development policy.

Sources and methods for estimating consumption of energy by industrial sector

Data for estimating fuel consumption by broad sector are collected by BERR and are published in DUKES. However, the figures shown in Table 13.3 differ from those given in DUKES in that:

- fuels used by the UK fishing fleet, UK international shipping and aircraft operators and ships and aircraft used for UK military purposes are included, whether or not they were purchased in the UK, whereas fuels purchased in the UK by non-resident operators are excluded;
- purchases of petrol and diesel abroad by UK motorists and road hauliers are included;
- non-energy uses of fuels for example, chemical feedstocks, solvents, lubricants and road-making material, are excluded. However, energy lost through gas leakage etc is included;
- the classification of industrial sectors used in environmental accounts differs from that used in DUKES. In particular, the transport sector is defined to include only enterprises that

provide transport services to other consumers (that is, public transport operators, freight haulage companies, etc.). The energy consumed by households' use of private cars is allocated to the domestic sector.

Atmospheric emissions (Tables 13.4 and 13.5)

Tables 13.4 and 13.5 give estimates of pollutants directly emitted to the atmosphere by each sector. The figures are on a National Accounts basis and differ from the basis used to monitor progress against the Kyoto Protocol in that they include estimated emissions from fuels purchased abroad by UK residents[5], including those used by international shipping and aircraft on international flights. Emissions from fuels purchased in the UK by non-UK residents are excluded. Detailed estimates of pollutants from each sub-sector are given on the National Statistics website at

www.nationalstatistics.gov.uk/statbase/Product.asp?vlnk=3698.

The website also gives details of emissions from acid rain precursors such as Sulphur Dioxide, other pollutants like Benzene and heavy metals including Lead and Zinc.

Pollutants and environmental themes

Atmospheric emissions can be aggregated according to their contribution to environmental themes such as greenhouse gases and acid rain. A description of the pollutants covered and the methodology used to calculate environmental themes is given in the annex to these notes.

Attributing emissions to industrial sectors

The disaggregation of national estimates of emissions to industrial sectors is based upon an initial disaggregation provided by the National Environmental Technology Centre (Netcen)[6] which maintains the National Atmospheric Emissions Inventory (NAEI)[7]. Emissions are estimated by multiplying fuel consumption by emissions factors and adding releases unrelated to fuel use such as methane arising from landfill.

The NAEI data is used to identify the main processes and industries responsible for the emissions, which are then allocated to individual sectors on the basis of information from a variety of sources. For example, emissions from diesel use by Heavy Goods Vehicles are allocated to sectors using vehicle mileage data from the Department for Transport. Expenditure information is also used, for example to allocate emissions arising from the use of various industrial coatings (e.g. general industrial, heavy duty and vehicle refinishing) to relevant sectors in proportion to each sector's expenditure on paints, varnishes and similar coatings, printing ink and mastics, using the National Accounts supply-use tables as the main source. A full description of the methods and sources used in these accounts is available on request from the ONS Environmental Accounts branch.

There are a number of formats for the reporting and recording of atmospheric emissions data. These include the Intergovernmental Panel on Climate Change (IPCC) and United Nations Economic Commission for Europe (UNECE) measures both published by Defra and the National Accounts consistent measure published by the ONS. For further details please refer to *Environmental Accounts* on the National Statistics website.

Table 13.4, shows latest estimates of air pollutants directly emitted by each sector. Emissions generated by the electricity supply industry have not been reallocated to their customers in this analysis. Emissions from road haulage are given on an 'own account' basis, i.e. attributed to the sector owning the transport rather than to the sector of the goods being transported. Similarly emissions from households' use of private cars are allocated to the domestic sector. Figures for total road transport emissions are provided separately.

Table 13.5 shows estimates of greenhouse gases and acid rain emissions by industrial sector.

Material flows (Table 13.6)

Economy-wide material flow accounts record the total mass of natural resources and products that are used by the economy, either directly in the production, distribution and consumption of products and services, or indirectly through the movement of materials which are displaced in order for production to take place.

A material flow account balances the inputs (extraction of natural resources from the UK environment, and imports of goods) with the outputs (wastes, emissions to air and water, exports) and accumulation (in terms of new buildings etc) within the economy. This mass balance concept is based on the principle that matter can neither be created nor destroyed.

The direct input of materials into the economy derives primarily from domestic extraction, that is from biomass (agricultural harvest, timber, fish and animal grazing), fossil fuel extraction (such as coal, crude oil and natural gas) and mineral extraction (metal ores, industrial minerals such as pottery clay, and construction material such as crushed rock, sand and gravel).

The direct input of materials from domestic sources is supplemented by the imports of products, which may be of raw materials such as unprocessed agricultural products, but can also be semi-manufactured or finished products. In a similar way the UK produces exports of raw materials, semi-manufactured and finished goods which can be viewed as inputs to the production and consumption of overseas economies.

Water is used so widely and in such quantities that its inclusion in the accounts tends to obscure other resource use. For this reason, the accounts only include the water that is contained in products (e.g. agricultural produce and imported beverages). Water for other consumptive uses (cleaning or irrigation) and *in situ* uses (such as hydroelectric power) is excluded from these accounts.

Hidden flows measure the quantity of material displaced by the process of extraction but not actually used in the production of goods and services. Indirect flows measure the quantity of material associated with imports of raw and semi-processed goods into the UK. Both hidden and indirect flows are measured indirectly by applying coefficients for particular materials and goods to estimated levels of mass associated with domestic and overseas extraction. Therefore, there is a direct relationship between hidden flows and actual extraction. Levels are sensitive to assumptions embodied in the particular hidden or indirect flow coefficient used. Examples of hidden flows are unused extraction from mining and quarrying (also known as overburden), discarded material from harvesting (for example, wood harvesting losses such as timber felled but left in the forests), and soil and rock moved as a result of construction and dredging.

Recycling of materials is not treated either as an input or as an output in the material flow accounts because the waste is not viewed as leaving the economic domain. However, the amount of recycling is included in the accounts both to ensure that double counting is avoided and because it is the subject of considerable policy interest in its own right.

Indicators

There are a number of indicators which can be used to summarise the flows of materials into and out of the economy. Table 13.6 includes three of the main indicators used to measure inputs. There are also a number of output and material balance indicators, which cannot yet be calculated because of lack of data. The output indicators are potentially more useful as they provide a better link with the environmental impact of resource consumption.

Direct Material Input (DMI) measures the input of materials directly used by the economy, that is all materials that form part of products or are used in production and consumption activities. DMI equals used extraction in the UK (including that which is used or contained in the production of exports) plus imports.

Domestic material consumption (DMC) measures the total amount of material directly consumed by the economy, that is, it includes domestic extraction and imports but excludes exports. For this reason, it is the input indicator which is most closely related to the consumption activities of the economy, as measured in monetary aggregates such as Gross Domestic Product (GDP).

The **Total Material Requirement (TMR)** measures the total material basis of the economy, that is the total direct and indirect resource requirements of all the production and consumption activities. TMR includes the amount of used extraction in the UK, the imports into the UK and the resulting indirect or hidden flows associated with extraction in the UK and imports from other countries. Although TMR is widely favoured as a resource use indicator, the estimates of indirect flows are less reliable than those for materials directly used by the economy, and it can also be argued that it double-counts trade flows, in that materials used both in the production of imports and in the production of exports are included. The indicator therefore needs to be considered alongside other indicators.

In summary:

Direct Material Input (DMI) = used domestic extraction + imports

Domestic Material Consumption (DMC) = DMI – exports

Total Material Requirement (TMR) = DMI + indirect flows from domestic extractions + indirect flows associated with imports

The concept of **material productivity** is used to assess progress towards sustainable development. It is presented in terms of the relationship between material use and economic activity. This is calculated by dividing GDP in real terms by Domestic Material Consumption (DMC) that is the mass of domestic extraction plus the mass of imports and less the mass of exports.

Sources and methods

Data on the yields of agriculture, forestry and fishing come from the Food and Agriculture Organization (FAO)[8]. Mineral extraction data have been taken from the *UK Minerals Yearbook*[9] and information on the mass of imports and exports has been taken from trade information compiled by HM Revenue and Customs[10].

Factors applied to give estimates of the amounts of unused material moved for each tonne of used material have been taken from research carried out by the Wuppertal Institute on behalf of the Department for Environment, Food and Rural Affairs (Defra)[11] and by the University of Manchester on behalf of the ONS[12]. The methodology used to compile the account is also based upon the Wuppertal Institute's research.

More information about the material flow accounts is available in Economic Trends[13,14] and in the National Statistics website at:

www.nationalstatistics.gov.uk/statbase/Product.asp?vlnk=3698

Government revenues from environmental taxes (Table 13.7)

Definition of an environmental tax

An environmental tax is defined as a tax whose base is a physical unit (or a proxy for it) that has a proven specific negative impact on the environment. By convention, in addition to pollution related taxes, all energy and transport taxes are classified as environmental taxes. This definition has been agreed by international experts and adopted by the Statistical Office of the European Communities (Eurostat) and Organisation for Economic Co-operation and Development (OECD). It enables analysis to be based on the **effects** of taxes rather than the aims behind their introduction, i.e. the aim of a tax for raising government revenue rather than reducing environmental degradation does not preclude it from being defined as an environmental tax.

Nevertheless, the interpretation and use of measures of environmental taxes need care. In particular, the levels of revenues from environmental taxes do not necessarily indicate the relative importance or the success of environmental policy. High environmental tax revenues can result either from high rates of taxes or from high levels of environmental problems (e.g. pollution) leading to a large tax base. The broad measure of revenues can also fail to capture the effect of the differential rates that encourage a shift away from higher impact behaviour (such as the use of leaded petrol).

Taxes on energy products include duties on hydrocarbon oils used in road vehicles, the main ones being ultra low sulphur petrol and ultra low sulphur diesel. Taxes on energy products also include those used for non-transport purposes (such as industrial gas turbines and heating installations, with a reduced rate for energy saving materials) and the fossil fuel levy, which is levied on sales of electricity from fossil fuels and used to compensate companies producing electricity from non-fossil fuel sources such as nuclear or renewable energy.

The climate change levy, which is a tax on non-domestic use of energy, was introduced in April 2001. The levy applies to the industrial and commercial supply of the following energy types: electricity, natural gas as supplied by a gas utility, petroleum and hydrocarbon gas in a liquid state, coal and lignite, coke and seem-coke of coal or lignite, and petroleum coke consumed by businesses. The rates of the levy are based on the quantity of fuel supplied. There are separate rates for each type of fuel: which from 1 April 2007 stand at £0.00441 pence per kilowatt-hour (kWh) for electricity, natural gas £0.00154 pence per kWh, solid fuel e.g. coal and coke £0.01201 pence per kilogram and liquid petroleum gas for heating £0.00985 pence per kilogram.

There are some reliefs and exemptions available to business users of energy. Supplies exempt from the levy include: energy supplies not for burning or consuming in the UK (that is, UK exports); resale of taxable commodities other than gas or electricity; supplies used to produce taxable commodities other than electricity; and supplies of electricity from renewable sources.

VAT on duty is calculated as a fixed proportion (in most cases 17.5 per cent) of the duty paid on hydrocarbon oils. In practice much of this VAT will be reclaimed by business, but it could be argued that the total will eventually be paid when the final product or service is purchased.

Vehicle Excise Duty is paid by owners of motor vehicles on either a six monthly or annual basis. There have been various changes to this duty over recent years. Most recently, as from 1 April 2006, private cars, taxis and light goods vehicles registered before 1 March 2001 with an engine size up to and including 1549cc are subject to a tax of £115 per annum and a higher rate of £180 per annum for engine sizes greater than 1549cc. The same vehicle types registered on or after 1 March 2001 are taxed according to the level of carbon dioxide emissions. There are seven bands of carbon dioxide emissions, each with a different duty, so that the rate of duty increases in line with emissions from zero for cars with the lowest emissions level to £300 (annual rates) for those in the highest category. The rate of duty is also dependant on the fuel source used, for instance petrol, diesel or alternative fuels. Car tax was payable on purchases of new cars, up until 1993 when it was discontinued.

Air passenger duty was introduced on 1 November 1994. It applies to the carriage from a UK airport of chargeable passengers on chargeable aircraft at two different rates. The lower rate is charged where passengers are travelling to a UK destination or within the European Economic Area (EEA), and the higher rate applies in all other cases. Since 1 February 2007 the rate also differs depending on the class of travel. From 1 April 2001, standard rates of £10 for EEA destinations and £40 for other destinations were applied. From 1 February 2007 the rates have been set at £10 for the lowest class of travel within the EEA and £40 for travel elsewhere. Duty for travel in other than the lowest class is £20 within the EEA and £80 elsewhere.

Landfill tax was introduced in October 1996 and aims to encourage waste producers to produce less waste, recover more value from waste e.g. through recycling or composting and to use more environmentally friendly methods of waste disposal. The tax applies to active and inactive (inert) waste disposed of at landfill sites. Types of waste excluded from this tax include dredgings, disposals from mines and quarries and also waste resulting from the clearance of contaminated land.

A standard rate of tax is levied on active waste, this was introduced at the rate of £7.00 per tonnes and has since risen to £18 per tonne in 2005-06. This rate rises by £3 to £24 per tonnes in 2007-08 and will be £32 per tonne from 1 April 2008. A lower rate of tax is levied on inert waste, which has remained at £2.00 per tonne from the year of introduction, this rate will rise to £2.50 per tonne from 1 April 2008.

The **aggregates levy** was introduced on 1 April 2002. The objective of this tax is to address the environmental costs associated with quarrying operations (noise, dust, visual intrusion, loss of amenity and loss to biodiversity), by reducing the demand for aggregate and encouraging the use of alternative materials where possible e.g. the use of waste glass and tyres in aggregate mixes. The tax applies to the commercial exploitation of sand, gravel and rock and includes aggregate dredged from the seabed within UK territorial waters. It is a specific tax, charged at £1.60 per tonne. From 1 April 2008, this rate will increase to £1.95 per tonne.

There are a wide range of exemptions for some quarried or mined products e.g. coal, metal ores, industrial minerals and for minerals used in the production of lime and cement and for exports of aggregates. Imports of aggregates are taxed upon first sale or use in the UK.

In 2006, ONS conducted a review of environmental taxes in the United Kingdom. A summary of this review was published in the October 2006 edition of *Economic Trends*[15]. This review identified several new environmental taxes and reassessed other taxes that are currently considered environmental taxes. Due to data availability problems it has not been possible to implement the results of the review for this data release.

Environmental taxes breakdown by 13 industries (Table 13.8)

Sources

It is based on general government environmental taxes data and unpublished Supply-Use data for taxes on products and production, that are informed by latest available Supply-Use tables. From these sources it is possible to estimate allocations of environmental taxes to individual industries. A more detailed account of the methods used in this analysis are published in the August 2004 and October 2006 editions of *Economic Trends*[16] .

Environmental protection expenditure (Tables 13.9, 13.10 and 13.11)

Definition of expenditure

Environmental protection expenditure is defined as capital and operational expenditure incurred because of, and which can be directly related to, the pursuit of an environmental objective.

Spending on installations and processes which are environmentally beneficial, but which also produce revenue (or savings) exceeding expenditures, are excluded on the grounds that they are likely to have been carried out for commercial not environmental reasons. Also excluded are expenditures on natural resource management (e.g. fisheries and water resources), on the prevention of natural hazards (e.g. flood defence), on the provision of access and amenities to National Parks etc, and on the urban environment. The spending has been classified by the following groups of environmental concerns:

- Protection of ambient air and climate
- Waste water management
- Waste management
- Protection of biodiversity and landscapes
- Other abatement activities such as on the protection of soil and groundwater, protection against radiation, and noise and vibration abatement
- Other environmental expenditure, on research and development, education and administration.

Public sector spending shown in Tables 13.10 and 13.11 has also been classified by the following types of expenditure:

- current costs, including staff costs (compensation of employees), other on-going expenditure on purchases of goods and services and the estimated consumption of fixed capital
- capital expenditure or investment including outlays on land and on the additions of new durable goods to the stock of fixed assets for environmental protection
- income from sales, fees and charges for the provision of current or capital goods and services, such as fees for waste removal, but excluding taxes
- current and capital transfers to other sectors of the economy
- net transfers to and from the Rest of the World.

Sources

Table 13.9 gives figures for spending by the extraction, manufacturing, energy production and water supply industries. They are drawn from a survey for 2004 carried out on behalf of the Department for Environment, Food and Rural Affairs (Defra) by URS Dames and Moore.[17] Information for 2005 is available from the Defra website bit it has not been possible to incorporate this into this publication. The estimates should be regarded as approximate **orders of magnitude only**. Because of this qualification the estimates shown fall outside the scope of National Statistics. Tables 13.10 and 13.11, which give estimates for expenditures by the public sector, are based on information obtained from the Public Expenditure Database produced by the HM Treasury.

Comparisons with previous surveys

The information on spending by industries in 2004, which is summarised in Table 13.9, comes from a regular series of surveys. The estimates from this survey and the earlier surveys should be regarded as very approximate and any comparisons between the results should be treated with care.

Annex: Atmospheric pollutants and environmental themes

Greenhouse gases

There is a growing consensus that the rise in concentrations of greenhouse gases in the atmosphere has led to changes in the global climate system. The greenhouse gases included in the atmospheric emissions accounts are those covered by the Kyoto Protocol: carbon dioxide (CO_2), methane (CH_4), nitrous oxide (N_2O), hydrofluorocarbons (HFCs), perfluorocarbons (PFCs) and sulphur hexafluoride (SF_6).

The main source of **carbon dioxide (CO_2)** is from the combustion of fossil fuels, but it is also produced in some industrial processes such as the manufacture of cement. Carbon dioxide is a long-lived gas remaining in the atmosphere for between 50 and 200 years. It is the main anthropogenic greenhouse gas.

Methane (CH_4) is produced when organic matter is broken down in the absence of oxygen. Large quantities are produced by enteric fermentation in cattle and sheep, by the spreading of animal manure and from organic waste deposited in landfill sites. Methane is also emitted in coal mining, oil and gas extraction and gas distribution activities. Methane is a significant greenhouse gas.

Nitrous oxide (N_2O) is released in a few industrial processes and from the soil when nitrogenous fertilisers are applied in agriculture and horticulture. These are the main anthropogenic sources. It is a long-lived pollutant, lasting about 120 years in the atmosphere and is a potent greenhouse gas.

Hydrofluorocarbons (HFCs), perfluorocarbons (PFCs) and sulphur hexafluoride (SF_6) are artificial fluids that contain chlorine and/or fluorine. Because of their low reactivity and non-toxicity they were widely used as refrigerants, foam blowing agents, aerosol propellants and solvents.

To aggregate the greenhouse gases covered in the accounts, a weighting based on the relative global warming potential (GWP) of each of the gases is applied, using the effect of CO_2 over a 100 year period as a reference. This gives methane a weight of 21 relative to CO_2 and nitrous oxide a weight of 310 relative to CO_2. SF_6 has a GWP of 23,900 relative to CO_2. The GWP of the other fluorinated compounds varies according to the individual gas.

Greenhouse gas emissions are sometimes shown in terms of carbon equivalent rather than CO2 equivalent. To convert from CO_2 equivalent to carbon equivalent it is necessary to multiply by 12/44.

Acid rain precursors

The term 'acid rain' describes the various chemical reactions which acidic gases and particles undergo in the atmosphere. The gases may be transported long distances before being deposited as wet or dry deposition. When deposited, hydrogen ions may be released, forming dilute acids, which damage ecosystems and buildings. The gases covered are sulphur dioxide (SO_2), nitrogen oxides (NO_x) and ammonia (NH_3).

The emissions are weighted together using their relative acidifying effects. The weights, given relative to SO_2, are 0.7 for NO_x and 1.9 for NH_3. This is a simplification of the chemistry involved, and there are a number of factors which can affect the eventual deposition and effect of acid rain. There may be an upward bias on the weights of the nitrogen-based compounds in terms of damage to ecosystems.

Sulphur dioxide (SO_2) is produced when coal and some petroleum products containing sulphur impurities are burnt. Sulphur dioxide is an acid gas that can cause respiratory irritation. It can damage ecosystems and buildings directly and is a major contributor to acid rain.

Nitrogen oxides (NO_x) arise when fossil fuels are burnt under certain conditions. High concentrations are harmful to health and reduce plant growth. Like sulphur dioxide, nitrogen oxides contribute to acid rain; nitrogen dioxide (NO_2) also plays a part in the formation of ground ozone layer.

Ammonia (NH_3) is predominantly emitted from spreading animal manure and some fertilisers.

Other air pollutants

PM_{10}s are smoke particles whose diameter is less than 10 microns. They are regarded as responsible for some physiological damage and have been linked to premature mortality from respiratory diseases.

Carbon monoxide (CO) is produced in small quantities when fossil fuel is burnt with insufficient oxygen for complete combustion. At high concentrations carbon monoxide is toxic.

Non-methane volatile organic compounds (NMVOCs) cover a variety of chemicals, many of which are known carcinogens. Emissions of NMVOCs arise from the deliberate and incidental evaporation of solvents (for example, in paints and cleaning products), from accidental spillage and from non-combustion of petroleum products. The environmental accounts include natural emissions of NMVOCs from managed forests. NMVOCs play a role in the formation of ground level ozone, which can have an adverse effect on health. The NMVOC emissions include benzene and 1,3-butadiene.

Benzene is released largely from the distribution and combustion of petrol. It is a carcinogen which has also been found to cause bone-marrow depression and consequent leukopenia (depressed white blood cell count) on prolonged exposure.

1,3-Butadiene is a colourless, gaseous hydrocarbon. It is produced by dehydrogenation of butene, or of mixtures of butene and butane; it may also be made from ethanol. 1,3-butadiene is believed to be a carcinogen, for which the safe level is not known. Emissions of 1,3-butadiene arise from combustion of petroleum products and in its manufacture of synthetic rubber, nylon and latex paints in the chemical industry. 1,3-butadiene is not present in petrol but is formed as a by-product of combustion. The increasing use of catalytic converters through the 1990s has caused a significant reduction in emissions from the road transport sector.

Heavy Metals

Lead (Pb) is a heavy metal that is emitted from the combustion of petrol, coal combustion and metal works. Emissions of lead continued to fall in 2000, mainly as a result of the ban on the sale of leaded petrol from 1 January 2000. Lead has been found to inhibit the development of children's intelligence. If the levels of lead are sufficient, lead can cause degenerative processes such as osteoporosis, inhibit many enzyme reactions in the body and cause reproductive disorders such as sterility and miscarriages.

Cadmium (Cd) is a normal constituent of soil and water at low concentrations. Industrially, cadmium is used as an anti-friction agent, in alloys, semi-conductors, control rods for nuclear reactors and PVC and battery manufacture. The main sources of cadmium emissions are from waste incineration, and iron and steel manufacture. Emissions of cadmium have declined over recent years; this is mainly attributable to the decline in coal combustion.

Environmentally, cadmium is dangerous because many plants and some animals absorb it easily and concentrate it in tissues. Cadmium competes with calcium in the body, and if levels are sufficient, it will displace calcium, causing embrittlement of bones and painful deformations of the skeleton. Cadmium also competes with zinc in the body, and if levels of cadmium are high enough, cadmium will also displace zinc from enzymes in the body.

Mercury (Hg) emissions are generated by waste incineration, the manufacture of chlorine in mercury cells, non-ferrous metal production and coal combustion. Emissions of mercury have declined over recent years due to improved controls on mercury cells and their replacement by diaphragm cells and the decline of coal use. Due to the volatility of mercury, if levels are sufficiently high, compounds containing mercury attack and destroy various parts of the body, particularly teeth, lung tissues and intestines.

References

1 Office for National Statistics (2007) *Environmental Accounts* Spring 2007 edition, ONS

www.nationalstatistics.gov.uk/statbase/Product.asp?vlnk=3698

2 Business Enterprse and Regulatory Reform (formerly know as Department of Trade and Industry). *Development of UK Oil and Gas Resources* (the 'Brown Book'). Various issues (title has changed over the years). HMSO/TSO.

www.og.dti.gov.uk/information/statistics.htm

3 European Commission (2000). *Accounts for subsoil assets: Results of pilot studies in European countries, 2000.* Office for Official Publication of the European Communities, Luxembourg.

4 Business Enterprse and Regulatory Reform (formerly know as Department of Trade and Industry). *Digest of United Kingdom Energy Statistics.* Various issues. HMSO/TSO.

www.dti.gov.uk/energy/inform/energy_stats_overview/index.shtml

5 Office for National Statistics (2002). *Adjustments to the UK's atmospheric emissions and energy accounts to bring them on to a National Accounts "Residents" basis.* Report to Eurostat, April 2002.

www.nationalstatistics.gov.uk/downloads/theme_environment/Adjustments_UK_atmospheric_emissions_energy_accounts_national_accounts_residents_basis.pdf

6 National Environmental Technology Centre (Netcen)

www.airquality.co.uk/archive/index.php

7 Department for Environment, Food and Rural Affairs.

www.defra.gov.uk/environment/statistics/globatmos/gagccukem.htm

8 Food and Agricultural Organization (FAO), available at:

http://apps.fao.org

9 British Geological Survey (2005). *UK Minerals Yearbook 2005.*

www.bgs.ac.uk/mineralsuk/commodity/uk/ukmy.html

10 HM Revenue and Customs trade data, available at

www.uktradeinfo.com

11 Department for Environment, Food and Rural Affairs (Defra) Resource Use and Efficiency of the UK Economy: A study by the Wuppertal Institute

www.defra.gov.uk/news/2002/020617a.htm

12 Office for National Statistics (2003), UK Material Flows Review

www.statistics.gov.uk/statbaseProduct.asp?vlnk=3698

13 Sheerin C (2002), UK Material Flow Accounting. *Economic Trends,* **No. 583,** 53 – 61.
www.statistics.gov.uk/CCI/article.asp?ID=140

14 Gazley I and Bhuvanendran D (2005, Trends in UK Material Flows between 1970 – 2003, *Economic Trends*, No. 619 39 – 47

www.statistics.gov.uk/cci/article.asp?ID=1174

15 Gazley I (2006), UK environmental taxes: classification and recent trends, *Economic Trends*, No 635, 15 – 64
www.statistics.gov.uk/cci/article.asp?ID=944

16 Lin E and Francs P (2004), An Industrial Analysis of Environmental Taxes, *Economic Trends*, No 609 54 – 59

www.statistics.gov.uk/cci/article.asp?ID=944

17 URS Dames and Moore (2006). *Environmental Protection Expenditure by Industry: 2004 UK Survey.* [July] 2006.

www.defra.gov.uk/environment/statistics/envsurvey/ expn2004/index.htm

13.1 Estimates of remaining recoverable oil and gas reserves

Million tonnes

		1994	1995	1996	1997	1998	1999	2000	2001	2002	2003	2004	2005
Oil (Million tonnes)													
Reserves													
Proven	JKOV	575	605	665	690	685	665	630	605	593	571	533	516
Probable	JKOW	920	765	690	700	575	455	380	350	327	286	283	300
Proven plus Probable	JKOX	1 495	1 370	1 355	1 390	1 260	1 120	1 010	955	920	857	816	816
Possible	JKOY	580	520	670	625	540	545	480	475	425	410	512	451
Maximum	JKOZ	2 075	1 890	2 025	2 015	1 800	1 665	1 490	1 430	1 344	1 267	1 328	1 267
Range of undiscovered resources													
Lower	JKNY	480	380	285	285	275	250	225	205	272	323	396	346
Upper	JKNZ	3 140	2 920	2 700	2 680	2 550	2 600	2 300	1 930	1 770	1 826	1 830	1 581
Range of total reserves													
Lower[1]	JKOA	1 055	985	950	975	960	915	855	810	865	894	929	862
Upper[2]	JKOB	5 215	4 810	4 725	4 695	4 350	4 265	3 790	3 360	3 115	3 093	3 158	2 848
Expected level of reserves[3]													
Opening stocks	JKOC	1 965	1 975	1 750	1 640	1 675	1 535	1 370	1 235	1 160	1 192	1 180	1 212
Extraction[5]	JKOD	–127	–130	–130	–128	–132	–137	–126	–117	–117	–106	–95	–85
Other volume changes	JKOE	137	–95	20	163	–8	–28	–9	42	149	94	127	35
Closing stocks	JKOF	1 975	1 750	1 640	1 675	1 535	1 370	1 235	1 160	1 192	1 180	1 212	1 162
Life expectancy[4] (years)	JKOG	16	13	13	13	12	10	10	10	10	11	13	14
Gas (billion cubic metres)													
Reserves													
Proven	JKOH	660	700	760	765	755	760	735	695	628	590	531	481
Probable	JKOI	855	780	660	620	585	500	460	445	369	315	296	247
Proven plus Probable	JKOJ	1 515	1 480	1 420	1 385	1 340	1 260	1 195	1 140	998	905	826	728
Possible	JKOK	400	435	540	600	455	490	430	395	331	336	343	278
Maximum	JKOL	1 910	1 915	1 960	1 980	1 795	1 750	1 630	1 535	1 329	1 241	1 169	1 006
Range of undiscovered resources													
Lower	JKOM	430	395	440	500	440	355	325	290	238	279	293	226
Upper	JKON	1 602	1 412	1 585	1 700	1 595	1 465	1 440	1 680	1 386	1 259	1 245	1 035
Range of total reserves													
Lower[1]	JKOO	1 090	1 095	1 200	1 265	1 195	1 115	1 060	985	866	869	824	707
Upper[2]	JKOP	3 517	3 327	3 545	3 685	3 390	3 215	3 065	3 215	2 714	2 500	2 415	2 041
Expected level of reserves[3]													
Opening stocks	JKOQ	1 735	1 945	1 875	1 860	1 885	1 780	1 615	1 520	1 430	1 235	1 184	1 120
Extraction[5]	JKOR	–65	–70	–84	–86	–89	–99	–108	–104	–102	–102	–95	–86
Other volume changes	JKOS	275	–	69	111	–16	–66	13	14	–93	51	31	–80
Closing stocks	JKOT	1 945	1 875	1 860	1 885	1 780	1 615	1 520	1 430	1 235	1 184	1 120	954
Life expectancy[4] (years)	JKOU	30	27	22	22	20	16	14	14	12	12	12	11

1 The lower end of the range of total reserves has been calculated as the sum of proven reserves and the lower end of the range of undiscovered reserves.
2 The upper end of the range of total reserves is the sum of proven, probable and possible reserves and the upper end of the range of undiscovered reserves.
3 Expected reserves are the sum of proven reserves, probable reserves and the lower end of the range of undiscovered reserves.
4 Based on expected level of reserves at year end and current extraction rates (source: ONS).
5 Negative extraction is shown here for the purposes of the calculation only. Of itself, extraction should be considered as a positive value.

Source: ONS and Department of Trade and Industry

13.2 Oil and gas monetary balance sheet

£ million

		1994	1995	1996	1997	1998	1999	2000	2001	2002	2003	2004	2005
Oil													
Opening stocks[1]	JKPA	13 715	19 691	30 341	36 226	34 691	19 003	23 016	43 382	59 673	51 836	50 008	63 806
Extraction[2]	JKPB	–1 723	–2 957	–3 707	–3 461	–2 144	–2 905	–5 566	–7 577	–6 445	–5 813	–6 711	–8 396
Revaluation due to time passing	JKPC	785	1 328	1 523	1 365	962	1 185	2 213	2 945	2 377	2 380	2 971	4 120
Other volume changes	JKPD	1 011	–1 234	338	2 654	–69	–360	–239	1 689	5 146	3 053	4 958	1 786
Change in extraction	JKPE	1 355	216	–11	–91	187	220	–924	–1 107	–	–1 217	–1 830	–2 895
Change in rent	JKPF	4 338	12 749	6 698	–3 034	–15 546	5 446	24 577	19 398	–10 754	–1 834	13 109	23 988
Nominal holding gains	C3OC	211	547	1 044	1 033	921	428	304	942	1 839	1 603	1 300	1 430
Closing stocks	JKPG	19 691	30 341	36 226	34 691	19 003	23 016	43 382	59 673	51 836	50 008	63 806	83 840
GAS													
Opening stocks	JKPH	8 919	15 359	23 961	28 388	33 624	25 416	30 483	43 556	50 849	46 803	44 084	50 015
Extraction[2]	JKPI	–887	–1 479	–1 962	–2 329	–1 989	–2 704	–4 275	–5 088	–5 117	–4 961	–5 550	–7 412
Revaluation due to time passing	JKPJ	577	978	1 141	1 334	1 259	1 554	2 170	2 533	2 478	2 156	2 474	3 402
Other volume changes	JKPK	1 236	3	677	1 278	–135	–803	259	361	–2 514	1 417	1 010	–3 911
Change in extraction	JKPL	325	943	1 998	208	409	1 288	1 352	–557	–357	–37	–1 056	–1 888
Change in rent	JKPM	5 052	7 730	1 749	3 936	–8 644	5 159	13 166	9 096	–103	–2 742	7 907	22 268
Nominal holding gains	C3OB	137	427	824	809	893	572	402	946	1 567	1 448	1 146	1 121
Closing stocks	JKPN	15 359	23 961	28 388	33 624	25 416	30 483	43 556	50 849	46 803	44 084	50 015	63 596

1 The estimated opening and closing stock values are based on the present value method -see *Environmental Accounts* on the National Statistics website for more detailed descriptions of the methodology used. The estimates are extremely sensitive to the estimated return to capital and to assumptions about future unit resource rents.

2 Negative extraction is shown here for the purposes of the calculation only. Of itself, extraction should be considered as a positive value.

Source: ONS

13.3 Energy consumption

Million tonnes of oil equivalent

		1990	1995	1996	1997	1998	1999	2000	2001	2002	2003	2004	2005
Direct use of energy from carbon fuels													
Agriculture	JKPO	2.3	2.3	2.3	2.3	2.2	2.2	2.1	2.1	2.1	2.2	2.2	2.1
Mining and quarrying	JKPP	3.9	4.9	5.6	5.8	6.4	6.3	6.7	7.6	7.5	7.6	7.5	7.3
Manufacturing	JKPQ	42.3	42.1	43.3	43.3	42.3	42.7	42.8	40.9	39.0	39.6	38.2	38.0
Energy, gas and water supply	JKPR	56.8	51.9	52.8	50.2	52.3	51.5	55.2	57.7	56.8	59.5	60.3	60.7
Construction	JKPS	3.0	3.1	3.2	3.3	3.3	3.3	3.3	3.4	3.4	3.5	3.6	3.7
Wholesale and retail trade	JKPT	5.1	5.6	5.8	5.6	5.7	6.0	6.0	5.7	5.5	5.6	5.9	5.8
Transport and communication	JKPU	22.0	24.7	26.9	27.5	28.8	28.6	29.6	30.9	31.1	32.2	34.3	35.4
Other business services	JKPV	2.5	2.6	2.7	2.5	2.6	2.7	2.7	2.8	2.4	2.4	2.4	2.5
Public administration	JKPW	3.8	4.1	4.1	4.0	3.8	3.7	3.4	3.7	3.8	3.5	3.6	3.6
Education, health and social work	JKPX	4.7	4.8	5.2	5.2	5.3	5.4	5.2	5.2	4.5	4.6	4.9	4.8
Other services	JKPY	2.4	2.2	2.3	1.9	1.9	1.9	1.9	2.0	1.7	1.8	1.8	1.8
Domestic	JKPZ	54.0	54.4	60.5	57.7	58.5	58.7	59.2	60.5	60.0	60.4	61.4	59.3
Total use of energy from carbon fuels	JKQA	**202.9**	**202.7**	**214.6**	**209.2**	**213.1**	**213.2**	**218.0**	**222.9**	**218.1**	**222.9**	**226.0**	**225.0**
Energy from other sources[1]	JKQB	17.7	23.1	24.0	23.8	25.0	24.0	21.4	22.1	21.3	20.6	19.4	19.8
Total energy consumption of primary fuels and equivalents	JKQC	**220.6**	**225.9**	**238.5**	**233.0**	**238.1**	**237.1**	**239.3**	**245.0**	**239.4**	**243.5**	**245.4**	**244.8**
Direct use of energy including electricity													
Agriculture	JKQD	2.6	2.6	2.7	2.7	2.6	2.6	2.5	2.5	2.5	2.5	2.5	2.4
Mining and quarrying	JKQE	4.1	5.1	5.8	6.0	6.6	6.5	6.9	7.8	8.0	8.3	8.2	8.2
Manufacturing	JKQF	49.1	49.9	51.4	51.3	50.1	50.7	50.7	48.4	46.8	47.1	45.8	45.7
Electricity, gas and water supply	JKQG	52.6	50.3	51.2	48.4	51.5	49.4	50.0	53.2	51.1	52.8	52.3	52.5
of which - transformation losses by major producers	JKQH	46.5	45.1	45.2	44.0	45.3	43.7	44.0	46.3	44.9	46.4	45.6	46.5
distribution losses of electricity supply	JKQI	2.1	2.5	2.4	2.5	2.4	2.4	2.5	2.7	2.6	2.6	2.6	2.6
Construction	JKQJ	3.1	3.3	3.4	3.4	3.4	3.5	3.5	3.5	3.6	3.7	3.7	3.9
Wholesale and retail trade	JKQK	7.1	7.8	8.1	8.2	8.3	8.6	8.7	8.5	8.4	8.6	8.9	8.9
Transport and communication	JKQL	22.7	25.6	27.8	28.5	29.8	29.7	30.6	32.1	32.2	33.4	35.5	36.6
Other business services	JKQM	4.2	4.5	4.6	4.6	4.7	4.9	5.0	5.2	4.8	4.8	4.8	4.8
Public administration	JKQN	4.4	4.8	4.7	4.6	4.3	4.3	4.0	4.3	4.4	4.2	4.4	4.3
Education, health and social work	JKQO	5.8	6.0	6.5	6.4	6.6	6.7	6.4	6.8	5.7	5.6	5.9	5.9
Other services	JKQP	2.9	2.8	2.7	2.3	2.3	2.2	2.1	2.3	2.0	2.2	2.2	2.1
Domestic	JKQQ	62.0	63.2	69.7	66.7	67.9	68.2	68.8	70.3	69.9	70.3	71.3	69.4
Total energy consumption of primary fuels and equivalents	JKQR	**220.6**	**225.9**	**238.5**	**233.0**	**238.1**	**237.1**	**239.3**	**245.0**	**239.4**	**243.5**	**245.4**	**244.8**
Reallocated use of energy													
Energy industry electricity tranformation losses and distribution losses and allocated to final consumer													
Agriculture	JKQS	3.2	3.1	3.2	3.1	3.1	3.1	3.0	3.0	3.0	3.0	3.0	2.9
Mining and quarying	JKQT	4.5	5.4	6.1	6.3	6.8	6.7	7.2	8.1	8.7	9.2	9.2	9.5
Manufacturing	JKQU	62.5	61.9	63.3	62.6	61.5	61.6	61.5	59.4	57.3	57.8	56.2	56.3
Electricity, gas and water supply	JKQV	11.1	11.6	12.3	11.1	13.5	12.9	13.5	14.5	13.9	14.2	14.4	13.6
Construction	JKQW	3.3	3.5	3.6	3.6	3.6	3.7	3.7	3.7	3.8	3.9	3.9	4.1
Wholesale and retail trade	JKQX	10.4	11.3	11.7	12.0	12.1	12.3	12.5	12.6	12.5	12.7	12.9	13.2
Transport and communication	JKQY	23.9	27.0	29.2	30.0	31.3	31.1	32.1	33.7	33.7	35.0	37.1	38.2
Other business services	JKQZ	7.2	7.4	7.5	7.7	7.8	8.0	8.3	8.7	8.1	8.2	8.1	8.1
Public administration	JKRA	7.2	6.1	5.8	5.5	5.2	5.2	4.9	5.1	5.1	5.2	5.4	5.4
Education, health and social work	JKRB	7.7	7.9	8.6	8.3	8.5	8.5	8.0	8.5	7.4	7.1	7.4	7.5
Other services	JKRC	3.8	3.7	3.4	2.9	2.7	2.6	2.5	2.8	2.4	2.7	2.7	2.6
Domestic	JKRD	75.9	77.1	83.9	79.9	81.9	81.5	82.2	84.7	83.5	84.4	85.1	83.4
Total energy consumption of primary fuels and equivalents	JKRE	**220.6**	**225.9**	**238.5**	**233.0**	**238.1**	**237.1**	**239.3**	**245.0**	**239.4**	**243.5**	**245.4**	**244.8**
Energy from renewable sources[2]	JKRF	1.9	2.3	2.1	2.3	2.6	2.8	2.8	3.0	3.3	3.5	4.1	4.6
Percentage from renewable sources	JKRG	0.9	1.0	0.9	1.0	1.1	1.2	1.2	1.2	1.4	1.4	1.7	1.9

1 Nuclear power, hydroelectric power and imports of electricty.
2 Renewable sources include solar power and energy from wind, wave and tide, hydroelectricty, wood, straw and sewage gas. Landfill gas and municipal solid waste combustion have also been included within this definition.

Source: Netcen, Department of Trade and Industry, ONS

13.4 Atmospheric emissions, 2005

Thousand tonnes

	Greenhouse gases[1]	Acid rain precursers[2]	Emissions affecting air quality							
			PM10[3]	CO[4]	NMVOC[5]	Benzene	Butadiene	Lead (tonnes)	Cadmium (tonnes)	Mercury (tonnes)
Agriculture	51 302	556	22.298	49.073	83.3	0.230	0.088	0.407	0.030	0.032
Mining and quarrying	29 155	87	12.803	38.751	111.9	0.373	0.016	0.264	0.064	0.021
Manufacturing	119 745	437	32.951	573.555	347.3	2.372	0.469	86.698	2.049	3.586
Electricity, gas and water supply	188 216	639	10.089	75.010	49.2	0.522	0.006	9.657	0.709	2.272
Construction	11 302	50	9.504	59.636	65.1	0.248	0.120	0.371	0.042	0.020
Wholesale and retail trade	18 809	54	6.660	75.675	60.9	0.282	0.176	12.901	0.096	0.035
Transport and communication	104 466	1 004	68.972	160.507	58.9	3.617	0.734	4.856	3.716	0.211
Financial intermediation	7 066	14	1.986	52.400	4.7	0.114	0.042	0.144	0.034	0.006
Public administration	9 226	40	2.012	44.452	5.0	0.283	0.055	0.536	0.030	0.044
Education, health and social work	11 029	15	1.096	13.134	2.3	0.059	0.008	0.430	0.021	0.039
Other services	27 159	44	1.507	97.313	29.0	1.798	0.203	0.359	0.030	1.352
Domestic	155 972	271	36.893	1 258.947	257.2	7.345	0.761	4.843	0.439	0.135
Total	**733 446**	**3 212**	**206.770**	**2 498.454**	**1 075**	**17.243**	**2.677**	**121.5**	**7.261**	**7.752**
of which, emissions from road transport	128 057	415	34.336	1 139.791	121.095	2.942	1.637	2.1	0.420	0.004

1 Carbon dioxide, methane, nitrous oxide, hydro-fluorocarbons, perfluorocarbons and sulphur hexafluoride expressed as thousand tonnes of carbon dioxide equivalent.
2 Sulphur dioxide, nitrogen oxides and ammonia expressed as thousand tonnes of sulphur dioxide equivalent.
3 PM10's are carbon particles in air arising from incomplete combustion.
4 Carbon monoxide.
5 Non-methane Volatile Compounds, including benzene and 1,3-butadiene.

Source: Netcen

13.5 Greenhouse gas and acid rain precursor emissions

Thousand tonnes

		1990	1995	1997	1999	2000	2001	2002	2003	2004	2005
Greenhouse gases - CO2,CH4,N2O,HFC,PFCs and SF6[1]											
Agriculture	JKRH	60 737	58 581	59 719	57 797	55 581	52 603	52 938	52 545	52 326	51 302
Mining and quarrying	JKRJ	40 554	37 103	36 581	32 462	31 958	31 118	31 578	30 891	30 279	29 155
Manufacturing	JKRK	173 414	159 153	164 436	140 790	136 609	130 999	122 466	123 796	120 037	119 745
Electricity, gas and water supply	JKRL	216 921	177 712	162 955	158 571	170 305	181 971	177 093	185 228	185 453	188 216
Construction	JKRM	8 973	9 513	9 943	10 217	10 249	10 429	10 523	10 750	10 964	11 302
Wholesale and retail trade	JKRN	13 834	15 807	16 806	18 638	19 064	18 433	18 281	18 401	19 248	18 809
Transport and communication	JKRO	64 757	72 296	80 667	83 759	86 581	90 644	91 654	95 001	101 425	104 466
Other business services	JKRP	6 627	7 037	6 783	7 252	7 315	7 745	6 718	6 839	6 816	7 066
Public administration	JKRQ	10 814	10 787	10 389	9 664	9 006	9 680	9 724	8 977	9 232	9 226
Education, health and social work	JKRR	11 821	11 583	12 223	12 738	11 974	12 670	10 499	10 489	11 071	11 029
Other services	JKRS	58 089	52 242	46 924	40 640	38 379	34 823	31 693	28 724	27 326	27 159
Domestic	JKRT	141 774	141 856	151 633	155 007	155 461	158 921	157 939	158 470	160 663	155 972
Total greenhouse gas emissions	JKRU	**808 315**	**753 669**	**759 059**	**727 536**	**732 481**	**740 035**	**721 105**	**730 112**	**734 839**	**733 446**
of which, emissions from road transport	JKRV	111 824	114 693	122 215	123 915	123 363	123 477	126 205	126 249	127 489	128 057
of which, emissions from water transport[2]	F8ZP	17 015	17 014	19 764	16 630	16 138	20 551	22 279	23 789	27 442	27 234
of which, emissions from air transport[3]	F8ZQ	20 374	24 658	28 045	33 845	37 350	36 825	36 122	37 361	40 382	42 843
Acid rain precursor emissions - SO2,NOx,NH3[4]											
Agriculture	JKRW	719	669	680	659	611	597	575	557	562	556
Mining and quarrying	JKRX	101	83	91	82	84	74	77	92	88	87
Manufacturing	JKRY	934	760	663	562	511	490	443	432	438	437
Electricity, gas and water supply	JKRZ	3 277	1 937	1 284	981	1 052	994	914	935	752	639
Construction	JKSA	71	67	65	62	60	58	55	53	51	50
Wholesale and retail trade	JKSB	99	84	76	72	68	61	60	57	58	54
Transport and communication	JKSC	793	778	855	740	716	835	872	911	1 017	1 004
Other business services	JKSD	38	33	27	24	22	21	17	17	14	14
Public administration	JKSE	79	67	63	52	48	48	44	36	41	40
Education, health and social work	JKSF	61	44	39	28	23	22	17	16	15	15
Other services	JKSG	77	68	59	50	48	50	46	46	44	44
Domestic	JKUK	700	564	530	461	411	377	346	321	302	271
Total acid rain precursor emissions	JKUL	**6 950**	**5 154**	**4 433**	**3 773**	**3 653**	**3 629**	**3 466**	**3 472**	**3 383**	**3 212**
of which, emissions from road transport	JKUM	997	844	774	685	619	566	524	483	452	415

1 Carbon dioxide, methane, nitrous oxide, hydrofluorocarbons, perflurocarbon and sulphur hexafluoride expressed as thousand tonnes of carbon dioxide equivalent.
2 Emissions from the water transport industry (EA code 69)
3 Emissions from the air transport industry (EA code 70)
4 Sulphur dioxide, nitrogen oxides and ammonia expressed as thousand tonnes of sulphur dioxide equivalent.

Source: Netcen, ONS

13.6 Material flows

Million tonnes

		1970	1975	1980	1985	1990	1995	1997	1998	1999	2000	2001	2002	2003	2004	2005
Domestic extraction																
Biomass																
Agricultural harvest	JKUN	42	38	47	47	46	47	53	51	52	51	45	51	48	48	47
Timber	JKUO	3	3	4	5	6	8	7	7	7	8	8	8	8	8	8
Animal grazing	JKUP	49	49	49	48	47	45	45	44	43	43	43	43	43	43	43
Fish	JKUQ	1	1	1	1	1	1	1	1	1	1	1	1	1	1	1
Total biomass	JKUR	96	92	101	100	101	100	106	103	104	102	97	102	100	101	99
Minerals																
Ores	JKUS	12	5	1	1	–	–	–	–	–	–	–	–	–	–	–
Clay	JKUT	38	33	25	23	21	18	15	16	15	15	14	14	14	15	13
Other industrial minerals	JKUU	14	11	11	11	11	10	10	8	8	8	9	8	9	8	8
Sand and gravel	JKUV	122	131	110	112	128	106	103	103	105	106	105	98	95	102	100
Crushed stone	JKUW	156	169	150	160	212	200	182	181	179	176	183	173	170	175	169
Total minerals	JKUX	342	349	298	307	373	334	310	309	308	305	311	293	288	300	291
Fossil fuels																
Coal	JKUY	149	129	130	94	94	53	48	41	37	31	32	30	28	25	21
Natural gas	JKUZ	11	37	39	37	43	71	86	90	102	111	109	106	106	96	88
Crude oil	JKVA	–	2	80	128	92	130	128	132	137	126	117	116	106	95	85
Total fossil fuels	JKVB	161	168	249	259	229	254	262	264	276	268	257	252	240	217	193
Total domestic extraction	JKVC	**598**	**608**	**648**	**666**	**702**	**688**	**679**	**676**	**687**	**676**	**665**	**648**	**628**	**618**	**583**
Imports																
Biomass	JKVD	38	33	30	31	38	40	41	42	42	42	46	47	49	50	50
Minerals	JKVE	30	32	24	34	41	50	51	54	50	51	54	55	55	60	58
Fossil fuels	JKVF	123	111	74	76	89	73	79	76	71	83	99	95	102	127	137
Other products	JKVG	6	7	14	15	19	23	29	31	30	34	34	32	34	36	35
Total imports	JKVH	**197**	**184**	**141**	**157**	**187**	**188**	**200**	**203**	**193**	**210**	**232**	**228**	**240**	**273**	**280**
Exports																
Biomass	JKVI	3	5	8	11	13	15	18	17	16	17	13	15	19	18	19
Minerals	JKVJ	17	20	26	22	25	39	43	46	42	44	43	42	44	48	48
Fossil fuels	JKVK	23	19	60	102	67	103	106	103	108	115	118	120	104	98	88
Other products	JKVL	5	7	8	11	12	17	18	20	21	21	21	20	21	21	21
Total exports	JKVM	**47**	**51**	**101**	**146**	**117**	**173**	**185**	**186**	**187**	**198**	**194**	**197**	**189**	**185**	**177**
Indirect flows																
From domestic extraction (excl soil erosion)[1]	JKVN	576	575	633	627	693	634	634	589	620	567	573	564	549	547	518
Of which;																
unused biomass	JKVO	25	23	32	35	37	37	42	40	40	40	35	40	38	39	37
fossil fuels	JKVP	169	202	287	274	309	276	281	245	260	231	241	225	209	204	178
minerals and ores	JKVQ	185	155	120	120	144	116	104	103	98	97	95	101	100	104	101
soil excavation and dredging	JKVR	197	195	195	199	203	204	206	201	222	199	202	199	202	201	203
From production of raw materials and semi-natural products imported	JKVS	394	395	368	423	457	527	541	597	562	614	711	648	671	692	752
Key indicators																
Physical trade balance (exports - imports)[3]	DZ76	–150	–133	–40	–11	–70	–14	–15	–17	–6	–13	–38	–32	–52	–88	–103
Direct Material Input (domestic extraction + imports)	JKVT	796	792	789	822	889	876	879	879	881	886	898	876	869	891	864
Domestic Material Consumption (domestic extraction + imports - exports)	JKVU	748	741	688	677	772	703	694	693	694	689	704	679	680	706	686
Total Material Requirement (direct material input + indirect flows)	JKVV	1 765	1 762	1 790	1 872	2 039	2 036	2 054	2 065	2 063	2 067	2 182	2 089	2 089	2 130	2 134

1 Indirect flows from domestic extraction relate to unused material which is moved during extraction, such as overburden from mining and quarrying.
2 Components may not sum to totals due to rounding.
3 A negative physical trade balance indicates a net import of material into the UK.

Source: ONS

13.7 Government revenues from environmental taxes

£ million

		1993	1995	1996	1997	1998	1999	2000	2001	2002	2003	2004	2005	2006
Energy														
Duty on hydrocarbon oils	GTAP	12 497	15 360	16 895	18 357	20 996	22 391	23 041	22 046	22 070	22 476	23 412	23 346	23 448
including														
Unleaded petrol[1]	GBHE	4 242	5 901	7 043	8 073	9 897	11 952	11 841	1 936	–	–	–	–	–
Leaded petrol/LRP[2]	GBHL	4 502	4 088	3 716	3 393	2 984	1 630	1 115	653	310	320	75	20	15
Ultra low sulphur petrol	ZXTK	–	–	–	–	–	–	1 121	10 560	12 721	12 158	12 447	11 999	11 435
Diesel[3]	GBHH	3 484	5 127	5 888	6 528	7 088	1 274	32	60	–	–	–	–	–
Ultra low sulphur diesel	GBHI	–	–	–	146	806	7 338	9 130	8 815	9 316	9 756	10 482	10 992	10 812
VAT on duty	CMYA	2 187	2 688	2 957	3 212	3 674	3 918	4 032	3 858	3 862	3 933	4 097	4 086	4 103
Fossil fuel levy	CIQY	1 331	1 306	978	418	181	104	56	86	32	–	–	–	–
Gas levy	GTAZ	240	161	198	181	32	–	–	–	–	–	–	–	–
Climate change levy	LSNT	–	–	–	–	–	–	–	585	825	828	756	747	711
Hydro-benefit	LITN	22	27	30	32	32	35	42	46	44	44	40	10	–
Road vehicles														
Vehicle excise duty	CMXZ	3 482	3 954	4 149	4 334	4 631	4 873	4 606	4 102	4 294	4 720	4 763	4 762	5 010
Other environmental taxes														
Air passenger duty	CWAA	–	339	353	442	823	884	940	824	814	781	856	896	963
Landfill tax	BKOF	–	–	113	361	333	430	461	502	541	607	672	733	808
Aggregates levy	MDUQ	–	–	–	–	–	–	–	–	213	340	328	327	325
Total environmental taxes	JKVW	**19 755**	**23 835**	**25 673**	**27 337**	**30 702**	**32 635**	**33 178**	**32 049**	**32 695**	**33 729**	**34 924**	**34 907**	**35 368**
Environmental taxes as a % of:														
Total taxes and social contributions	JKVX	9.0	9.3	9.6	9.4	9.7	9.7	9.3	8.6	8.7	8.5	8.3	7.7	7.3
Gross domestic product	JKVY	3.1	3.3	3.3	3.4	3.5	3.6	3.5	3.2	3.1	3.0	2.9	2.8	2.7

1 Unleaded petrol includes superunleaded petrol.
2 Lead Replacement Petrol (the alternative to 4-Star leaded petrol introduced in 2000) is lead-free.
3 Duty incentives have concentrated production on ultra low sulphur varieties.

Source: ONS, DTI

13.8 Environmental taxes breakdown by 13 industries 2004

£ million

	Energy	Transport	Pollution	Resources	Total
Agriculture	95	64	1	–	160
Mining and quarrying	78	4	2	326	410
Manufacturing	2 439	82	71	–	2 592
Energy, gas and water supply	178	5	5	–	188
Construction	1 329	110	7	2	1 448
Wholesale and retail trade	2 151	232	54	–	2 437
Transport and communication	5 977	152	28	–	6 157
Other business services	820	187	60	–	1 068
Public administration	237	2	109	–	348
Education, health and social work	164	7	82	–	253
Other services	422	41	253	–	717
Households	14 065	4 490	–	–	18 555
Rest of the world	349	243	–	–	592
Total	28 305	5 619	673	328	34 924

Source: ONS, Environmental Accounts

13.9 Environmental protection expenditure in specified industries 2004

£ million

	Protection of ambient air and climate	Waste water management	Waste management	Protection of bio-diversity and landscape	Other abatement activities	Research and development education and adminstration	Total environmental expenditure
Mining and quarrying	22	51	48	3	22	3	149
Food, beverages and tobacco products	64	294	161	4	51	6	580
Textiles, clothing and leather products	7	25	26	–	8	1	67
Wood and wood products	3	4	28	–	4	1	40
Pulp and paper products, printing and publishing	9	44	97	1	12	2	165
Coke, petroleum and nuclear fuel	34	104	37	39	151	1	366
Chemicals and man made fibres	47	313	121	1	45	39	566
Rubber and plastic products	10	20	84	–	30	7	151
Other non metallic mineral products	25	15	30	1	14	1	86
Basic metals and metal products	113	64	75	1	35	4	292
Machinery and equipment	19	47	78	1	42	15	202
Electrical, medical and optical equipment	6	11	17	–	9	1	44
Transport equipment	20	32	61	3	34	24	174
Other manufacturing	6	18	43	–	6	2	75
Energy production and water	124	23	16	61	50	2	276
Total expenditure in extraction, manufacturing, energy and water supply industries	**509**	**1 065**	**922**	**115**	**513**	**109**	**3 233**

The figures in these tables fall outside the scope of National Statistics and components may not sum to totals due to rounding.

Source: Department for Environment, Food and Rural Affairs

13.10 Environmental protection expenditure by public sector 2003

£ million

	Protection of ambient air and climate	Waste water management	Waste management	Protection of bio-diversity and landscape	Other abatement activities[1]	Research and development education and adminstration	Total environmental expenditure
Staff costs	84	143	614	307	37	149	1 334
Other running costs[2]	49	82	2 557	228	29	316	3 262
less							
Current income	–1	–2	–11	–1	–	–1	–15
Net operating costs	**132**	**223**	**3 160**	**534**	**67**	**464**	**4 581**
Capital payments[3]	26	17	143	87	262	58	594
less							
Capital receipts	–	–	–11	–	–	–1	–12
Net capital expenditure	**26**	**17**	**133**	**87**	**262**	**57**	**582**
Current grants and subsidies							
to industry	25	–	2	31	–	25	83
to households	–	–	–	–	–	9	9
Capital grants and subsidies							
to public corporations	–	31	–	–	–	–	31
to industry	–	–	–	–	1	–	1
to households	130	–	–	–	1	–	131
Net transfers to the rest of the world	–	–	–	3	–	–	4
Net expenditure[2]	**313**	**271**	**3 295**	**656**	**331**	**556**	**5 422**

1 Includes expenditure on the protection of soil and groundwater, on noise and vibration abatement, on protection against radiation and on other environmental protection activities.
2 Includes an allowance for the consumption of fixed capital.
3 Includes outlays on land.

Source: ONS

13.11 Environmental protection expenditure by public sector 2004

£ million

	Protection of ambient air and climate	Waste water management	Waste management	Protection of bio-diversity and landscape	Other abatement activities[1]	Research and development education and adminstration	Total environmental expenditure
Staff costs	90	153	656	328	40	160	1 426
Other running costs[2]	50	84	2 621	234	30	324	3 343
less							
Current income	–1	–4	–22	–1	–	–3	–32
Net operating costs	**138**	**232**	**3 255**	**561**	**70**	**481**	**4 737**
Capital payments[3]	43	29	238	145	435	97	987
less							
Capital receipts	–	–	–9	–	–	–1	–10
Net capital expenditure	**43**	**29**	**229**	**145**	**435**	**96**	**977**
Current grants and subsidies							
to industry	25	–	2	31	–	25	84
to households	–	–	–	–	–	8	8
Capital grants and subsidies							
to public corporations	–	71	–	–	–	–	71
to industry	–	–	–	–	3	–	4
to households	43	–	–	–	–	–	43
Net transfers to the rest of the world	–	–	–	1	–	–	1
Net expenditure[2]	**250**	**332**	**3 486**	**738**	**509**	**610**	**5 926**

1 Includes expenditure on the protection of soil and groundwater, on noise and vibration abatement, on protection against radiation and on other environmental protection activities.
2 Includes an allowance for the consumption of fixed capital.
3 Includes outlays on land.

Source: ONS

Supplementary Information

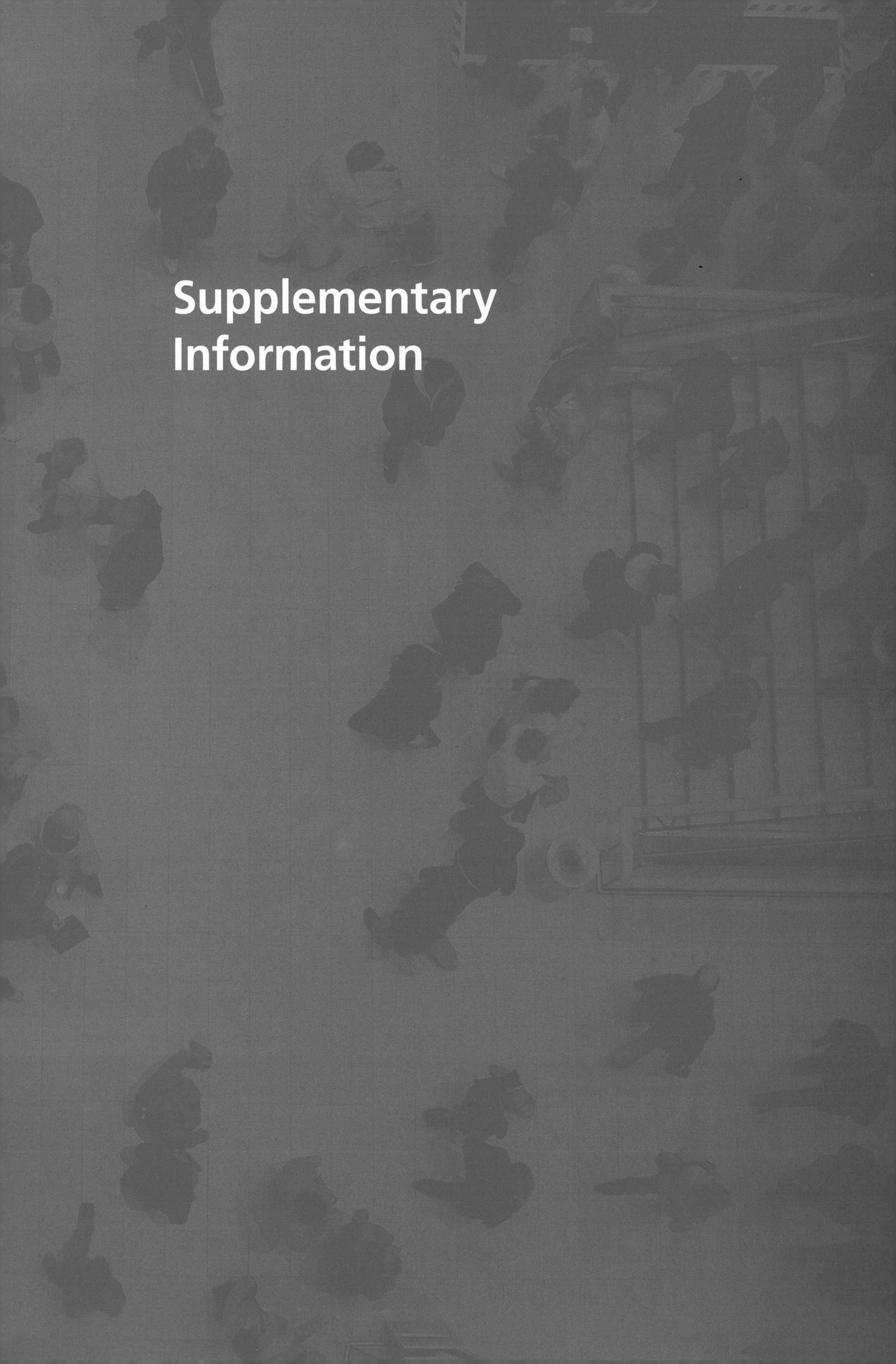

Glossary

Above the line

Transactions in the production, current and capital accounts which are above the Net lending (+) / Net borrowing (financial surplus or deficit) line in the presentation used in the economic accounts. The financial transactions account is below the line in this presentation.

Accruals basis

A method of recording transactions to relate them to the period when the exchange of ownership of the goods, services or financial asset applies. (See also cash basis). For example, value added tax accrues when the expenditure to which it relates takes place, but Customs and Excise receive the cash some time later. The difference between accruals and cash results in the creation of an asset and liability in the financial accounts, shown as amounts receivable or payable (F7).

Actual final consumption

The value of goods consumed by a sector but not necessarily purchased by that sector. See also Final consumption expenditure, Intermediate consumption.

Advance and progress payments

Payments made for goods in advance of completion and delivery of the goods. Also referred to as stage payments.

Asset boundary

Boundary separating assets included in creating core economic accounts (such as plant and factories, also including non-produced assets such as land and water resources) and those excluded (such as natural assets not managed for an economic purpose).

Assets

Entities over which ownership rights are enforced by institutional units, individually or collectively; and from which economic benefits may be derived by their owners by holding them over a period of time.

Assurance

An equivalent term to insurance, commonly used in the life insurance business.

Balancing item

A balancing item is an accounting construct obtained by subtracting the total value of the entries on one side of an account from the total value for the other side. In the sector accounts in the former system of UK economic accounts the term referred to the difference between the Financial Surplus or Deficit for a sector and the sum of the financial transactions for that sector, currently designated the statistical discrepancy.

Balance of payments

A summary of the transactions between residents of a country and residents abroad in a given time period.

Balance of trade

The balance on trade in goods and services. The balance of trade is a summary of the imports and exports of goods and services across an economic boundary in a given period.

Balance sheet

A statement, drawn up at a particular point in time, of the value of assets owned and of the financial claims (liabilities) against the owner of these assets.

Banks (UK)

Strictly, all financial institutions located in the United Kingdom and recognised by the Bank of England as banks for statistical purposes up to late 1981 or as UK banks from then onwards. This category includes the UK offices of institutions authorised under the Banking Act (1987), the Bank of England, the National Girobank and the TSB Group plc. It may include branches of foreign banks where these are recognised as banks by the Bank of England, but not offices abroad of these or of any British-owned banks. An updated list of banks appears in each February's issue of the Bank of England Quarterly Bulletin. Institutions in the Channel Islands and the Isle of Man which have opted to adhere to the monetary control arrangements introduced in August 1981 were formerly included in the sector but are not considered to be residents of the United Kingdom under the ESA. Banks are included in the Monetary financial institutions (S.121/S.122) sector.

Bank of England

This comprises S.121, the central bank sub-sector of the financial corporations sector.

Bank of England - Issue Department

This part of the Bank of England deals with the issue of bank notes on behalf of central government and was formerly classified to central government though it is now part of the central bank sector. Its activities include, inter alia, market purchases of commercial bills from UK banks.

Basic prices

These prices are the preferred method of valuing gross value added and output. They reflect the amount received by the producer for a unit of goods or services minus any taxes payable plus any subsidy receivable on that unit as a consequence of production or sale (i.e. the cost of production including subsidies). As a result the only taxes included in the basic price are taxes on the production process - such as business rates and any vehicle excise duty paid by businesses - which are not specifically levied on the production of a unit of output. Basic prices exclude any transport charges invoiced separately by the producer.

Below the line

The financial transactions account which shows the financing of Net lending(+) / Net borrowing (-) (formerly financial surplus or deficit).

Bond

A financial instrument that usually pays interest to the holder, issued by governments as well as companies and other institutions, e.g. local authorities. Most bonds have a fixed date on which the borrower will repay the holder. Bonds are attractive to investors since they can be bought and sold easily in a secondary market. Special forms of bonds include deep discount bonds, equity warrant bonds, Eurobonds, and zero coupon bonds.

British government securities

See Gilts.

Building society

Those institutions as defined in the Building Society Acts (1962 and 1986). They offer housing finance largely to the households sector and fund this largely by taking short term deposits from the households sector. They are part of the monetary financial institutions sub-sector.

Capital

Capital assets are those which contribute to the productive process so as to produce an economic return. In other contexts the word can be taken to include tangible assets (e.g. buildings, plant and machinery), intangible assets and financial capital. See also fixed assets, inventories.

Capital formation

Acquisition less disposals of fixed assets, improvement of land, change in inventories and acquisition less disposals of valuables.

Capital Stock

Measure of the cost of replacing the capital assets of a country, held at a particular point in time.

Capital transfers

Transfers which are related to the acquisition or disposal of assets by the recipient or payer. They may be in cash or kind, and may be imputed to reflect the assumption or forgiveness of debt.

Cash basis

The recording of transactions when cash or other assets are actually transferred, rather than on an accruals basis.

Central monetary institutions (CMIs)

Institutions (usually central banks) which control the centralised monetary reserves and the supply of currency in accordance with government policies, and which act as their governments' bankers and agents. In the UK this is equivalent to the Bank of England. In many other countries maintenance of the exchange rate is undertaken in this sector. In the United Kingdom this function is undertaken by central government (part of the Treasury) by use of the Exchange Equalisation Account.

Certificate of deposit

A short term interest-paying instrument issued by deposit-taking institutions in return for money deposited for a fixed period. Interest is earned at a given rate. The instrument can be used as security for a loan if the depositor requires money before the repayment date.

Chained volume measures

Chained volume measures are time series which measure GDP in real terms (ie, excluding price effects).

C.i.f.

The basis of valuation of imports for Customs purposes, it includes the cost of insurance premiums and freight services. These need to be deducted to obtain the f.o.b. valuation consistent with the valuation of exports which is used in the economic accounts.

COICOP (Classification of Individual Consumption by Purpose)

An international classification which groups consumption according to its function or purpose. Thus the heading clothing, for example, includes expenditure on garments, clothing materials, laundry and repairs.

Combined use table

Table of the demand for products by each industry group or sector, whether from domestic production or imports, estimated at purchaser's prices. It displays the inputs used by each industry to produce their total output and separates out intermediate purchases of goods and services. This table shows which industries use which products. Columns represent the purchasing industries: rows represent the products purchased.

Commercial paper

This is an unsecured promissory note for a specific amount and maturing on a specific date. The commercial paper market allows companies to issue short term debt direct to financial institutions who then market this paper to investors or use it for their own investment purposes.

Compensation of employees

Total remuneration payable to employees in cash or in kind. Includes the value of social contributions payable by the employer.

Consolidated Fund

An account of central government into which most government revenue (excluding borrowing and certain payments to government departments) is paid, and from which most government expenditure (excluding loans and National Insurance benefits) is paid.

Consumption

See Final consumption, Intermediate consumption.

Consumption of fixed capital

The amount of capital resources used up in the process of production in any period. It is not an identifiable set of transactions but an imputed transaction which can only be measured by a system of conventions.

Corporations

All bodies recognised as independent legal entities which are producers of market output and whose principal activity is the production of goods and services.

Counterpart

In a double-entry system of accounting each transaction gives rise to two corresponding entries. These entries are the counterparts to each other. Thus the counterpart of a payment by one sector is the receipt by another.

Debenture

A long-term bond issued by a UK or foreign company and secured on fixed assets. A debenture entitles the holder to a fixed interest payment or a series of such payments.

Depreciation

See Consumption of fixed capital.

Derivatives (F.34)

Financial instruments whose value is linked to changes in the value of another financial instrument, an indicator or a commodity. In contrast to the holder of a primary financial instrument (e.g. a government bond or a bank deposit), who has an unqualified right to receive cash (or some other economic benefit) in the future, the holder of a derivative has only a qualified right to receive such a benefit. Examples of derivatives are options and swaps.

DIM (Dividend and Interest Matrix)

The Dividend and Interest Matrix represents property income flows related to holdings of financial transactions. The gross flows are now shown in D.4.

Direct investment

Net investment by UK/overseas companies in their overseas/UK branches, subsidiaries or associated companies. A direct investment in a company means that the investor has a significant influence on the operations of the company. Investment includes not only acquisition of fixed assets, stock building and stock appreciation but also all other financial transactions such as additions to, or payments of, working capital, other loans and trade credit and acquisitions of securities. Estimates of investment exclude depreciation.

Discount market

That part of the market dealing with short-term borrowing. It is called the discount market because the interest on loans is expressed as a percentage reduction (discount) on the amount paid to the borrower. For example, for a loan of £100 face value when the discount rate is 5% the borrower will receive £95 but will repay £100 at the end of the term.

Double deflation

Method for calculating value added by industry chained volume measures; which takes separate account of the differing price and volume movements of input and outputs in an industry's production process.

Dividend

A payment made to company shareholders from current or previously retained profits. See DIM.

ECGD

See Export Credit Guarantee Department.

Economically significant prices

These are prices whose level significantly affects the supply of the good or service concerned. Market output consists mainly of goods and services sold at 'economically significant' prices while non-market output comprises those provided free or at prices that are not economically significant.

Enterprise

An institutional unit producing market output. Enterprises are found mainly in the non-financial and financial corporations sectors but exist in all sectors. Each enterprise consists of one or more kind-of-activity units.

Environmental accounts

A satellite account describing the relationship between the environment and the economy.

Equity

Equity is ownership or potential ownership of a company. An entity's equity in a company will be evidenced by ordinary shares. They differ from other financial instruments in that they confer ownership of something more than a financial claim. Shareholders are owners of the company whereas bond holders are merely outside creditors.

ESA

European System of National and Regional Accounts. An integrated system of economic accounts which is the European version of the System of National Accounts (SNA).

European Investment Bank

This was set up to assist economic development within the European Union. Its members are the member states of the EU.

European Monetary Cooperation Fund

Central banks of member states of the European Monetary System deposit 20 per cent of their gold and foreign exchange reserves on a short-term basis with the European Monetary Cooperation Fund in exchange for ECUs. The Fund is the clearing house for central banks in the EMS.

Exchange Cover Scheme (ECS)

A scheme first introduced in 1969 whereby UK public bodies raise foreign currency from overseas residents, either directly or through UK banks, and surrender it to the Exchange Equalisation Account in exchange for sterling for use to finance expenditure in the United Kingdom. HM Treasury sells the borrower foreign currency to service and repay the loan at the exchange rate that applied when the loan was taken out.

Exchange Equalisation Account (EEA)

An account of central government held by the Bank of England in which transactions in the official reserves are recorded. It is the means by which the government, through the Bank of England, influences exchange rates.

Export credit

Credit extended overseas by UK institutions primarily in connection with UK exports but also including some credit in respect of third-country trade.

Export Credits Guarantee Department (ECGD)

A government department whose main function is to provide insurance cover for export credit transactions.

Factor cost

In the former system of national accounts this was the basis of valuation which excluded the effects of taxes on expenditure and subsidies.

Final consumption expenditure

The expenditure on goods and services that are used for the direct satisfaction of individual needs or the collective needs of members of the community as distinct from their purchase for use in the productive process. It may be contrasted with Actual final consumption, which is the value of goods consumed but not necessarily purchased by that sector. See also Intermediate consumption.

Finance houses

Financial corporations that specialise in the financing of hire purchase arrangements.

Financial auxiliaries

Auxiliary financial activities are ones closely related to financial intermediation but which are not financial intermediation themselves, such as the repackaging of funds. Financial auxiliaries include such activities as insurance broking and fund management.

Financial corporations

All bodies recognised as independent legal entities whose principal activity is financial intermediation and/or the production of auxiliary financial services. However, the United Kingdom currently treats financial auxiliaries as non-financial corporations.

Financial intermediation

Financial intermediation is the activity by which an institutional unit acquires financial assets and incurs liabilities on its own account by engaging in financial transactions on the market. The assets and liabilities of financial intermediaries have different characteristics so that the funds are transformed or repackaged with respect to maturity, scale, risk, etc, in the financial intermediation process.

Financial leasing

A form of leasing in which the lessee contracts to assume the rights and responsibilities of ownership of leased goods from the lessor (the legal owner) for the whole (or virtually the whole) of the economic life of the asset. In the economic accounts this is recorded as the sale of the assets to the lessee, financed by an imputed loan (F.42). The leasing payments are split into interest payments and repayments of principal.

Financial Services Adjustment

Now renamed FISIM (see below) this is a feature temporarily carried over from the previous system. The output of many financial intermediation services is paid for not by charges, but by an interest rate differential. The value added of these industries is shown including their interest receipts less payments, in effect imputing charges for their services. However, GDP in total takes no account of this, and an adjustment is necessary to reconcile the two. For the treatment in the new SNA (to be implemented fully in the EU at a later date) see FISIM. Since most output of these industries is intermediate consumption of other industries the difference between the two methods in their effect on total GDP is relatively small.

Financial surplus or deficit (FSD)

The former term for Net lending(+)/Net borrowing (-), the balance of all current and capital account transactions for an institutional sector or the economy as a whole.

FISIM

Financial Intermediation Services Indirectly Measured. The output of many financial intermediation services is paid for not by charges but by an interest rate differential. FISIM imputes charges for these services and corresponding offsets in property income. FISIM, an innovation of the 1993 SNA, has not yet been fully implemented in the UK economic accounts; the earnings are not yet allocated to the users of the services.

Fixed assets

Produced assets that are themselves used repeatedly or continuously in the production process for more than one year. They comprise buildings and other structures, vehicles and other plant and machinery and also plants and livestock which are used repeatedly or continuously in production, e.g. fruit trees or dairy cattle. They also include intangible assets such as computer software and artistic originals.

Flows

Economic flows reflect the creation, transformation, exchange, transfer or extinction of economic value. They involve changes in the volume, composition or value of an institutional unit's assets and liabilities. They are recorded in the production, distribution and use of income and accumulation accounts.

F.o.b.

Free on board, the valuation of imports and exports of goods used in the economic accounts, including all costs invoiced by the exporter up to the point of loading on to the ship or aircraft but excluding the cost of insurance and freight from the country of consignment.

Futures

Instruments which give the holder the right to purchase a commodity or a financial asset at a future date.

GFCF

See Gross fixed capital formation.

Gilts

Bonds issued or guaranteed by the UK government. Also known as gilt-edged securities or British government securities.

Gold

The SNA and the IMF (in the 5th Edition of its Balance of Payments Manual) recognise three types of gold:

- monetary gold, treated as a financial asset;
- gold held as a store of value, to be included in valuables;
- gold as an industrial material, to be included in intermediate consumption or inventories.

This is a significant change from previous UK practice and presents problems such that the United Kingdom has received from the European Union a derogation from applying this fully until the year 2005.

The present treatment is as follows:

- In the accounts a distinction is drawn between gold held as a financial asset (financial gold) and gold held like any other commodity (commodity gold). Commodity gold in the form of finished manufactures together with net domestic and overseas transactions in gold moving into or out of finished manufactured form (i.e. for jewellery, dentistry, electronic goods, medals and proof - but not bullion - coins) is recorded in exports and imports of goods.
- All other transactions in gold (i.e. those involving semi-manufactures such as rods, wire, etc, or bullion, bullion coins or banking-type assets and liabilities denominated in gold, including official reserve assets) are treated as financial gold transactions and included in the financial account of the Balance of Payments.

The United Kingdom has adopted different treatment to avoid distortion of its trade in goods account by the substantial transactions of the London bullion market.

Grants

Voluntary transfer payments. They may be current or capital in nature. Grants from government or the European Union to producers are subsidies.

Gross

Key economic series can be shown as gross (i.e. before deduction of the consumption of fixed capital or net (i.e. after deduction). Gross has this meaning throughout this book unless otherwise stated.

Gross domestic product (GDP)

The total value of output in the economic territory. It is the balancing item on the production account for the whole economy. Domestic product can be measured gross or net. It is presented in the accounts at market (or purchasers') prices.

Gross fixed capital formation (GFCF)

Acquisition less disposals of fixed assets and the improvement of land.

Gross national disposable income

The income available to the residents arising from GDP, and receipts from, less payments to, the rest of the world of employment income, property income and current transfers.

Gross value added (GVA)

The value generated by any unit engaged in production, and the contributions of individual sectors or industries to gross domestic product. It is measured at basic prices, excluding taxes less subsidies on products.

Hidden economy

Certain activities may be productive and also legal but are concealed from the authorities for various reasons - for example to evade taxes or regulation. In principle these, as well as economic production that is illegal, are to be included in the accounts but they are by their nature difficult to measure.

Holding gains or losses

Profit or loss obtained by virtue of the changing price of assets being held. Holding gains or losses may arise from either physical and financial assets.

Households (S.14)

Individuals or small groups of individuals as consumers and in some cases as entrepreneurs producing goods and market services (where such activities cannot be hived off and treated as those of a quasi corporation).

Imputation

The process of inventing a transaction where, although no money has changed hands, there has been a flow of goods or services. It is confined to a very small number of cases where a reasonably satisfactory basis for the assumed valuation is available.

Index-linked gilts

Gilts whose coupon and redemption value are linked to movements in the retail prices index.

Institutional unit

Institutional units are the individual bodies whose data is amalgamated to form the sectors of the economy. A body is regarded as an institutional unit if it has decision-making autonomy in respect of its principal function and either keeps a complete set of accounts or is in a position to compile, if required, a complete set of accounts which would be meaningful from both an economic and a legal viewpoint.

Institutional sector

See Sector.

Input-Output

A detailed analytical framework based on Supply and Use tables. These are matrices showing the composition of output of individual industries by types of product and how the domestic and imported supply of goods and services is allocated between various intermediate and final uses, including exports.

Intangible assets

Intangible fixed assets include mineral exploration, computer software and entertainment, literary or artistic originals. Expenditure on them is part of gross fixed capital formation. They exclude non-produced intangible assets such as patented entities, leases, transferable contracts and purchased goodwill, expenditure on which would be intermediate consumption.

Intermediate consumption

The consumption of goods and services in the production process. It may be contrasted with final consumption and capital formation.

International Monetary Fund (IMF)

A fund set up as a result of the Bretton Woods Conference in 1944 which began operations in 1947. It currently has about 180 member countries including most of the major countries of the world. The fund was set up to supervise the fixed exchange rate system agreed at Bretton Woods and to make available to its members a pool of foreign exchange resources to assist them when they have balance of payments difficulties. It is funded by member countries' subscriptions according to agreed quotas.

Inventories

Inventories (known as stocks in the former system) consist of finished goods (held by the producer prior to sale, further processing or other use) and products (materials and fuel) acquired from other producers to be used for intermediate consumption or resold without further processing.

Investment trust

An institution that invests its capital in a wide range of other companies' shares. Investment trusts issue shares which are listed on the London Stock Exchange and use this capital to invest in the shares of other companies. See also Unit trusts.

Kind-of-activity unit (KAU)

An enterprise, or part of an enterprise, which engages in only one kind of non-ancillary productive activity, or in which the principal productive activity accounts for most of the value added. Each enterprise consists of one or more kind-of-activity units.

Liability

A claim on an institutional unit by another body which gives rise to a payment or other transaction transferring assets to the other body. Conditional liabilities, i.e. where the transfer of assets only takes place under certain defined circumstances, are known as contingent liabilities.

Liquidity

The ease with which a financial instrument can be exchanged for goods and services. Cash is very liquid whereas a life assurance policy is less so.

Lloyd's of London

The international insurance and reinsurance market in London.

Marketable securities

Securities which can be sold on the open market.

Market output

Output of goods and services sold at economically significant prices.

Merchant banks

These are monetary financial institutions whose main business is primarily concerned with corporate finance and acquisitions.

Mixed income

The balancing item on the generation of income account for unincorporated businesses owned by households. The owner or members of the same household often provide unpaid labour inputs to the business. The surplus is therefore a mixture of remuneration for such labour and return to the owner as entrepreneur.

Money market

The market in which short-term loans are made and short -term securities traded. 'Short term' usually applies to periods under one year but can be longer in some instances.

NACE

The industrial classification used in the European Union. Revision 1 is the 'Statistical classification of economic activities in the European Community in accordance with Council Regulation No. 3037/90 of 9th October 1990'.

National income

See Gross national disposable income and Real national disposable income.

National Loans Fund

An account of HM Government set up under the National Loans Fund Act (1968) which handles all government borrowing and most domestic lending transactions.

Net

After deduction of the consumption of fixed capital. Also used in the context of financial accounts and balance sheets to denote, for example, assets less liabilities.

Non-market output

Output of own account production of goods and services provided free or at prices that are not economically significant. Non-market output is produced mainly by the general government and NPISH sectors.

NPISH

Non-profit institutions serving households (S.15). These include bodies such as charities, universities, churches, trade unions or member's clubs.

Operating surplus

The balance on the generation of income account. Households also have a mixed income balance. It may be seen as the surplus arising from the production of goods and services before taking into account flows of property income.

Operating leasing

The conventional form of leasing, in which the lessee makes use of the leased asset for a period in return for a rental while the asset remains on the balance sheet of the lessor. The leasing payments are part of the output of the lessor, and the intermediate consumption of the lessee. See also Financial leasing.

Ordinary share

The most common type of share in the ownership of a corporation. Holders of ordinary shares receive dividends. See also Equity.

Output for own final use

Production of output for final consumption or gross fixed capital formation by the producer. Also known as own-account production.

Own-account production

Production of output for final consumption or gross fixed capital formation by the producer. Also known as output for own final use.

Par value

A security's face or nominal value. Securities can be issued at a premium or discount to par.

Pension funds

The institutions that administer pension schemes. Pension schemes are significant investors in securities. Self-administered funds are classified in the financial accounts as pension funds. Those managed by insurance companies are treated as long-term business of insurance companies. They are part of S.125, the Insurance corporations and pension funds sub-sector.

Perpetual Inventory Model (or Method) (PIM)

A method for estimating the level of assets held at a particular point of time by accumulating the acquisitions of such assets over a period and subtracting the disposals of assets over that period. Adjustments are made for price changes over the period. The PIM is used in the UK accounts to estimate the stock of fixed capital, and hence the value of the consumption of fixed capital.

Portfolio

A list of the securities owned by a single investor. In the Balance of Payments statistics, portfolio investment is investment in securities that does not qualify as direct investment.

Preference share

This type of share guarantees its holder a prior claim on dividends. The dividend paid to preference share holders is normally more than that paid to holders of ordinary shares. Preference shares may give the holder a right to a share in the ownership of the company (participating preference shares). However in the UK they usually do not, and are therefore classified as bonds (F.3).

Prices

See economically significant prices, basic prices, producers' prices.

Principal

The lump sum that is lent under a loan or a bond.

Private sector

Private non-financial corporations, financial corporations other than the Bank of England (and Girobank when it was publicly owned), households and the NPISH sector.

Production boundary

Boundary between production included in creating core economic accounts (such as all economic activity by industry and commerce) and production which is excluded (such as production by households which is consumed within the household).

Promissory note

A security which entitles the bearer to receive cash. These may be issued by companies or other institutions. (See commercial paper).

Property income

Incomes that accrue from lending or renting financial or tangible non-produced assets, including land, to other units. See also Tangible assets.

Public corporations

These are public trading bodies which have a substantial degree of financial independence from the public authority which created them. A public corporation is publicly controlled to the extent that the public authority, i.e. central or local government, usually appoints the whole or a majority of the board of management. Such bodies comprise much the greater part of sub-sector S.11001, public non-financial corporations.

Public sector

Comprises general government plus public non-financial corporations.

Purchasers' prices

These are the prices paid by purchasers. They include transport costs, trade margins and taxes (unless the taxes are deductible by the purchasers from their own tax liabilities).

Quasi-corporations

Unincorporated enterprises that function as if they were corporations. For the purposes of allocation to sectors and sub-sectors they are treated as if they were corporations, i.e. separate units from those to which they legally belong. Three main types of quasi-corporation are recognised in the accounts: unincorporated enterprises owned by government which are engaged in market production, unincorporated enterprises (including partnerships) owned by households and unincorporated enterprises owned by foreign residents. The last group consists of permanent branches or offices of foreign enterprises and production units of foreign enterprises which engage in significant amounts of production in the territory over long or indefinite periods of time.

Real national disposable income (RNDI)

Gross national disposable income adjusted for changes in prices and in the terms of trade.

Related compa nies

Branches, subsidiaries, associates or parents.

Related import or export credit

Trade credit between related companies, included in direct investment.

Rental

The amount payable by the user of a fixed asset to its owner for the right to use that asset in production for a specified period of time. It is included in the output of the owner and the intermediate consumption of the user.

Rents (D.45)

The property income derived from land and sub-soil assets. It should be distinguished in the current system from rental income derived from buildings and other fixed assets, which is included in output (P.1).

Repurchase agreement (Repo)

A deal in which an institution lends or 'sells' another institution a security and agrees to buy it back at a future date. Legal ownership does not change under a 'repo' agreement. It was previously treated as a change of ownership in the UK financial account but under the SNA is treated as a collateralised deposit (F.22).

Reserve assets

The UK official holdings of gold, convertible currencies, Special Drawing Rights, changes in the UK reserve position with the IMF and European currency. They include units acquired from swaps with the European Monetary Co-operation Fund (EMCF).

Residents

These comprise general government, individuals, private non-profit-making bodies serving households and enterprises within the territory of a given economy.

Residual error

The term used in the former accounts for the difference between the measures of gross domestic product from the expenditure and income approaches.

Resources and Uses

The term resources refers to the side of the current accounts where transactions which add to the amount of economic value of a unit or sector appear. For example, wages and salaries are a resource for the unit or sector receiving them. Resources are by convention put on the right side, or at the top of tables arranged vertically. The left side (or bottom section) of the accounts, which relates to transactions that reduce the amount of economic value of a unit or sector, is termed uses. To continue the example, wages and salaries are a use for the unit or sector that must pay them.

Rest of the world

This sector records the counterpart of transactions of the whole economy with non-residents.

Satellite accounts

Satellite accounts describe areas or activities not dealt with by core economic accounts. These areas/activities are considered to require too much detail for inclusion in the core accounts or they operate with a different conceptual framework. Internal satellite accounts re-present information within the production boundary. External satellite accounts present new information not covered by the core accounts.

Saving

The balance on the use of income account. It is that part of disposable income which is not spent on final consumption, and may be positive or negative.

Sector

In the economic accounts the economy is split into different institutional sectors, i.e. groupings of units according broadly to their role in the economy. The main sectors are non-financial corporations, financial corporations, general government, households and non-profit institutions serving households (NPISH). The Rest of the world is also treated as a sector for many purposes within the accounts.

Secondary market

A market in which holders of financial instruments can re-sell all or part of their holding. The larger and more effective the secondary market for any particular financial instrument the more liquid that instrument is to the holder.

Securities

Tradeable or potentially tradeable financial instruments.

SIC

Standard Industrial Classification. The industrial classification applied to the collection and publication of a wide range of economic statistics. The current version, SIC92, is consistent with NACE, Rev.1.

SNA

System of National Accounts, the internationally agreed standard system for macroeconomic accounts. The latest version is described in System of National Accounts 1993.

Special Drawing Rights (SDRs)

These are reserve assets created and distributed by decision of the members of the IMF. Participants accept an obligation, when designated by the IMF to do so, to provide convertible currency to another participant in exchange for SDRs equivalent to three times their own allocation. Only countries with a sufficiently strong balance of payments are so designated. SDRs may also be used in certain direct payments between participants in the scheme and for payments of various kinds to the IMF.

Stage payments

See Advance and progress payments.

Stocks, stockbuilding

The terms used in the former system corresponding to inventories and changes in inventories.

Subsidiaries

Companies owned or controlled by another company. Under Section 736 of the Companies Act (1985) this means, broadly speaking, that another company either holds more than half the equity share capital or controls the composition of the board of directors. The category also includes subsidiaries of subsidiaries.

Subsidies (D.3)

Current unrequited payments made by general government or the European Union to enterprises. Those made on the basis of a quantity or value of goods or services are classified as 'subsidies on products' (D.31). Other subsidies based on levels of productive activity (e.g. numbers employed) are designated Other subsidies on production (D.39).

Suppliers' credit

Export credit extended overseas directly by UK firms other than to related concerns.

Supply table

Table of estimates of domestic industries' output by type of product. Compiled at basic prices and includes columns for imports of goods and services, for distributors' trading margins and for taxes less subsidies on products. The final column shows the value of the supply of goods and services at purchaser's prices. This table shows which industries make which products. Columns represent the supplying industries: rows represent the products supplied.

Tangible assets

These comprise produced fixed assets and non-produced assets. Tangible fixed assets, the acquisition and disposal of which are recorded in gross fixed capital formation (P.51), comprise buildings and other structures (including historic monuments), vehicles, other machinery and equipment and cultivated assets in the form of livestock and trees yielding repeat products (e.g. dairy cattle, orchards). Tangible non-produced assets are assets such as land and sub-soil resources that occur in nature over which ownership rights have been established. Similar assets to which ownership rights have not been established are excluded as they do not qualify as economic assets. The acquisition and disposal of non-produced assets in principle is recorded separately in the capital account (K.2). The distinction between produced and non-produced assets is not yet fully possible for the United Kingdom.

Taxes

Compulsory unrequited transfers to central or local government or the European Union. Taxation is classified in the following main groups: taxes on production and imports (D.2), current taxes on income wealth, etc (D.5) and capital taxes (D.91).

Technical reserves (of insurance companies)

These reserves consist of pre-paid premiums, reserves against outstanding claims, actuarial reserves for life insurance and reserves for with-profit insurance. They are treated in the economic accounts as the property of policy-holders.

Terms of trade

Ratio of the change in export prices to the change in import prices. An increase in the terms of trade implies that the receipts from the same quantity of exports will finance an increased volume of imports. Thus measurement of real national disposable income needs to take account of this factor.

Transfers

Unrequited payments made by one unit to another. They may be current transfers (D.5-7) or capital transfers (D.9). The most important types of transfers are taxes, social contributions and benefits.

Treasury bills

Short-term securities or promissory notes which are issued by government in return for funding from the money market. In the United Kingdom every week the Bank of England invites tenders for sterling Treasury bills from the financial institutions operating in the market. ECU-denominated bills are issued by tender each month. Treasury bills are an important form of short-term borrowing for the government, generally being issued for periods of 3 or 6 months.

Unit trusts

Institutions within sub-sector S.123 through which investors pool their funds to invest in a diversified portfolio of securities. Individual investors purchase units in the fund representing an ownership interest in the large pool of underlying assets, i.e. they have an equity stake. The selection of assets is made by professional fund managers. Unit trusts therefore give individual investors the opportunity to invest in a diversified and professionally managed portfolio of securities without the need for detailed knowledge of the individual companies issuing the stocks and bonds. They differ from investment trusts in that the latter are companies in which investors trade shares on the Stock Exchange, whereas unit trust units are issued and bought back on demand by the managers of the trust. The prices of unit trust units thus reflect the value of the underlying pool of securities, whereas the price of shares in investment trusts are affected by the usual market forces.

Uses

See Resources and Uses

Use Table

See Combined Use Table.

United Kingdom

Broadly, in the accounts, the United Kingdom comprises Great Britain plus Northern Ireland and that part of the continental shelf deemed by international convention to belong to the UK. It excludes the Channel Islands and the Isle of Man.

Valuables

Goods of considerable value that are not used primarily for production or consumption but are held as stores of value over time. They consist of precious metals, precious stones, jewellery, works of art, etc. As a new category in the accounts the estimates for them are currently fairly rudimentary, though transactions are likely to have been recorded elsewhere in the accounts.

Valuation

See Basic prices, Purchasers' prices, Factor cost.

Value added

The balance on the production account: output less intermediate consumption. Value added may be measured net or gross.

Value Added Tax (VAT) (D.211)

A tax paid by enterprises. In broad terms an enterprise is liable for VAT on the total of its taxable sales but may deduct tax already paid by suppliers on its inputs (intermediate consumption). Thus the tax is effectively on the value added by the enterprise. Where the enterprise cannot deduct tax on its inputs the tax is referred to as non-deductible. VAT is the main UK tax on products (D.21).

Index

Figures indicate Table numbers. The letter "**G**" indicates that the item appears in the Glossary. Where the item is discussed in the section introductions, the appropriate page number is given.

Key for this index

References are either to pages of text or to table numbers.

S - appears in sector tables which are numbered using the following system:

The table numbering system for the Blue Book shows the relationships between the UK, its sectors and the rest of the world. A 3-part numbering system (e.g. 1.7.2) has been adopted for the accounts drawn directly from the ESA95. The first two digits denotes the UK sector, the third digit denotes the ESA95 account. They are as follows:

0 Goods and services account

1 Production account

2 Generation of income account

3 Allocation of primary income account

4 Secondary distribution of income account

5 Redistribution of income in kind account

6 Use of income account

7 Accumulation account

8 Financial account

9 Financial balance sheet